# THE MEMOIRS

OF

# JAMES, MARQUIS OF MONTROSE.

Swan Electric Engraving Co.

*Montrose*

# The Memoirs of James
## MARQUIS OF
# MONTROSE
1639—1650

BY THE
### REV. GEORGE WISHART, D.D.
(BISHOP OF EDINBURGH, 1662-1671)

TRANSLATED WITH INTRODUCTION, NOTES, APPENDICES, AND THE
ORIGINAL LATIN (PART II. NOW FIRST PUBLISHED)

BY THE
### REV. ALEXANDER D. MURDOCH
F.S.A. SCOT., CANON OF ST. MARY'S CATHEDRAL, EDINBURGH
EDITOR AND TRANSLATOR OF THE GRAMEID MS.

AND

### H. F. MORLAND SIMPSON
M.A. CANTAB., F.S.A. SCOT.: FETTES COLLEGE

The Naval & Military Press Ltd

in association with

The National Army Museum, London

*Published jointly by*

**The Naval & Military Press Ltd**
Unit 10 Ridgewood Industrial Park,
Uckfield, East Sussex,
TN22 5QE England

Tel: +44 (0) 1825 749494
Fax: +44 (0) 1825 765701

www.naval-military-press.com
www.military-genealogy.com
www.militarymaproom.com

*and*

**The National Army Museum, London**
www.national-army-museum.ac.uk

*In reprinting in facsimile from the original, any imperfections are inevitably reproduced and the quality may fall short of modern type and cartographic standards.*

# ERRATUM.

### CRITICAL INTRODUCTION, p. xlv.

*Translations*—should have included a Quarto (pamphlet) Edition, 1648, pp. 119. The Translation is the same as that of 1649. Two copies, bound up with other contemporary pamphlets, are in Advocates' Library. Robert Mylne's MS. note on Montrose's invasion, 1650, has unfortunately been partially destroyed by the binder.

# The Editors' Preface.

HE amount of historical matter brought together in our notes and appendices (much of which is printed for the first time, and was unknown to ourselves at the beginning of our undertaking) obliges us to limit our Preface to a brief memoir of the author, with a passing glance at his times, mainly in special reference to the career of Montrose and his biographer. The difficulty of collecting even the few fragmentary elements for such a notice has been increased by confusion with the life of another Wishart.[1] The times were out of joint; the ancient family to which he belonged was breaking up; hence data sufficient for a complete biography have eluded our search.

George Wishart, born in 1599, was the younger son, as is generally assumed, of John Wishart of Logie Wishart[2] in the county of Forfar, and grandson of Sir John Wishart of that ilk. The family had long been in possession of the estates, having held charters from Gilbert de Umphraville, Earl of Angus, in 1272.[3] In 1526 John Wishart, on resigning his charter from the

---

[1] Following Keith (Catalogue of Scottish Bishops) most writers identify George Wishart with William Wishart, parson of North Leith, who suffered in the same cause.

[2] Inq. Spec. Forfar, 188, 189.

[3] Nisbet's Heraldry, and Jervise' Mem. of Angus and Mearns, ii. 132. The distinguished family of Wishart, according to Jacob Vanhassan, quoted by Nisbet, originated in Robert, a natural son of David, Earl of Huntingdon, who, from a slaughter of Saracens, got the sobriquet Guishart (a derivation not clear). He was the founder of the noble family of Brechin, whose

Earls of Angus, then under forfeiture, received a royal charter[4] converting the estates into a free barony, to be called "the barony of Wishart." This John was perhaps the great-grandfather of our author.

Wishart's father did not come into the property till Sir John died in 1629. Probably, therefore, he had sought other fields than those of Angus, and is said to have made his home in East Lothian. Here George Wishart was born, and according to the same authority the University of Edinburgh was his Alma Mater. But a careful review of the Laureate Roll shows that he did not there take his degree. As at St. Andrews we find a Georgius Vyshart entered in 1612 as a student in St. Salvator's College, and taking his degree in 1613, it is probable that the alumnus of St. Salvator's who became M.A. in one year's time, had received part of his education elsewhere.[5] Did Wishart study first at Edinburgh and take his degree at St. Andrews?

In 1612 the University of St. Andrews was weak at its centre, though things were beginning to improve. Andrew Melvill, who had held rule up to 1608, though a good scholar, was more

---

blazon, "Argent, three piles in point gules," is identical with the shield of the two Wisharts of Pitarrow and Logie Wishart. Nisbet, in describing the Queensberry arms, gives as part of the Douglas contribution to that shield "Argent three piles in point gules for Wisharts of Brechin," the right to carry these "three Passion Nails" having passed to the Douglasses, Earls of Angus, with the heiress of Brechin. From the Brechin stem sprang the two families of Pitarrow and Logie about the same time. The earliest charter evidence is supplied when John of the Mearns witnesses local charters about 1200, and in 1242, when Adam, Abbot of Arbroath, conveys to Pitarrow the mills and lands of Conveth, Scotston, &c. From that time the Pitarrow branch takes a prominent place in Scottish history. William Wishart, Bishop of St. Andrews, was an eminent statesman and prelate, 1256 to 1278. He rebuilt in stately manner the east end of his cathedral, after it had been thrown down by a tempest; Robert, Bishop of Glasgow, one of Edward's regents, joined Wallace, and from his own wardrobe supplied Robert Bruce with coronation robes; John Wishart, Archdeacon of Glasgow, a patriot sent to the Tower of London, released in 1322, became Bishop of Glasgow; Sir James Wishart, Justice-Clerk in 1513, whose son George is supposed to have been the famous Protestant martyr; and lastly, the greedy comptroller of Queen Mary, Sir John, of whom Scotstarvet said, "the laird of Petteraw was an earnest professor of Christ, but the meikle devil receive the comptroller." This was the highest position in wealth and importance attained by the family. From that time it began to decay. The property was sold in 1622 to Sir John Carnegie. See Grub, Eccl. Hist. i. 345 n; Jervise, Mem. of Angus and Mearns, with References, ii. 174-178 and 132.

[4] Acts Parl. Scot., ii. 379, where see charter at length.

[5] Mr. Maitland Anderson, the obliging keeper of the *Acta Rectorum*, in his letter to us says, "It is rather unusual to find a person graduating in the year immediately after his entrance, and the customary explanation is that he may have had a year or more of study at another university before coming here."

a party leader than an administrator. Robert Howie,[6] his successor, was a vicar of Bray, determined, whatever happened, to live and die Principal of St. Mary's. James Martin, Provost of St. Salvator's, was engaged in lifelong struggle with the "proud plunderers who, contrary to justice," had seized the college revenues. Students were few and very young.[7] There was, however, a dawn of hope. King James founded and enriched the library, and sought to restore something of its ancient glory to the ecclesiastical metropolis of Scotland. The titular archbishopric had been revived in the person of George Gladstanes, "a man of good learning, ready utterance, and great invention, but of an easy nature,"[8] on whom anti-Prelatists such as Row, and even Calderwood, lavished foul calumny without stint.[9] His son Alexander, the newly appointed minister of the town church, was a figure likely to impress our youthful scholar. "Handsome, genteel, of a competent estate, an excellent scholar, very eloquent, wise and discreet, free of vice, and in favour with king, court, and country."[10] Alas, that his end should have proved unworthy of this beginning!

For nine years after taking his degree, Wishart's life has left no record, save that he married Margaret Ogilvy, and had two sons, Thomas and Patrick. The lady's name may perhaps account for the glow which tints his narrative of all that concerns the house of Airlie, but her origin is as yet unrecovered history. His opportuneness in writing a book which at once obtained European attention, and his alacrity in printing it, may be some evidence of a touch with continental feeling and with the foreign publisher, gained by travel. In any case, the book is evidence that his youth was not wasted. A degree at fourteen leaves a good deal of time for the education of the Master of Arts, and foreign travel was a natural and ordinary method for obtaining it. Search in the Baptismal Register of St. Andrews shows that that city was

---

[6] Rothes, in his Relation, calls him "the fearfull Robert Howie," meaning timid. St. Mary's still bears his device in stone. He appears frequently in Baillie's letters.

[7] Our author, like the Admirable Crichton, took his M.A. degree at fourteen.

[8] Spottiswoode, History, iii. 227.   [9] See Row, Calderwood, Index, and Book of Pasquils.

[10] See Scott's Fasti, St. Andrews.

not his home when his sons were born, but where it was has yet to be disclosed. Kirk-session records will some day tell. It may be a fair conjecture, from his subsequent intimacy with Spottiswoode and his family, and from his appointment to Monifieth and ordination at Dairsie, that he was well known to the archbishop before 1625. Was he engaged in secretary or librarian work for the metropolitan in St. Andrews, or at Dairsie, his favourite abode?

On Tuesday, September 20, 1625, Wishart received ordination at the hands of Spottiswoode, in his new church of Dairsie, " built at his own cost after the English forme, which," as is quaintly said, " if the boisterous hand of a mad reformation had not disordered, was one of the beautifullest pieces of work that was left to our unhappy country."[11] Wishart had been appointed by the King to the parish of Monifieth in place of Patrick Durham,[12] who died on 23rd August 1624. The date of the appointment is given as August 26, 1624, but this must be a clerical error for 1625, three days being insufficient even for communicating Durham's death to the King. The kirk-session of Monifieth thus notes the ordination and appointment. "The quhilk day, 18th Sep 1625, the Archbishop his Edict was servit at the Kirk doore for admissione of Mr George Wishart to the ministrie of Monifieth on Tuysday nixt the 20th of Sep instant. The 20th of September the said Mr George resavit ordinatione in Dairsey."[13] The ordination was by the "New Ordinal," issued with authority in 1620. There was then no order of deacon in the Church of Scotland, those bearing the name being only lower members of the kirk-session, and exercising secular callings. The ordaining of ministers and consecrating of bishops alone fell within the scope of the Ordinal, and gave to the former power and authority to preach the Word of God, to minister His holy Sacraments, and exercise discipline.

---

[11] Spot. Miscel. i. 7. (The words were written in 1678.) The church had but a short lease of its beauty. In 1641 its "superstitious monuments" were subject of inquiry by the Synod of Fife, and in 1645 an order was given for "the levelling of the queer." The portion of it still standing, seen among its trees, takes one back beyond its date to the architectural spirit of pre-Reformation times. See Sibbald's Fife and New Stat. Account, ix. 773.

[12] Doubtless a relation of the Durhams of Grange, a leading family in the parish. He was thirty-five years of age, and had been only eight years minister. He married the daughter of his predecessor, Andrew Clayhills, in whose time the "mans and gleib were perfyte." Synod Records, Fife, 69.   [13] Parochial Registers (in Register House), Co. of Forfar, vol. ii. (1624-26).

Apparently there had been no service in Monifieth from June 27, 1624, till Wishart's arrival on September 25, 1625, save once in January. The old church [14] was meanwhile being repaired with stones brought down the Tay from the ruins of Balmerino, and carted from the shore by the various heritors. Elders and deacons took charge of such matters, and when Wishart entered upon the incumbency, he found himself in all parochial matters limited to his seat as chairman of the kirk-session. In his preaching he was free. The breakdown of the Church under Roman supremacy had been mainly in morals, and in such an emergency of pastoral failure, common-sense, acting with the democratic spirit of the Reformation, made the parishioners themselves judges of parish morality. The eighth head of the first Book of Discipline laid down that men of "best knawledge in Goddis Word, of cleanest life, men faithfull, and of most honest conversation that can be fund in the church, must be nominat to be in electioun." From these elders and deacons were chosen. Supervision of parochial morals extending to power of divorce, and of the minister to the extent of deposing him, was included within the extensive jurisdiction of these parish magnates.[15] Monifieth could at one time boast of twelve elders and twelve deacons in its session. During Wishart's short tenure of office—from 20th September 1625 to April 3, 1626—the session was occupied with the repairing of the chancel at the expense of the parish.[16] Masons, skleiters, glassen, wrichts, had all to be satisfied, and the work was finished just as Wishart left. The "church yaird" was used, under pretence of "shearing" (*i.e.*, cutting the grass), as a pasture-ground. A sharp penaltie repressed "this abus of beastis," and the whole parish was gathered for getting good walls put round the sacred enclosure "after the bairseed." A high price was put upon "kirk burial" (*i.e.*, burial within the kirk), "lest it ouirgo the hole kirk." Sunday desecrations, as working of mills, playing "gouff," ale-drinking in

---

[14] The ancient church was on the site of a Culdee chapel, which had replaced a pre-Christian sacred enclosure. See Sculptured Stones of Scotland, Anderson's Early Christian Times, and New Stat. Account, Scotland.

[15] See Kirk-session Register of St. Andrews, Pref. xxii.

[16] A point which indicated the settlement of an old dispute as to whether the parson should not repair the chancel at his own expense. See Dunlop Paroch. Law, 4.

time of service, slackness in church attendance on the part of the ferry-people, are dealt with; and in the case of the ale-drinking two elders were dispensed from service that they might perambulate the town. The poor were seen to out of the collections and fines, and even "Inglish" supplicants, such as John Bull and Richard Ives, are generously supplied, the latter getting 24s. Scots. The bulk of the session's work, however, lay in dealing with unhallowed unions, some of them "inveterate." Michael Ramsay and a frail Euphemia were well acquainted with all the stages of "citation," "appearance," "repentance," and "penalty;" and their relatives, after frequent forfeiture of bail for future good behaviour, gave them up. Michael was on his way to the higher court, the Presbytery, when we part with him in these records.[17] The "presumful abus" of drunkenness does not much appear in this part of the record. Perhaps the memory of the culprit who, in the first vigour of the session, had been sentenced to be "brankit, stockit, dukit, and banisit ye heile paris," had still survived as a warning against the "vyce." We may hope too that the vigour of Wishart's sermons obviated the necessity experienced by the session in the time of his successor, in 1643, of keeping the women awake. "Five shillings for tar to put upon the women that holds the playds about their head in the church"[18] is surely an indefensible barbarity perpetrated on the poor sufferers under long sermons. Sermons were by this time regarded as wholesome penalties. Poor Helen Scott, for "sclandering and flyting," got a daily attendance on the preaching, and that in a visible part of the church, within sight of the minister. She had a choice which some might have preferred, viz., "the jougs" and banishment. William Carmichael, in Wishart's time, called Isobel Webster a "thief," and stuck to his guns for one session, but satisfied by penalty and repentance in the next. The only matter of personal interest to our author appearing in these records[19] is the baptism

---

[17] Grissel Kid is cited for her fornication with William Durham, a reversal of the order we should have expected. Was the session tuned by the rage of the laird of Grange, who would naturally regard Grissel as the seducer of his son, and not *vice versâ*? Durham does penance, however.

[18] See Aberdeen Eccl. Records for notice of like and other extraordinary customs.

[19] The Parochial Registers of Monifieth in the Register House, though decayed in parts, are, on

of his daughter Jean, on Friday, December 23, 1625. The witnesses were Thomas Wishart of Ballindarg,[20] Wishart's second cousin; John Durham,[21] minister of Monikie, who died father of the Church in 1639, "an aul agit man" (his memory went back to the proceedings of 1560); and William Maule, in Giuldie.[22] This was his third child. She shared the vicissitudes of her father's fortunes, and appears in his will as the spouse of William Walker, minister of North Berwick.

Wishart's last service in Monifieth was on April 3rd, 1626, and on April 10th he took up his duties in the Town Church of St. Andrews as colleague to Alexander Gladstanes. John Rutherford, from Dairsie, now more given to physic than to theology, succeeded him at Monifieth.

The change to St. Andrews no doubt meant more money, but it also brought him into the society in Scotland most agreeable to a man of scholarly tastes. The policy of strengthening the bishops had had a wholesome effect in rousing a movement for restoration of things befitting the name and ancient glory of the first cathedral and university city of Scotland. There were plans for rebuilding the cathedral and repairing the colleges. The New Library was being enriched day by day. Dairsie was a pattern for parochial churches. Liturgical revision, and restoration of church and college costume, were accompanied with the solid good of restored tithes. Church, college, and castle were all putting on something of a brighter garb under the new régime. Sir Robert Spottiswoode had returned with his spoils recovered from foreign libraries, whither flying ecclesiastics had carried them on the first outbreak of the Reformation. In especial, the Black Book of Paisley was restored to Scotland by his hand. His and his father's books were reckoned to be worth £6000 sterling. The number of students increased, and the sons of the great families of Scotland naturally sought

---

the whole, in a good state of preservation. They go back to 1552, and indicate zeal for morals from the start. We are indebted to the Rev. W. Macleod for transcript of portion belonging to Wishart's time, and to Dr. Young the present minister of the parish for valuable notes.

[20] Ballindarg was originally included in the barony of Wishart, but had passed to a branch of the house. See Inq. Spec. and Gen. Forfarshire.

[21] Scott Fasti, Monikie.

[22] We cannot identify this place. The word may be Dundee badly written.

education at St. Andrews. Montrose entered Wishart's old college on January 26, 1627, and he was preceded by Lord Lorn (his future enemy, Argyll), the Earl of Morton, the Earl of Wemyss, Lord Robert Douglas, and a host of other good Scottish names are his contemporaries. Hunting, hawking, horse-racing, archery, golf, and tennis provided the recreations represented by the outdoor pastimes of the modern undergraduate. Classics, poetry, romance, chess, and cards, with frequent visits to country houses, in Montrose's case, and doubtless in that of others, filled up the time stolen from severer studies.[23] The Golf Links and Archery Butts brought together gay gatherings, when the silver arrow[24] or the championship had to be won. The important, though sometimes despised, culinary art was well forward in those days in Scotland. As Napier says, "they knew how to live as well as how to die. Their domestic records of the larder, the pantry, and the cellar, whether in reference to the funeral, the wedding, or the sick chamber, might create an appetite under the ribs of death." He is referring to the accounts of expenditure kept by the young Montrose's purse-bearer.[25] These accounts suggest scenes of deep interest, when they tell of the hiring of "three extra horses for my Lord's visit to the Archbishop of St. Andrews at Dairsy." The scaffold and exile ended the days of the home party and their guest, and probably of many more who were wont to meet in the hospitable mansion. Montrose himself, his friend Sir Robert "the good President," and young Dairsy died by the hand of the executioner. The Archbishop died in exile, and Sir John, his eldest son, escaped only by the loss of his property. There was east wind at St. Andrews of more than one kind, and much anxiety from the vigorous sombre spirits of the first Reformation, who were preparing for the second, when an opening should appear. Yet on the whole

---

[23] For the facts of this picture compare Lyon's Hist., Napier Mem., Sprott's Scottish Liturgies, Connell on Tithes, Billing's Baronial Remains, Preface to Sir Robert Spottiswoode's Practicks.

[24] Napier gives an engraving of Montrose's medal as a winner of the silver arrow in 1628, and a facsimile of his name as entered by himself in the Matriculation Roll, Jan. 26, 1627, "Aetat 14. Jacobus Gramus, Comes Monterouse."

[25] Napier, Mem., Chap. iv., &c.

it was a pleasant place for a man who loved books, good society, and (no doubt) good wine.

Mr. John Lambye's accounts show that Montrose stood on terms of intimacy with Wishart. On leaving St. Andrews for his early wedding, his trunks were intrusted to the minister's care. "Item given to the minister, Mr George Wishart his servants, who had kept and transported the furniture and trunks, twenty four shillings."[26] The numerous entries we have found in the St. Andrews Register[27] of the baptism of Wishart's children evince a comfortable relationship with Church, college, county, and city, inasmuch as the sponsors are the Archbishop, Sir John and Sir Robert Spottiswoode, Sir James Sandilands, Dr. Martyne, Gladstanes the Archdean, Dr. Howie, the Provost John Carstairs, and the eminent citizen Hew Scrymgeour, who so took to heart the death of Sir Robert Spottiswoode, his old master's son, that the sight of the scaffold, some days after the event, sent him home to die on his own threshold. The child to which he was sponsor was named Huego after him.

Such a family and such society in St. Andrews required means, but happily there was an improvement in ministers' stipends. The admirably conceived and courageously executed policy of Charles First to restore the tithes of the Church was the one statesman-like and successful act of his reign of lasting benefit to the stipends of the present Presbyterian Establishment. It was an Act, however, resented by the nobility, the great impropriators of tithes, who dreaded the threatened Act of Revocation, a still more drastic measure.[28] Yet with the immense boon conferred on every other class, and with the relaxing of the Articles of

---

[26] Napier, Mem., 70.

[27] Register House. The names of Wishart's children were Thomas and Patrick, born before 1625. Jean, baptized Monifieth, December 23, 1625. Margaret, baptized St. Andrews, May 26, 1628. Robert, baptized October 14, 1629. Marie, baptized June 16, 1631. Huego, August 10, 1632. A child unnamed, baptized January 15, 1634. James, baptized February 3, 1637. All the children who came after Robert died before their father's imprisonment in 1644. He had then only five children, and the names above, including Robert, appear in Wishart's will shortly before his death. The Provost's descendant was the well-known Principal William Carstares.

[28] See Connell on Tithes, *passim*, also his quotation from Vigneul Marville of remarks of Clarendon on the importance of the tithes question in bringing about the Revolution. Cf. Burnet, Dukes of H., "the whole progress of the design for the resumption of the Tithes into the crown

Perth, Charles could afford to despise their opposition, and might have done so to the end had his next measures been conceived with the same common-sense. But they insulted the self-respect and the religious sense of the nation, made opposition patriotic, and undid their author and his friends. The nobles now saw their chance, coalesced with the opposition ministers, gained many of the moderate sort, and roused the nation.

In 1629 John Wishart succeeded his father Sir John in his estates, and this event may have improved Wishart's position. He became a D.D. of St. Andrews,[29] and appears in the dignity on the roll of the Court of High Commission, Oct. 21, 1634. The storm was now, however, brewing which was to cast down crown and mitre, and Wishart with them. He was, however, to see both restored, and was himself to become a bishop.

Our want of space forbids any attempt to tell again the story of the rise of the Covenant and fall of the King. Loyalty in Scotland had not risen much beyond devotion to feudal chief or head of clan, and the King as King at no time had focussed the national life. In Charles' case, he was unknown in his native land, and report of his English contempt for Scotland made him suspected. His representatives in the kingdom were mostly self-seeking, weak, or treacherous, and the nobles were on the defensive, while a deep undercurrent of repressed religious feeling pervaded the nation. Here surely was a most unhappy time in which to try experiments in absolute government in Church and State. Many were his mistakes in the experiment—his long deferred coronation, with the insulting proposal for bringing the Scottish regalia to England; the prominence of Laud in Scottish Church affairs and coronation ceremonies; the King's appearance with pencil in hand to note opponents in his first Parliament; the Balmerino trial on the *Infamous Libel;* the replacing of peer and lawyer by bishops in offices of state; the Book of Canons,

---

and the restoring them to the church" had much influence. See also Large Declaration; Acts Parl. Scot. v. 189-219; Gardiner, Hist. Eng. vii. 277, where story of Act of Revocation is condensed. Grub, Eccl. Hist. ii. 336, 337. Gard. quotes Poetical Remains, *ed.* Maidment.

[29] James brought in the "noveltie," says Calderwood, "without advice or consent of the Kirk," yet in 1569 he records an Act of Assembly as to proceeding by degrees in schools to the degree of "Doctor of Divinitie." Ch. vii. 222, ii. 478, and Lyon's St. Andrews, ii. 193-198.

issued without ecclesiastical countenance; and the Prayer Book, imposed by Royal authority alone—these mistakes, had the King's purposes been ever so beneficial for the country, would have ruined them. The stool of Jenny Geddes (whether she existed or no) symbolised that which discharged a deep mine of discontent in Scotland. Laud's policy had alienated Spottiswoode and the bishops from touch with the nation, and made them merely servants of the King. They failed to make a stand, and lead the nation against the royal claim to dictate without the Church in Church affairs. Alexander Henderson stepped into the deserted position, and fought the battle of Kirk freedom till it became exaggerated into the license of ecclesiastical tyranny. His petition against the "bookes," though careful and judicious, yet sounded the note which gathered the people. Its echo in our own time founded the Free Kirk. Rothes, Loudon, and Balmerino had neither brains nor religion enough for a great struggle; Henderson had both, and his accession to their party resulted in the *General Supplication* which, for their personal safety, brought the Privy Council to their knees before the supplicants—the riots of September and October 1637 had convinced them of their strength. The cry of "Poperie at the door," maintained on English pamphlets, which, new every day, did "adde oyl to this flame," made dangerous any stand for the King. "I think our people to be possessed of a bloody devil far above anything that ever I could have imagined though the masse in Latin had been presented. The ministers who has the command of their mind does disavow their unchristian humour, but are noways so zealous against the devill of their furie as they are against the seducing spirit of the Bishops."[30] Rothes and the minister of Methven, by "travail" and "canniness," brought Montrose (*aetat. ca.* 24) to the great meeting of November 15th, which resulted in *the Tables*, and gave the future champion of the King a place on the committee of four nobles in that body so deadly to the throne. The *National Covenant* gave them an enthusiastic backing from the bulk of the nation. Below we shall say something on this important

---

[30] Baillie, Letters, i. 23.

bond, but here we may give in David Mitchell's words the situation as it affected the loyal clergy, and our author among them. "It (the Covenant) is the oath of the King's House 1580, with strange additions, a mutual combination for resistance of all novations in religion, doctrine, and discipline and rites of worship that have bin brought in since that tyme; so as if the least of the subscrivers be touched (and there be some of them not 10 yeers of age, and some not worth 2^d·) that all shall concurre for their defence, and for the expulsion of all papists and adversaries (*i.e.*, all that will not subscribe) out of the Church and Kingdome, according to the lawes, whereof a hundred are cited in the Carta. This goes on apace. The true Pastors are brought in to Edin^r. to cry out against us wolves; and they with our brethren here—Ramsay and Rollock—and your whilome friend the Principall (crying out that they are neither good Christians nor good subjects that do not subscribe, nay, nor in Covenant with God) have made us so odious, that we dare not goe on the streets. I have been dogged by some gentlemen, and followed with many mumbled threatnings behind my back, and then, when I was up staires swords drawne, and 'if they had the Papist villaine, O.' Yet I thank God I am living to serve God and the King and the Church and your Lordship. Your chiefe (Rothes) is the chiefe in this business. There is nothing expected here but civill warre!"[31]

The archbishop saw the work of thirty years cast to the ground, and with other bishops and nobles went southward at the beginning of April. Wishart, with Dr. Panter and Andrew Learmont[32] fled from St. Andrews and joined Spottiswoode at Morpeth, our author proceeding with him to Newcastle, and perhaps to London. There is a gap in the session records of the kirk of St. Andrews at this time, but the official has done his best, though not successfully, to give unity to his fragments.[33] That Wishart left St. Andrews

---

[31] Baillie, Letters, i. App. xxvii. p. 464. Letter to John Lesly, Bishop of Raphoe.

[32] Howie, Bruce, Martin, and Baron subscribed the Covenant, and Gladstanes allowed it to be read in church, but preached no more himself. Baillie, Letters, i. 98.

[33] "After 1 April no session kept; ther omissions was becaus off the Magistratis elders and deacons of this session their subscryving of the Covenant agaynst their ministeris myndis or consent so that they did not concurre together for keeping of the Session as likwyis the whole citie except some verie few did subscryve the said confession of faith contained in the said Covenant" (Marriage

with a good character and against the wishes of his people, is proved beyond contradiction by the action of the Glasgow Assembly towards him. That body, as the legitimate expression of the Divine voice, summoned before them all the bishops and uncovenanted clergy. The bishops indiscriminately were accused of horrible crimes and frivolous offences, the word *respective* being inserted in the common charge to save decency, without diminishing vulgar odium.[34] Quite gleefully Baillie tells us "This day we put sundrie of the Bishops through our hands . . . pronounced him [Edinburgh] to be deprived and excommunicat; . . . we decreed him [Aberdeen] to be excommunicat," and so on. This body, which dealt with the superiors they had promised to obey with all the recklessness of an irresponsible tribunal, had Wishart's case before them on December 4, 1638. "The toun of St Andrews complained that their minister Dr Wishart had deserted them above 8 months; they seemed content enough with the man's life and doctrine if he would returne, and acknowledge

---

Reg. vol. $\frac{453}{5}$). After entries of baptisms, ending 9th April 1638, is a note to the effect that the baptisms preceding that date had been performed by Dr. Alex. Gladstanes, archdean, and Dr. George Wishart, minister" (Bap. Reg. vol. $\frac{453}{1}$). Gladstanes, however, baptizes June 4th, 1638, the son of Robertson of Clermonth. After entry of 4th September 1638 we have the following:—"All this tyme Bygone was no Session holdin nather haid the Presbitrie gevin out any ordinance theranent till Wadinsday the 12 of Sept it was ordaneit that everie minister that preached here, in their course about, suld convene the Session and moderat the samyn till it pleased God to procure a settled ministerie for this citie" (vol. $\frac{453}{5}$). After entry July 1st, 1638, "Nota—About this tyme and before our last ministeris preaching for the Covenant and uthoris supplied as you see they ar partlie here insert and moir particularlie and specially are insert in the booke of the poores common collection at the Kirk doores with the ministeris that baptized the bairnis I mean collation the dayis together of the moneth and the year" (*ibid.*). By October the overthrow of King's and Archbishop's work is thus indicated:—"*Sunday 21st October* 1638.—Quhilk day the Holie Communion was celebrat with great Solemnitie in the old fashion sitting, My old Lady Marquess of Hamilton, my Lord Lyndesay, and sundrie utheris baronis Ladyes and gentlemen strangers being present thereat, the bellis rang at three houris to the mornyng service. The ministeris thereof wer, Mr George Hamilton haid the preparatioun sermon, Mr Andrew Auchinlek the mornyng, and Mr Alexander Hendersone the foirnoone service, and Mr David Forret the sermone of Thanksgiving. The Magistratis and cheiff of the Session attending the services, the brodis, basonis [? alms dishes, patens, and chalices] and Elements." (Reg. of Marriages, vol. $\frac{453}{5}$).

[34] The unreality of these charges is evinced by the appointment of the three bishops who afterwards took the Covenant to cure of souls, without more ado, though they had lain under these horrible charges. Baillie's account of the Assembly should be read to understand the situation. How Montrose could continue to sit in such an assembly is unaccountable.

the Assemblie: howbeit malitious desertions so long a tyme be sufficient for deposition yet we referred the case to farder consideration. We deposed Dr. Gladstanes with one mouth."[35] Again, under December 14th, we read, "St Andrews Complaint against Dr Wishart who had deserted them for manie moneths was heard; their supplication also that they might have Mr A. Henderson for minister." The case was still left over, and not till 1639, after being absent eighteen months, was he deposed. The charges then were heavy enough, but there was no bringing an action for libel at that time against the judicatories of the Assembly, and the only remedy now is to appraise their valuelessness. Judgment was the main thing, evidence a trifle of secondary importance.

Early in May 1637 Spottiswoode, in London, took part in a conference with the King, Laud, Bishop Maxwell, and Hamilton, and presented the complaints as to bad treatment of the bishops left in Scotland and their clergy, brought up by Andrew Learmont.[36] Hamilton was decided on as the peace-maker, and the bishops were advised to return to Scotland under his safe keeping. They went to Newcastle, but were too wise to go farther on the strength of the promises of that weak and shifty guardian. The archbishop took up his abode in Newcastle early in 1639, and we find Wishart appointed to a lectureship in All Saints there on 19th October of that year.[37] Spottiswoode returned to London, where he died 26th November 1639,[38] worn out with the troubles of his age, and oppressed with the gloomy prospects of his Church.

For sequence of events in Scotland our dates at page 18 may be consulted, to which we shall refer in speaking of Montrose's earlier and later attitude. Meanwhile we note the few facts known as to Wishart's life at this time. The King's

---

[35] Baillie, i. 151.
[36] Burnet, Dukes of Ham., 41.
[37] Brand's Hist. of Newcastle, i. 387. Robert Jennison, S.T.P., had been lecturer from 1622. In 1631 a subscription had been raised for his "better encouragement." For nonconformity he was suspended in 1639. W. took his place, and with him was associated (December 17, 1639) Robert Bonner, who suffered suspension and imprisonment in the Royal cause during the Civil War.
[38] Preface to Spottiswoode's History, cxxx., where see his confession of faith and his will.

failure with his subjects both north and south, and the good understanding between the revolutionary parties in both kingdoms, made the position of a "malignant" clergyman very trying, even in Newcastle. It would seem, however, that in 1640[39] Wishart was appointed to an afternoon lectureship at St. Nicholas, which he could hold with his other preferment. He was in the enjoyment of these offices when his old enemies the Covenanters, with his young friend Montrose still in their ranks, though now sick of the connection, disturbed his peace. Doubtless he aided the good citizens and Astley's force in repairing the fortifications as best they might against the advancing Scottish army, but with Gateshead unfortified, their work was of little avail. Leslie made for the open side of the town, meaning to cross the Tyne at Newburn. Conway left half his force in garrison, and with the remainder marched out to guard the ford where all should have been. On 30th August Leslie was in Newcastle, drinking the King's health, to the Mayor's surprise. Wishart retired with the garrison, having lost all but life. Doubtless Wishart kept away till Leslie recrossed the Tweed, which was not till September 25, 1641. On his way to Edinburgh the King was entertained at Newcastle by the rough old soldier, to whom he promised an earldom.[40] Wishart returned to his duty in Newcastle, and though the journal of the House of Commons, June 18, 1642, records his dismissal from his preferment as a frequenter of taverns, it is probable that the occupation of the town by the Earl of Newcastle, June 17th, made this order a *brutum fulmen*.

On May 12, 1643 we have the notice "Afternoon Lectureship," St. Nicholas, "Dr. Wiseheart, or Wishart, was appointed to this Lectureship."[41] The Vicar of Newcastle from 1630 was Yeldard Alvey.[42] Prynne calls him the Arminian and superstitious vicar of Newcastle. In Wishart he found a fellow-worker. The

---

[39] Scott's Fasti, Wishart.

[40] In the records as given by Brand we have the following notices of the Scottish occupation of Newcastle. St. Andrews Parish, Oct. 25, 1640, "one of the Redshanks buried of the Scottes army. Feb. 9, 1640 (? 41), Thomas Karr and Jane Lanton married—one of the Scottes army and would pay nothing to the church."

[41] Brand, i. 312.

[42] May 26, 1645, he was removed by order of Lords and Commons.

King set up the Royal Standard at Nottingham, Aug. 22, 1642.[43] The Scottish army, bought by the English Parliament's submission to the new Solemn League and Covenant (wherein Vane nevertheless outwitted Henderson), again crossed the Border, 20,000 strong, "in a dismal snowie season," 15th January 1644. The snow was knee deep, "and blowing and snowing so vehemently that the guides could with great difficulty know the way, and it was enough for the followers to discern the leaders." With the snow there came "a frost so great (the like whereof we had not seen) that in two nights the river of Twede freesed so strong that our army and ammunition, which was at Kelso, marched over upon the ice, which otherwise could not have come over."[44]

On Saturday, Feb. 3rd, Leven drew up before Newcastle; but the Marquis of Newcastle had thrown himself with a strong force into the town, and the summons of the Scots met with a spirited answer from the Mayor, Sir John Marley, and the common council. The circuit of the walls was "2 miles 239$^{yds}$ 1$^{ft}$."[45] A considerable number of houses lay outside the walls, and these were all burned down, so as to deprive the besiegers of cover. By the 22nd February the siege slackened, and Leven moved on Sunderland, leaving about Newcastle six regiments of foot and some horse. Then began the manœuvring about Bowden Hill and Hilton, and Montrose came upon the scene demanding help from the struggling Marquis.[46] By the 8th of April, Leven, who had acted on the defensive, resolved in concert with Fairfax, to attack, and marching from Easington to Quarrendon Hill, drew up within two miles of Durham, where Newcastle lay. Pursued by Leven, the Royalist general fell back on York, which he entered, April 19th, taking with him a strong contingent from the garrison of Newcastle town. Montrose having failed at Dumfries, made with Crawford a diversion in the north of England by the siege of Morpeth in the early part of May,[47] and he was then in free communication with Newcastle, and doubtless with Wishart, who was pursuing his clerical duties within the well defended walls.

---

[43] Gardiner, Hist. Eng. x. 219, where see interesting notes.
[44] From "The Siege and Storming of Newcastle," p. 5.
[45] Ibid. 9.    [46] See p. 42.    [47] P. 46, n. 4.

THE EDITORS' PREFACE. xxi

The battle of Marston Moor was fought on 2nd July, and Leven turned northward again. Callander, with a fresh army from Scotland, had crossed the Tyne at Newburn, taken Lumly and Stockton Castles and Hartlepool, and turned back to the Tyne. Gateshead was his first point of attack, which he carried in two days, and obtained command of half the Tyne bridge. This was in the beginning of August. Meantime Leven was approaching to take up the siege in earnest. To oppose him were some "1700 men made up of 800 of the train-band and 900 volunteers, forest-men, colliers, keilmen, and poore tradesmen. In the town also were the Scottish Lords Crawford, Rea, and Maxwell. These, taking a different side to the great bulk of their countrymen, fought for the king behind the walls." [48] Throughout the siege George Wishart continued to deliver his lectures, inspiriting the defence. Some of these have come into the possession of the Rev. W. D. Macray, Assistant-Librarian of the Bodleian, who, on learning our interest in the matter, has most kindly allowed us to make extracts from the interesting volume. The note [49]

---

[48] Lithgow quoted in "The Siege and Storming of Newcastle," 19.

[49] The quarto volume, bound in calf, has the book plate of George Chalmers, Esq., F.R.S.S.A., and a note by Mr. Macray, giving some account of its history. It appeared in "Part III. of Chalmers' Auct. Cat., 1842, as No. 1695, and in Part IV. of the Cat. of Jos. Lilly's stock (the London Bookseller), at whose sale it was bought by Salkeld, bookseller, of Orange Street, Red Lion Square, for 3s., of whom I bought it in March 1873 for 5s. All the three catalogues described the volume as containing sermons of the latter part of the 16th century." Mr. Macray proceeds: "These anonymous sermons for Saints' days and Ascension Day are written in a Scottish hand. They were preached at a lecture by one who had been recently appointed lecturer in a town then besieged by Parliamentary forces. It had been besieged for some months, and successfully defended by a handful. The Mayor had been elected to that office for a third time. Two gates are mentioned, Westgate and Sandgate ; a shot fired from the former slew 'a whole crew of enemies,' and at the latter a blow had been averted. Mention is also made of a narrow escape of the blowing up of the powder magazine, and of a shot passing between the Mayor and his sword-bearer on the day of his election.

"It appears from the foregoing allusions that the town was Newcastle-upon-Tyne, and the preacher George Wishart, chapl : to the Marq : of Montrose, and afterwards Bishop of Edinburgh. For Newcastle was besieged by the Scottish army from Feb. to Oct. 1644, when it was taken ; and Sir John Marley was Mayor for the 3rd time in that year. There were gates of the abovementioned names there. Wishart was appointed lecturer at S$^t$ Nicholas, 12 May 1643, as stated in Brand's Hist. of Newcastle. He had been lecturer at All Saints' from 1639. (For the authorship of the one sermon in a different hand, there does not appear to be any clue.)

"The writer of the sermons says that he had written on the question of the original language of St. Matthew's Gospel."

So far Mr. Macray's note. We have ourselves remarked the following, and made an extract

xxii                    THE EDITORS' PREFACE.

below will give the history of the volume and a sketch of its contents.

---

from the sermon on St. Michael and All Angels, as specially interesting to our readers in the "canny town."

On a spare leaf at the beginning is written, Auxilium nostrum sit in nomine Domini qui fecit cœlum et terram! Also, in darker ink—

> Raro aconita bibuntur
> fictilibus, tunc illa time cum pocula sumes
> Gemata, et late setinum ardebit in auro.

---

Dicite pontifices in sacris quid facit aurum?

---

The sermons are on—1. S. John the Baptist; 2. S. Matthew and the Apostles; 3. S. Peter; 4. S. James; 5. S. Bartholomew; 6. S. Matthew the Publican; 7. S. Michael and All Angels. A sermon in another hand, on the text, "When He was come near, He beheld the city and wept over it." In the original handwriting, fourteen lines on the text, "These are they which came out of great tribulation,"—evidently part of a sermon for All Saints' Day. Was it cut short by the taking of the town, October 19th?

In the second handwriting the text for a sermon, Prov. xx. 1 : "Wine is a mocker, and strong drink is raging, and whosoever is deceived thereby, is not wise." A long sermon in original hand on Gal. iv. 4. Next comes a short sermon on the Ascension, Mark xvi. 19. A sermon on the Coming of the Spirit, having a reference to the previous discourse, follows, the text being Cor. iii. 16, 17.

The following extract from the Lecture on St. Michael and All Angels will present the reader with some features of Wishart's character and style.

"Come I now then to my exhortation, and I shall deliver it in the very words of Joab to Abishai his brother, and to the Host of Israel, when they fought against the children of Ammon. 'Let us be of good courage and play the men, and behave ourselves valiantly, and God will do what seemeth Him best;' and let no man say 'Oh our help is far from us,' for if our eyes were but opened we might perhaps see all the mountains about us full of those fiery chariots and horses, so that they were more that were for us, than all that are against us. I attest the consciences of you all when you look back again to the weeks and months of this siege which are already passed, and call to mind your own opinions and judgements; what thought you that this handful of ours could not only have resisted that equally mighty and malicious enemy; but also so often beaten, killed, and taken them in their very forts and works, in so far that our friends are stricken with admiration and joy, our enemies with amazement and fear, and ourselves more encouraged and strengthened than at the first hours? and from whom is this I pray you? I will not definitely say from the present and ready ministry of the Angels, for I know that God is not tied to use their services but when and where He pleaseth (and yet I think the ministry of the Angels the most likely and probable means that can be alledged) but sure I am it is from the Lord of Angels who as He creates, so He also ruleth, and disposeth all things *verbo omnipotentiæ suæ*, and that is enough. Let Him but say the word as the faithful Centurion witnessed, and we his servants shall be saved. I know the minds of many, and the very speeches of some. 'O say they when cometh our help from such or such great men,' and I know not what princes, 'they stay too long, we shall not be able to await their coming,' &c. What impatient murmuring is all this? What distrust and diffidence! What tempting of God! for first I tell you that I am of good hope that that very human help, those same noble princes are nearer than we are aware, and may come in a good time ; but are we Christians, and do we not look higher, to the King of kings and princes, whose sure forces are always present, and ready, whose arms are ever on them, whose armies fly with wings swifter than the wings of the wind, who in a night, in an hour, in an instant, can, and will, deliver us, and defeat greater armies than our enemies, if we be not wanting to ourselves.

By Michaelmas things were getting very serious. "Colliers of Elswick and Benwell were employed under John Osbourn, a

---

First we being faint-hearted and discouraged, that is to say distrustful infidels who have no faith, next in being needy and avaricious wretches, we will not open our garners, our cellars, our purses, to the needy soldier and the poor neighbour; that's again to say, worse than infidels and to deny the faith. I know that many of you would take it in a great huff and indignation if I should say that you were very cowards who would not hazard your persons and limbs in so good a cause; and what a miser art thou, who will give thy life, and will not give thy loaf of bread; who will give thy person, and will not give thy purse in that same cause. If we had but hearts of men in us, the poorest of the town needed neither want meat nor clothes yet for a long time, even until the Lord should give us help from his holy place. Neither let any man say that I preach and press this doctrine much upon others, but am as backward from the practice of it as any else, saying I am like the Pharisee who laid heavy burthens upon other men's shoulders &c. Nay I hope I am not so base. Most of you know very well that I am a man who cannot brag much of my riches, yet will I not complain much of my poverty, but as I am, I am ready to lay down at the feet of our rulers, as much spare clothes as will help to apparel, as much good plate as will help to maintain half-a-dozen of soldiers until we get what help the Lord shall send us; neither shall I keep up a spoon or a blanket unbestowed, before any poor soldier or neighbour wants, but bestowed in the hands of our rulers, to be dispensed in an orderly way, and I take God to witness that if I had either spare corn or coin, it should all go that same way. For to lay aside all argument taken from humanity, from country, from Christianity I pray you what will your corn and coin avail you if yourselves, and your town, and all that you have, come into the hands of those bloodgales (*sic*) who after so many great spoils, cannot yet say *satis?* And lastly, if we be not wanting in humbling ourselves, and seeking the Lord's face, in turning from our wicked ways, and making prayers and supplications with strong crying and tears until he have mercy upon us, and in offering unto Him the sacrifice of praise, &c. . . .

"But I now endeavour to raise up your hearts to remember a recent experience or two of this, that our souls may be the better quickened to bless and praise the God of angels for some singular services of this kind. Who amongst us was so wise and vigilant as to foresee and so prevent that blow intended against us by blowing up of our own powder, whereby many of us had been miserably massacred, and the rest made an easy prey and spoil to our cruel enemies? When a great part of the match was burnt, when the fire was come within a finger length of the powder, and we all sleeping secure, who was there so ready with water to quench that fire, to prevent that blow, and not only to preserve us, but that same powder, to work much vengeance upon our enemies? Sure I am, God Himself was the Author of that deliverance, and if by the ministry of any second cause, surely none so likely as this of our text, that of some holy angel at His charge and command. And blesséd be His name for it, for evermore. So yet more recent amongst many notable experiences of that kind since the beginning of this siege, on Monday last, the day of the election of our Magistrate, when that thundering shot came between the sword-bearer and our chiefest Magistrates, who pulled them back, and made them halt the while? Who interposed his shield to receive it, or his dagger to divert, and put it by? Who did it? Sure I am it was only God, and likelier no means than this same ministry of the angels, at His charge and command. So, who took the aim, who gave the fire, to that our piece at West gate, whose breach was covered with their pieces which caw'd (Scotch for knocked) a crew of our enemies to the ground at once? Surely He who directed the stone of David's sling against the brain pan of Goliath, who maketh His arrows sharp in the hearts of the king's enemies; and by no ministry more likely than that of His Angels at His charge and command.

"And now howbeit this be a general doctrine, and a duty belonging to all men, yet must I tell you, and I pray you advert unto it, that it more especially concerns you that are Magistrates whom God hath also made liturgical persons, howbeit not spirits, and sent you also forth to minister for His people, to whom He hath given charge to keep, to nurse, to lead, to rule the same in all their

false rebellious Scot, to undermine the walls, which they did, and blew them up and so got and plundered the town."[50] The eloquence of Wishart, the fighting determination of the Mayor, and the reputation of Crawford were all needed to maintain spirit in the defence. Wishart's cassock scarce concealed the soldier within him. The fatal day arrived, the 19th October, when Leven carried the town, and Wishart, with the Mayor and Scottish lords, sought refuge in the Castle, which they held out till the 22nd. He had begun to prepare an All Saints' Day lecture in a spirit prophetic of earthly woe and heavenly consolations, his text being, "These are they which came out of great tribulation" (Rev. vii. 14); but he had only written a few lines when his quarters were beaten up for the third time by the Covenant. He had established a home in Newcastle, and doubtless it was cleared of all his possessions—his third loss of all things.[51] Leven gave no terms, and Sir John Marley and his companions surrendered at discretion. The noblemen and the clergyman, with the prisoners from Ribble Bridge—Lord Ogilvy[52] and others—were, after a little delay, sent to Edinburgh, where the prisons were already choked with captives. The Thieves' Hole received our author.

Imprisonment had its degrees in Scotland as elsewhere. To be "wardit" in your own house with a long purse and plenty of friends might not be altogether unpleasant; to be "wardit" in the house of a criminal officer had alleviations which money or friends could purchase; to be sent to the Castle meant some air and exercise; but the Thieves' Hole meant bad company, scanty food, foul bedding, dim light, and a stench even worse than the stench of the neighbouring close through the Luckenbooths, named the "stinking style." Wishart's experience of the Hole for nearly

---

ways, and joined in that same service with the blesséd Angels of Heaven, to whom as He hath committed the name and dignity, so hath He much more the service and duty."

Then follows, after some scriptural quotations, a strongly worded exhortation to the magistrates, and especially to the mayor, who is addressed as " our thrice repeated Mayor and Governour."

Sir John Marley escaped from prison after the surrender of Newcastle; and after the Restoration was twice elected mayor. His neck was to have met with " Straffords Courtesie," but he died in his bed in 1670.

[50] Brand, Hist. Newcastle, 467 n.

[51] Who took possession of the precious MS. vol. in which Wishart had just begun his All Saints' lecture?   [52] See pp. 48 and 49, n. 9.

twelve months made him a friend of prisoners for ever. In the days of his episcopate he could not enjoy the good things of his table till he had sent some of them up to the Tolbooth to alleviate the hunger pangs of his Covenanting successors in the place of suffering.

We gather that Wishart's family had gone with him to Newcastle, as he speaks there of a house, blankets, and plate; but they soon followed him to Edinburgh in woeful plight. At the end of 1644 the poor man, counting on a kindly side in the Covenanting heart for a kindly Scot, petitioned Parliament for something for himself and his family with this result, 28th January 1645:—

"*Prayeres said. Rolles called.*

"*Reference in favoures of M[r] George Wisharte.*

"The Estates of Parliament Haveing heard and Considdered the petitione Givine in be M[r] George Wishart Minister Desyreing some reas[ll] mentenance to him his wyfe and fyve childrine so longe as he is Detenit in prisone be the estates in the Tolbooth of Ed[r] where he remaines incarcerat wanteing meanes to menteane themselves And craveing warrand that his wyffe and childrine may have accese to visite him at all occasiones The estates Remittes the foir[d] supplicatione and Desyre thereof to the committie appoynted for provyding of moneyes To grant modificatione to the supplicant for interteaneing of him his wyfe and childrine Dureing his aboade and deteineing in waird be the estates And that according as that committie shall thinke ffitt."

By this time Montrose had won his battles of Tippermuir and Aberdeen, and was ravaging Argyll, but Kilsyth was yet far distant. The spring and summer of 1645, with their pestilence and misery for the Scottish capital, had to wear away over the heads of the surviving Royalist sufferers in the loathsome prisons; but at last, on the 15th of August, among the Kilsyth hills, Montrose struck the blow which opened their doors. Kilsyth had a wonderful effect, as Wishart experienced, in changing the estimation in which prisoners were held. They became at once the arbitrators of the fate of Edinburgh and its inhabitants.[53] The delivered captives at once sought Montrose's "Leaguer" at Bothwell, and Wishart soon found himself in congenial employment as

---

[53] See p. 131.

secretary and chaplain in the household of the Governor-General of Scotland, and once more in friendly intercourse with his old friend Sir Robert Spottiswoode, who had brought down the great commission for the hero of Kilsyth. It was a gay time for him after all his sufferings, when nobility and gentry were pouring into the camp, and "passes and securities" were being given out without number. We may fancy his enjoyment as, in critical vein, he scanned for Montrose the lines of adulatory literature [54] which now came in from unexpected quarters, and in anticipation of restored peace contemplated a share in "putting to the press" Drummond's "Irene" and such like. Alas for Montrose and the King, Philiphaugh lay in the immediate distance, and Wishart's elaborate sermon at Cranston Kirk could not be heard, for time was more precious than exhortation [55] as the little army moved to its doom. From this time our author's memoir is the work of an eye-witness. He appears to have followed Montrose throughout the remainder of the campaign, and put to sea with him and his companions on September 3, 1646, when all hope was for the present gone.[56] They landed in Norway, September 10th, and, after some wandering, the Hague became the headquarters of the exiles. By October 1, 1647, Wishart had written the Dedication of his important "Commentarius," and by the beginning of 1648 it was spreading through Europe, and had come before the Commission of the General Assembly in Scotland. Mr. Alexander Petrie, their informant in Holland, had intimated its appearance, and their reply to him, March 13th, is preserved in their minutes. "For that you wrytt concerning a treatise, De rebus gestis M. Montis Rosarii, we shall be glad you send some of them to the

---

[54] We are reluctantly compelled to give up our quest for the "pieces" alluded to by Wishart at p. 131.

[55] In his Covenanting days Montrose had listened "attentivelie and reverentlie" to the longer discourses of the Rev James Rowe, his chaplain. One notice of this is under May 6, 1637, when he was marching his force to join Leslie at Duns Law. See Churches of St. Baldred, 90.

[56] What had the parsons being doing in the Mearns or Aberdeen before they sailed, or what influence had they left behind them for working trouble to the Commission of Assembly? "It is this day recommended that particular informations with the evidences therof be given to the Clerk concerning the malignant carriage of Mr George Wishart, Mr James Wood and Mr Andro Sandilands, that the Com$^n$ may tak course for their excommunication." Records Gen. Assembly, Dec. 22, 1646, p. 158.

Moderatour, that after sight therof we may accordingly take such course in it as shall be found fitting."[57] The curious letter which we print at page 7 from Prince Charles, refusing the Dedication of the work, and asking for its suppression, does not seem to have had a serious purpose, or mean a lasting alienation of the author from court favour. Clarendon is responsible for the following notice :—

"A learned and worthy Scotch divine, Dr. Wishart, being appointed to preach before the king, they [the Scotch Commissioners] formally besought the king that he would not suffer him to preach before him, nor to come into his presence, because he stood excommunicated by the kirk of Scotland for having refused to take the covenant, though it was known that the true cause of the displeasure they had against that divine was, that they knew he was author of that excellent relation of the Lord Montrose's actions in Scotland—which made those of his Majesty's council full of indignation at their insolence; and his Majesty himself declared his being offended, by using the Marquis of Montrose with the more countenance, and hearing the Doctor preach with the more attention."[58]

The scene with Montrose on the arrival of the news of the King's execution argues a great intimacy, coupled with mutual respect on the part of the hero and his historian; and this subsisted to the end. Wishart was doubtless absorbed in all the negotiations of the time, and remained in connection with Montrose's household while it held together. A separate purse was, however, necessary, and Wishart sought and obtained the chaplaincy of a regiment of Scots in the pay of Holland, quartered at Schiedam, the Colonel of which would appear to have been in sympathy with Wishart's politics. "My Colonel had been on his journey before now, but that the Prince of Orange took him with his Highness in a progress that he is making towards Guelderland. I know he will make

---

[57] Records of Gen. Assembly, 391. See Baillie to Spang, Glasgow, March 27 [1648], "That book you wrote of, *Res Gestae Marchionis Montis Rosini,* let us have it." Did the Kirk supply the copy hung about Montrose's neck at his execution?

[58] Clarendon, quoted in W.'s Montr. (1819), 4.

the speediest return that may be." So writes Wishart from Schiedam to Lord Napier at Hamburg, Jan. 1, 1650.[59] The letter has a cry of anxiety in it as to the expedition upon which all loyal exile hearts were set. "Oh, the God of armies and giver of victory, bless the same to the end." Here Wishart's stout heart met the blow of his hero's failure and death. The Anniversary poem tells something of the love that could not die (pp. 486-491). His military charge was converted into a civil one, and Wishart became minister of the Scottish Congregation at Schiedam. The differences between Episcopal and Presbyterian forms at this time were trifling, and there was no question of a bishop's authority in Schiedam. Wishart as a kindly Scot, good companion, and well-read clerk and politician, was sure to win his way were he let alone. But again, the Covenant beat up his quarters with persecution. The Queen of Bohemia was his friend with the States, and aided him in holding his post against the representations of the bitter Kirk at home. He is said to have been her chaplain, we know not on what evidence. The statement, as in the similar representation of his relations with Lord Napier, may only mean that he secured a place in her favour, and obtained her help and protection. The amount of hostility of the Kirk, and the measure of its success against our author at Schiedam, have yet to be brought to light. We may presume that Wishart's family shared part of his exile.

The Restoration brought return, and was promptly effective in establishing our author in Newcastle as lecturer at St. Andrews, in room of Mr. Stephen Dochray, who died August 11, 1660. In September the Common Council appointed him on "the Kings letter" at a salary of £80. This disposes of the story of his return with the Queen of Bohemia, who did not visit

---

[59] Napier, Mem., 730. In the Napier charter-chest is a bond for 1000 merks, borrowed by Archibald Lord Napier, and Mrs. Lilias Napier, our sister, from Mr. James Weems, lawful son of Dr. Ludowich Weems, payable "thirty days after this our bond shall be shown and intimated tô Lady Elizabeth Erskine, Lady Napier." It is dated "Shiedam in Holland 7-17th of October, 1652," and witnessed by "Dr. George Wiseheart, minister of the Scots Congregation there, and writer thereof." Napier, Mem., 810.

England, and her ungrateful nephew, till May 26, 1661.[60] In 1660 Wishart, without having drawn this salary, passed to St. Nicholas on a stipend of £150. Did he here complete in another MS. the sermon on those who came out of great tribulation?

The "valetudinarie" condition of Wishart at this time no doubt prevented him from taking part in the State funeral of his great hero or visiting his remains as they lay in state at Holyrood from January 7th to May 11th 1661. Early in April of that year he applied to the Parliament of Scotland for some support out of vacant stipends, and obtained a grant of £300. The petition throws some light on his history, and is given below.[61]

---

[60] After forty years of exile in Holland, and nearly fifty of absence from England, the brave bright daughter of James I. landed at Gravesend, only as the guest of Lord Craven. She hired Lord Leicester's House, where now is Leicester Square, and there sitting in her chair in the early morning of February 13-23, 1662, the Queen of Hearts passed away in full possession of all her powers. See Mrs. Green's "English Princesses," ii. 82. Her chaplain was George Beaumont.

[61] WNTO his Maiesties Commissioner his Grace, And the honourable Estates of Parliament,
The Supplicatione of D$^r$ George Wiseheart, sometyme Minister of Gods word at S$^t$ Andrews,

Humblie sheweth

Whereas your Lo$^s$, has ordaind (for encurageing of others to loyaltie heirafter) That all vacand Stipends shall be conferred upon such Ministers (or the wyfes and children of such of them as are dead) who during these lait trowbles, Have suffered for their loyaltie; And seing your Lo$^s$, Petitioner, for his loyaltie suffered as earlie, as much, as long, as constantly and patiently, as any of his statione in the Kingdome; Being in Anno 1637 for'ct to flie to another Kingdome, from his charge at S$^t$ Andrews, and since, once and againe rob'd, of all his goods, Imprisond, banisht, and for persisting in his knowne avowed loyaltie, and in that christiane deuty of holdeing up his Majesties conditione, and just cause, to Almightie, in publick worshipe, followed with Persecutione, even beyond Seas, by the late Usurpers, and that even till the blessed day of his sacred Majesties wonderfull restitutione. Theirfor and becaus your Lo$^s$, Petitioner is not only valetudinarie, and past sixtie alreaddie, bot also in regaird your Petitioners poor wyfe and children (In caice Providence should remove him) should be vnable to defray some litle burden, the contracteing wheirof being inevitable, by any in your Petitioners conditione, these tuentie zeirs by gone.

May it Please your Grace, and the Honorable Estaits of Parliament To take your Petitioners former Sufferings, upon account of his loyaltie, and his present burdens theirby contracted, to your consideratione, And in regaird theirof, and that your Petitioner is valetudinarie, past sixtie, and so affrayed of not being able to attend the Privie Councell, To determine at present, what your Lo$^s$, shall think fitt to allow your Petitioner, And grant a precept upon M$^r$ John Wilkie Collector of the said vacand stipends, for paiment of what shall be allowed, out of the first and readdiest of the said vacand stipends, that are or shall be thereafter receaved be him or his deputies, And your Petitioner, as bound in deuty, shall ever pray &$^c$.

Ed$^r$ 15 Apryle 1661.

The Lord Com$^r$ and Estaitts of Parliament doe ordain ane precept to be drawen upon M$^r$ Jo$^n$ Wilkie Collector of the vacand stipends for pay$^t$ to the petitioner of the sowme of Thrie hundreth punds sterling mo$^ey$ out of the first & reddiest of the vacant stipends.

GLENCAIRNE Can$^{ll:}$rius I P D Par.

The warrant for payment is dated May 14th 1661. **Acts Parl. Scot,** vii. 240, and App. 59, 76. See grants to widow of William Wishart, "person" of Leith, ibid. 384, and App. 84.

Scotland meanwhile was in doubt and anxiety as to the effect of the Restoration on its ecclesiastical future. Presbyterianism was no longer a unity. Resolutioners and Protesters divided the Kirk. The former were the Moderates of a later date, "the wise men of the *via media*," as a living professor [62] of Church History calls them, "the peaceable, liberal, constitutional" majority, who had abolished the Act of Classes in 1651. The Protesters were more infected with Puritanism and the energetic piety of the sects, and resisted the restoration of the Engagers to public trust. Strange to say, Dickson (the reputed author of the paean, "The wark goes bonnily on"), Douglas, and Baillie were the preachers of moderation. Rutherford led the minority of perfervid Puritans. Sharpe was the agent of the Resolutioners, first with Cromwell, then with Monk, and lastly with Charles. His letters are perfectly open with his employers, and little by little the party submitted to the inevitable. The grand idea of a Solemn League and Covenant to bind the three kingdoms was surrendered, and they fell back on a *covenanted Scotland*. This too was given up for a simple maintenance of Presbyterianism. The Rescissory Act opened their eyes, and the execution of Argyll and Guthrie made many tremble. In September 1661 the restoration of Episcopacy was proclaimed, and on November 14th a writ passed the great seal, nominating Sharpe to the primatial see of St. Andrews in succession to Spottiswoode. Two other Resolutioners were at the same time appointed, Fairfoul to Glasgow and Hamilton to Galloway. Leighton was preferred to the see of Dunblane. They were consecrated together in Westminster Abbey on December 15th. Edinburgh was offered to Douglas, but declined, and Wishart was appointed. David Mitchell,[63] his fellow-sufferer, got Aberdeen, and Sydeserf, the surviver of Charles I.'s bishops, exchanged his old seat of Galloway for the better endowed and peaceful Orkney. Resolutioners obtained all the other sees. On June 1, 1662, at St. Andrews, "in the communion isle," Wishart was consecrated by Sharpe and two transformed Covenanters,

---

[62] See Rev. R. H. Story's William Carstares, p. 10.

[63] Mitchell in his poverty during the Commonwealth had lived by skill in watchmaking. He died in 1663. Lauderdale wished to translate Wishart to Orkney, "if it can be with his good liking." Orig. MS. letter, 4th Feb. 166¾ in Episcopal Chest.

Haliburton of Dunkeld and Murdoch Mackenzie of Moray (the latter had been ill to guide under the Covenant). The bishops took their seats in Parliament as of yore, and we find Wishart in his place in 1662, 1663, and 1665 taking his share in committee work as to articles, taxation, and supply, and on commissions for universities and "planting kirks." The Court of High Commission was revived in 1664, but died a natural death before two years were out.[64] The lower courts of Presbyterian discipline, synod, presbytery, and kirk-session, remained, and a General Assembly was always possible. Their relations with the bishop are illustrated by the document printed below,[65] in which the name Andrew Cant, once familiar on the Covenant side, reappears in an Episcopal license to a descendant who became a bishop. At first Wishart had difficulties with the ministers of Edinburgh, three of whom[66] refused to join with him in discipline, and were

---

[64] See Grub, iii. 209, on misrepresentations of this court under the Restoration.

[65] The subjoined license has been kindly put at our disposal by the Bishop of Edinburgh. It is from the "Episcopal Chest," and bears Wishart's autograph as bishop. It is docketed "5 License, upon trial had, by ye Bp of Ed$^r$ to Mr Andrew Cant, to preach March 15$^{th}$ 1670. O. 5."

"We the Moderator and Remanent Brethren of the Presbytery of Ed$^{h:}$ Doe Testify to the Right Reverend George Lord Bishop of Ed$^{r:}$ that the Bearer M$^{r:}$ Andro Cant younger (upon the Recommendation of M$^{r:}$ W$^{m:}$ Keith, Professor of Divinity) hath been tryed in the Ordinary pairts of tryall taken of such who are to be licenssiat to preach in publick, and in all of them did abundantly satisfy us and was by us Well Approven. So that Wee cannot bot Recommend him to your Lordship for obtaining of License to preach in publick whensoever he shall be Lawfully called thereunto being confident that he by Earnest prayer and Diligence shall prove a profitable Instrument in the Vineyard of the Lord whensoever it shall please the Master of the Harvest to call him forth to be a Labourer therein—And in Witness of the premisses, these presents are Written at our Command and subscrived in Our names At Ed$^r$ the second of March One thousand six hundred three score and ten years by

AR: TURNER *Moderator*
CHARLES LUMISDEN *Clerk*."

"In consideratione of ye premyss within written and in regard ye within named M$^r$ Andrew Cant y$^{or}$ has owned and acknowledged ye Kings Majestys dutie and subjection be his subjects togedder with due obedience to ye p$^{nt}$ (present) Church governnment by Archbyshops and Byshops as ye same is now established be law—Theirfor We witt ye us to have granted licence as be these presents we grant full Libertie and Licence to ye said M$^r$ Andrew Cant y$^{or}$ to preach the word of God in any church within our Diocese of Ed$^n$ where he may be lawfully desired—Given under our hand att Cannogait the fyfteen Day of March 16 hundred three score and ten yeirs

GEO: EDINBURGEN."

[66] James Hamilton, John Smith, and George Hutchieson. Douglas and the remaining ministers, except Andrew Laurie, who became Dean, were forbidden to preach. Their places were supplied by sufferers, or sons of sufferers in the Rebellion, such as James Kid, who had £100 given him by Parliament and the parish of Holyrood, John Paterson of Ellon, son of the late Bishop of Ross, and

deposed by Parliament. The Protesters thus obtained some support from divisions among the Resolutioners. Fanaticism began to manifest new vagaries,[67] and the broken Covenant became a rallying cry for the pious peasantry of the West, with Rullion Green as the termination of their rising. The prisoners, after the fight, met with Wishart's sympathy, and from his table in his Canongate lodging a good portion of the bishop's dinner went daily up to the Tolbooth. Compulsory worship at an Established shrine had the same effect under Episcopacy as under Presbytery: the young and independent would not go to church; but now the "fervid Covenanters" gave them a reason why, and an opportunity of seeking pastures new. The situation called for discretion and spiritual zeal as well as authority. Authority unfortunately took too readily to force as a remedy for the trouble. Our conception of Wishart's character suggests that he would have dealt much more successfully with delinquents, had the state machinery not so hampered his action. There was no prayer-book now or difficulty as to worship, but there was Middleton and Lauderdale, and the Privy Council and statecraft, and the Bishop of Edinburgh was only a wheel in the machine. Innovations in worship and observance were, however, inevitable, and we find the laird of Brodie noting, August 15th 1662, "Yesterday the Bishop of Edinburgh did baptis the Advocat's son, and us$^d$ som of the ceremonies, and Service Book. I desird to spread this befor God and committ it to him."[68]

The Bishop's family consisted of Thomas, Patrick, Robert, Jean, and Margaret. Thomas and Patrick were married, and in 1667 the Rev. William Walker, parson of North Berwick, a

---

Wm. Annand. Lamont names John Robertson of Kirkcaldy, and three Fife ministers as admitted by Wishart to charges in Edinburgh. William Colville became Principal of the college. Hutchieson and Douglas were "indulged" in 1669, and their people flocked to hear them; but as they only preached morality, and "not to the times," they were called "dumb dogs."

[67] See Sir George Mackenzie's Vindication, &c., for "Solemn League," "West Kirk Declaration of 13 Aug. 1650," Exact copy of Treasonable and Bloody Paper, called "The Fanaticks' New Covenant," "The True Presbyterian Anti-Prelatick Declaration," "Blasphemous and Treasonable Paper emitted by the Phanatical Undersubscribers." Also see Turner's experiences among the Covenanters of this time, Mem., 158 ff.

[68] Brodie's Diary, 270. See also p. 239, "I did see Dr. Burnet, and heard that the Bishop of Edinburgh (then at Newcastle, January 27, 1662) was a stomacked proud man. Oh Lord! bring forth good out of the euels, sins and corruption of men."

young widower (he was only forty-three when he died in 1682), carried off Jean for his second wife. Margaret married Mr. James Aikenheid, and their son, the Bishop's namesake, comes in for 1000 merks in his grandfather's will. Two men and two maid-servants seem to have formed the Episcopal establishment. They each get £20 by the will, and an additional £20 is given to William Littlejohn, "our servitor." He left to the poor of Holyrood parish £500 Scots, "to be disponed at the sight of M$^r$ James Kid, Minister, and George Herriot, balzie of the Canongate." Wishart made his will on his deathbed within his house in the Canongate, on July 1st 1671. There is no mention of his wife in it, and it is probable, notwithstanding Scott's statements to the contrary in the Fasti, that she predeceased Wishart. Patrick is appointed sole executor, with ample powers. The deed is drawn by George Haliburton, son of the late Bishop of Dunkeld, a writer in Edinburgh. The witnesses were Patrick Forbes Bishop of Caithness, son of the distinguished minister of Alford, and John Wiseheart, "one of the Commissars of Edinburgh," who obtained the barony of Balgavie, and bought back Logie Wishart, the old family possession, which had been lost to the family in the troubles.[69] Thomas Wishart, the Bishop's eldest son, became "caution" when the deed was registered. The Bishop, knowing death to be certain and the hour uncertain, and wishing while his memory lasted to adjust his affairs, leaves his soul to God, hoping to be "saved throughe the onlie merits of our dear Saviour Jesus Christ, and ordanis our bodie to be decentlie and honestlie buried amongst the faithfull when and where it sall pleas God to call us out of this mortalitie." He died 25th (?) July 1671, in the 72nd year of his age.

He was buried "within the Kirk of Halyroodhous upon the

---

[69] The poor commissar who thus won back the estate, lost his two sons, and again the property went into the market. It is now held by Colonel Kinloch of Logie.

On the death of Wishart's father, the estate was found to be deeply involved, and Moncrieff of Moncrieff and others held bonds over it which they put in force. Wishart's brother, William, stuck to the place and is charged "with troubling them and dispossessing them furth of their lands and barony, and doing certain other outrages. He does sitt and dwell in the maner place and principal mansion situat upon the maines of the said barony." They have a bad time with him in the barn-yard and mills, and even in the courts of law, till a committee of parliament reports, and he is ousted, May 17, 1661.

north side on Satterday the 29th July," where his epitaph—becoming illegible—may still be seen; we give it as a note below.[70] The following contemporary "character" of the Bishop will be read with interest.

"*A character of D$^{r\cdot}$ George Wishart Bishop of Edinburgh who died in July 1671.*"

"Here are consigned the ashes of That Reverend Prelate George Bishop of Edinburgh; in whome did meet the Innocence and persecution of the Primitive Christians; worthy of better times, but necessary for ours: his practice, having been in the midst of so many distractions one of The Clearest Rules for discovering Clouded Truth; to whose breast it fled for sanctuary in an age wherein almost every man els got up his owne designe or caprice of religion: so yt while Aaron's rod was a serpent in the hands of others it blossom$^{d:}$ in his as in its Ark. On many accounts the miracle of his age: for he was the best churchman even then when thrown out of the church: the best subject, when declar$^{d:}$ Traitor; and the best country-man when he was rail$^{d:}$ upon as its barbarous enemy. But thereafter he had wearyed the cruelty of his enemys, and starvd their malice, then upon him as a center did rest the praise of all opposite partys who agreed in nothing but in admiring of him, and said his Principles were the best since all men thought they were so near each to his owne. A churchman who was reverenc$^{d:}$ as a Bishop while he was a minister, and desired to be esteemed but as a Minister when he was a Bishop; wishing to be higher than his bretherin in nothing

---

[70] EPITAPH ON THE MURAL TABLET, WISHART'S TOMB, IN HOLYROOD ABBEY CHURCH.

Hic recubat celebris Doctor Sophocardius alter,
    Entheus ille Σοφος καρδιαν Agricola
Orator fervore pio, facundior olim
    Doctiloquis rapiens pectora dura modis.
Ternus ut Antistes Wiseheart, ita ternus Edinen.
    Candoris columen nobile, semper idem.
Plus octogenis hinc gens Sophocardia lustris,
    Summis hic mitris claruit, atque tholis:
Dum cancellarius regni Sophocardius, idem
    Praesul erat fani, Regule Sancte, tui.
Atque ubi pro regno, ad Norham, contendit avito
    Brussius, indomita mente manuque potens;
Glasguus Robertus erat Sophocardius alter,
    Pro patria, qui se fortiter opposuit.
Nec pacis studiis Gulielmo, animisve Roberto
    Agricola inferior, caetera forte prior;

Excelsus sine fastu animus, sine fraude benignus,
    Largus opis miseris, intemerata fides.
Attica rara fides; constantia raraque, nullis
    Expugnata, licet mille petita, malis.
In regem, obsequii exemplar, civisque fidelis,
    Antiquam venerans, cum probitate, fidem.
Omnibus exutum ter, quem proscriptio, carcer,
    Exilium, lustris non domuere tribus.
Ast reduci Carolo plaudunt ubi regna secundo,
    Doctori Wiseheart insula plaudit ovans.
Olim ubi captivus, squalenteque carcere laesus,
    Annos ter ternos, praesul honorus obit.
Vixit Olympiadas ter quinas; Nestoris annos
    Vovit Edina: obitum Scotia moesta dolet.
Gestaque Montrosei, Latio celebrata cothurno
    Quantula (proh!) tanti sunt monumenta viri

The Register of Burials, Canongate, has the entry of burial but not of death.

more than in Devotion, nor to be richer than they in nothing but in Virtue; who never invaded the secular power, nor ever yealded to their invasion upon the Church, the Churchis Athanasius in Religion and its Ambrose in government, A subject who thought his duty his reward and made the Law his Reason. A soldier who retained the innocence of an Hermite in a Barbarous camp and who brought with him the valour of a Martyr to a barbarous barr thus he was neither afraid of his Enemys Courage in the field nor of their Malice upon the bench And was still at once reddy to shed his blood against them and his tears for them. His revenues were the Poor's Exchequer his discours his Enemys best Apology, his conversation one of the best arguments for Episcopacy and his life the most preferable paterne for a geneous and Pious Churchman. But as he desir$^{d:}$ no other witness to his best actions than his own conscience so he needs no other monument but his own fame for he Lived much nearer to what he ought to have been than to what I can Discribe him."[71]

We do not think it necessary to refute the misrepresentations of Wodrow; they are destitute of any semblance of evidence, and are contradicted by the tenor of Wishart's life, and his reputation among his contemporaries. He was a genial, kind-hearted, free-spoken man, unconcerned as to how he looked in Puritan eyes, as he mingled with kindly Scots in feast or fray; but his comfortable relations with the best men of his time, and women too, whether Episcopalian or Presbyterian, evince that his standard was at least as high as that of his age.

As to his children we have been unable to trace their history. Jean's husband died and left her a good library, which, however, did not meet his debts. Captain Patrick took a good position in the army, and is noted by Lauderdale for promotion. His daughter Jean married Thomas, fifth son of James Dundas of Morton and Philipston. Thomas Dundas acquired the lands of Drumcross in West Lothian. His son Thomas, by Jean Wishart, was the father of the Thomas Dundas who, in Douglas's time, was the male representative of the Dundases of Newliston.[72] A Colonel Wishart of Cliftonhall appears later on in the Acts of Parliament.

---

[71] From Episcopal Chest. It is docketed with another paper thus: "Dr Tillotson's Letter to the Lord Russell dated July 20$^h$ 1683. Also A character of Dr George Wisehart Bishop of Edinburgh."

[72] Douglas Baronage, Dundas of Newliston.

A few words on the literary merits of Wishart's Latin work will not be out of place in this sketch of his life. Bearing in mind the haste of travel and anxieties of exile, under which the book was composed, and hurried through three editions in a twelvemonth, we venture to think that occasional slips of grammar and inelegancies of expression will be lost sight of in admiration for the author's vigour and command of language. The personal interest of the narrative is deepened by the knowledge that, behind the author, stood his subject. Montrose was in fact so completely identified with the work that it came to be known as "his book," and as such was his proudest ornament on the scaffold. At times there is in it a clear Caesarean terseness of *Commentary*, in which we seem to trace Montrose's own trenchant phrase. As a party manifesto and personal vindication, its success was immediate, and is gauged by the animosity it roused in the extreme section of Scottish rebels. In the main it is just, temperate and faithful, as the reader may assure himself by reference to our notes. And these are qualities not generally conspicuous, even in writers whose heat might have been tempered by time. In spite of its frank strictures on those whose selfishness and shifty *loyalescence* it exposes, probably, no book or pamphlet of the period, except, perhaps, the "Eikon Basilike," did more service to the exiles in rousing interest abroad and winning sympathy for their cause. Latin was naturally chosen as the fittest medium, in an age when it was still a living language; in courts, camps, and trading marts the common tongue among the polite of all nations. But the very circumstance which then ensured a wider circulation for the book tended in later days, as the spoken language fell into disuse, to obscure its merits and narrow the circle of its readers. Nor have previous translations adhered so faithfully to the meaning and spirit of the original as to justify its reputation among contemporaries. The merits of our own version are submitted to the reader's judgment. By reprinting the rare Latin, we challenge criticism, but discharge ourselves of a debt due to earnest students, and due to the author's fame.

## Montrose, Argyll, and the Solemn League and Covenant.

Montrose is a historical paradox; the victorious Covenanting leader of the Bridge of Dee is the champion of the King unto death; the friend of Spottiswoode is a ruling elder in the Glasgow Assembly which excommunicates him.

Montrose, a soldier by nature, with true patriotic principles of constitutional government working within him, and religious toleration more than latent, returned, aged 24 years, to Scotland, by way of the English Court, and there found his country and religion practically at the mercy of Hamilton, a contemptuous Scot whom he despised, and of an Englishman, Laud, whom he suspected. His own reception by Charles no doubt intensified the interpretation he was already giving to the situation, and he came down to Scotland in revolt. His political idea was practically a Reform Bill, which would give representation and influence to the People as represented by the lesser Barons, gentry, and educated Classes. The elevation of the Masses was not then in view. In revolt, and with reform in his mind, he was ready to fall in with the National Movement, when presented to him with the skill of Rothes and the zeal of Robert Murray. As a soldier he should have seen more of the field and known his comrades better, before he engaged, but he was young and impulsive. He found himself at war with the King and constitutional principle, when he thought himself engaged only in sweeping from Scotland the domination of such as Hamilton, and the religious tyranny of the Court as exemplified in the rule of Bishops. When, however, he engaged, he did so thoroughly; the Covenanters rejoiced, the Bishops feared. In the corrupt state of the times, his union with politics was like a breath of pure Highland air sweeping through the closes of Edinburgh. His more than ordinary pride made him ill to guide, and he would not bear the shackles which the real leaders of the party sought to fasten upon the spirited young nobleman. He was not long in discovering, that he was only exchanging Hamilton and a misguided King for Argyll without a King at all, and the rule of the Bishops[73] for a Presbyterian intolerance, that was preparing to force its system on the three kingdoms at the point of the sword. Hence his readiness at Aberdeen to accept signatures to the Covenant with loyal qualification; hence the Cumbernauld Bond, in which so many noblemen and officers joined against the Argyll policy; hence "the Plot" to bring the King down to Scotland, and the undying antagonism between Montrose and Argyll.

Montrose was a leader in constitutional reform, and sought the Nation's deliverance from the oppressive influence of the three Scottish magnates—Hamilton, Huntly,[74] and Argyll.

The triumph of the Royalists at the Restoration was too short-lived to establish Montrose in tradition as a hero whose deeds, genius, and character should have been his country's pride. That triumph was marred by gross cruelty and folly of administration. When the reaction followed, and Presbyterianism emerged triumphant from fifty years of strife, inevitably, with the fall of the house of Stuart, popular sympathy was estranged, not only from the ardent partisans of that house, but also from the men of moderate counsels, who fought and died for those noble principles of constitutional government in state and tolerance in religion which the

---

[73] It is a matter of dispute whether Montrose was an Episcopalian or a Presbyterian. The disputants should agree first as to a "definition of terms," and understand the significance of these during the period in question. Episcopacy was only assuming its distinctive features, and taking up in some cases what Presbytery was laying down. It is a common mistake to suppose that "Read Prayers" and "Book Devotions" were Episcopal innovations. They were in use from the time of John Knox, on week-days and Sundays, and Laud's Prayer-book was an English supplanter of a liturgy developed out of the Book of Common Order by Committees of Assembly, and presented to King James for royal approval. It was thrown aside for Laud's book, which put read prayers out of fashion with Presbyterians, and into favour with Episcopalians. There was little religious in the early features of Reformation Episcopacy. Episcopacy was first revived to save for the Church the relics of her property, then to superintend a Presbyterian organisation, and only later for the conveying of Holy Orders. Montrose was a religious man, but we should say he was indifferent as to the form of Church government. He would certainly never have expressed himself in the words of Lord Napier's Remonstrance (Napier, Mem., App. iii., xliv.), and there is no evidence that he ever saw it. The Rev. P. Simson cannot be relied on as to the words on bishops with which he credits Montrose, but they may fairly enough represent his attitude. *Ibid.* 185-189.

[74] For Huntly we must refer our readers to the notes in the text. Had he been able to get over the sense of his own greatness, and fall in loyally with the King's lieutenant, the campaign of Montrose would have had a successful ending, and Huntly might have died with honour in his bed.

common-sense of the two nations has finally established. Popular sympathy is still bestowed mainly on those who stood forth as champions against the arbitrary abuse of prerogative. The ignorance of English writers, and the ignorance and latent bigotry of some Scottish writers have tended to perpetuate a view of Montrose which repeats the sneers of his enemies, and represents him merely as an erratic genius, whose mainspring was vanity, pique, and vulgar ambition. To repeat such imputations is vastly more easy than candidly to recognise the essential difference, the broad line of cleavage which first separated Montrose and the Banders, and afterwards the mass of the nation in the Engagement, from the extreme clerical fanatics and the powerful handful of noblemen, headed by Argyll. (See p. 205.) The Covenant of 1637 united the nation in just opposition to the King's and Laud's arbitrary interference in matters of Church government in Scotland. The King gave way, and in the words of his Parliament, he left Scotland a contented king of a contented people. The Solemn League of 1643 was an unprovoked invasion of England on the part of Presbyterian propagandists, seeking by help of a faction in England to impose on that country an alien form of Church discipline—the very thing which had aroused such vigorous and successful opposition in Scotland in 1637. It was an attempt to force Presbyterianism on England and Ireland at the sword's point. As such it stands condemned by the common-sense of modern times, happily expressed in the *practice* of all denominations. It is not necessary to go further than this, and point out the essential difference in the royal prerogative as established by law and custom in England and the limits of the royal prerogative in Scotland. For the course pursued by the Solemn Leaguers of 1643, we can find no moral justification that would not entitle their defenders at the present day to invade England and Ireland with the same absurd demands.

The Marquis of Argyll identified himself with this party of irreconcilables. Fanaticism, reasoning with severe logic from narrow premises, is in its nature essentially unreasonable. Had Argyll remained consistent to the principles on which he established his triumph in 1648, we should have regarded him as a dangerous fanatic, but entitled to respect for sincerity of life. Between such a man, if sincere, and the sectaries of England with their professions of toleration, there could have been nothing in common. Yet to his personal interest he sacrificed the party which had climbed to power by his support; and it is impossible to account for his acceptance of Cromwell in 1648, and after Worcester, on any theory but that of personal aggrandisement. We do not condemn him so much for accepting the seemingly inevitable, and acquiescing in Cromwell's Protectorate, as for his support to principles which should have made that acquiescence impossible, and for his cruel treacherous conduct to those who dissented from those principles. Making every allowance for that self-deception which sees in personal success the Divine sanction, we cannot regard Argyll as a martyr to any motive but that of selfishness. Presbyterianism, triumphant under a new dynasty, has swelled its roll of martyrs with a motley array of men who, in their lives, were not merely (though not always) fiercely opposed to the Stuarts, but also fiercely opposed to one another. The true representatives in 1660 of those who had condemned Montrose were the "Supplicators," a section represented later on by the rigid Cameronians and other irreconcilables. For such men all government not based on the sanctions of Old Testament law (narrowly misread) was an impossibility. On conspicuous occasions, such as that of the Sanquhar Declaration, they stood condemned even by writers like Wodrow, who from their ranks recruited the heterogeneous martyrology of the Kirk. And certainly such enthusiasts in their stern unbending consistency, seem far more deserving of our sympathy or pity than the weaker or craftier bigots who veered to shifting gusts and flaws in the storm of politics and religion. Of such was Archibald, Marquis of Argyll. Driven on by the force of public opinion, he had acquiesced in the proclamation of Charles II. as King, yet continued to intrigue with and derive help from that party in England which refused to acknowledge the King. Later on he repudiates and oppresses the party of his own countrymen whose voice had been loudest in that proclamation; and having illegally constituted his own section a Committee of Estates, proceeds by votes of that committee to execute the King's commander-in-chief. Occasions may arise when armed resistance to the royal authority becomes a duty. But this pretext of making war on the King in the King's name, however well it may have served the rebels as a legal quibble, was beneath their professions of sincerity, and inconsistent with their conduct to the King's supporters. We do injustice to Argyll's penetration as a statesman if we imagine for a moment that he was imposed on by Charles II.'s wry-faced acceptance of the Covenant and League. Yet this acceptance was the *sine quâ non* of government in Scotland to Argyll and his clerical supporters. If it was impossible to accept Charles and his loyal supporters without it in 1650, how was it possible to accept Cromwell without it in 1652? And why, before Charles had repudiated his bad bargain, did Argyll not only decline to support Glencairn in 1653, but actively sought to prevent his son Lorn from doing so? Such was the man to whose malice and ambition Montrose fell a victim. Both perished the victims of a heartless monarch. Yet there the likeness ceases. Let those who crawl on the base level of so-called expediency defend Argyll's statesmanship if they will, and condemn his victim as an impracticable visionary in politics. Yet Montrose's principles have triumphed, even in the Church whose misguided zeal has condoned Argyll's practices. Set the men side by side, action by action, face to face—" Hyperion to a satyr!"

# CRITICAL INTRODUCTION.

## PREVIOUS EDITIONS, TRANSLATIONS, AND MANUSCRIPTS.—THE PRESENT TEXT.

### Part I. Editions of the Latin.

1. *First Edition.* Title-page, dated 1647, without place. 8vo. Size $5\frac{8}{10}$ in. by $3\frac{8}{10}$; pp. 248, the last two pages in smaller type, to save another sheet. The Dedication is dated October 1, 1647, at which time Montrose, and doubtless Wishart with him, were at the Hague. The style of the book and printing are Dutch. The Signet and University Libraries contain copies, the latter with a fine frontispiece portrait of Montrose. The Bishop of Edinburgh also has a copy (lacking the portrait), which he kindly allowed the present Editors to send to the British Museum for comparison with their "first edition," with which it was found to be identical. In the British Museum Catalogue the place of printing is conjecturally assigned as Amsterdam (*v.* Ed. 3 below); but the English translation of 1647 (?) was printed at the Hague. The British Museum possesses two copies of this edition, one in the Grenville and one in the General Library. It consists of 135 leaves 8vo, $5\frac{8}{10}$ in. by $3\frac{8}{10}$.

2. *Second Edition.* Paris, *Ex Typographia Ioannis Bessin, prope Collegium Remense. Cum privilegio Regis* 1648. The most beautiful of all the editions, 8vo, pp. xxiv. and 563, finely printed on good paper, in large thick type, 18 lines to the page, with broad margins. Date of Dedication October 1, 1647. On p. xxiv. is the French *Imprimatur*, as follows:—

Extraict du Privilege du Roy

Par Grace et Privilege du Roy donné à Paris le 28. jour de Janvier 1648. Signé par le Roy en son Conseil, BERAUD: il est permis à IEAN BESSIN Maistre Imprimeur & Libraire à Paris, d'imprimer, vendre & distribuer un Livre intitulé, *De Rebus auspiciis Serenissimi Caroli Dei gratia Magnæ Britanniae Regis* &c.

pendant le temps et espace de cinq ans, à compter du jour qu'il sera achevé d'imprimer, et defenses sont faites à toutes sortes de personnes de quelque qualité & condition qu'ils soient de l'imprimer, vendre ny distribuer sans le consentement dudit Suppliant, à peine d'amende arbitraire, comme il est plus amplement porté par les Lettres de Privilege.

Of this edition the Editors have two copies.

3. *Third Edition.* Amsterdam, *impensis Ioannis Crosse*, 1648. *Editio secunda quam antehac locupletior et longe accuratior*, namely, the second *Dutch* edition: 4 in. by 3, 12mo.; pp. xiv. and 221. A few typographical errors in the first edition have been corrected, but a great many fresh ones introduced, and there are absolutely no additions to the text. The above note on the title-page is a mere flourish. The Dedication is dated "7 Febr. 1648." The Editors possess the only copy known to them.

4. Edition of 1649 (?), mentioned in the Publisher's Pref., in 1756 translation.

5. The present edition is the first to give the complete Latin of *both* parts, so far as it has been possible to ascertain from the existing MSS. what Wishart actually wrote in Part II. The spelling of the Latin has been slightly modernised, and obvious errors corrected. The punctuation is revised, but on the whole the text is conservative. Wishart's punctuation, as shown in previous editions of Part I., was "heavy" and inaccurate. As a specimen of his orthography and punctuation the present edition contains an exact copy of the Dedication and Author's Preface, reproduced as a clue to the identification of the lost original MS. of Part II.

The Latin of Part II. will be more fully discussed below, in the section on the MSS.

### Date and Place of Composition.

After the battle of Kilsyth, August 15, 1645, Wishart was liberated from the Tolbooth, and joined Montrose, probably before the month was out. From that time he appears to have accompanied him till the Marquis left France for Austria in April 1648. Following Montrose, in his camp at Bothwell, throughout the remainder of the campaign, and on his journeys abroad, till April 1648, Wishart stands foremost as an authority in the events he describes. Of much he was himself an eye-witness. For events prior to his release, he had the best opportunities in the camp, and among the exiles, of acquiring information at first hand, from officers and men, and from Montrose himself. His information in Part II. was doubtless derived from many who had shared in the campaigns of the Hamiltons and Montrose. His authority for the expedition of the Engagers is in the main supported by the Memoirs of Turner, who shared in the Preston campaign. But there seems to be a subtle difference in the Latin of Parts I. and II. This does not appear in the diction, nor even in minute peculiarities of punctuation, in which our MSS., especially D, have retained traces of the characteristics of Part I. In the latter there is a vivid force and soldierly brevity of style, which suggests that in the Latin *we are frequently reading Montrose's own words translated*. Montrose himself is said to have been an accomplished scholar. Latin was then the common medium of intercourse with foreigners, and probably he was familiar enough with it to fully appreciate what his biographer was writing. Part II., on the other hand, with many turns of phraseology sufficient to establish the identity of authorship, shows a greater tendency to rhetoric and long periods, in a somewhat pulpit-controversial style. Where, however, the author describes events, his narrative is succinct and clear. His account of Monro's dash at Stirling and Argyll's flight, recall the historian of the march from Dundee; and the story of Montrose's trial and death is told with a simple force and elegance worthy of the great tragedy. For the source of this, see English, Pt. II., Ch. x. nn. 1, 10, 20, 33, &c.

We have seen that Wishart accompanied Montrose to Norway in September 1646. The travellers reached Hamburg, probably in October. There they stayed "for some time," till about February 1647. The first edition is dated October 1, 1647. Probably, therefore, most, if not all, of Part I. was composed during their residence at Hamburg; for Montrose seems to have made no great stay in Holland on his way to Paris, which he reached about the end of March, and remained there till he went to Austria in April 1648. Unless, therefore, Wishart had already commenced his narrative before they left Scotland, it must have been composed mainly between October 1646 and February 1647, at Hamburg. It was not till the receipt of Montrose's letter from Geneva (in April or May ?) that Lord Napier retired to Brussels. Napier's letter to his wife, beginning "I did forbear these two months to write unto you, till I should hear from my Lord Montrose . . ." is dated Brussels, 14th June 1648 (*v.* Napier, Life of M., Ed. 1840, p. 433). Probably Wishart was among the "gentlemen belonging to my lord" who accompanied Napier by "Haver-de-grace" and Middelburgh to Brussels. But at no time prior to the publication of the first edition do we find Wishart making any considerable stay in Holland, unless we suppose that when Montrose went on to Paris, Wishart remained behind, a conjecture without any evidence but the fact of publication in Holland, in October 1647, when Montrose was at Paris. In any case, the

# CRITICAL INTRODUCTION.

work was most probably written between October 1646 and the end of September 1647, during which period the exiles made no permanent stay except at Hamburg, and after their arrival at Paris. Possibly the arrangements for printing the work in Holland were made during their short halt there in March 1647,[1] when Montrose waited for Ashburnham's visit (pp. 190, 191).

## TRANSLATIONS.

1. *The First Translation* is said to have been printed in 1647. But the Editors have been unable to see or hear of any copy with this date. The information rests on the authority of the editor of the 1720 Translation, but appears doubtful, as he dates the first Latin edition in 1646, and the second in 1647. He adds, "I have not seen any in Latin of a later date, and am apt to think there has been none since." These errors in dates might lead us to suppose that he had not seen the Latin at all, were it not that his preface does show some slight acquaintance with it.

Mr. W. Y. Fletcher of the British Museum, to whom the Editors are indebted for valuable information on the copies there, informs them that they have two copies of the second edition of this translation, undated, printed by Samuel Rogers, an English bookseller residing at the Hague.

This translation, identical with the Redivivus (see below), was reproduced in 1649 under the title, *The History of the Kings Majesties Affaires in Scotland, Vnder the Conduct of the most Honourable James Marques of Montrose, Earl of Kincardin, &c. and Generall Governour of that Kingdome, In the Years, 1644, 1645 and 1646. Printed in the Year,* 1649. Small 8vo, 192 pp. (last leaf in smaller type to save another sheet), with an atrocious portrait, *Earle of Montros*, signed þ. At the end of the preface "to the reader" are Montrose's verses *Vpon the Death of King Charles the First*. A copy of this edition was kindly lent to the Editors by the Rev. Fr. G. Congreve of Oxford.

In 1652 the same translation was reproduced in the MONTROSE REDIVIVUS, *or the Portraicture of James late Marquess of Montrose, Earl of Kincardin &c.* 1. *In his Actions, in the years* 1644, 1645, *and* 1646, *for Charles the First.* 2. *In his Passions, in the years* 1649. 1650. *for Charles the Second K. of Scots. London, printed for Jo. Ridley, at the Castle in Fleet-street, neer Ram-alley,* 1652. 8vo.; 'pp. viii., 202; $5\frac{9}{16}$ in. by $3\frac{1}{2}$. With a rude portrait of the Marquis holding a baton.

The Advocates' Library and the British Museum have copies of this

---

[1] The Queen's letters to Montrose (Napier's Life, pp. 422, 423) are dated Paris, February 5th, and Paris, March 15th. In the latter she says she had just been "apprised of your arrival in Holland."

work. Besides the translation of Part I. of Wishart's Commentary, it contains, (1) *The Continuation of Montrose's Historie*, pp. 167–188, which appears to be independent of Wishart's Part II., and was probably by an English writer, as it contains errors in Scottish names similar to those in the first translation of Part I. (2) *A true and perfect Relation, of all the passages concerning the Examination, Tryall and Death of the most Honourable James Marquesse of Montrose, Earl of Kincardin, Lord Graeme, Baron of Montdieu, &c. Knight of the most Honourable Order of St. George, Lieutenant Governour, and Captain Generall for his Majestie in the Kingdom of Scotland*, pp. 189–198. Of this, pp. 189–196 are from the same sources as Wishart's Part II. after the great lacuna, and beginning *Conjurati proceres* . . . (Ch. x. in our translation). It is quite impossible that a scholar of Wishart's skill should have had anything to do with the first translation of Part I., which is not only written in wretched style and full of errors, but in the Latin of names makes blunders such as no Scot could have fallen into. Pages 197–199 contain some interesting details of Montrose's personal appearance, character, and accomplishments. (See pp. 521–2.) (3) Pages 199 to the end contain *The Speech of Collonel William Sybbald intended by him to have been spoken on the Scaffold at time of his Execution at Edenborough, Jan. 7. 1650, but hearing that libertie would not be given him to speak so freely, he gave a Copie of it to a speciall friend.* (See pp. 244, *n.* 2.)

Between 1647 and 1660 "there were several editions in 4to and 8vo," according to the editor of the 1720 Translation.

2. *Second Translation.*—*A Complete History of the Wars in Scotland; Under the Conduct of the Illustrious James Marquis of Montrose, in two Parts. The 1st Part describing the wars in the Years 1644, 45, 46. The 2d Part containing an Account of Montrose's Negotiations Abroad, and the State of Affairs in Scotland, from the Year 1647, to the Year 1650 Inclusive. This 2d Part being never before published, is now first done into English, from the Latin of the Right Reverend Father in God, Doctor George Wisheart, Bishop of Edinburgh. With an Appendix, containing 1st, A Description of Montrose's pompous Funerals in the Year 1661. 2dly, A Character of King Charles the 1st, by the famous Mr. Alexander Henderson, on his Death-Bed. 3rdly, Montrose's Declaration when he returned to Scotland, Anno 1650. 4thly, The Declaration of the Commission of the Kirk in Answer to it. 5thly, Two Poems done by Montrose. As Also, Fifteen letters to Montrose, from King Charles the 1st., His Queen, King Charles the 2d, and Prince Rupert. Now first published from the Originals, in the Hands of the Publisher. Printed in the Year*, 1720.

The Editors' copies are 8vo, 5¾ by 4⅛ in., with a poor portrait, "W. Elliot, sculp.," pp. xvi., 200, and (Appendices) lvi. and 24. There is no place of printing or name of editor. In the 1756 Tr. it is said to have been printed at Edinburgh, 12mo, 1720, edited by Mr. Adams. The references on p. 9 of the Publisher's Preface to that edition show that the number of pages and size were different. There must then have been two editions of it in 1720. The book is rare. Neither the Advocates' nor Signet Library contains a copy. Part I. in this translation is a reprint of the old 1647 or *Redivivus* translation, with a few errors corrected, chiefly in names.

This edition contains the first translation of Part II. (referred to as Tr. 1 in our Crit. Notes to the Latin of Part II.) as far as the great lacuna (*v.* Lat. c. vi., n. 15). The remainder is taken from the Redivivus. The editor, in his Preface, speaks of "the Original," but gives no information as to the MS. or MSS. he used. He is accused by the editor of the 1756 Tr. of "inexcusable inadvertency" in his omission of entire sentences and paragraphs, and perhaps he was to blame. But it is quite clear, not only from his omissions, but also his *additions* (viz., cap. i., nn. 5, 6), that he did not use either of the MSS. now in the Advocates' Library, and from his note at "the great chasm" it seems that his MS. terminated there. His ch. vii. (p. 188, 8vo Edn.) was taken, as his note testifies, from the "true and perfect Relation" appended to the Montr. Rediv. (*v.* above). Either, then, his MS. was not the original, or it was the original, but more mutilated than the copies in the Advocates'. From the evidence in c. i. n. 5, it seems likely that the Editor of the 1756 Tr. had access to this MS. or to the original. Otherwise he would hardly have substituted *Maelstrand* for *Malstrand*. (See p. 435, n. 5, and Index.) There cannot be a shadow of doubt that Wishart wrote *Marstrand*, perhaps with a looped *r*, mistaken for an *l* by copiers or translators. Unhappily the Advocates' folio (D) lacks c. i., and the smaller MS. (E) has a blank of one word to the name. Either, then, E was written before 1720, or the copier, Robert Wodrow, was unacquainted with this edition. For the discussion of these MSS. *v.* below.

3. *Third Translation* (referred to as Tr. 2 in our Crit. Notes to the Latin of Part II.).—*Memoirs of the Most Renowned James Graham, Marquis of Montrose. Translated from the Latin of the Rev. Doctor George Wishart, afterwards Bishop of Edinburgh. With An Appendix, Containing many curious Papers relating to the History of these Times; several of them never hitherto published. Edinburgh: printed for W. Ruddiman jun. and Company &c.* 1756. This is a small 4to, 5¾ in. by 4⅜ in.

In this translation the whole text has been revised; but the editor was largely indebted to his predecessor. In Part II. "the original MSS." have been used and omissions supplied; but the editor's alterations of the 1720 Tr. are not always made with taste and judgment. He was, in fact, saturated with the false notion of "the dignity of history," and models his style on the "Johnsonese" style of the period. He makes many serious errors of omission and commission. His reproduction of the previous editor's note at the great lacuna, "Here the Bishop's narration stops," is mere carelessness, as his chapter vii. shows that he had access to a Latin MS. Perhaps his worst mistake is that noted to p. 436, n. 8, where he reproduces the absurd translation "to whom they were obnoxious," which occurs in the 1720 Tr., but is one of three Errata corrected by that editor: "Page 136. *Obnoxious*, read *obliged*."

4. The 1756 edition was reproduced with the fresh matter added in notes and appendix, by A. Constable & Co., Edinburgh, 1819—8vo., 8½ in. by 5¼, pp. xvi. and 530—as a result of revived interest in Montrose, aroused by "the last series of the Tales of My Landlord." The frontispiece portrait was "from a rare print published in the year 1648," the original of which appears to have been the portrait prefixed to the 1647 edition— probably cut out by one of those detestable people who plunder old books for the framing and print shops. The top left-hand corner bears the Montrose arms, and in the top right corner is a gauntlet issuing from a cloud and grasping a hedgehog, with the motto, "Col senno e con la mano."

5. On the merits of the present edition, which completes the series, it is not for the Editors to pronounce any opinion. They venture, however, to hope that a less pretentious style of English and greater fidelity of translation will commend it to the reader. The Introduction, Notes, and Appendices will be found to contain much information now first collected; and scholars will welcome the first appearance in print of the original Latin of Part II. Part II. Chapters vii. viii. ix. contain their own addition to complete the narrative omitted in the great lacuna.

### Of the Manuscripts of Part II.

Of these only two are known to exist, both in the Wodrow collection of the Advocates' Library, quoted as D and E in our Critical Notes.

*MS.* D is a folio, roughly stitched in quires of eight pages. The pages contain thirty lines each, and are numbered up to 60, the last word on p. 60 being *sacrosanctum*, the catch-word of the next page. Probably

# CRITICAL INTRODUCTION.

therefore four pages have been lost (*v. c. vi. n.* 96). The first quire, containing the whole of c. i., is also missing, the first page being numbered 9. In c. vi. pp. 49–52 are also wanting (*v. c. vi. n.* 15). This gap occurs at the great lacuna noted in all editions. As p. 48 has space for a few more lines, it seems probable that the missing pages here were blank, purposely left so, to be filled in by what the writer supposed to exist in the original. If so, we may suspect that he either did not copy from the original, or did not recognise it as such. In the main the text is sound, punctuated in the same style as Part I. in the printed editions, and written in a clear round hand. In the few instances where its readings have seemed inferior to those of D, the errors are mostly of the nature of "slips" and omissions, or due to obscurity of writing in the MS. copied (*v.* especially cap. ii. n. 37; iii. nn. 32, 86; iv. n. 20, where both are wrong; but D is nearer the true reading suggested by Tr. 1, &c.). In general where Tr. 1 affords a clear indication of the true reading, it supports D. In the mass of *variae lectiones* which the reader will find in the Critical Notes, the readings of D are so manifestly more correct, that in any case of doubt its authority is almost always to be preferred. The readings noted do not by any means exhaust the divergencies in minutiae of spelling and punctuation. In the latter respect it is particularly bad. In our text the spelling is slightly modernised, in conformity with that adopted in our text of Part I. But for the critical valuation of these two MSS. the Editors hope that no varieties of importance are omitted, and enough given to justify their estimate and choice.

*MS.* E. On the title-page of E we find "MSS. vol. $\frac{33}{V}$ (with v scored out). 1. Extracta de Chronicis Scotiae. 2. Historia Montisrosana from Bh (?) Brisbans papers written by Bishop Wishart 1651 Collated by," and then follows a monogrammatic signature for "Robert Wodrow." The handwriting appears to be certainly his, on the evidence of his vast correspondence, entombed in the Library. It is beautifully neat and clear, and in a style similar to that of D, namely, early eighteenth century. On the inside of the cover are the words μη ὑπερφρονεῖ παρ ὁ δεί φρονεῖν ἀλλα φρονει εἰς τό ϛοφρονενειν (*sic*), a quotation from Rom. xii. 3, which possibly is Wodrow's comment on Montrose's character, and shows him to have been as ignorant of Greek as he was of Latin at the period when he transcribed this MS. The writing shows that the errors were not due to hasty copying. Making every deduction for obscurity of writing in the MS. or MSS. he "collated," we are forced to conclude that Wodrow was lamentably ignorant of Latin in its simplest rules of grammar and orthography, and seems to have copied with astonishing fidelity, considering his apparent ignorance of the sense. But bad as the MS. is, it remains the more valuable of the two. For, excepting such stray hints as the 1720 and 1756 translations afford, it is our only authority for the text of c. i., part of c. vi. (x. in our translation), and the Latin poem by Wishart.

Strictly speaking, the expression "collated" should mean the use of more than one MS. But the text affords no clear evidence of more than one. The note to the great lacuna (v. c. vi. n. 15) shows that one of Wodrow's MSS. was a folio. This cannot have been our folio D. For D, which shows the same lacuna, has 4 pages blank, and Wodrow could scarcely have written "a page" for "a sheet." It is inconceivable that many of the errors of E could have been made by the most careless copier, with D before him. It is impossible that the *additions* and few superior readings of E should have occurred to a copier of D, especially to so poor a Latinist as Wodrow. But the strongest internal evidence against such a supposition is the omission, with lacunae, of a few words, *e.g.*, *mulctator* and *palam facta* (v. p. 460, nn. 74, 75), where the reading of D is clear as day. Happily, Wodrow has himself left a record that his folio was not our D. On a loose scrap of paper in the volume the editors found the following, in Wodrow's hand :—

M. R. W.<br>Lacunae.

| Book. | my own. |
|---|---|
| Sheet 2 p. 1 lyn 39 | sh: 2. p. 1. lyn ii. |
| Sheet 2 p. 1 lyn 41 | sh: 2. p. 1. lyn 13. |
| Sh: 2 p. 2 — lyn 28 | sh: 2. p. 4. lyn 13. |
| Sh: 3 p. 4 lyn 28 — | sh: 3. p. 13. lyn. 2. |
| Sh: 4 p 4 lyn 12 | sh: 4. p. 14. lyn 2. |
| Sh: 4 p 4 lyn 16 | sh: 4 p. 14. lyne 9. |
| 2 pag of ye verses | 4 page of ye verses |
| lyn penult: ye first | ye same word is |
| w$^d$ yrof wanting | left blank at ye |
|  | foot of y$^e$ page. |

That the "Book" was a folio is shown by the absence in the above references of any page higher than 4 to the sheet. That it was the "folio" referred to in the text of E, is probable from the absence of quotations from any other MS. That it was not our folio D is evident from the fact that the "Book" contained at least 41 "lynes" to the page, and secondly, the references do not agree with the paging of D, and thirdly, the lacunae in E of the words *mulctator* and *palam facta* do not occur in D. We conclude, therefore, (1) that the "Book" was a *folio MS., now lost;* and (2) that as it contained lacunae, it was *not the original*.[2]

From the English of the 1720 Tr. it is evident that the editor did not use either E or the "Book." His translation supplies the lacunae in E, and some of them, especially the names, in c. i. (*v*. nn. 5, 6), are such as no editor would *guess*. In the absence of c. i. to D it is not easy to say whether he had access to that MS.; but his additions and omissions in the text (*v*. c. i., n. 8, &c.) render this highly improbable, even if we suppose, with the editor of the 1756 Tr., that he was "inexcusably inadvertent." It is difficult, on such a supposition, to account for his curious error in writing "Malstrand" for "Marstrand" (c. i. n. 5) unless he was using a MS. written in a difficult crabbed hand, such as Wishart himself wrote, whereas the writing of D is very clear. On the other hand, his note in ch. vi. (n. 15) shows that he was unacquainted with any MS. which continued the narrative beyond the great lacuna, and probably therefore *did not use the original*, or else found it in a mutilated condition.

The editor of the 1756 Tr. speaks of "MSS.," but gives not the slightest direct clue to their nature, contents, or whereabouts. But as he has altered "Malstrand" to "Maelstrand" (which is equally incorrect), and supplies direct from the Latin that portion of ch. vi. for which the 1720 translator depended on the *Montr. Rediv.*, he must either have had the original or D in a more perfect condition than that in which it now exists, or, as he seems to assume, he used the MS. or MSS. used by the former translator. His correction of Malstrand supports the last hypothesis. In c. i., n. 17 is an indication that for that chapter at least the editor had only one MS.

To sum up the conclusions to which the present Editors incline, D and E are entirely independent MSS., the former perhaps copied from the original, the latter from a lost folio, not the original, and apparently not used since Wodrow handled it. The translator of the 1720 edition used a fourth MS., probably not the original, and certainly neither E nor the lost folio; probably also not D, even when less mutilated than at present. The translator of the 1756 edition assumes that his "MSS." were those used by his predecessor, but we incline to think this doubtful, or true, perhaps, of only one of them, namely, that in which "Marstrand" appeared (to him) to be "Maelstrand." The omissions he supplies are drawn

---

[2] For the actual lacunae in E, *v*. Lat. text, c. i. notes 5, 6, 24; c. iii. notes 74, 75; c. iv. n. 45; c. vi. n. 25; besides the greater gaps; c. vi. nn. 15 and 104.

perhaps from D (less mutilated than at present). Neither of these editors, nor the editor of the 1819 reprint, seems to have known anything of the poem appended to E—indirect evidence that this MS. was unknown to them. *The lost Latin MSS. of Part II. are therefore the original, the folio copied by Wodrow, and one or more others, used by previous editors.*

For fuller evidence on this subject the critical reader is referred to the notes on the Latin text. In the hope that this summary may stimulate a search for the missing documents they will not apologise for claiming so much of the reader's attention to many seemingly trivial points of verbal criticism.

## POSTSCRIPT.

Herr Oberlehrer August Seraphim, of Mitau, Courland, has favoured the Editors with valuable notes and transcripts of 32 letters, accounts and documents in the Ducal Archives at Mitau, which throw much light on the relations of the Stuarts to the House of Kettler, and Sir John Cochran's movements and negotiations with James, Duke of Courland, and the King of Poland in 1645–1647, and 1649–1650. These copies are only an instalment of what Herr Seraphim finds there, and he has kindly promised to continue his researches. The Editors regret that the papers arrived too late to embody in this work. In the main they confirm with interesting details the account given in the text of the aid accorded by Duke James to Montrose, and throw much light on the allusions to this in the Montr. Redivivus, and in Sir John Maclear's letter. These, with Sir John Cochrane's report to Charles II. on his mission in 1649 to Hamburg, and some fragments kindly communicated by the keeper of the Royal Archives at the Hague, will appear in the forthcoming miscellany of the Scottish Historical Society.

ON SOME CONTEMPORARY PRINTED PAPERS IN THE BODLEIAN LIBRARY, OXFORD.

We regret that our notes on Part I. should appear without the additional light which the various contemporary pamphlets

## POSTSCRIPT.

enumerated below would have contributed, had we discovered their existence in time. Mr. Firth called our attention to the first, and the proximity on the Bodleian Catalogue of another reference to Montrose led us to a second volume full of interesting papers. A hasty inspection gave us the following titles and some matter bearing on our subject. How much truth may underlie these relations remains to be seen—

I. "A True Relation of the happy successe of His Majesties Forces in Scotland under the conduct of the Lord James Marquiss of Montrose His Excellencie, against the Rebels there;——Also Causes of a Solemne Fast and Humiliation kept by the Rebells in that Kingdom according to a copy printed formerly at Edinburgh.
Printed in the yeare 1644."

It credits Montrose with the taking of "Morpeth Castle and the Fort of South Sheele," and with "driving the rebels out of Durham, Lumly Castle, Blythnooke and all other places beside Sunderland." It contributes additional details as to Tippermuir, and the murder of Lord Kilpont, giving the words of the victim which brought on him the "durk" of Stewart, "Lord forbid man, would you undoe us all." "Fourteen stobs" followed to make sure he should not speak again. Stewart, we are told, "fell mad and so still continueth seeking by all means to murther himself." Aldbar, Dun, and Crathes Castles are mentioned *en route*, and some spirited passages of the battle of Aberdeen are noted. "The laird of Innerwharity was run in the thigh with a lance, Sir Thos Ogilvy dishorsed, the Earl of Kinnoul had his horse shot with a canon, Sir John Drummond was wounded in the head. Montrose orders Major Lachlan to bid his men throw away their pikes and guns and take to swords and durks, saying 'resolution must do it.'" "Montrose hasted into the town to save it from being plundered whereby it had little loss save by those who were killed in the battle." Some of the fighting men were pursued into the town and killed. The soldier who parted with his leg so bravely is mentioned. Later on Lord Carnegy killed two straggling Irish, and fled before Colonels Hay and Gordon to Dundee. They burnt some houses at the Town End. "The news" only covers the events up to Fyvie. To prove its truth it quotes in full a document calling a Solemn Fast for four causes, of which the fourth is, "By the breach already made by a contemptible crew, naked and unarmed, upon our dear brethren in Stratherne, Fyfe, Aberdeen and other parts of the north." The document is signed "A. KER."

There are two copies of above, *Bodleian* 40. *L.* 73.

> II. "Chancellor Loudon's speech before a grand Committee of both Houses of Parliament.
>
> Published by authoritie.
>
> Printed at London by E. P. for Hugh Perrey in the Strand 1645."

It is a vigorous appeal to the English on the claim of the mutual League and Covenant for aid to meet the catastrophe of Kilsyth.

It gives his views of the battle.

> III. "Montrose totally Routed at Tividale in Scotland on Saturday last by Lieutenant General Lesly where were taken and killed Two thousand Foot, Eight hundred Horse, and nine Knights; and all the King's Papers and Writings sent to Montrose are taken.
>
> Sent to a Member of the Honorable House of Commons, and appointed to be forthwith printed.
>
> London, Printed for Edward Husband Printer to the Honorable House of Commons, Sep 18$^h$ 1645."

*"To the Worshipfull Edmund Prideaux Esq., One of the Honorable House of Commons.*

Sir—I think it my duty to give you notice at present, of the good News come hither this night out of the North by Sir James Hachet, of a Battell fought in Tividale, on Saturday last in the morning betwixt Montrose, and Lieutenant General David Lesly, where Montrose, after a short dispute, was totally Routed, his army consisting of one thousand Horse, and Two thousand of his prime Foot, of which not twenty escaped.

# POSTSCRIPT.

About Two hundred of his Horse with himself saved themselves by flight. There are 9 Knights taken Prisoners amongst which Sir David Murray, Sir Alexander Lesly, Sir William Rog, Sir William Tewes slain, with whom is found all the Writings from the King to Montrose.

We had this News about nine this night, and to second it, we Received yours about eleven at night of the taking of Bristoll, which was welcome News here, for which I expresse my thankfulnesse and rest your humble servant

HULL, 15 *Sept* 1645
11 *at night*.

WILLIAM THOMPSON.

*For Yourself.*

Sir—In few words Montrosse had this day One thousand four hundred Foot and One thousand horse or thereabouts in the Field; the Foot are most of them killed many of the Horse are escaped; Lanerick took Spotwood prisoner, with the Seal of Secretary in his pocket: One thousand four hundred Foot and Horse were sent by Monroe into the Highlands, and six hundred another way, being confident that Lieutenant Generall Lesly was south of Newcastle when in truth he was in Scotland. All Montrosse his Papers are taken: Two thousand two hundred Scottish sent for into Ireland, are landed in the North of Scotland. We hear no further News of a Meeting about our businesse; My Service to your Master from Your Servant.

The good service of some English in Commissary Generall Middleton's Regiment is much spoken of.

BARWICKE, 13*th Sept* 1645.

FINIS."

The above is the entire sheet.

IV. "The Great Victories"
"Commanded to be printed, and published according to order. London Printed by Jane Coe 1645."

The great victories are 1st, at Chester by Col. Jones, 2nd, at "Divizes" by Cromwell, and 3rd, Philiphaugh. The account of Philiphaugh is supplied by David Lesly himself to Leven.

"Here followeth the copie of a Letter from Lieut Gen David Leshly to Generall Leshly his father (sic); of his great Victory against Montrosse on Saturday and Sonday Sep the 13th and 14th 1645.

For his Excellency the Earl of Leven, these present.

*May it please Your Excellency;*

It hath which God to give us (sic) a Notable and unexpected Victorie highly begun on the 13 of Sept between 11 and 12 a clock and was pursued the next day. All Montrosse's forces which were Irish and Highlanders, killed upon the place, the strength of horse and dragoones were about 2000, which are all fled severall wayes. I protest I never fought with better horsemen and against more resolute foote who were drawn up amongst the closes. The commanded horsemen, and Middleton's Regiment were put once back but advanced againe and did most gallantly." Then follows commendation of Nobles and officers by name, and he states his purpose of going to Glasgow to keep "Colekintoe" in the west. It is dated "From the place where the Battle was fought 15th of Sept 1645."

Then we have a

"List of the particulars of this great Victory obtained by Lieut Gen Leshly against Montrose Sep 17th.

3 Barons slain upon the place, 2500 killed upon the place, 300 killed in pursuit, 500 run to their own homes.

Taken prisoners—Earle of Tarquire, Lord Linton, Lord Seaton, Lord Dunnould, Lord Grey, Lord Ogleby, 1700 taken prisoners. Montrose fled with not 20 men with him, 200 Irish shot to death against posts after they were taken straggling in the country."

There is then a note to the effect that "the Scots have not lost one Nobleman," only Middleton's father whom Montrose "murdered (before the fight too) in his bed a grave ould gentleman, that never took up armes at all."

V. "A True Relation of the totall Routing of the Lord George Digby and Sir Marmaduke Langdale by the Scottish Forces under the Command of Sir John Browne of Fordell, Knight.

Published by Authority.

Printed by M. B. for Robert Bostock at the Kings Head in Pauls Churchyard 1645.

The Papers from II. to V. inclusive are in one Vol. in the Bodleian, Ash. 1071.

In the first named vol. there are 33 pamphlets besides the "True Relation," several of them having reference to Scotland. No. 22 is a collection of Letters from Argyll, Lanark, Warriston, and others, "now at Edinburgh, to their friends at London, intercepted by Sir Rich. Willys, Governour of Newark" printed at Oxford 1645.

Two of our Illustrations claim a special note, the Frontispiece and the Seal on our Title.

The Frontispiece is a reproduction of Faed's engraving for the Maitland Club of the beautiful portrait of Montrose by Gerard Honthorst (*Gherardo dalle notte*), now at Brechin Castle. Mr. Mark Napier brought the picture to light, and has given a full account of it both in the Memorials and in the Memoirs of Montrose. It was painted in 1649, immediately after the death of Charles the First, and presented, it would seem, to the Queen of Bohemia by Montrose himself. She hung it in her cabinet "to fright away the Brethern." "The figure appears clad in black armour, significant of the profound but menacing grief of the warlike mourner for his martyred King; the right hand grasps the (red) baton of the Empire; the left rests on a helmet overshadowed by funeral plumes; and a background of sombre scenery, illuminated by a single gleam, supports the dignity of the composition, and marks the genius of Gherardo." These are the words of Lord Napier, in an article in *Fraser's Magazine*, June 1851.

The Seal which adorns our title-page was found attached to some of the last private letters written by Montrose. A Lion crouches on the pinnacle of a precipice in act to spring across a deep ravine to a higher precipice beyond. The motto is NIL MEDIUM—the "win or lose it all" "of his wild ballad." The device and motto appear on Montrose's own standard in his last expedition. "That he was wont to write the fatal sentiment to Prince Rupert, that in his troubadour vein he sang it to an imaginary mistress, that he bore it on his banner, and had it engraven on his signet, all shows how deeply it was graven on the hero's heart. The trammelled Lion, tripped by the treaty of Breda, missed its spring, and fell in the yawning gulph." So writes the chivalrous yet laborious historian of Montrose, Mr. Mark Napier, to whose work the Editors owe, and gladly record, great indebtedness.

They have also to express their obligations to his son, Lieutenant Napier, R.N., for permission to use these engravings, as likewise to his publisher, Mr. Thomas Stevenson, for ready aid and concurrence.

Special thanks are due to Keepers of Archives, Herren C. F. Bricka, Copenhagen;

## POSTSCRIPT.

C. F. Oedhner, Stockholm; Friedländer, Berlin; Dr. Hagedorn, Hamburg; Gabriel Gustafson, Bergen; Kr. Koren, Throndhjem; Baron Bühler, Moscow; Arneth, Vienna; Mons. Servois, Paris; Th. H. F. van Rienndyk, The Hague; and Mr. W. G. Fletcher, British Museum, for their researches in our favour: also to Dr. Joass, Golspie; the Rev. W. D. Macray, and Mr. Firth, Oxford; Mr. Slight, Court of Justiciary, Edinburgh; Mr. William Mackay, Inverness; Mr. W. W. Graham-Watt, Skaill, Orkney, for valuable information; and the Advocates for leave to use the MSS. and Wodrow letters in their library.

Mr. A. Graham Murray, M.P., by the loan of the Acts of Parliament of Scotland and other books of difficult access, has greatly lessened our labour, and Mr. Alex. T. Y. Simpson, Newcastle-on-Tyne, has rendered great assistance in compiling the Index. The courtesy of librarians has been unfailing. Our thanks to others for material aid has been in most cases expressed in our notes, but want of space forbids the recognition of much for which we are grateful.

A. D. M.<br>H. F. M. S.

*May* 1, 1893.

## AUTHORITIES REFERRED TO IN THIS EDITION.

Aberdeen, Description of, in 1661 (Spalding Club). 1842.
—— Extracts from Burgh Records of (Spalding Club). 2 vols. 1844.
—— Extracts from Ecclesiastical History of (Spalding Club). 1846.
—— Records of University of (Spalding Club). 1855.
Anderson, Joseph, "Scotland in Early Christian Times." Edinburgh. 1881.
Antiquaries, Proceedings of Society of, of Scotland. Index vol. 1893.
Assynt MS. (see Taylor), "History of the Parish." 1832. In the Dunrobin archives.
Ayton, "Life of Alexander Henderson."

Baillie, Rev. Robert, "Letters and Journals." 3 vols. Edinburgh. 1841.
Balcanquall. See "Large Declaration."
Balfour, Sir James, "Annales of Scotland." 4 vols. Edinburgh. 1825.
Bates, T., "Elenchi motuum nuperorum."
Billings and Burns, "Baronial Remains of Scotland."
Black, David D., "History of Brechin." Brechin. 1839.
Blackhal, "Narration" (Spalding Club). 1844.
Brand, John, "History of Newcastle-on-Tyne." 3 vols. 1789.
"Britane's Distemper," by Patrick Gordon (Spalding Club). 1841.
Brodie, Diary of Lairds of (Spalding Club). 1852.
Bryce, James, "Confessions of Faith, Catechisms, Collection of Acts, &c." Glasgow. 1761.
Burnet, Bishop, "Lives of James and William, Dukes of Hamilton." London. 1677.
—— "History of his own Time." London. 1883.
Burton, J. H., "The Scot Abroad." Edinburgh. 1881.
—— "History of Scotland."

Calder, "History of Caithness." Glasgow. 1861.
Calderwood, "History of the Kirk of Scotland." 8 vols. Edinburgh. 1844.
Carlyle, "Cromwell's Letters and Speeches." 3 vols. London. 1857.
Chambers' "History of the Rebellion in Scotland under Montrose." Edinburgh. 1828.
"Chanut, Memoires de." 1677.
"Churches of St. Baldred" (A. J. Ritchie). Edinburgh. 1880.
Clarendon, "History of the Rebellion." 6 vols. Oxford. 1717.
"Cloud of Witnesses" (see Naphtali).
"Confessions of Faith." Glasgow. 1761.
Connell, Sir John, "Treatise on Law of Scotland respecting Tithes." 3 vols. Edinburgh. 1815.

lx  AUTHORITIES REFERRED TO IN THIS EDITION.

"Coronation of Charles I." (Henry Bradshaw Society). London. 1892.
Craven, Rev. J. B., "History of the Episcopal Church in Moray." London. 1889.

Danske Magazin.
"Douglas Peerage" (Woode). 2 vols. Edinburgh. 1813.
Dunlop, Alexander, "Parochial Law." Edinburgh. 1841.

Evelyn, John, "Memoirs and Diary of" (Ed. W. Bray). 5 vols. London. 1827.

Fife, Extracts from Minutes of Synod of (Abbotsford Club).
Forbes, Bishop Robert, "Journals," by Rev. J. B. Craven. London. 1886.

Gardiner, S. R., "History of England." 10 vols. 8vo. London. 1886.
—— "History of the Great Civil War." 3 vols. London. 1886.
Gordon (of Sallagh), continuation of "History of Earls of Sutherland." Edinburgh. 1813.
Gordon ("Parson of Rothiemay"), "History of Scots Affairs" (Spalding Club). 3 vols. 1841.
Grameid, James Philp (Scottish History Society). 1888.
Grub, George, "Ecclesiastical History of Scotland." 4 vols. 8vo. 1861.
Guthrie, James, Life of (Free Kirk General Assembly Committee). Edinburgh. 1846.
Guthrie, Bishop Henry, "Memoirs." Glasgow. 1747.
Gwynne, "Military Memoirs" (Ed. Sir Walter Scott). Edinburgh. 1822.
Green, Mary A. E., "Lives of Princesses of England." 2 vols. London. 1854-55.

Heath, John, "Chronicle of the Late Intestine War." Second Edition. London. 1676.
Henderson, Alexander, Life of, by Free Kirk General Assembly Committee. Edinburgh. 1846.
Henderson, John, "Caithness Family History." Edinburgh. 1884.
Hutchinson, "History of Durham." 2 vols. Newcastle. 1785.
—— "History of Northumberland." 2 vols. Newcastle. 1778.

Innes, Family of (Spalding Club). 1864.

Jervise, Andrew, "Land of the Lindsays." Edinburgh. 1882.
—— "Memorials of Angus and Mearns." 2 vols. 1885.
—— "Epitaphs" (vol. ii.). 1879.

Keith, "Catalogue of Scottish Bishops." Edinburgh. 1824.

Lamont, John, "His Diary, 1649-1672." Edinburgh. 1810.
"Large Declaration, The King's." Dr. Balcanquall. London. 1638.
Lyons, "History of St. Andrews." 2 vols. Edinburgh. 1843.
Mackay, William, in "Transactions of the Gaelic Society of Inverness" (vol. xvi.) 1889-90.

## AUTHORITIES REFERRED TO IN THIS EDITION.

Mackenzie, Sir George, "Vindication of the Government in Scotland during the Reign of King Charles II." London. 1691.
Mackenzie, "History of the Macdonalds."
—— "History of the M'Leods."
M'Dowall, William, "History of Dumfries." Edinburgh. 1867.
Mahon, Lord, "Essay on Montrose" ("Quarterly Review," p. 157, Dec. 1846).
Maidment, "Book of Scottish Pasquils, 1568–1715." Edinburgh. 1868.
Maitland, "History of Edinburgh." Edinburgh. 1753.
Masson, David, "Drummond of Hawthornden." London. 1873.
Maxwell, Alexander, "History of Old Dundee." Edinburgh. 1884.
"Memorie of the Somervilles." Edinburgh. 1815.
"Mercurius Aulicus," 1643–44 (Advocates' Library, Edinburgh).
"Mercurius Britannicus," 1643 and 1659 (Advocates' Library, Edinburgh).
"Mercurius Caledonius," 1648 (Writers' Library, Edinburgh).
Mitchell, Prof. Alexander F., D.D., "Catechisms of the Second Reformation." London. 1886.
—— "Records of the Commissions of the General Assemblies" (Scottish History Society). 1892.
Monteith, Robert, of Salmonet, "History of the Troubles of Great Britain," Translated by J. Ogilvie. Second Edition. London. 1738.
—— "Histoire des Troubles de la Grande Bretagne." First Edition. Paris. 1661.
"Montrose Routed at Tividale," and numerous contemporary pamphlets in Bodleian Library. 1 vol.
Morris, Mowbray, "Montrose." London. 1892.

"Naphtali and Cloud of Witnesses." 8vo. Glasgow. 1846.
Napier, Mark, "Memoirs of Dundee." 3 vols. 8vo. Edinburgh. 1859.
—— "Life of Montrose." 1840.
—— "Memoirs of Montrose." 2 vols. 8vo. Edinburgh. 1856.
—— "Memorials of Montrose" (Maitland Club). 2 vols. 4to. 1850.
"Newcastle, Siege and Storming of." Compiled by Thos. Allan. Newcastle. 1889.
"New Statistical Account of Scotland." 15 vols. Edinburgh. 1845.

"Ormonde Papers," Edited by Thomas Carte. 2 vols. London. 1739.

Pococke, Right Rev. Richard, "Tours in Scotland" (Scottish History Society). 1887
"Presbytery Book of Strathbogie" (Spalding Club). 1843.
Public Records, "The Forty-Seventh Annual Report of Deputy-Keeper of."

Ritchie, A. J., "Churches of St. Baldred." Edinburgh. 1880.
Rothes, John, Earl of, "Relation of Proceedings concerning the Affairs of the Kirk of Scotland" (Bannatyne Club). 1830.
Roundhead Officers, Letters of (Bannatyne Club). 1851.
Row, "History of the Kirk of Scotland" (Woodrow Society). Edinburgh. 1842.
"Rupert, Prince, Memoirs of," Edited by Warburton. 1849.

"Ruthven Papers" (Roxburgh Club).
Scot, Hew, "Fasti Ecclesiæ Scoticanæ." 6 vols.
Sculptured Stones of Scotland (Stuart). 2 vols. fol. Spalding Club. 1867.
"Seaforth Archives."
"Seton, Memoirs of Chancellor." Edinburgh. 1882.
Shaw, Lachlan, "History of Moray." 3 vols. Glasgow. 1882.
Shiels, Rev. Allen, "Hinde let Loose." Edinburgh. 1744.
"Siege and Storming of Newcastle" (told by eye-witnesses). Newcastle. 1889.
Skinner, "Ecclesiastical History of Scotland." 2 vols. London. 1788.
Spalding, "Memorials of the Troubles" (Spalding Club). Aberdeen. 1851.
"Spalding Club Miscellany." Aberdeen. 1852.
"Spottiswoode Club Miscellany." 2 vols. 1844.
"Spottiswoode Club Miscellany." 2 vols. Edinburgh. 1845.
Spottiswoode, Sir Robert, "Practicks of the Laws of Scotland." Edinburgh. 1706.
—— Archbishop, "History of the Church of Scotland" (Spottiswoode Club). 3 vols. 1851.
Sprot, Rev. G. W., "Scottish Liturgies of the Reign of James VI." Edinburgh. 1871.
"St. Andrews and Cupar, Selections from Presbyteries of" (Abbotsford Club). 1837.
"St. Andrews Kirk-Session, Records of" (Scottish History Society). 2 vols. 1889-90.
Stephen, "History of the Church of Scotland." 4 vols. London. 1844.
"Stirlingshire, History of," by Nimmo. 2 vols. 8vo. 1817.
Story, Rev. R. H. "Career of William Carstares." Edinburgh. 1874.

"Thurloe Papers," Edited by J. Birch. 7 vols. London. 1742.
"True Relation of Happy Success in Scotland." 1644. With 33 other contemporary pamphlets in Bodleian Library. 1 vol.
Turner, Sir James, "Memoirs" (Maitland Club). 1829.

Urquhart, Sir Thomas, "Memoirs." (From Burton's "Scot Abroad.")
"Universal Kirk, Booke of."

Walker, Clement ("Theodorus Verax"), "Anarchia Anglicana, or History of Independency." First Edition. 1649.
—— John, "Sufferings of the Clergy." London. 1714.
"Wardlaw MS.," by Mr. John Fraser, in Dr. R. Carruthers' "Highland Note-Book." Edinburgh. 1843. Reprint.
"Westminster Confession of Faith." Edinburgh. 1889.
"Whitelocke's Journal."
"Wigton Papers." Miscellany, Maitland Club.
Wilson, Daniel, "Memorials of Edinburgh." 2 vols. Edinburgh.
"Wodrow MSS.," fol. lxvii. (Advocates' Library). Edinburgh.
—— fol. MS. of Wishart, Part II.
—— 4to MS. of Wishart, Part II.

# LIST OF SUBSCRIBERS.

## A

HER GRACE THE DUCHESS-DOWAGER OF ATHOLE.
THE LORD BISHOP OF ABERDEEN AND ORKNEY.
THE LORD BISHOP OF ARGYLL AND THE ISLES.
THE RIGHT HON. LADY ADDINGTON, Winslow, Bucks.
The Rev. F. L. M. ANDERSON, North Berwick.
R. ROWAND ANDERSON, Esq., LL.D., Colinton.
EDWARD G. ALLEN, Esq. (for Library of Parliament), Ottawa.
JOHN RAMSAY ANDERSON, Esq., Edinburgh.
THOMAS and GEORGE ALLAN, Newcastle-on-Tyne.
ARCHIBALD ANDERSON, Esq., Oxford Square, London.
THOMAS ANDREW, Esq., Doune.
Miss ADDIE, Birkenshaw, Edinburgh.
JAMES ALLAN, Esq., Helensburgh.

## B

THE RIGHT HON. LORD BLYTHSWOOD.
The Rev. G. STEWART BURNS, D.D., Glasgow.
The Rev. JAMES BEALE, Duns.
The Rev. S. GILBERT BEAL, Darlington.
JOSEPH BELL, Esq., M.D., Edinburgh.
F. T. BARRET, Esq. (Mitchell Library), Glasgow.
ROBERT BLAIR, Esq. (Secretary, Society of Antiquaries of Newcastle).
J. P. M. BLACKETT, Esq., B.A., Elstree, Herts.
Miss BLACK, Glencairn Crescent, Edinburgh.
JOHN S. BLACK, Esq., Oxford Terrace, Edinburgh.
JOHN BLAIR, Esq., W.S., Ettrick Road, Edinburgh.
ROBERT FITZROY BELL, Esq., Heriot Row, Edinburgh.
J. W. BOWHILL, Esq., B.A., Trinity, Edinburgh.
JAMES BRUCE, Esq., W.S., St. Bernard's Crescent, Edinburgh.
Miss MARY BURTON, Liberton.
JOHN WILLIAM BURNS, Esq., Cardross.
JAMES BROOKMAN, Esq., W.S., Ravelstone Park, Edinburgh.

## LIST OF SUBSCRIBERS.

R. P. BRERETON, Esq., M.A., Oundle.
WILLIAM BARRIE, Esq., St. Vincent Street, Glasgow
JAMES H. BISSET, Esq., Burnside House, Aberdeen.
G. W. BRUCE, Esq., Leven.
CHARLES B. BALFOUR, Esq., Newton Don, Kelso.

### C

Sir THOMAS D. GIBSON CARMICHAEL, Bart., Peeblesshire.
T. CRAIG-CHRISTIE of Bedlay, Esq., Glasgow.
The Rev. J. B. CRAVEN, Kirkwall.
The Rev. HUGH C. R. CUNNYNGHAME, Edinburgh.
J. T. CLARK, Esq. (Advocates' Library), Edinburgh.
JOSEPH COWEN, Esq., Blaydon-on-Tyne.
Mrs. J. H. CHAPLIN, Pen-y-wern Road, London.
ALASTAIR CURRIE, Esq., Trinity, Edinburgh.
JAMES CURLE, Esq., junr., W.S., Melrose.
Mrs. COCHOT, Gibson Square, London.
THOMAS A. CROAL, Esq., London Street, Edinburgh.
ROBERT CARFRAE, Esq., George Street, Edinburgh.
Miss C. H. CHARTERS, Gillespie Crescent, Edinburgh
Miss CULLEN, Panmure Place, Edinburgh (2 copies).
Miss JANE BOTHWELL CURRY, Montpelier, Edinburgh
DUNCAN CAMERON, Esq., Tain.
JAMES COWAN, Esq., 35 Royal Terrace, Edinburgh.

### D

LADY DOUGLAS, Edinburgh.
LADY DOUGLAS, Watford, Herts.
Mrs. HOME-DRUMMOND, Stirlingshire.
ARTHUR DICKSON, Esq., Montrose.
DOUGLAS & FOULIS, Edinburgh (3 copies).

### E

THE LORD BISHOP OF EDINBURGH.

### F

The Rev. HENRY FYFE, Fraserburgh.
The Rev. W. Y. FAUSSET, M.A., Ripon.
J. R. FINDLAY, Esq., Rothesay Terrace, Edinburgh.

## LIST OF SUBSCRIBERS.

W. HOWDEN FERME, Esq., Haddington.
R. B. FINLAY, Esq., Phillimore Gardens, London.
J. B. FLEMING, Esq., Kelvinside, Glasgow.
E. G. FRAENKL, Esq., Osborne Villa, Dundee.

### G

THE LORD BISHOP OF GLASGOW.
The Rev. J. STEWART GAMMELL of Drumtochty, Fordoun.
Lieut.-Col. R. C. GRÆME, Naval and Military Club, London.
Lieut.-Col. G. GARDYNE, Forfar.
JOHN GRAHAME, Esq. (Sheriff-Substitute), Perthshire.
THOMAS GRAHAME, Esq., St. Enoch Square, Glasgow.
Mrs. GRANT of Kilgraston, Bridge of Earn.
HENRY O. OGILVIE GRANT, Esq., Blythswood Square, Glasgow.
GEORGE GRAY, Esq., Glasgow.
NORMAN J. N. GOURLIE, Esq., Wardie, Edinburgh.
JAMES L. GREIG, Esq., B.A., Oxford Terrace, Edinburgh.

### H

(The late) Sir JOHN D. HOPE, Bart., Pinkie House.
The Rev. W. A. HEARD, M.A., Fettes College.
The Rev. J. W. HUNTER, Callander.
The Rev. C. G. HENDERSON-HAMILTON of Dalserf, Hamilton.
W. J. HAGGERSTON, Esq. (Public Libraries), Newcastle-on-Tyne.
R. HARRISON, Esq. (London Library).
JOHN HOWKINS, Esq., Queensberry Lodge, Granton Road, Edinburgh.
G. C. HARRISON, Esq., M.A., Fettes College.
JOHN HURD, Esq., Lenzie.
E. A. HANSELL, Esq., M.A., Oundle.
W. C. HENDERSON & SON, St. Andrews.

### I

The Rev. R. MITCHELL-INNES, Edinburgh.
(The late) ALEXANDER FORBES-IRVINE, Esq., of Drum.

### J

GEORGE AULDJO JAMIESON, Esq., W.S., Drumsheugh Gardens, Edinburgh.
HENRY JOHNSTON, Esq., St. Colme Street, Edinburgh.
Mr. GEORGE P. JOHNSTON, George Street, Edinburgh (2 copies).
Mrs. JOHNSTONE, Moray Place, Edinburgh.

## LIST OF SUBSCRIBERS.

### K

The Rev. Canon KEATING (for Episcopal Theological Library), Edinburgh.
Mrs. W. DOUGLAS KIRKPATRICK, Leck, Kirkby Lonsdale.
KEGAN PAUL, TRENCH, TRÜBNER, & CO., London (2 copies).

### L

JAMES LYMBURN, Esq. (for Glasgow University Library).
THOMAS G. LAW, Esq. (for Signet Library), Edinburgh.
B. P. LASCELLES (for Harrow School Library).
Miss J. D. LANGLANDS, Strathearn Place, Edinburgh.
FREDERICK T. C. LINTON, Esq., Leith.

### M

Sir W. A. MACKINNON, K.C.B., London.
The Rev. A. GRAY MAITLAND, Dudley.
JOHN MACKENZIE, Esq., Manor Place, Edinburgh.
HENRY DUNNING MACLEOD, Esq., Oxford and Cambridge Club, London.
ALEXANDER MACPHERSON, Esq., Kingussie, N. B.
DAVID MACBRAYNE, Esq., Royal Exchange Square, Glasgow.
ALEXANDER W. MACDOUGALL, Esq., Wantage.
J. E. SWINTON MAXWELL, Esq., Canning Street, Liverpool.
J. W. MORKILL, Esq., M.A., Killingbeck, Leeds.
IAN MACINTYRE, Esq., M.A., Albany Street, Edinburgh.
R. C. H. MILLAR, Esq., Montrose.
Mrs. MORETON MACDONALD, Largie.
JOHN METHUEN, Esq., Ross-shire.
Mrs. MACINNES, Great Stuart Street, Edinburgh.
DAVID MURRAY, Esq., West George Street, Glasgow.
Mrs. MEAKIN, Adamson Road, London, N.W.
WILLIAM MACKAY, Esq., Inverness.

### N

THE RIGHT HON. LORD NAPIER AND ETTRICK, Selkirk.
The Rev. W. S. NICHOLSON, Dundee.
ROBERT T. NORFOR, Esq., Morningside Drive, Edinburgh.
Miss ANNE NAPIER, Alva Street, Edinburgh.

# LIST OF SUBSCRIBERS.

## O

Sir REGINALD OGILVY, Bart., Inchture.
HENRY T. N. HAMILTON OGILVY, Esq., Biel.
Sir DAVID F. OCHTERLONY, Bart., St. Andrew Square, Edinburgh.

## P

GEORGE A. PATERSON, Esq., M.D., Coates Crescent, Edinburgh.
FREDERICK PITMAN, Esq., Great Stuart Street, Edinburgh.
HOWARD PEASE, Esq., Newcastle-on-Tyne.
R. Y. PICKERING, Esq., Montgomery Quadrant, Glasgow.
J. PARSONS, Esq., Ann Street, Edinburgh.
Mrs. R. O'B. PRICHARD, Edinburgh.
Miss PLATT, Kirkby Lonsdale.
T. L. PATON, Esq., M.A., Rocester, Stafford.

## R

JOHN RAMSAY, of Barra, Esq., Aberdeen.
COLIN G. ROSS, Esq., Newcastle-on-Tyne.
J. S. REID, Esq., Litt.D., Cambridge.
J. C. ROGER, Esq., Essex.
W. BROWN ROBERTSON, Esq., Dundee.
CECIL REDDIE, Esq., M.A., Ph.D., Abbotsholme, Derbyshire.

## S

THE (late) LORD BISHOP OF ST. ANDREWS.
THE RIGHT HON. THE EARL OF SOUTHESK, K.T., LL.D.
Sir JOHN R. SINCLAIR, Bart., of Dunbeath, Wick.
The Rev. C. E. SEARLE, D.D., Pembroke College, Cambridge.
The Rev. W. STEPHEN, Dumbarton.
The Rev. C. PRESSLEY SMITH, Edinburgh.
W. S. THOMSON-SINCLAIR, of Freswick, Esq., Dunbeath Castle, Caithness.
THE SECRETARY OF THE ANTIQUARIAN SOCIETY, Newcastle-on-Tyne.
PATRICK STIRLING, of Kippenross, Esq., Dunblane (3 copies).
H. SCOTT, of Brotherstone, Esq., Johnshaven.
DAVID STEWART, Esq., Banchory House, Aberdeen.
FRANCIS R. SANDERSON, Esq., Galashiels.
J. STRUTHERS, Esq., Drumsheugh Gardens, Edinburgh.

# LIST OF SUBSCRIBERS.

Mrs. SINCLAIR (of Barrock), 11 St. George's Road, London
Miss STUART, Torphichen Street, Edinburgh.
Mr. THOMAS G. STEVENSON, 22 Frederick Street, Edinburgh (4 copies).
JAMES S. STURROCK, Esq., Bruntsfield Place, Edinburgh (2 copies).
Herr OBERLEHRER A. SERAPHIM, Mitau, Courland, Russia.

## T

Sheriff GEORGE H. M. THOMS, Edinburgh.
D. W. TANQUERAY, Esq., M.A., Fettes College.
EDWIN TEMPLE, Esq., M.A., Glenalmond College.
W. TOMLINSON, Esq., Victoria Villas, Whitely-by-the-Sea.
Mr. JAMES THIN, South Bridge, Edinburgh (3 copies).

## W

The Rev. H. A. WILSON, Magdalen College, Oxford (2 copies).
The Rev. J. WISEMAN (Diocesan Library), Aberdeen.
Messrs. D. WYLLIE & SON (University Library), Aberdeen.
RICHARD WELFORD, Esq., Gosforth, near Newcastle-on-Tyne.
GEORGE W. WATSON, Esq., Walker Street, Edinburgh.
CECIL WHITE, Esq., Drummond Place, Edinburgh.
W. L. WATSON, Esq. (of Ayton House), Perthshire.
LOUSON WALKER, Esq., Greenock.
Miss WINGATE, Park Circus, Glasgow.

## Y

J. S. YEO, Esq., M.A., Fettes College.

# CONTENTS.

## ENGLISH TRANSLATION.

|  | PAGE |
|---|---|
| THE AUTHOR'S DEDICATION | 1 |
| THE AUTHOR'S PREFACE | 9 |

### PART I.—(1644–1646.)

#### CHAPTER I.

Pretexts of the Covenanters—Montrose detects their designs, 1639—They invade England and seize Newcastle, August 1640—Montrose's correspondence with the King betrayed—He forms an Association for the King—Charles's letters intercepted and Montrose imprisoned—Parliament at Edinburgh, July 1641—Montrose released . . . . . . . . . . . . . 13

#### CHAPTER II.

Conduct of the English malcontents, 1642—Montrose in England—Meets the Queen at York, February 1643—His advice rejected for that of Hamilton—Convention of Estates at Edinburgh, June 1643—Montrose's conference with Henderson, from whom he learns the designs of the Covenanters . . . 24

#### CHAPTER III.

Montrose joins the King at Gloucester—His plan approved, December 1643—Antrim promises help from Ireland—Hamilton and Lanark arrive at Oxford, December 1643—Arrest of the Duke and flight of Lanark to London—Montrose sets out for Scotland—Interview with the Marquis of Newcastle . . . 34

#### CHAPTER IV.

Montrose at Dumfries—The English soldiers desert—He returns to Carlisle—His movements in Northumberland—Interview with Prince Rupert—State of Scotland—Montrose enters Scotland in disguise, and reaches Graham of Inchbrakie in Perthshire . . . . . . . . . . . . . 45

#### CHAPTER V.

Arrival of the Irish—Montrose meets them in Athole—Is joined by Lord Kilpont and Sir J. Drummond—Battle of Tippermuir and surrender of Perth . . 54

## CONTENTS.

### CHAPTER VI.

March from Perth to Cupar in Angus—Assassination of Kilpont—Montrose joined by the Earl of Airlie and his two sons—March to Dundee—Defeat of Lord Burleigh at Aberdeen . . . . . . . . . . . 63

### CHAPTER VII.

Huntly prevents the Gordons from joining—Montrose retires into Badenoch—His illness causes rumours of his death—Returns to Athole and Angus, and crosses the Grampians to Strathbogie—Surprised by Argyll and Lothian at Fyvie—Beats his assailants off and retreats to Balveny . . . . . . 70

### CHAPTER VIII.

Montrose lays Argyleshire waste—March north to Loch Ness—Seaforth's levies to oppose him—Montrose turns back and crushes the Campbells at Inverlochy—Sir Thomas Ogilvy is killed . . . . . . . . . . 79

### CHAPTER IX.

Return northwards—Surrender of Elgin—Lord Gordon joins—Montrose enters the Mearns and defeats Hurry near Fettercairn—Offers battle to Baillie and Hurry on the Isla—Lewis Gordon deserts with most of his clan—Montrose retires north—Seizes Dundee—Extraordinary march to evade Baillie and reach the Grampians . . . . . . . . . . . . 87

### CHAPTER X.

Montrose at Crieff—Attacked by Baillie—Retreat by Strathearn—Joined by Aboyne—Pursues Hurry across the Spey to Elgin, Forres, and Inverness—Battle of Auldearn, May 1645 . . . . . . . . . . . 96

### CHAPTER XI.

Hurry joined by Baillie—They challenge Montrose—March up to Badenoch—The enemy retreat to Inverness—March southwards to attack Lindsay—Desertion of the Gordons—Battle of Alford—Lord Gordon killed . . . . 104

### CHAPTER XII.

March southwards to the Dee—Strong reinforcements from the Highlands—Convention of the Covenanters at Perth—Attack on Montrose's camp at Methven Wood—Montrose retreats to Little Dunkeld—Joined by the Gordons and Ogilvies—March into Strathearn . . . . . . . . 113

### CHAPTER XIII.

The Fife men join the Covenanters—Montrose marches to Kinross—Crosses the Forth—Battle of Kilsyth, and utter rout of Baillie, August 1645 . . . 119

## CONTENTS.

### CHAPTER XIV.

Flight of the Covenanting Lords—Montrose enters Glasgow—Joined by many noblemen—Edinburgh surrenders and releases the Royalist prisoners—Settlement of the west country . . . . . . . . . . 126

### CHAPTER XV.

Intrigues of Roxburgh, Home, and Traquair—Montrose appointed Commander-in-Chief and Lieutenant-Governor in Scotland—Macdonald and the Highlanders retire home, followed by Aboyne and his men—The King orders Montrose to march to the Borders and join Traquair and Roxburgh, who deceive him . 135

### CHAPTER XVI.

March to Selkirk, September 1645—Surprised by Leslie at Philiphaugh, and overpowered—Cuts his way through, and with half his forces regains Athole . . 142

### CHAPTER XVII.

Montrose joined by four hundred men of Athole—Butchery of prisoners by the Covenanters—Huntly refuses aid—Aboyne joins Montrose, but soon leaves him—March to Perthshire—Death of Lord Napier . . . . . 149

### CHAPTER XVIII.

Montrose in Lennox—The Covenanters execute Rollock, Alexander Ogilvy, Nisbet, O'Kean, and Lachlan—Montrose marches to Athole—His overtures again declined by Huntly, whom he surprises into an interview—They concert a plan to reduce Inverness and gain over Seaforth . . . . . . . 157

### CHAPTER XIX.

A party of Argyll's men invade Athole, but are defeated at Callander—Convention at St. Andrews—Lord Ogilvy escapes—Nathaniel Gordon, Sir Robert Spottiswood, Andrew Guthrie, and William Murray are executed . . . . 165

### CHAPTER XX.

Montrose refuses to retaliate on his prisoners—Huntly disappoints him—Montrose obliged to raise the siege of Inverness and retreat before Middleton—Huntly again shuns a conference—Huntly pillages Aberdeen . . . . . 174

### CHAPTER XXI.

The King at Newcastle orders Montrose to disband—The order is repeated, with terms for himself and friends—He disbands—The Covenanters try to prevent his departure—He escapes with his friends to Norway, September 1646 . . 182

# CONTENTS.

## PART II.—(1646–1650.)

### CHAPTER I.

Montrose in Norway—His journey to France—The Queen's courtiers endeavour to keep him from Court—Lord Jermyn's opposition—Montrose's advice to the Queen—The Queen accepts the overtures of the Presbyterians—Montrose leaves Paris . . . . . . . . . . . . 189

### CHAPTER II.

Character of the Presbyterians and Independents—The latter seize the King—The Presbyterians invoke Scotch aid—The Scotch raise an army—Hamilton appointed General—Factions of Hamilton and Argyll . . . . . 199

### CHAPTER III.

Hamilton invades England—Joined by Musgrave, Langdale, and others, who hand over Berwick and Carlisle—Defeated by Cromwell at Preston—Flight and surrender—A new army raised in Scotland under Lanark—Monro defeats Argyll at Stirling—Lanark's loyalty suspected—He concludes a dishonourable peace with Argyll—Cromwell and Argyll in Edinburgh . . . . . 208

### CHAPTER IV.

1649.—The King's execution—Conduct of the Scotch Commissioners in London—Montrose's journey to Prague and reception by the Emperor—He reaches the Hague, where he hears of the King's death—Attends Charles II. at the Hague—His advice opposed by Lanark and Lauderdale—Execution of the Duke of Hamilton . . . . . . . . . . . . . 224

### CHAPTER V.

Message to the Hague from the Estates, with their proclamation of Charles II. as King of Scotland—Arrival of Cassilis and the Commissioners—Huntly executed—The Commissioners present their demands—The opinion of the Scotch Peers—Charles leaves for France, attended to Brussels by Montrose . . . 235

### CHAPTER VI.

Montrose prepares for his descent on Scotland—State of affairs in Scotland and Ireland—His prospects of assistance from foreign courts thwarted by Scotch intrigues . . . . . . . . . . . . . 244

### CHAPTER VII.

1649.—Preparations for a descent on Scotland . . . . . . . 249

# CONTENTS.

## CHAPTER VIII.

State of Scotland in 1649-1650—Parliament, Courts, Kirk, Army—Affairs in Orkney—Montrose at Kirkwall—Orders to Hurry—Lands in Caithness—Declaration at Thurso—Caithness gentry—Effect of the news in the North—Dunbeath Castle taken—March to Carbisdale—Preparations at Edinburgh—Negotiations at Breda (Livingstone's Letter)—Lieutenant-Colonel Strachan; his letter to James Guthrie—Council of War at Tain—The local levy (Monroes and Rosses)—April 27, Strachan surprises Montrose at Carbisdale and cuts his army to pieces . . . . . . . . . . . . . . . 289

## CHAPTER IX.

Montrose's flight, capture, and journey south . . . . . . . 310

## CHAPTER X.

Sentence passed on Montrose—His entry into Edinburgh—Speech in the House—Last words and execution . . . . . . . . . . 322

English of Latin poem on the death of Montrose . . . . . . 335

## LATIN TEXT.

Part I. . . . . . . . . . . . . . . . 341
Part II. . . . . . . . . . . . . . . . 439
Wishart's poem on the death of Montrose . . . . . . . . 486

## APPENDICES.

I. Battle of Carbisdale—List of those killed and taken—Sequel of the expedition . 493
—Fate of the detachments left in Dunbeath, Strath Naver, and Orkney . 496

Rewards to the victors . . . . . . . . . . . . 501

II. (1.) Two letters from Montrose, Doune, Ap. 20, 1645, and Cullen Aboyne, 17 May 1645, extracted from the *Mercurius Aulicus* . . . . . . 501

(2.) News from his Majesty's army in Scotland, to be presented to the Most Honourable the Lord Lieutenant-General of Ireland; written at Inverlochy in Lochaber the 7th of February 1644 [1645] by an Irish officer in Alexander Macdonald's forces. (Carte's Ormonde Papers.) . . . . . 503

III. Verses written by the Marquis of Montrose upon the murder of King Charles I. 505
—Dr. Wishart's Latin version of Montrose's verses . . . . . 506

## CONTENTS.

|     |     | PAGE |
| --- | --- | --- |
| IV. | Two letters from the Berlin archives. Montrose to the Marquis of Brandenburg, Hague 22 Jul: 1649, and the reply thereto, Cleves, 27 July, 1649 | 506 |
| V. | Commission from Charles II. to Montrose, for settling the differences with the town of Hamburg and borrowing a sum of money from the Senate. St. Germains, 5th Sept. 1649 | 507 |
| VI. | Letter from Montrose to Frederick III., King of Denmark, Copenhagen, 19 Oct. 1649. From the royal archives in Copenhagen | 508 |

Letters and extracts from the royal archives in Stockholm

| VII. | Proposals on behalf of Charles II., submitted by Robert Meade to Queen Christina | 509 |
| --- | --- | --- |
| VIII. | Correspondence concerning Montrose at Gothenburg, 14 Nov. 1649—22 Feb. 1650, between Per Lindormsson Ribbing, Provincial Governor, Field-Marshall Count Linnart Torstensson, Governor-General, and Admiral Thyssen-Ankerhielm. (Eleven letters or extracts.) | 510 |
| IX. | List of the papers found in Dunbeath Castle, when taken by Leslie. Advocates' Library, Edinburgh | 515 |
| X. | Terms offered to Charles II. by the Scottish "Estates." Thurloe, State Papers | 516 |
| XI. | Extracts from records of the Presbytery of Dingwall, and letter from Smyth of Braco | 518 |
| XII. | Letter from Louis XIV. of France to the Estates of Scotland, and personal details on appearance of Montrose | 520 |
| XIII. | Did Neil Macleod betray Montrose? | 522 |
| XIV. | Relics of Montrose | 534 |

INDEX . . . . . . . . . . . . 538

# LIST OF ILLUSTRATIONS.

| | |
|---|---|
| PORTRAIT OF MONTROSE IN 1649 BY GERARD HONTHORST | *Frontispiece* |
| MONTROSE'S SEAL | *Title-page* |
| FACSIMILES, ORDERS SIGNED BY "GEORGE DRUMMOND;" "MARCH 8, 1650, KINNOULE" | *to face page* 292 |
| MAP, MONTROSE'S MARCH AND JOURNEY SOUTH (1650), WITH VIEW OF ARDVRECK CASTLE, ASSYNT | ,, ,, 294 |
| BATTLEFIELD OF CARBISDALE, APRIL 27, 1650 | ,, ,, 306 |
| RELICS OF MONTROSE; HIS FOREARM AND SWORD | 537 |

# The Author's Dedication.

To the Most High and Mighty

## CHARLES

*Of Scotland by the Grace of God, and Prince of Wales,*

*Duke of Rothesay,*

*Heir of Britain, France, and Ireland, &c.*

ITH all humility, most exalted Prince, this slight sketch of your most admirable servant Montrose is presented to your Highness. Though a rude, unpolished portrait, and clad in barbarous Latin, it will not fear the light, nor shrink from inspection, if your Highness will deign to receive it with that gracious favour you are wont to bestow on strangers introduced into your presence.[1] He may claim audience the more boldly as not wholly foreign to your notice,[2] but a true son of your paternal kingdom, though disowned, as it were, by the deadly wrong of the times, and reared and nurtured in a foreign land. Nor are there wanting many strongly marked features to reveal his fatherland and race. He is come of Scotland, your own country, the kingdom of a hundred and nine of your ancestors, whose sacred blood and lives survive in you. Receive, then, the son of that ancient realm, the humble servant of your beloved sire, his most gracious lord, and, amidst all the chances of adversity, your most devoted liege.

---

[1] As to the Prince's reception of the work, see a very curious letter printed at the end of this Dedication. It has not appeared in print before, as we believe. Burnet refers to the subject (Dukes of Hamilton, 344). "To oblige the Duke the more, a book being dedicated to his Highness containing some passages much to the Duke's dishonour, he refused to accept of it, and ordered it to be called in." At least *three* editions appeared in 1647-8 (*v.* Crit. Introd.).

[2] There is some confusion in the Latin between the portrait and the subject of it.

Yet if this suffice not to win your favour and induce you to bestow life upon our feeble offspring, deign at least in your great mercy to grant this poor little portrait, though sketched with unskilled pencil, some recognition of its lineaments and form. Even so endow it with life, if not with immortality. For who would despise the image of Alexander, Cæsar, Scipio, or of your grandsires, James the Peaceful, or Henry the Great, because it had been hewn by the hand of some obscure and clumsy artist? Montrose will not, I predict, want his Apelles or Leucippus, nor perchance a Homer to recite his deeds.[3] Meantime may it please you, gracious Prince, to accept this work of ours until their advent. Nor heed the roughness of our speech, but yield a generous audience to deeds of true Roman heroism, such as in fame and difficulty far transcend the crowd of common souls. The blots and errors you may detect, you will attribute, as is but just and fair, not to his genius, but rather to our lack of it. I can with confidence promise that your Montrose will fail neither to gratify nor be of service to your Highness.

What could be more gratifying to a Prince, second only to his sire, so nobly born and royally educated, accustomed from his cradle to all that savours of heroism, than to behold, embrace, and honour a hero, who, without boasting, is to be esteemed inferior to none of our age—

"*Quem sese ore ferens, quam forti pectore et armis!*"

Under the best of kings, your most gracious father, by his conduct in war he foreshadowed, as it were, the vigour of your own manhood. His achievements have won the admiration of the present, and the unceasing praises of all posterity. Envy attends on glory and dogs its footsteps. But envy is transitory and perishable; it will never overtake or obscure a firm and imperishable fame. Here, however, illustrious Prince, we show you no

"*Antiphaten Scyllamque, et cum Cyclope Charybdin;*"

no fabled monsters or specious miracles, but enemies, monsters in very semblance, and victories over them gained by a miracle. For what arrogant attempt of the Giants in the legends of "false Greece" have not these plotting "Sons of Earth" dared against God, religion, faith, law, and right in opposing your most august parents, yourself, and all your loyal subjects? By heaping up mountains of lies and calumny they have erected

---

[3] Prophetic of Aytoun, of the magnificent monument in St. Giles', Edinburgh, by Dr. Rowand Anderson, and the many efforts to give his features, culminating in Faed's reproduction of Honthorst's portrait (*v.* Frontispiece).

those strongholds from which they have made war on heaven with their impious force. What storied deed is told of Apollo, Pallas, or Mars in overthrowing those giants, which our hero has not undertaken, with no less valour, and accomplished with like success? That he has not entirely overthrown those whom he had conquered, is, we think, wholly to be attributed to your destiny, unwilling that your country should owe its glorious salvation to any but yourself. For the Enceladus and Titans who kept the sire in chains are destined to be hurled into the caves of Etna by the thunderbolts of the son alone.

And what could be more profitable to your Highness, in an undertaking to which you are bound by laws both human and divine, the rescue of your sire and country from a cruel tyranny, than ever to have before your eyes, as your forerunner and guide, him who first detected the secret plots, wiles, and treachery of the rebels, and almost alone showed how to overthrow their impious boldness and shatter their forces, grown to a head before they were recognised. Certainly you will not find in him mere " force without soul." For he is not more brilliant in the field than in the council. He advised (would to God his advice had prevailed!) that the monster should be throttled in the cradle; and when it had grown to maturity, only failed to crush it, that your valour might not be deprived of so glorious an exercise. In addition to his lofty courage and rare skill in war, you will find in him proofs of distinguished statesmanship, which though, to our misfortune, too little trusted, is destined hereafter to be of service to you and posterity. He urged that the rebels, who relied on the exceeding mercy of a most excellent sovereign, on his clemency to offenders, his trust in the unworthy, his generosity to ingrates, his indulgence to all, rather than on their own powers, should at once be assailed and quelled by righteous force of arms, the only possible remedy, ere their power, grown strong by forbearance, had surpassed all bounds. If only this had been done, Britain would not have shuddered with civil bloodshed, the splendid temples of our Lord would not have been impiously desecrated, our market-places would not have reeked with the blood of nobles and priests, your sire and brothers would not have languished in ignoble durance, nor would you and your mother, so widowed, as it were, now be exiles on a foreign though a kindred and a friendly shore.

> "*Quis talia fando*
> *Temperet a lachrimis?*"

But though in achievements glorious even beyond envy, the hand of God Almighty is most brilliantly made manifest, that to Him alone the whole undivided glory may be given, who would not recognise, honour, extol, and love him whom God in His great mercy hath deigned to appoint as His agent? Had Montrose been forced to contend with a single enemy, face to face, his achievements might have seemed less considerable. But though exposed to attack from two, and often even three hosts, in front, in flank, and rear, the least of them far superior to all his forces in numbers, arms, and ammunition, he always extricated himself with boldness and success. His only store of powder, arms, and other munitions was what he wrested from the conquered enemy. In one year he gained six brilliant and complete victories, and utterly expelled the Covenanted lords from Scotland. During a winter of exceptional severity he lived for the most part in the open air, without quarters, without even tents. He endured all war's hardships with nothing to appease his thirst and hunger but icy water or melted snow, without bread and salt, and with only a scanty supply of lean and starveling cattle. But his greatest difficulty was to contend with those who wished to seem his Majesty's most eager champions, slothful cowards, flown with insolence, mean waverers, soiled with avarice or abominable treachery. Certainly he could never have borne and overcome all these difficulties without the most invincible constancy and indomitable love towards his dearest sovereign.

Unlike other generals, he was unable to restrain his troops by the severity of law or punishments. He had neither the power nor right. They received no pay; they fought solely for love of their king and affection to their leader. At any moment they could desert to the rebels, if offended by the smallest injury, or subject to the least appearance of disgrace—men, for the most part, insolent and factious, prone to mutiny on the slightest provocation. To maintain his influence and authority in such an army was of all tasks the most difficult. His most anxious thought was how to adapt his plans and actions to the measure of others, or at least to seem to comply when compelled to feign compliance.

But, to advance the royal cause, he looked down with indifference and lofty contempt on the hatred of the enemy, the envy of rivals, the calumnies of courtiers, the complaints of friends, the abuse of the vulgar herd, and—what was more bitter than all, and served more to terrify the superstitious commons—denunciations and curses of frenzied ministers: a general altogether worthy of a nobler war and a happier age.

Finally, these memoirs of Montrose will show your Highness what is our greatest hope for your future fortunes—that the Scots have never all been rebels to their most excellent king. To say otherwise is grievously to misrepresent our nation, a cruel and malicious slander of our enemies, as unjust to men of honour, ready to suffer any hardship in His Majesty's cause, as they have been treacherous and disloyal to your sire and yourself. Their sole aim is to discredit and cripple your friends, servants, and most faithful subjects, whose loyalty and courage fills them with evil terror, lest those wicked conspirators should, through them, be forced to pay the due penalties of treason. Let no caviller declare that we think or speak ill of the most noble nation of England, a charge we abhor with our whole soul. Many of them have aided their king with loyalty and courage, to their own eternal glory. This we gladly recognise and declare, and congratulate them for it. Only let them treat us with the same justice and candour, and not impute to our whole race the crime of a mere faction, however powerful and great. Let them do to others as they would be done by, and not deny that there have been Scots, the most distinguished men of every rank, who in the most desperate times have willingly shed their blood in upholding and vindicating the royal majesty against a conspiracy of scoundrels, both Scotch and English. This is, in truth, so manifest, that, without boasting, they can confidently declare that, with no pay or recompense beyond their loyalty and affection to a most gracious king, they have suffered and inflicted on their foes far greater losses in proportion to their means, and have gained over them more famous victories, than those who, when the king's treasure was utterly exhausted, reduced him to such complete destitution, that he was, in effect, compelled to surrender to the conspirators. Alas! how much better had it been, as the event shows, had he betaken himself to his trusty Scots; not to those rebels who opposed him on behalf of the English conspirators, but to those duteous, brave, loyal subjects who were fighting his battles under Montrose. Those who, under his viceroy and lieutenant, dared such deeds and achieved such victories as we have faithfully described in these memoirs, would assuredly have held nought too dangerous or difficult, had they been animated by the presence of so dear a pledge. Nor would any one, not ignorant of Scottish affairs, doubt that his presence would easily have attracted to his cause the hearts of a people naturally disposed to favour so excellent a king. This those rebel lords knew right well, and were earnest in their endeavours to close the way to his native soil, when he was scarce forty miles from the border.

And indeed, the Scots, though at that very time subject to a most harsh yoke of slavery under their tyrants, did not fear to pursue with the most dreadful imprecations the authors and accomplices of that shameful plot to betray the King of Scots to the English. Nay, even those who had so far agreed with the federates in all else, spoke out at peril of their lives, and declared that the kingdom of Scotland alone by itself had sufficed for the King's predecessors, and their ancestors had sufficed to defend and protect them against their powerful and warlike enemies, especially the English, over whom, as long as they stood by their kings, they had gained many glorious victories. Though they had experienced many vicissitudes in war with various peoples, both abroad and in Britain, they had never been forced to hand over their kings to the will of others. To do so now, the spirits of their ancestors, the sacred reverence due to royal authority, their honour and duty, their reputation here and hereafter, every law, human and divine, forbade. It was, in short, a flagrant violation of their own treaty. They had invoked the Everlasting God, to bear witness, and punish them, if they fought not to the last gasp against all men, to protect their king, his dignity, prerogative, and life. Indeed, except those rebellious and profane men, who by their evil arts had raised and commanded an army, and were ready to cut the throats of those who were without arms, without a leader, almost all Scots longed beyond all things for a time to prove their loyalty, and even seal it with their blood. Doubtless the victims of that most cruel tyranny will return to a mild and righteous government, so soon as ever the longed-for light of your sire's countenance or your own hath shone upon them like a healing star.

It is for you, then, most noble and mighty Prince, to bend all your powers of mind and body to succour your distressed fatherland and sire. To this end all earnestly demand, entreat, and expect your active aid, and pledge their own. By right of birth and inheritance this land is yours. The eyes of the nation—of the whole world—are on you. All devout men pray that, with God's help and good fortune, you may undertake with energy the task of restoring the Church, which lies prostrate and polluted by the filth of abominable sects, of establishing anew your father's kingdom, and recovering the ancient prosperity and glory of the realm, and that you may successfully terminate the work of restoring peace and order. They pray that hereafter, in God's good time, this, the most ancient realm in Europe, may acknowledge, love, and venerate you as its lord and master, and that the same prosperity may ever attend your offspring,

"*Et natis natorum, et quæ nascentur ab illis.*"

Wherefore, most gracious Prince, deign to raise, embrace, and cherish your faithful Montrose, and use him, whether as general in warfare, or councillor in peace, as one who, we hope and dare affirm, will never put so great a prince to shame.

*1st October* 1647.

## THE AUTHOR'S DEDICATION.

The following curious letter of Prince Charles against Wishart's book occurs in a copybook of the Prince's letters in July–Sept. 1648, in Bodl. MS. 895, p. 49. It is kindly supplied by the Rev. W. D. Macray of the Bodleian, who had never seen it noticed by historians.

"CHARLES P.,

"Right trusty and right entirely beloved cousen, Wee greet you well. Wee have seen a booke which hath beene published and dedicated to us, conteyning a relation of your proceedings in the late unhappy warre in Scotland, and are well pleased that your actions and conduct therein bee made knowne to the world with such advantage as they deserve; but finding a liberty used by the Author of that discourse concerning y<sup>e</sup> actions and carriage of severall persons of Quality whereby they are respectively charged with many crimes of a high nature, wee conceive wee cannot in justice afford our Patronage to accusations which render persons of honour infamous before they be heard, and wee therefore desire that the said booke be suppressed, and that there bee no further publication made thereof; and to y<sup>e</sup> end that our desire herein may bee accordingly effected, wee thinke fitt to recommend the doing of it to your care and endeavours, rather than to send [to] y<sup>e</sup> Author, being a person altogether unknown to us. Given at St. Germaines, y<sup>e</sup> 5th of March 164$\frac{7}{8}$.

"To our right trusty and right entirely beloved cousen
    James, Marques of Montrose."

This disclaimer was so tardy that we may reasonably suspect the Prince himself regarded it as merely formal, and never intended it to be acted on.

# The Author's Preface.

HERE are a few things of which it is desirable to inform the reader of these slight memoirs, whereof some relate to the Marquis of Montrose, whose actions in his own country for the space of two years are the subject, and others respect the author himself.

As to the Marquis, he is chief of the Grahams, a most ancient and famous family in Scotland, called in the old Scotch tongue *Graham-More*, or the Great Graham. He is descended from that Graham,[1] so famous in the histories of the realm, who was father-in-law to Fergus II., King of the Scots, and was the first who in the reign of his son-in-law attacked and demolished the wall built by Severus from the Firth of Forth to the mouth of the River Clyde, which is the narrowest part of Britain, and was the utmost limits of the Roman Empire; and by this exploit checked the growth of the Roman province. Hence the ruins of this wall, which may still be clearly traced, retain his name to this day, and are called by the natives *Graham's Dyke*. This same Graham, who was the founder of this noble family, having survived his son-in-law, Fergus, was, on account of his great civil as well as military skill, appointed Regent of the kingdom and Guardian to his grandson. When he had restored the teachers of the Christian religion, who had been banished by the late wars, and established both Church and State by excellent laws, he voluntarily resigned the government into the hands of his grandson, when he came of age. He lived in the times of the Emperors Arcadius and Honorius, about the year of our Lord 400. From him, through a long and prosperous line, sprung this noble family, who by imitating the valour of their ancestor, have grealty distinguished themselves through succeeding ages. Eminent among these was the bold Graham who, with Dunbar, brought such timely aid to his country when threatened by the Danes, who were already masters of England,

---

[1] Our author had read Buchanan and Fordun.

and had more than once made unsuccessful attacks on Scotland with very powerful armies. In later times the reputation of the family for courage and renown was maintained by the noble John Graham, who, after the death of Alexander III., in the interregnum, while Bruce and Baliol disputed for the crown, was, with that famous viceroy, William Wallace, a foremost champion of his country's freedom against the unjust tyranny of Edward, King of England, and after many heroic deeds died on the field of honour, fighting gallantly in its defence. His tomb may still be seen in a little chapel called Falkirk or Valkirk[2] (*Fanum Valli*), which takes its name from Graham's Dyke above mentioned, near which it stands. Near it the Marquis of Montrose owns a large and fertile estate, inherited from his ancestor, the first Graham.

But that I may not seem to derive the nobility of our illustrious hero's race only from the faint traces of remote antiquity, I must not omit his grandfather,[3] Earl of Montrose, who almost in our own memory was advanced to the highest offices, and discharged them with the greatest success. He was Lord Chancellor of Scotland when King James VI., of blessed memory, succeeded to the crown of England, and was made his Lord High Commissioner in Scotland, and enjoyed that highest honour bestowed on a subject, with the love and affection of both king and people, till his death. The father of the Marquis was a man of singular gifts of mind and body, distinguished both at home and abroad. After having performed many honourable embassies for King James, he was appointed President of the Council by King Charles, but was snatched away by an untimely fate from the service of his country and all good men, to the great grief of all.[4] As to their descendant, the Marquis, his actions during a year and a half, when as yet he has hardly attained the thirty-sixth year of his age, are left to the reader's judgment to commend our opinion and expectation of him.

One thing I beg leave to add. There have been three periods which have almost proved ruinous to the realm of Scotland. The first by the oppression of the Romans, whose yoke our ancestors cast off under the leadership of the first Graham, a son of the noble British family of the Fulgentii; the second by the Danes, who were repulsed by the signal valour of the second Graham we have mentioned; and the third by the English and Normans, whom the third Graham twice drove out of Scot-

---

[2] See true derivation of Falkirk in Skene, Books of Wales, vol. i. p. 93. The monument is frequently noted by travellers, and is still to be seen.
[3] John, third Earl, Chancellor 1598-9, Viceroy of Scotland 1604.
[4] See the Dyet of his Burial, Napier, Mem., p. 25.

land, inflicting on them many severe defeats. So that what was said of the Scipios of old in Africa seems to be true of this family, that the Grahams are destined to relieve their country in its hour of direst need; and that it is not without the special will of Providence that the Marquis in these worst of times has arisen to preserve the royal prerogative, the peace, lives, and ancient liberties of the subject, and the ancestral glory and splendour of his own house. So much I have thought necessary to premise concerning Montrose.

As for the author,[5] he professes no great skill in such studies, and expects no reputation for genius, of which he has little or none, nor profit and advantage, which are to many writers their chief incentive. His sole object in putting hand to this slight work has been to spread the truth among other nations and transmit it to posterity. He has learned by recent and lamentable experience in a similar case, that prosperous villany finds many friends, while truth in distress has but few to plead its cause. When the confederates in both kingdoms had by their usual arts of lies and calumnies overthrown the Church, to sate their greed with the sacrilegious spoils of its revenues, and heap a curse upon posterity, there were many to extol them to the skies for it, as men who had deserved well of their country, of the Church itself, and even of mankind in general; while they excommunicated the most revered servants of God, confessors and martyrs, and loaded them with reproach and blasphemy, because they steadily opposed their designs. There was, therefore, no reason to doubt that these persons, who are practising the same artifices to uproot and destroy the royal authority, that they may enjoy the prerogatives which they have seized by treason and treachery, would find many to use the like freedom in railing, and rave against this excellent nobleman and his most brilliant deeds, and instil their venom into the unwary and ignorant; like wasps, which are said from the most sweet and wholesome herbs to store up poisonous juices in their tongue and sting. To remedy this evil, the writer gladly offers this brief and simple little narrative, as a timely antidote, to lovers of pure truth. The truth he has resolved to defend stubbornly, undeterred by the heavy load of hatred and malice sure to fall upon him, without flattery and without vague and ambiguous phrase. Born and bred in freedom, he has resolved to lose it only with his life. Though he makes no claim to the applause bestowed on a great historian for his genius, skill, or elegance of style, yet he thinks himself justly entitled to claim credit for the plain truth. In the defence and spread of this he has despised what are held to be the most cherished of worldly goods. Thrice

---

[5] See Preface, Life of Author.

he has been stripped of all he had. Thrice he has been imprisoned in most foul and squalid jails. And now for the third time he is an exile in the same cause. The consciousness, however, of innocence, and the satisfaction of being thought by God worthy to endure so much for truth and justice, fill him with joy and gladness. Therefore, candid reader, love the truth at least that is in him, and kindly excuse his faults. Farewell.

# PART I.

## NARRATIVE OF THE DEEDS

OF

## JAMES, MARQUIS OF MONTROSE,

IN SCOTLAND IN THE YEARS 1644–1646.

### CHAPTER I.

*Pretexts of the Covenanters—Montrose detects their designs, 1639—They invade England and seize Newcastle, August 1640—Montrose's correspondence with the King betrayed—He forms an Association for the King—Charles's letters intercepted and Montrose imprisoned—Parliament at Edinburgh, July 1641—Montrose released.*

JAMES, MARQUIS OF MONTROSE,[1] had hitherto sided with the Covenanters in Scotland, and employed his energies in the cause only too vigorously and successfully. Their specious pretexts were the maintenance of religion, the honour and dignity of the King, the laws of the land, and the freedom of this ancient realm, which had been valiantly and happily defended against their most powerful enemies—the Romans, the Saxons, Danes, and Normans—by the sweat and blood, the lives and fortunes, of our ancestors. Their own false inventions they spread among the people by means of suitable ministers. It was given out that the sole object of the English Court was to reduce a free race to the condition of a conquered province, and enslave them to the empire of their ancient foes. Meantime they had bound themselves by public declarations and a solemn oath not to

---

[1] For Montrose's "first siding" with the Covenanters, and for an account of the *National Covenant* and *Solemn League and Covenant*, see Preface. For sequence of events, dates, &c., with notice of Banders, Plotters, and the "Incident," see *n.* at end of chapter.

engage in any attempt by force or arms, or otherwise than by petitions, to induce the King to assent graciously to the humble supplications of his subjects, and interpose his authority to save the religion and liberty of their dearest native land.

But at length, in the year 1639, Montrose found out that these fair tales were invented to steal the hearts of the silly and superstitious multitude, and alienate them from the King, as an enemy to religion and liberty. For the Covenanters did not dissemble to him their opinion that Scotland had been too long ruled by kings; that it would never be well with them as long as one of the royal house of Stuart survived, and that in extirpating that family they ought to begin with the King. Montrose perceived that His Majesty's person and royal authority were aimed at. Filled with loathing for so horrible a crime, he resolved to abandon the Covenanters, frustrate their designs, reduce their resources, shake their power, and with all his might preserve the King and kingly power entire and inviolate. But as the Covenanters, by force or fraud, had brought over almost the whole nation to their side, he judged himself too weak alone to check their power. He therefore determined not to declare his purpose too suddenly or rashly. Among them he had many friends, men of great power in the number of their followers and clansmen, in influence and wealth. These he resolved to detach from them, and recall them to the King's service. By this means he might gather a considerable body to secure the King's safety and his own.

Meantime the Covenanters raised a strong army against the King, and in a solemn convention at Duns, at which Montrose was not present, they determined to invade England. This resolution had been taken by their leaders six weeks before in their secret conclave. With this end in view, they had been at pains to disseminate many apologetic pamphlets throughout the whole of Britain, in which they laboured to explain the reasons of the expedition. When Montrose returned, as he could not prevent their resolution, he determined to give it his approval in appearance. He commanded in this army two thousand foot and five hundred horse. Five thousand more were under the orders of his most intimate friends, who had solemnly engaged to help him in this business for the King. Had the greater part of them kept their word, they would have brought the whole army over to the King, or at all events would easily have baffled the Covenanters. The camp lay at the river Tweed, on the border. The officers and nobles cast lots, and it fell to Montrose to be the first to cross. This he did on foot, at the head of his own infantry, and with great readiness, the better to conceal his design and allay suspicion. Indeed, his influence in the army and his frank honest disposition began to be so much dreaded by those guilty rebels, that they kept a strict watch on all his behaviour, words, and deeds.

Four miles above Newcastle they crossed the river Tyne, and seized that town by the treachery of the English commanders, who fell back on York with the King's army, though it was very strong. Commissioners were appointed on both sides to settle the terms of peace, and a truce was agreed on. During the truce Montrose had written to the King to assure him of his loyalty, duteous obedience, and readiness to serve His Majesty. This was the entire substance of his letters. Some gentlemen[2] of the King's bedchamber, in whom the King placed the fullest confidence, and whose practice it was every day to communicate to the rebels the King's most secret plans, of which they themselves were often the advisers or promoters, stole these letters by night, and transmitted copies to the Covenanters at Newcastle. Some of the most forward of the rebels were not ashamed to tax Montrose sharply with this correspondence. They dared not make an open quarrel of it or call him publicly to account, because of his great power and influence in the army; but among the common people they loaded him with slander and reproach.

---

[2] "Word came here that the King was under some suspicion of his *cubicularies* (bed-chambermen) that they were revealing what they heard him say, to the Scots, which I believe was not far by, so long as he keeped the Marquis of Hamilton beside him" (Spalding, i. 246). "Queen Henrietta Maria in 1642 advised her husband to be careful of his pockets, where he then kept the key of the cipher used between them" (Gardiner, Hist. Eng., viii. 361). The gentleman suspected by Montrose (Guthrie's Memoirs, p. 117) was William Murray of the bed-chamber, afterwards Earl of Dysart. He was suspected of betraying the King's intention to arrest the five members. Clarendon, quoted in Gard., Hist. Eng., x. 135. For note on Murray see Ch. iii.

Throughout the kingdom most of the preachers were devoted to their interests, and their venal tongues were employed to sway the people's minds. Nothing has contributed more effectually to promote and foster the present rebellion than the virulence with which these worthy orators in their public assemblies revile the King and all his faithful subjects as "the enemies of Christ," to quote their favourite phrase—men who are themselves a scandal and reproach to the name of Christian.

On his return to Scotland, Montrose bent his whole attention to avert from His Majesty the impending storm of rebellion. Finally, he determined to bind a large number of the leading men and nobility in an engagement, a solemn compact to defend His Majesty, with all his privileges and ancient and lawful prerogatives, against all enemies, foreign and domestic, with their lives and fortunes, to the last gasp. Matters had gone so far that there would have been an open division, which was his aim, when some of the associates, through fear, fickleness, and irresolution—the worst sort of men to keep a secret—betrayed the whole affair to the Covenanters.[3] They made a great stir and hubbub about it, but for a while things were accommodated, for they durst not yet resolve on any open violence to Montrose.

Soon afterwards the Covenanters contrived a new oath,[4] to secure the obedience of the army. They also entered into a very close league[5] with the English Parliament. They now thought themselves sufficiently secure from the plots of any private man. But Montrose's unbending sense of honour, and lofty enterprising genius were intolerable to them, and they began seriously to deliberate how to make away with him.

To pave the way for their wicked purpose, they bribed some

---

[3] See note on Cumbernauld Bond at end of chapter.

[4] We do not know of any special oath imposed at this time. Leslie had his regulations for the army, which may have been stiffened. The General Assembly reimposed the Covenant from time to time, and was supported by the Estates. Is Wishart, who was in England at the time, reading here his English experiences into those of Montrose, and confusing dates? The imposing of the Solemn League and Covenant on soldiers met with prolonged opposition in England.

[5] M'Crie (Life of Henderson, p. 43) speaks of the effect of the treatment of their Commissioners at Oxford as being that the Scots soon after entered into a very close alliance with the Parliament of England. There is no doubt that the leaders of the party in England and Scotland were in close relations.

of the people about Court with promises and rewards to give information of some letters written by the King to Montrose. Through them they learnt that they were sewn in the saddle of the messenger, a man named Stewart,[6] a dependent of the Earl of Traquair. As soon as the messenger crossed the border, he was seized, his saddle ripped open, and the letters discovered. They contained nothing that the best of kings might not command, or the best of subjects perform. Nevertheless, these master-craftsmen in the art of slander set their suitable ministers to work to spread the most tragic reports, that they had at last discovered the plots of the King and Montrose to overthrow religion and ruin their country. Even then they shrank from an open trial. Without warning, and when he had no suspicion of their design, they arrested him, along with Lord Napier of Merchiston and Sir George Stirling of Keir, his relatives and most intimate friends, and thrust them into the Castle of Edinburgh.

On the conclusion of peace between the two nations, though in fact there had been no war between them, but an agreement to wage war on their most just and gracious sovereign, a Parliament[7] was summoned to Edinburgh, at which the King himself was

---

[6] Captain or Lieutenant-Colonel Walter Stewart, prominent in the history of the plot (see note at end of chapter), was a cousin and domestic of Lord Traquair, who describes him as a "fool, or at least a timid, half-witted body," whom men of common-sense like Montrose and Napier would never have trusted with the secrets of a plot. He was an officer in the army under Leslie, spoke to treasonable language of Sir Thomas Hope of Kerse at Newcastle, employed by Sir Thomas Stewart of Grantully to report Argyle's words at Balloch Castle, and later to convey to the Duke of Lennox the desires of Montrose and the others with him for the King's presence in Scotland. On his return journey, between Cockburnspath and Haddington, he was captured "by one sent expressly to meet him," and conveyed to Balmerino's lodgings at nine o'clock at night. Sir Thomas Hope of Kerse was "the first that came in after him," and in a letter, dated 7th June (Napier, Memoirs, 308-309), gives the account of the ripping of the saddle and finding the King's letter to Montrose, and fixes the date of the capture of Stewart as Friday the 4th. Spalding gives different date, place of arrest, and Christian name of Stewart; but Hope's letter is the more direct evidence. See Napier.

[7] Second Parliament of Charles I. Sat from 15th July to 17th November 1641, the King being present from 17th August to the end. He had come determined to satisfy the Scots, in the hope of at any rate reducing the number of his foes, if he could not gain them and their army as allies against his southern opponents. Charles grew in confidence. "You may assure every one," he wrote to Nicholas, September 3, "that now all difficulties are passed here." On September 25 Sir Patrick Wemyss writes, "There was never King so much insulted over; it would pity any man's heart to see how he looks, for he is never quiet amongst them, and glad he is when he sees any man that he thinks loves him; yet he is seeming merry at meat" (Carte's Ormond Papers, i. 4; Gard., Hist. Eng., x. 19-21). Besides guaranteeing all previous concessions, he gave authority for Par-

present. In vain Montrose entreated to be tried before the King and Parliament. The Covenanters, conscious of his innocence and their guilt, were resolved to detain him in prison without a trial, until the King had left Scotland and conceded all their demands in Parliament. They were greatly afraid that his wisdom, courage, and influence with the peers and commons would induce the great majority to adopt his plan for the safety and preservation of the throne. On the return of the King to England, Montrose and his friends were at last set at liberty. As an order in Parliament had been passed that he should hold no intercourse with the King, he retired for a while to his own house. This was towards the end of the year 1641.

---

## SEQUENCE OF EVENTS WITH DATES EMBRACED UNDER CHAPTER I.

### 1639.

Jun.18-19. Montrose heartily on the side of the Covenant, fought the battle of the Bridge of Dee and took Aberdeen.

„ 21. News of the Pacification of Berwick reached Aberdeen on 20th.
Montrose disbanded his forces, returning south with Earl Marischal.
"They went to Duns to have their part of the joy, as weell they did deserve in the common peace; where they were made most welcome both to their commerads and their King" (Baillie, Letters, i. 223).

„ 24. Riots in Edinburgh; Hamilton jostled and denounced.

July 3. "Tumult of women invaded Traquair, Kinnoull, and Lord Aboyne in their coaches."

„ 16. Rothes, Montrose, Lothian, Johnston, and others went to the King at Berwick as Covenanting leaders. Argyll, Loudon, and others excused themselves, though sent for.

„ 29. King went south from Berwick without going to Edinburgh, owing to distrust shown.

Aug. 12. Traquair as Commissioner opened General Assembly and closed it, after sanc-

---

liament to meet every three' years without royal assent, and resigned all right of appointment to offices of state, justice, and law. His chief opponents received honours and good posts, while his friends got at most a bare toleration. Argyll was made a Marquis, and General Leslie received an Earl's coronet, placed on his head by the King's own hands in open Parliament. They told him on his going away that he was leaving them "a contented King of a contented people." Guthrie, 108; Balfour, iii. 165; Act. Parl. Scot.

| | | |
|---|---|---|
| Aug. | 30. | tioning its abolition of Episcopacy "as contrary in itself to the Word of God." |
| ,, | 31. | Opened Parliament, and eventually succeeded in proroguing it. |
| Nov. | 14. | Parliament prorogued under protest. Montrose fell under suspicion of the extreme men. |
| Dec. | — | The King invited him to Court. |
| ,, | 26. | He courteously declined by letter of this date from Edinburgh. |

### 1640.

| | | |
|---|---|---|
| Jan. | 3. | Letter from Johnston of Warriston to Lord Johnston, commending the example of Montrose to him in declining to go to Court. |
| ,, | 31. | Loudon, Dunfermline, and other Commissioners sent up to London owing to growing troubles. |
| Feb. | — | Preparations for war going on in England, and the same in Edinburgh. |
| Mar. | — | Lord Southesk and twenty-three Royalists put in prison or in ward in Edinburgh. Loudon sent to the Tower, and other Commissioners in London put under ward. |
| May | 1. | Four citizens, in the operations against the Castle, killed by the cannon of General Ruthven—first blood of new Civil War. |
| ,, | 28. | Aberdeen and the North, under Monro, compelled to take the Covenant. |
| June | 2. | Parliament sat without royal authority. |
| ,, | 11. | Parliament adjourned till November 19th. Leslie ordered to muster the army at Dunglass and march to Duns. |
| ,, | 18. | Argyll, with commission of fire and sword against Athole and the Braes of Angus, mustered at Inverary. |
| ,, | 27. | Loudon delivered from the Tower and sent down to Scotland. Montrose went into Perth and Angus to raise two regiments for the Covenanting army. |
| ,, | 30. | By the 30th he had taken over Airly Castle, and, having placed in it Colonel Sibbald, marched south with his force to join Leslie. |
| July | 7. | Before July 7, Argyll had dishonourably got the Earl of Athole and other Royalist chiefs of the district into his hands, removed Sibbald, and destroyed Airlie Castle. |
| ,, | 13. | Leslie marched to Duns and encamped at Choicelee Wood, four miles south of Duns. His strength was 24,000 foot and 2500 horse. The prevailing feature in the way of uniform was the blue bonnet with the bunch of blue ribbons—"Montrose's whimsies." The cavalry included a contribution from the "Parliament House," in the shape of a "College of Justice troop," commanded by Sir Thomas Hope, younger. Three undated manifestoes were issued at this time :— 1. Six considerations of the lawfulness of the expedition. 2. Intentions of the army declared to their brethren in England. 3. Information frae the Scottish Nation to all the true English. |
| ,, | 31. | Before this date Montrose was asked to sign a paper to support the making of Argyll dictator, or at least supreme beyond Forth, but said "he would die or he did it." |
| Aug. | — | Montrose came to Edinburgh, and found Lord Lindsay not averse to the dictator idea. |

At Cumbernauld House (Lord Wigton's) he was instrumental in getting the Conservative Covenanters to join in a "Band" early in August. The following is the CUMBERNAULD BAND:—

"The copy of the bond subscribed by Montrose and the rest of these noblemen:—

"Whereas we under-scribers, out of our duty to Religion, King, and Country, were forced to join ourselves in a Covenant for the maintenance and defence of eithers, and every one of other, in that behalf: Now finding how that, by the *particular and indirect practising of a few*, the country, and cause now depending, does so much suffer, do heartily hereby bind and oblige ourselves, out of our duty to all these respects above mentioned, but chiefly and namely *that Covenant already signed*, to wed and study all public ends which may tend to the safety both of Religion, Laws, and Liberties of this poor kingdom; and, as we are to make an account before that Great Judge at the last day, that we shall contribute one with another, in a unanimous and joint way, in whatsoever may concern the public or this cause, to the hazard of our lives, fortunes, and estates, neither of us doing, consulting, nor condescending in any point, without the consent and approbation of the whole, in so far as they can be conveniently had, and time may allow. And likeas we swear and protest by the same oath, that, in so far as may consist with the good and weal of the public, every one of us shall join and adhere to others (each other) and their interests, against all persons and causes whatsoever, so what shall be done to one, with reservation foresaid, shall be equally resented and taken as done to the whole number. In witness hereof," &c.

"The subscribers of the principal bond, and in this order:—

| MARSCHELL. | STORMONT. |
| MONTROSE. | SEAFORTH. |
| WIGTON. | ERSKINE. |
| KINGHORN. | KIRCUBRYCHT. |
| HOME. | AMOND. |
| ATHOL. | DRUMMOND. |
| MAR. | JOHNSTON. |
| PERTH. | LOUR. |
| BOYD. | D. CARNEGY, *Master of Lour*." |
| GALLOWAY. | |

These are names on the principal bond, but "Napier," "Keir," and others were added. See Napier, Mem., 269–270; Guthrie, Mem., 90.

Aug. 17. The army moved to Coldstream.
 ,, 21. Crossed Tweed, Montrose leading.
     By Cornhill, Millfield, Middleton Haugh, Edglie Moor, Newton of Eglesham, Long Framlington, Netherwitten, and Trewick, they came in sight of
 ,, 27. Newcastle, August 27th.
 ,, 28. Conway defeated and Newburn ford taken.
 ,, 29. Conway and Ashley the Governor of Newcastle marched out early.
 ,, 30. Sir William Douglas presented himself at the gates later in the day, and Newcastle was occupied in force. The advance party dined with the Mayor, who was surprised at their drinking the King's health.

On the 29th Dumbarton Castle surrendered to the Covenanters.

Sept. 15. Edinburgh Castle surrendered by the brave General Ruthven.

Oct. 2. Negotiations begun at Ripon.

About this time Montrose wrote one letter to the King, which was communicated to Leslie "by some bedchamberman (as many deemed) who searched the King's pockets when he was asleep" (Guthrie, p. 87). "The coolness of the General cast water upon the spunk which was beginning untimeously to smoke" (Baillie).

Nov. 19. Lord Boyd, one of the Banders, died, revealing in his illness the existence of the Bond.

Argyll, hearing of this, visited Lord Almond, who with Montrose had come north, and from him gathered the story of the agreement. The Banders were immediately cited and the paper ordered to be burned; but though some pressed for their lives, it was thought best to "pack up the business."

Dec. 16. Bond burned, according to Spalding.

1641.

Jan. 16. Bond burned, according to Guthrie.

Montrose with army at Newcastle.

Feb. — Montrose in Scotland, bent on thwarting Argyll. His paper on sovereign power written about this time, and his views of the true policy for the King given in a letter to him written at this period (v. Napier, Mem., 280-311). THE PLOTTERS, Montrose, Napier, Stirling of Keir, and Stewart of Blackhall, met frequently, and determined to urge the King to visit Scotland, guarantee religion, liberty, and constitutional government, and so end Argyll's rule. Colonel Walter Stewart, going to London on his own account, took up missives from the Plotters to the Duke of Lennox, begging him to urge the King's visit to Scotland. Their schemes involved the ruin of Argyll, and their chief reliance was upon the unguarded language of that potentate at the Fords of Lyon and at Balloch Castle, and the jubilant songs of his followers about "King Campbell." John Stewart, younger of Ladywell, was the original evidence.

Feb. 28. About this time Montrose was at Scone on a visit to Lord Stormont, where the Earl of Athole, John Stewart, and others connected with the Balloch

Mar. Castle scenes were staying. Here came Mr. Robert Murray, minister of Methven, to whom Montrose was too free about his evidence against Argyll. Murray gave the story to Mr. John Graham, minister of Auchterarder, who by and bye used it in the pulpit against Montrose.

May 19. Graham, summoned to Edinburgh, gave Murray as his authority.

„ 27. Murray "taken off the street" and brought before the Committee of Estates, when Montrose accepted responsibility for the story, giving Ladywell and Lord Lindsay of the Byers as part of his authority.

„ 31. Stewart examined, and, in face of Argyll, stuck to the charge. Lord Lindsay cleared himself as to any special reference to Argyll.

Stewart sent to prison, and, being dealt with by "two profound men, Balmerino

June 5. and Durie," wrote next day to Argyll humbly craving an interview.

„ 6. Argyll took with him a deputation of other profound men at night, with the
„ 7. result that next day Ladywell withdrew his statements and declared them forgeries.

| | |
|---|---|
| June | 4. Colonel Walter Stewart, on his return journey from London, was arrested between Cockburnspath and Haddington. His pockets were searched and saddle ripped up. A letter was found from the King to Montrose, quite in general terms (Napier, Memoirs, 316), also many other papers, of which he gave confused accounts, but which were considered damaging to the Plotters. He was sent to prison in the Castle. |
| ,, | 10. John Stewart's declaration was sworn to. |
| ,, | 11. Montrose, Napier, Keir, and Blackhall arrested and imprisoned apart in the Castle. |
| ,, | 22. The Earl of Sutherland was sent to bring Montrose for a private examination to the Council, but he refused a private trial. |
| ,, | 23. He was taken down under guard of 400 men, but declined to answer, except in a public trial. |
| | Lord Napier, examined the same day, was offered liberty, but declined it till the disgrace was removed from himself and his friends. |
| | Montrose and the others made frequent petitions from their prison as to their affairs and trial. (See Wigton Papers, Mait. Club Misc., ii. 428-433, for important documents, and Acts of Parl. Scot., 1641.) |
| July | 15. Parliament met. |
| ,, | 27. Montrose before Parliament twice, and sent back to prison. |
| ,, | 28. John Stewart of Ladywell executed. |
| Aug. | 10. In London the King sanctioned the treaty with Scotland, securing payment to the Scots after their army had recrossed the Tweed. £220,000 still due. |
| ,, | 14. The King rode into Edinburgh at six o'clock at night. |
| ,, | 15. Heard Mr. Alexander Henderson preach in Holyrood. |
| ,, | 17. Attended Parliament in state. |
| | Montrose's case delayed till the 24th. |
| | Hamilton and Argyll at agreement. |
| | Strong feeling among the King's friends against Hamilton. |
| | Lord Ker challenged Hamilton (Baillie says, in drink), calling him "a juglar with the King and a traitor both to him and to his countrie." He sent Lord Crawford with the challenge. |
| Sept. | 10. An impeachment of Hamilton contemplated; an arrest, even an assassination, under certain circumstances, talked of. |
| Oct. | 11. Hamilton went to the King in the garden at Holyrood, and, after speaking "in a philosophicall and parabolicall way," ended in asking leave to retire from Court that night, because of the envy and malice which hatched plots against him, to which he would never believe the King "wer in aney wayes accessorey" (Balfour, Ann., iii. 95). |
| | About this time Montrose wrote three letters to the King, the last on the 11th, offering to prove treason against important men. The bearer of the letters was William Murray, groom of the bedchamber. |
| ,, | 12. The INCIDENT fully developed by the flight of Hamilton, Argyll, and Lanark to Kineil House, near Bowness. |
| | The names connected with the Incident are the Earls of Crawford and Carnwath, who, as alleged, spoke of assassination, the latter saying "there were three kings in Scotland, and two of them behoved to lose their heads;" Lieut.-Col. Alexander Stewart, Captain William Stewart, who betrayed him, Lieut.-Col. Hume, Col. Ludovicke Leslie, Colonel Cochrane, Captain Robert Kennedy, and Colonel Hurry. Lords Almond, Ogilvy, and |

Gray, at Lord Airth's house, are mentioned in the evidence. Through a slip in Clarendon's note, which escaped his editor, a story crept into history that Montrose offered to assassinate Hamilton and Argyll; but this is now given up. Montrose was a close prisoner in the Castle in the hands of Argyll and his party, and wrote his strongest letter only on the 11th, when the Incident had developed, and it merely indicated Hamilton, without naming him, as a traitor. (See Reports of Committee to Parliament, and other evidence in Balfour, iii. 94-137.) Gardiner (History of England, x. 26) acquits Montrose of the charge, and suggests that Clarendon in his blundering way had confused Montrose with Crawford, who might have made such a proposal.

Oct. 30. Sir Thomas Hope humbly entreats His Majesty to show the Committee Montrose's last letter. The King answered that at two o'clock he would show it.

Nov. 2. Montrose, Napier, Keir, and Blackhall petition for liberty on security. No answer to be returned till Montrose should say what he meant by his letter to the King. He was ordered to be examined by the Committee on the Incident at two o'clock.

„ 3. Committee reports that he declines to say more than he has already said to the King or Committee, an answer "which did not give satisfaction."

„ 17. Parliament ordered Montrose and his friends to be liberated under caution, and to appear before a Committee appointed by the King, January 4.

Parliament dissolved and feasted, and the King rode south on Thursday, November 18, at eight o'clock in the morning.

## CHAPTER II.

*Conduct of the English malcontents, 1642—Montrose in England—Meets the Queen at York, February 1643—His advice rejected for that of Hamilton—Convention of Estates at Edinburgh, June 1643—Montrose's conference with Henderson, from whom he learns the designs of the Covenanters.*

IN the year 1642 the Covenanters of both kingdoms began to lay aside the mask and carry on matters more openly. In England the rebels harassed the King with their unjust, foolish, and unreasonable complaints. They loaded him with calumnies, profaned his sacred name with scurrilous ballads, reviled him in infamous libels and pasquils, stirred up riots, and incited the scum of the people to assail him with arms, mob him in his very palace, and threaten him with the direst extremity. Though he might very justly have punished them by his own authority, he chose to refer the matter to Parliament, thinking by that means to secure their obedience. But it was vain for the gracious King to defer in this and other matters to ungrateful men, themselves the authors and abettors of these crimes. All his predecessors, from William the Conqueror downwards, had not done so much to lighten the alleged grievances of their subjects and secure their liberties. At last, much against his will, he was forced to withdraw from London,[1] for the safety of himself and family. For the Queen's security he sent her to Holland. He himself retired to York. The

---

[1] The King and Queen left Whitehall (to which they never returned, save he for his death and she as a widow) January 10, 1642. They went to Hampton Court in such haste, that, from want of preparation, the King, Queen, and three children had to sleep in one room. After short visits to Windsor and other royal residences, the King bade a tender and very touching farewell to the Queen and Princess Royal at Dover on February 23. They sailed for Holland, where the young Prince of Orange at Helvoetsluys received his bride and her mother. The Queen had crown jewels with her, to be converted into war material; and the King, to secure northern ports for its reception, moved to York, March 19. See Gard., Hist. Eng., x. 150; Green, Princesses of Eng., ii. 126-127, with their references.

Estates of Parliament, as they call themselves, at once flew to arms, and, under officers of their own nomination, employed the forces which the King had intended for Ireland, and which were then in readiness, against the King himself.

The rebels in Scotland, who knew well that the King had a sufficient force to reduce the English, resolved not to fail their brother allies in their need. Though the King, in the recent Parliament held at Edinburgh, had graciously conceded all that they could wish, as they have recorded in their public acts, yet now they prepared to wage war against him in England.

It was necessary to secure themselves at home. Montrose was almost the only man they dreaded, and they spared no efforts to win him again to their side. Of their own accord they offered to make him lieutenant-general of the army, and whatever else he might desire within their power. But perceiving that a terrible storm was lowering over the King's head, he set out for England to warn him of the danger, accompanied by Lord Ogilvy, who was in his confidence.

At Newcastle he heard that the Queen had returned from Holland, and had just landed[2] at Bridlington in Yorkshire. Thither he hastened, and gave her a detailed account of the state of affairs; but being fatigued and ill after a very stormy passage, she told him that she would advise with him more

---

[2] The Queen sailed from Scheveling on $\frac{19}{9}$ January, but was driven back by a tempest, in which she showed her courage, while her attendant ladies, in terror, were making loud confessions to her chaplain. "Comfort yourselves, my dears; Queens of England are never drowned," she said. After a stay at the Hague, where she got the better of the States-General, who had laid hold of one of her ships, she sailed again from Scheveling amid the adieus of a brilliant company, and, escorted by Van Tromp, landed at Bridlington, February 22, bringing with her much warlike store, and, it was said, £2,000,000 in money. Admiral Batten, for the Parliament, with four ships, says Monteith—with six, says Spalding—fired on her lodging in the town. Spalding, who errs somewhat in dates and distances, gives the scene in picturesque Scotch: "Hir Majestie, haveing mynd of no evill, bot glad of rest, now wiryt by the sea, is cruellie assaulted; for thir sex rebellis schipps, ilkane be courss, settis thair bred syde to hir lodging, batteris the houss, dings down the rooff or sho wist of hirself. Alwaies sho gettis up out of hir naiked bed in hir night walycot, bairfut and bairleg, with her maidis of honour (quhairof one, throw plane feir, went straight mad, being ane nobleman of Englandi's dochter), scho gettis saiflie out of the houss. Albeit the stanes war flisting about hir heid, yit couragiouslie scho gois out, thay schooting still; and scho escaipes, and gois to ane den, which the cannon culd not hurt, and on the bair fields scho restit, insted of statelie lodginges cled with curious tapestrie" (Spalding, ii. 233. See also Monteith's Troubles, 135; Gard. Civil War i. 108; and Green's Princesses, ii. 135.)

fully when they came to York.³ On her arrival there she sent for him, and he again laid the matter fully before Her Majesty, and showed her that the Scotch Covenanters were likely to prove as dangerous as the English, if not promptly suppressed. Being asked for his advice, he replied that force must be resisted by force; the King had many faithful, brave subjects in Scotland able and willing to resist the Covenanters, should they dare to make any attempt against the King; all they lacked was the King's warrant, without which they would attempt nothing; with it there was nothing they would not attempt, supported by his authority. The only risk was in delay, for the Covenanters, when once they had raised an army, would easily suppress any attempt at a rising. A stand should be made at the outset and the viper's egg crushed; it was too late to apply medicines when the poison had infected the whole body.

The advice was wholesome and seasonable, such as the wise Queen would doubtless have approved; but just as the project was fairly afloat, it was checked by the arrival of the Duke of Hamilton.⁴ He came from Scotland ostensibly to pay his respects

---

[3] After a stay at Boynton Hall, Sir William Strickland's house, where she "borrowed" all the family plate, leaving only her portrait in pledge, the Earl of Newcastle (created Marquis, October 27, 1643) conducted the Queen to York, where she arrived March 5. Her reception of the various proposals of Montrose and Hamilton, as given by Wishart, is supported by Burnet.

[4] James, third Marquis of Hamilton, was created Duke of Hamilton by patent dated Oxford, April 1643. The intimate friend and trusted kinsman of the King, who upheld him under circumstances of grave suspicion, Hamilton, perhaps without deliberate intention of treachery, proved himself as destitute of support as a breaking reed, and as capable of piercing the hand leaning upon it. With a great sphere and opportunity, he exhibited no elevated principle or practical skill, and the centre of consistency in his life, on any platform above present selfish convenience, is difficult to find. His affection for Charles, which was real, gave him no strength of sacrifice for his sake, nor could it hinder his contributing to his humiliations in the days when a staunch friend in such a position might have saved him. Secure in the King's affections and in his own influence with him, he used him as his own piece on the chessboard. His diplomacy, which was reckoned great in Scotland, ended in his going over to the opposite side, without his seeming to know it, and in his warfare he was chiefly anxious to avoid strife. His last efforts in the "Engagement" added no lustre to his policy or his skill in war, though it showed his heart was in the right place, and his death for his master, and faithfulness to his friends under great temptation to betray their names to Cromwell, imparted a sunset brightness to a dusky day of many promises.

Born June 19, 1606, at the age of fourteen he married Lady Mary Fielding, daughter of William, first Earl of Denbigh, and niece of Buckingham. In 1625 he succeeded his father, who died at the age of thirty-five; he carried the sword of state in that year at the coronation of Charles I. In 1628, though only twenty-two years old, he was Master of the Horse in place of Buckingham, Lord of the Bedchamber, and a Privy Counsellor of both kingdoms. In 1630 he was sponsor at the baptism of Prince Charles, as proxy for the King of Bohemia, and was made a Knight of the

to the Queen and congratulate her on her safe return; but in reality he had posted thither, with the knowledge and consent of the Covenanters, to thwart Montrose's plans. He did not, indeed, deny the danger from the Scotch Covenanters, but he endeavoured to extenuate it, and condemned Montrose's advice as rash, imprudent, and unseasonable. That stout and warlike nation, he said, was not to be reduced by force of arms, but by gentleness and good treatment. War, especially civil war, ought to be the last remedy, as even the conqueror had usually cause to repent it. The chances of war were uncertain. Were the King to conquer, it would be a sorry triumph over his own countrymen, while defeat would entail consequences which he shuddered to mention. Every effort should be made to preserve peace with that nation, and matters had not yet come to such a pass that they need despair of peace and reconciliation. In short, he would himself undertake the whole business, if the King would trust his loyalty and zeal as his Commissioner. Montrose

---

Garter. He carried over a force of 6000 men to Germany to assist Gustavus Adolphus, and met with some success and poor treatment. He was Commissioner of the King at the General Assembly of 1638 in Glasgow Cathedral, which he failed to control or to close. In 1639 he commanded the fleet in the Forth, which did nothing (it is said that it brought down Anne Cunninghame, his mother, to Leith, with a pistol for him in case he landed), and afterwards joined the King at Berwick, and acted for him after the pacification there. In 1641 he accompanied the King to Scotland, but fell much into the hands of Argyll, with whom he fled to Kineil on the scare of the "Incident." In 1642 he was in a measure the tool of Argyll and the Covenanters, and in 1643 Charles became convinced of the culpable conduct of Hamilton and his brother Lanark, and had them arrested at Oxford in December. Lanark escaped, but Hamilton was sent to Pendennis Castle, and afterwards to St. Michael's Mount in Cornwall, whence he was released by the Parliamentary forces, April 1646. In July he joined the King at Newcastle, and was employed by him to conciliate the Scots. He took the Covenant as Earl of Cambridge in the House of Lords and afterwards in Scotland. On 12th August he compeared before the Commission of Assembly, and on a "representation in write," presented on the 13th, he was forgiven his delay, and signed the Solemn League and Covenant. He entered England with an army of 10,500 men on July 8, 1648, and occupied Carlisle for the King; was defeated at Preston, August 17, and surrendered to Lambert on security of their lives and safety of their persons, August 25. For details see below, Part ii. Chap. iii. He was conveyed to Windsor and lodged in the house of one of the "poor knights." Here he had a short interview with the King as he passed through the town to Whitehall. He escaped, but was taken in Southwark, and after a lengthy trial, when he pleaded the quarter given at his surrender and his position under the Scottish Parliament, he was, as a peer of England, condemned to death. Resisting many tempting offers to betray to Cromwell the names of those who had invited him into England, he made a good end on the scaffold with Lords Holland and Capel, March 9, 1649. "Infelix Hamiltonius" is his pointed epitaph in Wishart's poem. See Burnet's Dukes of Hamilton, 405 and *passim*; Turner's Mem., 50-76; Monteith's Troubles, 504 and *passim*; Napier's Montrose, *passim*; Gard. Civil War, iii. 421-448 and *passim*; Records of Commissions of General Assemblies, Scot. Hist. Soc., 23-24.

replied that this advice could only serve to waste time, until the Covenanters raised an army and deprived the King of any chance of defending himself and his friends from their tyranny. His warning was only too true, as the melancholy catastrophe proved. But in this debate Montrose was borne down. He was not such an accomplished courtier, and the brilliant qualities which have now made him famous throughout the world were then unknown to the Queen. Hamilton returned in triumph to Scotland, and appeared to be leaving no stone unturned in the King's interest.

Meantime, the Covenanters, on their own authority, summoned a Convention of the Estates at Edinburgh,[5] June 22, 1643, in direct violation of the laws. All intelligent and loyal men foresaw that this would prove destructive to the King's affairs, and abhorred it so much that they resolved not to honour it with their presence; but Hamilton summoned them all by writs in the King's name and authority to attend; for that he did not doubt that they would have the majority of votes, if they did not fail His Majesty at this crisis; but, should they be out-voted, he was prepared with his friends to protest against the Covenanters and at once withdraw. Most of the nobility, excepting Montrose and the few who adhered to him, came up to the Convention, enticed by the King's name and the hopes held out to them. Thereupon Hamilton employed his friends to beg Montrose, by his allegiance and reverence for the King, to join the Convention. Montrose, who justly suspected all Hamilton's proceedings, replied that he was ready to face any danger at the commands of the King's Commissioner; but on this condition, that he must pledge his word of honour that, if they could not obtain just and reasonable terms

---

[5] "It was under Argyll's influence that on May 10th the various bodies which together acted as the Government of Scotland resolved to summon a Convention of Estates—a kind of informal Parliament—to meet on June 22, 1643, without the royal consent" (Gard., Civil War, iii. 205). Hamilton offered the King's sanction, if they abstained from military preparation. On the 26th they declared themselves a free Convention. On the 2nd August the General Assembly was opened in Edinburgh, Sir Thomas Hope being Commissioner, having the "honours" carried before him, and sitting in the "King's loft in St. Giles' Kirk." Mr. Alexander Henderson was the Moderator, the ablest man for the crisis. The Assembly and Convention had frequent consultations. The English Commissioners were received, and the Solemn League and Covenant was devised at this time. (See our Preface, and Guthrie, 135; Spalding, ii. 259.)

in the Convention, he would endeavour to gain them by force of arms. To this Hamilton replied that he would protest, but would not fight. After weighing the matter, Montrose retired to his own house, resolved to keep his hands clean and await the issue.

When the Convention met, the Covenanters had a majority of some seventy votes. They trampled on the royal authority, and arrogated to themselves the right of calling Parliaments, levying troops, and contracting treaties with foreign nations, with other powers as yet unheard of, except by consent of the King. To crown all, they resolved to raise a strong army against the King, and send it to the assistance of their English allies. To this end they burdened the people with subsidies and new taxes,[6] far heavier than a hundred and nine monarchs in their greatest straits had imposed, even were all they had levied for two thousand years reckoned together.

Montrose perceived that the King would be ruined by his own royal authority. But as he could not oppose both the power of the Covenanters and the King's commands, with sorrow and anxiety he was forced to disguise his views. The Covenanters, however, imagining that his heart was estranged[7] from the King by the repulse he had suffered at York and the preference shown to Hamilton, renewed their advances and employed friends to win or bribe him over.[8] They offered him places, money, and the highest offices, both civil and military. He appeared to listen to their proposals not altogether unfavourably, his object being to penetrate their secret designs. To satisfy his scruples more fully, and to cement and sanctify this friendship, they sent him Alexander

---

[6] See Spalding, ii. 267, as to the pressure of taxation :—"Whereof the like was never heard in any King's time, and now imposed without warrant of the King by subjects upon subjects. Let any discreet man judge how the loyal subjects of this poor kingdom were borne down and daily oppressed. . . . Besides, see the excise and other grievous and intollerable burdens." For the Act see Spalding, ii. 266.

[7] The Queen's letter to Montrose, dated York, 31st May 1643 (Napier, Memorials of Montrose, ii. 77-78, and Mem., 380), indicates a suspicion of the existence of this feeling in Montrose. After the interview with Huntly at the beginning of June (Spalding, ii. 252), there was a strong suspicion of a Royalist rising under Montrose.

[8] See Guthrie's Mem., 129, as to the offers of Argyll and the other leaders through Sir James Rollock and Sir Mungo Campbell.

Henderson,[9] that great apostle of their Covenant. Montrose was eager for a conference with this man, as he fully expected to fish all their secrets out of him. But lest a private meeting with such a man should give offence to the King's friends, he determined to take with him as witnesses the Lords Napier[10] and Ogilvy,[11] Sir

---

[9] Alexander Henderson. Baillie says of him: "He was most incomparably the ablest man of us all for all things" (Letters, i. 122). "Our best penman," "these dainty sheets of Mr. Henderson," 189-90. He was without doubt the ablest man all round among the Presbyterian leaders. Born about 1583, he studied at St. Andrews, and became a professor of philosophy there, when he was very Episcopal, taking Archbishop Gladstanes as his patron in a flattering dedication, which gained him the kirk of Leuchars. Guthrie adds that "for gravity, learning, wisdom, and state policy he far exceeded all" the others on his own side. Robert Bruce and William Scott are credited with influencing his change of view. The enforcing of the Prayer-book brought him out as the leader of the opposition in 1637. As Moderator of the Glasgow Assembly, he met all the difficulties of the situation with determination and dexterity, and carried every point of his party. From that time nothing was done without him. "He was so looked upon and reverenced by the generality of the ministry throughout the land, that they (the extreme party) could scarce have had them on their side without him" (Guthrie, p. 135). When the King came down for the Parliament of 1641, Henderson, then minister in Edinburgh, stood high in his favour, and had much influence with him. He received from him the rent of the Chapel Royal. As Moderator of the Assembly of 1643, he had a difficult part to play, and the Solemn League and Covenant was his creation, though subsequently modified by the skill of Vane and the influence of the Independents. He was one of the Commissioners from the General Assembly to England, took part in the Assembly of Divines at Westminster, and for three years was employed in London in all the negotiations affecting Scotland at that critical time. He visited the King at Newcastle in May 1646, and stayed there till the beginning of August. His health giving way, he returned to Scotland by sea, and arrived in Edinburgh August 11th, much exhausted. He died, enjoying much peace of mind, August 19th. He was buried, says Aiton, on the 21st, in St. Giles' Churchyard, near John Knox, but the remains were afterwards removed to the Greyfriars' Churchyard, where a monument detailing his virtues and triumphs was erected to his memory. It was defaced at the Restoration, it is said, and renewed at the Revolution. A rumour went out to the effect that Henderson before his death had gone over to the King's views and party, and that he died of a broken heart at sight of the misery he had brought on the country. Clarendon states this positively, and Dr. Barwick says he died *ex dedecore*. These reports had reached Holland, and had been quoted to Baillie before October, as in a letter to Spang of October 2nd (ii. 398) he contradicts the story. See also notes to the above reference. Shortly after Henderson's death a pamphlet appeared purporting to be "The Declaration of Mr. Alexander Henderson . . . made on his Death-Bed," in which the King is much lauded and the teaching of the Covenant rescued from disloyal interpretation. It was thought to be the work of some moderate Presbyterian among the "Engagers." The Assembly of the time condemned the pamphlet as forged, scandalous, and false. It is given as an appendix in the 1720 (English) edition of Wishart. See General Assembly Commission Records, Scot. Hist. Soc., p. 583, note, and for Henderson, see his Life by Aiton and by M'Crie.

[10] Lord Napier. See note end of Ch. xvii.

[11] James Lord Ogilvy, eldest son of James, first Earl of Airlie, born before 1616, at first held out Airlie Castle in the absence of his father, but afterwards surrendered it to Montrose. Disregarding the "taking in" of the "bonnie house" by Montrose, though both were acting under the same authority, Argyll destroyed it in 1640, acting throughout with much savage violence, and, if Gordon is to be believed (which Gardiner questions without giving sufficient reason), with great cruelty towards Lady Ogilvy in the house of Forther in Glen Isla, where she was expecting her con-

George Stirling of Keir,[12] and other staunch supporters of the King; and so they met on the banks of the river Forth, not far from Stirling.

Montrose professed himself very happy in the visit of so worthy a man, one on whose honour, integrity, and judgment he could rely in difficulties. He told him that in consequence of recent differences he had lived at home, in order to remove the jealousy of his enemies. He was ignorant of all that was going on in the Convention, and was quite at a loss how to act in so ticklish a state of affairs. He begged him, therefore, to inform him freely and with his usual candour of their intentions. Henderson, taking it for granted from these expressions that he was inclining to the Covenanters, in order to engage him more fully, answered plainly and without reserve that they were resolved to send as powerful an army as possible to the assistance of their brethren in England against the King's forces; and that all the Covenanters in both kingdoms were unanimously agreed either to die or force the King to order; that nothing was more earnestly desired than that he should join in favour and friendship

---

finement (Gordon, Scots Affairs, iii. 165). Lord Ogilvy acted loyally with Montrose throughout, was taken prisoner in Lancashire in July 1644, and sent to the loathsome prison of Edinburgh, where he lay till released by the victory of Kilsyth. As he was escaping from Philiphaugh he was taken prisoner under condition of quarter, but would have shared the fate of the other victims at St. Andrews, had he not been rescued by his sister. See Ch. xix. He survived the troubles, and died second Earl of Airlie at an advanced age in 1693. His wife was daughter of the first Lord Banff and granddaughter of Sir Alexander Irvine of Drum and Lady Marion Douglas. See Scot. Act. Parl., Index; Gordon, Scots Affairs, as above; Pref. to Sir George Mackenzie's Practicks; Napier, Index; Gard., Hist. Eng., ix. 167-168, and note 3.

[12] Sir George Stirling of Keir, born 1615, married Lady Margaret Napier, daughter of Archibald, first Lord Napier. Jamieson painted his portrait, now at Keir, in 1637, when he was twenty-two years of age. See Napier's Mem. for a reproduction of it. He was an Elder with Montrose in the Glasgow Assembly of 1638, and followed him afterwards in his Covenanting, Conservative, and Royalist sympathies. When in prison with Montrose for the plot (see note at end of Chap. i.) he declares his devotion to "the good cause," meaning the Covenant. He is said, after his liberation, to have ridden in 1642 with Montrose to the King at York, and been refused access to him in terms of treaty. See Spalding, ii. 141. He is in prison again in 1645 in Edinburgh Castle, and afterwards in Blackness, where he was allowed to take the air on the top of the tower. His wife was persecuted at the same time, and "wardit" in Edinburgh, in Merchiston, and in Linlithgow. Kilsyth freed them, with many others. On 21st November 1645 he was sent to prison in St. Andrews by the persecuting Committee, and on the 10th of December his wife is allowed to join him there "from out among the rebels." He was permitted to retire to Holland in 1646. In 1652 he was a deputy to Parliament for Stirlingshire, and a deputy of Parliament to England, and he was a J.P. for Stirling in 1663.

See Napier, Mem., *passim*, Act. Parl. Scot., and *n*. end Ch. x.

with his peers and the other estates of the realm; it would bring joy to all, and not only profit, but also honour to himself. His example would at once bring over the few, if there were any, who respected the empty shadow of royalty. As for himself, his most hearty thanks would be due to God, if He would deign to make him the minister and mediator of so great a work. He therefore earnestly entreated him to speak out his mind, and intrust his fidelity and diligence with what he would have the Convention do for his profit and honour, for he was sure he would be satisfied in all his heart's desire.

This was clear information, and exactly what Montrose desired to get. He was anxious still to keep them a while in suspense and doubt. What answer should he return? To declare himself openly their enemy would be of no service to the King, and might bring ruin on himself. On the other hand, his generous mind disdained to encourage their hopes. It was dishonourable to promise what he had resolved not to perform. He therefore adopted this course. Henderson at this conference was accompanied by Sir James Rollock,[13] the head of an ancient and wealthy family, who had married Montrose's sister, and after her death a sister of the Marquis of Argyll, the ringleader of the Scottish Covenanters. Being equally allied with both of them, he seemed a very fit mediator between them. Montrose asked him whether their offers were authorised by the Convention, or suggested merely by their own zeal. Sir James replied that he imagined Henderson had orders from the Convention. Henderson, however, denied it, but did not doubt that the Convention would make good his promises. Montrose declared that he could come to no definite conclusion, unless he could rely on the public faith, espe-

---

[13] Sir James Rollock, afterwards second Lord Rollo, was the eldest son of that Sir Andrew Rollock of Duncrub who on 10th January 1651 was created Lord Rollo by Charles II. Sir James was knighted by Charles I., and had a charter, as junior of Duncrub, of the lands of Duncrub, March 8, 1642. His mother was the Hon. Catherine Drummond, fourth daughter of the first Lord Maderty. Sir James married, first, Lady Dorothea Graham, the sister of Montrose, who died in 1638 without issue. He then married Lady Mary Campbell, youngest daughter of Archibald, seventh Earl of Argyll, and half sister of the Marquis of Argyll, chief opponent of Montrose. His brother, Sir William Rollock or Rollo, was a faithful friend of Montrose, captured at Philiphaugh, and executed at Glasgow, 21st October the same year. See *n.* on Sir W. Rollock, Ch. iv., and Wishart *passim*; also Douglas Peerage, "Lord Rollo," where Edinburgh is put by mistake for Glasgow.

cially as the messengers disagreed among themselves. Hereupon they began to blame one another, as usually happens in such cases, when they ought rather to have laid the blame on their own carelessness and neglect. Thus the conference was broken off. Montrose had gained his point, and they returned, as wise as they came, to give an account of their success.

## CHAPTER III.

Montrose joins the King at Gloucester—His plan approved, December 1643—Antrim promises help from Ireland—Hamilton and Lanark arrive at Oxford, December 1643—Arrest of the Duke and flight of Lanark to London—Montrose sets out for Scotland—Interview with the Marquis of Newcastle.

ON returning from the conference, Montrose related all that had passed to friends he most trusted. At the same time he entreated them to hasten with him to the King in a body, for so they were more likely to be believed, that His Majesty, on being fully informed of everything, might give ear to sounder counsels, and take timely measures to avert, if possible, the impending evil. Most of them exclaimed that the King's authority was ruined, and that it was beyond human power to reduce the kingdom to its proper obedience; for their own parts, they had acquitted themselves before God, their own consciences, and the world, by persisting so far in their allegiance, to their disgrace, loss, and peril. For the future they would be merely onlookers, earnestly imploring God Almighty for better times. Montrose, whom no considerations could ever discourage from persevering in an honourable purpose, communicated his design to Lord Ogilvy, his dearest friend, and set out straight for Oxford. When he came there, the King was gone down to the siege of Gloucester;[1] but he told the Queen what the Covenanters in

---

[1] Charles went to Gloucester on 8th Aug., and summoned it to surrender 10th Aug. 1643. He was there six days, and was called to Oxford. Montrose must have come first to Oxford about the 10th, and returned with the King. The letters of the King and Queen to Hamilton, 28th Aug. 1643, indicate that there were grounds of suspicion in their minds, and the official communications to Lanark and the Council, ending with the private letter to Hamilton, 28th Sep., make it clear that these suspicions had grown to an opinion adverse to the brothers. Recent events in Scotland and England strongly supported Montrose's contention. The Solemn League and Covenant, devised by Henderson and amended by Vane (see Preface), was adopted by the General Assembly, and was ratified by the Convention of Estates, 17th Aug. It reached London 26th Aug. After passing through the hands of the Assembly of Divines, the Lords, and Commons, it was ordered to be sworn to in St. Margaret's, Westminster, 25th Sep. It was

Scotland were plotting against His Majesty; but all to no purpose. Such was her confidence in the Hamiltons that she refused to believe a word.

Finding he could do nothing with the Queen, Montrose went down to Gloucester and laid the whole matter before the King himself. He informed him that a very powerful army was being raised in Scotland, and the day had been appointed for marching into England. He had penetrated their plans, and the highest command in the army had been offered him as a bait for his friendship. But as he detested so black a crime, he had hastened to inform His Majesty; if he could not apply a sufficient remedy in time, he might at least thwart and delay their designs till the King's affairs in England were settled. The rebels in either kingdom might be easily dealt with separately; but should they join forces, it would then be a matter of the greatest difficulty. There were very many people in Scotland ready to sacrifice all they had in their affection to the King; but when once the army had been raised, their loyalty would be of little service to the King, and probably destructive to themselves. The proud spirit of the rebels ought to be crushed and their forces broken at once, before they came to a head; neglect now would breed repentance when too late. Such advice he continued daily to press upon the King, but in vain. He had to struggle not only with the deeply rooted confidence which the King reposed in the Hamiltons, but also with a set of worthless courtiers, who continually buzzed into the King's ears Montrose's youth, rashness, and ambition, and his hatred and envy of the Hamiltons, whose integrity, fidelity, discretion, and power they enlarged on in the most glowing terms.

---

then returned to Scotland, and on 22nd Oct. was ordered, in the King's name, without his consent, to be sworn to and subscribed by all subjects. The mustering of the army was proceeded with under Leslie, and their pay was provided for by the English Parliament, Oct. 27th. Fifty thousand pounds was sent to Leith by sea, Nov. 4th. The Scots entered England Jan. 19th. Hamilton and Lanark left Scotland the end of Nov., arrived at Oxford Dec. 16th, and were confined to their chambers. Early in Jan. the Duke was sent to Pendennis Castle, and Ludlow Castle was fixed as a prison for Lanark, but he escaped to London the night before his removal. He is next found with the Covenanters in Scotland. On Feb. 1st Montrose received a commission as Lieutenant-General to Prince Maurice, who was named Captain-General of the forces in Scotland. Burnet, Dukes of Hamilton, 246-272; Gardiner, Civil War, i. 233, 207, 351.

Montrose was completely baffled. The King returned to winter at Oxford, and though he began to perceive, from the incessant rumours of the Scotch army, that Montrose had foretold him nothing but truth, his sacred Majesty was resolved to give his Scottish subjects not the slightest pretext for complaint unless they entered England. He was determined to keep the pacification religiously. Should they break it, he felt confident they should answer for it to God and himself.

During these discussions at Oxford the Covenanters in Scotland did just as they pleased, with none to oppose their wishes. They levied as large an army as possible, and already 18,000 foot and 2000 horse stood ready on the Borders.[2] At last the Hamiltons condescended to inform the King of the approach of this hostile force. In their letters they endeavoured to excuse their own conduct. According to promise, they had done their utmost to prevent this invasion from Scotland during the past summer; but now that winter was approaching they could hinder it no longer; but they assured him that they would presently be at hand with a very powerful army. When the King found his confidence thus openly abused, he sent for Montrose at last, showed him his letters from the Hamiltons, and, when too late, earnestly requested his advice.

Montrose replied that the King could at last perceive that his advice had proceeded neither from ambition, avarice, or hatred of the Hamiltons, but solely from a sense of duty and allegiance. For more than a year he had persistently warned both their Majesties of the impending danger. It had been his misfortune that his faithful service had found no credit with so good a master. The affair now seemed desperate, though it might easily have been cured, had His Majesty not yielded to the will of those who had used his authority to stop the mouths of some, and, under pretext of affection to the King, had seduced others, who had never intended it, unwittingly to favour the rebellion, and who, now that the army was ready, yielded everything to the rebels without a blow. The King complained that he had been

---

[2] See previous note.

most grossly betrayed by those to whom he had intrusted his secrets, his crown, his honour, and his life, and earnestly pressed for his advice. Montrose answered that though matters seemed in a deplorable state, yet if it pleased his royal master, he promised either to reduce the rebels to order, of which he did not yet despair, or lose his life in the attempt. The King, not a little cheered by Montrose's confidence, gallantry, and firmness, even in these desperate circumstances, desired him to take a day or two's grace for full deliberation, and so dismissed him.

At the time appointed he returned to the King and explained to him that the task was one of the greatest difficulty. All Scotland was under the yoke of the Covenanters; they had seized and garrisoned all the strongholds, and were abundantly supplied with men, money, arms, ammunition, and provisions—in short, every requisite for war. Moreover, the English rebels were joined with them in a very close league to defend each other against all the world. As for himself, he had neither men nor money, nor even arms, or anything to help his credit at the outset. Yet he would not distrust God's help in a righteous cause, and, if the King commanded, he would undertake it. It could do the King no further harm, for he himself would bear the hatred, envy, and danger of his attachment to the King, provided he would graciously accede to a few demands. In the first place, it was of the utmost importance that he should order some soldiers from Ireland to land in the west of Scotland. Secondly, he should order the Marquis of Newcastle (who commanded the royal forces in the north of England) to aid Montrose with a party of horse to enter Scotland, with the help of which he would penetrate into the heart of the kingdom. Further, that he should obtain some troops of German cavalry from the King of Denmark. And lastly, that steps should be taken to procure arms abroad and have them transmitted to Scotland. Nothing further was wanting but human energy; the rest must be left to God's good providence. The King approved of his plan, thanked him for not yet despairing, and encouraged him to undertake the matter promptly. He also promised that he would attend to his demands.

He immediately sent for the Earl of Antrim[3] and informed him of Montrose's plan. Antrim is of Scotch extraction, descended from the noble and ancient family of the Macdonalds, a man of great estate and power in Ireland, and allied to some of the highest nobility in England by his marriage with the Dowager Duchess of Buckingham. Having been driven out of his own country, he was living at the time in Oxford. He very readily undertook to raise the Irish force, and at the same time entered into a voluntary engagement with Montrose to make a descent with 10,000[4] men in Argyleshire, opposite Ireland, by the 1st of April 1644. These arrangements were made in December 1643.

For the foreign troops and arms the King despatched Sir John Cochrane,[5] his ambassador, with his commission and instruc-

---

[3] Randal MacDonell, Marquis of Antrim, a Roman Catholic involved in the Irish plots. He had been a prisoner at Carrickfergus, and escaped as a sick man carried out on a couch. In 1643 he was again captured by Major Ballantine, an officer of Monroe's, when landing a little above his old prison at Carrickfergus. Here he was again imprisoned. Letters were found on him from Aboyne and Nithsdale, indicating an extensive plot to employ the Irish rebels on the royal side. This gave much alarm in Scotland and intensified the feeling against the King in England. "A little Monsieur, some agent of the Queen," offered to the Scotch Council the renewal of a league with the French, and made the freedom of Antrim a condition. Antrim, however, escaped in October, and, with Nithsdale and Aboyne, was at Oxford when Montrose was urging his scheme (Baillie's Letters, ii. 73, 105, 116). Spalding, ii. 291-292, gives his own touches to the story of the "escape of this great Papist from Captain Wallace, as great a Puritan." Lieutenant Gordon, an officer under Wallace, son of Sir Alexander Gordon and uncle to the Earl of Sutherland, "crafftellie convoyit up unespyit in his breikis certaine towis, be the quhilk the erll escaipit and wan frielie away, to Wallass' gryte greif, and the lieut. follouit and fled also." See Spalding, ii. 242, for the letters of Aboyne, &c., and "The Declaration of the House of Commons on the Rise and Progress of the Grand Rebellion in Ireland."

[4] "Wishart gives 10,000 as the number of the men to be sent with Antrim. This appears from the correspondence in the Carte MSS. to be wrong, and is evidently transferred from the number planned to be sent to England" (Gard., Civil War, i. 350). All the Celts destined for Scotland were 2000 men.

[5] Sir John Cochrane was frequently employed in negotiation with foreign potentates. With Henderson, another Scotchman, he had been "commissioned in 1642 to visit the King of Denmark, to urge him to send arms for 12,000 men, 24 cannon, £100,000, a fleet of ships of war, 3000 German infantry, and 1000 horse" (Gard. Civil War, i. 45). In 1644 he is again employed thus, and Charles II. sent him on an embassy to the King of Poland in 1650. He was the eldest son of Alexander Blair, third son of John Blair of Blair, who, having married the sole heiress of William Cochrane of Cochrane, had assumed her name. Through a letter from the Queen of Bohemia particularly recommending him, Charles I. received him into his service, and he became a colonel in the army. He was made an unwilling recipient of Montrose's strong views about Argyll at Newcastle, and was afterwards mixed up in the history of the "Incident." The King in his evidence speaks of him as "having maney discourses, most of his auen praisses." Being arrested and ordered to be sent to John Smith's house, he, "at the going out of the Parliament Court for that

tions. The orders to the Marquis of Newcastle were conveyed by some of Montrose's own company. Montrose himself, having received the King's letters and commission to be lieutenant-governor of Scotland and general[6] of the forces, was on the point of starting for Scotland, when news was unexpectedly brought that the Duke of Hamilton[7] and his brother, the Earl of Lanark, were hastening to Oxford. To procure easier access to the King, who had always hitherto been led by their advice, and to recover their old favour with him, they gave out on their way, especially to the governors of shires and towns and commanders of the army, that they had been banished by the Covenanters and their estates plundered for their loyalty to the King, and they were flying for their lives to Oxford. Montrose and his friends maintained that these were but idle tales, invented to wipe out the stain of their late guilt. Trusting to the favour they had recently enjoyed with the King, and the influence of a powerful faction at Court, devoted to their interests, they made sure of retaining their position, could they but gain admission to the King's presence. Their sole object in posting thither was to defeat Montrose again, and quench the faint spark of loyalty that still flickered in Scotland. Montrose frankly declared that he would not stand by to see such doings. He therefore humbly begged His Majesty that, if the men who had so often cheated his hopes were to return to favour, he would give him leave to look abroad for employment; not that he desired any severity towards them, but entreated His Majesty to beware of further harm from them.

---

night, made ane escape at ane posterne." He afterwards surrendered and was sent to jail, but by and bye he was allowed to exchange the jail for John Smith's house (see for his evidence in the Incident, Balfour, Ann. iii. 98-107). He was again summoned for assisting to draw up the Oxford Declaration in 1644, and is among those exempted from pardon (Act. Parl. Scot.). He died before the Restoration without children. His wife was one of the Ormond family.

His younger brother William was raised to the peerage and became the first Earl of Dundonald. Douglas Peerage, "Dundonald."

[6] In Ruddiman's translation there is a note here ascribing a mistake to W. in speaking of Montrose as general of the forces, whereas he was only lieutenant-general under Prince Maurice. The Latin is *dux*, and may mean any kind of general. The mistake lay in translating *dux* "*commander-in-chief.*"

[7] See note on page 34. Hamilton and Lanark arrived at Oxford, December 16, 1643.

The King consented with reluctance to forbid their presence at Court, and, after all, he allowed the Earl of Lanark[8] to stay in the city. Lanark, however, at whose instigation I cannot tell, left Oxford for London, where he went to the English Parliament. Shortly afterwards he betook himself to the army of the Scotch Covenanters, who had now entered England, and from that time forth devoted himself heart and soul to their cause. The desertion of the brother struck the King so much that he saw it was high time to secure the Duke himself in prison.

Both in the Court and royal camp there were several Scotsmen who were suspected, and perhaps not without reason, of favouring the Covenanters and betraying all the King's secrets. To put them to the test, Montrose hit upon the following contrivance. He got a protestation,[9] drawn up by the King's command,

---

[8] William Hamilton, Earl of Lanark and second Duke of Hamilton, was brother of James, the first Duke. He was ten years younger than his brother, by whom he was educated, being about nine years old at his father's death. He studied at Glasgow College and in France, was well received at the English Court, and his interests were forwarded by his brother, who arranged his marriage at twenty-two with Lady Elizabeth Maxwell, eldest daughter of the Earl of Dirleton. He was created Earl of Lanark in 1639, and on the death of the Earl of Stirling in 1640 he was made Secretary of State for Scotland, being only twenty-four years of age. He was mixed up with his brother in all matters, and was deprived of the Seal at Oxford in 1643. He then joined the Covenanters, and gathered 1000 or 1500 men to attack Montrose at Kilsyth, but came too late. He was a Commissioner of the Parliament in the negotiations at Newark. In the "Engagement" he commanded in Scotland, while his brother marched into England. On his brother's death he became Duke of Hamilton. Eventually he died, Sep. 12, 1651, from a wound under the knee, received while bravely fighting at Worcester. Notwithstanding some slips in his faithfulness he had a character for honesty. Burnet says that "from a child he could never by any temptation be made to lie" (Burnet's Dukes of Hamilton, 417). Sir Philip Warwick quotes as his own opinion a saying of Montrose, that "when Lanark was in arms against him and against the King, he did it open-faced and without the least treachery." Wishart commends him for his honest refusal to join Montrose after Kilsyth (v. Ch. xv.; Napier, Mem., 98). When Lanark pleaded with the King for his brother at the Incident time, Charles said coldly that he believed that he was himself (Lanark) an honest man, and that he had never heard anything to the contrary; but that he thought his brother had been very active in his own preservation (Hardwicke's State Papers, ii. 299). After his pledge of quarter to, and kindly treatment of, Sir R. Spottisswoode he left him to the mercy of his enemies at St. Andrews, not even voting with the minority—a stain on his fame. Wharton, the English Commissioner, writing from Berwick to Parliament, notices as a curious thing that the Earl of Lanark took Sir Robert Spottiswood, his successor as Secretary for Scotland, prisoner, "and in his pocket the Seal the King took from him, so as he is possessed of it again" (see Records of Com. of General Assemblies, Scot. Hist. Society, Introd. xxi.). Lanark was the last Duke of Hamilton in the male line. Duchess Anne, his brother's daughter, carried the title to a Douglas.

[9] See Bond with corrected signatures in Napier's Memorials of Montrose, ii. 119-121; also Baillie's remarks on it in letters of Feb. 18 and Ap. 2, 1644.

to be subscribed by all the Scots who wished to be esteemed loyal, professing therein their abhorrence of the Covenanters' designs, and especially condemning their invasion of England against the King and laws of the land as an act of high treason. Further, they solemnly pledged themselves to avenge that crime on the offenders at the hazard of their lives and fortunes. This protest was eagerly subscribed by men of worth and honour. Yet the two men in whom, next to the Hamiltons, the King had most confidence, the Earl of Traquair[10] and William Murray,[11] a gentleman of the bedchamber, were induced, or rather compelled, to put their hand to it with great reluctance and through

---

[10] John Stewart, first Earl of Traquair, though commended by Clarendon for his ability, and loyalty to King and Church, was yet generally denounced by his contemporaries on both sides of politics. Wishart, Montrose, Balfour, Baillie, Scotstarvit, and the pasquil writers of the time all condemn his conduct, and his character is painted as mercenary and deceitful. Clarendon's panegyric on his "affection for the Church, which was so notorious that he never deserted it till both it and he were overrun and trode under foot," would hardly have been so warm had he seen Traquair's petition, 26th December 1646, "to be allowed to prove himself, in the sight of God and man, at the sacrifice of life and fortune, a faithful Covenanter" (Napier, Mem., 580; quoting Rescinded Acts; see Wishart, chaps. xv., xvi., on his treachery at Philiphaugh). He was a man of great ability, but relied on by few except the King. He ended in begging for a copper in the streets of Edinburgh, and died in 1659 smoking a pipe of tobacco.

"Thy face, thy tongue, thy heart are at a strife
Which of them to thy lies should add most life.
Bold brows attend thy double tongue, with eyes as bold," &c.
"Book of Scottish Pasquils," Edinburgh, 1868, p. 113.

[11] William Murray, son of the minister of Dysart, and nephew of Thomas Murray, the preceptor of Charles in his youth, and afterwards, when Prince of Wales, his secretary. Another uncle was Robert Murray, minister (sometimes, from his church being an old collegiate church, called Provost) of Methven, who played an important part in bringing Montrose into the Covenant and sending him to prison for the plot. By Thomas Murray's influence William was made the Prince's whipping-boy, and grew into great intimacy and trust with Charles. In a former edition of Wishart a note here describes him as one of the worst characters of that perfidious age, and he seems to deserve the condemnation to a large extent. See *n.* p. 15 as to his supposed betrayal of trust when groom of the bedchamber, in more than one direction. Notwithstanding all the suspicion attaching to him, the King created him Earl of Dysart in 1643, though the patent did not pass the Seals till his daughter, the clever but ill-famed Duchess of Lauderdale, got the precedency of the old patent when she was made Countess of Dysart. At Breda he acted for the Covenanters, and was in their confidence from the beginning. Burnet, who disliked him, says of him, "His Lordship had one particular quality, that when he was drunk, which was very often, he was on a most strict reserve, though at other times pretty open" (Burnet, "Own Times," i. 224; Douglas Peerage). Charles II. seems to have given a new patent in 1651 to the Covenanting Commissioner. Lamont (37, an. 1651) says, "This year ther were sundrie of the gentrie nobilitat, as the Laird of Kleish made Lord Colvin; Will Murray, of the bedchamber, Lord of Dysert; the Laird of Frieland, Lord Ruthven, with severall others." He was on the Roll of Parliament in 1670, 1672, 1673 (Act. Parl. Scot.).

fear of being discovered traitors. Yet even they too promised on their oath to meet Montrose in Scotland with some assistance by a certain day. In this matter too they broke their oath most foully.

Montrose then set out for Scotland; but he had hardly turned his back, when the friends of the Hamiltons and other faithless courtiers began to represent him as a vain, ambitious man, who had undertaken more than he could possibly perform; and, to frighten any who might be disposed to share in so noble an enterprise, they were extravagant in praise of the forces and power of the Covenanters, and took every opportunity of maliciously declaring that no good could be expected from such a man.

Unmoved by the calumnies of such worthless creatures, Montrose proceeded to York[12] and Durham, where he sent off the King's instructions to the Marquis of Newcastle, and the next day they met in conference. Newcastle told him that the army was in absolute want of everything. The rebel Scots, in the depth of winter, had unexpectedly broken in and spoiled his recruiting, and were now within five miles, threatening his camp with far superior numbers. In short, he could not spare him any of his horse without a downright risk to the whole army. Montrose, on the other hand, urged that nothing could contribute more to the success of the war, than to send a part of his horse, in which he was strong, with him into Scotland, to divert, or at least divide,

---

[12] Feb. 1. Montrose commissioned as Lieutenant-General to Prince Maurice for Scotland.
,, 13. Commission changed into one as Lieutenant-General to the King for Scotland.
Mar. 1 (or thereabout). Montrose set out from Oxford, accompanied by Lords Crawford, Reay, Nithsdale, Ogilvy, and Aboyne, Colonel Innes, Colonel Cochrane, John Macbrayre, and others. Lords Crawford and Reay went off with a squadron towards Shrewsbury.
,, 8. Colonel Cochrane sent on to the Marquis of Newcastle at Durham to prepare him for the demands of men, money, &c., to be made on him.
,, 13. Montrose writes to Spottiswoode, giving Newcastle's refusal.
,, 15. Montrose went on to Durham.
,, 24. Took part in the second affair at Bowdenhill, and thought Newcastle and General King "slow."
Apr. 13 or 14. With his own party of 200 Cavaliers, 100 more from Newcastle (the Duchess says 200), on worn-out horses, a few Westmoreland horsemen, and 800 foot and two guns, he crossed the Border and marched by Annan to Dumfries. See Napier, Mem., 389-396, for interesting letter of John Macbrayre and letters of Montrose, with the evidence at inquiry in Scotland as to Montrose at Bowdenhill; also Turner, Mem., 35-36.
May 6. Date of Montrose's patent as a Marquis.

the enemy, and by striking at them in their own homes force them back to defend themselves. Newcastle[13] courteously replied that as soon as he was free from the present danger he would not fail Montrose. As he was a man of honour and approved loyalty, he would undoubtedly have kept his word, had he remained longer in the command of those parts, and been but once convinced of Montrose's honour and nobility of purpose. In the meantime all the aid he could afford him in his present straits was about a hundred troopers, but mounted on lean, ill-appointed horses (through no fault of his, but owing to the envy of some men), with two small brass field-pieces. He also sent orders to the King's officers and commanders of the militia in Cumberland and Westmoreland to attend Montrose in his journey into Scotland with all the force they could muster, and give him every assist-

---

[13] William Cavendish, Earl of Newcastle, created Marquis in reward for his victory at Adwalton Moor, by patent dated October 27, 1643, commanded in the northern counties, which he had drawn into an Association, and to which he was imparting a unity promising well for the future of the Royalists. The appearance of Leven's army in Northumberland on 19th January in aid of the Parliament disconcerted his plans. He was able to give Montrose scarcely any help. Newcastle was "a very fine gentleman," according to Clarendon, and his second wife, in her Life of him, describes him thus: "His shape is neat and exactly proportioned; his stature is of middle size, and his complexion sanguine. His behaviour is such that it might be a pattern to all gentlemen, for it is courtly, civil, easy, and free, without formality or constraint, and yet hath something in it of grandeur that causes an awful respect for him" (Life of Duke of Newcastle, London, 1667; but see Dict. of National Biography). His sumptuous entertainments of Charles I. and the Queen at Bolsover and Welbeck, on their going to Scotland and returning, were without parallel, and cost over £20,000. Ben Jonson wrote the masque "Love's Welcome to Welbeck." The Marquis was a great patron of literature, and himself wrote plays, of which "The Triumphant Widow, or the Medley of Humours," a comedy, has a prominent place in notices of its author, though critics such as Pepys ridiculed it. His great book, with the remarkable illustrations by Diepenbeke, entitled *Le Methode et Invention Nouvelle de Dresser les Chevaux*, is a sumptuous folio, published at Antwerp, 1657, at a cost of £1300. It was translated by John Brindley, and published in two grand volumes, London, 1743. His real interests lay in the refinements and in the cultured paths of life. In war, though not a brilliant leader, he was safe, and on the whole successful, till Prince Rupert at Marston Moor disgusted him with the war. He drove off to Scarborough and shipped for Hamburg, where he stayed a year. He then went to Paris, and married his second wife, a daughter of Sir Thomas Lucas, and maid of honour to Queen Henrietta. Afterwards he settled at Antwerp, where he was very popular, and his Riding-House there became a centre of all well-bred and courtly visitors to the Low Countries. After the Restoration he recovered part of his property. In 1664 he was created Duke of Newcastle. His losses through the rebellion were computed by the Duchess at £940,000. He died Dec. 25, 1676, and was succeeded by Henry, his second son, with whom the title became extinct in the Cavendishes. See Hume's estimate of the first Marquis, Hist. of Eng., vii. 13; Gard., Hist. of Eng., quoting Con the Jesuit, viii. 243; literary references are given in Dict. of Nat. Biog. Pepys' Diary, 18th March 1668, has a critique of the Duchess and of him. See also Doyle's Extinct Peerages.

ance. Accordingly, on his road to Carlisle Montrose was met by the Cumberland and Westmoreland men to the number of eight hundred foot and three troops of horse, who, in obedience to Newcastle's orders, were to accompany him into Scotland. He himself had two hundred horse, most of them nobles and gentlemen, who had served as officers in Germany, France, or England. With these scanty and not over-trusty forces he entered Scotland on the 13th of April, in haste not to fail the Earl of Antrim at the time appointed.[14]

---

[14] Namely, April 1.

## CHAPTER IV.

Montrose at Dumfries—The English soldiers desert—He returns to Carlisle—His movements in Northumberland—Interview with Prince Rupert—State of Scotland—Montrose enters Scotland in disguise, and reaches Graham of Inchbrakie in Perthshire.

HAVING entered Scotland, Montrose had reached the river Annan, when a mutiny broke out among the English soldiers, occasioned by the servants of Richard Graham,[1] and almost all deserted and fled in haste to England. Nevertheless he marched forward with his own men to Dumfries,[2] which was surrendered by the inhabitants. There he waited for some little time, expecting to meet Antrim with his Irish auxiliaries. But the time agreed on was already long past, without any message or rumour of their coming. The Covenanters were gathering from all sides, and he would certainly have been surprised and cut off, had he not beaten a timely retreat. However, he managed to reach Carlisle without loss. It was now evident that he could get no assistance from England. There was no prospect of speedy help from abroad. Hope of the Irish was almost gone. He found too that the Earl of Callander[3] had raised a new army to

---

[1] Richard Graham. See note below, p. 51.

[2] Montrose was peaceably received by the people of Dumfries, though his force was small. Sir James Maxwell, Provost of Dumfries, was executed at Edinburgh in July this year "for receiving of some of the Banders within the towne." "He was a true King's man and hater of his enemies, for the whilk he sufferit" (Spalding, ii. 391). But see M'Dowall, Hist. of Dumfries, 410, where Spalding is quoted (with a wrong reference) to the above effect, yet in the Appendix, 910, list of Provosts, *John Corsane* is given as Provost in 1643.

[3] The Hon. James Livingstone, third son of Alexander, first Earl of Linlithgow, acquired a great reputation in military affairs in Bohemia, Germany, Holland, and Sweden. In 1633 Charles made him Lord Livingstone of Almond. Lord Almond was second in command to Leslie in the army of 1640, and one of the Cumbernauld Banders. He was made Earl of Callendar when Charles was dispensing honours to his enemies and half friends in 1641. In 1643 he hung back from the Scotch army, but in 1644 he marched against Montrose at Dumfries with 5000 men, and eventually joined Leven in the siege of Newcastle. The Scotch Committee gave him an Act of approbation and exoneration, July 13. He joined in the "Engagement," and was second in com-

reinforce Leslie, who, with the English Covenanters, had by this time laid siege to York. He determined, therefore, to waste no time in inactivity, but join the King's forces in Northumberland and Durham. This resolve was neither unprofitable to them nor dishonourable to himself. He drove a garrison of the Covenanters out of Morpeth,[4] and took the castle by storm. All the booty he gave to his English soldiers. The garrison he dismissed without punishment, on parole never again to draw sword against the King. His next enterprise was against a fort at the mouth of the river Tyne,[5] from which the Covenanters had recently expelled an English garrison. This he recaptured, and sent the prisoners back to Scotland on the same conditions as at Morpeth. He then got together a large quantity of provisions from Alnwick and the neighbourhood, with which he relieved Newcastle. After these exploits he was summoned by letters from Prince Rupert, Count of the Rhine Palatinate, who was hastening to raise the siege at York. He obeyed with all possible despatch, but did not come up with the Prince till he was falling back on York the day after that unfortunate battle.[6] At first the Prince freely offered

---

mand to Hamilton. On the failure of that expedition he fled to Holland, when Cromwell dealt with his estates. He returned at the Restoration, and died without issue in 1672, the title going to his brother. See Douglas Peerage; Turner, Mem.; Guthrie, Mem.; Napier, Mem., *passim*. He was a nobleman who, between war and politics, was much put to it in steering a course for himself, but on the whole succeeded. In Montrose's cypher key he is represented by "Almanak," probably from his study of the signs of the times.

[4] The siege of Morpeth was commenced by Montrose and the Earl of Crawford about the 10th of May 1644. He led his attacking party from Newcastle. The castle was defended by Lieutenant-Colonel James Somerville and Captain John M'Culloch, who repulsed the first assault with great loss to the assailants. Trenches were next made and six guns brought up from Newcastle. The attacking party was assailed in the rear by Welden's horse, but notwithstanding, Montrose carried the place. For interesting evidence as to the affair see the deposition of Captain J. M'Culloch in Napier, Mem., 400. The son of the governor, Somerville, wrote an account of the siege in his "Memoire of the Somervilles." In 1666 Captain John M'Culloch was executed for high treason after the battle of Pentland. Spalding, ii. 379, adds a touch to Wishart's account of the treatment of the prisoners. "Thair was ane fight about Morpot, quhair divers of our Scottis foot soldiouris were overcum by the Banderis, strippit out of thair clothis and armes, and send hame naikit about this tyme." See letter from the English Commissioners on Montrose's activity, dated Sunderland, 8th May, quoted by Napier, Mem., 398.

[5] Tynemouth. Montrose's activity held Callendar back from Newcastle, and enabled the town to be provisioned. "The delay of Callendar's incoming so long has given time to the Marquis of Montrose to make havoc of the northern counties, which will make the siege of Newcastle the harder" (Baillie, Letters, ii. 196). Wishart himself was in Newcastle at this time.

[6] Marston Moor, fought July 2, 1644. See Gard., Civil War, for full account of the battle, and Rupert's relations with Newcastle and Montrose.

him a thousand horse to lead into Scotland; but some of the people about the Prince, who had too much influence with him, induced him to change his mind, so that the day after he had made the promise Montrose could not obtain a single trooper. Although disappointed by all from whom he could expect any assistance, Montrose never lost heart. Returning to Carlisle with those few but trusty, gallant men, his staunch adherents, he despatched Lord Ogilvy with Sir William Rollock[7] into the heart of Scotland, meanly disguised to elude the enemy. They returned within a fortnight with word that in Scotland all was lost. The passes, castles, and towns were garrisoned by the Covenanters. None dared to speak of the King with the least reverence or affection. Struck with these gloomy tidings, many of those who had hitherto adhered to Montrose began to cast about for their own safety. In this they were instigated to desert mainly by that worthy nobleman, the Earl of Traquair,[8] who forgetting all the vows and imprecations he had made before the King, undertook, in the name of the Covenanters, to offer indemnity, and even rewards in money and preferment to deserters, just as if he were an agent for the rebels, and not, as he pretended, for the King. Yet this man stood higher in the good King's favour, and was more trusted than any man, excepting Hamilton.

Montrose upon this called his friends together to advise with him upon this miserable state of things. Some were of opinion

---

[7] Sir William Rollock, now spelt Rollo, was the younger brother of Sir James of Duncrub (see *n.* p. 32). He was lame from infancy, but a brave soldier. Resigning his position as captain in General King's "lifeguard of horse" at Newcastle, he took service with Montrose as major, and with Colonel Sibbald accompanied him in his ride to Tullybelton. After the battle of Aberdeen he fell into Argyll's hands, as he was carrying despatches to the King. (See Chap. xviii. and Napier, Mem., 459, for Argyll's proposing the assassination of Montrose to Rollock.) He was taken prisoner at Philiphaugh, and beheaded at Glasgow Cross, 21st October 1646. The date of his death has been in dispute, but it is now decided by the discovery of the warrant of the Estates for the execution. The sederunt, held at Glasgow, 21st October 1645, consisted of Crawford (Lindsay) pres., Lanark, General David Lesly, Cessnock, Tullibardine, Elphinston, Finlater, Kirkcudbright, Kilbirnie, General Baillie, Kowdoun, and George Porterfield. Rollock was called in, and sentenced to be beheaded that afternoon. The Glasgow bailie, Robert Burns, who presided, gives four o'clock as the hour. See Chap. xviii. *n.*; also Guthrie, Mem., 208; Nap., Mem., index; Acts Parl. Scot., vi. pt. i. 587.

[8] See *n.* p. 41.

that he should go to Oxford and inform His Majesty that affairs in Scotland were past recovery; that Antrim had not come with the Irish forces, and there was no prospect of their coming; that little or nothing had been got from the English; no news of the men or arms from abroad had arrived, and accordingly it was no fault of his that he had failed in his appointed task. Others advised him to resign his commission to the King at Oxford, with letters of excuse, and retire abroad until it should please God to grant a more favourable opportunity. All were fully agreed that nothing further should be attempted in Scotland. Montrose stood alone in the lofty, undaunted view he took of matters, intent on very different plans from these. He considered himself bound, even at peril of his life, never to forsake his dearest lord and King, never to despair of so just a cause. Should he attempt some daring exploit beyond the reach of common souls, he foresaw that it would redound to his own honour, and perhaps also the interests of the King. God in His mercy might still turn the King's misfortunes into joy; and should he fall in some great enterprise, he would die with honour and renown. So resolved, and commending the matter earnestly to the care and protection of Almighty God, he performed such exploits, without men, without money, and without arms, as fill us who have heard of them, seen them, and been present at them, with astonishment, and will deservedly arouse the envy and imitation of the greatest generals hereafter. What these were will appear in the course of our narrative.

He now transferred to Ogilvy the few who had remained constant in their fidelity to him, to be conducted to the King; and as he had always communicated his plans to him, he informed him of his present design, and charged him to press the King earnestly to have a supply of arms at least, if not of men, sent at once from abroad. For two days he accompanied them on their return, and then withdrew privately, leaving with them his horses, servants, and baggage, and returned to Carlisle with the utmost expedition. Not suspecting his departure, as Ogilvy and his most intimate friends were still with them, the party continued their march to

Oxford. But they never reached it,[9] for most of them, including Ogilvy, Sir John Innes,[10] colonel of a regiment of horse, Henry Graham,[11] his brother, a youth of great promise, James, John, and Alexander Ogilvy,[12] Patrick Melvin,[13] and other gallant gentlemen,

---

[9] See letter of Fairfax in Napier, Mem., 405, and instructions for Lord Ogilvy, ibid., 406-408, with extract from Rushworth giving an account of the affair at Ribble Bridge. Colonel Doddington and Colonel Shuttleworth achieved these captures. The prisoners were sent first to the army before Newcastle, and, at the end of the siege, to Edinburgh, some to the Castle and some to the "Thieves' Hole." A former editor of Wishart says that our author was among the prisoners. This is a mistake; he was lecturing in Newcastle with regularity during the siege, and only became their fellow-prisoner at its conclusion.

[10] "Sir John Innes" we have not been able to identify as to his parentage. He signed Montrose's bond at Oxford, and went with him to York and Durham. See Napier, Mem. of Mont., ii. 119, and Macbrayre's letter, Napier, Mem., 389. He is sent with Sir John Hurry to invite Huntly to a conference, they being "two persons of the most eminent character in his (Montrose's) army, and who would be acceptable to Huntly" (Chap. xxi. *infra*). Several of the cadet families of Innes were King's men, such as Leuchars, Coitts, and Coxton, though Innes of Innes was a supporter of Argyll, and a Lieutenant-Colonel John Innes commanded a regiment of horse on the Covenant side (Spalding, ii. 432). Alexander Innes of the Leuchars family, connected with Buckingham and Strafford, and engaged in communicating with the Queen, writes from Oxford, June 27, 1643, saying that his brother Robert has been committed by Parliament, and that James is a prisoner at Windsor. John Innes of Leuchars signs the Kilcummin Bond. There are several Innes names in the long list of those receiving "assurances" from Middleton in 1646, where "Harie Graham" and more than one John Ogilvy and James Ogilvy occur in Act. Parl. Scot., vol. vi. pt. i. 669. "John Innes, a rebel," submits, 15th May 1647, to the Commission of the General Assembly at Aberdeen (Gen. Assemb. Rec., 249), where may be seen submissions of many others of the name. See also "The Family of Innes," edited by Cosmo Innes, Spalding Club, 235 and *passim*; also Spalding, ii. 450 and 467, &c.

[11] Henry Graham, a natural brother of Montrose, was detained as a prisoner before Newcastle, and sent to the Tolbooth of Edinburgh, and afterwards to the Castle. He accompanies the other refugees from Stonehaven to Norway (Chap. xxi.). In the last expedition of Montrose he took part, but being left in charge at Kirkwall, escaped the disaster at Corbiesdale. In "the true funerals" of the Marquis in 1661 we have "Sir Harry Graham, in complete armour, on horseback, carrying on the point of a lance the colours of the house. This noble gentleman accompanied his Excellence in all his good and bad fortunes, both at home and abroad." The watchfulness of the Argyll government in Scotland is shown in two extracts from Balfour, Ann., iv. 32 and 53, as to Captain Hall's frigate, in which Henry Grahame escaped from Orkney. Hall and Sir Henry Grahame "being themselves aland, were taken and imprisoned by the people of Norway after the shipe was surprised; bot they were released therafter, in respect no Scotchman would receave them off ther hand." . . . "The housse ordaines the Provost of Edinburgh to causse searche and try anent thesse shipes that cam last from Norway, and refussed to take Sir Henrey Grahame, Captain Hall, and others who were offered to be delivered to them."

[12] We have not been able to identify the two first-named Ogilvys. More than one John and James Ogilvy were out with Montrose. John of Baldovey appears at Kilsyth, and in the pardon list of 1647. After the Restoration he became a justice of peace for Forfarshire. John of Gela or Gella and his son John are also on the pardon list. There is also a John and a James in Littlekeny on the same list. Is the Alexander Ogilvy mentioned here the same as Alexander Ogilvy, the young son of Sir John of Inverquharity, who joined Montrose before Aberdeen and Kilsyth, and became one of the victims of the Covenant on the scaffold at Glasgow after Philiphaugh? (see p. 118 and Ch. xviii.). If so, he could not have been more than sixteen years of age at this time. Apparently an Alexander Ogilvy signed the Oxford Bond.

[13] Patrick Melvin or Melvill appears as Major Melvin in the preparations for the descent upon Orkney. Napier, Mem., 729. See also *n*. at end of Part I.

much esteemed by Montrose, fell into the hands of the enemy. They were all subjected to a long and loathsome imprisonment, until set at liberty by Montrose himself next year, after which they did him faithful service.

Having returned to Carlisle, he imparted his design to the Earl of Aboyne.[14] He was anxious that he might not have the least cause to complain that he had undertaken an affair of such importance without the knowledge and advice of one whose help he might afterwards require in its prosecution. But as that young nobleman was lacking in steady perseverance, he did not urge him to share the hardships of the journey. He found no difficulty in persuading him to stay at Carlisle till summoned by the news of his success. It would then be more seasonable for him to return to his own country.

Being now prepared for his journey, he made choice of only two men as his companions and guides,[15] Sir William Rollock, a gentleman of tried honour, prompt in action and advice, and one Sibbald,[16] whom Montrose held in no less honour and esteem on account of his reputation for courage. This man, however, afterwards deserted him in his greatest need. Disguised as a groom in the service of Sibbald, Montrose was mounted on a lean jade, and led another horse in hand. In this guise he reached the Border, where he found all the ordinary safe passes strictly guarded by the enemy. Here an accident happened which gave

---

[14] Lord James Gordon, Viscount Aboyne, second son of George, second Marquis of Huntly. See Chap. xii. *n.*

[15] See previous note on Sir William Rollock or Rollo. Spalding repeats more than once that "Crouner Hay and Crouner Sibbald cam with Montrois from England." Montrose and his companions left Carlisle August 18, 1644.

[16] Colonel William Sibbald, attached early to Montrose, was left by him in charge of the "Bonnie House of Airlie" on its surrender by Lord Ogilvy, and was ejected from it by Argyll, preparatory to its destruction; see note at end of Chap. i. As to his later desertion of Montrose at Fyvie, see Chap. viii. As a messenger of Montrose from Holland, he was captured, and threatened with torture by the Scotch Parliament (see Acts vi. pt. ii. 564), "if he give them not satisfaction in his examination." He was afterwards executed, January 7, 1650. His dying speech, as he intended to deliver it, is given in various editions of Wishart as an appendix. Sir James Turner has this characteristic notice of Colonel Sibbald :—" I went by land to Holland, accompanied with Colonel Sibbald, who carried letters from Montrose both to Scotland and Ireland. From Rotterdam I wrote with him to my wife at Edinburgh to furnish him with a considerable peece of money (for he was not well stored), which she did; and he had his heade chopd of not long after at the Crosse of Edinburgh; so I lost both my friend and my money."—Turner, Mem., 92.

him still greater concern. Not far from the Border they fell in with a servant of Richard Graham,[17] who taking them for Covenanters of Lesly's army, who were scouring the country in those parts, assured them in frank confidence that his master was on excellent terms with the Covenanters, and had undertaken, as though he were their spy, to inform them of all who came that way, if suspected of favouring the King; an unworthy act of a shameless villain, a man whom Montrose used to hold in the highest esteem, one who had been raised from the dunghill, of the lowest class, to say no worse of him, to the dignity of knighthood, and an estate which was the envy of his neighbours, by the favour and misplaced bounty of the King.

They had not parted long from this man when they met a soldier, a Scotsman, who had served in England under the Marquis of Newcastle. Passing by the other two, he came to Montrose and saluted him. Montrose, to maintain his disguise, did not acknowledge the salute; but the man was positive, and in the most respectful humble manner exclaimed, "Do not I know my Lord the Marquis of Montrose well enough? But go your way, and God speed you!" When he saw that the soldier recognised him, he dismissed him with a few gold pieces, and the man did not betray the confidence put in his fidelity.

Montrose was greatly alarmed by these circumstances. He therefore resolved to push forward with the utmost speed, to anticipate the rumour of his coming, and spurred on without

---

[17] Lord Nithsdale's opinion of Sir Richard corresponds with that of our author. In his letter from Carlisle to Lord Antrim at York, May 2, 1643, he says:—"Good Sir Richard Grahame and a number of roundheads in these parts, upon your servant coming post, have spread report that you and I are upon ane plot to bring forces from Ireland to take in this country, in so much as I have been forced to affirm the contrary with oaths, as I might justly do. This much is given out by him, one Dalstoun, and others, as in aquitall to your lady, for raising him out of the dunghill, which my Lord her husband did. He will be at York within two or three days, he will shift it off upon the puritans of this country, whereof he is the head; but upon my word your Lordship is little beholden to him to my knowledge."—Spalding, ii. 245; copy of letters found in Antrim's pocket when he was taken by Monro. Antrim's "lady" was the widow of the Duke of Buckingham.

Sir Richard had been confidential attendant to Buckingham and Master of the Horse in his establishment. He accompanied Charles and Buckingham when, as Tom and John Smith, they set out in 1623 on their wild excursion to Spain to see the Infanta. James I. created him a baronet in 1629. He distinguished himself at Edgehill, and founded the family of Esk, from which sprang other well-known families of Graham on the Borders.

sparing his horse, and scarcely drew rein for four days, when he entered Perthshire near the Highlands, and reached the house of his cousin,[18] Patrick Graham of Inchbrakie, not far from the river Tay. Inchbrakie was descended from the illustrious family of Montrose, and worthy of his noble parentage. Montrose, therefore, deservedly put the greatest confidence in him. There he staid for some days, passing the day in an obscure cottage, and the night in the neighbouring mountains alone, for he had sent his companions away to his friends to get intelligence, and bring him an exact account of the state of the kingdom.

After spending some days in busily collecting information, they returned with nothing but dismal news—all honest, loyal subjects were crushed and prostrate under the tyranny of the rebels. Of those who had dared to defend themselves by force, some were fined, others put to death,[19] and others in prison, daily expecting the worst. The Marquis of Huntly[20] had risen prematurely, but had surrendered at the first trumpet blast of the enemy, though his forces were large and only lacked a fit commander. His friends and followers were now exposed to the implacable hate and vengeance of their enemies, while he himself had fled to

---

[18] Patrick Graham, the elder, of Inchbrakie, had been one of the guardians of Montrose on the death of his father, and was still in possession of the property of Inchbrakie, though a George Graham of Inchbrakie appears in 1641 as a justice for the suppression of broken men in the Highlands. See Napier, Mem., 21-25, for some interesting notices of Patrick's care of Montrose's books, &c. His son Patrick, called "Black Pate," was a very vigorous ally of Montrose throughout the campaign; gained him even after Philiphaugh a slight return of victory in his defeat of Argyll's men in Menteith. He was excepted from pardon for some time after his forfeiture, though at length he got an assurance of safety from Middleton. He was in custody in 1650 along with Graham of Gorthie under the charge of Colonel Pitscottie, who is directed to put them "to liberty" (not "to death," as the Index of the Acts has it), Act. Parl. Scot., vi. pt. ii. 575. We afterwards find him with his son George taking important places in the great funeral, he himself carrying the Order of the Garter, and George carrying the great mourning banner. He held several commissions in the country after the Restoration. The house which Montrose visited was not Inchbrakie on the Earn, but Tullybelton, nearer the Tay. It lies about four miles south of Dunkeld and five north of Methven. It has passed out of the hands of the Grahams.

[19] Gordon of Haddo, and Logie, had been executed on the 19th July, while Maxwell and others suffered about the same time. There were many Royalists in prison and in exile, such as Irvine of Drum in exile and his son in jail in Edinburgh, and the whole of Huntly's lands and those of the other Royalists in the north were under most severe exaction. Spalding, ii. 317, and *passim*.

[20] George Gordon, second Marquis of Huntly (see *n.* Ch. vii. and preface), had taken the field in April, but immediately retired to Strathnaver, Lord Reay's country, where he remained in seclusion for some time. Lord Reay himself was shut up in Newcastle along with Wishart and Lord Crawford.

the uttermost corner of the island, where he lay concealed on another man's land.

Montrose was much troubled by this news, especially of Huntly's mistake and the ruin of the Gordons; and not without reason; for as they were famous for loyalty, courage, and renown in arms, he lamented that they had suffered such signal calamity through no fault of their own. However, he now began to consider how he might induce them to join himself, and again take up arms for their beloved King, but under another general.

## CHAPTER V.

Arrival of the Irish—Montrose meets them in Athole—Is joined by Lord Kilpont and Sir J. Drummond—Battle of Tippermuir and surrender of Perth.

IN the meantime vague rumours began to spread among the shepherds on the hills that some Irish had landed in the north of Scotland, and were wandering about the Highlands. Montrose thought it not unlikely that these were some of the auxiliaries promised four months ago by Antrim. But he remained in doubt, till he received letters from some Highland friends, and also from Alexander Macdonald,[1] whom Antrim had appointed to command this small body of Irish. These letters had been sent to one of their friends, an ardent Royalist, to be forwarded, if

---

[1] Alastair M'Coll Keitache Macdonald was the son of the fierce old Coll Keitache MacGillespick Macdonald of Colonsay. The nickname Keitache means *ambidexter*. Corrupted into "Colkitto," it was applied to both chiefs. Alastair was Antrim's cousin, and had served under that incapable leader in Ireland. With Antrim's promised aid, 1600 men, he landed at Ardnamurchan early in July, wasted the country for forty miles, and seized Mingary and Loch Alyne. Getting no support from his kindred, he prepared to return to Ireland. The Campbells meanwhile had burnt his three ships, and he was obliged to march eastwards through Lochaber, but failed to raise any strength for the King. Even the loyal clans doubted his commission, or would not serve under a Macdonald. After trying the Mackenzies in Ross, and nearly coming to blows with them, he came down upon Badenoch, and there, through the influence of the Gordon connection, raised 500 men. Down the Spey he was stopped by the Laird of Grant, and turned towards Athole, where his force would probably have been destroyed by the Robertsons and Stewarts but for the timely appearance of Montrose. A messenger from these clansmen sent towards Perth with the fiery cross encountered Montrose in Methven, and informed him of the situation. Within twenty-four hours Montrose united the opposing forces. After Kilsyth Macdonald was knighted by Montrose, but deserted him before Philiphaugh. He maintained himself with a force in Kintire, and refused to lay down arms even on the King's command. He was attacked by David Leslie, and "like a fool (for no sojor he was, though stout enough), put in 300 of his best men in a house at the top of a hill called Dunavertie, environed with a stone wall, where there was not a drop of water but what fell from the clouds. Then leaving Kintire he went to Islay, where he played just such another mad prank, leaving his old father with 200 men in a castle called Dunneveg, where was no water." . . . "Not without stain on Leslie's honour, the old man coming out on some parole was hanged, and every mother's son except one put to the sword" (Turner, Mem., pp. 45-48). Alastair had gone to Ireland, and in an affair in Munster, after quarter given, was basely stabbed in the back by an officer of Inchiquin's, and died on the ground (Gordon's Britaine's Distemper, 65-75 and *passim*; Turner, 45-48; Napier, Mem., *passim*; Act. Parl. Scot., Spalding, Gardiner, &c.).

possible, to Carlisle, where they thought Montrose still was. This gentleman, without the faintest inkling of Montrose's return to Scotland, though he lived in the neighbourhood, decided, by a lucky chance, to inform Patrick Graham of these letters. The latter promised to take charge of them, and undertook to deliver them faithfully to Montrose, even if he had to go all the way to Carlisle. Thus, by the manifest favour and guidance of Providence, they came to hand much sooner than was expected.

He returned answer as though still at Carlisle, and bade them be of good courage, as they should not want timely help and a general to lead them. At the same time he ordered them to come down into Athole as soon as possible. The men of Athole were under many obligations to Montrose, who esteemed them highly for their remarkable loyalty, devotion, and constancy to the King, as well as for their distinguished bravery. And certainly they fully justified his high regard to the very end of the war.

The Irish, and a very few Highlanders, almost all from Badenoch, on receipt of these orders hastened to Athole. As this was not more than twenty miles distant, Montrose set out on foot, in Highland dress, accompanied only by his cousin, Patrick Graham, as his guide, and joined them so unexpectedly that the Irish could scarce be persuaded that the man before them was Montrose himself. But when they saw that he was saluted by the Athole men and others who knew him well and almost worshipped him as a guardian angel, they were transported with joy. He came to them in the very nick of time, for they were in the utmost danger. Argyll was in their rear with a strong and well-appointed army. The Lowlands were in arms, ready on their coming down into the plains to trample them under their horses' hoofs. The vessels that had brought them over had been burned by Argyll to cut off their escape. The Athole[2] men too and other Royalists refused to join them in any perilous enterprise, as they were strangers, and apparently supported by no royal authority. Moreover, they were not commanded by any person of ancient nobility, a thing much

---

[2] The Athole men were preparing to attack the Irish and Badenoch men (Patrick Gordon, Britaine's Distemper, 65-69).

respected by the Highlanders; and they would never have fought under Alexander Macdonald, whom they looked upon as an upstart. And lastly, their number was very small, not more than eleven hundred, though ten thousand [3] had been promised.

Next day the Athole men to the number of 800 took up arms and offered their service to Montrose with the greatest readiness. With this band, and earnestly commending his most righteous cause to the protection of Almighty God, he now wished for nothing more earnestly than to be in the thick of the enemy. Impatient of further delay, he marched that very day through the plains of Athole towards Strathearn, in order that his friends and supporters, if any should rise on the news, might have an opportunity of joining him before they could be prevented by the enemy, and also that by this sudden movement he might strike terror into the enemy and fall upon them before they could collect their scattered forces. Passing by Weem,[4] a castle of the Menzies', as they had maltreated a trumpeter, whom he had sent to them in a friendly manner, and attacked his rearguard, he ordered their lands to be laid waste and their houses and cut corn to be fired, that on the very threshold of the war he might terrify others. On the same night he crossed the Tay, which is far the largest river in Scotland, with part of his forces; the rest followed early on the following day. On the point of marching he gave the command of the Athole men, at their own earnest request, to Patrick Graham,[5] whom we shall often have occasion to mention, and never without honour, and despatched him to scout with a picked body of the most active Athole men. He returned with intelligence that he had seen a body of armed men on a hill at Buchanty.[6] They were commanded by Lord Kilpont,[7] son of the

---

[3] See Chap. iii. *n.* 4.

[4] Weem Castle is Castle Menzies. The laird was Alexander Menzies. In 1645 with several neighbours, allies of Argyll, he petitioned Parliament to remedy their starving condition and compensate their losses. He was allowed £10,000 Scots (Act. Parl. Scot., vi. pt. i. 387 and 791).

[5] See Chap. iv. *n.* 18.

[6] Buchanty on the Almond. His route doubtless lay from Castle Menzies by Aberfeldy, Amulree, and the Sma' Glen to Buchanty.

[7] John, Lord Kilpont, was the eldest son of William Graham, seventh Earl of Menteith, then known as Earl of Airth, by Agnes, daughter of Patrick, Lord Gray. His father claimed the Earl-

Earl of Menteith, a nobleman of very ancient lineage, descended from the illustrious family of the Grahams, and by Sir John Drummond,[8] son of the Earl of Perth, also a kinsman of Montrose. They had been summoned by the Covenanters to join in opposing the Irish as public enemies, and had with them 500 men, all foot, and as yet had heard nothing certain about Montrose. He marched straight up to them, resolving to surprise them, and either bring them over to his side or overwhelm them. But as soon as they understood that Montrose was in command, they sent some of their chief friends to demand his intentions. He replied that he acted by the King's authority, and had undertaken to defend it to the utmost against an abominable rebellion. Further, he required them, by the affection they owed him, not to refuse their aid to the best of kings. Such service became their birth, and would be acceptable to the King; it would redound to their present advantage and future honour both at home and abroad, should they hasten to be the first to support a tottering throne. Without a moment's hesitation they gladly came over; for both of them were at heart ardent Royalists.

From them Montrose learned that the Covenanters had gathered in great numbers at Perth (the second city of Scotland next to Edinburgh) and were there awaiting his descent from Athole. As he knew that Argyll with his army was close on his heels, to avoid being hemmed in between two armies, he

---

dom of Strathearn by virtue of descent from David, eldest son of Robert II., by Euphemia Ross, and secured the title by patent, July 31, 1631. This concession revived a possible claim to the crown, turning on the question whether Elizabeth More or Euphemia Ross was first wife to Robert II. Some indiscreet boast that his blood was the reddest in Scotland gave offence. He was deprived of his offices and titles and retired into private life, retaining only his title of first Earl of Airth. In 1644 the Menteith lands were secured to him and his heirs, and he was styled Earl of Airth and Menteith. In 1611 he married Agnes, daughter of Patrick, Lord Gray, and had four sons and three daughters. John, Lord Kilpont, married Lady Mary Keith before 1633, and left a son. William, second Earl of Airth and Menteith, disposed of his whole property to the Marquis of Montrose and Graham of Gartmore in 1694 (see Red Book of Menteith; Douglas Peerage, "Airth").

[8] Sir John Drummond, fourth son of John, second Earl of Perth, founded the family of Drummond of Logie Almond. He was distantly connected with Montrose. His brother is reckoned among the nine nearest of kin to the deceased at the grand funeral of the hero. Sir John accompanied Montrose to Strathbogie, but on Argyll's pass, with many others, went south before the winter set in. In 1652 we find him Commissioner for Perthshire.

determined to march on Perth, and either force the enemy to fight, or take the town and reduce it to obedience. Accordingly he advanced three miles from Buchanty, and, after a very brief halt to rest his men, resumed his march at early dawn. Not more than three miles from Perth he saw the enemy drawn up for battle on a broad open plain called Tippermuir.[9] They were commanded by Lord Elcho,[10] who had no great reputation as a soldier. With him were the Earl of Tullibardine[11] and Lord Drummond,[12] the latter, it was reported, against his will, he and all his father's family being at heart favourable to the King. There were also very many knights, of whom the most distinguished officer was Sir James Scott,[13] who had served with credit in the Venetian army. Their forces consisted of 6000

---

[9] Gardiner gives a good account of the battle, drawn from Wishart, Patrick Gordon, Spalding, and the Depositions in Napier's Memorials, ii. 149. It was fought Sunday, September 1, 1644.

[10] David, Lord Elcho, eldest son of John, first Earl of Wemyss. He succeeded to the earldom 22nd November 1649, his father dying on the day of Lady Elcho's funeral. "He built a commodious harbour for Methil and greatly improved the place of Wemyss." His third wife was the lady who holds a most important position in Scottish genealogy as ancestress, through her three marriages, of many noble families, including Buccleuch, Leven, Wemyss, Sutherland, &c. (Book of Earls of Leven and Melville, Lamont's Diary, Douglas Peerage).

[11] James, fourth Earl of Tullibardine, was son of Patrick, Lord Murray of Garth and third Earl of Tullibardine. He was a staunch Covenanter. His brother, the Hon. William, followed Montrose, and suffered after Philiphaugh with Sir Robert Spottiswoode. The Earl declined to use his influence for him since he had joined that wicked crew (see Chap. xix.; Guthrie, Mem., 206. Cromwell in his "act of grace" fined him £1500 for his connection with the Engagers. He died without issue, "being ane old man," and his title passed to the first Marquis of Athole (Lamont's Diary, 270).

[12] James, Lord Drummond, eldest son of the Earl of Perth and brother of Sir John above mentioned. His sympathies were with the Royalists, as he signed the Cumbernauld Bond and joined Montrose in August 1645, and was taken prisoner at Philiphaugh. Baillie does not hesitate to attribute the defeat at Tippermuir to the "villany of Lord Drummond." He succeeded to the Earldom in 1662 and died in 1675. His son James, fourth Earl, was the well-known Chancellor of James VII.

[13] Sir James Scott of Rossie, in Fife, Knight and Colonel, appears frequently in the civil history and military affairs of the time. In 1633 he assigns to David Beaton, the King's physician, the liferent of the feu-duties of Kingsbarns, and in 1641 he appears as a "gentleman of the privy chamber," receiving with his wife, Dame Antonetta Willoughby, a pension of 1000 merks Scots. He was a commissioner in the negotiations at Ripon, and in 1644 on the Commission of War for the North. Was this the Colonel James Scott who, with Colonel Ludovic Leslie, in 1661 obtained a monopoly for making saltpetre, tanning without bark, making iron without coal, making soap, raising water out of pits, improving ground, making ploughs, saltpans, and making crystal? He is supposed to have a first right to "inventions hitherto vnknowne for draining of myns, coallpits, and other things opprest with water, and for makeing of all sorts of milnes, which being put in motion shall continew of itselff without the force of a river, strenth of men, horses, or wind, weiks, moneths, yea yeirs, or vntill materialls weir or breake, which then can speedily be repaired. In which motion the same may be stopt when requisite and againe made to begin and continew as aforsaid, altho no liveing creature be present" (Act. Parl. Scot., vii. 127).

foot and 700 horse, and, trusting to their numbers, they had already in anticipation devoured their enemy. It was Sunday, the 1st of September, and their ministers were specially charged to encourage the soldiers in their sermons and animate them for battle by reminding them of their (so-called) Holy Covenant. And, to give them their due, they performed their part stoutly at the expense of their lungs, promising them in the name of God Almighty an easy and bloodless victory. Nay, one of them, Frederick Carmichael,[14] esteemed by the ignorant people a man of great learning and holiness, did not hesitate to declare in his discourse, "If ever God spoke certain truth out of my mouth, in His name I promise you to-day a certain victory."

Having finished their devotions duly, as they thought, they drew up their army in order of battle. Elcho himself commanded the right wing, Sir James Scott the left, and the Earl of Tullibardine the centre. The cavalry were posted on the wings, by which they confidently expected on such open ground to surround the enemy. When Montrose saw the superior numbers of the enemy, and especially their strength in horse, as he himself had not a single trooper, and not more than three horses altogether, lean, sorry jades, he had reason to fear he might be surrounded, and attacked in front, rear, and flank. He therefore extended his line as much as possible, in files only three deep, with orders to discharge all at once, those in the front rank kneeling, the second stooping, and the rear rank, in which he placed his tallest men, standing erect. They were to waste no powder, of which they stood in great need, and not to fire a single shot till face to face

---

[14] Frederick Carmichael, minister of Markinch in Fife, a forward Covenanter. He preached before the King at Holyrood, Sunday, September 26, 1641, on the text, "Let him kiss me with the kisses of his mouth; for thy love is better than wine" (Cant. i. 2). In 1641 he complains that ministers sent out with the army did lack necessary maintenance (Balfour, Ann., iii. 77 and 175). He was on the Commission for reforming St. Andrews and Aberdeen Universities, a Commissioner of Assembly, and frequently Moderator of Presbyterian gatherings in Fife. Under 1655 Lamont has the following:—"Mr. Frederick Carmichael, to helpe to build the walls of his house, did cause tak some stones out of the churchyeard deike; the place is yet visibell, being on the south-west syde of the church deike, over against Walter Mutray's house in Markinshe." The minister died "att his dwelling house at Markinshe, and was interred att the said church, the 7th of May, in the day time."—Ibid. 248. See also Act. Parl. Scot., vi.-vii. 198-394, &c.; Scot's Fasti, Markinch; Records of Commissions of General Assemblies, Index.

with the enemy; then after one discharge, to fall on bravely with drawn swords and muskets clubbed; and the enemy, he assured them confidently, would never stand their charge. Montrose himself took command of the right wing, facing Sir James Scott. The left he assigned to Lord Kilpont, and the centre to Macdonald with his Irish. This was an excellent arrangement, for the Irish, who had neither long pikes nor swords, if placed on the wings would have been exposed to the enemy's cavalry.

Montrose had sent Drummond,[15] Lord Maderty's eldest son, a very accomplished young nobleman, to the leaders of the enemy, to declare, in his name, that he, as well as his royal master, whose commission he bore, had the utmost abhorrence of shedding his countrymen's blood, and most earnestly desired a bloodless victory. Such a victory both armies might gain if they would return to their duty and allegiance without the hazard of war. He was neither covetous of honours for himself nor envious of other men's preferment, and had no designs against the lives of his fellow-countrymen. All he desired was that in God's name they would at length give ear to sounder counsels, and trust to the clemency, faith, and protection of so good a King. Hitherto His Majesty had fully complied with all the demands of his Scotch subjects, both in civil and religious matters, though to the very great prejudice of his royal prerogative, and was still ready, like a most indulgent father, though provoked by unspeakable injuries, to embrace his penitent children with open arms. If, notwithstanding, they persisted in rebellion, he called God to witness that their stubbornness forced him into the present strife.

To this they made no reply. Contrary to the law of nations, they seized the envoy, who had undertaken that office solely out of love to his country, and sent him under guard to Perth, to be imprisoned like a malefactor, impiously vowing that after their

---

[15] David Drummond, Master of Maderty, afterwards third Lord Maderty. His father and he were staunch Royalists, and suffered imprisonment and fine in the cause. David Drummond's second wife was Lady Beatrice Graham, the sister of Montrose—"the bairn Beatrix" (Napier, Mem., 430). Patrick Maxwell, sheriff-clerk of Perth, depones to seeing the Master of Maderty led into Perth before the battle as a prisoner "by Bachiltoun and Balmedy." After the battle he saw him free in the gallery of Margaret Donaldson's house (*id.*, 437). In 1645 he paid a fine of £2000 Scots; was pardoned in 1647, and died in 1684.

victory they would cut off his head. But God was more merciful, and provided otherwise than they intended for the safety of this noble and accomplished man.

As soon as they were within cannon-shot,[16] the enemy, under Lord Drummond, sent out some picked men to skirmish with Montrose and harass his line. To check them he despatched a small body, who at the first onset threw them into disorder, routed them, and drove them back in panic on their own line. Montrose seized the decisive moment to charge; nothing could animate his men and strike terror into the enemy more effectually than an immediate attack, while they were still confused and dismayed at this first blow, before they had time to rally or recover courage. With a loud cheer he hurled his whole line upon them. The enemy discharged their cannon, which were planted in front, but at such a distance, that they produced more noise than execution. They then advanced, and their horse moved forward to attack. But Montrose's men, though their powder was spent, and few of them were armed with pikes or even swords, received them boldly with such weapons as fell to hand, namely, stones, no less, of which they poured in heavy volleys with such force and spirit that they compelled them to sound a retreat and trouble them no more. The Irish and Highlanders, in gallant rivalry, behaved with the utmost courage, and pressed so hard on their retreat that at last they broke and fled. On the right wing the engagement lasted longer. Here James Scott for some time made a desperate effort to gain the higher ground. But Montrose's men, who were superior in strength of body, and especially in speed and agility, seized the position. Then the Athole men charged down with drawn claymores, and, unchecked by a hail of bullets from the musketeers, they closed with them, slashing and cutting down all before them. Unable to stand the shock, the enemy at last fairly fled away. Most of the cavalry saved themselves by the speed of their horses, but among the foot there was a very great slaughter, as the conquerors pursued them for six or seven miles. Two thousand

---

[16] Lat. *globi tormentarii jactum*. In the 1652 trans. "musket-shot;" but for "musket-bullets" Wishart uses *globulum* above, and *tormenta*, &c., regularly of cannon.

Covenanters are said to have been slain, and a larger number captured. Some of them took the oath of service and enlisted with the victor; but nearly all of them broke their word and deserted. The rest were set at liberty on parole never afterwards to fight against the King or his generals. On the same day Montrose took Perth, without inflicting any damage,[17] though most of the inhabitants had fought against him in the battle. By this act of signal mercy he hoped to win them to the King, the sole end and aim of all his plans.

---

[17] See Depositions, Napier, Mem., 434–444.

## CHAPTER VI.

*March from Perth to Cupar in Angus—Assassination of Kilpont—Montrose joined by the Earl of Airlie and his two sons—March to Dundee—Defeat of Lord Burleigh at Aberdeen.*

FOR three days Montrose halted at Perth, in the vain hope that many gentlemen of those parts, who boasted much of their zeal for the King, might be roused by news of the victory to take arms and join him with their friends and followers. But none came in except the Earl of Kinnoul,[1] with a few gentlemen of Gowrie, and most even of these did not remain very constant to him. By this time Argyll[2] was drawing near with a strong army of foot, and a body of horse drawn from the south. Montrose therefore crossed the Tay, and encamped in the open fields (his usual quarters) near Cupar, a small town in Angus, once the site of a famous monastery, now in ruins.[3] Here he was met by that gallant youth, Sir Thomas Ogilvy,[4] son of the Earl of Airlie, with

---

[1] George, third Earl of Kinnoul. W. is premature in giving him the title. His father *d.* Oct. 5, 1644, at Whitehall. At this date he was Lord Dupplin. He accompanied Montrose to the north, and was with him at Crathes, as deponed Jan. 31, 1645, by the Master of Spynie. In 1645 the process against him and his servants is stopped—he had had Argyll's pass. In 1646, on his mother's petition, he is allowed to be brought from France to be "bred and brocht up as his ain son" by his cousin, the sumptuous Earl of Carlisle. In 1649 the Queen of Bohemia, from Rhenen, $\frac{1}{1}$ Aug., writes to Montrose, "I am grown a good archer, to shoot with my Lord Kinnoul." In Sept. 1649 he landed in Orkney with the advance body of Montrose's force, and reports to his commander in a long letter from Kirkwall. He died suddenly in Orkney. Douglas errs in omitting this Earl from his roll, and it is a question whether he has not ignored another Earl, who is said to have perished in the wilds of Corbiesdale. William Hay appears as the gallant ensign who rescued the royal standard at Philiphaugh, and who later on escaped from Edinburgh Castle by sheets and blankets tied together. Douglas gives him as third Earl. He was either fourth or fifth.

[2] Argyll. See p. 76, *n.* 20, and Preface.

[3] The ruins of the abbey of Cupar in Angus still remain. It was founded by Malcolm the Maiden, 1164 for Cistercians (Wyntoun-Cronykill, ii. 200). The rental-book of the Abbey (Grampian Club, 1879) gives its history. The lands became a temporal lordship Dec. 20, 1607. The Lord Cupar at this time was James Elphinston, second son of Lord Balmerino. See Maxwell's "Old Dundee" for amusing account of Lord Cupar's efforts to recover a "great aquavyte pot spulzeit," and sold cheap, by the Highlanders on this occasion.

[4] Sir Thomas Ogilvy, second son of first Earl of Airlie, *b.* Aug. 23, 1616. For his character and death, æt. 39, *v.* p. 85 and *n.* 16. He married Patricia, daughter of the brave old Lord Brentford. "Your Majesty had never a truer servant, nor there never was a braver, honester gentleman" (Montrose's despatch from Inverlochy to the King, Feb. 3, 1645).

other noble gentry of Angus, who readily proffered their service. He received them with courtesy and thanks, and dismissed them to prepare for the campaign. Very few of them, however, except the Ogilvies, followed his march.

Next day at early dawn, before the drums had beat to march, the whole camp was in an uproar, the men all running to arms, shouting and storming like madmen in their rage and indignation. Hearing the disturbance, Montrose, who thought that it was some brawl between the Highlanders and Irish, threw himself into the thickest of the throng. There he found that a most horrible murder had just been committed. On the ground lay the noble Lord Kilpont,[5] foully slain. The villain who had done the deed was one Stewart,[6] his own retainer, whom this nobleman had distinguished with great familiarity and friendship. On that very night they had even shared the same bed. It is reported that the base slave had resolved to make away with Montrose himself, and counting on his great influence over Kilpont, hoped to induce him to share his crime. For this purpose he took him aside to a solitary spot and disclosed his design. Kilpont, however, received the proposal as it deserved, with loathing. Whereupon the wretch, fearing betrayal, suddenly fell on his unsuspecting friend and master, and stabbed him to death with several wounds. The abandoned assassin killed a sentinel at the gate of the camp and made his escape, the night being dark, and his pursuers scarcely able to see the length of their pikes. Some said that the traitor had been bribed by the Covenanters, others that he was

---

[5] See p. 56, n 7.

[6] On the motive for this murder see the Postscript, Introd. to "Legend of Montrose." Some details in the letter cannot be correct. In the Act ratifying Stewart's pardon it is said that having repented of joining the rebels, and abhorring their cruelty, he resolved to desert, and carry his friends with him. When he tried to win Kilpont, they fell into a quarrel and "struggle, and Stewart, for his own relief, was obliged to kill him at the kirk of Collace, with two Irish rebels who resisted his escape." He and his friends went straight to Argyll. Their conduct was approved by the Committee of Estates, Dec. 10, and it was declared that "the said James Stewart did good service to this kingdom in killing the said Lord Kilpont and twa Irish rebels, . . . and the Committee approved of what he did" (Act. Parl. Scot., vi. pt. i.). By Bishop Guthrie, p. 166, he was explicitly charged with the intention to assassinate Montrose and Macdonald. He became a major in Argyll's force. Ardvoirlich is south of Loch Earn. See Gard., Civil War, ii. 90; Napier, Mem., 447. The proclamation of £20,000 Scots for Montrose, dead or alive, was dated 12th Sept. 1644, namely, a week after this murder.

merely allured by the hope of reward. Be that as it may, it is certain that he is in high favour among them to this very day; and though the man was no soldier, Argyll immediately promoted him to very high commands in the army. Montrose was deeply distressed at the fate of this nobleman, who had been a devoted friend to the King and himself, as learned in polite literature, philosophy, divinity, and law, as he was famous for truth and courage. Embracing the lifeless body again and again, he delivered it with sighs and tears to his sorrowing friends and followers, to be carried home to his parents, that it might be committed to the grave in a manner suitable to the dignity of that honourable family.

With the rest of his forces he then marched to Dundee. This town, confident in its numbers and a reinforcement to the garrison from Fife, refused to surrender. He therefore resolved not to hazard the reputation of his late victory on a siege, and turned away towards the river Esk. Most of his friends and kinsmen in those parts were men of wealth and powerful following; and as they used to boast loudly of their power and loyalty, he hoped they would join him. But on the news of his approach they all withdrew, except Ogilvy, Earl of Airlie,[7] who, though sixty years of age, came in with his sons Sir Thomas and Sir David, and some of their friends and vassals, all men of tried courage, and adhered to him firmly, with admirable perseverance and fidelity, in spite of all misfortunes, to the end of the war. Amidst the almost universal defection, Airlie and Montrose were all that remained to honour and adorn the Scotch nobility.

Meantime he received intelligence that Commissioners of the Covenanters, with Lord Burleigh,[8] their chief and president, lay at

---

[7] James, eighth Lord Ogilvy, "for the loyalty and fidelity of his ancestors," created Earl of Airlie April 2, 1639. He did honour to those ancestors. Excepting Huntly, he was the only Scottish noble who refused the Covenant, and fought the matter out on Scottish soil. For his constancy see Ch. vii.; his conduct at Kilsyth, Ch. xiii. Excommunicated and excepted from pardon in 1646, he yet clung to his own glens, and in 1647 his forfeiture was rescinded, and he appears to have lived in peace and quiet. His gallant sons, Lord Ogilvy, Sir Thomas, and Sir David were worthy of their race.

[8] Robert Arnot of Ferney, married the heiress of Burleigh, and acquired the title of Lord Burleigh. He was much in the hands of Argyll. Lord Burleigh was twice president of the Scotch Parliament, and took care to have his acts condoned in succeeding Parliaments. He was on commissions of war, and a colonel of Fife regiments, but no soldier. On Aug. 10, 1663, "being ane old man, he depairted out of this life att Burley, and was interred att his parish church the 12th Aug., in the night time" (Lamont).

Aberdeen with an army, and were labouring hard, by entreaties, bribes, or force of arms, to win over the northern parts, on which Montrose chiefly relied. He resolved to drive them out at once, before Argyll could join them with his army, and hastened thither by forced marches. Seizing the bridge of Dee, he approached the city, and found the enemy drawn out before it in battle array. Lord Burleigh commanded 2000 foot, and 500 horse which he stationed on the wings. He occupied a strong position, and, with his cannon well placed in front, was ready for battle.

Montrose's army numbered only 1500 foot, for Kilpont's men had gone to escort the body of their dead leader to his parents, and most of the Athole men, after the victory at Perth, had gone off laden with booty to their own country, which was not far off. His horse, numbering only forty-four, he divided and posted on the wings, strengthened with some of his most active musketeers and archers, who in agility and speed were almost as good as horsemen.[9] Their duty was to prevent the enemy's horse from surrounding him, a task they accomplished gallantly beyond all expectation and belief. The right wing he assigned to James Hay[10] and Nathaniel Gordon,[11] the left to Sir William Rollock,[12]

---

[9] This mingling of active and disciplined musketeers with cavalry was the saving of the little force more than once. Archers formed part of Claverhouse's host, and were not unknown in Prince Charlie's army. See end of Ch. *n.* 17 on battle of Aberdeen.

[10] Col. James Hay is probably the same who joined Montrose in Orkney, and was taken at Corbiesdale. He appears in the "list of prisoners" as "Nachton's brother." At this time he had followed close behind Montrose from England. In 1646 a Col. James Hay, in company with Lord Gray, gave much trouble to the General Assembly, but he may have been Col. J. H. of Linplum, since the Presbytery of Haddington had charge of the case. See Part II., Ch. vi., and Records of Com. of General Assembly.

[11] Col. Nathaniel Gordon, son of John Gordon of Ardlogie. Spalding's notices of him from 1633 contain the elements of a historical romance. With his father and brother, or other gay Gordons and Irvines, he lives in fray or foray, or other more serious military service. If the magistrates of Aberdeen are to be kidnapped and hidden away in Auchindoon, a herring prize seized off the harbour, or—"desperat courss—the Cartowis at Montrose to be carried off," or "Andrew Cant fleyit to the hairt and causit to remove out of the toun," or "Dundee and Aberdeen harmless merchants cuming to Elgin fair to be reft and spulzeit," or the Marquis of Huntly, or Lord Gordon, wants a gallant lieutenant, Nathaniel Gordon is the man. He joined Montrose on his approach to Aberdeen with "30 weill horsit gentilmen." He accepted Argyll's pass, of "deip policie," that by his aid he might get rid of the excommunication resting on him. On Feb. 19, 1645, with Lord Gordon, "he lap quicklie on horss" and came again to Montrose at Elgin, where they were made welcome. For his capture at Philiphaugh and death at St. Andrews, see Ch. xix. For details as to his monetary transactions and his will, see Act. Parl. Scot., vi., Index.

[12] See p. 47, *n.* 7.

all men of conspicuous courage. The left wing of the enemy was directed by Lewis Gordon,[13] son of the Marquis of Huntly, a bold, fiery, but fickle youth, who had forced his father's friends and clansmen, much to their distaste, to take up arms against Montrose. The ground he occupied being a level plain suited to a cavalry engagement, he charged Montrose's right wing. Observing the danger, Montrose sent Rollock with his twenty horse to their assistance. Ably supported by the courage of their officers and the activity of the picked footmen, they gave the enemy such a warm reception, that, though only forty-four to three hundred, they threw their ranks into disorder, and repulsed them with heavy loss. But being themselves so few, they did not dare to pursue them further. The great prudence of their officers on this occasion contributed largely to the victory; for the enemy now charged Montrose's left wing, exposed for want of the horse. With admirable promptness he at once transferred his horse, after the rout of Lewis Gordon, to his left. As they were too few to show front to the enemy's more extended line, by a flank movement they avoided their first onset; then wheeling with great dexterity, they charged their flank, fell on them sword in hand, cut them down, and scattered them in flight. Forbes of Craigievar,[14] a man of rank among the enemy, and Forbes of

---

[13] Lord Lewis Gordon, third son of George, second Marquis of Huntly, afterwards third Marquis. In 1639, when only thirteen, he went secretly to the Highlands "and tooke the guiding of the ruide hylanders upon him, shewing thereby . . . how this sparke was like to growe to a great and ardent burning flame" (Pat. Gordon, 19). In 1641 he went off to Holland from London, "with his father's haill jewells in a cabinet, being of great worth, leaving his father sorrowful for his bad miscarriage" (Spalding). In 1644 he was in Edinburgh under the care of Lady Haddington and in alliance with Argyll, his uncle. He next appears in Aberdeen, and is received by Lord Gordon, who gives him a command. In disgust at a Forbes being put over him in command of his own men, Lord Gordon left for Strathbogie, but Lewis remained. They were both afterwards led about by Argyll, and saw the destruction of their fine estates. At this time Lewis married the Laird of Grant's daughter. See his conduct, Ch. xx.; and Pat. Gordon, 184, and Index. He was banished for a time, but in 1651 was restored to his honours and estates.

[14] Sir William Forbes of Craigievar. In contempt of the cavalry tactics of the day, used by Lord Lewis Gordon—an advance with pistols, discharge in ranks, and retreat in caracole—Craigievar charged through the main battle of the Irish; but they only opened up to receive him and closed again, swallowing up his troopers and himself. He broke his parole "to the no small prejudice of his reputation." He was again a prisoner, and sent by Huntly to Auchindoon in 1646. His name appears prominently in all the Covenanting schemes, and at constant feud with the Gordons and Irvines. Having no house fit to dwell in, the house of Drum is given to him for a time by the Argyll powers. Bolls of meal are paid to him in 1648, but there is a "tutor of Craigievar" in 1649. Craigievar is one of the very picturesque old houses in Aberdeenshire.

Boyndlie[15] were taken prisoners. The rest they permitted to retreat in safety, as they were too few to venture on pursuit. The leaders of the enemy's horse were more enraged by this second disgrace than dismayed by their loss; and imputing their defeat to the light musketeers who had been stationed among the horse, they sent for infantry from their own centre, intending to renew the fight with greater spirit. Montrose foresaw this, but was unwilling to expose this handful of brave men to a fresh attack, especially as their horses were spent with the two previous encounters, while the enemy were now reinforced by infantry. He had already observed that the enemy's horse were still in confusion and at a considerable distance from their foot. He therefore rode up to his own foot, who were exposed to a galling fire from the enemy's cannon, and addressed them as follows: "We shall gain nothing, my men, by fighting at a distance. Who can distinguish the strong from the weak, the coward from the brave? Get to close quarters with yon craven feeble striplings; they will never withstand your valour. Fall on them with sword and musket-butts. Crush them; drive them off the field, and take vengeance on the traitor rebels." Scarce had he given the word when they charged, and hurling them into confusion, put them to utter rout. Their horse also, who were waiting for the foot to help them, when they saw them flying, galloped off the field. The victors, unable to pursue, much less to come up with them, let them escape in safety. But the foot they dealt with very differently, few of them escaping with their lives; for, as they had nowhere to fly to except the city, the victors and vanquished rushed in pell-mell through the gates and posterns, and the streets of the whole town were heaped with the slain.

This battle had lasted for four hours without a decisive result. Montrose had some cannon, but they were of no service to him, the advantage of ground being, as we have said, on the side of the enemy, whereas their cannon made no small havoc of our

---

[15] Alexander Forbes of Boyndlie, in Buchan, one of the active Covenanting barons of the shire, and influential as "tutor of Pitsligo" and able to bring to the field the Pitsligo tenants.

men. Among others, an Irishman was observed trailing his leg, so shattered at the thigh by a cannon-ball that it hung by a mere shred of skin. Observing his comrades somewhat dismayed at his misfortune, he hailed them with a loud, cheery voice, " Ha, comrades, such is the luck of war; neither you nor I should be sorry for it. Do your work manfully. As for me, sure my Lord Marquis will make me a trooper, now I am no good for the foot." With these words he coolly drew his knife, without flinching cut away the skin with his own hand, and gave the leg to a comrade to bury. Eventually he recovered of his wound and was actually made a trooper, in which service he afterwards showed great fidelity and courage.[16] This battle was fought at Aberdeen on the 12th of September 1644. Montrose having recalled his men to their colours, entered the city and allowed them two days' rest.[17]

---

[16] It is to be regretted that the name of this heroic Irishman has not been preserved. The discipline, courage, endurance, cheerfulness, and fun of the Irish through this campaign are evidenced by all contemporary authorities, and should have secured for them the treatment due to true soldiers.

[17] The true date seems to have been the 14th Sept. The battle was fought across the present Hardgate. Montrose's letter to the magistrates and their reply still exist (facsimile in Spalding). That of Montrose is blurred at the sixth line by a drop of rain, and the letter of the magistrates betrays their agitation. The magistrates were not in harmony with the politics of the citizens, but were forced on the city by the Covenanting leaders. Wishart passes lightly over the results of the battle to this poor, loyal city. For best account of battle, see Patrick Gordon; and for details as to cruelty following, see Spalding. Gardiner gives a map and a good description of the battle, with a note on the letter.

## CHAPTER VII.

*Huntly prevents the Gordons from joining—Montrose retires into Badenoch—His illness causes rumours of his death—Returns to Athole and Angus, and crosses the Grampians to Strathbogie—Surprised by Argyll and Lothian at Fyvie—Beats his assailants off and retreats to Balveny.*

IN the meantime news arrived that Argyll was drawing near, with far stronger forces than any they had yet met. The Earl of Lothian[1] accompanied him with 1500 horse. Montrose, therefore, removed from Aberdeen to Kintore, a village ten miles off, that the Gordons, Huntly's friends and clansmen, and others who were thought to be devoted Royalists, might have an opportunity of joining him. From that place he despatched Sir William Rollock to Oxford, to inform the King of his successes, and obtain help from England or elsewhere. He was to tell him that though he had gained two victories, he was beset on all sides with so many powerful armies, that they would be unable to hold out without speedy relief.

Nothing meanwhile gave Montrose so much anxiety as that not one of the Gordons, of whom he had conceived great hopes, came in to him. Some of them did indeed profess their great willingness, but were, they said, all restrained by the example and influence of Huntly, the chief of the family and clan, who secretly thwarted Montrose; and though skulking in the farthest corner of

---

[1] William, third Earl of Lothian, son of Robert, Earl of Ancrum, who bemoaned his politics. The Acts of Parl. show that he was frequently employed in military and civil business. He was colonel of his own regiment, two companies of which were made up of his tenants in Teviotdale, and he was Lieut.-General of the Scots army in Ireland. He was a successful commissioner to France on Scotch business; but on reporting himself at Oxford, in Nov. 1643, and refusing to swear that he would never bear arms against the King, he was sent a close prisoner to Bristol. Shortly after he was "enlarged" he was sent to strengthen Argyll at Aberdeen. In 1646 he met the King at Southwell, and imperiously demanded his signature to the Covenant, the establishment of Presbyterianism in England and Ireland, and a command to "James Graham" to lay down arms. Charles refused all demands, retorting "he that made you an Earl made James Graham a Marquis." For his opinion of Montrose see Correspondence of Earls of Lothian and Ancrum, i. 121-126. After the Restoration he was fined £6000 Scots for his previous politics.

the island, he envied another the glory which he himself had failed to acquire. He had forbidden his friends and clansmen, even with threats, to have anything to do with Montrose, or help him by word or deed.[2] When Montrose perceived that this was the case, he determined to withdraw into the wilds of the Highlands, where he knew that the cavalry of the enemy, in which their main strength consisted, would be useless. As to their foot, however numerous, he had no fear of them, trusting to his good cause and the courage of his men. He therefore buried his cannon[3] in a bog, and divested himself of all his heavy baggage. When he reached the river Spey he encamped not far from the old castle of Rothiemurchus,[4] with an army very few in numbers, but rapid, cheerful, and accustomed now to victory.

On the opposite bank he found the men of Caithness, Sutherland, Ross, and Moray, with others, to the number of five thousand,[5] all in arms to prevent his crossing the river, which is

---

[2] George, second Marquis of Huntly, had reason to distrust Montrose. As leader of the Covenanters, Montrose had defeated the Gordons and imposed the Covenant in the north; and his shabby conduct in arresting Huntly and Gordon in 1639, after safe conduct given, fully accounts for his estrangement. Huntly, however, stood aloof too long, and acted too late for the King's good or his own safety. No doubt things would have worn a very different complexion had he shown the same devotion as his son Lord Gordon. See Preface. P. Gordon, who writes many pages of defence of him from W.'s attacks, admits as faults among his shining virtues, "self-will, obstinacy in opinion once adopted, and great distance from all beneath him." "Service done and not to doe was forgotten, and old servants for whom there was no use must be brusht or rubt off as spots from cloathes; so as this falt, if it may be tearmed a falt, was truelie a noble one, for it attendeth allwayes on nobilitie" (p. 229). Is he severe or simple in this criticism on the Marquis and his class? He draws a close parallel between the Marquis and the King in person, mind, career, and fate. The Covenanters, for their own encouragement, were wont to say they had but two to deal with, Charles and Huntly, and both were unfortunate. He figures in all the contemporary writings, but see specially P. Gordon, Spalding, Blackhall's Narration, Genealogy of House of Sutherland.

[3] These cannon were appropriated by Huntly in 1645 (v. Ch. xviii.). Gardiner says they were buried at Rothiemurchus. The march from Kintore was by Strathdon, Glenavon, and Tomintoul to Strathspey.

[4] The ancient castle, which stands on the island in Loch-an-Eilan, is of considerable dimensions. The island being scarcely larger than the foundations, the castle appears to rise in some places immediately out of the water. The laird was once styled Thane. Shaws, Mackintoshs, and Grants were successive owners. See Shaw's Hist. of Moray, i. 261, and Grameid, 182.

[5] It is not to be understood that these forces had actually taken the field. They were to be counted on against Montrose. The Laird of Grant with the others "had no intention to tempt him too far, and therefore had agents with him daily upon termes of capitulation, assuring him that in their heartes they were royalists, and indeed the Laird of Grant was thought to be really so, . . . for his lady, as a sweet charming nightingall, did never cease powerfullie to agent the justice of the King's cause with her husband" (P. Gordon, 85). "The 5000 men" are omitted in the last translation (v. Introd.).

the most rapid in Scotland, until Argyll, who was pressing on his heels, should fall upon him in the rear. Hard pressed and besieged, as it were, by so many enemies on all sides, to shake off their cavalry at least he made for Badenoch, a rugged, mountainous country, almost impassable for horse. Here he fell sick, and was very ill for some days, to the unbounded joy of the Covenanters, who, without hesitation, gave out that he was quite dead, and ordained a day of public thanksgiving to God for this deliverance.[6] Their fine prophets did not fail to improve the occasion. As if they were the oracles and mouthpiece of the divine decrees, they proclaimed that he had fallen, slain by the hand of the Lord of Hosts Himself. But their joy did not last long, for he soon recovered, and, like one risen from the dead, terrified his enemies more than ever. As soon as his illness permitted, he returned to Athole,[7] and despatched Macdonald with a party to the Highlanders, to urge them to join, and force such as refused. He himself marched back to Angus, hoping either to wear out Argyll and his horse by these forced marches, and compel him to go into winter quarters, or to leave him as far behind as possible. Argyll continued to follow him, but so slowly and at such a distance that it was very evident he had no heart at all to try the chance of battle.[8] Therefore, passing through Angus, Montrose crossed the Grampians, a continuous range of hills running east to west, which divides Scotland into two nearly equal parts, and returned to the north country.

As soon as he thought he had left Argyll behind far enough to give his men a rest, he set out for Strathbogie,[9] to have a personal interview with the Gordons, and persuade them to join. But it was all to no purpose. Huntly had forestalled him by his orders, and following their chief's example, they hid themselves in secret lurking-places. As men of spirit and bravery, though they did not dare to challenge the displeasure of their chief, they were ashamed of their own inglorious inactivity. The Lord Gordon

---

[6] Is there other evidence of this thanksgiving?
[7] Oct. 4, 1644. Guthrie, 168.
[8] See Guthrie, Mem., 169-172.
[9] Strathbogie Castle had been embellished, and the grounds laid out with taste by the Marquis, but Monro had cut down all the plantations to make huts for his troops, and Argyll followed him with an unsparing hand.

also, Huntly's eldest son, a man of worth and power, to his shame was prevented by Argyll, his maternal uncle. The Viscount Aboyne, his second son, was confined in Carlisle, which was then besieged, and Lewis had joined the enemy. Thus there was none of Huntly's family to head a rising.

Montrose, however, made their country his headquarters for a considerable time.[10] During the interval, almost every other night, he marched parties of light foot, for he had few or no horse, seven, eight, and sometimes even ten miles, to beat up the enemy's quarters, and rout them in the small hours of the night, and never failed to capture men and horse. As he always brought his men off safe, they became flushed with confidence; however few their number, there was nothing they would not dare and do, with him to lead them. At length, giving up all hope of the Gordons, he left Strathbogie at the end of October,[11] and marched to Fyvie Castle, which he seized.[12] Here he was reduced to the most imminent danger by utterly false intelligence of the enemy from his spies, in whom he had put great confidence. Suddenly, while he thought they were still beyond the Grampians, they encamped about two miles from him. Argyll and Lothian commanded, with 2500 infantry and 1200 horse, whereas he himself had only 1500 foot and not more than 50 horse, Macdonald having been detached with a party. It would have been the height of madness to have descended into the plain with so small a force, while to shut himself up in the castle, which was poorly fortified, was, he thought, dishonourable and derogatory to the reputation he had gained by his late victories. He therefore adopted another course, and led his men out to somewhat higher ground on a hill overlooking the castle. The ground was rugged, broken with ditches, and dikes raised by the farmers to fence their fields, in appearance like a camp. But before he had got them all into position the small

---

[10] Spalding says "for a week."

[11] He left Strathbogie Oct. 24. Argyll in pursuit had only reached Athole on the 14th.

[12] Fyvie. This magnificent house still stands, one of the glories of Scottish baronial architecture. Part of the structure dates from 1400, but most of it is the work of Chancellor Seton and a French architect at the beginning of the seventeenth century. In Montrose's time it was in its new glory, less baronial and more domestic than of old. See Billings, and Memoir of Chancellor Seton by George Seton.

party of Huntly's men who had joined him at Strathbogie fled before their very eyes.[13]

The enemy attacked the height with spirit and carried a considerable part of it. Had they been able to maintain it with the same courage and obstinacy, Montrose would have been crushed. His soldiers, dismayed by the flight of their allies and the numbers of the enemy they had to face, were on the verge of despair; but he at once restored them by his presence, cheering them with the memory of their past achievements and native valour. Calling to a young Irishman, Colonel O'Kean,[14] he bade him go with what men he could get together and drive those fellows from their dikes, that they might be troubled no more with them. He had often had occasion to note and commend O'Kean's extraordinary courage; and the brave man fulfilled his general's expectations. Though the enemy were far superior in numbers and supported by cavalry, he drove them headlong from the dikes and captured some bags of powder which they had left behind in their hurried flight. This booty was very seasonable, as they were in great want of powder. Nor must I here omit to mention a striking instance of ready wit in one of the men. Seeing the bags, he exclaimed, "What, have they served us out no ball? Well, we shall have to go after those stingy storekeepers and fetch it ourselves," just as though the enemy had nothing to do but provide them with all the necessaries of war.

Meanwhile, as his horse, which were but fifty in all, were too much exposed, he brought up his light musketeers just in time. Lothian had sent five troops of horse to charge them; but before they had half crossed the intervening field, they were so galled by the fire of our musketeers that they wheeled and fell back in confusion. Elated with their double success, Montrose's men could hardly be restrained from charging the whole army of the enemy with a cheer. Montrose praised them, as they deserved, without rebuke, but bade them remember their duty and wait the word. At last, towards evening, Argyll, having failed in his

---

[13] Just before the battle he had 200 horse; later on he has only 50. Did the Gordons number 150?

[14] O'Kane, O'Kean, O'Kyan, or O'Cahan; Lat. *O Caenus*. For his fate, *v*. Ch. xviii. *n.*

attempt, withdrew his men to a distance of about two miles and passed a sleepless night. On the morrow, hearing that Montrose's men were in want of powder, he led his army out to the same ground and made a show of renewing the attack on the hill and dikes. But his heart failed him, and nothing of note happened beyond some light skirmishes of flying parties, while the main bodies kept their ground. Montrose, meanwhile, had all the dishes, flagons, pots,[15] and other pewter vessels that could be got together melted down into bullets. Even this supply was not sufficient for his men; but the inconvenience did not damp their ardour. One of them, in particular, whenever he fired his musket—which always hit, as he supposed—turned to his comrades and shouted merrily, "Sure as a gun, I have broken another traitor's face with the pot." It is, in truth, little wonder that Montrose's men were often in want of powder and other stores, considering that the only supplies they got were from the enemy they conquered.

Towards the close of the second day Argyll again retired across the river[16] by the road he had come, to a distance of three Scots miles (equal to one German mile).[17] Several days were thus spent at Fyvie, Argyll with his powerful army gaining nothing but disgrace among his party and contempt among the enemy. His cowardice was blamed for not having finished the war on the spot.[18]

At last Montrose marched back to Strathbogie by night, afraid of exposing his rear in the daytime to be harassed on the retreat by the enemy's horse. There he resolved to halt for sometime, as the rugged country secured his men from the enemy's horse; and it was also near the Highlands, from which he daily expected Macdonald with reinforcements. Next day the enemy pursued him, intending to force on an engagement in the open field. As soon as they came in sight they drew up in line of battle, as though ready to charge in full force. Argyll first sent out some Highlanders to skirmish, but they met with a stout resistance

---

[15] Latin, *matulas*.
[16] The Ythan.
[17] Equal to about four English miles.
[18] The 1752 translation is very loose here.

and were repulsed. Montrose was thus enabled to take up more advantageous ground, and Argyll returned to more cautious but less honourable strategy. He requested a truce, and proposed a conference on mutual pledges of assurance; yet he not only began to tamper with Montrose's men by offers of reward and indemnity, but even, to his shame be it spoken, was mean enough to put a high price on Montrose's head as the reward for his murder or assassination.[19]

Montrose, who well knew the man's cunning and natural propensity to intrigue and treachery rather than fair open fight, saw through this design, and felt the urgent necessity of withdrawing his scanty forces as far as possible from the enemy's horse and Argyll's knavery.[20] He therefore called a council of war and laid his plan before them. All approved of its wisdom, and promised to continue with unshaken loyalty in his service. He resolved therefore on a forced march next night to Badenoch; and to lighten his men for a march of such difficulty, he sent his baggage forward under convoy, and ordered his men to hold themselves ready for battle on the morrow. The baggage was already in motion, when suddenly word was brought that Forbes of Craigievar, his prisoner, whom he had allowed to live at large

---

[19] See p. 64, *n.* 6.

[20] Archibald, eighth Earl of Argyll, first Marquis, born in 1598, obtained possession of his father's estates while yet Lord Lorn, his father Archibald having declared himself a Roman Catholic. Charles, disregarding the old Earl's advice to throw his son into prison lest he should "wind him a pirn," let him go down to Scotland. His appearance at the Glasgow Assembly of 1638 gained him the confidence of the active Presbyterians. Baillie, i. 144, says, "Argyll craved leave to speak, and at that tyme we did not well understand him, but his actions since has made his somewhat ambiguous speeches plain. . . . It has been the equity of our cause which has been the only motive to make that man, in that necessare tyme, to the extreame hazard of his head and all he possesses, to encourage us openlie by his assistance" (*Ib.* 146). There can be no question as to the able strategy of Argyll and profound knowledge of the materials he had to deal with in this most puzzling time. He never lost his presence of mind in any complication, and even on the scaffold he was able to enhance his reputation. He was destitute of physical courage, but his coolness in circumstances of hopeless entanglement shows a master of moral nerve. Though he was bound up with the religious movement of the Covenant, it is evident that he used it, not it him. Montrose at Strathbogie had grown in knowledge of his adversary since he talked so freely at Scone. See Clarendon, Biographia Britannica, Dict. of Nat. Biography, and contemporary history generally for the character of this remarkable man; see also, for redeeming feature, ref. in Grameid, 129. "The Thane of Cawdor," "Family of Innes," and other Spalding Club vols. give interesting traits of this nobleman in original letters.

in his camp on parole, and Sibbald,[21] who, besides Rollock,[22] was the only person who had shared his counsels and accompanied him from England, with several others, had deserted to the enemy. Alarmed at their treachery, he justly suspected that they would betray his plans in order to ingratiate themselves with the enemy. Immediately he recalled the baggage and convoy and appeared to have changed his resolution entirely. But this was a mere ruse, the delay being intended to discredit the information of the deserters. At last, after waiting four days, he again sent off the baggage; and lighting fires through all the camp, he stationed what horse he had in the rear in sight of the enemy, as if on picket duty, until his infantry were out of all danger. He then withdrew his horse in safety, and the whole army arrived about daybreak at Balveny.[23] Finding that they were here safe from the cavalry, and no longer pursued by the enemy, as it was now about midwinter, he allowed his men a few days' rest.

The effects of Argyll's craft now began to appear. Most of the nobility, gentry, and experienced officers (for, excepting the Irish and Highlanders, Montrose had more officers than privates) took Argyll at his word and deserted. Some of them pleaded ill-health, others declared themselves unequal to such winter marches, through wild, pathless mountains, beset with rocks and thickets, and mostly buried in snow, where the foot of man never trod; and therefore unwillingly, they said, and only through absolute necessity, they begged to be dismissed. He refused leave to none that asked it, but more with an air of indignation and scorn for their degeneracy than indulgence and approval. Indeed, it is difficult to estimate the effect their example had in weakening his forces, and discouraging many who were on the point of joining his standard. Only Lord Ogilvy, Earl of Airlie, though sixty

---

[21] *i.e.*, on the journey from Carlisle. The 1752 translation errs in implying that this confidence was continued and exclusive. See p. 50, *n.* 16.

[22] *v.* Ch. iv. Rollock, we may assume, was still in the hands of Argyll, being pressed to assassinate Montrose, if the story be true.

[23] Balveny, an important castle on the west bank of the Fiddich. See Shaw's Moray, i. 128, and Grameid, 186.

years of age and in feeble health, with his two sons, Sir Thomas and Sir David,[24] worthy of such a father, remained. Nothing could ever induce them, even at the utmost danger, to tear themselves from him.

---

[24] Sir David Ogilvy of Clova, third son of the Earl. Excluded from pardon, forfeited, and at length pardoned, he survived the troubles, and is found in Parliament and in the Commisson of the Peace for Forfarshire after the Restoration.

## CHAPTER VIII.

*Montrose lays Argyleshire waste—March north to Loch Ness—Seaforth's levies to oppose him—Montrose turns back and crushes the Campbells at Inverlochy—Sir Thomas Ogilvy is killed.*

FROM Balveny Montrose returned to Badenoch, where he received sure intelligence that Argyll had sent his horse into winter quarters and was lying with his infantry at Dunkeld, from which place he was using every artifice to persuade the Athole men to desert. Though confident of their loyalty and steadiness, Montrose marched down to Athole with incredible speed, and in one night traversed with his army twenty-four miles, through a wild, desolate, and snow-clad tract.[1] His object was to fall upon Argyll while he had no horse with him. But the mere rumour of his approach was enough. While he was still sixteen miles distant, Argyll in terror bade his men shift for themselves, and himself fled headlong to Perth, which was held by a strong garrison of Covenanters.[2]

Macdonald had now returned and brought along with him the Chief of the Macranalds[3] with 500 of his men. To these Montrose

---

[1] No doubt by the route now followed by road and rail from Kingussie to Blair Athole.

[2] Argyll went on to Edinburgh, where he was taking credit for a "bloodless" conclusion to the campaign when he heard of the concentration in Breadalbane. He then set out for Inveraray to muster his clansmen in readiness for the spring.

[3] John Macdonald was Captain of Clanranald at this time. He is entered on the Kilcummin Bond, as given by Chambers, as "J. Macronald of Eyellandtirrem (fiar of Moydart) and Captain of Clanronald, father of Donald Moydartach." See Mackenzie's Macdonalds of Clanranald.

Eneas Macdonell, afterwards Lord Macdonell and Aros, was the leader of the Glengarry clan, though his grandfather Donald, the chief, was still alive. Donald died a very aged man on the 2nd of Feb. 1645, the very day of the battle of Inverlochy, at which his grandson was leading the clansmen against the Campbells. Eneas signs the Kilcummin Bond, and is described as "apirand of Glengerry" (Mackenzie's Macdonalds of Glengarry, Chambers' Rebellions). Three uncles of Eneas went with him, Donald Gorm, John Mor, John Og. Donald Glas Macdonald of Keppoch, with the Lairds of Glencoe and Glen Nevis, afterwards joined. M'Leans, Stuarts, Camerons, Robertsons, all join about this time. See the same names, with many others, in the rising under Claverhouse, as given in rich detail (Grameid, Book iv.).

added Patrick Graham with some picked Athole men; and with this body he marched to the loch from which the Tay issues, with the intention of passing through Breadalbane[4] to Argyleshire, convinced that he could attack his enemy nowhere more successfully than in his own land. There were many strong reasons for this resolution. In the first place, Argyll's authority and power in the Highlands made him formidable to his peers and neighbours; and he was therefore the life and soul of the whole rebellion in its rise and growth. The least resistance to the Covenanters and their commands was sure to bring down Argyll with a tumultuous army of Highlanders, five or six thousand strong, many of them, too, forced to serve against their will,[5] and his wretched victim was crushed. It was therefore good policy to shatter the power of a man so seditious, greedy, and cruel. Moreover, the Highlanders who favoured the royal cause, and hated Argyll like poison, had often felt his tyranny, and were afraid to give help until his power was overthrown. And lastly, as the Covenanters held the Lowlands with strong garrisons and numerous bodies of horse, Montrose had nowhere else for his troops to winter, unless he had a mind to exhaust and ruin the resources of his friends.[6] Urged by these considerations, he hastened forward by long, difficult marches, and with incredible speed swooped down into Argyle.

Argyll was at that time busy enlisting soldiers in his own country, and had appointed the day and place of rendezvous. He was living in his castle of Inveraray without a thought of danger, imagining that the enemy was a hundred miles and more away. Till now he had always believed it impossible for an

---

[4] Much of Breadalbane was in possession of Sir Robert Campbell of Glenurquhy, an active Covenanter. His brother, Patrick of Edinample, was with Montrose, and signs the Kilcummin Bond. Macgregors and M'Nabs joined soon after. For a picturesque account of the M'Nabs' service to Montrose, see P. Gordon, 97.

[5] For notices of smaller clans forced to serve under the Campbells, and sometimes to take their name, see Skene's Highlanders, and Grameid, iv.

[6] There is no doubt that the Macdonalds urged the winter campaign in Argyleshire on Montrose, who was indisposed for it. He expressed opposition and questioned whether there was food enough in the country for his army; but Angus MacAlain, a Glencoe man, satisfied him as to that, saying, "I know every foot of every farm or half farm under MacCailein; and if good water, tight houses, and fat cows will do for you, there is plenty to be had" (Mackenzie, but see Chambers' Rebellions, ii. 5).

army to penetrate into Argyle even in the middle of summer. He had often been heard to boast that he would rather lose a hundred thousand florins than that any mortal should know the passes by which an armed force could invade his country. It was the last thing he dreamt of, when the panic-stricken drovers from the mountains brought word that the enemy were scarce two miles distant. Irresolute and well-nigh beside himself with dread, he scrambled into a fishing-boat and saved himself by flight, abandoning his friends, clansmen, and the whole of his country to fate and the mercy of the enemy. Argyleshire is a rough, mountainous country, with a meagre, unproductive soil, but well adapted for breeding cattle, its chief source of wealth. Montrose divided his army into three parties, the first commanded by the Chief of the Macranalds, the second by Macdonald, and the third by himself. With these he descended on the enemy's fields and ravaged the whole district from end to end. Wherever they fell in with armed men hastening to the appointed rendezvous, they put them to the sword, sparing none that were fit to carry arms, and did not desist until they had hunted every man fit for service out of the country or driven them into secret lurking-holes. They then gave their villages and cots to the avenging flames and burnt them to the ground, an act of retaliation on Argyll, who had been the first of all to wage this cruel war of fire and sword upon his countrymen. Lastly, they drove all their cattle. Nor did they deal more gently with Lorn and the neighbouring parts which acknowledged Argyll's authority. These proceedings lasted from December the 13th, 1644, till about the 28th or 29th of January.[7]

Montrose used to acknowledge that never had he experienced the singular providence and fatherly mercy of God in a more remarkable manner than at this time in bringing him and his men safe out of those parts. Had the passes been defended by

---

[7] Montrose marched from Loch Tay by Glendochart, much in the line of the Highland Railway. The Macdonalds extended far and wide among the glens. The writer of the Red Book of Clanranald boasts that the party under John Muidartach, which penetrated the length of Kilmartin Glassery, slew 895 persons without battle or skirmish; but this is unsupported. John brought in on one occasion 1000 head of cattle. See Mackenzie, Chambers, Napier, and Burton.

only 200 resolute men, his forces would either have been annihilated or easily prevented from invading the country.[8] If only the herds had driven their cattle out of reach, as they might easily have done, they would have perished with hunger in that barren land. Had the winter proved as hard and stormy as usual in those parts, they would have foundered in snow or been frozen to death. But God had deprived his enemies of courage and the season of its usual severity; and in place of bread, had given them great abundance of cattle.

Leaving Argyle at last, and passing through Lorn, Glencoe, and Lochaber, he came to Loch Ness.[9] He had now grounds for hoping that all the Highlanders, terrified by his treatment of Argyll or freed from the fear of him, would join him in defence of the King's righteous cause against the rebels.

But there was no lack of employment for his indomitable spirit. Word was brought that the Earl of Seaforth,[10] the most powerful chief in those parts, of whom he had formed the highest hopes, was on his way to attack him with an army of 5000 horse and foot, consisting of the garrison of Inverness, veteran troops, and the levies of Moray, Ross, Sutherland, Caithness, and the Fraser Clan. Montrose had only 1500, for the men of Clanranald and most of the Athole men, unaware of this approaching force, had obtained leave of absence, and returned home laden with the booty from Argyle, intending, however, to return when summoned. Montrose, however, did not hesitate to encounter Seaforth's disorderly army. Though he knew that Seaforth was supported by veteran soldiers, yet the rest of his force

---

[8] "Prevented their retreat," 1752 translation.

[9] He rested for a time at Kilcummin, now Fort Augustus. Here he drew up the "Bond subscryvit at Killiewheimen, the penult dayes of Jan. 1645." Some fifty-three signatures are attached to it, many of which, as those of Seaforth, Gordon, Nath. Gordon, &c., must have been affixed after Inverlochy. It also bears the signature of Lord Graham, Montrose's eldest son, then about sixteen years old. Not long after the battle he died at Gordon Castle. See full copy of Bond from Montrose charter-chest, with notes on it, in Napier's Memorials of Montrose, ii. 172-174.

[10] George, second Earl of Seaforth, is one of the many characters of the time whose position is hard to define. He is with Montrose in the Cumbernauld Band; he commands the forces north of Spey against Montrose in 1644, joins Montrose at Elgin after Inverlochy, and signs the Kilcummin Bond; deserts, and fights at Auldearn in the force of Sir John Hurry; in doubtful position at the Hague, but urges Montrose to attempt his last enterprise. See Act. Parl. Scot.; Douglas, Napier, &c.

was a mere rabble of new levies, peasants, drovers, shopmen, servants, and camp-followers, altogether raw and unfit for service.

He had made up his mind to give them battle, when a trusty messenger[11] overtook him with news that Argyll, having raised a force of Lowlanders and such of the Highlanders as still adhered to him, had made a descent on Lochaber, and was then at the old Castle of Inverlochy, on the shores of Loch Eil.[12] Montrose, who saw through Argyll's crafty but cowardly disposition, guessed his plan, which was to follow him at a respectful distance till he had engaged with this army from the north, and then to reap the advantage of the battle, though determined not to risk a decisive engagement himself, if he could avoid it. He therefore thought it a matter of more importance and less danger to attack Argyll, and show that he could be beaten even in the Highlands, where he was adored like some awful god by the simple people. If he succeeded, he expected that Seaforth's army, terrified by the report of the victory, would easily be brought to order.

Montrose was then thirty miles from Inverlochy. Leaving the beaten track, on which he placed guards to prevent intelligence reaching the enemy, he struck off straight through the wild pathless mountains of Lochaber.[13] No army had ever yet traversed that region. The country was known to none but drovers and

---

[11] The messenger is said to have been Ian Lom, the Bard of Keppoch. From Keppoch he might have reached Montrose by Glen Roy, and the track which Montrose followed in descending on Inverlochy. Guthrie gives Allan MacIldowie of Lochaber as the messenger; such a message was probably intrusted to more than one. Montrose was at his best in such a crisis—an army before and behind him on the one practicable road. He struck by a route unsuspected at the army which expected him least.

[12] Flying from Inveraray, Argyll went to Dumbarton, where he met General Baillie with regular troops, 1100 of whom were lent to him to supplement the Clan rising. Campbell of Auchinbrech was recalled from Ireland, and the Campbells began to follow on the track of Montrose, burning and destroying, through Glencoe and Lochaber, till they reached Inverlochy, the strategical centre in Highland warfare. Its importance was afterwards recognised in the erection of Fort William.

[13] The route was up the Tarff to the lofty pass of Corrieyairack, thence down upon the sources of the Spey, crossing into Glen Roy, from the far end of which the descent by Roy Bridge and Keppoch to the Spean is well known. A few miles farther along this shoulder of Ben Nevis brings you to Inverlochy. The ordinary route would have been straight down the great valley now traversed by the Caledonian Canal. A surprise would have been impossible by this track. This extraordinary march was begun on Friday morning, January 31. On Saturday night they were close to the field of Sunday's battle, Feb. 2nd, and Argyll had taken refuge in his barge with Sir James Rollo. For Claverhouse's marches over the same route see "Grameid."

hunters in pursuit of the deer, vast herds of which roam the mountains. The enemy's scouts were surprised and killed, and before they were aware of his approach he was upon them. Undismayed, however, by the surprise, they ran to arms and prepared for battle.

When Montrose saw that they were ready, he halted awhile for his rear, which had fallen behind through the fatigue and difficulty of the march, to come up. It was night, but the moon shone almost as clear as daylight. All that night they lay under arms, and by the faint light harassed each other incessantly with light skirmishes, so that neither side had time for repose. All waited eagerly for day, except Argyll alone, more anxious for his own than others' safety,[14] who sneaked off at dead of night, and taking boat, again saved himself from the peril of the battle. His part was to be the umpire and spectator of other men's prowess. At daybreak Montrose drew out his men in line of battle.[15] The enemy did the same with alacrity; for, as the prisoners afterwards admitted, they thought that Montrose himself was not present, but only one of his principal officers, with a part of his forces.

At length, about sunrise, on the 2nd of February, the day of the Purification of the Blessed Mary, mother of God and ever Virgin, the trumpet gave the signal. It was a sound of terror to their enemy, not only as showing they had horse with them, a thing unusual in those parts, but that Montrose himself was in command. Nevertheless the chieftains of the Campbells (which is the name of Argyll's clan), stout and gallant men, well worthy of a better chief and a juster cause, began the battle with great personal courage. But their soldiers in the first rank, after a single discharge, fled before the furious onset of Montrose's men, who fell on them with a loud cheer, and followed them up with

---

[14] All the Latin editions give "*aliis consultior*," which could only mean "more careful for others," the opposite of the obvious sense, which requires *sibi ipsi quam aliis, &c*. The repetition of the error is proof that the later editions underwent little or no revision. Below and at end of Ch. vi. we have in all editions *nec hostes impigre*, where the obvious sense requires *et impigre* or *nec pigre*. These errors are marks of hasty composition.

[15] These men had tasted little or nothing for two days. Montrose and Airlie's breakfast that morning, says P. Gordon, was but a "little meal mixt with cold water, which, out of a hollow dishe, they did picke up with there knyves for want of spoones."

such impetuosity that with a single charge they swept their whole force into irretrievable ruin. Then ensued a terrible slaughter of the fugitives for nine miles without cessation. Of the enemy 1500[16] were slain, among them many distinguished gentlemen and chieftains of the clan Campbell, who fell on the battle-field fighting too courageously for their craven chief. Enemies though they were, Montrose lamented their fate, and used his authority to save and give quarter to as many as he could. Argyll himself, on board his boat, rowed away from the shore to where he could watch the slaughter of his men from a safe distance. Some officers, whom Argyll had brought with him from the Lowlands, took refuge in the castle, but surrendered on a promise of quarter, and were treated with kindness by Montrose, who set them at liberty, and loaded them with many proofs of his mercy and generosity.

In this battle, though a number of his men were wounded, Montrose lost only three private soldiers. But the joy of a brilliant victory was clouded by the death of the gallant Sir Thomas Ogilvy, son of the Earl of Airlie, who died of his wounds a few days afterwards. He had won distinction in the King's service under his father-in-law, Ruthven, Earl of Forth and Brentford, an officer of world-wide renown. On the outbreak of war in Scotland he had attached himself to Montrose, who esteemed him among his dearest friends. Accomplished both as a scholar and soldier, he added fresh glory and lustre to the ancient name of Ogilvy, and by his noble death for King and country he contributed mainly to that day's victory. Montrose, who was deeply afflicted by his loss, ordered the body to be conveyed to Athole,

---

[16] P. Gordon says 1700. The general, Auchinbreck, with fourteen barons of the name of Campbell, were killed and twenty men of quality taken (P. Gordon, 102). His account of the march and battle is more vivid, personal, and full than that of our author. O'Kean or O'Cahan, the Irishman, appears again in command of the left wing, giving orders to fire only into the breasts of the enemy, which order was so perfectly obeyed that by their first discharge "they fyred their beardes." Montrose had managed to bring with him some fifty horse, commanded by Sir Thos. Ogilvy. When 200 of the fugitives made for Inverlochy Castle, Sir Thomas "afrontes them and forced them to flee with the rest up the side of the lake or firth. In this conflict the brave gentleman receaued a shote whereof he died soone after, to the no small regrait of the whole armie" (*ib.* 102). See also Spalding, Napier, and Gardiner. The latter (ii. 104) by mistake calls Sir Thomas Ogilvy Lord Ogilvy. Lord Ogilvy was a prisoner in Edinburgh.

and interred as magnificently as the time and place allowed. For many centuries the power of the Campbells in the Highlands had been the terror of their neighbours, but it was utterly broken by this overthrow. Montrose's designs had now free course; for the Highlanders, who are a very warlike race, being freed from the hated tyranny of Argyll, were more eager to offer their service in the King's cause.[17]

---

[17] See Montrose's important despatch to the King, and discussion of it (Napier, Mem., 484).

## CHAPTER IX.

Return northwards—Surrender of Elgin—Lord Gordon joins—Montrose enters the Mearns and defeats Hurry near Fettercairn—Offers battle to Baillie and Hurry on the Isla—Lewis Gordon deserts with most of his Clan—Montrose retires north—Seizes Dundee—Extraordinary march to evade Baillie and reach the Grampians.

AFTER some days' rest from the immense fatigue of their recent march, Montrose led his men back over the mountains of Lochaber to Loch Ness; thence he passed through Errick, Dearn, and Nairn,[1] and crossed the river Spey, where he received news that a considerable body of the enemy were at Elgin, the chief town of Moray, a district beyond the Spey. Montrose hastened to them, either to draw them over to his side or reduce them by force of arms. But the very news of his approach dispersed this little cloud, and they fled in terror to their lurking-holes. However, he continued his march, and on the 14th of February the town of Elgin surrendered.[2]

At this time Lord Gordon,[3] eldest son of Huntly, a man whose

---

[1] Straths Errick, Nairn, Dearn, and Spey lie more or less parallel. There must have been much cross-country climbing from strath to strath before the roads were made which cross the Findhorn and Nairn rivers. Fraser, Grant, Mackintosh, and Macpherson are the chief names of these regions.

[2] The Northern barons met at Elgin under Lord Seaforth on 17th Feb. to provide for the safety of the North, but they fled on Montrose's approach. He entered Elgin on 19th. W. is mistaken in giving 14th. Here Lords Gordon, Lewis Gordon, with Col. Nathl. Gordon, freed from excommunication (see p. 66, *n*. 11), joined Montrose from the Bog of Gight, now Gordon Castle. Seaforth came in, and "the sweet nightingale," the laird of Grant's wife, prevailed in sending that chief to Elgin, where, with Seaforth, he signs the Kilcummin bond. March 4th, Montrose moved to Gordon Castle, where Lord Graham, his eldest son, overtaxed with the winter's campaign, died, and was buried at Bellie.

On Feb. 12 Argyll appeared in Edinburgh with his left arm in a sling, "as if he had been at bones breaking." Generals Baillie and Hurry, with the inevitable ministers, were deputed to put down the growing rebellion.

[3] George, Lord Gordon, eldest son of the Marquis of Huntly. He had served in Alsace and Lorraine under Marechal de la Force. With his father he had suffered at the hands of Montrose, having been imprisoned in Edinburgh in 1639. He was induced by his uncle Argyll to side with the Covenanters while his father was in hiding, but they did not trust him. Inverlochy decided him, and unreservedly he threw himself into the royal cause. For a time it looked as if Montrose

excellent good qualities deserve the highest praise, left his uncle, Argyll, by whom he had been detained against his will, and openly espoused the King's cause, voluntarily offering his service and obedience to Montrose, as the King's general and vicegerent. He brought with him not many followers, but those he had were picked men, his personal friends and dependents. Montrose welcomed him with courtesy and warmth. Afterwards, when he came to know him thoroughly and had proved his honour, the two men became knit together in the most sacred bonds of friendship.

As most of the inhabitants of Moray were devoted to the Covenanters, and had hid themselves in their lurking-places, he had no hope of any help from a people so hostile to his cause. He therefore led his forces across the Spey, in order to raise the shires of Banff and Aberdeen by the presence, example, and influence of Lord Gordon. Having levied there what forces he could, with 2000 infantry and 200 horse he crossed the river Dee and Grampian Hills, descended into the Mearns, and encamped not far from Fettercairn.[5]

About seven miles distant lay a body of Covenanters under Sir John Hurry,[6] an active, gallant officer, who had won distinction

---

was to have the united support of the Gordons. As it was, they now furnished him with a body of good horse. Lord Gordon brought in Lord Lewis with him, and Lord Aboyne was meditating in Carlisle his ride north to join Montrose. On the character and death of Lord Gordon see W. below, and P. Gordon, 131. The latter, after stating that Gen. Baillie left 1600 of his best men dead at Alford, adds, " But alas! what were all those in comparisone of that noble and magnanimius youth, that heavine dasleing sparke of true nobilitie, that miracle of men, the matchless Lord Gordon, who was there slain after he had totallie defeate and routed Baccaras." " He was a man in all perfection, altho he died before time or nature had granted him a beard."

[4] Hurry before this had made a raid upon Aberdeen, where Donald Farquharson, the pride of Braemar, and Nath. Gordon, with other Cavaliers, were enjoying themselves carelessly. Donald was killed in the street, to the great grief of all, and Gordon barely escaped, losing Huntly's best horse, which he had been riding. Hurry also from Ald (? Alt) Montrose, carried off James, now Lord Grahame, and his tutor, who were imprisoned in Edinburgh Castle. Lord Airlie was taken ill, and was escorted to Strathbogie by a strong detachment. See Spalding, P. Gordon, and Napier. W. says nothing of the burning (about March 21st) of Stonehaven, Cowie, Ury, and Drumlithie, with Marishall's lands, or the killing of the aged father of the future Earl of Middleton, " as he sat in his chair in the castle of Caldhame." The parish records of Menmuir and other kirks in the Mearns and braes of Angus show grievous interruptions of worship through the presence of Montrose. The house of the minister of Fettercairn, Mr. James Strachan, was burnt on this visit to Fettercairn (Jervise, Land of Lindsay and Angus and Mearns).

[5] Sir John Hurry's ambush lay in the wood of Halkerton Castle, the property of Sir Alexander Falconer, who was made a peer in 1647.

[6] Sir John Hurry was a townsman of Aberdeen, where the name appears on Council records

abroad, and was now colonel of a regiment of horse and general of all their forces. With 600 troopers he advanced to reconnoitre Montrose's strength, and thinking that Montrose had but few foot and no cavalry, he hoped to draw him down into the plain and give a good account of him. In any case, he felt confident of a safe retreat. To draw him on, Montrose concealed his forces in a glen, and showed front with the 200 horse only, but these he had as usual lined with the most active of his musketeers. Hurry, seeing they were so few, led his men to the charge. When too late he observed the foot, who were following briskly at the horses' heels, and sounded a retreat, which he himself covered with great gallantry. As they fell back Montrose's men pressed on with great eagerness, and drove them across the river Esk; nor did they feel themselves safe even when sheltered by nightfall, but fled with precipitation to Dundee, twenty-four miles distant. Those who had pursued them so far then returned to Fettercairn, and next day marched to Brechin. Here Montrose was informed that Baillie,[7] a general of great reputation, had been summoned from England to take supreme command of the enemy's forces, and had been joined by Hurry with his horse; besides which, he

---

some way back. In the Incident he appears as Capt. Hurry. He joined the Parliamentary army, but deserted to Rupert, and informed him that £21,000 was being conveyed to Thame, thus bringing on the affair at Chalgrove Field and the death of Hampden. After this engagement he was knighted by Charles. Taken prisoner in Lancashire, July 1644 (see *n.* p. 31), and perceiving how matters were going, he changed sides in August; but by and bye he is in the service of the Estates and commands at Auldearn. Changing again, he joins Montrose, and leaves the country with him. He had a commission in the army of the Engagement, and at Preston "got a dangerous shot on the left side of his head, whereof, though he was afterwards taken prisoner, he recovered" (Turner, 65). He acted as Montrose's major-general on his landing in Scotland; was taken prisoner at Corbiesdale, and beheaded at Edinburgh. Rev. J. Fraser noticed Colonel Hurry at Inverness on his way to Edinburgh, "a robust, tall, stately fellow, with a long cut on his cheek." Spalding, P. Gordon, Napier, and Gardiner, *indices*.

[7] General William Baillie of Letham was a natural son of Sir William Baillie of Lamington, who, after the death of his wife, married the mother, but failed to legitimatise the son. He served under Gustavus Adolphus, and was one of the "experimented" soldiers called into Scotland by the Covenanters in 1638. He was at the affair at Newburn, commanded the Scots garrison at Durham, and was at Marston Moor. He might have done better in Scotland had he been free from the ministers and the committee. In later life he endeavoured to oust the young laird of Lamington from his possessions, but failed. Two of his sons married daughters of Lord Forrester of Corstorphine, and by an arrangement between the General and Lord Forrester they were to come into the title. James, who assumed the title, was afterwards stabbed with his own sword by his wife's niece in the garden-house at Corstorphine. She was sentenced to death, escaped, was retaken, and beheaded.

had a number of veteran troops recalled from England and Ireland. The Covenanters were now resolved to prosecute the war with greater vigour. Henceforth he would have to deal with very different soldiers, commanded by generals of great experience.

To extricate himself from their cavalry, in which they were always superior, he kept upon the most advantageous ground, and marched towards the Tay by the foot of the Grampians, intending, if possible, to cross the Forth, where he expected numbers to rise for the King. But the enemy saw through his design, and sent these commanders with a very strong force to prevent it. As soon as they came in sight, Montrose offered battle, but they had not the least intention of risking an engagement, and did not even attempt to harass his rear as he retreated. He marched on to the Castle of Inverquharity,[7] and next day to the village of Alyth.[8] Thence he again marched down into the plain, leaving the mountains far behind, and challenged Baillie by a trumpeter to fight. Between the armies ran the river Isla, which neither of them could cross with safety, if the passage were disputed. Montrose therefore requested permission to cross with safety; but if Baillie did not approve of that, then he would give him a free and safe passage, on condition that he would pledge his honour to fight without further delay. To this Baillie replied that he would mind his own business himself, and would fight at his own pleasure, and not another man's commands.

Several days were thus passed in face of the enemy, who made no sign of coming to the attack; while Montrose himself, through want of cavalry, had no hope of forcing a passage. He therefore marched on to Dunkeld,[9] and was on the point of attempting to cross the Tay, when he was almost ruined by an

---

[7] Inverquharity—the Latin gives the pronunciation. Sir John Ogilvy, the first Baronet of this very ancient branch of the Clan, lived very quietly, and engaged as little as possible in the troubles (Napier). The old castle with its "iron yet" still remains, and the licence to erect the *yet*, from James II. or III., 1444 or 1467, was in the possession of the late Sir John Ogilvy, but the property of the castle has passed away from Ogilvy of Inverquharity. See Jervise, "Land of the Lindsays," 345-346, and Appendix.

[8] *Eliota* is no doubt Alyth. Eliot, near Arbroath, is out of the district and not a *vicus*.

[9] *Duncaledonia*, ancient Latin name, now abbreviated into Dunkeld.

unexpected misfortune. Lewis Gordon,[10] son of Huntly, who had fought against him at Aberdeen, by the mediation of his noble brother Lord Gordon, had been received into favour by Montrose. On the plea of some letters, real or pretended, from his father, written in his place of concealment, he prevailed on almost all the Gordons to desert, without his brother's knowledge, and abandoned his brother and Montrose in the hour of danger. Indeed, it is very doubtful to which of the two he bore the greater grudge.

Montrose was seriously disconcerted by this unlooked for desertion. He was now obliged to retreat to the north to recruit his forces. But, in spite of this, he still made as though he would march to the Forth.[11] In consequence, all his spies agreed in reporting that the enemy to their last man had crossed the Tay[12] to seize the fords of the Forth and oppose his passage. That his attempt might not seem altogether ineffectual, he resolved to make a brilliant dash at Dundee and surprise it on his march. That city was a hotbed of sedition and a sure refuge for the rebels in those parts, whose cause it largely contributed to foster; and was at the time feebly garrisoned by the townsmen. His weaker troops and those who were lightly armed were sent with the baggage to skirt the foot of the mountains, their orders being to meet him at Brechin. With all his cavalry, 150 in number, and 600 light-armed musketeers, he himself set out from Dunkeld about midnight, and by a march of extraordinary speed reached Dundee about ten o'clock on the morning of the 4th of April. He immediately summoned the townsmen by a herald to surrender, if they wished to save themselves and their city; otherwise he threatened them with fire and sword. They endeavoured to gain time and did not at once reply; at last they threw his herald into prison. Incensed at this affront, Montrose stormed the town in three different quarters. The townsmen for awhile

---

[10] On the question whether Lord Lewis left Montrose at Dunkeld or after fighting at Dundee, see Gardiner. The forthcoming Huntly Book, edited by Sir W. Fraser, may contribute evidence to settle the dispute.

[11] Montrose had received a letter from the King not long before this, urging a descent upon the Lothians, and promising the aid of 500 horse under Musgrave. Gard., Civil War, ii. 176.

[12] Baillie had gone no farther than Perth. Montrose was badly served with intelligence.

made some show of resistance on the walls, but in vain. The Irish and Highlanders charged with fury. Some of them drove their opponents from the works,[13] manned the cannon, and turned them against the town; others burst open the gates and seized the church and market-place; while others, again, fired the houses in several places. And had not the common soldiers, in their ill-timed greed and intemperance, turned aside to plunder and drink, this wealthy city would there and then have been wrapped in flames. It was as well for the conquerors as for the vanquished city that it was not so. The news of the scouts that the enemy had crossed the Tay was altogether false. Some squadrons, certainly not many, had been seen to cross. These they had taken for the whole army of the enemy, a mistake which nearly proved the ruin of themselves and their party.

Montrose was standing on elevated ground [14] which overlooks Dundee, watching the progress of the fight in the city below, when breathless scouts came up with word that Baillie and Hurry were scarcely a mile distant with 3000 foot and 800 horse. Instantly he recalled his men out of the city, but not without the greatest difficulty. Secure of their victory, flushed with drink, and eager

---

[13] In 1645 Dundee within its walls might be regarded, speaking roughly, as a parallelogram, the market-place and church at the centre converged upon by four streets—two from the west, two from the east. At the north-west corner, within the walls, stood the Corbie Hill, with its platform of guns commanding the town. On Ap. 4 the wall outside the hill was under repair, and there had been two plans as to the work, that of John Mylne, a local mason, and that of Henry Young, afterwards a famous engineer. Mylne, after proceeding so far, had given way to Young, whose plan was only adopted Ap. 1. At this weak point Montrose dashed in and captured Corbie Hill. The defenders of the West Port and Nethergait Port were taken in the rear by their own guns, and the way was open to the Highlanders. A rush for a hundred yards or so would bring them to the Kirk and Market-place. From Corbie Hill Montrose could look along the Overgait and see most of what went on in the centre of the town, and there he would get the first alarm of Baillie's approach. On the alarm he and his officers, moving eastwards through the town, could carry their men out by the Seagait and East Port in a straight course. The difficulties of the present city did not exist in the little town of 1645. See Maxwell's "Old Dundee" and map. The walls cost £162, 10s. to repair after this event, and the town, for its losses, received the sympathy of Estates with a grant of £57,477 Scots, of which £20,000 only was paid. See Dundee Charters, Accounts, 1645-47, and Act. Parl. Scot. VI. i. 579. For interesting details, see Evidence of John Gordon, Napier, Mem., 495, and of the Master of Spynie, *id.* 448.

[14] Corbie Hill, as we consider. It has now been quarried away, but in 1645 it was the principal eminence within the walls, not excepting the Castle Hill. The Law, or any part of it, is out of the question, with Dudhope and its grounds and West Chapel Shade, and much open country between, to say nothing of the tall trees on the sides of the Scouring Burn. It would not have given even a bird's-eye view, and a leader on the top of it would not have been of much use.

for the rich booty, his men could hardly be induced to abandon their prey. The enemy were actually within gunshot before they could be torn away. Montrose's council, as is usual in moments of supreme danger, were divided in opinion. Some pressed him to look to his own safety and ride away. It was impossible, they urged, to bring off the foot, fatigued with their morning's march of over twenty miles, exhausted by the day's fighting, and now laden with plunder and heavy with drink.[15] They would have to march twenty, perhaps thirty, miles farther before they could halt with safety. It was the chance of war, a thing to be borne with courage. He had often inflicted far greater losses on the enemy than this. None could doubt that if he were saved he would soon recruit his forces; but should any disaster befall him, the case would be desperate and everything lost. Others exclaimed that all was now utterly lost. Nothing remained but to die with honour. Let them charge the thickest of the enemy and perish on the field of glory. Montrose concurred with neither. Nothing could ever induce him to abandon his bravest men in their hour of utmost peril. He preferred an honourable death among his men to a base regard for his own safety. On the other hand, for such a handful of men to charge the enemy and dash their heads, so to speak, against a rock, was the last resource of despair, and not to be used rashly; and as God Almighty ought not to be tempted by cowardly neglect, neither should His aid be despaired of by brave Christian men. He therefore encouraged them to do their duty manfully, and leave the issue to God and the means to his own care.

Immediately he sent off 400 foot with orders to march as rapidly as possible without breaking their ranks. Two hundred of his swiftest men were commanded to follow, while he himself brought up the rear with the horse. The troopers rode in open order, with intervals to admit the light musketeers, should occasion arise. He believed that the enemy's foot could not overtake them;

---

[15] Gardiner, as against Napier, questions the power of drunken men to march as these did. But there are degrees in drunkenness. Fright and hard work would soon clear their heads.

and should their horse alone attack them, which he thought they would hardly venture to do, he expected to dispose of them without much difficulty. As the sun was now setting, he foresaw that the darkness would favour their retreat. When the enemy, who had received information of their numbers from some captives, presently confirmed by their own observation of the forces in retreat, saw that they were preparing to march off without a battle, they divided their forces and gave chase. Their object was not merely to attack him simultaneously in flank and rear, but also to cut off every road to the Highlands. To encourage their men to a hot pursuit, their generals put a price of 20,000 gold pieces on Montrose's head. By this time their cavalry were in advance, pressing hard upon the retreat, when those excellent musketeers who accompanied the horse shot down three of the most forward, one after another. The rest, taking a lesson from their fate, grew much less eager in pursuit. As soon as Montrose's men perceived that they could outmarch the enemy's foot, they regained their nerve and confidence, and, turning on their horse, skirmished stoutly until night put an end to the fighting. To shake off the enemy at all hazards, they marched for many miles eastward along the coast. This was not the route they intended to follow. Their real object was to make northwards to the Grampian hills, so as to relieve themselves of the enemy's horse, who continued to harass them; but Baillie had stationed far the greater part of his army between them and the Grampians, to cut off every avenue of retreat. About midnight, therefore, when not far from Arbroath, Montrose ordered a halt, but only for a brief interval. Suspecting that all direct routes and passes to the mountains were occupied by the enemy's horse, in which his judgment was not at fault, he ordered his men to face about and march rapidly to the south-west. In this way, but with incredible fatigue, he eluded his pursuers, whom he passed that very night, and soon afterwards turned northwards, and at sunrise next morning crossed the river Esk, not far from the castle of Careston. Thence he sent to Brechin to fetch up the party with the baggage; but having received timelier notice of Baillie's advance, they had chosen a safer route, and gained the mountains. While he halted at Careston[17] his scouts suddenly brought word that the enemy's cavalry were in sight, and that their foot, refreshed with food and sleep, were also hard in pursuit. Montrose, being now within three miles of the mountains, had little to fear; but his men, who had spent three days and two nights without sleep, marching or fighting incessantly, were so overwhelmed with drowsiness that pricks and wounds could hardly stir them up. The enemy were checked by light skirmishing, and suffered him at last to gain the foot of the hills, when they abandoned their fruitless pursuit, after all their trouble, while Montrose and his men made their way to Glenesk.[18]

Such was his memorable march from Dundee, discreditable to his scouts for their blunder, but almost unparalleled for the general's courage, endurance, and presence of mind in extremity of danger. The resolution and hardiness of his men were likewise marvellous. For sixty miles they marched incessantly, often engaged with the enemy, without food, without sleep, and without a moment's pause to rest. Whether such an account will be believed abroad or in after ages I cannot pretend to say; but it rests on the most certain information and the best of evidence. In fact, I have often heard officers of experience and distinction, not in Britain only, but also in Germany and France, prefer this march of Montrose to his most famous victories.

---

[17] Supposing Montrose had reached Eliot Water, near Arbroath, and doubled back as far as Panbride, he would there find a good track past Panmure House to Carmyllie, and thence to Guthrie, Melgund, and the fords at Careston. Gardiner's map should be consulted, though his placing Forfar so directly south of Careston and on the line of march is misleading. Compare Ordinance Survey Map. Careston belonged to Sir Alexander Carnegie, a relative of Montrose. Ochterlony, writing *circa* 1682, says of it, "A great and most delicat house, well built, brave lights, and of a most excellent contrivance, without debait the best gentleman's house in the shyre; extraordinare much planting, delicate yards and gardens with stone walls, ane excellent avenue, with ane range of ash trees on every syde, ane excellent arbour, for length and breadth none in the countie lyke it." Spottiswoode, Misc., i. 334. See also Jervise, Land of Lindsays, 297. On the lawns of Careston the weary men sought a little rest after a march of two nights without sleep, the storming and sacking of a town, with the fighting that followed.

[18] Glenesk is the glen of the North Esk. Gardiner's map is here misleading. The Laird of Edzell and Glenesk makes sore moan for his losses at this time, and the burning of the kirk and other depredations are credited to Montrose in the history of the glen. Jervise, "Land of Lindsays," *passim.*

## CHAPTER X.

Montrose at Crieff—Attacked by Baillie—Retreat by Stratheam—Joined by Aboyne—Pursues Hurry across the Spey to Elgin, Forres, and Inverness—Battle of Auldearn, May 1645.

MONTROSE having thus made good his retreat beyond all expectation, ordered his men to rest. Meanwhile he resolved on the following measures for prosecuting the war. He sent Lord Gordon away to his own country, with such of his men as had continued loyal and obedient after his brother Lewis's desertion, in order to bring back those whom his brother had seduced, and raise new levies to recruit his forces. This he executed with diligence and cheerfulness, punishing some of them, especially those who had advised and helped his brother in that crime. In this he was the more earnest that he might remove all shadow of blame from himself. Indeed, neither Montrose nor any one else loathed the treachery of Lewis more heartily than his own brother, Lord Gordon. Meanwhile Montrose, with a small detachment—for he had retained only 500 foot and 50 horse—marched through Angus into Perthshire, to distract the enemy by a diversion, until he could recruit his army by forces gathered from every quarter. The movement was well judged. The Covenanters had despatched Hurry, the lieutenant-general of their horse, to the north with a detachment of 600 veteran infantry and 200 horse, to support their friends and crush Lord Gordon; while Baillie himself halted with the army at Perth, in the heart of the kingdom, ready for any emergency. Montrose had reached Crieff, a village twelve miles from Perth, where, as Baillie was informed, he was quartered carelessly with a small band. On the watch for every opportunity, Baillie set out from Perth early in the night, with his whole army, and marched with great haste, thinking by daybreak to surprise and overwhelm Montrose. But he found him fully on his guard, with his infantry drawn up under arms, ready to fight or march. Montrose himself rode out with the horse to reconnoitre the number and strength of the enemy, and finding that they were 2000 foot and 500 horse, he ordered his men to march off with all speed, and keeping along Strathearn, to occupy the passes leading into it. With his handful of horse he covered their retreat, to save them from being ridden down by the enemy. They charged with spirit, but met with so warm a reception that they were thrown into disorder, and forced to fall back with some loss. Meantime his foot, after a march of six miles, made themselves masters of the pass of Strathearn,[1] so that the enemy were obliged to return from their fruitless attempt. Montrose lay that night, which was the 18th of April, at Lochearn, and marched next day to Balquhidder, where he was met by the Earl of Aboyne with a few others,[2] whom the reports of Montrose's success had encouraged to escape out of Carlisle, and return at last to their native country.

From Balquhidder they proceeded inland to Loch Katrine, where they received word that Hurry had raised a strong force in the north, and was threatening Lord Gordon. There was imminent danger lest this experienced and active officer should overpower that gallant young nobleman. Montrose therefore decided to oppose Hurry with all speed, as much to save so dear a friend from the impending peril, as to attack the enemy in detail and crush them piecemeal, knowing well that he was no match for their united forces. By a series of forced marches he passed through Balquhidder, along Loch Tay, which is twenty-four miles in length, through Athole and Angus, over the Grampians, and

---

[1] Which is the pass intended? Montrose retreated up the Earn by Comrie, and south of the Loch to Lochearnhead. No doubt the tradition of a raid on Ardvoirlich owes its origin to this march through the property. At the head of Lochearn three ways lay open, by Glen Ogle, Strathyre, or Balquhidder. By the last he recruited from the Macgregors' lands.

[2] Aboyne with sixteen horse broke out of Carlisle, and after much danger and a bad accident to his shoulder, met Montrose at the ford of Cardross. The Master of Napier, confined with his father in Holyrood, also escaped at this time and joined Montrose. Spalding gives young Keir as his companion, but this is probably a mistake, as Sir George Stirling does not appear to have had any family. John Alexander, a young son of the Earl of Stirling, joined Montrose from Keir along with Napier.

down through the strath of Glenmuick[3] into the very heart of Mar. There he was joined by Gordon with 1000 foot and 200 horse, and at once marched on to the Spey to seek the enemy and force him to a battle. Hurry was still in the belief that he had not yet crossed the Grampians, when he was not more than six miles off; for by a vast effort he had marched with such amazing rapidity as to outrun the news of his approach. Having no mind for an engagement till reinforced by a very strong body of troops and numerous auxiliaries, Hurry hastened across the Spey and marched to Elgin on his way to Inverness, which he had appointed as the rendezvous of all his forces. Montrose at once followed him to Elgin. Hurry hastened on to Forres, hotly pursued by Montrose, who pressed him so closely for fourteen miles, that even under shelter of night he had much ado to reach Inverness.

Next day Montrose encamped at the village of Auldearn.[4] Hurry, as he had expected, found the Earls of Seaforth and Sutherland, the Clan Fraser, with most of the men of Moray, Caithness and the neighbourhood, assembled in arms at Inverness. With these and the veterans of the town garrison he marched straight for Montrose. The force under his command numbered 3500 foot and 400 horse. Montrose, who had not more than 1500 foot and 250 horse, was now very anxious to retire. But Hurry pressed him so hard that retreat was almost out of the question. Moreover, Baillie with the southern army, which was still more formidable in cavalry, had already crossed the Grampians,[5] and was now far on his way to the Spey, marching in great haste. What was to be done? Either Montrose must fight with

[3] Glenmuick could be reached from Angus by Glenisla, by Clova, or by Glenesk and Glenmark. Gardiner and Napier differ as to the route after this; the former takes Montrose into Strathspey, and the latter brings him down the Dee at the end of April to an encampment at Skene, about ten miles from Aberdeen, and half-way between Dee and Don. Aboyne's raid with eighty horse on Aberdeen to seize twenty barrels of gunpowder and return the same night to his leader was possible only from the latter position.

[4] The village of Auldearn (corruption of Altdearn or High Dearn; the Dearn gives its name to the great Strath, and appears also, *e.g.*, in Darnaway, and in Findhorn, *i.e.*, Finn Dearn) lies on the road from Forres to Nairn and Inverness. For a careful account of the battle, drawn from P. Gordon and Wishart, see Gardiner, who gives the various positions after personal inspection of the ground.

[5] Guthrie says that Baillie, having burned Athole, set out for Aberdeen, but heard the news of Hurry's defeat before the end of the march.

Hurry, or take the far more serious risk of being hemmed in between the gathering forces of the enemy. He therefore resolved to risk a battle at once, leaving the issue to Providence, and chose an advantageous position to await the enemy. The village stood on a low ridge and covered a neighbouring hollow. Behind it are some hillocks, which conceal it from the view of all but those who are close upon it. In the hollow he drew up his forces, which were quite invisible to the enemy. In front of the village he stationed a few picked foot-soldiers, men of experience and prompt to act, along with his cannon, masked by some dykes which had been cast up there. The right wing he intrusted to Alastair Macdonald with 400 foot, stationed on ground which happened to be defended by dykes and ditches, brushwood and rocks.

These he ordered to reserve themselves, whatever happened, and not to quit their position, which formed a strong natural fortification, secure from any attack either of horse or of foot. To this division was consigned the well-known royal standard, broadly displayed, which used to be carried only before Montrose,—an admirable ruse, calculated to draw the main attack upon that impregnable position, so as to give him an opportunity for a successful attack upon the left. With this object he transferred all the rest of his men to the opposite wing, himself taking command of the foot, and Lord Gordon in charge of the horse. His main centre was left to the imagination of the enemy. In fact, he had none, but a small body stationed under cover of the dykes before the village made a show of one. With so small a force a reserve was out of the question.

As Montrose by this skilful arrangement had foreseen, the enemy no sooner observed the royal standard, than they sent the best part of their horse, with the veterans who formed their main strength, against that point, and commenced the assault upon the right wing and those who were posted before the village, keeping up a determined attack by constant relays of fresh men. This Montrose, with so few men, could not do. He therefore resolved to charge at once with the whole weight of his left. Just as he was on the point of giving effect to this resolution, a messenger, on whose fidelity and prudence he could rely, whispered in his ear,

"Macdonald and his right wing are routed." To prevent a panic among his men at the bad news, with admirable presence of mind he at once called out, "Come, my Lord Gordon, what are we waiting for? Our friend Macdonald on the right has routed the enemy and is slaughtering the fugitives. Shall we look on idly and let him carry off all the honours of the day?" With these words he hurled his line upon the enemy. The shock of the Gordons was irresistible.[6] After a brief struggle Hurry's horse wavered, recoiled, wheeled, and fled, leaving their own flanks naked and exposed. Though deserted by the horse, the infantry, being superior in numbers and much better armed, stood their ground bravely,[7] until Montrose came to close quarters, and forced them to fling down their arms and make a desperate but vain attempt to save themselves by flight. Montrose, however, did not forget the news his trusty messenger had brought. Followed by some of his promptest men, he wheeled to the right, where he found matters in a very different condition.

Macdonald, a brave man, but readier with his hand than his head, hasty in battle and bold to rashness, stung by the taunts and scoffs of the enemy, disdained to shelter himself behind dykes and bushes, and, contrary to orders, threw himself with his men outside of their strong position. His rashness cost him dear. The enemy, who were far stronger both in horse and numbers, and most of them veteran troops, drove his men back pell-mell, and had he not withdrawn them to a neighbouring enclosure just in time, they would every one of them have been lost, and the royal standard with them. Rash as he had been, he atoned for his error by his splendid courage in bringing off his men. The last to retire, and covering himself with a huge target, single-handed he withstood the thickest of the enemy. Some of the pikemen, by whom he was hard pressed, again and again pierced

---

[6] The slaughter of Donald Farquharson in the streets of Aberdeen by Hurry's men, and the murder of James Gordon of Struders in the house of a friend, where his wounds were being tended, made the Gordons "take the fewer prisoners and give the less quarter." Their battle-cry was "Remember Donald Farquharson and James Gordon." The charge was made after Cromwell's tactics, a rush sword in hand. See P. Gordon, Gardiner, and Napier.

[7] See Gardiner as to the discovery of the skeletons in Deadman's Wood, supposed to be those of the men who fell at this point.

his target with the points of their weapons, which he mowed off with his broadsword by threes and fours at a sweep.[8] But when those who were assailing the enclosure saw Montrose coming to the rescue, and their own men on the left put to rout, the horse fled headlong, but the foot, mostly veterans from Ireland, fought on doggedly, and fell man by man almost where they stood. The victors followed the fugitives for some miles. Of the enemy there fell about 3000 foot, of whom the veterans had fought with conspicuous bravery. Most of the cavalry escaped by a flight more timely than honourable. Even Hurry himself, with some of his best men, who were the last to quit the field, would not have escaped, had not the Viscount Aboyne carelessly displayed some ensigns and standards which he had captured in the rout, and instead of pursuing the fugitives turned to his own men, who took him for a fresh force coming on to renew the attack. The mistake lasted long enough to give the enemy's horse, though broken, time to scatter and fly by such paths as they happened to know or hit on. A few of them made their way with Hurry to Inverness before next morning.

The most distinguished of the enemy who fell were Campbell of Lawers,[9] colonel of one of the old regiments, Sir John Murray,[10] Sir Gideon Murray,[11] and some other brave men, whose loss might have been deplored, had they not stained their valour by the infamous crime of rebellion. In this they had not followed their own judgment, but the impulse of the mob or the ambition and

---

[8] For other details of Macdonald's prowess, and similar marvels performed by Ranald Og Macdonald of Mull, see Clanranald MS., quoted by Napier, Mem., 503-504.

[9] Sir Mungo Campbell of Lawers, "a good Christian and expert commander." For notices of his character and of his services in Ireland and England, with the provisions made for his widow and children, see Act. Parl. Scot., VI. i. 468. The notices are full and sympathetic. Lord Gordon buried him with much respect (P. Gordon, 127).

[10] Sir John Murray. We presume this is the son of Sir John Murray of Philiphaugh, who, in his supplication in 1649, says, "It is notorious how I lossed a hopefull gentleman that was my son at the battle of Auldairne, who was the staff of my old aige, in the north, againes the said rebel James Grahame, which many of your number can testifie." Act. Parl. Scot., VI. ii. 704.

[11] Sir Gideon Murray. We have not been able to trace the family of this soldier. Gideon was a common name in the Elibank family, but Patrick, second Lord, who joined Montrose, had no brother of the name. The same Christian name appears among the Murrays of Sudhope, and a Gideon Murray is authorised to fish in Shetland. Act. Parl. Scot., Index, Murray.

avarice of their chiefs. Of those who fought with Montrose on the left, he lost one only, a private soldier. On the other wing, where Macdonald commanded, he lost fourteen, also common soldiers, but a very large number were wounded. Montrose himself took care that these should be safely housed and receive medical attention. As for the prisoners, he consoled them with courtesy and gentleness. Those who repented of their rebellion he set at liberty or enlisted in his own service. The stubborn he lodged in various prisons.

Not long before, young Napier,[12] son of Lord Napier of Merchiston, by Montrose's sister, had stolen away from Edinburgh without the knowledge of his father or wife, and flown to join his uncle. In the battle of Auldearn his bravery shone forth with signal lustre, and he gave a fine proof of youthful promise, and laid the firm foundation of a most noble character. Enraged at this, the leading Covenanters at Edinburgh seized his aged father, who was now nearly seventy years old, and as noble a man as any Scotland had bred in this age,[13] and his lady,[14] the Earl of Mar's

---

[12] Archibald, Master of Napier, afterwards second Lord, was not of age in 1644. At seventeen he married Lady Elizabeth Erskine, daughter of the Earl of Mar, and he was at this time the father of several children. His portrait by Jamieson, in the possession of Lord Napier, and reproduced in Napier's Memoirs, shows a face of much sweetness and refinement, but with a firm mouth and chin, indicative of the courage exhibited by the young man. His letter to his wife, dated Brussels, June 14, 1648 (Napier, Mem., 665), though full of political matter, begins " My dearest Heart," and ends " My dearest Life, only yours," and professes, with evident sincerity, that he would go through all dangers imaginable " only to see you." " I confess I have satisfaction in nothing whilst we live at such a distance." " I should be more contented to live with you meanly in the deserts of Arabia, than without you in the most fruitful place in the world, plentifully and with all the delights it could afford." He fortified Montrose's castle of Kincardine, and held it with fifty men against Middleton for a fortnight, a military feat worthy of the courage displayed at Auldearn. He was included in Middleton's capitulation with Montrose, and, with certain restrictions on communications with him, he was permitted to go abroad. An interesting letter from Wishart to him, Jan. 1, 1650, is preserved in the Napier charter chest, as is a bond for a thousand merks borrowed by Lord Napier, and written and witnessed by Wishart in Schiedam, $\frac{7}{17}$ October 1652. Napier, Mem., 730–810, q.v. for many biographical details. See also Introd. to Napier's " Dundee."

[13] See Ch. xvii.; but in this connection see Lord Napier's remonstrance and petition addressed to Lord Balmerino, Napier, Mem., 507.

[14] Lady Elizabeth, eldest daughter of John, eighth Earl of Mar. The marriage contract was signed May and June 1641. Lord Napier, her father-in-law, was in prison for the plot, and signs the contract in Edinburgh Castle, July 20, 1641, witnessed by Colonel Lindsay of Belstane, the keeper of the castle. On the 7th May 1645 " the Master of Napier's lady " and his sister Lilias are committed close prisoners to the same prison, but with the benefit of a serving-maid. A few days later the ladies are permitted to have the " benefit of the air " once or twice in the day, provided the constable of the Castle be with them, and Lord Napier and Keir be kept close in their chambers at

daughter, Stirling of Keir,[15] his brother-in-law, a gentleman of great worth, the chief of the name, and one who had suffered many heavy penalties for his affection to the King, together with his two sisters, one of them an excellent lady, the wife of Keir,[16] and the other yet unmarried, and threw them into a deep dungeon, where they lay till set at liberty by Napier himself under the victorious auspices of his uncle.

This battle at Auldearn was fought on May 9, 1645.[17]

the time. On 30th July an order was given to remove the ladies to the care of the Earl of Mar, under heavy caution. It would appear that for some reason this order was not carried out entirely, for these ladies, with other members of the family, were in prison at Linlithgow when the Master of Napier set them free after Kilsyth. While her husband was abroad, Lady Elizabeth, now Lady Napier, lived with her five children at Merchiston, saving what she could of their ruined property. She was there in 1650, and is thought to have provided the embroidered linen "with pearlings about" which Montrose wore on the scaffold. It was she who obtained the heart of Montrose and had it embalmed. See Napier, Mem., *passim*.

[15] See p. 31, *n*. 12. Stirling of Keir was at this time in Edinburgh Castle, and later on at Blackness.

[16] Lady Margaret, eldest daughter of Lord Napier by Lady Margaret Graham, wife of Sir George Stirling of Keir, was Montrose's niece. She was devotedly attached to Montrose, and suffered much in the troubles. Her portrait by Jamieson is preserved at Keir. It shows her brother's firmness of mouth and chin, but an expression of more humour and shrewdness. She was summoned before a Committee of Estates on the 9th May, when her brother was fighting so bravely at Auldearn, confined to her lodging on May 16th, but in consideration of the plague in the city, allowed on the 22nd to go to Merchiston, and keep within the house and yards thereof. She was afterwards a prisoner in Linlithgow, whence she was delivered by her brother and Nathaniel Gordon. She was with her father at his death, but was recalled by the Estates, and required to join her husband at St. Andrews. With him she was in exile in Holland.

[17] The 1756 edition gives 4th May, but see the Latin. Guthrie gives 4th, following *M. Redivivus*. Gardiner adopts 9th. See letter to Gordon of Buckie from Montrose, dated 10th May, the day after the battle. Napier, Mem., 596.

## CHAPTER XI.

*Hurry joined by Baillie—They challenge Montrose—March up to Badenoch—The enemy retreat to Inverness—March southwards to attack Lindsay—Desertion of the Gordons—Battle of Alford—Lord Gordon killed.*

AFTER allowing his men a few days' rest Montrose marched to Elgin, the chief town of the district, where he made a longer stay for the sake of his wounded men, who were here better supplied with surgeons and suitable medicines than it was often possible to procure in the field. They then crossed the Spey, and advanced through Keith and Frendraught to Strathbogie. Here Baillie, who had been joined by Hurry with the cavalry which had survived the slaughter at Auldearn,[1] encountered him, and endeavoured to provoke a battle. But Montrose restrained his men, though eager to fight, as they were spent with their vast labours, and far inferior in numbers, especially in cavalry, until he could raise new levies and recruit his forces. He therefore chose a position of great advantage, and contented himself with skirmishes at the outposts till the evening, when he marched off to Balveny, pursued by the enemy. From Balveny he passed through Strathdon[2] and Strathspey up into Badenoch. The enemy kept pace with him along the opposite bank of the river, and again endeavoured to force a battle on him, but without avail. But though he resolutely declined to risk a pitched battle, he harassed them by frequent skirmishes, and especially by night alarms, and so far weakened their power and courage, that those

---

[1] Baillie says that Hurry joined him with about 100 horse.
[2] Baillie says Glen Livet, which was the natural course. Strathdon would have meant a great detour. "We came in sight of them in Glen Livet, but that night they outmarched us and quartered some six leagues from us. On the next day we found they were dislodged, but could find nobody to inform us of their march, yet by the lying of the grass and heather we conjectured they were marched to the wood of Abernethy on Spey."

who but a short while before had been so proud and insolent, officers and men alike, were seized with panic, and at night retreated in disorder to Inverness, though none pursued.[3]

Montrose was not a little glad to have shaken them off, especially as the Earl of Lindsay,[4] who, next to his rival Argyll, was the chief leader of the Covenanters, being brother-in-law to the Duke of Hamilton, had been in the habit of declaring that Argyll, whether through want of care or courage, or for some other cause, had always failed. He had himself, therefore, taken command of the newly raised army, expecting to manage matters to better purpose under his own control. He had already crossed into Angus with his army, intending to act as a reserve to Baillie, and should Baillie fail, ready at least to prevent Montrose from crossing the Forth. They were, in fact, always in great fear that Montrose should come south of the Forth, and transfer the seat of war nearer to Edinburgh. Hearing that Lindsay was still in Angus, near the castle of Newtyle, Montrose resolved to crush him at once, as he was an inexperienced general, and his men as yet raw and unaccustomed to the hardships of war.

With this plan he set out from Badenoch, and crossing the Grampians through the Braes of Mar, reached the river Airlie[5] by difficult and long marches, intending to surprise the enemy. This could easily be done, as he had outmarched the news of his approach. Everything was ready for the attack, and Lindsay not more than seven miles distant, when the north-country forces, almost to a man, deserted, and returned home by the road they had just come. The reason of it was uncertain.[6] Lord Gordon

---

[3] Baillie gives no hint of these alarms, but says that while Montrose was getting meal from Ruthven and flesh from the country, he got none, and his horsemen professing that they had eaten nothing for forty-eight hours, he was compelled to march northwards to Inverness for supplies. Baillie's letter, quoted in Napier, Mem., 524.

[4] Lord Lindsay of the Byers, who had assumed the title Earl of Crawford by consent of the Estates, the veteran Earl having been attainted.

[5] The river Airlie must be the Isla. There is an old drove road from the Braes of Mar through the glen to the lower river, which is only about seven miles distant from Newtyle. Baillie says Montrose went as far south as Cupar in Angus. From Cupar by Blairgowrie and the Spital of Glenshee he marched into Mar.

[6] Did the Marquis of Huntly mean to hold to his commission as Lord-Lieutenant of the North, and fight only north of the Grampians, or was he alarmed at Baillie's movement on Gordon Castle

was in the camp, and no one was more deeply incensed at this treachery, in so much that Montrose could with difficulty restrain him from punishing with death those of his own followers who had deserted. Some, however, were of opinion that they had been seduced by the orders of Huntly, secretly transmitted to his son Aboyne, who was then absent from the army on sick-leave. Huntly's proud envious nature was wrung by the news of Montrose's success. He was evidently annoyed at the close friendship of his eldest son with him. Be that as it may, Montrose was so downcast by this unexpected misfortune, that he abandoned his intention of attacking Lindsay, and was forced to bear with patience the loss of a brilliant victory, thus snatched, as it were, from his grasp.

Obliged to change his plans, he sent off Colonel Nathaniel Gordon, a brave faithful gentleman, to his own country, where he had great influence, and himself followed him. By this time Baillie and Hurry had returned from Inverness, and were encamped by the river Dee in Lower Mar. Montrose marched through Glenshee and the Braes of Mar into the heart of the country called Cromar. On the road, as he passed through the Braes of Mar, he despatched Macdonald with a party into the most remote Highlands to bring the forces which were being raised there with the utmost speed to his camp. He then sent off Lord Gordon, who had great influence and authority in those parts, to help Nathaniel Gordon and hasten his levies. This he performed with diligence, and among others brought back his brother Aboyne. While this was going on in Cromar, Lindsay joined Baillie in Lower Mar. Montrose being much inferior to them in the absence of Gordon and Macdonald, with the greater part of his forces, fell back before them to the ruined castle of Kargarf, that the enemy might not catch him in an open country and overpower him with their multitude of horse and foot. Here he felt himself safe, being near the mountains. At this place Aboyne again fell sick, and went off to Strathbogie. Under pretence of requiring a guard, he took with him a considerable troop of horse, which his brother Gordon afterwards with no small difficulty induced to rejoin the colours.

Meantime Lindsay took from Baillie 1000 of his veterans in

exchange for some of his own raw recruits.[7] With these, as if bent on some brilliant exploit, he returned through the Mearns to Angus, but the only result of his grand effort was to range through Athole with his army, ravaging and burning the whole district. In this he imitated Argyll, who was the first to introduce that cruel dreadful practice of wreaking his fury on houses and crops, with more spirit to fire than fight, especially where he came on unprotected towns and fields.

Baillie at that time was on his way to besiege Huntly's castle of Bogie, the finest in all the north country,[8] intending, if he could not reduce it, to plunder and burn the lands of the Gordons in that neighbourhood. Montrose, though Macdonald was absent with a large part of his forces, was anxious to secure the favour of Huntly and his friends by any service in his power, and hastened to their assistance. Learning that Baillie's army consisted mostly of new levies (as he had transferred part of his veterans to Lindsay), he was eager to fight him at once, and marched straight towards him. He had not proceeded more than three miles when the enemy's advanced scouts came in sight. He therefore despatched a flying party, acquainted with the country, to reconnoitre the strength, position, and bearing of the enemy. They returned at once with information that the infantry were stationed on a hill two miles distant, and their horse had occupied and advanced beyond a narrow difficult pass, which lay about midway between the two armies.[9] Against these Montrose sent off what horse he had at hand, with some light musketeers. The enemy at first received them with light skirmishing at a distance, but presently fell back behind the pass, which they had strongly fortified with artillery.[10] Montrose then brought up his foot to dislodge them if possible, but without effect, for the combatants were separated by the approach of night, which both armies spent under arms. Next

[7] Baillie says he got only 400 recruits in exchange for some 1500 at least. The exchange was rendered necessary by discontent among the old soldiers. Gardiner's note as to Wishart here needs correcting.

[8] John Gordon of Buckie commanded at Gordon Castle, and had a hundred men nightly on the watch.

[9] The position was at the Kirk of Keith.

[10] Translated in former editions "musketeers," but this W. renders by *sclopetarii* above, and here uses *tormentarii*.

day Montrose sent a herald to offer them battle, but Baillie replied that he would not take his orders to fight from his enemy. As it was evident he could not drive them from the pass without great risk, he withdrew to Pitlurg,[11] to entice him out. Thence he turned off to the Castle of Druminnor,[12] belonging to Lord Forbes, where he halted two days. Here at last he was informed that the enemy had quitted their pass and were marching to Strathbogie; so at daybreak he proceeded towards the village of Alford. Baillie meantime, having received certain information that Macdonald was away in the Highlands with a considerable detachment, now gave chase, imagining that Montrose was in retreat, and came in sight about noon. Montrose, as they seemed to be advancing, resolved to await them on rising ground; but as they turned aside about three miles to the left, he continued his march to Alford, where he spent the night, some four miles distant from the enemy.

Early next morning Montrose ordered his men to get under arms ready for battle, and stationed them on a hill overlooking Alford. He was himself engaged with a troop of horse in observing the enemy's movements and bearing, and examining the fords[13] of the Don, which runs by Alford, when he was informed that their horse and foot were hastening to a ford a mile distant from Alford, to cut off his retreat in the rear, imagining that he was in full flight. Their fine precautions lured them on to their own destruction. Montrose left his squadron near the ford, with some picked men of experience, to bring him intelligence of all that happened, and returned alone to order his battle. His first care was to occupy the hill above Alford, where he meant to receive the enemy's charge, if they fell on briskly. Behind him was a marsh, intersected by ditches and pools, which secured him in the rear from cavalry. In front was a steep hill, which concealed him from the enemy, so that they could hardly see his front ranks.

---

[11] Pitlurg, a few miles south of Keith.

[12] Druminnor, some fifteen miles south of Pitlurg, the seat of Lord Forbes before Castle Forbes was built. By crossing Suie Hill, Alford was reached in seven or eight miles.

[13] See Gardiner, ii. 251 *n.* on fords of Don at Alford, with his criticism of W.'s account of the position. Is he quite sure of the hill on which Montrose was posted, or as to which ford he was facing?

Scarcely had he finished his dispositions, when the troop left at the ford returned at a gallop with intelligence that the enemy had crossed the river, so that neither army could now retreat without certain loss. It is reported that Baillie, who was an experienced and wary general, was forced into this engagement much against his will by the rashness of Lord Balcarras,[14] who commanded a regiment of horse, and precipitated himself and his regiment into the very danger Baillie strove to avoid, so that he could not be extricated without risking the whole army.

Montrose gave the command of his right wing, which was opposed by a superior force of the enemy's cavalry, to Lord Gordon, assisted by the veteran Colonel Nathaniel Gordon. The left he assigned to the Viscount Aboyne, supported by Sir William Rollock. The main body was commanded by the gallant Glengarry[15] and young Drummond of Balloch,[16] assisted by the quartermaster, George Graham, a skilful officer.[17] The reserve, completely concealed behind the hill, were intrusted to his nephew Napier. Montrose took his stand upon the rising ground, and the enemy halted in the hollow, protected by ditches and pools. For a while both sides paused; the one side deeming it unsafe to storm the hill, the other unwilling to attack an enemy intrenched among deep ditches and marshes. In infantry they were nearly equal, each having about 2000; but in cavalry Baillie was superior, having 600, while Montrose had only 250.[18] These, however,

---

[14] Alexander Lindsay, second Lord and first Earl of Balcarras, a dashing cavalry officer, who displayed much courage here and at Kilsyth. He was one of the sederunt of Scotch peers who sentenced Montrose to death.

[15] Angus Macdonald was now chief of Glengarry. His aged grandfather died at home on the day of the battle of Inverlochy. See Ch. viii. *n.* 2.

[16] Nephew of the first Lord Napier. Turner names him as the messenger sent from friends at Keir to Montrose on his first entry into Scotland, before the failure at Dumfries, to tell him that if he would come to Stirling "he would find town, castle, and regiment all for him, and Perth likewise." With Graham of Inchbrakie he defeated a party of Campbells stationed in Menteith (Ch. xix.), and with his cousin, the second Lord Napier, gallantly held Kincardine Castle against Middleton (p. 102, *n.* 12). He escaped to Norway with Montrose. See Index.

[17] George Graham, in terms of the capitulation of 1646, was included in the pardon list.

[18] See Gardiner on the number engaged. His note and the authorities he quotes tend to confirm W.'s estimate, though in the text he says it is impossible to speak of the numbers with even an approach to accuracy. It may be noted too, that while W. places Napier and the reserve alone in concealment behind the hill, Gardiner says that the army was so placed that the front ranks even

were loyal gentlemen, who served as volunteers, proud in the justice of their cause, eager for glory in the King's service, and ready to die rather than be conquered; whereas Baillie's were hirelings, who fought for pay, enlisted from the meanest classes. Moreover, Montrose was well aware that most of the veterans were away with Lindsay, and judging that this raw militia would be terrified by the shout of his men and the clang of his trumpets, and scarce able to withstand the first shock, he gave the signal to begin by leading his men down, relying on their courage and the justice of his cause. In an instant Lord Gordon charged furiously, but was stoutly met by the enemy, confident in their numbers. They were now at close quarters, fighting hand to hand so obstinately that none could advance a foot or nail's breadth but over the body of his foe, while retreat was impossible, so great was the crush of men pressing on behind. Lord Gordon and Colonel Nathaniel were the first to cut a lane for themselves and their men by a great slaughter of the enemy. Immediately the Colonel called out to the light musketeers, who as usual lined the horse, "Come, my men, down with those useless muskets and stab or hamstring the rebels' horses with your dirks." They obeyed with alacrity, when just at this moment Montrose suddenly brought up Napier and the reserve, which had lain concealed behind the hill. The enemy, terrified by their unexpected appearance, now broke and fled. Aboyne, on the left, contented himself with light skirmishing attacks of small parties, till the enemy, seeing their right wing routed and flying, retreated without much loss. The foot, being thus abandoned by their horse, for some time fought on doggedly, refusing quarter, and were almost all of them cut down. Their flying horse owed their safety mainly to the fate of Lord Gordon, who, after the victory had been gained, charged too fiercely into the thickest of the enemy, and was shot down by a bullet from one of the fugitives.[19] His fall checked his men in the pursuit, their

could hardly be seen. The advance of the reserve, hitherto concealed by the hill, was the decisive movement in the battle, but G. speaks of Colonel Gordon's order to the musketeers as the deciding point. W. seems to reflect on Aboyne's inactivity in the battle. G. does not mention it.

[19] On Lord Gordon see p. 87, *n.* 3. He had determined to carry off Baillie from the centre of his men, and, it is said, was in the act of seizing him by the sword-belt when the fatal bullet struck him. See Napier, Mem., 528.

whole attention being now turned to their dying lord. Aboyne, too, was so deeply distressed at his brother's fate that he could not push the pursuit with vigour.

In this battle Montrose lost not one common soldier, and of gentlemen only two, Culcholy and Milton, whose names and families I should have been glad to mention had they been known to me, as they died gallantly in battle for king and country, liberty and law.[20] Nor must we omit due praise to some Scotch and Irish boys, scarcely fourteen years of age, who threw off their masters' baggage, and mounting their nags and sumpter horses, not only led the enemy to take them for cavalry, but, as if to rival their masters in courage, these slight striplings charged into the thickest of the fray. A few of them were slain, but not without selling their lives dearly. Young as they were, they thus left an example of a high and noble spirit, such as even men might imitate.

The death of Lord Gordon was such a heavy blow to all, that they seemed more like a beaten army than victors in the battle. At the first news they were struck dumb with grief. Then their sorrow burst through all restraint and found vent in a universal wail of lamentation, and with streaming tears the soldiers, as soon as they could command words, broke out into reproaches against heaven and earth for bereaving the King and kingdom, their age, themselves and their children of so gallant a nobleman. Conquest and plunder were forgotten as they crowded round his lifeless body, kissing his face and hands, weeping over his wounds, praising the beauty of his person even in death, and extolling a nature as noble and generous as his birth and fortune. They even cursed a victory that was bought so dearly. Nothing could have supported the victorious army under this immense loss but

---

[20] Spalding gives the names Mowat of Balwholly and Ogilvy of Milton, and adds that they were buried in the church of Alford. Investigation kindly undertaken for us by the Rev. James Gillan, parish minister, has hitherto failed to discover any trace of the burial places of these gentlemen. Balwholly was a small property near Turriff, and Milton is Milton of Keith in Banffshire. An Irish Captain Dickson was killed at Alford; George Douglas (the Earl of Morton's brother), who bore the standard (v. p. 145), Colonel Gordon, Gordon younger of Gight, Hay of Dalgetty, and some other Gordons were wounded.

the presence of Montrose, whose safety brought gladness and revived their drooping spirits. Yet Montrose himself could not control his grief, but mourned bitterly over the melancholy fate of his dearest, only friend. Grievously he complained that the pride of his race, the ornament of the Scotch nobility, the stoutest champion of the royal authority in the north, his best and bosom friend, should be thus cut off in the very flower of his age. At last, relying on time and reason to assuage his grief, he ordered the physicians to embalm the corpse, which he then escorted to Aberdeen, to receive a magnificent funeral, with all the honours of war. Under his personal care it was buried in the Cathedral Church in his own family vault.[21]

This battle of Alford was fought on the 2nd of July, 1645.

---

[21] Lord Gordon was buried beside his mother in the Cathedral at Old Aberdeen. "The Marquis of Montrose himselfe, with all or at least the greater part of the armie, did accompanie the corps to the inteirment. Nor did he forbear to showe himselfe the cheife murner, and indeid their was reason for it, for never two of so short acquantance did ever love more dearlie. . . . After the funeral obsequies ware ended, there ware many that wreitt his praises." P. Gordon, 133-134, where see a specimen of the praises in verse. The funeral no doubt took place from the camp at Craigton, some eight or nine miles from Old Aberdeen. See Ch. xii. *n*. 3.

# CHAPTER XII.

March southwards to the Dee—Strong reinforcements from the Highlands—Convention of the Covenanters at Perth—Attack on Montrose's camp at Methven Wood—Montrose retreats to Little Dunkeld—Joined by the Gordons and Ogilvies—March into Strathearn.

ON the evening of the very day on which Montrose gained the battle of Alford, he marched to Cluny Castle,[1] where he allowed his men only a few hours' rest, and proceeded to the banks of Dee. Thence he despatched Viscount Aboyne,[2] who by his brother's death had succeeded to his title, into Buchan and the neighbourhood to raise recruits; for most of those who had been at the battle, being Highlanders, and not far from their own country, had gone home with their booty. As Macdonald had not yet returned, he encamped for some time at Craigston,[3] to

---

[1] Cluny Castle, the seat of Sir Alexander Gordon, a cousin of the Marquis of Huntly. Sir Alexander was at this time a prisoner in Edinburgh.

[2] James, Viscount Aboyne, was the second son of the Marquis of Huntly. When the title Viscount Aboyne was created for his father, the terms of the patent settled the succession on James and his heirs-male upon his father's death or succession to the Marquisate of Huntly. (See Douglas.) A steady Royalist, yet, as an officer of the King's Lieutenant, most untrustworthy and capricious, he seems never to have got over his defeat at the Bridge of Dee, and his conduct generally partakes of the Gordon puzzle. More than once he deserted Montrose at critical moments, and his departure before Philiphaugh ruined the cause in Scotland. In 1648 he was excepted from pardon, but made his escape to France, where he died of grief a few days after hearing of the death of the King. See Act. Parl. Scot., P. Gordon, Spalding, *passim*.

[3] The editor of Ruddiman's Wishart says that there was no Craigston on the Dee, and suggests Crabston as the site of the camp. Napier sought to remove this difficulty by making Montrose suddenly alter his route, and taking him thirty miles north to Craigston Castle, in Buchan, in three days, burying Lord Gordon with solemnity in Aberdeen within the time, and despatching Aboyne to raise recruits in the district, to which he himself would, according to the theory, be advancing. Gardiner has been misled by Napier.

"Craigston" is doubtless Craigton on the Dee, seven miles from Aberdeen, commanding the passage of the river between Peter Culter and Mary Culter, a strong position on the road south, and surrounded by the houses of Drum, Kincausie, and other friendly Irvines. The place is mentioned in a charter of 1526, when "Walter Caidyow de Cragtoune and Petyrcultyr" sold both properties to Alexander Irvine of Drum. See "Antiquities of Aberdeen and Banff," iii. 346. The minister of the parish informs us that it appears in the Kirk Session Records of Peter Culter in the seventeenth century. Montrose, writing from the place on the 6th, calls it Craigtoun. It is now the site of the

wait for him and Lord Aboyne; but finding, to his disappointment, that the recruits were not sent up as speedily as he had expected, he grew impatient of further delay at such an untimely moment, and crossing the Dee and the Grampians, he marched down into the Mearns, and halted at Fordounkirk, famous in olden times as the seat and burial-place of St. Palladius.[4] At the same time he ordered Aboyne, who had reached Aberdeen, to meet him in the Mearns with the levies he was reported to have raised. Aboyne obeyed, but brought very few forces with him. He therefore sent him back north, to get together all the forces he could, and bring them to his camp with all speed. He himself marched through Angus, where he met his cousin, Patrick Graham, with his Athole men, ready for everything, under his command. Macdonald also joined him with a fine body of Highlanders, among whom was Maclean,[5] a brave and most loyal man, with about 700 choice foot of his friends and clansmen; and also the chief of the Macranalds,[6] a man of renown among

---

Board school of the district. It lay directly in Montrose's route to the south from Cluny by the Loch of Skene and the Culter ferry and ford. On the south side of the river a road lay in front of him over the spur of the Grampians from Mary Culter to Stonehaven, which he could traverse till he branched off south of the hills towards Fordoun. If there is evidence of his army crossing at Mills of Drum (see Gardiner's map), he would have had to march some three or four miles farther up the river, which would not have increased the length of his march to Fordoun. Accepting Craigton as the site of the camp, all difficulties are removed concerning the funeral of Lord Gordon, the despatch of Aboyne, the waiting his return, the date of the letter to Inver, and the meaningless sudden rush to Buchan. See P. Gordon, p. 136, as to arrangements with Aboyne.

[4] Fordoun, a place of much interest in Scottish history. Roman camps succeeded Celtic circles, and St. Palladius is said to have settled here in the fifth century, "and his church occupied nearly the same romantic site as the present parish kirk. A copious well in front of the manse still preserves his name, as does also an annual market in the neighbourhood, commonly called Paddy fair" (Jervise, "Angus and Mearns," i. 142). Wishart had special cause for thinking of St. Palladius. "Wishart of Pitarrow (a branch of his family), the selfish and sacrilegious comptroller of James V., is said to have enriched his own coffers by seizing the holy casket (containing the saint's relics), and scattering its still more revered contents to the winds. But from that time, says an old writer, the family never prospered."—*Ibid*. It was the birthplace (*ca*. 1350) of John de Fordun, the celebrated author of the "Scotichronicon;" also of George Wishart, the reformer and martyr.

[5] Sir Lachlan Maclean of Duart, the brave chief of the clan. Maclean of Lochbuy and the Captain of Cairnburgh accompanied Duart. In a list of the clans, said at the time to have been verified by Lord Brentford, the Macleans are reckoned able to muster 2000 for the Royal cause (Napier, Mem., 654). Sir Lachlan received a "remission" in 1647, but in 1648-49 he was again in difficulties through his raid upon Maclean of Torloisk, whom he shut up in Cairnburgh.

[6] See p. 79, *n*. 3. In the list referred to in preceding note, Clanranald is credited with power to raise 1300 men, while Antrim and Sir James Macdonald were expected to bring of the name 4000 more to the field. *Cf*. later lists given in "Grameid," Book IV.

the Highlanders, and devoted to the King's cause, with over 500 men; and the Macgregors and Macnabs, inferior to none in courage and endurance, who, after the custom of their country, followed their leaders and chieftains; but I am unable to give their exact numbers. Glengarry,[7] too, who deserves the highest praise for his bravery, loyalty, and devotion to Montrose himself, whom he had never left since the expedition into Argyle, had summoned about 500 through his uncles and others subordinate to him. Besides these, there were a number of the Farquharsons from the Braes of Mar, excellent men, of approved valour; and also some from Badenoch, few, but energetic and prompt in action.

Montrose, thus strongly reinforced, resolved to penetrate into the heart of the kingdom, not only to hinder the enemy's levies in Fife and south of Forth, but also to disperse the Convention of Estates, which the Covenanters had summoned, with great solemnity and ostentation, to meet at Perth.[8] There was now nothing to stop him but the want of cavalry, which almost always rendered it unsafe for him to descend into the Lowlands; but as he expected Aboyne and Airlie soon with a considerable body of horse, he crossed the Tay at Dunkeld, and approached the Almond, to the great dismay of the enemy at Perth. He then advanced still nearer, and encamped in the wood of Methven.

The enemy's foot, with the exception of the garrison of Perth, were encamped south of the River Earn.[9] The horse, appointed to guard the town and Convention, observing Montrose's scouts, rode back in hot haste with word that he was close at hand, and would soon be at the gates, and without doubt intended to besiege and storm the town. The nobility and members of the Convention were therefore urged to save themselves at once by flight, although Montrose had scarcely 100 horse, and they over 400. Next day, to increase their panic, he himself approached the town with these

---

[7] For Glengarry and his uncles see p. 79, *n.* 3.

[8] The adjourned Parliament could not sit at Edinburgh for the plague, but assembled in Stirling Castle, July 2nd, where General Baillie and Balcarras gave an account of their defeat at Alford. On the 12th signs of plague at Stirling caused an adjournment to Perth for the 24th, when all "noblemen, gentlemen, and heritors whatsoever were ordered to be there in person well mounted." Guthrie, Mem., 189-190.

[9] The chief position was at Kilgraston, near Bridge of Earn, on level ground.

horsemen, and the like number of light musketeers mounted on baggage horses, and displayed his men to advantage, so as to give them the appearance of a considerable body. As the enemy kept within the gates, he turned off towards Dupplin, and scoured the whole of the strath, as though he had horse enough to command the whole district. By this stratagem, the enemy were led to suppose that he was as strong in horse as in foot. They therefore gathered all the forces they could to oppose him, should he attempt to cross the Forth. But as it was unsafe for him to descend into the plains, both parties kept their positions for several days, the Covenanters awaiting levies from Fife, the country south of Forth, and from the west, and Montrose expecting reinforcements from the north. As Aboyne, whom he awaited with impatience, was too slow in coming up with his men, he sent to hasten his movements before they should lose this favourable opportunity. He complained, but in gentle, courteous language, as to a friend, that his delay and hesitation had caused him to forego a brilliant victory over the rebels, which might possibly have finished the war; but he did not doubt that they might yet atone for this loss, if he would act with speed and energy.

When the enemy discovered that he had deceived them with a sham muster of horse, and as their levies from all sides had come in, and they were now far superior in infantry as well, they required no further invitation to fight, and resolved to force him to a battle. He therefore decided to retire for a while to the mountains, knowing that the enemy would never dare to follow him, or, if they did, it would cost them dear. Accordingly, as they approached Methven in full force, he ordered his baggage to hasten secretly to the hills, while he himself drew out his army as if to fight, strengthened the approaches by very strong guards, and disposed his horse in front. The enemy felt confident that he meant to risk a battle, but it was only a feint to gain time till the baggage was out of danger. He then ordered his army to close up and march off rapidly in a single column. The horse, and some of the most active musketeers, were charged with the duty of bringing up the rear and covering the retreat from the enemy's cavalry. The enemy, who had expected that a battle was imminent, when they saw them suddenly retreating, pursued, at first briskly, but without effect, for Montrose's men occupied the passes in their line of march, and easily repulsed them. Thus, without the loss of a single man, they made good their retreat to high ground, inaccessible to the enemy's horse, where they were also safe from any attack of their foot.

It is worthy of mention that as Montrose's horse were approaching the passes, the enemy, well aware that they could pursue them no farther, that they might not, with all their efforts, seem to have accomplished nothing, charged with 300 of their bravest and best horse, who came up with a loud shout and jeering. Observing them, Montrose picked out twenty of his Highlanders, accustomed to hunting and excellent marksmen, and ordered them to check their insolence. Scattering at first, they crept forward with their guns concealed, and took such good aim that they brought down the most forward of their pursuers. As these were men of some note among them, the rest took a lesson from their fate, and were glad to fall back. But those good huntsmen, flushed with their first success, now followed them into the open ground and resolutely attacked the party, who, spurring furiously, fled headlong like a herd of deer before the hunters.

The enemy on their return encamped in the wood of Methven, on the same spot which Montrose had quitted. As they had done nothing of note in their expedition, and could not face men, they wreaked their rage upon women, most foully and shamefully butchering all they could lay hands on of the wives of the Irish and Highlanders, who followed the camp for love of their husbands.[10]

Montrose took up his quarters at Little Dunkeld,[11] the ground there being unfit and impassable for horse, and also because it was the most convenient spot to wait for the recruits whom he daily expected from the north with Lord Aboyne. During this time

---

[10] W. seems the sole authority for this tale of massacre, for Monteith is scarcely to be reckoned original, with W. before him. W.'s account implies a hurried retreat. Guthrie, 151, says Montrose "retired at his leisure, without loss or affront." The conduct of the Irish shortly afterwards at Tullybody (*ib.* 152) shows great exasperation. *Cf.* Ch. xiii. *n.* 5.

[11] South of the Tay, opposite Dunkeld.

the two armies lay at no great distance from each other, watching one another without any attempt at active hostilities.

At last Lord Aboyne and Colonel Nathaniel Gordon arrived at Dunkeld with their northern levies. They were fewer than had been expected, but their stoutness and true courage made some amends for the lack of numbers. They brought only 200 horse and 120 musketeers mounted on pack-horses or ponies, but no infantry besides. With them came the Earl of Airlie and his son Sir David, with eighty horse, most of them gentlemen of the family of Ogilvy; among whom was Alexander, the eldest son of Sir John of Inverquharity,[12] a youth who was not only distinguished for his handsome person and noble race, but famous beyond his years for courage and success in arms. With these reinforcements Montrose determined to lose no time in marching on the enemy; but when he reached the river Almond,[13] he heard a vague rumour that many of their late auxiliaries had deserted their quarters and gone home. To test the truth of these reports, he resolved first to reconnoitre. He therefore ordered his foot to rest, and before sunset rode up with his cavalry into full view. The enemy, taken by surprise, kept within their lines. Early next morning he again rode out to reconnoitre, and was informed that they had hastily decamped from Methven at dead of night, and crossed the river Earn[14] in disorder. Instantly he marched his men forward, and crossing the river by a stone bridge[15] six miles farther up, he lay that night in Strathearn.

---

[12] If not eldest born, he was eldest living, and styled "Younger of Inverquharity" in Act. Parl. David, second baronet, was his junior. Alexander joined Montrose at the Law of Dundee (p. 65), and was wounded at the battle of Aberdeen. See deposition of James Ramsay of Ogill, who "saw him in the morning of the conflict," and was afterwards sent for in Angus "to pans him (dress his wound), and he affirmed to me he had gotten the wound at Aberdeen." Napier, Mem., 457.

[13] Logie Almond, lying directly between Little Dunkeld and Methven Wood, was the ford for passing the Almond.

[14] They retreated on their main position at Kilgraston, which they intrenched (Guthrie, Mem., 161).

[15] Between Dupplin and Forteviot. He would cross Tippermuir to reach the bridge.

## CHAPTER XIII.

*The Fife men join the Covenanters—Montrose marches to Kinross—Crosses the Forth—Battle of Kilsyth, and utter rout of Baillie, August 1645.*

THE shire of Fife is the most populous and richest in Scotland, with more towns, villages, and hamlets than any other. The inhabitants are far from warlike, being mostly merchants, shopkeepers, sailors, and farmers. Of all men they are the most addicted to the new superstitions. Seduced by the example and influence of the nobility, and fascinated by the seditious sermons of their preachers, they had early, almost to a man, gone over to the Covenanters. The county is a peninsula, bounded on the south by the Firth of Forth, on the north by the river Tay, which admits ships of the greatest burden, and on the east by the ocean. The only entry by land is therefore on the west side, a narrow strip of land, in which both armies were at this time stationed.

The whole country was now in an uproar. Their fine ministers were especially busy thundering out excommunications. Some were raising the country in arms, without regard for age or rank. Some flocked in numbers to their call; others ran about in distraction to hide themselves, each as he was moved by superstition, confidence, or fear.

Montrose was eager to fight a decisive battle, before the levies from Fife should swell their numbers; but owing to the nature of the ground and the narrowness of the passes, the enemy were so strongly posted, that it was quite impossible for him to get at them or draw them out. Accordingly, after twice offering them battle, he resolved to push on into the heart of the country, and advanced to Kinross,[1] his object being to hinder the levies of this district,

---

[1] He passed between Kilgraston and the hills to Dron, where he lay in a strong position between the enemy and their Fife levies. He marched through Glen Farg to Kinross.

and draw the enemy out of their fastness to help their distressed friends. They allowed him to march past without daring even to harass his rear, and immediately turned off and hastened to the east part of Fife, keeping close along the rivers Earn and Tay.

On the march Montrose sent Nathaniel Gordon and Sir William Rollock forward with a small troop of horse. This party separated and scoured the country to obtain more accurate information, so that only ten men remained with the Colonel and Sir William. Suddenly they fell in with a recruiting party of the enemy, 200 strong, many of them mounted. Retreat was impossible; so these twelve men charged the 200, put them to flight, killed several, and took others prisoners.[2]

Montrose reached Kinross that evening. As the people of Fife were extremely adverse to the King, enslaved by superstition and their zeal for the Covenant, he made no doubt that they were now all in arms. As it would be imprudent to engage with such a multitude of horse and foot, he decided to cross the Forth. His object was to wear out the men of Fife by long fatiguing marches without a battle, rightly guessing that nothing but force could induce them to follow beyond their own boundaries. Most of them, being born and bred artisans, shopmen, and sailors, would, he expected, prove unfit for hard service, and soon grow sick of it. Moreover, the rebel noblemen, as soon as they saw, to their dismay, the war transferred to the Forth, began with greater zeal than ever to enrol soldiers in the Borders and west of Scotland. Foremost amongst these were the Earls of Lanark, Cassilis,[3] and

---

[2] This story, together with that of the last chapter, where twenty Highland hunters put 300 cavalry to flight, is by some considered fabulous. See Napier, Mem., 537, *n.*

[3] John, sixth Earl of Cassilis, called the Solemn Earl, was one of the first members of the Covenanting party. He joined in 1633 with Rothes in the petition which the King returned, saying, "No more of this, my Lord, I command you." He was an ardent Presbyterian, a ruling elder, and commissioner to the Westminster Assembly in 1643. He and the Rev. R. Baillie were sent to the Hague in 1649, where they delivered their message to the King. The language of it concerning Montrose is atrocious. He became Justice-General in 1649. After the Restoration he was named one of the four extraordinary lords; but as he insisted on taking the oath of allegiance with a caveat, he was superseded in 1662. He moved an address to the King that he should marry a Protestant, but had only one vote on his side. For himself and his family he is said to have secured a promise under the King's hand that they should not be disturbed in serving God any way he pleased. The Earl died in 1668. Douglas' Peerage, Baillie's Letters, Guthrie, &c.

Eglinton.[4] To prevent their levies, or prevail on them to join his cause before they could unite with Bailie and the men of Fife, were the objects to which Montrose turned his attention. He therefore set out from Kinross, and marched towards Stirling,[5] where he halted for the night, three miles from that town. Next day he sent his foot on in front, and followed slowly with his horse, suspecting that the enemy were pressing on his steps. In this his judgment was not at fault. The scouts in his rear brought word that Baillie was not far off, with the most powerful army he had ever had. Immediately afterwards the foremost scouts of the enemy came in sight. One of them, advancing incautiously, was taken by Montrose's horse and brought to him. Being examined, he told them freely and frankly that he believed Baillie intended to march all that night, to force him to an engagement before the Fife men were sent home, as they were already tired out, and could, he thought, scarcely be forced to cross the Forth, as they were satisfied with the retreat of the enemy from their own borders.[6] Montrose at once resolved to cross the Forth, and urged his men to march apace. Passing by Stirling, with its strong royal castle, which was then held by a powerful garrison of the enemy, he crossed the river that night by a ford four miles above the town. At dawn next day he made a brief halt six miles from Stirling,

---

[4] Alexander, sixth Earl of Eglinton, called Grey Steel, was associated with Cassilis and Rothes in the early movements of the party. He took part as a ruling elder in the Assembly which framed the Solemn League and Covenant, and voted in the Parliament which surrendered the King to the English. He fought at Marston Moor with the Scots, while his son and successor, Hugh, was fighting as a Royalist. He opposed the Engagement, siding actively with Argyll. To Charles II., as King of Scots, he became captain of horse guards. In 1651 he was surprised at Dumbarton by a party of English, and remained in prison till the Restoration. He died in 1661, aged seventy-three. Douglas' Peerage, Baillie's Letters, Index, &c.

[5] In reprisal for Argyll's doings in Mull, Maclean ravaged the parishes of Muckart and Dollar and burnt Castle Campbell. Macdonald's Irish plundered Alloa from Tullibody Wood, where they were quartered. Montrose and his cavalry officers received hearty hospitality from Lord Mar and his family at Alloa Castle, and Macdonald moved on towards Stirling. The point of passage of the Forth is uncertain. Guthrie, who was minister of Stirling at the time, says Montrose passed over Teith and Forth two miles above Stirling, avoiding the town on account of the plague. Menstry and Aithry were burned by Argyll, and Alloa threatened. The march of both armies to Kilsyth was by Denny.

[6] Guthrie, 153. They were on the point of mutiny, when "their leaders set their ministers to deal with them, who told them jolly tales" of the expected reinforcements from the West. (Guthrie is not altogether an independent authority. His errors of date follow the *M. Redivivus*, and show that he used it in his Mem.)

where he was informed that the enemy had not crossed the Forth that night, but had bivouacked about three miles from Stirling on the other side of the river. He resumed his march, and encamped at Kilsyth, on the field of the desperate battle. Here he ordered his men to rest, but to be ready to fight or march at a moment's notice. Meanwhile, the enemy crossed the Forth at Stirling Bridge, and towards evening encamped about three miles from Kilsyth.

During this, the Earl of Lanark, brother of the Duke of Hamilton, had gathered a force of 1000 foot and 500 horse from the friends and vassals of the Hamiltons in Clydesdale and the neighbourhood, and was now not more than twelve miles from Kilsyth. The Earls of Cassilis, Eglinton, and Glencairn,[7] and other rebel noblemen, were also busy raising the people of the west for the same unholy war. As these places had hitherto escaped the horrors of war, they were ready enough to take up arms. After weighing the matter, Montrose deemed it absolutely necessary to fight a decisive battle with Baillie and his present army, though superior in numbers, before they could unite with Lanark and the rest of their forces. Delay would either involve him in a much more desperate struggle, or compel him to abandon the fruits of his toil, and retreat to the Highlands, with the loss of the prestige gained by so many victories. On the other hand, the enemy, proudly confident in their numbers, and imagining that Montrose had for some days been marching in hot haste to escape, and had crossed the Forth through fear and not design, were determined to fight on the spot, and attack him in the strong positions he had chosen. Flushed with vain hopes, their chief

---

[7] William, ninth Earl of Glencairn. Though he voted for the Solemn League and Covenant, he opposed the sending of an army into England to assist the Parliament. He voted for the surrender of the King to the English, but heartily joined the Engagement. In 1649 the Parliament annulled his patent. When Scotland was in the hands of Cromwell, Glencairn received a commission from the King to command all the forces in Scotland, and raised a Highland army in 1653 which gave much trouble to General Monk. General Middleton was put over him in 1654. Soon after his arrival Glencairn fought his famous duel with Sir George Monro, and afterwards retired to his house. He was excepted from pardon by Cromwell in 1654, but was one of the peers called to convention by Monk on his way south in 1659. After the Restoration he succeeded Loudon as Chancellor, and died at Belton, in East Lothian, in 1664. Douglas' Peerage, Guthrie, Mem., Index, and Gwynne Mem. (Ed. Sir W. Scott, 1822).

anxiety was to cut off all retreat, or prevent his return to the Highlands. Some, however, have asserted that Baillie himself had resolved not to fight, but was obliged to yield to the authority and influence of the Earl of Lindsay and other noblemen[8] in the army, who compelled him, much against his will, to draw up his men. Be that as it may, at dawn they marched straight up against Montrose. Seeing this, he remarked that this was just what he most desired; the advantage of ground now made up for the want of men. He therefore hastened to seize the commanding points. He also ordered all his men, horse and foot, to throw off their heavier garments, and fight in white, stripped to their shirts.[9] They obeyed with cheerful alacrity, and thus disencumbered, they stood ready for battle, determined to conquer or die.

On the battlefield were some cottages and country gardens, a point of vantage which Montrose had occupied with a small guard.[10] The first effort of the enemy was to dislodge them, and they came on resolutely, but were received with courage. As the vigour of

---

[8] After his defeat at Alford, Baillie was controlled by a committee consisting of Argyll, Lindsay, Burleigh, Tullibardine, Balcarres, and Elcho. Baillie, impressed with the thought that the loss of the day would be the loss of the kingdom, would have approached with caution, but the noblemen feared only the escape of Montrose. Could they from the east reach a hill which sloped down upon Montrose's left flank in the west, they thought they might reckon with their foe. Baillie knew the danger of moving an army across an enemy's front, and protested, but obeyed. His hopes then lay n keeping out of sight while the operation was in progress. He endeavoured to conceal the movement behind the crest of the hill, but some of his men, by attacking an advance post of the enemy, drew a party of Highlanders upon them, and the rivalry of the Macleans and Macdonalds for the lead brought on a general attack before Baillie could reach the proposed position. The headstrong conduct of the Highlanders would have proved fatal to Montrose but for the indiscipline of the Covenanters and the brilliant charge of Lord Airlie. As it was, the Highlanders cut through the centre of Baillie's army, while the Gordons and Ogilvies routed the van. By this time the reserve were beginning to consult safety in flight. See Gardiner, Civil War, ii. 269-272; Napier, Mem., 539, with their authorities; P. Gordon, 139; Baillie, 420.

[9] For light on vexed questions of Highland costume see Skene's "Highlanders," and Notes in "Grameid." It should be understood that the main covering of the Gael, when employed in active work, was a strong coarse linen shirt—the material called *haaren*—steeped in a solution of tar or cow-dung. Philip, in the "Grameid," constantly describes the appearance of a body of Highlanders as a "saffron host," from the yellow hue of this garment. See Grameid, p. 54. They wore over this a waistcoat, and when travelling, or at kirk or market, a plaid, which, when belted, gave the appearance of the modern kilt. They never fought with a plaid about them, and generally cast off their shoes for the fray. If the ground were rough or covered with brush, or a race was to be run, like that at Kilsyth between Macleans and Macdonalds, the long shirt tails could be tied up out of the way, as the Clanranald MS. says they were on this occasion. *Cf.* the supporters in the Arms of Cluny Macpherson.

[10] Maclean of Treshnish, called Captain of Cairnburgh, held the post with a hundred men. They were in sight of the main body of the Macleans under Duart, and young Donald Moydartach of the rival Clanranald was near at hand, jealous of the opportunities of the Macleans.

their attack began to slacken, the defenders in their turn attacked and routed them, cutting them down without resistance. Animated by this success, the Highlanders who were near, without waiting for the word of command, charged up the hill, and fell headlong [11] on the entire army of the enemy. Montrose, though somewhat disconcerted by their untimely boldness, felt obliged to support them; and indeed it is hard to say whether their safety was due more to the cowardice of the enemy or the promptness of this aid. His whole army consisted of only 500 horse and 4400 foot, of whom 1000 or more by their own error had exposed themselves to the enemy, whose forces numbered 6000 foot and 800 horse. But as their rear were slow to advance, while their van halted till they should close up, Montrose had time to bring assistance to his men in peril. At last, however, he observed three troops of horse, followed by 2000 foot, despatched against the reckless detachment, whose fate seemed sealed. Several of his officers flatly refused the task of supporting them. He turned to Airlie. "You see, my Lord, those rash men of ours have plunged into desperate danger, and will soon be cut to pieces by the cavalry, unless at once supported. All eyes and hearts are upon your Lordship, as the only man fit for the honour of beating back the enemy, saving our comrades, and repairing by your cool veteran courage the error of their headstrong youth." With the utmost cheerfulness Airlie undertook this most difficult service, and at once rode off with a troop of his own horse, commanded by John Ogilvy of Baldovie,[12] a gallant and experienced officer, who had formerly been a colonel in the Swedish service. The enemy charged the Ogilvies. There was a fierce struggle, but they could not long withstand their bravery, and faced about, hotly pursued by the Ogilvies, who drove them back upon their own foot, and in one sweeping charge hurled the whole mass into confusion and rode them down. The splendid example of Airlie and his Ogilvies inspired Montrose's men with increasing courage. They could be held in no longer.

---

[11] "They leapt over the dyke, and with down heads fell on and broke these regiments."—*Baillie's Narrative.*

[12] John Ogilvy of Baldovie. He was eventually pardoned, and after the Restoration became a J.P. for Forfarshire. His house was about four miles from Dundee.

With a mighty shout, as though they had already won the day, they fell upon the enemy. The rebel horse could not long resist the onset, and scattered like chaff, leaving the foot to shift for themselves. The foot, after a faint resistance, soon threw down their arms and fled for their lives. In vain they sought to escape. The victors pursued them for fourteen miles, and cut them down. Of their entire force scarce a hundred foot are said to have got off safe. Their horse did not escape unpunished. Many were killed, others taken, and the rest scattered in every direction. Their whole baggage and arms fell into the hands of the conquerors. Montrose lost only six men, three of whom were Ogilvies, gallant gentlemen,[13] who sealed with their blood the brilliant victory to which they had cut the way.

Of the Covenanting nobles, who were present in large numbers at this battle, some saved themselves by a timely flight, and, thanks to their good horses, reached the strong castle of Stirling. Others slipped away to the Firth of Forth, and got aboard some vessels at anchor near the shore. Among these was Argyll, who now, for the third time, took boat and escaped aboard a ship. Even then he did not think himself safe till they had weighed anchor and stood away far out to sea.

Among the prisoners were Sir William Murray of Blebo,[14] James Arnot,[15] brother of Lord Burleigh, and Colonels Dick[16] and Wallace,[17] with very many more, all of whom Montrose treated with generosity and dismissed on parole.

This is the famous victory at Kilsyth, which was fought on the 16th of August 1645.[18] Of the rebels 6000 are said to have fallen in the battle.

---

[13] Inquiry has not been able to rescue the names of these gallant gentlemen from oblivion.

[14] Sir William Murray of Blebo does not appear under that designation in any authority we have consulted. Blebo, in Fife, belonged at one time to the Bethunes.

[15] James Arnot of Fernie, in Fife, the father-in-law of the Lyon King, Sir James Balfour of Denmylne.

[16] A Colonel William Dick was successful in gaining payment of arrears to the extent of £3732 in 1647, and gets a letter to the English Parliament asking for some consideration for his past services. Act. Parl. Scot., VI. i. 756.

[17] A Colonel Wallace petitions in 1650 for reparation of losses. In 1669 he is summoned as a rebel. Was he the Colonel James Wallace who commanded the Covenanters at Rullion Green?

[18] The date was August 15. W. is often inaccurate in his use of the Latin calendar.

## CHAPTER XIV.

Flight of the Covenanting Lords—Montrose enters Glasgow—Joined by many noblemen—Edinburgh surrenders and releases the Royalist prisoners—Settlement of the west country.

THE victory at Kilsyth changed the face of affairs throughout the whole kingdom. The Covenanting lords dispersed in the greatest terror, some to Berwick or Carlisle, others to Newcastle, and others to Ireland. Those who had hitherto concealed their favour to the King's cause no longer feared to show themselves openly, with protestations of loyalty, public prayers for the King's safety, and offers of help. Those who had fought for the Covenant began to beg for pardon, pleading in excuse that the violence and cruel tyranny of the rebels had forced them to it; they now submitted themselves and their estates to the victor, humbly beseeching his protection, and imploring his wonted clemency. Commissioners were also sent from the most distant shires and cities,[1] to profess their allegiance to the King, their duty and service to his vicegerent, and also to offer help in arms, provisions, men, and other necessaries of war. The nobility of the realm and chiefs of clans hastened in great numbers to pay court to the Lord Governor, and were loud in their congratulations on his brilliant success. He received them all with courtesy, and granted them his protection, a free pardon and immunity for the past, and words of kind encouragement. The utmost penalty he imposed on them was to exchange the rapacious and cruel tyranny

---

[1] According to Guthrie, the shires of Linlithgow and Renfrew and the towns of Irvine and Ayr sent commissioners, and Glasgow within two days of the battle sent Sir Robert Douglas and Mr. Archibald Fleming to congratulate Montrose on his victory. See also letter to the magistrates of Glasgow from Kilsyth (Napier, Mem., 553). Macdonald, who was sent to secure the peace of the south-west, met with a hearty welcome, even at Loudon Castle, where the Chancellor's lady embraced him, and having entertained him very sumptuously, sent her servant John Halden with him to present her service to the Marquis.

of the rebels for the gentle government and protection of his most gracious Majesty. He entreated them to forget their former animosities, and observe for the future more religiously their loyalty and duty to the best of kings, and not allow themselves again to be embroiled in the plots of seditious traitors, whose only aim was to satisfy their own lusts, to gratify which they had set the King and his subjects against each other, and well nigh ruined both. "For his own part," he said, "his sole object and desire had ever been to rescue, by force of arms, since no other means remained, their religion, king, and liberty, to free his peers and all the people from the tyranny of rebels, and restore the ancient peace, prosperity, and splendour of the realm. Should he succeed, he would give Almighty God, the author of all good things, his everlasting thanks. Should he fail, he was resolved at any rate to do his duty to God, to the King, his vicegerent on earth, and to all good men, and by his sincere endeavours stand clear in conscience and credit with all men, both now and hereafter."

The whole kingdom now rang with Montrose's praise. His lofty character, towering above all equals, his gallantry in war, endurance in toil, patience in difficulties, wisdom in counsel, his good faith with those that submitted, his rapidity in action, and his clemency to prisoners, in a word, the heroism which shone through all his deeds were the theme of every tongue, in every rank of men. Most were sincere in their admiration, though some, it is true, merely feigned applause. Some even, according to their wit or skill, expressed their admiration in poems and panegyrics.[2] Such are the changes and chances of human affairs, and, above all, the fickleness of popular esteem, that men now openly dared to curse Argyll, Balmerino, Lindsay, Loudon, and the other ringleaders of the Covenanters, whom they had lately revered and courted as deities, but now reviled as the authors of all their miseries.

Everything was thus succeeding to Montrose's wish. The

---

[2] Have any of these come down to us? See Preface. Montrose invited Drummond of Hawthornden to come to his leaguer at Bothwell, and bring with him his loyal "Pieces," and his "Irene," that he "might give order for the putting them to the press." For this letter and the poet's reply see Napier, Mem., 564. Zachary Boyd wrote "Carmina in Iac. Montirosam."

northern parts of the kingdom were secured behind him. The road to the south lay open. Everywhere the strength of the Covenanters was broken. Their leaders, whose guilty consciences despaired of pardon, were driven from the realm. But though they had now no regular army, the west was still in commotion. There the Earls of Cassilis and Eglinton and other promoters of the Covenant were engaged in inciting the counties to renew the war, and were reported to have raised a tumultuous body of about 4000 men. Montrose therefore, the day after the battle of Kilsyth,[3] led his forces to Clydesdale, where the Earl of Lanark had been levying soldiers, but on tidings of the victory he disbanded his men and fled. This position Montrose chose as the most advantageous for his affairs, both in the south and west. Thence he went to Glasgow, the chief town of the county, which surrendered. Amidst the joyous acclamations of the people he entered the city, having first ordered his men to refrain from acts of violence. Offenders were dealt with severely;[4] flagrant disobedience was punished with death, as a warning to others. As a favour to the inhabitants, he then left the town on the second day after his arrival, intending to camp at Bothwell. As this was only about six miles from the city, he allowed the citizens a garrison of their own, to guard them against any outbreak of military license. By such acts of clemency and favour he hoped to win the hearts, not only of the people of Glasgow, but also of other towns, more effectually than by force of arms.

He remained a considerable time at Bothwell,[5] where he received many of the nobility, some in person, others represented by their friends and deputies. The counties and towns, which were now eager in professions of loyalty and obedience, were reassured. Among the first to wait on him with offers of assist-

---

[3] Guthrie says two days. He left on the 17th, according to both authorities, if W. means what he says in dating the battle on the 16th.

[4] This agrees with Montrose's dying speech. Ruddiman's translation is fearfully wrong here, implying that his entry into Glasgow was followed by severe dealings and execution of suspected rebels.

[5] Montrose was at Bothwell from Glasgow on August 20th, when he gives his order to the Master of Napier and Col. Nat. Gordon for the release of prisoners in Linlithgow and Edinburgh. He broke up his camp there on Sept. 4th.

ance were the Marquis of Douglas,[6] chief of the noble and ancient family of that name, the Earls of Linlithgow,[7] Annandale,[8] and Hartfell,[9] the Lords Seton,[10] Drummond,[11] Fleming,[12] Maderty,[13] Carnegie,[14] and Johnston;[15] Hamilton of Orbiston,[16] Charters of

---

[6] William, eleventh Earl of Angus, created Marquis of Douglas in 1633. He maintained at Castle Douglas, with his numerous family about him, a grand hospitality worthy of the great house of which he was the chief. Whether from disinclination or from his settling into Roman Catholicism, he became estranged from politics. In 1639 he was expected to rise for the King, but on the approach of the Covenanters, says Baillie, "the courage of the Marquis failed him, and he fled; so without din the house was rendered and manned by us." He came back to Douglas Castle, "but kept himself out of the broils of those times as much as any of his quality in the kingdom" (Crawford's Peerage). After Philiphaugh he compounded with the ruling authority, was later on fined £1000 by Cromwell, and died in 1660, in his seventy-first year. For a sketch of his life see Masson's "Drummond of Hawthornden," 313.

[7] George, third Earl of Linlithgow, b. 1616, d. 1690, is doubtless meant by *Limmucensis*. Did W. coin this Latin word for Linlithgow? *Llyn* in Welsh means a lake. The Earl was colonel of a regiment, but was held in some suspicion by the Covenanters. Douglas says he suffered much hardship for his attachment to the royal family. He was keeper of Linlithgow Palace. The inventory of furniture in his use in the palace (Spottiswoode, Miscellany, i. 370) is a curious and interesting document. He was a witness against Argyll and Warriston at their trial. At the Revolution he was deprived of the office of Justice-General, which he had held from 1681.

[8] James Murray, second Earl of Annandale, succeeded his father in 1641. He joined with Morton, Carnwath, and others in a letter to the Queen on Scotch affairs. For this he was summoned to appear before the Estates, but the business was made up. After Philiphaugh he fled to England, where he lived privately till his death in 1658.

[9] James Johnston of Johnston was raised to the peerage by Charles I. at his coronation in 1633 as Lord Johnston of Lockwood, and in 1643 he was created Earl of Hartfell. He was imprisoned in 1644 as a favourer of Montrose. After Philiphaugh he was sentenced to death at St. Andrews, but escaped through the favour of Argyll. He was nephew of the potent Johnston of Warriston. He died in 1653.

[10] George, eldest son of George, third Earl of Winton, styled Lord Seton. He had been imprisoned in May, and fined £40,000 Scots for his loyalty, involving a sale of part of his estates, Winchburgh and Niddrie. After Philiphaugh he was imprisoned at St. Andrews and Edinburgh, and only liberated on his father giving a bond of £100,000 Scots for his appearance when called. He died in 1648, *æt.* 35. His son George became fourth Earl of Winton in 1650.

[11] James Lord Drummond, eldest son of the Earl of Perth, who had commanded the Covenanters' horse at Tippermuir.

[12] John, eldest son of John, second Earl of Wigton. He escaped from Philiphaugh, and, on the security of the Earl of Callendar, he was allowed "to repair home to his own dwelling-house" in Feb. 1646. For documents regarding his case, see Wigton Papers, Maitland Club Miscellany, ii. 444-447. He became third Earl, and died in 1665.

[13] John, second Lord Maderty, imprisoned after Philiphaugh, but released on his assurance of peaceful behaviour. He became security for Patrick Grahame of Inchbrakie under a penalty of £50,000. See p. 60, *n.* 15, and Douglas' Peerage—Strathallan.

[14] Was this Montrose's brother-in-law, James, Lord Carnegie, afterwards second Earl of Southesk? He was reputed a careful man, and must have felt sure as to Montrose's success.

[15] Presumably James, eldest son of Lord Hartfell. He married a daughter of the Marquis of Douglas, and became second Earl of Hartfell.

[16] John Hamilton of Orbiston was some time Justice-Clerk, busy in planting kirks and trying delinquents, in which he met with approval. He cannot have been grateful to W. for this notice. He retained office, however, till he joined the Engagers.

Amisfield,[17] Towers of Inverleith,[18] a man of great merit, who afterwards died bravely on the battlefield, Stuart of Rosyth,[19] and Dalyell,[20] brother of the Earl of Carnwath, knights, and very many more, whose names I have either forgotten or omit to mention, lest my thankless and unseasonable commendation should do more harm than honour to men now groaning under the heavy yoke of tyranny.

Montrose's first care after the victory at Kilsyth was for his friends in prison. His generous heart was filled with pity for their condition. On no other charge but the sin of loyalty to the King, they were seized and miserably lodged in the wretched filthy Tolbooth of Edinburgh, where they lived in daily expectation of death. He therefore sent his nephew, Napier, with Nathaniel Gordon and a flying squadron to Edinburgh, to summon the city to surrender, demand the liberation of the prisoners, and receive assurance of the loyalty and obedience of the citizens. Should they refuse submission, they were to threaten them with fire and sword. Four miles from Edinburgh they halted, and decided to approach no nearer, unless compelled by the stubborn obstinacy of the inhabitants. They wished to save the wretched citizens from the fury and insolence of the soldiers, who hated the city as the mainspring and fountainhead of the whole rebellion, and in their

---

[17] Charters or Charteris of Amisfield, also called Hempisfield, in Dumfriesshire. For his connection with Montrose in 1644 he had been tried, along with Lord Hartfell and the Provost of Dumfries, and imprisoned in Edinburgh Castle. His freedom, for two miles round, was soon allowed him, and the circuit was increased to six. He at length got rid of the process against him. The estate was acquired by the family in 1175, and the Tower of Amisfield, standing four miles north-east of Dumfries, is, according to Chambers, without exception the most curious specimen of the baronial tower existing in Scotland. Newmills, near Haddington, was acquired later on by a member of the family, who changed the name to Amisfield. M'Dowall's Hist. Dumfries; Douglas' Peerage—Wemyss. Capt. Charters was executed after Corbiesdale, v. Ch. viii., Part II.

[18] Sir John Towers of Inverleith died before 1649, as there is evidence that his widow, Lady Jane, daughter of the first Earl of Wemyss, married again in that year. He was killed probably at Philiphaugh. Their son, Sir John, was alive in 1662, after Wishart had written. Monteith's Hist., 224; Lamont's Diary.

[19] The old castle of Rosyth is to be seen from the Forth Bridge, a little way up the river on the Fife side. Stuart was imprisoned as a delinquent in 1645, and paid a fine of 3815 marks. Part of his punishment was to see his fine wood Hairshaw cut down to repair the houses in Muckart and Dollar damaged by the Macleans on their way to Kilsyth. He was afterwards on the Commission of Peace for Fife.

[20] Robert, second Earl of Carnwath, who, according to Clarendon, caused the catastrophe at Naseby, had one brother, John Dalyell of Glenae. See below, Ch. xvi.

headlong wrath and vengeance might set it in flames and reduce it to ashes. They had received express orders from Montrose to avoid this by every means. They were also anxious to preserve their men from the contagion of the plague, which then raged in the city and neighbourhood, and every day cut off large numbers of victims.

On the news of their approach, the citizens were filled with universal consternation and despair, howling as if the sword were already at their throats and their homes in flames. In their guilty terror many freely accused themselves as the most ungrateful, sacrilegious, perjured traitors, past all pardon. Standing outside, or by means of secret messengers,[21] they applied privately to the prisoners to beg and implore their protection, entreating them to have mercy on the wretched plague-stricken populace, and pacify the righteous anger of the conqueror. All their hopes, they said, lay in them; nought else could avert their utter ruin. They vowed also that, if he would spare them this once, they would atone for their past rebellion by stricter loyalty and more earnest obedience. The prisoners, so lately exposed to the bitter abuse and contempt of the vilest of the mob, eager to have them tortured and gibbeted, forgot all their sufferings and wrongs, and, with emotions of pity rather than revenge, rendered thanks to God Almighty for His gracious gift of freedom and unexpected preservation. Then, turning to their bitterest enemies, they bade them be of good cheer, as his gracious Majesty and Montrose, his lieutenant, sought only the safety and welfare of the penitent, not their ruin and extermination. They advised them to send delegates at once to Montrose to implore his pardon and protection. Nothing would be so likely to appease the conqueror as immediate surrender. As for themselves, they would not fail to intercede with him, and did not doubt that his great and lofty soul, invincible in war, would yield to the prayers and cries of the miserable city.

Comforted with this hope and helpful advice, the people of Edinburgh at once convened their Town Council to choose their delegates. Among the prisoners were two specially marked out

---

[21] Wishart was one of the prisoners, and an eye and ear witness.

by their birth, and influence with Montrose. One of these was Ludovick, Earl of Crawford,[22] head of the very ancient and noble family of the Lindsays, who had gained honour abroad in the Swedish, Austrian, and Spanish services. The Earl of Lindsay, his cousin, thirsting for the honours and titles of Crawford, had plotted to have his life, and by his cunning and influence had so worked on the Covenanters as to secure his doom. The only charge they could allege was that, as a soldier and man of action, he had served his royal master with diligence and fidelity, and they feared he would still do so, if allowed to live. The other was James, Lord Ogilvy,[23] son of the Earl of Airlie, a very dear friend of Montrose, formidable to the rebels both for his own and his father's courage and power. In consequence of ancient feuds and recent injuries, he was the declared enemy of Argyll, and was therefore accused on the same charge as Crawford and involved in the same peril. These men were selected by the Edinburgh Council from among the prisoners, at once restored to liberty, and besieged with supplications to use their influence with the Lord Governor, and assist their delegates to save a city already so heavily scourged by the hand of God. They called down every curse upon themselves and their offspring, if they should ever forget the favour or prove ungrateful to their benefactors.

In compliance with the universal wish, these two noblemen undertook this office. Escorted by the delegates, they set out to meet Napier. On his way to Edinburgh, Napier had the pleasure

---

[22] Ludovic, sixteenth Earl of Crawford, the last in the direct line, a gallant soldier. See, for his life, "Lives of the Lindsays." "The Incident" was probably due to his action and words, and his arrest following gave opportunity for Lord Lindsay of the Byers to make terms for his release, which were the changing of the succession of the Earldom in his favour, though three Lindsay houses had a preferable claim, viz., Spynie, Edzell, and Balcarres. This transaction was completed on 15th January 1642, and the Earl joined the King at Nottingham with a large troop of cavalry in August. He fought at Edgehill, Lansdown, Newbury, and Reading, and cut his way out at Poole. He defended Newcastle, and, with Wishart, was there taken prisoner, and they were together sent to Edinburgh. After Philiphaugh he continued with Montrose. He escaped to Spain, where he took up his old service; was at Badajoz in 1649. It is supposed he ended his career in France, when or how is not known. See "Lives of Lindsays;" Jervise, "Lands of Lindsays."

[23] See p. 30, *n.* 11. Brought down to Edinburgh, after the fall of Newcastle, with Crawford, Wishart, and other prisoners, he was kept in the loathsome Tolbooth. For his sufferings, see his wife's petition and other notices in Act. Parl. Scot., VI. i. 467. An order had been given to remove him to the Bass, but Kilsyth freed him.

of releasing his father and wife, Stirling, his brother-in-law, and his sisters from the prison at Linlithgow,[24] to which they had been removed from Edinburgh Castle by the Covenanters. With these liberated captives and the city delegates, having accomplished his mission, he returned with his forces to his uncle. Montrose, who had been deeply grieved by the long separation from such dear friends as Crawford and Ogilvy, embraced them warmly, congratulating them on their safe deliverance, and bestowed on them every honour and possible consolation for their long imprisonment. They in their turn, as was natural, extolled their deliverer and avenger by their thanks and praises, to the great joy of all who witnessed the meeting.

The Edinburgh delegates were then admitted to audience, and delivered their message from the Council and people of the town. The sum of it was, that they freely surrendered to the Governor, supplicated for pardon, promised loyalty and obedience for the future, and committed themselves and their estates to his patronage and protection, which they humbly implored. They promised also, in obedience to his orders, immediately to release the prisoners still in their custody, and begged him to feel assured that they would perform every duty according to his wish. Though the town, they said, had been so terribly drained by the plague that it could raise no soldiers, they were ready to pay their share for levies raised in other places. Above all, they implored him, in conclusion, to intercede for them with their most gracious lord the King not to be too severe on their city, which had been instigated to rebellion by the craft, influence, and example of a seditious dominant faction. Montrose reassured them on all points, and imposed no heavier penalty than the sacred obligation of allegiance to the King their master; they were faithfully to renounce all correspondence with rebels in arms, whether in Scotland or elsewhere; to surrender the Castle of Edinburgh (which was known to be then in their power) to the King and his officers; and lastly, as soon as the delegates returned, the prisoners were to be liberated at once and sent to his camp.

---

[24] See pp. 102-3, *nn.* 12-16.

On their return the prisoners [25] were immediately released, but as to the other articles, not one of them was performed. In this they acted with their usual perjury and falsehood, for which, if they do not come to their senses, the avenging God of truth and justice will hereafter punish their base ingratitude and repeated perfidy.

While this was going on at Edinburgh, Montrose despatched Alexander Macdonald and John Drummond of Balloch, a brave gentleman, with part of his forces to the west coast to suppress the disturbances there and frustrate the efforts of Cassilis and Eglinton. However, they did not wait their coming, but dispersed home in the greatest terror at the mere news of their approach. Some of the Earls and nobles hastened to Ireland, others slunk off to various lurking-places. All the western shires, and the towns of Ayr, Irvine, and others,[26] strove which should first submit, with ready offers of obedience, loyalty, and service. In fact, contrary to expectation, Montrose nowhere found men better affected to the King than in the west. A very large number of knights and gentlemen, the heads of families, and even some of the leading nobility, were glad to join him. But it is advisable at present, as they would probably desire, to omit mentioning their names with the praise they might claim in happier times. It is not our wish to make the King's most honourable and devoted subjects a mark for the cruel vengeance of their deadly enemies.

---

[25] The following were among the prisoners set free by Montrose :—The Earl of Crawford, Lords Ogilvy, Grahame (with his tutor), Napier, and Reay, Sir Alexander Irvine of Drum, Alexander Irvine, younger of Drum, and two servants, Alexander Irvine of Artamford, Sir Alexander Gordon of Cluny, Gordon of Gight, Sir George Stirling of Keir, Sir Philip Nisbet of Nisbet, Ogilvy of Powrie, Henry Graham, Dr. George Wishart, Lady Elizabeth Napier, Lady Lilias Graham, and Lady Stirling of Keir. Robert Irvine of Federate had just died in prison. The condition of these prisoners, as described in the petitions of Lady Ogilvy and Lady Mary Irvine, was most deplorable and disgusting. Wishart is said to have carried the marks of the rats' teeth to his grave.

[26] P. 126, *n.* 1.

## CHAPTER XV.

Intrigues of Roxburgh, Home, and Traquair—Montrose appointed Commander-in-Chief and Lieutenant-Governor in Scotland—Macdonald and the Highlanders retire home, followed by Aboyne and his men—The King orders Montrose to march to the Borders and join Traquair and Roxburgh, who deceive him.

MONTROSE now turned his attention to the south Borders. Messengers were sent to the Earls of Home,[1] Roxburgh,[2] and Traquair,[3] inviting them to join him in matters of peace and war, and all that concerned the royal cause. These noblemen had a very powerful retinue of friends and followers in that country, and were anxious to be thought zealous champions of the King's authority. Besides the bond of allegiance which they shared with others, they lay under very great obligations to his Majesty. He

---

[1] Sir James Home of Coldingknows became third Earl of Home in 1633 by right of succession, on the death of James, second Earl. W. errs in saying the King made him an Earl, but he secured to him all the honours, privileges, and precedencies enjoyed by his two predecessors. The Earl was a Cumbernauld Bander and an Engager, but his conduct towards Montrose was of a very doubtful loyalty. With Leslie so near and Naseby so recent, Border Earls were not convinced by Kilsyth. A royal army marching north to join Montrose would have confirmed the waverers. The Earl of Home died in 1666. Douglas' Peerage. See Gard., Civil War, ii. 334 *n.*

[2] Sir Robert Ker of Cessfurd, born about 1570, is mentioned by Sir Robert Cary, his opposite Warden on the Border, as a brave, active, young man. The Archbishop of York, to whom he had been committed prisoner, says of him, "I understand that the gentleman is wise and valiant, but somewhat haughty and resolute." About 1600 he was made Lord Roxburgh, and in 1616 Earl of Roxburgh. He was with the King at the Pacification of Berwick in 1639, along with his son, Lord Ker. The latter "quitted the royal army and joined the Covenanters at Duns Law, in sight of the King, which it was thought he would not have done without his father's connivance, he being such an awful man." His second wife was appointed governess to the Princess Elizabeth, daughter of James VI. Her funeral in 1643 was made the excuse for a rendezvous of Royalists to attack the Covenanters, but the attempt failed. On the Earl's death, his third wife, a daughter of the Earl of Morton, married James, second Marquis of Montrose, who was sixty years younger than her first husband, and was the mother of the third Marquis. The old Earl became an Engager, and was deprived of the Privy Seal. He died 18th January 1650. Douglas' Peerage—Roxburgh; Green's English Princesses. *v.* Index.

[3] See p. 41, *n.* 10. Traquair's treachery is scarcely to be doubted. He knew that Montrose's army had melted away, and was aware of the King's weakness in England. He also knew that Leven commanded the Border. Kilsyth did not really deceive him, though it constrained him to treat Montrose with courtesy.

had raised them to the highest honours from the order of simple knighthood, and had also appointed them lieutenants of very wealthy counties—a position in which they had amassed great riches beyond their station, and to the prejudice of the King. In reply they sent some of their most distinguished friends to Montrose, with assurances of their readiness to run all risks under his command and leadership in the service of their most bounteous lord the King. They promised to raise all the forces they could, and added that there was nothing to prevent them from joining, if he would only advance into their country with ever so small a party. His presence and authority would rouse and animate not only their friends and followers, but all the people of those shires to join him cheerfully, and those who refused could be compelled or reduced to order. In conclusion, they earnestly entreated him to aid them in this matter, and in all else he should find their most faithful ready service. Fine words, and at first sight honourable, but uttered with the faith usual among those favourites of the King who had tasted most liberally of his bounty.

Possibly the Earl of Lanark, brother of the Duke of Hamilton, ought not to be blamed on the same score; for when Montrose earnestly invited him, through some friends, to join the King's cause, though he had a fair prospect of pardon for the past and his brother's release, he replied, in plain, outspoken terms, that he would have nothing to do with their party, and would not pretend a friendship which he did not mean to cultivate.[4] Would that all in whom the King has trusted too implicitly had from the beginning of these troubles spoken always with the same candour and directness.

About the same time Montrose sent the Marquis of Douglas and Lord Ogilvy over into Annandale and Nithsdale to join the Earls of Annandale and Hartfell in raising all the forces they could, especially cavalry. With these troops they had orders to march to Traquair, Roxburgh, and Home, and oblige them, without further double-dealing, to take part in the war. Montrose, who had had a taste of the ways of courtiers, began to suspect

---

[4] See p. 40, n. 8.

their contrivances for delay. He had already often experienced their shifts and fickleness, especially Traquair's. Douglas, with the prompt aid of Hartfell and Annandale, soon levied a considerable body of men as far as numbers went, but they were mostly raw ploughmen and shepherds, unused to discipline, ready enough at the outset, but they soon lost heart, and could not be kept to their colours. When Douglas and the rest of the commanders observed this, they wrote repeatedly to Montrose to hasten to meet them at the Tweed with his veterans, as his presence and authority, and the company and example of his tried soldiers, would force them, willingly or unwillingly, to do their duty. Meanwhile, according to his orders, they advanced to Strath Gala, to give Roxburgh and Traquair the opportunity, and help if necessary, to raise their men. But these good men were in no haste to comply; they were deep in the plots of the Covenanters, and well aware that David Leslie and all his cavalry were on the march from England, and would soon be at hand.[5] They had resolved to betray the King in their usual way, and to draw Montrose, whose glory they envied, into the hands of his enemies by fraud, as they could not succeed by force. To this end they poured in messages by friends and frequent messengers, not only to Douglas and his party, but even to Montrose himself, to assure him that they were ready to face the most imminent dangers, but that they were quite unable to raise their friends, clansmen, and followers, unless Montrose himself came to rouse and animate them by his presence. To confirm their declarations the more fully, they imprecated the most dreadful curses on themselves if they did not stand firm and true to their promises. Montrose, however, remained unshaken by their adjurations, and continued still at Bothwell, thinking, if they were really upright and sincere in their professions, that Douglas and his men, who were still in their neighbourhood, were quite sufficient to encourage and compel their friends and followers.

Montrose had now continued for some considerable time in

---

[5] For Argyll's efforts at Berwick to withdraw supporters from Montrose, see Lord Ogilvy's letter to Aboyne. Napier, Mem., 567.

quarters at Bothwell, when many of the Highlanders, being loaded with spoil, deserted secretly and returned to their own country. Their officers, too, now pressed openly for a brief leave of absence. They pretended that, as the enemy had no longer an army within the kingdom, there was no immediate occasion for their presence. They complained that their houses and crops, on which their parents, wives, and little ones depended for the coming winter, had been burnt and destroyed by the enemy without any reparation. They, therefore, earnestly begged a few weeks' furlough, to make some provision for their families against cold and starvation, and offered solemnly to pledge themselves to return within forty days in greater strength and numbers. Montrose, seeing that he could not detain them, as they were volunteers without pay, in order to secure their gratitude more firmly, resolved not only to sanction, but even to order their absence. He therefore publicly commended the soldiers, and in the King's name thanked the officers. He urged them to settle their affairs with diligence, and appointed their countryman and kinsman, Alexander Macdonald (who was only too forward in craving that office), to accompany them as leader, and bring them back to camp by the day appointed. Macdonald, in a formal speech, returned thanks in the name of all to the Lord-Governor for his great condescension, and, as though he were their bail or surety, solemnly promised their speedy return. Yet he had resolved not to return; and he never again set eyes on Montrose. Not content with the force of Highlanders, more than 3000 of his bravest men, he secretly seduced 120 of the best of the Irish, whom he carried off with him also as a body-guard.[6]

Just at this time messengers from the King at Oxford reached Montrose by various roads. Among these was Andrew Sandilands,[7] a Scotsman, but educated in England, where he had entered holy orders, an upright, loyal man, much esteemed by Montrose, with whom he remained till the end of the war. Another was Sir

---

[6] The Latin *scilicet* is ironical.

[7] He had been imprisoned for some time before 1650, for in that year Mr. Andrew Sandilands and two other clergymen were set at liberty, but bound to quit the country, and not to return under pain of death. Act. Parl. Scot., VI. ii. 580.

Robert Spotiswoode,[8] formerly the distinguished President of the High Court of Session in Scotland, and at this time his Majesty's Secretary for that kingdom. He came from Oxford through Wales, and passed over the Isle of Man, from which he landed in Lochaber and made his way to Athole, whence he was conducted by the Athole men to Montrose. Almost all the messengers, among other matters, brought orders for Montrose to join Roxburgh and Traquair, and take their assistance and advice, without question of their loyalty and zeal. Further, he was to hasten to the Tweed, on the Borders, where he would meet a body of horse, which the King would at once send to his aid from England. With these he might confidently venture to encounter David Leslie, should he march, as was suspected, to meet him with the Covenanters' horse. Such were the King's positive commands, repeated in every letter from the King, the result of his generous but misplaced confidence. Montrose was obliged to comply, and decided to set out to the Tweed.

On the day before he began the march,[9] he assembled the army. Macdonald and the Highlanders had not yet left him. Under the royal standard, Sir Robert Spotiswoode on his knee delivered to him his Majesty's commission, signed with the Great Seal, which Montrose handed to Sir Archibald Primrose,[10]

---

[8] Sir Robert was the second son of Archbishop Spotiswoode of St. Andrews. A memoir of him by his grandson will be found at the beginning of his edition of Sir Robert's "Practicks of the Laws of Scotland," with a full account of his trial and death. An address of Sir Robert to the Faculty of Advocates may be read in the Spottiswoode Miscellany, vol. i., which also contains much information as to the President and his family. See also there notice of his influence on Lochiel, which soon bore fruit in the royal cause. Sir Robert arrived at Bothwell September 1st. The 1652 edition translates Mona "Anglesea."

[9] September 3, 1645.

[10] Archibald Primrose of Carrington and Chesters succeeded his father James in the office of Clerk to the Privy Council, and had served as Clerk to the Estates. He joined Montrose after Kilsyth and was taken at Philiphaugh. On his release from prison in the end of 1646, he went to the King (then in the hands of the Scottish army), who knighted him. Owing to his connection with the Engagement, he lost his offices, which he had hitherto managed to retain. Charles II. made him a baronet before Worcester. At the Restoration he became Lord Clerk Register, and acquired much wealth, purchasing, among other properties, Barnbougle and Dalmeny. To get him out of the Clerk Register's post he was made Justice-General, and Sir George Mackenzie soon succeeded him in that office. In late acknowledgment of his services, his grandson James was created Viscount Primrose. On the death of Hugh, third Viscount, the line failed. Archibald, son of Sir Archibald by his second marriage, became first Earl of Rosebery. See Act. Parl. Scot., and Douglas' Peerage—Rosebery.

clerk of the Supreme Council, to be read aloud by herald. Then in a short but stately speech he commended the valour and loyalty of his soldiers, and assured them of his warm esteem. Before the whole army he singled out Macdonald for special praise, and by virtue of his royal commission conferred on him the honour of knighthood. At that time not only Montrose but all who favoured the King's cause held the highest opinion of Macdonald, which he belied, not only to the great detriment of the King, but to the utter ruin of himself and friends.

On the second day after Montrose had begun his march and had reached Calder Castle,[11] the Viscount Aboyne left the army,[12] and not only withdrew his own men, but seduced all the rest of the northern forces to desert. The Governor in vain opposed this step. Neither the arguments nor entreaties of his friends, who were heartily ashamed of his conduct, could induce Aboyne to stay even for one week longer, though assured that he would then be dismissed, not only with the General's leave, but the goodwill and esteem of all honest men.

Passing by Edinburgh, Montrose led his forces, now much reduced, through Lothian to Strath Gala, where he met Douglas and the other commanders, whose forces were much diminished by daily desertions. Here Traquair himself, with an unusual show of alacrity and joy, hastened to join him, professing the greatest devotion not only to the King, but also to Montrose himself. Next day he sent his son, Lord Linton, with a fine troop of horse, as if to fight under his standard, using him as a sort of pledge, to blind Montrose to the snares he was spreading for his destruction. This was not the first time that most ungrateful wretch Traquair had played spy for the Covenanters, to whom he intended to betray Montrose, and even the King himself.

He was now within twelve miles of Home and Roxburgh. Still they sent no message, and showed not the least sign of doing

---

[11] The seat of Lord Torphichen, near Mid-Calder. By Limphoy he went to Cranston, and by Torwoodlee to Kelso, and thence by Jedburgh to Selkirk. Wishart was to have preached at Cranston Kirk on Sunday, September 6th, but the sermon was stopped by the hurried march south. *v.* Practicks, p. 10.

[12] This and Macdonald's defection ruined the cause. See p. 138.

their duty. He was much disturbed, and resolved to march into their country and force them to join. This they had foreseen, and with consummate craft prevented his design. David Leslie[13] had now reached Berwick with his whole cavalry and many English volunteers. They were aware of his plan, in which they took their part. They sent to him, therefore, and proposed that he should send a party and make a show of taking them prisoners. This was done the day before Montrose's arrival. By this artifice that cunning old fox, Roxburgh, who carried Home with him, expected to curry favour with the Covenanters by a voluntary surrender to their protection. At the same time he would not lose favour with the King, as he could pretend that he had fallen into their hands against his will. This was Leslie's first exploit, after which he crossed the Tweed and marched into the eastern parts of Lothian.

Montrose saw through their treachery to the King and himself. He had now lost all hopes of that party of horse which the King was to have sent to his assistance. His retreat northwards to the Highlands was cut off by the enemy in great force. He resolved therefore, with the few men he had with him, to march into Nithsdale, Annandale, and Ayrshire to raise what horse he could; for though he had no certain intelligence of the enemy's strength, yet he conjectured that it consisted chiefly of horse.

---

[13] General David Leslie, afterwards first Lord Newark. For a good summary of his career see Douglas' Peerage—Newark. He proved himself a better soldier than Cromwell in his defence of Edinburgh, and but for meddling ministers would have avoided the disaster at Dunbar. His treacherous cruelty at Philiphaugh, Dunavertie, and Dunaveg, after quarter given, leaves an indelible stain on his memory. See Turner, pp. 45-48, and W., Ch. xvi., with Guthrie and P. Gordon.

## CHAPTER XVI.

*Montrose marches to Selkirk, September 1645—Surprised by Leslie at Philiphaugh, and overpowered—Cuts his way through, and with half his forces regains Athole.*

FROM Kelso Montrose marched to Jedburgh, and thence to Selkirk. There he quartered his horse in the village and his foot in a neighbouring wood,[1] resolving to occupy the favourable positions, lest he should have to fight at a disadvantage with an enemy whose strength was quite unknown to him. He ordered his captains of cavalry to send out numerous trusty and active scouts, set guards in suitable places on every side, and look well to their watch. It was his custom to see to all this in person, but that night he was unable to do so, having despatches to write to the King, to be sent off before daybreak by a trusty messenger he had fallen in with. He therefore requested them the more earnestly to have a care that the enemy, who were very strong in horse, should not surprise them unawares. The officers promised all care and diligence, and trusting to their vigilance he spent the whole night on his despatches. In the course of the night vague rumours of the enemy's approach reached him. These he transmitted to his officers, men of great military experience and reputation, acquired in foreign service. But whether deceived by the indolence of their men and spies, or blinded by fate, they confidently returned word that there was no enemy there or in the neighbourhood.[2] At daybreak some of the best and most experienced troopers were again sent out to reconnoitre. On their return they declared that they had scoured the country for ten miles round,

---

[1] Harehead Wood.

[2] "About the shooting in of the night, Hempsfield with his troop were beat out of Sunderland, four miles from Selkirk, eleven of his troop slain, the rest yielding themselves prisoners. Only Hempsfield himself and two with him escaped, and were come to inform him; but they were thought to have brawled among themselves in a drunken fray" (P. Gordon, 158). Ogilvy of Powrie made the second report.

and carefully examined all the by-roads, and rashly wished they might be cursed if there was a man in arms within ten miles. But it was afterwards found, when too late, that the enemy in full force was not above four miles from Selkirk, and had passed the night under arms.[3]

On the same day that Montrose marched from Jedburgh, Leslie mustered his men on Gladsmuir, a plain in Lothian, and in a council of war with the chiefs of the Covenanters, it was resolved to march to Edinburgh and the Forth, so as to oppose Montrose's retreat to the north, and force him to fight before he was again joined by the Highlanders. Suddenly Leslie changed his plan, and ordered his whole army to wheel to the left and march off with all speed. All who were not in the secret were surprised by this rapid change of route, for they were now marching by way of Strath Gala. But the reason for this afterwards transpired from the enemy's own account. Letters had reached him containing accurate information of Montrose's strength, which consisted only of 500 Irish foot and a few raw undisciplined horse. Victory was certain if they seized the opportunity of attacking him near the Tweed. Leslie at once acted on this advice, and, as we have said, spent the night about four miles from Selkirk. It has commonly been reported that Traquair was the source of this information. This I cannot assert for truth; but it cannot be denied that he ordered his son Linton[4] that very night to withdraw from the Royalists as fast as he could, a command he obeyed with great satisfaction, an instance of blackest ingratitude, to forsake a King to whom they were deeply indebted, and a disgrace to their posterity.

The morning was shrouded in darkness and dense fog, which favoured the enemy's approach.[5] They were already within half a mile, and marching up in order, when Montrose's scouts came flying in with the tidings. Mounting the first horse he could find,

---

[3] Leslie passed the night at Sunderland village, from which he drove Amisfield.
[4] Afterwards second Earl of Traquair, d. 1666. P. Gordon says he was recalled by his father four days before.
[5] Captain Blackadder returned with his men in a great fright, and reported to Montrose at breakfast "that a great armie was advancing within a mile of the toune" (P. Gordon, 158).

he galloped into the field appointed for the morning's rendezvous. There he found all in uproar and confusion. The cavalry, unused to command, were dispersed up and down the fields, more intent on baiting their horses than maintaining their lives with honour. On the first blast of the enemy's trumpet, they scattered in a panic, and rode about at random, so that they took no share in the fight; but a few, mostly nobles and knights, flew to the point of attack, and, though not more than 120 in number, bravely undertook to cover the right wing. The foot, too, in all 500, were in much the same plight; many of them at this unlucky moment were bent on saving their private property among the baggage, to their own ruin. To crown the catastrophe, many of the officers were absent, and never reached the field. The enemy's cavalry were 6000 strong, mostly from England. They advanced rapidly. Not a moment was left for deliberation. Twice they charged furiously on Montrose's right wing; twice they were gallantly met and repulsed with heavy loss. Finding they could make no impression on that noble squadron, they wheeled and broke in on the left wing, where there was no horse, riding down the few foot who offered resistance. At the same time 2000 of their horse, who crossed the river, threatened those gallant gentlemen in the rear. In danger of being surrounded, and cut to pieces where they stood by a galling fire, they made the best retreat they could, each for himself. For the foot there was little hope in flight; they stood firm and fought resolutely, till offered quarter, when they threw down their arms and yielded. But, notwithstanding the promise of quarter, these defenceless men were every one butchered in cold blood by Leslie's own orders, an indelible blot of savage cruelty and treachery on the glory and renown which he had gained abroad.[6] The enemy did not pursue those who had escaped, but fell to plundering the baggage, where they made a piteous slaughter of the poor women, boys, and camp-followers, without distinction of age or sex.

---

[6] "Quarter, it was said, by a vile equivocation, had been granted to Stuart, the adjutant, alone, not to his men" (Gardiner, ii. 337). For a recent effort to extenuate these atrocities after the battle, see Introd. to Records of Genl. Assemblies, by Dr. Mitchell. Even the equivocation would not have saved Stuart, who was condemned, but he managed to escape. For many details as to these massacres and the discovery of remains in Slain-Man's Lee, see Monteith, Guthrie, P. Gordon, and Chambers.

It is not easy to estimate the number of slain. Almost none of the horse, and very few of the foot, excepting those who had surrendered on terms, fell in fight. As they were not more than 500 in all, and of these, 250 rejoined Montrose before the next day, all armed with their swords, we may conjecture that those who were missing did not exceed that number. Very few prisoners were taken, and those mostly by the country people while straying in strange roads after their horses were tired out. The peasants, unmindful of the benefits and protection they had lately received from Montrose, delivered them up to their cruel enemies, to be slaughtered like beasts of sacrifice for demons.

Both the royal standards were saved from capture; that of the foot by a brave Irishman, who, with the greatest presence of mind amid the general confusion, when he saw the enemy masters of the field, stripped it from the staff and wrapped it round his body. With no other covering, he forced his way, sword in hand, through the midst of the enemy, and brought it to Montrose that night. To reward his valour, Montrose gave him charge of it for the future, and promoted him to be one of his life-guards. The other standard was saved by William Hay,[7] brother to the Earl of Kinnoul, a youth of fine character, who had been appointed standard-bearer in place of his maternal uncle, Douglas, son of the Earl of Morton, who had been disabled by many severe wounds in the battle of Alford. Stripping the flag from the staff, Hay carried it to England, where he lay for a while in hiding, until the country about Tweedside had become somewhat settled, when he set out, with Robert Towers[8] as his sole companion and guide, a brave, faithful friend and a soldier of experience, who had served with distinction for some time as a captain in France. Travelling through byways, and mostly at night, he made his way northwards, and had the pleasure of restoring the royal standard to his general.

[7] William Hay, afterwards fifth Earl of Kinnoul. He was imprisoned in Edinburgh Castle by the English in 1654, but, with six others, escaped, May 28th, "over the wall upon the sheets and blankets which did cover their beds." Colonel Montgomery was killed in the attempt. The Earl was recaptured after a three days' pursuit through the snow. He died in 1677. Lamont, 91, and p. 63, *n.* 1.

[8] Probably a member of the loyal family of Towers of Inverleith.

When Montrose perceived that the day was lost and his men scattered in flight, a sight he had never yet witnessed, for a while he thought only of selling his life dearly. Having rallied about thirty of the scattered horsemen, he resolved to die with honour, rather than fall alive into the hands of the enemy. He was surrounded by their squadrons in such dense numbers that he could not break through. Notwithstanding, he repeatedly charged them on every side. Of those who ventured out of their ranks, many were slain and the rest driven back. But as all was in vain, calmer counsels providentially prevailed in that brave and noble spirit; he reflected that his loss that day had been slight, and might easily be repaired. Only a small part of his forces had been engaged. The Highlanders, who were the strength of the kingdom, and all the northern parts, were still safe and untouched. Moreover, very many of the leading nobility, gentry, and heads of clans, who had now openly joined him, would be disconcerted by his death, and fall away, to the utter ruin of the King's cause in Scotland. His fall might prove a far greater loss to his dearest lord the King, than a single defeat. The cause was just, and he ought not to despair. The Marquis of Douglas, Sir John Dalyell, and a few brave and trusty friends, came very seasonably to second these reflections. They implored him with tears, wrung from them by their deep affection, by the memory of his past achievements, for the sake of his friends, his house, his sweet wife and children,[9] for the King, country, and Church, to have a care for his life. Next to God he was their only hope; with him they must live or die. Overcome by their entreaties, Montrose charged, and cut his way through the enemy, who were now more intent on plunder than pursuit. Those who ventured to follow, were either killed or taken prisoners. Among these was a captain of horse named Bruce,[10] and two cornets with their standards. They

---

[9] This is the only reference in W. to the Marchioness. She died in November of this year. James Burns, the Glasgow Bailie, says: "In November 1645 Montrose's lady died. He came and buried her at Montrose, and was pursued back again by Lieut.-Gen. Middleton." Crawford's MS. in Maidment's "Historical Fragments." The children then alive were James, Robert, and David. See Napier, Mem., 827, *n*.

[10] A Capt. Harry Bruce, son of Bruce, younger of Clackmannan, appears in the parliamentary papers of the time, petitioning for arrears of pay, and is appointed "rootmaster."

were treated with courtesy, and after a few days dismissed, on their promise to release as many officers of equal rank, a pledge they dishonourably neglected to redeem.

About three miles from Selkirk[11] Montrose overtook a number of his own men, who now made up a considerable force, and enabled him to proceed on his march, secure from the insults of the country people. In passing the Earl of Traquair's castle, whose treachery in betraying him to the enemy was as yet unknown to him, he sent a messenger requesting an interview with him and his son. For reply he was informed that they were both away from home, though some gentlemen of honour and credit declared that they were both there. Nor was this all. That gallant courtier not only congratulated the Covenanters on their victory, but had the effrontery to declare with scornful laughter that Montrose and the royal forces had at last been beaten in Scotland. Even his own daughter, the Countess of Queensberry,[12] reproved him for it, as far as filial modesty would permit.

Near the little town of Peebles Montrose made a brief halt, to rest his men in preparation for their journey. Here many of the stragglers came in. At sunset the whole force marched boldly into the town, where they spent the night. Next morning at daybreak they forded the Clyde, guided by Sir John Dalyell. Here he was met by the Earls of Crawford and Airlie, who had escaped by another way. When they saw that he was safe, they thought nothing of their recent defeat, and Montrose was no less rejoiced by the safety of his friends, the more so as they joined him with nearly 200 horse, whom they had picked up on the way.

Though now secure from pursuit, he resolved to press on into Athole, and raise the Highlanders and other friends in the north. He therefore crossed the Forth and Earn, and marched

---

[11] They went up the Yarrow, crossed Minch-Moor, and drew bridle at Traquair House, ten miles from the field, one of the most ancient of Scottish castles.

[12] Lady Margaret Stewart, married to James, second Earl of Queensberry, and mother of the first Duke. Her husband was on his way to join Montrose after Kilsyth, but was arrested by the Glencairn men. Traquair, Linton, and Lady Queensberry must have seen this story in print, but, as far as we know, it remained uncontradicted.

through Perthshire along the foot of the hills.[13] On his way he despatched Douglas and Airlie with a party of horse into Angus, and Lord Erskine[14] into Mar, to rouse their friends and vassals in those parts. Sir John Dalyell, who had recently contracted an alliance with Lord Carnegie,[15] was sent to him on the same mission. He also wrote to Macdonald to order him, according to his pledge, to rejoin him with the Highlanders on the day appointed. But above all, he begged Aboyne by letters and messengers to return with his friends and clansmen, who were ready enough of themselves, and wanted only his authority and example to rouse and encourage them.

---

[13] He was at Buchanty, in Glenalmond, on 19th September. See his letter to John Stewart of Sheirglass. Napier, Mem., 605.

[14] John Erskine, afterwards ninth Earl of Mar. His taking the Covenant was a great source of delight to the Rev. R. Baillie, but soon afterwards he signed the Cumbernauld Bond and remained loyal. He suffered much from fire and confiscation, and till the Restoration lived in a cottage near his own gate at Alloa. He died in 1668.

[15] "Margaret Carnegie the elder daughter of David, Lord Carnegie [who died October 25th, 1633, in his father's lifetime leaving no male issue] married—contract July 23rd 1637—Gavin, Master of Dalyell, who was afterwards third Earl of Carnwath. . . . Of this marriage there were two sons, James and John Dalyell, who were successively Earls of Carnwath, and a daughter Lady Jean Dalyell." Fraser, Hist. of the Carnegies, vol. i. 114.

## CHAPTER XVII.

*Montrose joined by four hundred men of Athole—Butchery of prisoners by the Covenanters—Huntly refuses aid—Aboyne joins Montrose, but soon leaves him—March to Perthshire—Death of Lord Napier.*

THE autumn was already advanced, but the harvest in that cold climate was not yet in. The houses and cottages destroyed by the enemy were still unrepaired against the approach of winter, often very severe in that country. The Athole men did not, therefore, show their usual promptness. Montrose, however, succeeded in obtaining from them 400 light foot to attend him northwards, where there was less danger to apprehend. They also promised faithfully that on his return, when he was to march southwards, the whole strength of the country should be at his service.

Meantime he received frequent assurances from Aboyne that he would at once join him with his forces. Macdonald promised the same for himself and the rest of the Highlanders. Erskine informed him that his men were already in arms, and only waited for Aboyne, who was near, or Montrose's orders to march.

About this time vague rumours prevailed that the King had sent him a strong body of horse. Many supposed that they were not far from the southern Borders.[1] Other reports spread of a very different nature and less questionable, that the captives had been brutally butchered without distinction of sex or age. Many of those who had fallen into the hands of the country folk had been savagely murdered. Those whom even these barbarous wretches had spared in pity, were driven together, and, by command of the Covenanting chiefs, thrown headlong from a high

---

[1] Digby, with 1500 horse, left Welbeck October 14, reached Dumfries about October 22, and had sought refuge in the Isle of Man by the 27th, whence he writes to Clarendon on that date. Gard., Civil War, ii. 354.

bridge and drowned in the river below,[2] men, women, and babes at the breast. As they struggled to the side they were beaten down with bludgeons and hurled back into the waters. The noblemen and gentlemen were confined in loathsome dungeons, to be exposed to the insolence of the mob, and then condemned to lose their heads.

Never had Montrose been so deeply grieved as by these melancholy tidings of his friends. Impatient of every delay that prevented him from flying to the rescue, he crossed the Grampians with extraordinary speed,[3] and marched through the Braes of Mar and Strathdon to Lord Aboyne. His presence he hoped would encourage him to hasten southward. His object also was to effect a junction with Erskine's and Airlie's forces, summon Macdonald and the rest of the Highlanders at once, and picking up the Athole men on his way, to march straight across the Forth to meet the royal cavalry. The enemy, dismayed by the imminent danger, would thus be deterred from murdering their prisoners. They would never dare, he thought, to vent their rage on those noblemen, while the issue of the war still hung in the balance. The news of his great preparations filled them with such anxiety

---

[2] By inserting "the Tweed" here, Ruddiman's translation has caused W.'s veracity to be questioned. The Tweed above Berwick was not then bridged. The river was the Avon, near Linlithgow, and the victims were straggling Irish picked up on the march from Philiphaugh. Sir George Mackenzie and P. Gordon support Wishart. The former, alluding to the two women put to death in the reigns of Charles II. and James II., says: "Our accusers should remember that these women were executed for higher crimes than the following Montrose's camp, for which four score women and children were drowned, being all in one day thrown over the bridge at Linlithgow by the Covenanters, and six more at Elgin by the same faction, all without sentence, or the least formality of law." "Vindication of the Government in Scotland," &c., published 1691, p. 20. Many straggling Irish were still in the country. See Montrose's order concerning them, September 19; Napier, Mem., 605.

[3] Some dates here may be of service:—1645, Sept. 13, Rout of Philiphaugh. Sept. 14, Montrose left Peebles and crossed Clyde. Sept. 19, writes to Stewart of Sheirglass from Buchanty in Glenalmond. Oct. 2, writes from Comrie. Oct. 7, replies from Drumminor to Huntly, who had sent congratulations by his son and Balloch from Gordon Castle. Oct. 21-22, Sir W. Rollo and others executed at Glasgow. Oct. 20, Montrose at Alford. Oct. 23, at Castleton of Braemar, but meaning to be in Glenshee that night. Oct. 25, at Lochearnside, where Captains Ogilvy and Nisbet announce Digby's approach to the Border. Digby was by this time in retreat from Dumfries. Montrose moved on Glasgow, but returned to Perthshire early in November. Nov. 9, he was at Kilmahog, near Callander. About this time Lord Napier died at Fincastle, and was buried by Montrose at Blair. In November also Montrose buried his wife at Montrose, and hurried back to Perthshire, pursued by Middleton. Ogilvy and Nisbet rejoin him in Athole, after a fruitless interview with Huntly.

and alarm, that they did, in fact, defer the execution of their prisoners.

On the march Montrose found that Erskine had been seized with a serious illness; but his vassals, whose loyalty and courage Montrose had more than once experienced, even in their master's absence, were all eager and ready, if Aboyne would do his part, as they relied much upon his example and authority.

Meanwhile the Marquis of Huntly, who had been lying hid for nearly a year and a half, roused by the fame of Montrose's victories and his recovery of the kingdom, or urged by some disastrous[4] destiny, had returned home. This man was as unfortunate as he was misguided in his judgment. Though he really was or wished to seem devoted to the King, a mean lurking envy of Montrose's glory urged him to try and lessen rather than emulate his fame. He was ashamed openly to admit the feeling before his own people, who had been eye-witnesses of Montrose's brilliant courage. Such a confession would seem a proof of estrangement from the King himself; but he gave out that in future he would himself lead them against the rebels. He therefore commanded his tenants and warned his friends and neighbours, not without threats, to serve under no standard but his own. They remonstrated; what answer should they return to the orders of Montrose, who was the Deputy-Governor, appointed by the King, with supreme command of all forces in the kingdom? He replied that he himself would not fail the King. Meantime it was to their honour as much as his own that the King and all men should know how much the Gordons contributed to the war in men and means. This could only be done, if they took the field by themselves. In magnificent terms he dilated on his own power and decried that of Montrose. He launched into extravagant praise of the glory and achievements of his own ancestors (who had, in fact, deserved all commendation). For many ages past the power of the Gordons had been, and still was, the terror of their neighbours. It would be most unjust to yield to another

---

[4] The Latin implies a belief in astrology, for which "disastrous" may be taken as sufficient rendering.

(meaning Montrose) the honour and glory acquired by their prowess and self-sacrifice. In future he would himself take care that neither the King should be robbed of the Gordons' aid, nor the Gordons of their due praise, influence, and reward.

To the ignorant such words seemed just and honourable. But thoughtful men among them, who knew the temper of the man, saw in them indications of an unjust bitterness and ill-will towards Montrose, and an intention to withdraw from him as many men as he could, not only to the utter ruin of the King and kingdom, but also of himself, as the event only too sadly proved. Among them there were not wanting men who had the sense and foresight to condemn his resolution as imprudent, ill-timed, and ruinous even to himself. They remembered that all his own enterprises had miscarried through bad conduct or bad fortune. Montrose was now more successful. They ought not to separate from him on a vain pretext that he appropriated the glory. United, their combined forces would suffice not only to defend themselves, but to reduce their enemies and restore the authority of the King, to their own eternal honour. Disunion would end in disgrace and ruin. Without the help of the Gordons, Montrose had gained many brilliant victories; whereas the Gordons without Montrose had achieved nothing of note. They therefore earnestly entreated him to adhere firmly to the Royal Governor, a service as agreeable to the King as it would be satisfactory to all good men and honourable to himself. Some of them did not hesitate to declare frankly that they would themselves risk their lives and fortunes to obey and serve Montrose, should Huntly obstinately persist in his determination. And in this they were as good as their word.

Huntly, however, rejected the advice of his friends, and continued to oppose Montrose's plans. Every proposal of his, however just, however honourable, fair, and advantageous, was thwarted or rejected. If, as often happened, Montrose deliberately agreed to his plan, he immediately changed his mind. At times, when Montrose was present, he was easy and compliant; but he never failed to cross him in his absence, and showed little consistency in his conduct.

Aboyne, however, was at last roused by frequent messages from Montrose and by the entreaties of his friends to make some show of keeping his word, and joined him at Drumminor,[5] a castle of Lord Forbes, with a considerable party, to the number of 1500 foot and 300 horse, all in good spirits and ready for any danger under Montrose's command. At their first meeting, he frankly declared that he and his men would march wherever the Governor should lead them, and that many more, whom he could not gather in so short a time, were to follow with his brother Lewis. Montrose highly commended his loyalty and zeal. At once he set out to retrace his steps, and to pick up the forces of Erskine and the men of Mar, intending to cross the Grampians and descend into Athole and Angus. He had no doubt that within a fortnight he should cross the Forth with a strong army.

Aboyne and his men performed the first day's march with cheerfulness; but on the morrow his brother Lewis, who had been put under the command of the Earl of Crawford, marched off home by night, as if to attack some squadrons of the enemy, and took with him a strong party of horse. Under pretext of a guard, he seduced as many soldiers as he could to accompany him. Crawford, on his return, reported that Lewis had gone home, but was to return next day. So Lewis had pretended, though he had no intention of returning. This was not the only instance of treachery by which that young man disgraced his name. On the third day they reached Alford. Here Aboyne's men showed signs of wavering. They were slow to muster, loitered on the march, straggled and fell out of line. Almost every night they deserted the camp by troops. At last Aboyne himself, their leader, had the effrontery to ask for leave of absence. Every one was taken by surprise. What, they demanded, could be the reason for so sudden a change of plan? In excuse he alleged his father's commands, which he could not disobey. His father would not, he said, have given such orders without good cause. The enemy's forces[6] lay in Lower Mar, and threatened them in the rear if

---

[5] Near Strathbogie. See Montrose's letter to Huntly from this place. Napier, Mem., 608.
[6] Some of Middleton's horse.

deprived of the protection of his own men. It was sheer folly to lead his men elsewhere, while himself involved in imminent danger. To this Montrose replied that he was well informed that the enemy mustered only a few troops of horse at Aberdeen, and no infantry at all. They were too few to attempt any serious enterprise. He felt confident that on the first rumour of his approach they too would be recalled by their generals to defend the Lowlands.[7] Huntly would consult his own interests far better by transferring the war to the enemy's lands than by waging it in his own domains. They ought therefore to hasten south in order to shift the burden of war from the north. Besides, he was daily expecting the reinforcements from England; he could not hope to effect a junction with them unless he crossed the Forth. Lastly, he described the piteous plight of the prisoners, many of whom were Huntly's own friends, relatives, and kinsmen. Unless they were rescued at once, they would all be barbarously murdered. These arguments were unanswerable. Aboyne therefore begged that the whole matter might be referred to his father. His request was granted. Two messengers were sent, likely to prove most acceptable to Huntly—Donald, Lord Reay,[8] in whose lands the Marquis had sought hiding, and Alexander Irvine,[9] the younger

---

[7] As the event showed.

[8] Donald, first Lord Reay. For his services abroad and his connection with the charge of treason against Hamilton, see Douglas, and Burnet, "Dukes of Hamilton." On his liberation from the Tower he went down to Reay, and by and by sailed for Denmark, whence he brought to Newcastle ships, arms, and money for the King's service. He served in the defence of the town, was there taken prisoner and sent to Edinburgh, whence Kilsyth delivered him. After this interview with Huntly he returned to the North. He died abroad, and was buried in Strathnaver in 1649.

[9] Alexander Irvine, son of Sir Alexander Irvine of Drum, Sheriff of Aberdeenshire, was early one of a band of restless Royalists in the North, led by Sir John Gordon of Haddo, nearly all of whom came to a violent end. Imprisoned and fined in 1640 for going to the King with a complaint, on regaining freedom he gave his enemies much trouble. In December 1643 he married Lady Mary, daughter of the Marquis of Huntly. In March 1644 he helped to carry off four magistrates of Aberdeen to Auchindoun, and in April he attacked Montrose, killed a magistrate, and plundered the town. With Huntly he was excommunicated, and a price of 18,000 merks set on him, "quick or dead." He escaped by sea from Fraserburgh with his wife, her two gentlewomen, his brother, and cousin, but was constrained by Lady Mary's illness to land in Caithness, where a relative, Francis Sinclair, son of Lord Caithness, made them prisoners in Keiss Castle, and delivered them for the price set on them to the authorities in Edinburgh. His brother Robert died there through ill-treatment. Kilsyth saved Alexander from a like fate, and he followed Montrose faithfully, keeping the field with him till the King commanded them to disband in 1646, when, with others, he was pardoned. Against the bitter persecution of the Covenanting clergy he and his father appealed to Cromwell's officers, and gained their support. Some of the best polemics of the time issued from Drum at this crisis. In 1658 Irvine succeeded his father in the now some-

of Drum, who had lately married Huntly's daughter. Both of them were deeply indebted to Montrose, who had recently restored them to liberty. Reay was so much affronted by his repulse that he was ashamed to return. Irvine, a brave young gentleman, who never afterwards forsook Montrose, returned with letters from his father-in-law. The answer was vague and unsatisfactory. Pressed to state his opinion of Huntly's real intentions, Irvine freely owned that he had got no certain reply, but he believed that nothing would divert Huntly from his perverse resolution. Aboyne declared that it was sore against his will to tear himself from Montrose; but affection required him to obey his father, who was besides in ill-health. He therefore earnestly pressed for leave of absence; it could last only a few days, till he had allayed his father's anxiety. He solemnly promised to follow him within a fortnight with far greater forces. This he affirmed on oath. A very reluctant permission was granted for the time required, and of his own accord he renewed his protestations.

After his departure Montrose marched down through the Braes of Mar and Glenshee into Athole. Thence, with some addition to his forces, he proceeded into Perthshire. Here his hopes from the North were revived by a messenger from Aboyne to assure him that he and his forces would join him before the day appointed. At the same time Captain Thomas Ogilvy, younger of Powrie,[10] and Captain Robert Nisbet,[11] reached him by different routes with

---

what ruined estates. He represented Aberdeen at the Restoration rejoicings in London. When offered the peerage which had been given to his father, but which had not passed the seals, he declined it, as it was shorn of the precedency of his father's patent. He is known in the family as the Entailer, and misfortunes following the deed have caused him to be well remembered. A portrait of the Entailer (good copy of a Vandyck by Cosmo Alexander), is preserved at Drum, but though a good picture, it cannot have been a contemporary work. He appears as a man of thirty, with auburn hair, a moustache, in a buff coat with a deep blue ribbon knot on his right shoulder, and a white lace necktie. Another portrait of him as an older man is preserved at Marischal College, Aberdeen. He is celebrated in the Deeside ballad, "The Laird of Drum." A History of the family, which before the Civil War was one of the most wealthy and important in the North, exists in MS., kindly lent us by Mrs. Anna Forbes Irvine. See Spalding, P. Gordon, and Antiquities of Aberdeen and Banff Shires, indices; also Buchan's Ballads and Deeside Guide.

[10] See p. 149, *n.* 1. Digby was already retiring to the Isle of Man. Captain Thomas Ogilvy, younger of Powrie, appears in the pardon list of 1646. He afterwards acted for Montrose at Kirkwall, and was killed at Corbiesdale. See letter to Montrose, Napier, Mem., ii. 413.

[11] Captain Robert Nisbet, doubtless the son of Sir Alexander and brother of Sir Philip. After 1646 he went abroad, and on his return with Montrose he was taken prisoner at Corbiesdale, and executed at Edinburgh in May 1650. See Pref., Nisbet's Plates, by A. Ross.

messages from the King. Their orders were to desire Montrose to make all haste to join Lord George Digby, son of the Earl of Bristol, whom he had sent with reinforcements of cavalry to meet him not far from the English Border. These messengers Montrose despatched to Huntly and Aboyne to communicate their instructions. At last, he thought, the King's authority and the hope of those succours would rouse them to hasten up their forces. Buoyed by this vain hope, he had already halted too long in Strathearn.

About this time Lord Napier of Merchiston died in Athole.[12] He was the head of a very ancient family, a truly noble gentleman, singularly upright in life, and of a most happy genius. In the sciences he equalled his father and grandfather, who were famous throughout the world for their skill in philosophy and mathematics; in jurisprudence he far excelled them. To their Majesties King James and King Charles he was a beloved and loyal servant, under whom he had held the office of Treasurer, and been ennobled for his loyalty and affection to the King. He had several times suffered imprisonment and sequestration at the hands of the Covenanters. Montrose in his boyhood had revered him as a most indulgent parent, in his youth as his wisest counsellor, in his manhood as his truest friend. His death affected him like the loss of a father. He was the author of some very learned dissertations on the right of kings and on the origin of the troubles in Britain, which, it is to be wished may some day see the light.

---

[12] Archibald, first Lord Napier. His father, referred to here, was the renowned inventor of logarithms. His grandfather, Master of the Mint, was a great authority on bullion, mines, and kindred subjects. Lord Napier himself was early an authority on agriculture. In 1598 he published a work on "gooding and manuring field land with common salt." When he was appointed Treasurer-Depute of Scotland, James VI. said of him that he was a statesman "free of partiality or any factious humour." In 1619 he married Montrose's sister, Lady Margaret Graham. In 1627 he was created a Scottish peer with the title of Lord Napier of Merchiston. Montrose and his sister Dorothea found a home at Merchiston. Though a strong Covenanter, and conscientiously opposed to liturgy and bishops, he was yet loyal to the King. His allies of the Covenant soon began to suspect him of "divisive courses." He was a "Bander" and a "Plotter," and suffered grievous oppression at the hands of his former friends of the Covenant. He was seventy years old when he died. Though buried carefully by Montrose at Blair, the Covenanters wished to lift his bones to pass forfeiture on them, but they were contented with a fine of 5000 merks. In addition to the works referred to by W. (some extracts from which may be seen, Napier, Mem., 102-107), he left behind him in MS. "A true relation of the unjust persute against the Lord Napier, written by himself," which was published in 1793 by Francis, seventh Lord. See Guthrie, Spalding, P. Gordon, and Napier's Mem. *passim*.

## CHAPTER XVIII.

Montrose in Lennox—The Covenanters execute Rollock, Alexander Ogilvy, Nisbet, O'Kean, and Lachlan—Montrose marches to Athole—His overtures again declined by Huntly, whom he surprises into an interview—They concert a plan to reduce Inverness and gain over Seaforth.

MONTROSE had already spent about three weeks on the march and in Strathearn, waiting for Aboyne and his forces from the north. The rebels were now beginning to wreak their fury on the captives. Impatient of further delay, he crossed the Forth and marched down into Lennox.[1] He halted on the estate of Sir John Buchanan,[2] a ringleader of the Covenanters in those parts. His hope was, that being near Glasgow, where the Covenanters were holding a Convention of Estates, he might scare them from murdering the prisoners. With this object he marched his cavalry out every day in sight of the city, and plundered the enemy's lands without resistance, though the Convention had a guard of 3000 horse in quarters to protect them and the city, while he had scarce 300 horse in all and 1200 foot. But before he had come into Lennox, the Covenanters had heard of the difference between Huntly and Montrose, and the desertion of Aboyne and his men in Braemar. Encouraged by this, they beheaded three brave gentlemen of distinction, as a prologue to the tragedy.[3]

---

[1] *Levinia*, Latin for old spelling, Levenax. The Vale of Leven bounds the district.

[2] From the Acts of Parliament it would appear that a Sir George Buchanan of Buchanan suffered greatly from this halt of Montrose. His son George had given occasion for this visit by breaking into Mugdock Castle in the previous year, and removing from it pikes, muskets, iron walls, and gates to Duntreath Castle. Buchanan got 20,000 merks compensation.

[3] The following is an extract from the Minute Book of the Committee of Estates, kindly furnished from the Register Office by Mr. Andrew Ross:—

"*Glasgow, 21st October* 1645.—Forsameikle as by decreit and sentence of parliament of the fyft and elevent of Februarie last, Mr. William Rollock, Alexander Ogilvie of Innerquharitie, and Sir Philip Nisbet are forfault and doome and sentence of law pronunced against them be a dempster for the cause conteaned in the said sentence as the same read and considered be the lords and others of the committie ordeanes the said Mr. William Rollock, Alexander Ogilvie, and sir Philip Nisbit, now prisoners in Glasgow, and who wer lately tane in rebellion with James Graham, to be

The first of these was Sir William Rollock,[4] who has often been mentioned in these pages with commendation. He was a gentleman of courage and experience, and from his earliest years much esteemed by Montrose, to whom he was faithful to his last breath. The chief crime imputed to him was that he had refused to pollute himself with a foul and villainous murder. After the battle of Aberdeen he had been sent by Montrose with despatches to the King. On his way he fell into the hands of the enemy, was condemned to death, and would certainly have suffered execution had not Argyll, who had shamefully set a price on Montrose's head, offered him great rewards, honours, and preferment to assassinate him. In fear of death he assented, and undertook a deed which in his heart he utterly abhorred. By this artifice he gained his life and liberty, and at once returned to Montrose, to whom he disclosed the whole affair, beseeching him at the same time to have a greater care for his own safety. Horrible as the crime was in his eyes, he was not the only man who had been tempted; many others had been lured by offers of a great reward, and most of them would use all their craft and energies to do the deed.

The next to suffer was Sir Alexander Ogilvy,[5] of whom we

---

brought before the comittie presently, and the sentence forsaid to be intimat and read to them and given out as doome of law be a dempster. Lykas the saids three trators being personally present before the comittie, the said sentence was read in their hearing and the doome therein conteaned pronounced be John Wilson, dempster. The execution wheroff the committie ordeanes to be upon the person of the said Mr. William Rollock this efternoone at the mercat croce of Glasgow, and upon the saids Alexander Ogilvie and sir Philip Nisbit at the same place upon the morne efternoone by straiking off thair heads from thair bodies, and ordeanes the provost and baillies of Glasgow to sic this sentence put in execution." For the "sederunt" see p. 47 *n.* 7.

[4] See p. 47, *n.* 7.

[5] In the Crawford Papers, Alexander Ogilvy is spoken of by Robert Burns, the Glasgow magistrate who presided at his execution, as a "lovely young youth." His courage, youth, and beauty are dwelt on by contemporary writers. A portrait of him, little more than half-length, by an unknown artist, is preserved at Baldovan. The picture is out of proportion, giving the hands of a child to the head of a lad of fifteen years. A high forehead, light brown eyes under rather thick eyelashes, a straight nose rather long, with somewhat full lips, a gentle expression, ruddy complexion, and long fair hair are the chief features. A short black jacket with sleeve turned back, showing blue lining, and disclosing a white shirt with full sleeves and a stiff white falling collar, give the costume, with the exception of indications of a black and red tunic, which would have appeared had the picture been continued below half-length. Though the eldest son alive at this time, he was the second son of the twelfth baron of Innerquharity, Sir John Ogilvy, first baronet. The young man's zeal, bravery, and precocity in warfare made his future to be feared, and his death was due to this as much as to Argyll's enmity to the name.

have also made mention before. He was the oldest son of Sir John Ogilvy of Innerquharity, an ancient family, famous in Scottish history. Though but a mere youth, scarce twenty years of age, he was brave beyond his years and firm in adversity. It is difficult even to guess what they could lay to his charge, except the new-fangled and unheard-of treason, namely, loyalty and obedience to the best of kings. But apparently it was necessary to sacrifice this intrepid youth to Argyll, the inveterate enemy of his family.

The third was Sir Philip Nisbet.[6] He too was of a very ancient family, of which, next to his father, he was the head. In England he had served with distinction under the King, and been promoted to the command of a regiment. Except the usual charge of treason, for lack of real cause, I can discover no reason for his death, but that he was a brave, active officer; and their evil consciences taught them to fear that he would one day avenge the atrocious injuries inflicted on his father and his family. All three suffered a noble death with courage and resolution,[7] as becomes honest men and good Christians.

To these we must add two Irish gentlemen, as distinguished for their courage as their birth, Colonel O'Kean and Colonel Lachlan,[8] who were odious to the Covenanters solely because they had often felt their prowess. These two were executed at Edinburgh. At Glasgow many more lay condemned to the same fate, but Montrose's sudden appearance within a few miles of the city obliged them to defer their execution.

The report of his friends' death was a great grief to the Governor. It is hard to say whether he was more incensed by the

---

[6] Sir Philip Nisbet, eldest son of Sir Alexander Nisbet of that ilk, head of the house. He left Scotland in 1638. He soon joined the King's army in England, was knighted, and made a colonel. He was governor of Newark-on-Trent, which he defended against the Scots. On the raising of the siege, he went to York with Prince Rupert, and eventually joined Montrose on his expedition into Scotland, when he raised the standard at Dumfries in 1644. When he rejoined Montrose, does not appear; with him he is included in forfeiture, February 11, 1645. With young Ogilvy, he was buried in "the churchyard of Glasgow," where those of the name in the town erected a tombstone to their young chief. Diligent search has failed to discover the stone. See Preface to Alexander Nisbet's "Heraldic Plates," by Andrew Ross.

[7] The occasion for David Dickson's exulting words, "The work goes bonnily on" (Guthrie).

[8] These brave Irish officers were hanged on the Castlehill, before Leslie and the Committee of Estates moved towards Glasgow. Argyll had special cause to remember them. O'Kean had led the attack at Inverlochy with his usual gay dashing gallantry.

cruelty of his foes or the cowardice of his friends. He had been disappointed by the Marquis of Huntly, whose forces under Aboyne had been so long expected in vain. Macdonald, too, of whom Montrose had formed the highest expectations, though repeatedly summoned, and encouraged by his presence in the neighbourhood, and though the day appointed had long passed, gave no hopes of a speedy return. Six weeks had now elapsed since Aboyne had engaged to rejoin with the northern forces. Winter was at hand, a winter more severe than any known to the present generation.[9] The reinforcements sent under Lord Digby by the King had been repulsed. All this might easily have been prevented, and the whole kingdom reduced to order, had not those fine champions of the good cause been false to their word.

At length, on the 20th of November,[10] Montrose retired from Lennox, and marching over the mountains of Menteith, which were buried in snow, he passed some glens and lochs, the names of which have escaped our memory, traversed Strathearn, crossed the Tay, and returned to Athole. Here he met Captains Ogilvy and Nisbet, whom he had despatched to Huntly with the King's commands. They reported that they had found the man obstinate and inflexible. He replied disdainfully that he put no faith in them and their royal commands. The King's whole mind, he said, was better known to him than to them or the Governor himself, with whom neither he nor his sons would have anything to do. The friends and vassals who had voluntarily pledged themselves to help Montrose, he rebuked with bitterness and threats, and treated more severely than rebels.

In spite of all this, the Governor thought it necessary to dis-

---

[9] Turner at Newark says "we past that winter with very much cold, bot very litle bloodshed."—*Mem.*, 41.

[10] Montrose's movements at this time are not easily dated. Perhaps they are best followed by taking for granted that he fixed his headquarters at Buchanan, the site of the present ducal mansion, about the end of October, and from thence made excursions round Glasgow. Leaving his main body there, he proceeded with a light party to take a "settled and solid course" for a levy in Athole and throughout the country. He is at Kilmahog, at the mouth of the Pass of Leny, on the 9th November, and means to be in Athole on the Friday following. About this time Lord Napier died, and was buried at Blair; and probably before the 20th the Marchioness was buried at Montrose. On the 20th he left Buchanan, and marched by Aberfoyle, Loch Ard, Loch Venachar, and the Pass of Leny, to Strathearn, and thence to Athole.

guise his feelings and act with patience. While employed among the men of Athole in organising the militia of their country, he again sent Sir John Dalyell to Huntly, thinking he would be more likely to arrange terms of friendship. Sir John's orders were to show him the danger to King and country, and the eminent risk to himself and every loyal subject; he was to lay before him clearly that it was only his and his son's fault that those brave and faithful prisoners had been slaughtered.[11] Unless he at last bestirred himself, others, including Huntly's most intimate friends, and some of the highest rank, would inevitably be butchered in the same way. He begged and implored him at least to consent to a friendly conference with his Majesty's Governor, and promised that he would give him ample satisfaction.

Huntly replied with his usual peevish obstinacy. He declined the proposed conference. Of all things it was the thing he most abhorred. He knew Montrose's ability. He dreaded to face his presence, his confidence, and wisdom. He knew he could not gainsay his arguments. Montrose, however, having settled affairs in Athole, determined to leave no stone unturned to bring him to reason. Regardless of the wrongs he had suffered in return for the benefits he had heaped on Huntly, he resolved to take him by surprise and force him to a reconciliation, and energetic action in the King's service. Accordingly he set out with his army in the month of December. The rivers and torrents were frozen, yet not sufficiently to bear their weight. But he struggled on, over mountain-tops and rocky crags buried in deep snow, and through Angus made his way northwards over the Grampians. Immediately he hastened with a few followers to Strathbogie, where Huntly was staying, and almost took him unawares. Huntly was dismayed at his unexpected approach. At the first news, to avoid the conference he dreaded, he fled in haste to his castle at Bog of Gicht,[12] near the mouth of the Spey, as though he meant to cross the river and himself attack the rebels in Moray.

Here it seems worth while to pause and briefly consider the

---

[11] For a letter from Montrose to Huntly to this effect, see Napier, Mem., 617. The text of the letter is from a pamphlet, "Blood for Blood," printed in 1661.

[12] "The Bog" was the ordinary name for Bog of Gicht.

origin of this sullen opposition to Montrose. Huntly had suffered no wrong at his hands. On the contrary, he had always been treated with an honour and courtesy for the most part undeserved. Indeed, I could never hear or guess any other cause than impotent envy—it cannot be called emulation—of his brilliant reputation. It cannot be said that he was alienated from the King so much as at feud with Montrose. Burning with unreasonable hatred, he plunged into a sea of foolish errors, preferring that everything should go to wrack and ruin rather than that Montrose should have the honour of the rescue. The knowledge of the injuries and insults which he had inflicted on Montrose added fuel to the flames of a mind smouldering with futile vanity. This, unless I am mistaken, was the chief reason why he so often shunned an interview. Besides the instances already mentioned, both father and son were guilty of frequent and serious offences against the Governor. It will not be out of place to mention a few.

In the preceding year Montrose, as we have related, had buried some heavy cannon.[13] Without his leave or knowledge they dug them up, and mounted them on their own castles with as much triumph as though they were trophies wrested from an enemy. They refused to restore them when demanded. Yet it was Montrose who had captured them in the battles of Tippermuir and Aberdeen; and at Tippermuir none of the Gordons was present, while at Aberdeen Lewis Gordon had fought in the ranks of the enemy. They behaved in the same way with the powder, arms, and other war material taken from the enemy, and stored for safety and convenience in their castles. These they appropriated to their own use, and refused to return a fraction of them. After the battle of Kilsyth, Aboyne on his return home liberated the Earl of Keith,[14] Lord Marischal of Scotland, the Viscount Arbuth-

---

[13] See p. 71, *n.* 3. P. Gordon (p. 171) controverts these charges, and gives a third locality as the burial-place of the cannon, viz., between Strathdon and Strathavon, Kildrummie and Rothiemurchus being the other hiding-places.

[14] The Earl Marischal and Lord Arbuthnot, with other friends, were consulting together at Halkerton, the house of Sir Alexander Falconer, in the Mearns, when Aboyne came on them as he was returning to the north with his troops after Kilsyth. They had not made their peace with Montrose, and Aboyne had them in his power. Irvine of Drum, who had inherited a long-standing

not,[15] and several other men of rank among the enemy, then his prisoners, without consulting the Lord Governor, and much against the advice of young Drum, his brother-in-law, who happened to be with him. On what terms he did this is uncertain; but apart from the insult thus offered to the Governor, apart from the loss of an important stronghold, Dunottar Castle, and other advantages gained in the war, it is at least certain that the Covenanters would never have dared to attack their prisoners so cruelly had their own friends been detained in custody. On his own private authority he levied subsidies and taxes—a thing the Governor himself had never done—under pretext of maintaining the war, but in fact for very different purposes, greatly to the detriment of the King's cause. Lastly, to crown their deplorable misconduct, the prisoners taken in the battles in the north, and committed to custody in their castles, were by them set at liberty, some at the enemy's entreaties, others for an insignificant ransom. To Montrose they refused the disposal of those captives whom Montrose himself had taken in battle, and had intended to keep solely with a view to exchanging them for his own gallant friends. Pricked in conscience by the knowledge of all these wrongs, Huntly always avoided Montrose like the plague.

But overlooking these injuries, and setting aside everything else, Montrose bent all his efforts to the King's cause. To this end he resolved to extort a conference from the Marquis, to engage his friendship on any terms, to agree to everything, refuse nothing to his caprice, if he could but soothe Huntly's morbid vanity. He therefore left his men in quarters, and attended by a few horsemen galloped off at early morning to the Bog of Gicht. So sudden and rapid was his approach, that the Marquis had no time for flight or

---

blood-feued with the Keiths, urged the detention of the noblemen. They pleaded that they were there arranging for coming in, and Aboyne let them go, Graham of Morphie interceding, on their promise to come into Aberdeen and settle terms. This they failed to do. William, seventh Earl, had fought with Montrose on the Covenant side, had been a Bander, and became an Engager, fighting at Preston. He was made prisoner at Alyth by a troop of English horse in 1651, and sent to the Tower, where he remained till the Restoration. He was made Lord Privy Seal, and died in 1661.

[15] Sir Robert Arbuthnot, made first Viscount in 1641. He was a ruling elder, opposed to the Engagement. He died 1655.

concealment. When they met, Montrose, forgetting the past, accosted him with gentleness and courtesy. He entreated him to join in defence of king and country. In everything he gave him such ample satisfaction, that Huntly, as if at last convinced, seemed to give way. He promised not only to send his forces, but to lead them to him in person and at once. They then discussed the plan of campaign. It was agreed that Huntly should cross the Spey and march to the right along the coast of Moray, while Montrose took the road to the left through Strathspey, which at that season was by far the most difficult route. Their object was to surround Inverness and attack the garrison. Meantime they would endeavour either to win over the Earl of Seaforth or force him to join. The garrison, however strongly fortified it might seem, was ill provided with victuals and other requisites, and supplies for a siege could not easily be brought up by land or sea in that severe and stormy winter. Everything seemed now arranged. Aboyne and his brother Lewis invoked every curse upon themselves, if they did not stand by Montrose in loyal, true, and devoted attachment, to the last gasp. As for the rest of the Gordons and Huntly's friends, they were overjoyed at this result, and cheered their lord and chieftain as if he had just returned from the dead.

## CHAPTER XIX.

*A party of Argyll's men invade Athole, but are defeated at Callander—Convention at St. Andrews—Lord Ogilvy escapes—Nathaniel Gordon, Sir Robert Spottiswood, Andrew Guthrie, and William Murray are executed.*

THINKING that Huntly's animosity was at last appeased, and that he was now earnestly resolved to join him, Montrose marched his forces through Strathspey towards Inverness.[1] But to keep the enemy in suspense on every side, he sent his cousin Patrick Graham, who has already on several occasions been mentioned with honour, and John Drummond, younger of Balloch, a gentleman of tried fidelity and courage, who had often done good service, with signed orders to raise the men of Athole, and seize any opportunity of crushing a rising in those parts. Roused by their influence and example, the Athole men showed themselves eager and ready to respond. They had not long to wait for an opportunity. The survivors of Argyll's men, driven by absolute want, or in terror of Macdonald's power and threats of annihilation, had left their own country and made a raid on the Macgregors and Macnabs, Montrose's friends. They were afterwards joined by the Stewarts of Balquhidder, the Menzieses, and other Highlanders who still followed Argyll's fortunes, and were said to have got together about 1500 men. They were even on the point of invading Athole, unless promptly opposed. Already they had taken an island in Loch Dochart,[2] which they ravaged with fire and sword, and proceeded to Strathample, where they

---

[1] Montrose struck up the Spey with 800 foot and 200 horse early in December. Huntly laid siege to Lethin House, with 1400 foot and 600 horse. There are letters from Montrose, dated Kennermony, December 23rd; Advie, 29th; Bala Castle (Castle Grant), 31st; from Strathspey generally, January 10th and 12th, 1646; Kylochy, in the valley of the Findhorn, January 25th, February 1st, 6th, 8th, 18th; Petty, March 15th. Graham and Drummond were despatched to Athole from Kylochy.

[2] The ruins of Dochart Castle still stand on the island.

laid siege to the castle of that name.[3] As soon as they heard of this, the Athole men determined to forestall their attack and prevent the raid into Athole. Though only 700 strong, they marched to meet them, led by Graham and Drummond. On the news of their approach, the enemy in alarm raised the siege of Ample and decamped towards Menteith. The Athole men, in pursuit, overtook them not far from Callander, a stronghold[4] in Menteith, where they found them drawn up for battle. They had occupied the river ford and manned the opposite bank on rising ground with a number of musketeers. When the Athole men saw this, and observed that their numbers were somewhat less than had been reported, not more, in fact, than 1200, though they numbered scarce 700 themselves, confident in their leaders and animated by their exhortations, they resolved not to wait the enemy, but be the first to charge. They therefore posted a hundred active men as though to hold the ford against the enemy on the opposite side. The rest dashed across the river by another ford near the castle. Seeing their resolution, Argyll's people at once fell back on Stirling. The party of a hundred men stationed at the lower ford at once crossed and seized the bank abandoned by the enemy. They then fell upon their retreating rear, which they severely handled, and the rest of the Athole men coming up, the whole force was put to flight with a loss reckoned at about eighty men killed. The rest escaped, owing to the fact that the Athole men had that very morning performed a long and difficult march of ten miles, and were quite without cavalry. After this success they returned home.

At that time the Covenanters held their Convention of Estates at St. Andrews,[5] which they profaned with blood that cries aloud

---

[3] The Ample falls into Loch Earn at Edinample, near the head of the loch. Patrick Campbell of Edinample, brother of Sir Robert of Glenurquhy, was a Royalist. Stewart of Ardvoirlich, the murderer of Lord Kilpont, being with the Campbells, was reported killed or taken in the battle which followed, but apparently without ground. As a near neighbour and enemy of Patrick Campbell, he probably instigated the attack upon this secluded Royalist house.

[4] Callander Castle (Latin *arx*) may mean the supposed Roman camp at the east end of the town. The Campbells retreated by Rusky, and some of them were drowned in the Goodie. This battle was fought February 13, 1646.

[5] November 26, 1645.

for vengeance, by the murder of several innocent men, whose virtues deserve eternal praise. The very hatred of the rebels is their highest glory; for their rage was directed against the noblest and best. Those from whom they had less to fear they thought it sufficient to punish with sequestration. Lord Ogilvy,[6] Sir Robert Spottiswood,[7] William Murray,[8] a noble young gentleman, and Andrew Guthrie,[9] a brave, active officer, were condemned to be executed at St. Andrews, as an atonement for the blood of so many of that district, of whom over 5000 were said to have fallen in various battles. As their proceedings were guided not by law but passion, they had recourse to their usual arts, and made religion the cloak for their savage cruelty. To this end they set up their prophets Cant,[10] Blair,[11] and other fanatics of the same spirit,

---

[6] Lord Ogilvy escaped at eight o'clock the night before his execution was to have taken place. £1000 was offered for him dead or alive. He joined Inchbrakie and Balloch in Menteith.

[7] For Sir Robert's "Information," *i.e.*, legal argument used to save his life, see Wigton Papers, and for his statement see Preface to Practicks. The scriptural argument is very curious and highly characteristic of the times. Quarter given was pleaded, and by the custom of Israel prisoners of war were spared, witness testimony to it given by Elisha: "Wouldst thou smite those whom thou hast taken captive?" &c. Replied—this was not the law of Israel, but a bad custom, the law being illustrated by the cases of Agag and Benhadad. Counter-replies and rejoinders followed. The plea was disallowed. The trial took place "where is now the University Library." Lyon's "St. Andrews."

[8] William Murray was not nineteen. His brother at first cast him off, did not appear at the condemnation on the 16th January, but on the 17th the intercession of his mother and sisters moved the Earl to plead his being under age and not *compos mentis*. A respite of two days was given. He died on the 23rd instead of the 20th. In his indictment he is charged with killing at Kilsyth Thomas Myreton of Cambo, a privy councillor, as also with the slaughter of Mr. Robert Brownlee, "a minister living peacefully in his own house." This was a day or two after Philiphaugh, when he was hiding on the Border. Murray made a speech on the scaffold full of spirit and good feeling. Act. Parl. Scot., VI. i. 525. See Guthrie; Spottiswood's Practicks; Napier's Mem., 597.

[9] His father had refused the Covenant and attempted to hold out Spynie. The Bishop was imprisoned in Edinburgh, but eventually allowed to retire to Guthrie Castle. Andrew Guthrie had fought at Aberdeen, Alford, Kilsyth, and Philiphaugh.

[10] Andrew Cant. Spalding in 1637 speaks of him as "a ringleader at the beginning of sorrow." He was minister of Pitsligo, but in 1639 was translated to Newbattle. With his wife and children he passed through Aberdeen about 1st March, when Spalding remarks—"a gryte covenanter, veray bussie in this alterationis, and mortall enemy touardis the beschoppis." He became minister of Aberdeen in August 1640, but "he first went preiching to General Leslei's camp at Newcastell." In March 1641 he took up his abode at Aberdeen, where he both gave and got much trouble. He was a great innovator on the usages of Aberdeen as to baptism, communion, preaching, and blessing, as well as in social custom. His son, who had been a bad boy at Aberdeen, became Principal of Edinburgh College, and his grandson Bishop of Glasgow. See Spalding, *passim*; Scottish Antiquary, Sept. 1892; Jaffrey's Diary, in Spalding, vol. ii. p. 505.

[11] Robert Blair had been expelled from Glasgow University for teaching that monarchical government was unlawful. About the Glasgow Assembly time he was placed at Ayr to counteract

to work on the people, and declaim their bloody oracles from the pulpit. God, they declared, demanded the blood of these men; only thus could the sins of the people be expiated and the wrath of the Lord turned aside. Most of the people, otherwise disposed to mercy, were by this artifice inflamed to regard them as accursed and devoted to destruction: those whom God Himself demanded had lost all title to the protection of human laws or advocacy. These worthy interpreters of the Divine will and secrets even presumed to doom them, body and soul, to eternal damnation. Having thus blinded the people, it was easy for those who were at once accusers and judges to condemn innocent men, with none to protect them, none to plead for them.

Lord Ogilvy, however, one of their most distinguished prisoners in rank and power, related to the Hamiltons on his mother's side, and a cousin of Lord Lindsay, contrived to escape by the following stratagem. He pretended to be sick, and applied for leave to have his mother, wife, and sisters to visit him in prison and attend him in his illness, a favour he obtained with difficulty. Out of respect to these noble ladies, the guards retired from his chamber. He embraced the opportunity to dress himself in his sister's gown and attire. At the same time she put on the nightcap he used in his sickness, and lay down in her brother's place. They then bade each other a tender, tearful farewell, and about eight o'clock in the evening were lighted out by the guards, who took him for his sister, and were completely deceived. Immediately he left the town. Horses were waiting in readiness. He at once mounted, and attended by two followers, before daybreak reached a place of safety. His keen-eyed guards did not discover their mistake till next day. Argyll was furious with rage and

---

the loyalty of Mr. W. Annan, in which he seems to have succeeded. He and Samuel Rutherford ousted Wishart and other loyal ministers from St. Andrews in 1638. Baillie supported his translation from Ayr on the ground of his experience of Blair's "great dexteritie, yea greater than any man I know living, to insinuate the fear of God in the hearts of young scholars" (Letters, i. 174). He became prominent among the advanced Covenanters. Charles II. as King of Scots visited St. Andrews and called on Blair, whose hurry to get him a chair was rebuked by his wife, saying that Charles was a young man and could "rax a chair for himsel." Blair grew rich and bought the estate of Claremont. "As he could not acquiesce with Episcopacy," he was ousted from his living at the Restoration. He died at Cawston near Aberdour in August 1666, and "was buried there in the day tyme." Lamont, 241; Lyon's "St. Andrews," index.

baffled malice, and shamelessly insisted, but in vain, on the punishment of those truly noble and loving ladies for the active part they had taken in the escape. They were protected by the justice of their cause, but still more by the power of the Hamiltons and Lindsay. Many even think that they connived at the part they had played; but on this I can pronounce no certain judgment.

Ogilvy's escape was a great blow to the Covenanters. They were filled with rage and madness, and determined to hasten the execution of the rest. The first to mount the scaffold was Colonel Nathaniel Gordon,[12] a man of excellent gifts, both of mind and body. When he saw death so near, he bitterly lamented the sins of his youth. Just before his death a paper was thrust into his hands to sign in attestation of his penitence. To this he readily put his name. At the same time he called God and his angels and all who were present to witness, that if there were anything in that document derogatory to the King and his authority, he utterly disowned it. He was then absolved from the sentence of excommunication laid upon him for an adultery he had committed long before. Amidst the profound pity of the spectators he laid his head upon the block. He had been guilty of a grave fault; but he was famous for his courage and military skill, of which he had given proofs both abroad and at home.

The scaffold was still reeking with the warm blood of Colonel Gordon when it was ascended by Sir Robert Spottiswood, a man worthy of everlasting renown. His singular virtues had earned the favour of King James and King Charles, who had advanced

---

[12] Colonel Nathaniel Gordon (see p. 66, *n.* 11), "one of the bravest and best soldiers in Europe" (Sir Walter Scott), was executed by the Maiden on Tuesday, January 20, 1646. It was sent for on the day of sentence, January 16. The magistrates of Dundee on that day are ordered "to delyver the Maiden to sic as sall be sent from the town of St. Androis for transportation thereof. Quhairanent thir presents sall be ane warrand." The execution took place at the Cross. For details, see Lyon's "St. Andrews."

Some of the peers who voted on the 16th for the death of these gentlemen made certain qualifications. The Earls of Dunfermline, Cassilis, Lanark, and Carnwath were not clear anent the point of quarter. Eglinton, Glencairn, Kinghorn, Dunfermline, and Buccleuch would have banished William Murray. Eglinton, Dunfermline, Cassilis, and Carnwath voted for banishment for the venerable President Spottiswoode. Lanark, who had given him assurance of quarter, did nothing for him. Napier, Mem., 596.

him to the highest honours. By King James he was knighted, made a Privy Councillor, and President of the Court of Session. Recently he had been appointed by Charles his Principal Secretary in Scotland. There was nothing in this great man's life which even his enemies could cavil at; but they charged him with treason, which is the more to be lamented, as he had never borne arms against them or meddled with warfare, his eminent reputation having been gained by the arts of peace. The only charge, therefore, which they could bring against him was that by his Majesty's command he had conveyed to Montrose his commission as Lieutenant-Governor and Captain-General of the kingdom. In defence he amply proved that he had acted in accordance with prescription and the law. All seemed convinced by his eloquence, all except the judges, appointed by the Covenanters as his mortal enemies and thirsting for his blood. Never would they have passed that lamentable sentence, had they held the least regard for equity and justice. The truth is, this excellent man was destroyed by a malice too strong to yield to innocence. When the Earl of Lanark, who had held the office of Principal Secretary for Scotland, deserted to the Covenanters, the King, who had treated the Hamilton family with the utmost kindness and bounty, had been obliged to deprive this ungrateful man, and bestow his dignity upon another. None more worthy than Sir Robert could be found for the honour. Hence that load of malice and revenge which crushed its helpless victim.

On the scaffold he appeared with his usual firmness and dignity. According to custom, he was about to address the people, but the impious Blair, who had thrust his company on him even to the scaffold, dreaded the effects of his eloquence, his composure, and his reputation. The secrets of the rebellion might be laid bare by those revered lips. The mob was ever eager to catch the utterances of the dying, and stored them in their memory. He caused the Provost,[13] formerly a servant of Sir Robert's father, to stop his mouth. Unmoved by his insolent

---

[13] Lyon gives only the names of Provosts after the Restoration.

discourtesy, he desisted from his address,[14] and gave himself up entirely to his devotions and prayers to Almighty God. Again he was rudely interrupted by Blair, who asked him with officious impertinence whether he would not have him too and the people to intercede with God for his soul. He replied that he desired the prayers of the people, but as for his blasphemous outpourings, they were abominable to God, and he would none of them. "Of all the plagues," he added, "wherewith the offended Deity hath scourged the nation, worse than fire, sword, and pestilence is this lying spirit, which God, for the sins of the people, hath put in the mouths of the prophets." The rebuke was keen but just. White with fury, Blair broke out into scurrilous abuse. He reviled his father in his grave; he reviled himself upon the verge of it. Such was the bearing of this fine preacher of Christian forbearance and long-suffering. All this Spottiswood, intent on higher thoughts, bore in serene silence. At last, undauntedly, without change of voice or mien, he bared his neck to the fatal stroke, with these last words, "Merciful Jesu, gather my soul unto thy saints and martyrs, who have run before me in this race." Truly, since men may suffer martyrdom not only for religion, but for every virtue by which a righteous man may seal his faith, we may not doubt that he received that crown.

Such was the end of this great man. All good men were filled with grief at his death, but to himself it did the highest honour. He was remarkable for his knowledge of things both human and divine. As a linguist he was famous for his skill in the European, Hebrew, Chaldaic, Syriac, and Arabic languages. He was deeply versed in history, law, and politics. His integrity, his fidelity, justice, and constancy were the honour of his country and his age. Ever consistent and even-tempered, no excess in his boyhood or youth had ever caused him to blush in riper years. In his heart he was a strict observer of the ancient worship, but without vain, superstitious ostentation. Friends he won with ease and retained with firmness. His death was much lamented even by many of the Covenanters.

---

[14] Sir Robert's written address may be read in Preface to Practicks, and in Ruddiman's and Constable's editions of Wishart. When he was stopped he threw copies of it to the multitude.

His body was taken charge of by Hugh Scrimgeour,[15] an old servant of his father, and buried privately, with such care as the times permitted. Nor did he long survive his beloved master. A few days afterwards, seeing the bloody scaffold not yet removed, he fell down in a swoon, and being carried home by his servants and neighbours, expired on his own threshold.

The fate of Sir Robert was shared by Andrew Guthrie, a son of the worthy Bishop of Moray, and for that reason hateful to the Covenanters. He was a youth of great courage in war, and showed no less resolution in his contempt for the death he suffered. He too was assailed by Blair with threats and abuse. He replied that he could not conceive of greater honour than to meet a glorious death for so good a King, in so just a cause. All present should see how fearlessly he would embrace it, and posterity would perhaps speak of it with praise. For his sins he humbly implored forgiveness of God's great mercy; but for the crime laid to his charge he had no fear. With such unshaken courage did this youth face death, who, if it had pleased Almighty God, was worthy of a longer life.

The closing scene to this tragedy was enacted two days later. William Murray, brother of the Earl of Tullibardine, a mere lad, was brought forward on the same bloody stage. All were amazed that his brother, who stood high in the service and favour of the Covenanters, did not intercede to save the life of his own only brother. Some imputed this to apathy, others to avarice, lusting for his brother's goods, and others to stolid superstition. All, even the Covenanters, condemned his base, ignoble silence. But noble and honourable to himself was the death of this youth, scarce nineteen years of age, and in the memory of history he has gained eternal fame and glory. He addressed the people briefly; then raising his voice he spoke as follows, in words reported to us by some who heard him:—" My countrymen, account this a new honour and distinction for the house of Tullibardine and the whole clan of Murray, that a youth of that ancient

---

[15] Hugh Scrimgeour, evidently a man of substance, for in 1650, Lamont tells us, Charles II. "lodged at umquhil Hew Scrimgeour's house, nire to the Abey." See note of him in Preface to Practicks.

race, in the flower of his age, willingly and gladly yields his soul, so far as man can take it, for his King, the father of his country, and the generous patron of our family. Let not my honoured mother, my dearest sisters, my kin, and friends lament my brief life. It has been long enough to die with honour. Pray for my soul, and God be with you."

## CHAPTER XX.

*Montrose refuses to retaliate on his prisoners—Huntly disappoints him—Montrose obliged to raise the siege of Inverness and retreat before Middleton—Huntly again shuns a conference—Huntly pillages Aberdeen.*

THE fate of his friends was a heavy blow to Montrose. But it could not shake or overwhelm his firmness and resolve. At no time did his lofty generous character reveal itself more nobly. Many, exasperated at the undeserved death of their friends, sought to goad him, while still bleeding with the sense of recent wrongs, to take immediate vengeance. Their grief was justifiable, and, in its first outburst, their demand for retaliation seemed to them not less just. They assailed the General with complaints and harassed him with their unseasonable reproaches. Their comrades, friends, and kinsmen, men of highest worth and courage, who had loyally served their country, their King, and the Governor himself, in spite of the quarter granted them, in spite of the usages of war, the law of the land, the rights of nations, the claims of nature, were being butchered with impunity. How could they bear to see the rebels taken in battle not only not imprisoned, but well lodged like friends, rejoicing, exulting, mocking at their grief? They were guilty, and they demanded their punishment. Only thus could the enemy be deterred from their monstrous cruelty, and their friends encouraged and confirmed. He received their complaints with gentleness, and commended their affection for their friends. "Yes," he said, "the lives of our noble, innocent countrymen must be avenged; but our vengeance must be such as it becomes honest, brave, valiant men to exact; not by crime and cruelties such as the rebels practise, but by true valour and in open war. Their crimes, their brutality must be conquered, not imitated." Let them look at the matter fairly. They would see the injustice of making their prisoners, who were therefore not even parties to the murder of their friends, pay the penalty, the innocent for the guilty. They had been promised quarter, a most sacred pledge, to be kept even to their foes. Never should they commit the crimes they loathed in their enemies. The time would surely come when the rebels would have to answer for their iniquities to the just God and to the King, His vicegerent on earth. "Meantime let them set a price on our heads, hire assassins, employ cut-throats, and break their plighted faith. Never shall they induce us to rival their crimes or seek to outdo them, except in valour and renown."[1]

Huntly, who had not the least intention of performing his promise to Montrose, had crossed the Spey and entered Moray, where he trifled away his time, far from Inverness, with neither honour nor advantage. Too intent on plunder, after wasting the country, he heard a vague rumour that the natives had concealed their gold, silver, and other valuables in some towers and obscure little castles. He laid siege to them, but without effect. But neither commands nor entreaties could prevail on him to desist. The delay gave the enemy time to throw provisions into Inverness on the side which he had undertaken to blockade, and every preparation was made for a siege. Had he kept his word with Montrose and prevented this, the garrison would speedily have been forced to surrender.

Montrose now received intelligence that General Middleton[2]

---

[1] *Cf.* "Humble remonstrance of the Commission of the General Assembly," in Napier, Mem. 593, also petitions from Synods and Provincial Assemblies of Merse, Teviotdale, Fife, Dumfries, and Galloway, laying before Parliament what "the Lord calls for" at their hands in the point of justice," *i.e.*, vengeance.

[2] John Middleton, the eldest son of John Middleton of Caldhame (see p. 88, *n.* 4), from trailing a pike in Hepburn's regiment in France, rose to command all the forces in Scotland for Charles II., and to an Earl's coronet. His first service in Scotland was under Montrose at Bridge of Dee. His treatment of Huntly and the Royalists was generous and courteous. In 1648 he served as an Engager, and was taken prisoner soon after Preston. He escaped to Scotland. In 1649 he joined Mackenzie of Pluscardine and seized Inverness, but surrendered to Leslie. He then made peace with the General Assembly. See Act. Parl. Scot., VI. Pt. ii. 505. In 1651 he commanded the Scotch horse, was captured at Worcester, and confined in the Tower, but escaped to France. In 1653 Charles sent him to command in the Highlands, and supersede Glencairn. Defeated by Monk, he again escaped in 1655, and remained with Charles till the Restoration, when he became ruler of Scotland as Commissioner till superseded by Lauderdale. He presided at the great funeral of Montrose, and carried out the doom on Argyll. To the joy of Scotland he was removed, and ended his days as governor of Tangiers. In "God's Judgments against Persecutors," he is said to have fallen down-stairs, and broken the bone of his right arm, which pierced his side, and thus fulfilled

had reached Aberdeen with 600 horse and 800 foot, and threatened to ravage the lands of Huntly and the Gordons. Colonel William Stewart[3] was sent with a message to Huntly, urging him to return to the siege of Inverness, as he had promised. But if he did not approve of this, with the enemy so near his own lands, he urged him at least to join forces with him and fall at once on Middleton, who, he doubted not, could easily be crushed. He returned a disdainful answer, that he would mind his own business himself, and needed no aid or help of Montrose to drive the enemy from his own domains. Finally, after ten weeks wasted in the siege of some paltry little castle,[4] after losing the pick of his men, he was forced to decamp, steeped in disgrace. In contempt not so much of Montrose as of his Majesty the King he fell back to the Spey without the Governor's consent or knowledge. It was the worst possible example to all, who were beginning to rise in great force, enthusiastic for the royal cause.

Among these, the most eminent for wealth and power and the number of their retainers and clansmen, were the Earl of Seaforth, Lord Reay, Sir James Macdonald[5] from the Isles, the head of a very ancient Highland family, Maclean, Glengarry, the Captain of Clanranald, and very many others. Some brought their men with them and others had sent for theirs. Before the end of March Montrose would have been able to descend on the Lowlands with a far greater army than had been seen in Scotland

---

his imprecation on taking the Covenant, "that his right arm might be his death if he broke it," *i.e.*, the Covenant. See Douglas, Turner's Mem., Lamont, Letters from Roundhead Officers, and Napier's Mem., 216.

[3] Colonel William Stewart, like Montrose, had been on the Covenant side, raised forces, and commanded them. He next appears in the Parliamentary papers as undergoing forfeiture for aiding Montrose in his invasion of the south. He became a Commissioner of the Peace. Act. Parl. Scot., VI. i., index. Colonel Stewart was among prisoners after Corbiesdale.

[4] This was Lethin, into which Brodie of Brodie had thrown himself. The place and its siege of three months are hardly noticed in Brodie's Diary, Spalding Club. P. Gordon says Huntly took the place, but apparently on very easy terms for the vanquished. See p. 165.

[5] Sir James Macdonald of Sleat, with his brothers and tenants, was pardoned in 1646 by Middleton's influence. He played a cautious game, and was trusted by neither party. The Covenanters appointed him in 1649 to put down Clanranald and the Irish, but his conduct in that business was not to their satisfaction. In 1656 Dempster, the agent for the King, says: "Sir James will swear or forswear for the saving of his estates," and he warns his correspondent against Colonels Smith and Borthwick as "gone by Sir James' means to do mischief" to the Royal cause. He became a J.P. after the Restoration.

Act. Parl. Scot., index. For the strength of the clan, see p. 114, *n*. 5, and "Grameid," index.

within the memory of man. But the unexpected defection of so great a man as Huntly not only encouraged the rebels to persevere, but hindered and dismayed the Royalists so much, that those who had already joined began to steal away, and others to invent excuses for hanging back.

Montrose was therefore obliged to change his method. As neither gentleness nor benefits could make any impression on men who were mostly fickle, wavering, unstable, and inconstant, he resolved to exercise his authority, and compel them to obey by force of arms and under severe penalties. With this object he determined to march into their country with a picked body of his trustiest men, and compel all the Highlanders and North-countrymen to take up arms. He well knew that many sheriffs and leading men of family, who were his friends, would welcome such a course. Nay, he did not doubt that the most powerful chiefs of the Gordons, who were heartily weary of their chieftain, would, if need be, give him their aid even in defiance of Huntly's express will. First, however, he resolved to use every gentle means possible, before he had recourse to this last stern remedy.

As Inverness was the most important garrison in all the North, and its harbour peculiarly suited for receiving foreign assistance, he wished above all things to reduce it. He therefore invested it with such forces as he had. Middleton with his troops was more than eighty miles distant. Huntly and the Gordons were in arms between them. Again he entreated Huntly not to fritter away time, but to fulfil his agreement and join him in the siege, or at least to hover about the Spey, where the enemy would have to cross, and prevent their passage, should they march to the relief of Inverness. Should they cross, he begged him to join him in crushing them. To all this his answer was so disdainful, that the Governor was compelled to give up all hope of him. He even thought it high time to look to himself for fear of treachery. Distrusting Huntly, he sent three troops of horse back to the Spey, to keep strict watch upon the enemy, and give him frequent and sure intelligence of their approach. These troops occupied the best positions for the purpose, and for some time kept strict guard. But at last Lewis Gordon, Huntly's son, who then commanded a garrison in Rothes Castle,[6] contrived a piece of villainy more shameful than all his previous guilt. He assured the officers in command of those troops at the fords of Spey that the enemy was at a very great distance, and had not the slightest intention of crossing the river to raise the siege. With the greatest show of civility, he invited them to leave their useless watching, and come to his castle to rest and partake of a banquet prepared in their honour. Relying on his friendship and good faith, they foolishly accepted the invitation. They were entertained with elaborate courtesy; costly dishes graced the board, with abundance of wine and whisky. With many jests and studied civility, he detained them till Middleton had crossed the Spey with a strong army of horse and foot and penetrated far into Moray. As soon as he was informed of this, he at last dismissed his guests with these jeering words: "Go to your general, Montrose, who will have hotter work now than when beaten at Selkirk."[7] Meantime the enemy were marching on Montrose with such speed that these horsemen passed them with difficulty, and arrived at Inverness almost at the same time. They seemed like the advanced guard of the enemy, as they were followed by the whole of Middleton's forces within cannon-shot. Most providentially, however, Montrose had already been warned, and concentrated his forces at a short distance from the town. As the enemy were far superior in cavalry, he avoided the plain

---

[6] Edward I. took up his quarters in this important fortalice. For two hundred years it has been a ruin.

[7] P. Gordon replies to this charge against Lord Lewis, that any one may see it to be false, as it would mean, if true, that he had forgot "his breeding, his birth, his place and qualitie, his love to the King's service, and the hatred he professed to his enemies," &c. He gives only two troops of horse as guarding the Spey, commanded by Captains Macdonald and Mortimer. According to P. Gordon, Middleton crossed the Spey at Garmouth, and Macdonald rode off to Inverness arriving there some five hours before Middleton. Mortimer made a detour, he says, to inform Lord Lewis at Rothes Castle that Middleton had crossed, and arrived at Inverness only two hours after Macdonald, which is impossible. Wishart was at this time very well acquainted with affairs, and as James Kennedy, Montrose's secretary, had been captured, perhaps he served Montrose for a time in that capacity. Lord Lewis was a bad character, and much favoured by Argyll. Gordon admits that Montrose, who could ill spare them, had to send men of his own to guard the Spey. This alone implies a grave suspicion, which the event justified. For Middleton, with only 1400 men, could scarcely have passed the Spey had it been loyally guarded by Huntly, who could call out four or five thousand men. Why should Lewis have been dependent on "two troops" of Montrose's men for such vital information?

ground, and fell back across the Ness. They charged his rear, but were received so hotly that they desisted.[8] The loss was very inconsiderable, and about equal on both sides. Montrose passed by Beauly into Ross, pursued by the enemy, eager to force him to an engagement on level ground, where he would have the disadvantage. Apart from the superiority of the enemy, the natives were treacherous and inconstant, and Seaforth's new levies were deserting by companies. He declined battle on such terms, and hastened to shake off the enemy's cavalry. With this purpose he passed by Loch Ness, marched through Strathglass and Errick and reached the Spey.

He had resolved to treat Huntly as a public enemy, unless he came to his senses, but first he would try every gentle method to bring him, if possible, to reason. Accompanied only by a single troop of horse as a body-guard, he rode with all speed to his castle at Bog of Gicht, a distance of twenty miles. On the way he sent a messenger to advertise him of his coming, and inform him that he came with such haste and without forces, only to greet him and consult with him on the King's service. The affair was urgent, as he had just received letters from his Majesty at Oxford, which he wished to lay before him. Huntly no sooner heard of his approach, than dreading to face the man, he scrambled on horseback, and, with a single attendant, galloped off without deigning to receive or converse with the King's Lieutenant-Governor. On learning this, Montrose rode back the twenty miles on the same day, which was the 27th of May.[9] He was the more anxious to conceal Huntly's obstinate resistance, as his evil example might infect others. But concealment was impossible. The Gordons themselves and other friends of Huntly, mostly gentlemen of honour, were filled with indignation. They openly cursed their chief, in their eagerness to disown the disgrace of his base conduct.

In truth, it is not easy to say how much that man's example shook others of the North. The Earl of Seaforth, who had

---

[8] Crawford, with some eighty men as a rearguard, kept the river with such captains as "the Laird of Dalgatie, younge Gight, and Harthill." P. Gordon, 186.

[9] Napier omits this effort at reconciliation.

recently been brought with the greatest difficulty to join, was thought to be wavering. It was said that he was still unsettled, and even then engaged in patching up a friendship with the Covenanters. But this I do not believe. Even Alexander Macdonald, on some pretext or other, though often earnestly entreated to return, made nothing but idle excuses from day to day. Dark rumours about him too began to spread. Bitter as was his hostility to Argyll, it was said that he relied on the friendly patronage of the Hamiltons, that he was bent on the private interests of the Macdonalds, regardless of the public welfare.

Reflecting on this, Montrose thought that no time was to be lost. Accompanied by a flying band of his most active men, he decided to make a tour in person through all the Highlands and the North, to raise new levies, encourage the loyal, compel the refractory to obey by the stern exercise of the laws and condign punishment, and treat them as sickly children are treated when constrained to take medicine for their health. There were many able and willing enough to help him in a course which they had themselves earnestly prescribed.

During the progress of events at Inverness, Huntly, anxious to retrieve himself from the imputation of never achieving anything himself without Montrose, besieged and took Aberdeen, which was then held by Middleton with a garrison of 500 men. But his own loss was heavier than the enemy's.[10] Besides throwing away the lives of many of his best men, he allowed his Highlanders to plunder the city. How far the harmless townsmen had deserved ill of the King or Huntly, let them judge who knew them best, knew that for loyalty and obedience to the King no city in Scotland stood higher than Aberdeen. He took many prisoners, some of them men of considerable note among the enemy. These he treated with fawning servility, more like a suppliant than a conqueror, and dismissed them freely without

---

[10] On the other hand, Gordon says the enemy lost 300, and Huntly lost not one (hundred) (p. 190.) The defence on the other points is very feeble. He describes the capture of Aberdeen in minute detail.

terms or promise. Among them were several colonels and knights who happened then to be in Aberdeen. Though many of his own friends were loaded with chains and languishing in close confinement both in Scotland and England, he made no efforts to exchange for any single one of them. Such was the man, always more ready to gratify the enemy than serve his friends.

## CHAPTER XXI.

*The King at Newcastle orders Montrose to disband—The order is repeated, with terms for himself and friends—He disbands—The Covenanters try to prevent his departure—He escapes with his friends to Norway, September 1646.*

WHILE Montrose was intent on his design, on the 31st of May a herald[1] arrived from his sovereign. An unaccountable fatality had induced the King to throw himself upon the Scotch Covenanters' army at Newcastle. By his orders Montrose was commanded to disband his army at once and withdraw to France, there to await his Majesty's further pleasure. Astonished by this unexpected message, he bitterly bewailed the King's sad fate, which had hurried him into the hands of his deadliest foes. He felt convinced that such an order from the King to disband his army must have been extorted from him by the craft, violence, and threats of those who had him in their power. What could he do? To obey would be to abandon the fortunes of his friends to sequestration, their lives to the axe and halter. If, in defiance of the King's express commands, he continued in arms, he would be guilty of rebellion, the very crime he had undertaken to suppress. And worst of all, it was to be feared that the rebels would impute his actions to the King, and having him in their power, treat him more severely in consequence. The King's despatches clearly hinted as much.

Montrose therefore decided to call a council of the nobles, chiefs, and knights.[2] The question concerned all, and ought to be settled by common consent. To this end, without considering the many wrongs he had received, he sent Sir John Hurry and Sir John Innes,[3] two of his most distinguished officers, to Huntly, to whom he thought they would be most acceptable, and invited

---

[1] Robin Car.

[2] Napier omits this conference and the correspondence with Huntly.

[3] Sir John Innes (see p. 49, *n.* 10). He was probably Sir John Innes of Leuchars. See Family of Innes, pp. 202-240.

him to so serious a consultation. The choice of day and place he left to Huntly himself. They were also to add that he was ready to come to Huntly's castle, should he wish it. Huntly replied that he had himself received letters from the King to the same effect, and had resolved to obey implicitly; the King's commands were such as to admit of no second thoughts, and left no room for further deliberation. The envoys remonstrated. Perhaps, they urged, Montrose was of the same mind, to yield prompt obedience to the King's mandate, if that mandate were given freely. Meantime it was the plain interest of all to provide at once for the safety of themselves and their men. Their weight and influence with the enemy themselves would be greater if they acted in concert. He merely replied that he had already acted for himself, and had nothing to do with others.

Montrose therefore wrote to the King, earnestly begging to be informed of his position among the Covenanters. Did he consider himself safe in their hands? Had he any further need of his service? If he had positively resolved that the army which fought in his defence should be disbanded, while the Covenanters in both kingdoms were still under arms and daily waxing in insolence, what guarantee should be demanded for the lives and fortunes of those brave, loyal men who had spent their blood and all that they held most dear for his sake? It would be horrible to hand such excellent men over to their savage foes, to be plundered and hacked in pieces.

The only answer his messenger brought was a list of articles drawn up by the Covenanters, with which Montrose was requested to comply. But as these articles were dictated by the enemy and most unreasonable, he rejected them with indignation. He would not deign to treat with them at all. Again he sent to the King, and vowed that as he had taken up arms only by the King's command, no mortal power but the King's should impose terms on him. He therefore humbly begged his Majesty, if it really were his pleasure that he should disband at once, not to hesitate, but himself prescribe and sign the terms. However hard they might prove, he promised the most implicit obedience. But the commands of every one else, be they who they may, he scorned.

The messenger at last returned with articles signed by the King's own hand, and orders, now repeated for the third time,[4] to disband his army without further delay, under pain of high treason if he hesitated a moment to obey. Other motives, besides the King's commands, urged him to acquiesce at once. Many who had joined him had begun to make their own terms with the rebels secretly and through their friends. He had clear evidence that this was so with the Earl of Seaforth and others. Huntly and Aboyne declared themselves openly against Montrose. They even went further, and threatened him with hostilities if he did not immediately obey the King's orders.[5] Antrim,[6] who had just come from Ireland into the Highlands without men or arms, was intriguing to seduce all the Highlanders, whom he called his kinsmen and allies, from Montrose, whom he termed in derision the Governor of the Lowlands. This desertion was most ill-timed, and ruinous to all their friends in those parts. After weighing these facts well, Montrose was compelled to obey the King's orders and disband his army.[7]

It was a sad day for all when he called his men together, and, after praising their conduct, said farewell. He did his best to cheer them with the fair prospect of the longed-for peace. Their present submission was, he told them, as essential to the King's cause as their past achievements. It was, however, obvious to all that the King's authority ended with that day. Every one felt

---

[4] To Montrose Charles repeated his orders to disband, June 15th, and wrote again on the 16th July to the same effect. "The last letter was, however, accompanied by secret instructions to spin out the operation as long as possible." Gard., Civil War, ii. 512.

[5] "They did not themselves obey the King's public orders, but Huntly had a private order countermanding the public one conveyed by Robin Leslie, David's brother." P. Gordon, 196.

[6] Antrim and Alexander Macdonald were planning a private war on the Campbells. Gard., Civil War, ii. 513.

[7] Montrose received the King's first letter, dated Newcastle, May 19, 1646, on the Spey, the last day of May. His answer is dated June 2nd. The King received it June 13th. Montrose also wrote privately by a separate messenger. He then left the Spey and crossed the Grampians to Glenshee. Then came the King's letters of June 15th and July 16th. Immediately after their receipt, Montrose and Middleton met alone on the Isla and arranged terms: Montrose, Crawford, and Sir John Hurry to be excluded from pardon, but were to be allowed to escape up to 1st September: Graham of Gorthie to have his life, but not his lands: all others on Montrose's side to be fully pardoned. Montrose assembled the remains of his force at Rattray, near Blairgowrie, July 30th, and disbanded. With Sir John Hurry, he rode off to Old Montrose. Charles' last letter was from Newcastle 1646—"Defer your going beyond seas as long as you may without breaking your word." For correspondence see Napier, Mem., 632–642.

convinced that the order to disband had been extorted from the King under fear of some evil more imminent. As for themselves, whatever terms might be made for their safety, they would rather have borne the worst, than stand by, idle, dishonoured spectators of the calamity which had befallen their dearest sovereign. Their generous hearts were wrung by the thought that foreigners, that posterity would think the Scots had all combined in one universal conspiracy, and unanimously deserted the best of kings. Their grief was greatly enhanced by apprehensions of the fate that awaited their brave, successful, and beloved general, torn from his king and country, from themselves and all true men. His soldiers fell at his knees, and besought him with tears, if the King's safety required him to quit the kingdom altogether, to take them with him where he would. They were ready to live, to fight, and, if it pleased God, to die under his command. In truth, not a few of them did resolve, to the manifest peril of their lives and fortunes, to follow him without his knowledge, even against his will, and among strange nations volunteer him services which they could no longer afford him in their own distressed country. According to the articles imposed by the King at the desire of the Covenanters, one of the chief conditions was that Montrose should quit Scotland before the 1st of September. Ships and provisions, with all the necessary stores, were to be supplied him. These terms were settled about the 1st of August.[8] The port of Montrose in Angus was fixed for his embarkation. To prevent all suspicion and grounds of complaint, he repaired thither to await the ships, accompanied only by his own servants and a small knot of friends.

Just at this time his implacable enemies employed certain suitable ministers to spread crafty false reports, asserted with confidence, that the Estates of the Realm, as they called themselves, would not permit so gallant a subject to be exiled: his presence would be urgently needed should their gracious lord the King, who had voluntarily put himself in the hands of the Scots, be unable to obtain justice from the English and obliged to appeal

---

[8] More probably before, as he disbanded July 30th.

to arms; and no age had ever produced a better general than Montrose. Such, indeed, were the earnest wishes of very many who failed to fathom the deep design of the rebels. It was a treacherous, deceitful plot. The sad event soon revealed their intentions to the King; and as for Montrose, they were laying a shameless snare to entrap him. Their object in these flatteries was to fill him with empty hopes, entice him to loiter beyond the appointed day, and by a breach of the treaty give them a fair pretext for crushing him.

The month of August was almost spent. Still there was no sign, nor the faintest rumour of either ships or provisions. Montrose therefore, though resolved to depart by the day appointed by the King, allowed some of his friends to treat with the Covenanters for further time. His object was to sound their intentions more fully. Their answer was vague and evasive. He therefore concluded, and with justice, that their words veiled nothing but treachery and guile. His suspicions were greatly increased by the arrival of a ship in the harbour of Montrose on August the 31st, the very last day allowed him. The master of the ship was a stranger, a boorish, stiff-necked champion of the Covenant. The crew and soldiers were of the same stamp, sullen, sour-visaged, scowling fellows. The ship was neither victualled nor seaworthy. In fact, when Montrose expressed his readiness to go aboard, and bade them get under weigh at once, the skipper told him that he must have a few days to caulk and rig the vessel before he durst go to sea. He then began to brag of himself and his ship, and showed a commission from the Covenanters ordering him to land his passengers at certain ports appointed by their enemies, and at no other.[9] At the same time several large English men-of-war were seen cruising for some days off the mouth of the river Esk, which forms the harbour of Montrose, ready to do the Covenanters a service, to cut off all escape from their toils, and pounce on the prey they longed to rend.

Montrose, however, saw through their treacherous schemes. Even among the Covenanters he had friends who warned him

---

[9] See Monteith, 245, who here supports W. from information apparently independent.

repeatedly that the sea swarmed with the English fleet: escape to France or Holland was impossible; his port of embarkation was almost blockaded; it was perilous for him to sail; his enemies' only object was to give the Scots Covenanters an excuse to destroy him for lingering in the country, or, if he did set out, that the English Covenanters might surprise him when unarmed and off his guard.

The friends who were with him were of opinion that it was best for him, with such danger staring him in the face, to make for the Highlands again and rally his men at once; better to trust the chances of war than a treacherous peace. But his affection for the King was too sincere and ardent to accept their advice. It was quite certain that a renewal of the war would be attributed to the King, however unjustly, and precipitate him into the most imminent danger. It might cost him his life. Pressed on all sides, with treachery to right and left against himself and against the sacred life of the King, he never faltered in his resolution to bear the brunt of all himself.

His determination, however, was not the effect of a sudden gust of passion and despair. Even in this extremity his measures for withdrawing himself were taken with prudence and deliberation. Some time previously, as soon as he saw through his enemies' designs, he had sent agents to search all the coast and harbours to the north, with orders, if they found a foreign ship, to offer the master a reward to be ready by a certain day to sail with some passengers who would appear, and convey them, please God, to Norway. By good fortune a small bark, owned in Bergen,[10] was found in the harbour of Stonehaven.[11] A bargain was soon struck, as the master was eager for an offer that promised considerable gain. Thither Montrose sent Sir John Hurry, John Drummond of Balloch, Henry Graham, his brother; John Spottiswoode,[12]

---

[10] *Actuarius lembus*, translated "pinnace" in Ruddiman, "bark" in "Montrose Redivivus." *Lembus* is also used below for the vessel in Montrose Roads. *Vide* Pt. II. Ch. i. p. 189, *n*. 2, on Thomas Gray.

[11] Latin *Stanhyvio*. The local pronunciation is still "Stanehyve."

[12] John Spottiswoode, younger of Dairsie, was executed in 1650. "He was a gentleman of great bravery, and though very young, gave proof of courage and conduct in the battles he fought with the Marquis." Pref. to Practicks, 40.

nephew of the great Sir Robert; John Lillie [13] and Patrick Melvin,[14] captains of distinguished courage and experience; George Wiseheart, doctor of divinity; David Guthrie,[15] a brave young gentleman; Pardus Lasound,[16] a Frenchman, formerly servant to the noble Lord Gordon, and afterwards taken by Montrose into his own service in grateful memory of his master; Rudolph, a German, an honest, trusty youth, with a few common servants besides. These he selected to share his wanderings, chiefly because he knew that they were so obnoxious to the Covenanters that they could not remain a moment safe in the country. On the 3rd [17] of September they put to sea with a fair wind, and began their voyage to Norway. The same evening Montrose himself, accompanied only by James Wood,[18] a worthy preacher, took a small cock-boat and got aboard a bark lying at anchor outside Montrose harbour. Disguised in a coarse garb, he passed for his chaplain's servant. This was in the year of our Lord 1646, and the 34th of his age.

---

[13] He afterwards, as Major Lillie, commanded the advance party at Corbiesdale, and died on the field.

[14] About the end of 1649, "Sir James Douglas, my Lord of Morton's brother, and one Major Melvin, with many gentlemen of quality from all places of the kingdom, arrived in a ship from Orkney to Denmark, who . . . . did intreat and press Montrose earnestly to go to Scotland." . . . Ormond Correspondent, *ap.* Napier, Mem., 729.

[15] David Guthrie, Major at Corbiesdale, was killed beside Menzies of Pitfoddels, the standard-bearer, close to Montrose. Monteith's "Troubles," 511.

[16] As to Lasound the Frenchman and Rudolph the German, nothing apparently is known.

[17] Monteith says 5th. "His friends put out to sea the 5th of Sept., having run the risk of being murdered by the country people, who cut the cable while the ship was at anchor, and put them in danger of splitting upon the rocks." Mem., 245.

[18] The Rev. James Wood is commended by Montrose to the care of Seaforth in a letter from Gottenburg, December 15, 1649. After the Restoration, in consideration of his sufferings in the royal cause, he received a grant of £100. Monteith gives the master of the vessel as "James Garden, a good friend of Wood's." Is this a mistake for "Jens Gunnersen"? It is probable that Jens brought his sloop down the coast from Stonehaven, and waited in Montrose Roads by appointment.

# PART II.

## CHAPTER I.

Montrose in Norway—His journey to France—The Queen's courtiers endeavour to keep him from Court—Lord Jermyn's opposition—Montrose's advice to the Queen—The Queen accepts the overtures of the Presbyterians—Montrose leaves Paris.

MONTROSE landed at Bergen,[1] in Norway, where he was kindly received and treated with the highest respect by Thomas Gray,[2] a Scotsman, then governor of the royal castle. A few days afterwards he made his way overland to Christiania, the capital of the kingdom, by a wild and difficult route, across high rugged mountain ranges buried in perpetual ice and snow. At Marstrand[3] he embarked for Denmark, having a strong desire to see the late illustrious King Christian, who had always been a

---

[1] September 10, 1646. See following note.

[2] Thomas Gray. Herr Gabriel Gustafson, conservator of the Museum of Antiquities in Bergen, supplies the following note:—"Lieut.-Colonel Thomas Gray came to Bergen in May 1641, with Colonel Laurence Blair and some officers, with wives and children, probably all Scotch. In June 1641 Gray was made commandant of the castle during the absence of the castellan, Henrik Thott;" hence *arcis regiæ pro tempore præfecto*. "The castle (*Bergenhus*) was in Henrik Thott's hands, 1641-48. In 1648 Thomas Gray received an appointment in Throndhjem, and in January 1649 was made Lieut.-Colonel of the Throndhjem regiment of infantry, with an annual salary of 800 rigsdaler. (See *Norske Rigs-registranter*, ix. 180; Nicolaysen's *Norkse Magasin*, ii. 211.) The royal castle was the Bergenhus, of which the present Walkendorf Tower was a part. The route Montrose followed to Christiania was most probably the Laerdal-way, from the head of the Sogne Fjord. His visit to Bergen is noticed in M. Hofnagel's 'Optegnelser,' 1596-1676, printed in the *Norkse Magasin*, ii. p. 212. The following is an extract: '1646, September 10.—A nobleman arrived from Scotland, the third in rank next to the King of England, named *James Montrose*, privately on Jens Gunnersen's *krejert* (sloop, old Scotch *craier* or *cruer*, v. Jamieson, Dict.): September 15th, he left to travel overland to Christiania. In June 1650 he was captured, hanged, and quartered.' The author of these 'Chronicles' was one of the town's schoolmasters, who lived at least 1620-64, and probably earlier and later." See p. 188, *n*. 18 and index.

[3] Marstrand, v. Crit. Introd.

steady friend to his nephew King Charles.[4] On his arrival, however, he found that the King was in Germany. To Germany, therefore, he hastened across the Baltic, and passing through Holstein by the most convenient road, rested for a short time at Hamburg.[5]

He foresaw that the conspirators among the Scots peers who commanded the army at Newcastle would soon come to terms with their fellow-conspirators in England to ruin the King or subvert his authority. He used to say that he so thoroughly knew the temper of those men, that nothing could ever induce him to change his opinion. It would be much to his interest, he thought, if news of their proceedings reached France before his own arrival.[6] The accomplishment of their wicked design would probably procure him a more favourable reception from those to whom the King had sent him. The enormity of their action might at last shock them into shaking off their blind confidence in the insidious promises of traitors. Experience had taught him that new enemies and new struggles awaited him. Courtiers and parasites, the plague of princes, on whom they fawn, with their glib slanders and insinuations, invented to please the rebels, would do their utmost to close every avenue to the Queen's presence and favour, to exclude him from her councils, and keep him in ignorance of the state of affairs. They feared he would detect their crafty intrigues, frustrate the efforts of the rebels, and disappoint them of the vile reward of their treachery.

At last the melancholy tidings arrived. Under pretence of pay due for their base service—so they would fain gloze over the infamy of their shameful crime—the chiefs of the Scots Covenanters had been paid their price. The bargain was struck, and the King

---

[4] Christian IV. of Denmark. He preceded Gustavus Adolphus as head of the Protestant League, and had helped Charles more than once with arms, though hard pressed in his war with Sweden. He died 1648.

[5] He stayed in Hamburg till March 1647, receiving there letters from the King dated Newcastle, January 21st, and the Queen, Paris, February 5th–12th. On his way through Flanders, he was met by Ashburnham, bearing a letter from the Queen, dated Paris, March 15th. In the letter of February 12th she refers to the full letter she had commanded Jermyn to write. See Napier, Mem., 655–657.

[6] January 2, 1647. The King wrote to the Queen saying that now he was a "prisoner" and escape impossible.

at once delivered over to the brutality of the English.[7] Montrose immediately hastened into Holland. It was high time for him, he thought, for the sake of the King and his own honour, to show himself in public, to do what he could to remedy this desperate turn of things. For the more these saints sought to crush the good King, and with him all royal authority, the more erect and firm he stood to restore the liberty and avenge the majesty of his sovereign. Their efforts served only to whet his loyalty and courage.

Mary, Queen of Great Britain, and daughter of Henry IV., King of France, had found a safe retreat for herself at Paris. But in vain she implored help for her royal consort. The rebellion in Britain might well have seemed the concern of all crowned heads. It was likely to prove the worst of examples to other nations. To France, especially, it was a direct menace. Yet very few could bring themselves to offer even the slightest aid to Charles in his distress. The French were estranged by the memory of their old enmity to England. They imagined, perhaps, that Britain had slighted their friendship for that of Spain. From whatever cause, they gloated over his misfortunes. They had kindled the flames,[8] and they were bent on feeding a conflagration destined, it may be, hereafter to rage among themselves.

Scarcely had the news reached Paris that Montrose was on his way through Belgium, when the crafty courtiers about the Queen, to whom his presence was the one thing they dreaded most, set to work and used every means to keep him off. They selected John Ashburnham,[9] a gentleman of the King's bedchamber, the same who had been his unhappy companion and guide, first to the Scots,

---

[7] The first £100,000 were paid January 30, 1647, and the Scotch Commissioners took leave; English replaced Scotch soldiers. Guthrie says the King was delivered over Thursday, January 28th, at 9 A.M. The second instalment of £100,000 was paid February 3rd, and by the 11th the Scots were out of England. Gard., Civil War, ii. 577. Hamilton and Argyll got each £30,000, and Argyll's friends £15,000. Napier, Mem., 655.

[8] An allusion to the alleged conspiracy of Pym and the Five Members to bring in French aid?

[9] John Ashburnham. In 1627 he had been employed by Buckingham, his kinsman, to make overtures for peace to the French, but without success. He became a trusted groom of the chamber, employed much in diplomacy. An intercepted letter of his to the King, urging him to hold out on hopes from the Dutch, influenced events. At Carisbrook he offered to murder Hammond to facilitate the King's escape. Gardiner, Indices.

and then to the Isle of Wight, to carry letters to him, and induce him to turn aside from France. When he met Montrose, he began to urge him to return at once to Scotland and renew the war, without men, money, arms, or attendants. Their object, in truth, as it appears, was to baffle all his efforts for the King's service, and expose him to risks so many and so great, that he would certainly perish.

Montrose had no difficulty in detecting their insidious designs. He replied that the service proposed would be most acceptable; but, as matters then stood, it was as yet impracticable. He lacked everything necessary for renewing the war, and the Queen offered no supplies. The spirit of his friends, even the most loyal to the King, was broken by their humiliating surrender on such disastrous terms. The whole kingdom was overrun by the rebels. Their army, well disciplined and well found, had been recalled from England. Huntly was crushed, the Gordons massacred, and the rest of the nation so cowed that none would dare to rise. Moreover, he was commanded by the King, whom he could not disobey, to wait in France for further orders. Those orders he was well assured the Queen could not intend him to slight and disregard. As soon as he had shown himself at Paris and paid his due respects to her Majesty, he should esteem it a new honour and distinction to undertake any task, however perilous and difficult, in the service of so excellent a Queen.

Ashburnham, failing in this attempt, set to work another way. He earnestly entreated him to have some regard at least for his own safety, to make his peace with the Covenanters, court their friendship, and save himself and friends for better times. On his own responsibility, he undertook to procure his Majesty's permission; nay, if he preferred it, his positive command,to treat with them on any terms. To this Montrose replied, that no man was readier to obey the King's instructions in all that was just and honourable; but not even the King should command his obedience in what was dishonourable, unjust, and destructive to his Majesty himself.

The Archduke Leopold[10] was at that time Viceroy of the

---

[10] The Archduke Leopold, brother of Ferdinand IV., whom he succeeded as Leopold I. in 1654, died 1715. He had lately been appointed to the Low Countries. *Vide* Ch. iv.

Spanish Netherlands. From him Montrose received a free pass through Flanders into France, and arrived in Paris. Most men thought that none could have been more welcome to the Queen's court. But the event showed how far they were mistaken. By the interest of the Presbyterians, and particularly of Lord Jermyn,[11] a powerful favourite at court, they did their utmost to lessen his influence and decry his merit. Lord Jermyn bore the Marquis a secret grudge. At the time when King Charles threw himself and all his fortunes on the Scotch Covenanters at Newcastle, to gratify them in everything, and win their hearts, he had commanded Montrose to disband his army. He replied that it would be most unjust, unless he and the other noblemen who had loyally fought for the King received full security for their lives, and unless their titles, lands, and estates were restored by decree of the King and Parliament. This was strenuously opposed by Argyll and other rebels, Montrose's open enemies, who dreaded his valour and coveted his rich estates. The King was in a dilemma. Montrose's demands were just, and the King wished to gratify him; but there could be no doubt that an effort to wrest displeasing terms from his enemies might cost him his life. He therefore turned to Montrose, and earnestly besought him not to cling obstinately to demands which would expose the life and safety of his Sovereign to imminent danger. He graciously promised that if ever he recovered his liberty and realms, he would remember his service. Meantime he had provided for his honour, dignity, and needs.[12] He requested him to retire to France, and act as his ambassador extraordinary to the Most Christian King. He had already despatched his commission and instructions, empowering him to take that office, and assured him that nothing should be wanting to maintain the dignity of his

---

[11] Henry Jermyn, son of Sir Thomas, Comptroller of the Household, and a well-known figure in the early struggles of the Parliament. Henry was first the life of the Queen's court and then her trusted counsellor, though in her Roman intrigues she was not open with her Protestant adviser. Even the ruin of Eleanor Villiers, her maid of honour, could not long banish the bright courtier. After the discovery of the Army Plot he fled to France, where he was the Queen's representative. He flouted Hyde and carried things with a high hand in the decaying court. He became Lord Jermyn and eventually Earl of St. Albans. For his character see Gardiner's History of England, vii. 339, and index.

[12] See the King's letter to Montrose, Newcastle, June 15, 1646. Napier, Mem., 636.

post, till, by the blessing of God, he should regain his ancient authority and recall Montrose to his own country. This appointment was highly displeasing to Jermyn, who was the King's envoy in ordinary at the French court. The intervention of so distinguished a man might, he greatly feared, strip him of some of his honours and emoluments; and nothing less than all would satisfy his rapacity. He laboured to keep Montrose away, employing the same court artifices by which he had ousted the Earl of Norwich not long before from the same appointment.[13]

According to the King's command, Montrose fully expected to receive the promised commission and instructions at once, but he was told that nothing had been heard of them at the Queen's court. No commands to that effect had reached them. Ashburnham, however, hinted to him privately that such indeed was the King's intention, and nothing could be more certain than that the court knew it. He had himself been despatched to France for that very purpose three months ago; but Jermyn's intrigues and influence got everything rejected that tended in the least degree to baulk his power or profit.

Montrose felt that the King's commands and his own most reasonable claims were slighted and despised; but his generous soul could not endure to soil and waste itself in such paltry court squabbles. He therefore addressed himself directly to the Queen, and humbly entreated her graciously to signify whether she esteemed his service in any way acceptable and useful to his Majesty. For as the King was now a prisoner, he was entirely dependent on her authority, ready to accept her orders with respect, to execute them with all fidelity and zeal, to shed his blood, to lay down his very life in her service. The Queen answered with a heavy heart, and failed to explain herself sufficiently. Whenever she was allowed to follow her own incli-

---

[13] The Earl of Norwich (1644) had been sent, when Lord Goring, in 1643, ambassador extraordinary to France, and there confirmed the alliances between the crowns of France and England. His intercepted letter to the Queen, giving details as to the success of his mission, was read in the House, January 10, 1644, and caused alarm. In 1648 he was forced into the command of the Royalist forces in Kent, and he aided in the defence of Colchester. He would have lost his head with Hamilton, Holland, and Capel, but it was saved by one vote. Monteith, "Troubles," and Gardiner, indices.

nations, she was always disposed to encourage and advance a subject so noble, and of such conspicuous loyalty and merit. But she was hemmed in with snares, and distracted by artful courtiers, who alternately cajoled and threatened her with tales of the Presbyterians' wrath and power; so that Montrose was at times perplexed by her shifting moods and inconsistency.

Something, however, must be attempted to terrify the rebels from plotting against the King's safety. Such was always his opinion, and the Queen was much of the same mind; but the courtiers took good care that he should not be supplied with money for pay, arms, or travelling expenses. Montrose repeatedly offered, if only they would furnish him with six thousand pistoles, to make a descent on Britain with 10,000 men,[14] and raise the King's subjects, who heartily abhorred the crime of detaining the King in captivity, and were eager to avenge him. He would stake his life, nay, more, his honour on the attempt. But all was in vain. The scheme was opposed by ravenous courtiers, to whom all that remained in the Queen's treasury seemed too little to glut their wanton luxury.

Meanwhile the rebel Covenanters, who had first entered into that horrible league against the King, who had armed the Scots and roused the English, then living peaceably, to share their wicked rebellion, who had reduced the King to such straits, and at last betrayed him to their fellow-conspirators in England, to his certain ruin, now attempted, without Montrose's knowledge, to impose a gross, impudent fraud on the Queen. They professed to be grieved at their King's imprisonment. The English had broken faith. They had promised that he should not be maltreated, that nothing should be determined without consulting the Scotch Covenanters. They were resolved, therefore, to take up arms and restore his liberty and former dignity, if only the Queen would not disdain their aid, but give her sanction and

---

[14] The Ruddiman trans. has altered this to 1000 men. It is difficult to account for the reading "*cum decem armatorum millibus*" if incorrect, and the Latin for 1000 men would have been "*cum mille armatis.*" In October Crawford and Montrose had good hope of raising 30,000 men in the North of Scotland. See Jermyn's and Culpepper's Letters, October 19, giving lists verified by Lord Brentford. Napier, Mem., 653.

authority to their designs for his Majesty's relief. They therefore humbly besought her to use the great influence which she deservedly had with her royal consort, to advise and persuade him to trust himself and all his fortunes to their faith and valour. They promised to leave no stone unturned, to spare neither blood nor toil, and never to sheathe their swords, until he were restored to his ancestral throne and dominions. The good but too credulous Queen, fascinated and blinded by their flattering words, was easily induced to trust them, and promise her assistance—a promise she fulfilled. They were anxious to conceal their design from Montrose; but their secret negotiations were not long hid. When at last it was necessary to divulge them, the Queen declared to him that both the King and herself were so much oppressed and wearied out by the troubles they had already suffered, and far greater calamities which beset and threatened them every day, that they had turned for help to the Covenanters. They were a second plank to cling to from the wreck: they must trust all to their honour. Such was their firm resolve, and nothing could shake it.

Montrose could never be induced to believe that those perfidious traitors, entangled in such a multiplicity of crimes, would deal honestly and loyally with the King. He could scarcely refrain from tears, when he saw his beloved Sovereign trusting to the insidious promises of open enemies and plunging into an abyss of misery. But he composed his countenance[15] as best he could, and replied to the Queen as follows: "It is for your serene Majesty to determine what is best for your interests. Our duty is to yield prompt obedience. Your Majesty shall find none more ready to obey than I. But I consider it my duty to give you timely warning of the perils likely to threaten the King and country, if he follows such a course; and to offer such remedies as the desperate state of affairs permits and demands. Your Majesty, I presume, is well aware how, from the beginning of the troubles, these honest men have persecuted the King with

---

[15] W. here evidently speaks of a *personal* conference with the Queen. It must, therefore, have taken place before April 1648; *v.* next note.

more than hostile hatred and ferocity. They were the first to detain him an unwilling prisoner in their army. They refused him entrance into Scotland. They betrayed him to the English. Even now they continue to butcher his faithful lieges, solely because they were faithful, and sacrifice them daily to their greed and cruelty. I cannot, in truth, think that rebels so utterly abandoned have come to their senses. Avarice, ambition, and a guilty conscience alike drive and goad them to the same course. They cannot but see that their sole hope of safety and impunity is staked on the total destruction of their injured Sovereign. There remains, in my opinion, one last way to curb and bridle their wanton fury, like a bit in the mouth of a vicious beast. And that is to permit me, whose former services to the King leave no room for friendship with the Covenanters, by royal authority and commission to raise an army chosen from those of my countrymen who justly suspect the wavering faith of the Covenanters, and will never, if they can help it, fight under their command. These forces would act as auxiliaries to those who have already entered England,[16] if they behave with honesty and truth. But if, as I greatly fear, they relapse into their natural ingrained temper, and seek to upset everything and again betray the King, the forces under my command will overawe them, and either keep them to their duty, or reduce them, if they mutiny or revolt. As for myself, I shall gladly yield them the command, the praise, the honour, the thanks and reward, if they will only at last heartily, earnestly, return to their allegiance. It will be recompense enough for my labour, pains and perils, to serve my Sovereign, the best of kings."

The Presbyterians, by solicitations and promises, flattery and

---

[16] The Engagers did not enter England till July 8, 1648. Montrose left Paris about the end of March that year. Hence this point in Montrose's proposals to the Queen cannot be history. About May 1647 Montrose had sent a sword to the King from Paris. When carried off from Holmby House by Joyce, the King managed to write to Montrose from Newmarket, June 19, 1647, and thanked him for the sword. There is a letter from Montrose to Sir George Stirling, dated "near Paris," July 26, 1647. See Napier, Mem., 660-664. Sir William Fleming brought the Engagers' propositions to Paris from the Isle of Wight, and on "March 25th, 1648, he landed at Leith with a message from the Queen and Prince, requesting to know what they might expect as to performance thereof." Guthrie, 265. A few days after, Hamilton and the others despatched him and William Murray with their answers.

boasts, had so filled the Queen's mind with vain hopes, that she utterly disregarded the sounder counsels of Montrose, and trusted the safety of herself, the King, and their children solely to those who had been the authors of all their misfortunes in the past, and were soon to bring on them still more numerous and heavier calamities. Montrose, that he might not seem the impious partner or idle spectator of such villainy, requested and obtained the Queen's permission to quit Paris,[17] and retire for a while to the country to recover his health and spirits.

---

[17] He left France in the beginning of April 1648, and travelled through Switzerland, Bavaria, and Austria. Lord Napier's letters to his wife give much interesting information as to Montrose at this period. Napier, Mem., 665.

## CHAPTER II.

Character of the Presbyterians and Independents—The latter seize the King—The Presbyterians invoke Scotch aid—The Scotch raise an army—Hamilton appointed General—Factions of Hamilton and Argyll.

AS we shall have frequent occasion to mention the Presbyterians and Independents, two new sects and new names, it will not, perhaps, be unacceptable to our readers, especially those who are foreigners, nor alien to our purpose, to premise a brief account of those men.

It usually happens that those who leave the right road and wander off the king's highway get lost in a labyrinth of devious and entangled by-paths. This, we find by sad experience, has been the case of those fanatical reformers. Under pretext of restoring religion, they have not only shaken but shattered both Church and State. After expelling the lawful rulers of the Church, trampling on its ancient discipline, mutilating Divine worship, and most impiously deposing the magistrates, they split off into innumerable sects and factions, with a legion of names, a legion of devices in mischief. But they may be all summed up under two heads or families, so to speak, Presbyterians and Independents, which include all the rest.

The former of these, the Presbyterians, affect to be so called from a new model of church government and discipline, an institution, or rather inquisition, unknown to former ages. This they commend to the vulgar under the specious but false name of the Presbytery. Into their meeting, which they call their presbytery, they co-opt such of the people as are most zealous for their way, chapmen, ploughmen, mechanics, sailors, tailors, colliers, cobblers, and the like, without Orders, and without instruction in sacred mysteries. These have the same right to vote as the ministers themselves. They are elected annually, and dignified with the title of lay or ruling elders. Among their ministers they pretend to maintain complete equality, a mere fiction, upset in practice. Their real rulers are a small clique, advanced by the popular applause and the giddy conceit of the rabble, who lord it most tyrannically, not only over their brethren, but over peers of the realm, and even the King himself. Ecclesiastical matters are all submitted to the presbytery, and not only so, but all matters, human or divine, under pretence of being scandals or stumbling-blocks, and *in ordine ad spiritualia.* Their provincial and national synods, which they call General Assemblies, are convened without the consent, and even against the will, of the supreme magistrate. These are a sort of superior presbyteries, cast of the same metal. In them they presume to deliberate and debate, and even to determine on the most important and weighty affairs of state. Against such as resist or gainsay their decrees they thunder out anathemas and excommunications, by which, according to their teaching, body and soul are damned and delivered to the devil. By these means they exercise a wonderful terror not only over the poor ignorant mob, but even over the nobility. They interdict all commerce and intercourse with the excommunicate, thus lightly tearing asunder and destroying the bonds that unite servants to masters, children to parents, wives to husbands, the people to their magistrate. Those who differ from them in religion, or even in the most trivial rite, are, in their judgment, to be pursued with exile and imprisonment, fire and sword, even to death. But their chief fury is directed against those who persist in denying the divine right of the presbytery. If they owe a neighbour a grudge, all his words and actions are narrowly scanned and scrutinised, so that very few can live safe among them. In their meetings they rail with the greatest bitterness against lords, princes, and even kings, to their very face, load them with abuse, render them odious and contemptible to the commons, and harass them with impunity. By such arts they win favour and power with the people, and persuade them that they are inspired with a spirit of prophecy. They preach that nothing, not even in Parliament, can be duly performed, unless approved by the vote of the presbytery; that presbyters can and ought to be judged by the presbytery only,—their divine privilege, as they never cease to assert; and further, that the civil magistrate has no right to call men to account for sedition and rebellion, until they have been first condemned by the presbytery. Such assertions are as widely at variance as it is possible to be with the "classes" of the Reformed Church in Belgium and the Palatine, and the Genevan Consistory. These yield due honour and respect to the civil magistrate and obey his commands; whereas the Presbyterians despise him, contradict, oppose, stir up riot, and hound on the populace to arms, whom they hold in bonds by dreadful superstitions and oaths. In a word, they are oppressive to all ranks of men by their insolence, greed, and self-conceit; and far more cruel and intolerable than the Druids of old, or Papal inquisitors of modern times.

To this account of the Presbyterians we add that of the Independents, their proper spawn and natural brood; for they are all of the same feather—all tarred with the same brush. They are called Independents, I suppose, because they acknowledge no dependence upon any superior. Emperors, kings, popes, bishops, presbyteries, synods, councils—however free and general—they reject, with cursings and anathemas, as anti-christian and devilish inventions. Separated from the rest of mankind, whom they consider as polluted and profane, they are divided and split among themselves into countless sects and parties, an inevitable consequence, where men violently rend asunder all bonds of union and society. In one point, however, they show a wonderful agreement; they tolerate one another, and inflict no heavier punishment on those who differ in matters of religion than seclusion from the congregation. In treachery, avarice, sacrilege, and cruelty, in hatred of magistrates who do not truckle to them, they agree and vie with the Presbyterians. Ecclesiastical orders, especially the laying-on of hands, of which the Presbyterians are willing to retain some show, they abhor as a magical rite, an invention of devils. The people elect their ministers. Those whom they set up one day they pull down the next. In their private meeting-houses they settle everything relating to divine worship and ecclesiastical government. Learning and learned men they hate like poison, as enemies of Christian piety. They give ear to no preacher who does not profess divine inspiration. In their babbling, random prayers, wordiness, magical gestures, distortions of the eyes and face, horrid bawling and general disorder are applauded and admired as infallible proofs of the Spirit's presence. Almost all of them are Anabaptists, and baptize by immersion of both sexes, naked, in rivers. The Eucharist they pollute in foul and abominable ways. Besides the Arian heresy and other impieties of the like nature, these notable reformers of the age have recalled from hell all the ravings and obscenities of the Carpocratians, Adamites, and Gnostics. Only Papists, and those who follow the form of divine worship prescribed by the Anglican liturgy, are by them held worthy of punishment by prison, exile, confiscation, fire, and sword; but they are more indulgent to Papists than to English Churchmen. All other heretics they tolerate, even Turks and Jews. They maintain that the people, meaning the lowest class only, excluding kings, princes, and peers, have by divine right absolute power over the lives and fortunes of all. In this, as in most other respects, they agree with the Presbyterians, except that the power they nominally ascribe to the people is in effect arrogated by the presbytery, to whose decrees the people are entirely subjected.

From the beginning of the troubles in Britain the Presbyterians have been at great pains to court the Independents, looking on them as their dearest sons and brothers. As they were more numerous, their assistance was considered likely to help them in subduing the public enemy, as they wickedly called the King. These silly and infatuated men would, they thought, at once join them in arms; or, if they refused, they could easily be brought over by force or fraud. Inflated by this vain hope, they did their utmost, without hesitation, to welcome, encourage, and advance the Independents. No favour was refused. Many of them were elected members of Parliament, others were promoted to positions of authority, and encouraged to aspire to the highest honours. They were made captains and colonels, intrusted with the command of cities, seaports, and castles, and even appointed to the richest provinces. Gradually they rose to such power that they became objects of suspicion and dread to their patrons, the Presbyterians, who found, when too late, that they had nursed in their bosom a viper which, by the just judgment of God, paid them their due reward. Thus the Independents deceived the most deceitful of mankind by well-earned treachery, and ventured to impose laws where they had hitherto received them. Among the sacred articles of that horrible confederacy which they impiously denominate their *Solemn League and Covenant*, not the least was an agreement, whereby both parties, with fraudulent interest, bound themselves to mutual toleration till the end of the war, as though they intended thereafter to discuss their controversies in an amicable spirit. The Presbyterians were resolved never to endure the Independents. The Independents were resolved never to submit to the tyranny of Presbyterians. The latter are more powerful in Scotland, the former in England; but the Scotch Presbyterians who favour the Independents, now that they have seized the government in England, are far more numerous than the English who favour the Presbyterians.

The King having been delivered up by the Scotch Covenanters to the English Presbyterians, was lodged in Holmby Castle,[1] and subjected to the indignity of a military guard. Here the Independents seized him by open force and carried him off,[2] a deed which at last opened their eyes to their power and daring. The Presbyterians were furious with rage and indignation. They appealed to their solemn pledge; they threatened vengeance for their breach of faith. The others, triumphant in the possession of their royal booty, insulted the Presbyterians like vanquished foes, and laughed their vengeance to scorn. They could afford to despise empty threats, for they were armed, and showed it. Extraordinary efforts were made by each party to deceive the other. Both pretended to defend the King's cause. Both

---

[1] The Earl of Pembroke received the King, and conveyed him to Holmby House, in Northamptonshire, February 3, 1647.

[2] Seized by Cornet Joyce, June 3rd (Guthrie says 4th). For his warrant to the King and Commissioners, Joyce pointed to his troopers. "A warrant," said Charles, smiling, "written in characters legible without spelling." The King in a kind of progress was carried at the head of the army to Hampton Court.

declared that his liberty and honour, his dignity and crown, should be restored on just terms. They bewailed his forcible detention by the others, whom they accused of maltreating the King and dealing dishonestly with themselves. They proclaimed that not only the King, but all his adherents should be restored to their favour and friendship. This was the only way to cement a firm, lasting peace, so ardently desired by all true men. In their public writings they made many protestations to this effect, especially the Independents. The chief among these was Cromwell,[3] the lieutenant-general of the army under Fairfax. But men of penetration saw through these professions, and perceived that no such intention had ever entered their mind. In fact, the object of the whole dispute between these parties was not which party should have the honour of liberating and restoring the King, but which should triumph over their sovereign, the captive of their bow and spear, which should wrest from him the reins of government. For some time the Independents actually treated him with less severity, so that many hoped they would make their peace with him. Numbers of his servants, particularly his chaplains and ministers of religion, were allowed access to him, a favour which his most pressing entreaties could not obtain from the Presbyterians. They permitted him to use the form of divine worship prescribed in the Liturgy, to which he was wholly and entirely attached, to his latest breath. The Scots were admitted to audience and conferences without the presence of witnesses. Several of the nobility and courtiers, even those who had adhered to him in the war, were allowed to visit him. In many matters he was treated with the respect due to royalty.[4] But the miserable catastrophe has proved that all these concessions were a treacherous scheme of the Independents to gain time till they had crushed their rivals, and established the power of their own faction on a broader, firmer basis, both in the army and in Parliament.

---

[3] Fairfax and Cromwell entered London August 6th, and took possession of the Tower and command of the militia, a popular movement. They expelled the eleven members.

[4] Hence the rumour that the King's full restoration was imminent. Montrose alludes to it in his letters to Keir, July 26, 1647. The chaplains were Sheldon and Hammond. The King was at Hatfield June 27th, at Windsor July 1st, at Caversham July 3rd, at Hampton Court August 24th.

The English Presbyterians, degraded, despairing, on the verge of political annihilation, turned for refuge to their old allies, the Scots. They implored their help. They promised that as soon as they took up arms and set foot in England, the vast bulk of the nation, now heartily sick of the tyranny of the Independents, would at once flock to their standard. The Scots, eager for a war in England, grasped at the opportunity, and laid the matter before their Parliament. The expedition was almost unanimously resolved on, but there was a difference of opinion as to the pretext for war and the choice of a general. Some would allege the perfidy of the Independents, their breach of the Solemn League and Covenant: the Presbyterian church government had not yet been established in England, though Episcopacy had long been utterly demolished, and the Independents were to blame. Argyll and his associates, who had drawn over all the most seditious ministers to their party, considered that this alone was sufficient pretext. Others, headed by Hamilton and his brother, though they acknowledged this as the principal cause of war, were for urging as additional cause, the unjust, shameful, and harsh detention of the King, contrary to the pledge given to the Scots at Newcastle. They considered it their bounden duty to take up arms and demand his liberation; to bring him to a "personal treaty," as they used to phrase it, with the Estates of his kingdom, in spite of the Independents. The Hamiltons were loud in such declarations, wishing to conciliate the Royalists and catch their votes. But Argyll and his creatures, those fine Presbyterians who boastfully term themselves the reformers of the world and the times, would not hear a word about the King. He was stiff-necked; he had hardened his heart in his wicked resistance to the presbytery. Let him be left to himself; let him be abandoned to his most cruel foes. Accordingly Argyll appealed to the General Assembly, and the Hamiltons to Parliament.[5]

The question divided the nation. Two supreme courts of appeal were set up, battling full tilt at each other. The General

---

[5] See General Assembly Records for important additions to history of Engagement, with pref. Sir James Turner, Guthrie, Hamilton Papers, Burnet's "Hamiltons," contain valuable information; see also Gardiner. Significantly Balfour in his Annals omits the events of the Engaging Parliament.

Assembly, on the one hand, thundered out curses and anathemas of excommunication; the Parliament, on the other, were loud in threats of imprisonment, banishment, forfeiture, fire and sword. Between fear and superstition the wretched commons were distracted. Even the nobles did not know how to act in such confusion. The Hamilton faction, who had a majority in Parliament, secured a vote to raise a very large army,[6] and appointed officers zealous for their party. They exacted pay, arms, and supplies from the people, and made every effort to hasten the preparations. In spite of the opposition of many who suspected his loyalty to the King, the Duke of Hamilton was nominated general, a sure omen of disaster. Argyll's faction, predominant in the Assembly, passed a decree denouncing and condemning the expedition sanctioned by Parliament. Not satisfied with using their spiritual artillery to terrify the people, they stirred up large numbers in the West to open riot and a reckless rush to arms. Their numbers gave them confidence. They were inflamed by their worthy preachers, whom they regarded as inspired; and though a raw, undisciplined rabble, it was not without difficulty that the rising was suppressed by Middleton.[7] Not a few of their ministers were taken prisoners, armed to the teeth,[8] and fighting desperately in the foremost ranks. But Hamilton, to curry favour with the presbyteries, gave them a free pardon for that and other treasonable crimes.

At the same time the members of the General Assembly, to draw reproach on the Parliament and render it odious, proclaimed and held a solemn fast[9] throughout all Scotland. The chief

---

[6] May 3, 1648.

[7] Middleton and Hurry were wounded in the head and forced to retire on this first attack upon the "Communicants" at Mauchlin. The "slashing communicants" fled on approach of Callendar and Turner. Sixty foot, five officers, and some ministers were taken. All were dismissed save three officers of fortune, who were sentenced to death, but spared on the intercession of some ladies. The ministers in charge of the rising were William Adair, William Guthrie, Gabriel Maxwell, and John Nevay, "old Cant's nephew." Nevay was Leslie's chaplain at Dunnavertie, "who never ceased to tempt him to bloodshed; yea, and threatened him with the curses befell Saull for spareing the Amalekites, for with them his theologie taught him to compare the Dunnavertie men." Turner, 47; Guthrie, 277.

[8] Lat. *caligati*, in jack-boots (?). The word implies equipped like soldiers.

[9] On March 10th, the Parliament was got to observe a "fast" in the Parliament House. The fast alluded to here was appointed for all kirks in the kingdom on the last Thursday of June and first Sabbath of July. The causes are set forth in Records of Assembly, 567.

reason alleged for this was the apostasy and defection of the Estates of the Realm from the truth and purity of religion, inasmuch as they were minded to restore the King upon too easy terms. The Duke of Hamilton openly professed himself a Presbyterian, and in several papers which he published,[10] declared and protested that it was his intention to uphold their solemn covenant and sacred league unimpaired against all mortals, and that the army which had been raised and put under his command would be employed before all things to that end. All Royalists, especially those who had served with Montrose, were carefully excluded from every post of honour and service, but secretly he gave them good hopes of promotion as soon as he entered England. By these means he thought he could please both parties, but succeeded in pleasing neither; for both suspected and hated him.

---

[10] A declaration of the Committee of Estates was issued, and other political papers are alluded to in Lanark's letter, April 13, 1648. See Burnet's "Dukes of Hamilton," and references to the Hamilton documents in Records of Assembly.

The General Assembly was by no means unanimous in support of Argyll's policy, for in July 1649 in the Assembly "maney ministers were deposed for manteining the last expeditione into England to be lawfull, for reliffe of our King.... They wold not dance to the play of the leaders, Douglas, Dicksone, Cant, Guthrie and Law." Balfour, Ann., iii. 418. See Baillie's Letters, especially iii. 31 *ff*. Spang, who saw the effects of this Kirk severity on the public mind abroad, gives Baillie excellent advice in his letters of March $\frac{4}{10}$, 1649, pp. 71-84.

## CHAPTER III.

Hamilton invades England—Joined by Musgrave, Langdale, and others, who hand over Berwick and Carlisle—Defeated by Cromwell at Preston—Flight and surrender—A new army raised in Scotland under Lanark—Monro defeats Argyll at Stirling—Lanark's loyalty suspected—He concludes a dishonourable peace with Argyll—Cromwell and Argyll in Edinburgh.

BESIDES the choice levies[1] raised in Scotland, Hamilton summoned from Ireland a considerable force of veteran troops under George Monro, an energetic officer. The Earl of Callendar, who had been trained in warfare from his earliest years, and acquired experience and distinction abroad, was appointed by Parliament his lieutenant-general, and accompanied him to England. Hamilton left his brother, Lanark, at home to bring up reinforcements, if required. Everything, in short, was settled to his mind: brave troops, a staff of skilled officers, great store of arms and provisions, the certainty of support in England; and yet one and all were astonished at his tardy, slow advance.[2] There were even some who loudly complained that he was wasting time: the enemy were getting under arms and in high spirits; the opportunity for striking a blow was slipping through his fingers; the English Royalists still in arms were being shamefully deserted, and the King himself again betrayed, all because of his shameful, ill-timed hesitation. It is indeed certain that large numbers in many counties of England, especially in Wales, Kent, and Cornwall, trusting to Hamilton's promises, and relying on stout support, had prematurely flown to arms, an error which in the end involved both themselves and the King in destruction.

---

[1] See for the history of Hamilton's expedition, Burnet, Turner, and Clarendon, the last named agreeing in much with Wishart. Gardiner, the historical specialist of the period, has given a clear narrative and abundant references. See our notes below, which are mainly gathered from his volumes.

[2] But see Turner, p. 61, &c., "This ill equipd and ill orderd armie." He blames Langdale for the route chosen, and attributes the want of preparation to the precipitancy of the rising in England.

At last he reached the Borders,[3] where he was met by a number of gentlemen from the North of England, eminent for courage and loyalty, and men of great weight in their own country. They joined the Scots as volunteers; and, as the surest proof and pledge of their fidelity and constancy, they delivered up Berwick and Carlisle, two strongly fortified towns, which they had lately wrested from the Independents. They withdrew their own garrisons, and admitted a Scotch governor and Scotch troops. Among those who joined were Sir Philip Musgrave[4] and Sir Marmaduke Langdale,[5] with many other gentlemen of birth, eminent for influence and authority, for their wealth, their following, and their achievements. These were usually admitted to public deliberations on matters mostly of slight moment; but were excluded from the secret councils, where serious business was transacted by a small conclave.[6]

The English, who knew the temper of their countrymen, the nature of their country and the roads far better than the Scots, were for marching through Yorkshire, the natives of which were better disposed to the King. But Hamilton, whose manner was to neglect Royalists and advance the interests of the Presbyterians, preferred to march through Lancashire, where he knew the inhabitants were more favourable to his sect. Unfortunately, he ordered Monro[7] to stay in Westmoreland with a very strong

---

[3] Hamilton entered England, July 8th, with 10,500 men, counting on 3000 more under Langdale. He took over Carlisle on the terms arranged with Sir P. Musgrave when the Royalists took Carlisle, April 29th. Sir M. Langdale had surprised Berwick, April 28th, and came under obligation to surrender it to the Scots when called on. Gard., Civil War, iii. 370. *Cf.* Walker, Hist. Independency, ii. 9.

[4] Sir Philip was to have joined Montrose with 500 horse in 1645 (see p. 61, *n.* 11). His failure evoked Montrose's letter to the King: "Had I but for one month the use of those 500 horse, I could have seen you before the time this could come to your hands with 20,000 of the best this kingdom can afford." Montrose to the King, April 20th. Merc. Aul., quoted by Gard., Civil War, ii. 160. He acted with Monro, and held out Appleby till about Sept. 30th.

[5] Sir Marmaduke served with distinction at Naseby, Rowton Heath, and Sherburn. He accompanied Digby to Scotland. At Preston, says Gardiner, "by the admission of friend and foe, Langdale and his Englishmen fought like heroes." He was captured, and imprisoned in Nottingham Castle. He escaped to the Continent before he was excepted from pardon, Nov. 21st. See Gard., Civil War, 510, and index.

[6] "Hamilton suffered himself to be bearded with impunity by Callander, and only escaped outward humiliation by assuming the appearance of being convinced."—*Ibid.* 416. These two, with Baillie and Middleton, formed the conclave.

[7] Sir George Monro from Ireland joined Hamilton at Kendal, but as Callander and Baillie would not treat him as a commander, Hamilton was obliged to leave him behind in the North, to

detachment of horse and foot. He also requested Sir Marmaduke and his men, who were, it is true, not very numerous, but Englishmen of courage and loyalty, to march and camp apart from the Scots. His own column he allowed to divide and straggle far and wide for more than twenty miles[8] across country, through the hamlets and farmsteads—a flagrant breach of all rules of military discipline. To excuse this madness, he pretended in this to consult the welfare of the yeomen and natives of a country so strongly favourable to the King, and give his men greater facilities for obtaining food, forage, water, and fuel. Meantime he neglected the enemy, who were most active and eager to seize on every chance of war.[9] Indeed, he carried carelessness so far, that though on other occasions he was, in the estimation of many, a man of wariness and foresight, and particularly skilful in laying traps for his adversaries, on this expedition he showed himself a general without aim, without skill, and without success, not to say worse of him, to the great misfortune of the King, the kingdom, and himself.

Meantime the Independents, who by violence and deceit had forced the King to fly to the Isle of Wight, had seized his person. They also snatched the city and Tower of London from the hands of the Presbyterians, and expelled them from both Parliament and army. As soon as they were absolute, they at last threw off the mask. Hating Presbyterianism as much as monarchy, they resolved to crush and trample on both. Their general, Fairfax, undertook to repress some Presbyterians who were in arms with the Royalists in Kent and Essex. This he easily effected, as they were ill-prepared and undisciplined, without officers, a raw rabble, unfit for war.[10] Colchester, however, though poorly fortified, held

---

form, with Musgrave's force, a separate army. He was nephew of Sir Robert Monro, commander of the Scots in Ulster.

[8] Here Clarendon agrees. Had he read Wishart? The army was depending much on plunder.

[9] Lambert fell back slowly, fighting wherever he got a good position. He quartered his men at Bowes and Barnard Castle, and left a garrison in Appleby Castle. Gard., Civil War, iii. 416.

[10] June 1st, Earl of Norwich with 7000 Kentish men moved on London and took Bow Bridge. June 4th, Lucas raised a force in Essex, and at Chelmsford, June 9th, united with Norwich. June 12th, they were in Colchester, preparing to hold it against Fairfax. It capitulated August 27th, and was occupied next day. Holland took the field at Kingston July 4th, and by the 10th was surprised and taken at St. Neots. Lingen in Hereford and Byron in Wales also proved failures. The Prince of Wales off Yarmouth and in the Downs was equally ineffective. *Ibid.* under dates.

out longer than was expected, owing to the courage and determination of the King's officers, especially Lucas[11] and Lisle.[12] Cromwell, the lieutenant-general, surprised the Scots under Hamilton in Lancashire, and met with much the same success. The English, commanded by Sir Marmaduke, were the first to be attacked. For a long time they held their ground with great bravery; but at last, borne down by numbers, almost surrounded, in want of powder, and despairing of the help from Hamilton, which they had implored in vain, they were forced to look to themselves and fly. Cromwell, accurately informed by deserters of the sort of order and discipline maintained by Hamilton, in the certain hope of a very easy victory, charged furiously on the centre of the Scots with his cavalry, in which he was pre-eminently strong. Hamilton, in his ignorance of military affairs, was confounded by this sudden onslaught. In aimless panic he fell back on Preston with what forces he had about him.[13] Even there he

---

[11] Sir Richard Lucas, a Colchester man, brother of Lord Lucas. His execution with Lisle on the capitulation was an act disgraceful to Fairfax. By two P.M. on the 28th they were sentenced to death and executed at seven o'clock. According to Colchester belief, the grass will not grow in the castleyard round the stone on which he stood to be shot. *Ibid.*, and Walker, Hist. Ind., ii. 14.

[12] Sir George Lisle, a good soldier, had held the important ridge at the battle of Cheriton which Waller gained. From London he joined Norwich, and shared in the defence of Colchester. As Lucas fell Lisle leaped forward, caught the body, and kissed the face. He then took his place on the fatal stone. The men said they would not miss him. He smiled, and said they had missed him before when he was nearer. *Ibid.*

[13] The dates of events (from Gardiner) may help to clear this somewhat vague account. About August 3rd Lambert took up a position between Knaresborough and Leeds to await Cromwell's coming, and check any movement of the Scots to relieve Pontefract. While Hamilton lingered at Kendal, Langdale, impatient, pushed on to Settle, hoping to win over the governor of Skipton. August 9th, Hamilton advanced towards Hornby, where he still was on the 13th, when Langdale rode over from Settle to tell him the Parliamentary forces were gathering in Yorkshire. Whether Langdale knew that Cromwell was near Lambert is not certain, but Cromwell joined forces with Lambert that very day. While Langdale was drawing in his forces from Settle towards Preston, Cromwell marched through Craven, and reached Gisburn on the 15th. On the evening of the 16th he fixed his quarters in Stonyhurst Park, while the Scottish cavalry were far south of Preston, towards Wigan. Hamilton arrived in Preston early on the 17th, and ordered Baillie to continue his march across the bridge. Meanwhile to the north-west of the town Langdale was already engaged with Cromwell. The Duke, surprised by this, stopped Baillie and sent for the cavalry. Callander overruled this decision, and Baillie crossed the bridge. Hamilton, however, fell back with a small body of horse to aid Langdale, outnumbered two to one. After four hours' heroic struggle they fell back on the town. The Ironsides soon cleared the streets. Langdale himself cut his way across to Baillie, but his infantry surrendered and his cavalry fled north to Monro. Hamilton crossed by a ford. Before night Baillie was driven over the Darwen, leaving the bridge as well as Ribble Bridge in Cromwell's hands. Turner was for fighting on the spot, but it was decided at a night council to slip away in the dark. On they went to Wigan, and next night on towards Warrington. Cromwell,

made no fight. Driven on by fear or fate, that very night he abandoned the town without waiting for the rest of his men, who, though summoned by no messengers and without orders, were promptly and cheerfully hastening in to his assistance on the first report of the action. He hurried across the river, leaving no guard to defend the bridge, which was immediately seized by Cromwell; and abandoning his infantry, he got to horse and fled, a leader only in disgrace and helplessness. The foot, following their commander Baillie's example and orders, shamefully threw down their arms and surrendered to the victorious enemy. Some of the horse joined Monro, but most of them followed and managed to overtake their flying general. He still had over 3000 light cavalry, who, after a march of three or four days, having recovered their strength and left the enemy far behind, were of opinion that something might still be done. Some were for cutting their way through to Monro, others thought they should push on to Wales, and there join the Royalists who were still in arms. All, with scarcely an exception, agreed that they should rather sell their lives with honour, than endure the misery and disgrace of captivity. The General was absolutely alone in declaring that it was the fortune of war, to be accepted with humility; they must not kick against the goads of fate; there was no hope in fighting, while there was not the least reason to despair of mercy from the enemy: surrender at once was the sole road to safety. Cromwell's officers had not come up, but the Duke's impatience brooked no delay. He hastened to treat with the governor of some obscure garrison,[14] and having obtained a promise of quarter, he agreed to surrender himself and his followers. This petty governor

---

on the 19th, was on them at Winwick, killed 1000 and took 2000 prisoners. Though still superior in numbers, Baillie with his 4000 foot surrendered at Warrington Bridge. Cromwell wrote that he had now 10,000 prisoners. Lambert continued the pursuit. On the 22nd Hamilton with his cavalry was at Uttoxeter. On the 25th he offered to capitulate to the governor of Stafford. Lambert then appeared on the scene, and articles of surrender were agreed on. Lord Grey of Groby rode in and seized Hamilton as *his* prisoner, but Lambert stuck to the terms of agreement—they were to be prisoners of war, "the lives and safety of their persons assured to them." *Ibid.*, but see Clarendon, Turner, and Burnet. Walker gives Colonel Wayte as the actual receiver of H.'s submission, and agrees much with W.

[14] Governor of Stafford. "Vitam," below in the singular seems invidious, but had W. meant only his own life he would have written "suam."

had hastily got together a rabble of some four hundred country people, to whom Hamilton with his three thousand finely-appointed cavalry was on the point of surrendering, when word came that the Earl of Stamford[15] (others say Lambert) was at hand. To his discretion he surrendered himself and his army on the same terms as the governor had prescribed, and was immediately led off to prison.[16] Callander,[17] his lieutenant-general, whom Hamilton's friends blame for the loss of the army and all their misfortunes, because the general had devolved on him the charge of the discipline and entire control in the camp, avoided this deep disgrace, and adopting a more honourable expedient, travelled in disguise through England, and having found a ship, escaped to Holland. Of the prisoners, the richer were set free on ransom. Some escaped by eluding or bribing their guards. The common soldiers were treated with barbarous and unchristian cruelty, and sold for paltry sums to slave-dealers, who sent them out to the most degrading, grinding slavery in the West Indies.[18]

Monro and those of his men who had survived the battle of Preston were at once recalled to Scotland by the Earl of Lanark. Near the Borders he was joined by a large number of his friends, vassals, and other Royalists. A number of English noblemen and gentry also volunteered to serve either in Scotland or England, ready to fight to the last against the rebels, and eager to share his fortunes. The nobles, most of whom were favourable to the King, gathered their forces from every side and came flocking in, or sent special messengers to assure him of their goodwill and readiness to help. Soon an army was gathered

---

[15] Lord Grey of Groby was commander of the Midland Association, and claimed Hamilton (*vide n.* 13). The Earl of Stamford was a Grey, hence the error. Lambert was first on the scene after the surrender. *Cf.* Walker, Hist. Ind., ii. 55 and 131.

[16] *Vide* p. 26, *n.* 4.

[17] Callander went first to London, and thence escaped. See Turner for account of his own misfortunes and the whole expedition.

[18] The mass of prisoners was a sore burden. A distinction was made between those who had taken service under compulsion and the volunteers. The former were released on parole, the latter sent to the Plantations. When the market there was glutted, the rest were sent to Venice to serve under the Republic. Gard., Civil War, iii. 448. In January 1649 many were sold to Cromwell's admirers, the Jews, "who kept a constant traffic with the Turks, Moores, and other Mahometans; the Barbadus and other English Plantations being already cloyed with Welch, Scottish, Colchester and other prisoners." Walker, Hist. Ind., ii. 62.

sufficient to oppose Cromwell should he invade Scotland, and to quash Argyll if he attempted to stir up trouble at home. But this army wanted a leader. A council of war was therefore held to appoint a new general in place of Hamilton, now a prisoner in England. Lanark, his brother, whose ambition exceeded his merits, claimed the appointment, and, in spite of the strongest opposition, assumed rather than received the command. The Earl of Roxburgh, a man of great experience and distinction in the country, and far the most powerful nobleman in those parts, opposed him in a grave, moderate speech, and earnestly implored him, for the sake of their dear sovereign and distressed country, to withdraw his untimely demand for that dignity. "Even before the late defeat," he said, "many were much offended at the disastrous expedition into England. It seemed in a manner foredoomed, and solely because your illustrious brother had been appointed general. Not a few denounced his want of loyalty in the King's business—unjustly, as I think. But no one would have denied his want of success. And on this success people's estimate of the conduct of generals does, in a great measure, though erroneously, depend. For my own part, I would rather ascribe the late loss of that very powerful army and the signal disgrace of our nation to the cowardice of others or the malevolence of fate. But it is evident enough that most of the people, whose favour at this crisis we must do our utmost to conciliate, differ widely from what I feel it proper to express. Their minds are now embittered and sore; and if you, my Lord, are substituted for your brother, they will at once cry out that King and country are undone; that the brothers are one in mind and motive, one in the objects they pursue, and will certainly experience one and the same fate. Among our nobles there are still many men of weight, courage, and ability, men whose ancestors have commanded royal armies with honour and renown. I propose that one of these be invited, and even obliged, if he hesitate, to assume the command. And I think, if it please this honourable council, that the command should be intrusted to the Earl Marischal, a man in the prime of life, possessed of great wealth, second to none in ancestry and family renown, untouched by the breath of suspicion or the cavils of faction, and, I must not omit to say, no canvasser for the honour of this office."

All the nobles and officers present voted for Roxburgh's proposal. But at last Lanark, after indulging in excessive compliments to his own merits, threatened that he would never endure to have the command wrested from his hands in the absence of his brother. Roxburgh, and others with him, who had the wisdom and foresight to perceive the end of such courses, retired home, full of sorrow and anxiety, and from that day forth abstained from meddling in affairs so utterly confused and so plainly rushing on their doom.[18b]

As soon as Lanark entered Scotland, his first care was to dismiss his honourable and valiant English allies. The reason he alleged was his unwillingness to offend and irritate his Scots by surrounding himself with strange foreign soldiery. Meantime he held out hopes of concerting some plan for mutual aid—a hope which they found at last to be as vain as it was false. Next, with great parade of business, he despatched messengers with letters to all parts of the realm, to encourage all men of every rank, especially the nobles and chiefs of wealthy leading families and clans, to rise boldly and at once. Part of his brother's army had, he admitted, been lost, in spite of their general's courageous resistance, by the cowardice of others, but the greater part was still safe and resolute under his command. He therefore earnestly begged them to gird themselves to share with him the glory and profit of certain victory. But as he was well aware that many considered him wavering in loyalty, he solemnly imprecated curses on himself, if he failed to pursue to his last gasp that most holy war, begun at first to rescue and restore his most gracious Majesty, with the additional motive now of his dearest brother's safety. Few were so steeled and hard of heart as not to be touched, few so incredulous as to doubt his sincerity and earnestness. All beyond Forth, not even Fife excepted, prepared to rise. The Earl of Seaforth brought up 4000 choice men from the Hebrides and farthest parts of Ross and Caithness. From

---

[18b] *Vide* p. 223, *n*. 36.

the uttermost Orkneys the Earl of Morton[19] was already in Lothian with about 1200 men; but they were unarmed, and to arm them was not the intention of their excellent general. There was also good reason to suspect that they would soon be joined by the Gordons,—whose chief, the Marquis of Huntly,[20] was then shamefully imprisoned at Edinburgh and in danger of his life,—by the Earl of Erroll,[21] hereditary Master of the Horse in Scotland, the Earls Marischal, Buchan,[22] Athole,[23] with all their men, Ogilvy, Spynie,[24] Carnegie, Scrimgeour,[25] Drummond, Tullibardine, Erskine, Fleming, Livingstone, Lindsay,[26] Sinclair,[27] Douglas, Queensberry, Hertfell, Galloway,[28] Dumfries,[29] Maxwell,[30] Annandale, Home, Linton, with very many other Earls, Barons and chiefs of clans, either devoted to the Hamiltons or ardent Royalists.[31] The Highlanders were ready to a man, Argyll alone

---

[19] William, seventh Earl of Morton, had just died in Orkney, August 7th. His son Robert was served heir in March 1649, and died that same year in Orkney. He probably was in Lothian with his retainers on succession questions. Orkney was granted to the seventh Earl to reward sacrifices for the crown which had involved the sale of Dalkeith. See Kinnoull's letter from Orkney below.

[20] Huntly had remained in arms off and on during 1646 and part of 1647. Some of his bravest followers, such as Young Leith of Harthill and Gordon of Newton, had suffered on the scaffold. He was captured in Strathnaver, and imprisoned in Edinburgh in 1647.

[21] Gilbert, tenth Earl of Erroll, was a colonel of horse in the Engagement, and raised a regiment for Charles II.

[22] James, seventh Earl of Buchan, fined by Cromwell's Act of Grace £1000 for this loyalty.

[23] John Murray, second Earl of Athole, was excepted from the Act of Grace for joining Glencairn against Cromwell. He was made Marquis in 1676, aided William of Orange at the Revolution, and died in 1703. His wife was a daughter of the brave Countess of Derby.

[24] George Lindsay, third Lord Spynie, suffered much in the cause as an Engager, and with Charles at Worcester, being imprisoned in the Tower and excepted from the Act of Grace. On the death of Ludovic, Earl of Crawford, he became head of the ancient family. The patent of the title of Spynie could not be found, and was never voted on.

[25] John Scrimgeour, third Viscount Dudhope, was at Worcester, out with Glencairn, and captured by Middleton. At the Restoration he was made first Earl of Dundee.

[26] John, tenth Lord Lindsay of Byres, afterwards Earl of Crawford-Lindsay, (v. index), stood for the Engagement, and suffered a long imprisonment in the Tower and Windsor Castle. He held high offices in Scotland after the Restoration, but his hatred of Episcopacy and refusal to make declaration shook his influence, and he retired from office, dying in 1676 at the age of eighty.

[27] John, sixth Lord Sinclair, an Engager, at Worcester, in the Tower till 1660, died 1676, æt. 66.

[28] Alexander, first Earl of Galloway, died in 1649, and the honours and penalties of loyalty fell to his son James, second Earl, whom Cromwell fined £4000 sterling. The second Earl "was a proper stately person, most courteous and affable, so that the meanest persons in the country might easily have got access to him . . . yet he knew well enough how to keep his distance" (Douglas).

[29] William, seventh Lord Crichton of Sanquhar, made Earl of Dumfries in 1633.

[30] Was this Robert Maxwell, restored in 1647 to his father's forfeited title as second Earl of Nithsdale, and commonly called the Philosopher? He had been out with Montrose.

[31] As to the other noblemen given here, see index.

excepted. Many of these had already drawn sword in the war, to their own great cost.

Argyll's faction, aided and abetted by the most fanatic of the ministers, had gathered a rabble from the West, made up of a few farmers, cowherds, shepherds, sailors, cobblers, and the like, utterly untrained to war and without arms, and sent them to Edinburgh to fight under David Leslie.[32] They were loaded rather than fitted with weapons they were quite unsuited to carry, and mounted on horses, or rather jades, long condemned to the mill, and equipped with pack-saddles and rude halters in place of saddles, bridles, and bits. Argyll himself followed with some 700 soldiers of the same sort, some of whom he intended to throw as a garrison into Stirling, the place being suitable to his design.

To Edinburgh Lanark was now advancing at the head of a powerful army, composed of 5000 very active cavalry and 6000 foot, mostly veterans. The men were cheerful, well drilled, well armed, and well officered, eager to engage the enemy, and confident of an easy, bloodless victory. The advanced guard had already reached Musselburgh, four miles from the city, where they attacked the bridge over the Esk,[33] and though much inferior in numbers, dislodged and routed the force stationed by Leslie to defend it, with some loss to the enemy and none to themselves. They reported to Lanark that the enemy showed no aptitude or spirit for fighting, and thought of nothing but flight or surrender.

---

[32] The Whigamore raid of Lord Eglinton and his son Robert moved on Edinburgh about September 5, accompanied by Loudon, the Chancellor, and David Dickson, and welcomed by the city magistrates and ministers. Leven held the Castle, which protected them. The Hamilton party in the town opened negotiations with them, and Lindsay and Glencairn rode south with proposals to Lanark. Monro crossed the Tweed September 8, and advanced by Haddington on Edinburgh, which they passed on the south side, and on the 11th ate the deserted supper of Cassilis and his raiders at Linlithgow. By the afternoon of the 12th, Monro with the cavalry was at St. Ninians, close to Stirling. Argyll entered Stirling at eleven o'clock that morning, and having set his posts and quartered his men, went to dine with Lord Mar, the governor. The meat " was setting on the table " when he heard of Monro's approach, and fled by the bridge to North Queensferry, where he took boat for the fourth time." Monro's slaughter of Argyll's men was condemned by his superiors on their arrival. On the night of the 12th Leslie and the Whigamores were at Falkirk. Monro offered to destroy them, but Lanark negotiated, and on the 16th concluded a treaty in effect harsh to Monro and his Irish. All the Irish ports to which they might have sailed were now in Monk's hands, and old Sir Robert Monro taken. Cromwell crossed the Tweed September 21, met Argyll on the 22nd, sent Lambert on to Edinburgh at once, and himself followed October 4. See Guthrie.

[33] The picturesque old bridge near the railway station.

A victory without bloodshed, and therefore without prejudice, was in their hands. The capital of the kingdom, the naval magazines of Leith, with immense stores of implements, cannon, powder, and ball, and a great supply of provisions, might easily be seized that very night, perhaps even before sunset, if they pushed on. There was no need for the whole army; a mere third of it would suffice to settle the whole business.

And in truth, had he given his assent, no one doubted that Scotland might have been regained and returned to its allegiance. Instead, he sounded a retreat, and ordered his victorious troops to cease fighting and retire. Then leaving the highway to Edinburgh, he marched off to the left. Officers and men were astounded at such a movement. Soon their astonishment gave place to murmurs of indignation at letting slip so grand a chance to finish the war in Scotland at once. His ill-timed hesitation would benefit their enemies and injure themselves. It gave them not only time to breathe, but time to collect forces both in Scotland and beyond the Borders, especially from Cromwell, for whom they were fighting. The capital, where the Estates were held, with all its stores, arms, and treasure, was being simply given away gratis to the enemy. To crown all, their own reputation, which is a matter of no small moment in a war, was being lost and passing to enemies who did not deserve the name of soldiers.

The more sagacious now began for the first time to suspect his drift. No sane person could suppose that Lanark, a man of keen intellect and much foresight, could be so foolish and so mad, without some object very different to what he professed. He had, in fact, long before this resolved on any terms to make his peace with Argyll's faction, and had made a show of arms to display his power, not his will, to do them a mischief, and to secure greater favour with them. It is now notorious that he had long been in secret negotiation with Argyll, utterly indifferent to the interests of his soldiers and comrades, whom he had summoned to his standard.

When the enemy saw to their joy that Lanark had turned away from Edinburgh and was marching through the Pentland Hills, they hastened to draw out their contemptible force of dummy soldiers; not that they put any confidence in them, but by making a show of force to keep up appearances and influence with the people, and fleer at brave men crippled by their leader's orders. The veteran officers and soldiers, pierced with sorrow, shame, and rage, could scarce brook the affront. Their general had great difficulty in restraining them from falling furiously upon their paltry foe; but his authority prevailed, and they were compelled to march towards Stirling.

On reaching Falkirk [34] the van with a few veterans was led by Monro, an honourable man, earnest in the King's service, and eager to serve him faithfully in a war which, as he imagined, had been undertaken in his cause. He had now got wind of Lanark's intrigues, dark and secret though they were. As he could not overthrow them, he resolved to thwart them or expose them by a skilful stratagem. The general was marching slowly, bringing up the rear far behind, when word was brought that Argyll with 700 Highlanders had that morning occupied Stirling. To Stirling, therefore, Monro and his men advanced with all speed, in order, if possible, to surprise him. The gates were shut and guarded; but he managed to gain access through a park which Scottish kings had constructed near a pleasant orchard as a deer preserve. Here he found a small postern, but too narrow and low to admit him on horseback. Dismounting, therefore, this active, indefatigable officer broke down the gate and burst in. The rest of his men followed slowly, one by one, as they could scramble through the narrow wicket, and scarce six came up with him before he was engaged. Argyll's men, confounded by the sudden attack, and at a loss what to do, with none to command them, scattered through the streets and wynds in disorder and confusion. Their leader himself, at the first news of the enemy's entrance, resolved, as usual, to make off, and headed the flight. Mounted on his swiftest steed, he passed the gate farthest from the attack, and made for the bridge over the Forth, hotly pursued by Monro. But his fleet horse carried him off like a deer from the fangs of a stag-hound; he gained the bridge and escaped.

---

[34] Lat. *Fanum Valli*, Wall Kirk, according to W.'s derivation, p. 10.

His men, however, were not so lucky. Nearly 200 of them were killed, and the rest taken prisoners.

At length Lanark came up, attended by Lords Lindsay and Glencairn, the sole confidants of his secret plans. They were vastly disgusted at this gallant action of Monro. Lindsay could not contain his annoyance, and angrily exclaimed, "Woe's me, that ever I should live to see this unlucky and disastrous day!" For they were sorely afraid that the exasperation on both sides would defeat their hope and eagerness for peace.

Lanark, however, disguised his feelings with profound craft both to the soldiers and those nobles who had not yet joined, and whom he teased continually with letters to that purpose. Monro, however, and others too, saw through his machinations. Among these were the men of Athole, rough Highlanders, but by no means lacking in sagacity. They had been in arms for some time, and had come down as far as Strathearn. Thence they sent their humble earnest petition to the general and nobility with him, praying them, if they were in earnest, to exert the authority intrusted to them by the King and last Committee of Estates, and proclaim those who resisted, and specially those who convened forces at Edinburgh, as rebels and traitors. Such a pledge would confirm the doubtful and wavering. "For though," as they said, "it were wrong to doubt your firmness, loyalty, and courage, yet there are many capable of greatly aiding your cause who are deterred by the fear that you may desert them, and contract a base peace with the enemy, dishonourable to yourselves and destructive to your allies. Should that which we mention with loathing really happen, what can we expect but curses and excommunications, imprisonment, exile, confiscations, and every form of death from our savage enemies?" Others too made the same and many more complaints, but without avail. They at first dallied and put off their just and honourable demands, and soon thought nothing of deceiving them outright. At last Glencairn, first cousin of the Hamiltons, and Lindsay, their brother-in-law, both of them bound like slaves to their interest, had the effrontery to speak of the necessity of demanding and accepting, not on fair terms, but on any terms whatsoever, a peace which they had already concluded unknown to the rest of their party. At this the soldiers were indignant, and began to murmur and storm. The general, with a skill that almost extorts admiration, welcomed this display of spirit and resolution, while he approved of the zeal for peace displayed by the others. In outward show he agreed with his soldiers; in his heart he was with his kinsmen. In a vague, rambling speech he accused Glencairn and Lindsay, and complained that they had begun to treat with the enemy without their general's knowledge or consent, and demanded a dubious and treacherous peace on very hard—almost intolerable conditions. At the same time he aimed a side blow of reproof at those who expressed such abhorrence of accommodation and seemed to rejoice in civil broils. And though he professed that he himself would never accept those hard terms thrust on them by the enemy, yet he implored others, by the perils to which they exposed their parents, wives, children, and friends, to acquiesce in those very terms. Few, however, were so foolish and infatuated as to believe that this brace of peace-makers, devoted to him on so many accounts, and in all else the creatures of his will, would have presumed to think, not to say treat, of peace without his orders.

Thus at last, in spite of much resistance on the part of soldiers, officers, and all the loyal nobility, the advice of Glencairn and Lindsay prevailed. These soldiers had been levied by authority of King and Parliament. On that same authority their officers had relied. Their supplies were abundant. Their force was continually growing by large and powerful accessions from every side. They were worn out by no fatigues, thinned by no disease, unassailed by even the slightest loss an enemy could inflict; in straits for nothing, unimpaired in health and vigour, well armed, and in high spirits. Yet they were compelled to accept the hardest and most iniquitous terms imposed by a few feeble un-soldierly rebels, without the King's mandate, without the vote of Parliament, without the support of any legal authority.

By the articles of this peace it was provided, firstly, that all officers and men who had served under the Hamiltons should lay down their arms,—those who were at Stirling and in the neighbourhood within two days,—their adherents in more distant parts within a fortnight. Those who refused were to be held guilty of rebellion. All noblemen who had shared in Hamilton's recent expedition, or in any way abetted it, were to present themselves before the next meeting of the Estates, to stand their trial. In those proceedings they were to have no voice or vote. Colonels, captains, and other officers were to be stripped of their titles and commissions, and excluded from any return to office, until penance done and satisfaction given to the Presbytery. The same enactment applied to the common soldiers. The Irish one and all were to quit Scotland, under pain of death if found there beyond a certain day. Finally, all were to submit to the judgment of the Presbytery, and cheerfully accept the penalties it imposed, under pain of excommunication.

On the day when these articles were published to the troops, it happened conveniently that they were almost all scattered in villages and hamlets. Otherwise it is certain there would have been a great mutiny. The few who were on the spot were filled with the bitterest indignation, and could scarce refrain from falling on those worthy peace-makers and tearing them limb from limb. Lanark, their general, did his utmost to clear himself of all blame. But, to his pain as much as shame, their fury found vent in a wild burst of Scotch lamentation. "Montrose! Montrose!" they cried, "who will give us back Montrose? Alas for the evil chance that keeps thee from thy distressed country! We, who to-day are treated as worthless cowards and pedlars, and, heaven help us! turned adrift like godless traitors, under thy command would have given peace to our country, stamped out the rebels, and, with God's good help, restored the King to his throne." The whole town rang with their complaints and cries, their curses on those who had betrayed their king, ruined their country, deserted their brave, loyal soldiers, and abandoned all true men to their enemies' lust. Thus, like mourners taking a last farewell, they turned away and went as chance or Providence directed. Amidst the general misery the most miserable of all were the Irish. Without food, and without money to pay their way and passage, in instant fear of death if they delayed a moment, they had to depart. Some of them while preparing to return were stripped of their clothes, others wounded or killed, all ill-treated, at the instigation especially of the Westland ministers, who urged their people to wreak on these poor innocent men an unjust, unchristian vengeance for the Irish massacre.

The Argyll faction having thus, without effort and bloodshed, gained a fine victory, and made themselves as absolute in Scotland as the Independents were in England, bent all their attention to their own interests. In the first place, even while the peace was being negotiated, they invited Cromwell into Scotland. On his arrival he was received at Edinburgh in the most friendly and magnificent manner by Argyll. After solemnly thanking him, as one who had conferred great benefits on Scotland by destroying Hamilton's army, he entertained him to a public banquet, and escorted him like a conqueror to the Castle amidst a roar of artillery. Before his departure he secretly entered into an accursed compact with Argyll and his partisans to destroy the good King,[35] then his prisoner, and all his race, and they engaged to help each other in rooting out monarchy throughout Britain. Of this Cromwell, on his return to England, was wont to brag among his party far more than of his victory at Preston.[36]

---

[35] "Lady Home's house in the Canongate became an object of mysterious curiosity, from the general report at the time that the design to execute the King was there first discussed and approved." Napier, Mem., 673. Gardiner says Cromwell was lodged in Lord Moray's house. Moray House, in the Canongate, was built by Mary, Countess of Home, at the beginning of Charles I.'s reign, who left it to her daughter Margaret, Countess of Moray. Wilson, Memorials of Edinburgh, 294. *Cf.* Notice in the "True Funerals," Appendix.

[36] As negative evidence of date of MS. of Part II., the statement as to Roxburgh on p. 215 is of value. Roxburgh in 1651 joined in the invitation to Charles to come to Scotland. See Crit. Introd.

## CHAPTER IV.

1649.—The King's execution—Conduct of the Scotch Commissioners in London—Montrose's journey to Prague and reception by the Emperor—He reaches the Hague, where he hears of the King's death—Attends Charles II. at the Hague—His advice opposed by Lanark and Lauderdale—Execution of the Duke of Hamilton.

THESE events have been described at somewhat greater length than the scope of our work perhaps required, chiefly for the benefit of foreigners, that they may see by what artifices not only Montrose but the King himself was opposed, and how these worthy men ruined themselves and enslaved their country.

Such was the state of Scotland towards the close of 1648. In the beginning of 1649 they suffered a calamity, the curse of which will last for ever. On the 30th of January the Independents, elated with their victories, maddened with frenzy, and blinded with ambition and avarice, contrary to all law, human and divine, impiously butchered their sovereign, that most holy, just, chaste, and gracious prince, responsible only to the tribunal of God. At this very time commissioners to the English Parliament, sent by the Argyll party, but nominally from the Estates of Scotland, were residing in London. The chief of them in power and influence was the Earl of Lothian, the most implacable and ungrateful enemy to the King, although his Majesty's signal munificence had raised him and his father to the highest honours and wealth. These men took no steps to oppose the sentence of death passed on the King, acquiescing in it as a just and legal procedure. Their instructions were, not to question the right of the English Commons to dethrone, and even punish the King with death, if so resolved.[1] However, they were willing to protest against his exe-

---

[1] *Cf.* Gardiner as to Lothian and his fellow-commissioners. "On the 6th, the 19th, and the 22nd they denounced, in the name first of the Committee of Estates, and secondly of the Scottish Parliament, the proceedings taken against the King." His authority is "a letter from the Commissioners of Scotland, E. 539, 11." But see Clarendon, who speaks of a "few men in Scotland who no doubt were as consenting to the parricide as Cromwell or Ireton." Clar. State Papers, ii. 474.

cution, that by a show of disapprobation on their return to Scotland they might have a ready excuse to throw dust in the eyes of the ignorant, as if that crime had been perpetrated against their will and intervention. Accordingly, on the day appointed for that accursed butchery they left the city, to return without compunction in a few days' time. Craftily those wicked, faithless men judged that they must turn their eyes from a spectacle that would shame the Christian world, though in their hearts they panted for it. Indeed, it deserves to be accounted one of this good King's greatest calamities that many of those on whom he or his father King James had showered the highest favour, enriched with the most profitable offices, and advanced to the most honourable positions of wealth and dignity, should of all men prove the most ungrateful, the very head and front of rebellion; whereas those whom he found most loyal were generally those who were furthest removed, and even repelled from the court, the Parliament, and every office of administration.

Montrose, who thoroughly knew the temper of the Covenanters, had not only foreseen, but openly predicted those disasters, and had laboured to prevent them, but in vain. The minds of the royal family were prepossessed by the specious, deceitful promises of the Presbyterians, and fascinated by the blandishments of the Hamiltons. For his wholesome counsels there was no room. When he observed this, worn out with grief and pain, he left France, where he found all his efforts useless to serve the King or himself.[2] This he did without the Queen's knowledge; but in writing he fully explained the reasons of his action and neces-

---

There is nothing either explicit or implied in the Instructions to the Scots Commissioners to bear out the words of W. as to the death or the dethroning of the King. In the Declaration given in 1819 ed. of W.'s "Montrose," p. 483, we read—they, the Scots Commissioners, "did expostulate with the Commons for taking away the King's life;"—a tardy proceeding, coolly worded, and thus bearing out W.'s account.

[2] As to opportunities of advancing his own interests in France, see Lord Napier's letter, Napier, Mem., 665. "Montrose was in treaty with the French, who, in my opinion, did offer him very honourable conditions, which were these:—First, that he should be General to the Scots in France and Lieutenant-General to the Royal army, when he joined with them, commanding all Mareschals of the field, as likewise to be captain of the gen-d'armes, with 12,000 crowns a year of pension, besides his pay, and assurance the next year to be Mareschal of France and Captain of the King's Own Guard, which is a place bought and sold at 150,000 crowns." The two last were only promised by Mazarin, not inserted in the terms.

sity for his departure, for which he humbly craved her pardon and generous construction.

In the beginning of April he arrived at Geneva, accompanied by two gentlemen of knightly degree. From Switzerland he passed by the Tyrol and traversed Bavaria and Austria. The Emperor,[3] to whom he was bound, with a view to the King's and his own interests, was then absent from Vienna; but at Prague he overtook him, and was very kindly and graciously received, both on account of his achievements in Scotland and his eminent loyalty and devotion to the King, which had spread his name and fame to the remoter parts of Christendom. After a few days his Imperial Majesty left Prague, taking Montrose with him, and distinguished him with signal marks of his favour and esteem. He appointed him one of his generals, with the honourable title of Marshal in the Imperial army,[4] by letters patent, and a commission to raise forces, with the sole command, under the Emperor himself. He allowed him to enlist and impress men in all parts of his Imperial Majesty's dominions, with power to have his own colonels and captains. The parts of Germany on the borders of Flanders were considered specially suitable for promoting and completing his levies. He therefore dispatched a letter to the Spanish ambassador, recommending Montrose in the most honourable terms to his Serene Highness Leopold, his brother, Archduke of Austria and Governor of the Spanish Netherlands, requesting him to use his authority and influence to advance Montrose's business. In this Montrose's plan was successful. His sole object being to serve the King, it was his wish to be near at hand, in order to take advantage of any opportunity that might occur. Indeed, he never ceased to apprehend that the King would be betrayed, and even destroyed, by those Presbyterians to whom he had intrusted himself and his fortunes.

Being honourably dismissed by the Emperor, as the shorter road through Germany was beset by the enemy, he was obliged

---

[3] Ferdinand III., 1639-58.

[4] The patent is dated from the Castle of Lintz, on the Danube, "12th . . . . . 1648." The month is torn off, but it was probably June or July. It mentions Montrose's "famous repute and experience in war." (Original in Montrose charter-chest.) Napier, Mem., 670, *n*.

to go from Vienna to Presburg in Hungary. Thence he descended by Tyrnau[5] to Poland, and passing through Cracow, made his way through Prussia to Dantzig, the busiest port on the Baltic. Here he took ship for Denmark, where he was kindly received by the King, and rested for some days after the fatigues of a most troublesome journey. He then passed into Jutland, took ship again for Groningen in Friesland, and so made his way to Brussels. The Archduke had fallen back on Tournay after his late defeat at Lens.[6] Thither Montrose hastened with the Emperor's greetings, and having delivered his credentials, besought his advice and assistance in the affairs of the Archduke's Imperial brother. But after the severe loss inflicted on that gallant army, such jealousies and disturbances prevailed in the provinces that nothing could then be done to help him, and the matter was deferred till their return to Brussels. On their arrival there, the Archduke laid it before the States to consider the best method of assisting the Emperor, and order the necessary steps to be taken.

During the progress of these deliberations at Brussels, Montrose received from his Royal Highness Charles, Prince of Scotland and Wales, who was then residing at the Hague, letters[7] full of esteem and confidence, and with an urgent invitation to come thither. Those who attended the Prince, and were devoted to his service, especially his Highness Prince Rupert of the Palatine, who had always agreed with Montrose's views of the Presbyterians, had induced Charles to follow his own natural inclinations, and send for Montrose. The Duke of Hamilton had just lost an excellent army in England, and in Scotland his younger brother had shamefully abandoned and dispersed a still better and more

---

[5] Lat. *Terranova*. Is this Tyrnau, about forty miles north-east of Presburg, on the railway to Cracow?

[6] August 20, 1648. The Archduke lost 7000 men, 32 cannon, and 100 standards. Lens is south-west of Tournay. As to the Lat. *Lansensem*, v. Crit. Notes.

[7] Montrose was at Brussels early in September. He writes to Prince Rupert from there September 7th, and he had before written to the Prince of Wales and the Duke of York. Some five letters from Prince Rupert, the first dated September 20, follow before the close of the year. The Duke of York answers on September 11th. The first letter from the Prince of Wales is dated January 20, 1649. In it he says Hyde was to meet Montrose in some place which the latter was to name, to discuss in secret the proposals that had been made. Napier, Mem., 676-692. This meeting took place at Sevenbergen.

powerful army. Presbyterians and Royalists alike, in both kingdoms, were now reduced to great straits. Montrose alone remained, the only man now with will and resolution to make any attempt in Scotland. He had been badly treated. His advice had been neglected, his assistance never called for except to lead a forlorn hope. Yet such, they felt confident, was his generosity, his loyalty and affection to his dearest lord and master, that in spite of all he would still be ready to face any peril in the King's service.

Montrose being thus assured of the Prince's esteem and confidence, obtained the Archduke's leave, and was hastening to the Hague,[8] when he was stricken by the doleful tidings that the good King, who had ever been dearer to him than his own eyesight, had been murdered by the English Independents. Good God, what horror seized him at the first uncertain rumour of his death! But when the news of this monstrous parricide was confirmed, and there remained no more room for hope, his grief became passion, his anger was heightened to fury, and his noble spirit was so overwhelmed that his limbs stiffened, and he fainted in the midst of his attendants, falling down like one dead. When at length he recovered, after many deep groans, he broke out into these words: "We must die, die with our gracious King. May the God of life and death be my witness, that henceforth life on earth will be bitterness and mourning!" Among those who stood round him, I, who write this history, happened to be present, and though grieved beyond measure, and unable to bear up against the blow which had stunned my own spirit, on hearing these exclamations I hastened to minister words of encouragement. "No," I said, "rather must brave men live, live, my noble master, and summon up all their courage and spirit to inflict vengeance on those impious and inhuman parricides, to take up arms in a just and holy cause, and restore his princely son and lawful heir to the throne of his ancestors. These are the obsequies due to the memory of the dead, a worthier aim for your affection, loyalty, courage, and reso-

---

[8] Montrose was on the point of leaving Brussels, or already on his way, when the news came. Probably it was conveyed by Hyde. On February 15 Montrose was at the Hague (Letter to Hyde).

lution, than weakly to despond and sink under the greatest misfortunes, even such as ours, to gratify our wicked enemies, and give them a new victory and fresh triumphs at our cost." Kind and gracious as he ever was, he heard me with patience at least, but as the sweeter thought of the vengeance he so ardently longed for recalled new life into his choking heart, he revived somewhat, and, with a calmer, more resigned mien, replied, "And for that I may endure to live henceforth, to avenge the martyred sire and raise the son to his father's throne: I swear it before God, angels, and men!" With these words he rushed into the most retired chamber of the house, and refused to see or speak with any one for two days. At length on the third day he permitted me to enter his bedchamber, and there I found a piece of paper on which he had recorded his solemn vow in a brief but elegant poem, breathing the spirit of his deepest heartfelt thoughts; for he was a man of most refined genius, and used to divert his intervals of relaxation from weightier cares with poetry, in which he had a very happy vein. A Latin version by myself will be found on the page which follows these additional memoirs. I cannot pretend to rival the author's fine point; but perhaps the rendering, such as it is, may not be unacceptable to those who are ignorant of the English tongue.[9]

Charles, the second of that name, and by royal right the lawful heir, on his father's death sent for Montrose, as soon as grief and decency would permit, and gave him many signal and encouraging proofs of his close friendship and esteem. In the first place, he gave him a commission to be Lieutenant-Governor of Scotland and commander-in-chief of all forces by land and sea, with much the same powers, expressed in the same terms, as in the commission he had previously held under his father. He likewise appointed him his ambassador to the Emperor, the King of Denmark, the Princes of Germany and others, his allied kinsmen and friends, with power to raise forces and procure the arms and money necessary to renew the war; and with full authority to make treaties and alliances, give pledges, and transact all business as he should

---

[9] For the lines and Latin see Appendix.

think fit, in the King's name. In the most pressing and honourable terms he recommended him to the various courts.[10]

Affairs were now in fine train. All were sanguine of the happiest results, when the younger Hamilton[11] interfered, as usual, to blast their fairest hopes. Accompanied by his creature Lauderdale,[12] he had sped to Holland, pretending that he had been obliged to fly from Scotland. But his real object was to oppose and thwart Montrose's sounder counsels, in which he and his brother the Duke had somewhat too often succeeded with the late King. Montrose's advice was that the King should go in person to Scotland[13] as soon as possible, and by his presence and example animate his faithful subjects, who were far the most numerous party, to rise in arms. The people, he urged, had now learned by experience the deadly shifts and tricks of the rebels. Most men now hated and despised the invectives against the King with which their fanatical ministers had hitherto blinded the people, enslaved them to superstition, and seduced them from their due allegiance. Men's hearts were hot with indignation, wrung with horror at the recent murder of the King, and eager for revenge.

---

[10] The first commission is dated at the Hague, March 4; the second at Brussels, July 6. Napier, Mem., ii. 388, *n.* The first was given after Lanark and Lauderdale had reached the King, but before the Commissioners from Scotland arrived, March 25th (O.S.) For some guiding dates see *n.*, end of chapter.

[11] Lanark had scarcely arrived in Holland when he heard of the King's death. Burnet's "Hamiltons," 421. In a letter to Ormond, March 30, 1649, Lord Byron says, "I came to the Hague ten days since, where, not long before, the Earl of Lanerick, now Duke Hamilton, was arrived. There I found likewise the Marquis of Montrose, the Earls of Lauderdale, Callendar, and Seaforth, the Lords St. Clair and Napier, and old William Murray. These, though all of one nation, are subdivided into four several factions. The Marquis of Montrose, with the Lords St. Clair and Napier, are very earnest for the King's going to Ireland. All the rest oppose it, though in several ways. I find Duke Hamilton very moderate, and certainly he would be much more were it not for the violence of Lauderdale, who haunts him like a fury. Callendar and Seaforth have a faction apart, and so hath William Murray, employed by Argyll." Napier, Mem., 695.

[12] John, second Earl of Lauderdale, at first a strong Covenanter, then an Engager. He was sent over to Holland to invite the Prince of Wales to Scotland when Hamilton marched into England. After the news of Preston he left Holland to employ his interest for the King, but finding the Engagers in trouble, he did not land, but returned to the Hague, carrying Lanark with him, at the beginning of 1649. He stayed there till Charles went to Scotland in 1650, and was only allowed to attend the King of Scots after penance in the kirk of Largo for his sins as an Engager. After Worcester he was nine years in the Tower, and soon after the Restoration he gained, with many offices, the chief administration of affairs in Scotland, and was made Duke of Lauderdale. He died August 24, 1682. He was an enemy of Montrose, but confessed that he knew of no death to be attributed to him but what was done in the field. Clarendon, Burnet, Douglas, Napier.

[13] But see Byron's letter above, and *n.* at end of chapter.

Delays were useless; they should not linger until their rage grew cool, but cut off from the conspirators every chance of increasing their strength by force and fraud. Many who had hitherto been opposed to monarchy were now softened, sensible of their folly, and returning to their senses. In short, the Prince's presence would be equal to a host. Let him therefore use all speed, and not delay his journey a single day or hour. At such a crisis every moment was precious.

This advice was strongly seconded by the Earl of Seaforth, Kinnoul, Sinclair, and other noblemen, who had purposely come from Scotland to Holland to impress this very advice upon the King. Hamilton, however, said that nothing should be done rashly. A new King ought to suspect everything, and must win men's affections before he exposed his life to such a risk. The clergy, the King's most bitter foes, had unbounded influence with the common people. The power of Argyll's faction was unlimited, and supported by the name and authority of the Estates. Everything, he declared, was unfavourable to the King. He must therefore deal kindly and gently with the Parliament, and attempt nothing not previously sanctioned by their votes. In the most tragic terms he repeatedly declaimed against the cruelty, treachery, and seditious tempers of those people who were incensed beyond measure against himself for the Prince's sake. Still his sole endeavour was to induce the King to depend entirely on them, and trust those who had brought his father to destruction. Charles himself inclined decidedly to Montrose's opinion. Seeing this, Hamilton, with the help of the courtiers, strove, but strove in vain, to alienate the youthful Prince's mind from Montrose, whom he represented as a headstrong, reckless, self-seeking adventurer, too eager for civil wars, and ready to promise more than he could perform. His insinuations so far prevailed that more time than Montrose cared to lose was wasted in discussions, which only added more delays and obstacles to his scheme.

The King loved Montrose, but feared Lanark. He wished to have them both devoted to his service; but he found it impossible to reconcile opinions so divided and minds so adverse and estranged. Montrose protested that he had never had any private quarrel with the Hamiltons. The difference, he said, had arisen and been perpetuated by their insincerity in the King's affairs. Under the cloak of duty they had always seemed to hurt the King more than his declared enemies. Their pernicious counsels had shattered his strength and energies. They had assisted and encouraged the rebels, with whom they had been careful to maintain the most intimate friendship. No arguments had ever prevailed, or could even now prevail on them, openly and entirely to break with the Covenanters in Scotland, under whatever name they put themselves up for sale, whether as Estates of the realm or Assembly of the Kirk—and heartily throw in their lot with their Prince. Their deeds had always belied their words, their pledges been mere shifts.[14] But if they were at length really sorry for the past, freely and frankly returning to their allegiance, and would promise that henceforth they would have nothing to do with the Covenanters, he was ready to forget their former misdeeds, and join them in a solemn pledge of friendship; but only on condition that they would sign and publish a bond to protest their abhorrence of the Scotch conspiracy with the English rebels, and of all leagues contracted by his subjects without the King's will and consent, particularly their so-called *Solemn League and Covenant;* and, further, denounce all wars against the King, whether in Scotland or England, and declare that those who were the authors and abetters in this crime were in their opinion impious and wicked persons, guilty of high treason; and that Charles the Second, by the grace of God King of Great Britain, etc., failing other means, might lawfully, and even ought to, take up arms to avenge his father's murder, and recover his ancestral throne; and lastly, that they would give their solemn promise that they would for that end afford him and his generals and vicegerents staunch and loyal aid, and venture life and fortune in his cause.

Hamilton and Lauderdale, who, in their private audience with the King, used to accuse the Estates of the Kingdom of treachery,

---

[14] See Montrose's formal argument and advice, read in Council, May 21, 1649, entitled, "My opinion to His Majesty upon the desires of the Scots Commissioners at the Hague." Napier, Mem., 705.

cruelty, rebellion, and the foulest crimes, yet took good care not to assail or offend them by any public document or declaration, in this anxious dilemma replied vaguely, without sufficiently explaining their views of the royal rights, which in casual conversations they extolled, but craftily declined to commit themselves in public. The name, authority, power, and resources of the Estates they proclaimed aloud and magnified. It was more, they said, to the King's interest to wait for their opinion, and be raised by their votes and influence to his father's throne, than to waste his country with fire and sword, and regain even a rightful crown at the cost of a bloody civil war. In short, they could not approve the opinion or accept the friendship of those who urged for civil wars, however just, least of all the friendship of Montrose, who, for his services in the field done with the late King's commission, had been banished, outlawed, and sequestrated.

Meantime the Duke of Hamilton, who, after his defeat at Preston, had been detained prisoner in England, was beheaded in London by the Independents.[15] Thus the justice of Heaven, by the unjust judgment of the regicides, brought him to the same scaffold as his murdered sovereign. Long before he had, it is said, consulted a wizard, whose answer was: "The King shall die a violent death, and the Fates have decreed that thou shalt succeed him." So perhaps some evil spirit deluded this ambitious man, who succeeded his Prince, not on the throne, but on the scaffold.

---

[15] March 9, 1649, see p. 26, *n.* 4; also Turner, 83–84. Walker, Hist. of Independency, ii. 131. "See *Digitus Dei* upon Duke Hamilton" is his marginal comment.

---

ADDITIONAL NOTES.

*Page* 229.—Hyde at the Hague writes to Rupert, February 28: "Montrose a gallant person, very impatient to be doing—the King entirely trusts M. . . . M.'s hopes of Germany. M. very friendly with Seaforth."—Rupert's Mem., 332. Scotch Commissioners' Instructions drawn out March 1. They contain no mention of Montrose, whose presence at the Hague was probably unknown in Scotland. Spang writes, March 9, "Montrose frequently at court," &c.—Baillie, iii. 78. Commissioners sailed March 17th, reached Rotterdam 22nd, and Hague 26th. These dates dispose of Clarendon's remarks, "When he (Montrose) heard of the Commissioners being come from Scotland, and of the other Lords' arrival there, he would no longer defer his journey thither, but came to the Hague . . . and presented himself to the King, who received him with a very good countenance." (Clar. v. 287.)

*Page* 230, *n.* 13.—Wishart, in writing the above, antedates Montrose's later policy. Ireland till September was almost entirely in Royalist hands. It was not till the news of Cromwell's landing at Dublin (Aug. 15) and rapid successes that the plan was abandoned. As late as Sept. 2 the Queen of Bohemia wrote to Montrose, "The King is constant in his resolution to go to Ireland." On Sept. 7 Baillie (iii. 102) wrote, "It seems Ireland is lost." On Sept. 11 Drogheda was sacked, and 2000 of the garrison massacred—"almost all their prime soldiers" (Cromwell's Letters, Carlysle, ii. 49). Baillie, iii. 100, on Sept. 14, "Now on the great change of the Irish affairs . . . The King's chief hope was Ireland. . . . It looked once prettie fair for him. . . . This was the King's great snare all this year to keep him off an agreeance with us." Queen Elizabeth wrote, Oct. 2, "The King went for Jersey upon Monday was sennight (*i.e.*, Sept. 24). . . . The King will go to Ireland if not stopped by Parl. ships." About the end of October Rupert broke out of Kinsale, and gave Ireland up as hopeless. Nov. 19 Queen Elizabeth writes, "All goes ill in Ireland."

## CHAPTER V.

*Message to the Hague from the Estates, with their proclamation of Charles II. as King of Scotland—Arrival of Cassilis and the Commissioners—Huntly executed—The Commissioners present their demands—The opinion of the Scotch Peers—Charles leaves for France, attended to Brussels by Montrose.*

DURING this period of suspense at the Hague, a messenger[1] arrived from those who styled themselves the Estates of Scotland, who assured the King of their sincere affection, and presented a proclamation, wherein they declared Charles the rightful heir of his father and successor to the throne of Scotland.[2] The Hamilton and Presbyterian faction seized the occasion not only to offer their congratulations, but to boast and exult over this as a special manifestation of Providence. They now openly inveighed against those who maintained that the King should not rely on men who had given such signal proof of loyalty and affection. In truth, had they been sincere, and actuated by a sense of allegiance, no one would have denied that they had done their duty and gave good hopes of its performance. But men of discernment recognised on the face of it a base plot, craftily aimed at the most vital interests of the King and monarchy. The people were eager to avenge the King's murder, and loud and threatening in their clamour to restore his son to the control of Government. To throw dust in their eyes, the intriguers issued this proclamation, not to establish the King, but to overturn the royal authority, root and branch, and grasp it for themselves. Not only had they

---

[1] Sir Joseph Douglas was the chief messenger. "He arrived at Rotterdam, March 2nd (N.S.)." Baillie's Letters. The letters from William Spang to Baillie at this time give the feelings and intrigues of Montrose's opponents. See specially the letter from "My dwelling-house," March 7th, and from "My chalmer at Hague," March $\frac{9}{19}$, iii. 67-84.

[2] The Chancellor Loudon, "in black velvet goune," read the proclamation at the Cross, Feb. 5, 1649. Balfour, Ann., iii. 387. The news of the execution of Charles arrived Feb. 4.

made great changes in the ancient form of words usual on such occasions, but had added new phrases of their own contrivance.[3]

As to the death of Charles, they were content to term it violent. There was not a word of regicide, not even of homicide; not a single mark to brand the wickedness and injustice of it, or to testify their abhorrence of the crime, or indeed of many other crimes which it is needless here to recount. Above all, it was intolerable, to loyal minds horrible, that the very Prince whom they acknowledged as their lawful and supreme sovereign should in almost the same breath be debarred from all exercise of his lawful authority, until he had given satisfaction to the Estates, which they call the Parliaments, of both kingdoms. This was not to declare him King, but to cite him to judgment in their own court. What else was this but to offer him a crown without security, to strip him of that supreme temporal authority, for which he was accountable to none but God—subjects trampling on their lord? What was it but to degrade their young, innocent, and harmless Prince before themselves, persistent rebels against the late King; nay, to expose him also to English traitors and regicides, still reeking with his father's blood, a fresh victim for the rage and hatred of men gone mad? Such just reflections and censures on their edict would soon have checked and abashed the empty boasts of the Presbyterians at Court about their Estates, had they not received from Scotland fresh supplies of the same grist to feed their assurance.

The news of Montrose's great influence and favour with the new King roused various feelings in Scotland. The Royalists were full of glad hopes. Their opponents heard it with no less sorrow and dismay. The Estates in particular were in great dread. They knew the man's innate courage; they had often proved it. Besides the old adherents of royalty, there were many who now repented their errors, and were ready to obey him. They thought therefore that they must do their utmost to prevent his return to Scotland, either alone as lieutenant-general, or even

---

[3] Charles II. was proclaimed "over the Cross of Edinburgh only conditionally till he did subscribe the League and Covenant . . . . and till that tyme not to have any exercise of his royal power." Lamont, p. 1.

in the King's train. In the present state of public feeling they foresaw that he would carry the country almost to a man with him, to the certain destruction of those who had consented to the King's murder. To meet this danger they sent the Earl of Cassilis,[4] one of the first nobility, with some creatures of inferior rank, as commissioners to the King in Holland. All of these were deeply in the toils of the new superstition, and inflamed with a bigoted hatred of monarchical government. Their commission, as they pretended and carefully proclaimed to all the world, was a free invitation to Charles to his ancestral realm of Scotland; but their real object was to baffle Montrose's plan, and by flattering the King with idle hopes of peace and obedience, to deter him from prosecuting the war until the chance of success had slipt away.

Meanwhile, lest these proceedings should arouse the suspicions of their English confederates, the regicides, they encouraged them with a melancholy proof of their intentions. As they had none of royal rank to butcher, they took the Marquis of Huntly, chief of the Gordon clan, as the nearest to the throne, and after a long imprisonment, passed on him a most iniquitous sentence, and beheaded him.[5] Huntly, besides the splendour of his birth, in which he was second to no subject, was of an ancient family, long dreaded by neighbours for its power in friends, vassals, clansmen, and the favours of fortune, as they are called. In person he was endowed with the highest gifts of mind and body. To his Prince

---

[4] The Commissioners Cassilis, G. Wynram of Liberton, Revs. Robert Baillie, of Glasgow, and James Wood, of St. Andrews, "shipped in at Kirkaldie in Ihone Gillespie's shipe, and loused on Saturday, the 17th March, at night. They returned to this kingdome the 11th of June 1649 mutch unsatisfied." Lamont, 2. See Baillie's speech "made in the King's bedchamber at the Hague, March 27th, Tuesday, three o'clock afternoon." Letters, iii. 84. For their railings against Montrose, see *ib*. 512-53. His temperate reply to their more serious proposal is given, Napier, Mem., 700-705. The Commissioners in their letter April 3rd describe the King as "of a very sweet and courteous disposition," and Baillie says "he is one of the most gentle, innocent, well inclyned Princes, so far as yet appears, that lives in the world; a trimme person, and of a manly carriage; understands prettie well; speaks not much; would God he were amongst us." *Ib*. 88.

[5] March 22nd. Lamont says "he was beheaded at the Cross of Edinburgh. He died blockishlie, not being relaxed of his excommunicatione; his corps afterwarde werre carried by sea to the North, to be interred there" (p. 3). Balfour says he was carried to Seton to be "interrid ther in the comon buriall of that family, from which himselve had issewed." Ann., iii. 393. The Commissioners in Holland, April 3rd, speak of the "supposed death of Huntly" as being wrested to their disadvantage. See Huntly's last speech, Wigton Papers, Maitland Club Misc., ii. 442.

he had been loyal from the very beginning of the troubles, and this alone rendered him so hateful to the Covenanters that they resolved to make away with him. Indeed, except for that unhappy quarrel he had with Montrose and the King and country, it will be hard to find his equal. The very day on which the Commissioners sailed from the Firth of Forth was appointed for his execution.[6] From this the King might easily have drawn an omen of what was to be expected at the hand of those who were daily slaughtering his best and most loving lieges.

When these fine Commissioners were admitted to the King, their solemn gait, mournful dress, downcast eyes, and dismal countenances were the picture of abject humility.[7] In fact, many who were unacquainted with the temper and habits of these men hoped that they were about to implore pardon and oblivion for the past, and promise loyal obedience for the future, with a full acknowledgment of the King's hereditary rights, and a sincere offer of lasting peace and concord. Their commission was twofold, from the Estates and from the Assembly of the Kirk. In both Cassilis was the spokesman, as a member of the Estates and as a lay elder. Introduced into the royal presence, they prefaced their address with deep sighs and many groans, as Vergil says of the sibyl, "To shake heaven's burden from the labouring breast."[8] At last they presented their papers, containing the oracles of the Estates and General Assembly. In these they protested that the terms of accommodation offered were honourable, respectful, and obedient, and absolutely necessary for the settlement of the State and the King's restoration. If he complied, he could be brought to Scotland by universal consent.

When the King had considered these papers in council, at the first glance they appeared a bogus contrivance to scare him from assuming the government, rather than an invitation to accept it. Their demands were unjust, a reproach to the late King his father, and a snare and pitfall for his son and successor. In a word, they

---

[6] But see p. 233.
[7] See the Queen of Bohemia's references to "the Brethern" and godly Windrum. Napier, Mem., 711-720.
[8] Vergil, Æn., vi. 78.

demanded three things: First, that the King should ratify not only the National Covenant, but also their Solemn League and Covenant of the three kingdoms; to be confirmed by his signature, oath, and sanction, extended in its ends and aims throughout all his dominions, and promoted to the utmost of his power. Secondly, that he should also ratify and confirm all acts and ordinances of the Estates of Scotland passed to establish that Covenant and League, the Presbyterian Church government, the rule of divine worship which they call the Directory, the Confession of Faith, and the Catechism; and that he should also freely and readily give his assent to all acts and ordinances already passed or hereafter to be passed by the other Parliaments of his dominions; that he should himself conform to them, especially in divine worship, both private and public; that he should renounce the old liturgy of the Anglican Church, and adopt the new Directory, with a solemn promise and oath never to oppose it or alter one tittle of its tenor. The third demand, which in itself would have sufficed, as it embraced all else, was that he would solemnly give and declare his assent to all civil enactments of the present and succeeding Parliaments; and that in ecclesiastical matters he would abide by the resolutions of the General Assemblies; which all ranks, it appeared, princes and subjects alike, were to submit to and cheerfully obey.

The King requested them, if they had orders to make any other demands, to produce them at once,[9] that he might answer them altogether. He begged them to modify their terms, and not cling too rigidly and obstinately to harsh expressions. He desired also to be informed, in clear, plain language, what help he might expect from them for the recovery of England and Ireland. Lastly, they had not made the faintest allusion to the horrible murder of the King, his father, of blessed memory, or to the cruel authors and instruments of that crime, on which he would have them openly before all the world express their thoughts and judg-

---

[9] "I do insist upon my former answer, and do desire and expect that you do deliver all the propositions or desires you or any of you are entrusted to present to me, before I make an answer to any particular one, being resolved to consider of the whole, before I declare my resolution upon any part." C. R., April 10 (N.S.), 1649. See also a like demand repeated April 16th. Baillie's Letters, iii. 513-515.

ment.[10] They replied that the sum of their commission was contained in those three articles. They had nothing to add but what was to the same effect, unless they received fresh instructions from the Estates. Their demands were not only just and honourable, but absolutely necessary, founded on divine right and Holy Writ. They could not therefore without impiety recede from them one hair's breadth or tittle. As for the assistance his Majesty demanded for the reduction of England and Ireland, he might expect the Estates to grant such succours as they shall deem fair and necessary according to the League and Covenant. Such were their vague involved replies to all questions. But as to the murder of the King they were in a wretched dilemma. They were ashamed to approve and commend it. They were no less loth to condemn it, and provoke the English to awkward revelations of their complicity in the crime. Though this was the main point on which the King was most urgent, he could extort from them nothing but complaints and expostulations on the suspicion with which he seemed to regard the Estates of Scotland.

Much time was frittered away in these debates. Meanwhile the Commissioners were busy making interest with the Prince of Orange[11] and notables of the United Provinces, as well as with the envoys of Denmark and other Princes, to use their mediation with the King, and induce him to accept their terms. To them they repeated in the same strain that the Estates of Scotland were devoted to the King, and ready to receive him with open arms, to restore him to his father's throne, to yield him due loyalty and obedience, provided only he would renounce Episcopacy and accept the Presbyterian form of church government. This was the same as that which prevailed in Holland, the Palatine, Geneva,

---

[10] "Our grief for this paper" (*i.e.*, the King's reply) "was great, it was much worse than anything we expected; not only the hand of the worst of the English counsell, but of James Graham also, and others of our evil countrymen, was visible therein." Report, Baillie, Letters, iii. 517.

[11] William of Nassau, Prince of Orange, married Mary, eldest daughter of Charles I. He died November 6, 1650, æt. 24. For an interesting and somewhat amusing account of how Spang prepared him to take up the case of the Covenanting Commissioners, see Baillie, *ib.* 71-80. "The Prince of Orange will again extremely press the King to grant the Commissioners' desires, and so ruin him through your sides," wrote the Queen of Bohemia in June 1649. The Princess of Orange sided with Montrose. "My niece is still of our side constantly," Queen Elizabeth writes to Montrose in November 1649.

and other reformed churches (though in reality they are very different and plainly at variance). If he refused, all hope of ever recovering the crown was lost. These suggestions would have availed little with most of them, had not Hamilton and Lauderdale insidiously seconded their efforts with their praise and approbation of all they said. It was chiefly owing to them that most men thought the King, considering the state of his affairs, could and ought to assent to their demands, however hard and difficult. Foreigners, indeed, in their ignorance of affairs in Britain, did not penetrate the dark designs of the rebels, and failed to see through the snares that beset the King and the very principle of kingly government.

That all the Christian world, and especially his friends and allies, might know that there was no sacrifice, consistent with justice, honour, and conscience, which Charles in his desire for peace and harmony would not make to satisfy his Scotch subjects, he turned to his Scots peers, many of whom were in Holland, and charged them on their duty and allegiance to give him their opinion separately, in writing, on these demands. Hamilton, Lauderdale, and their faction, with sullen disrespectful obstinacy, declined the task, though it was a duty established by the ancient law and custom of their country. Montrose, Seaforth, Kinnoul, Sinclair, and others complied.[12] They declared, and proved by many powerful arguments, that these demands were inconsistent with law, both human and divine, repugnant to the laws of Scotland, insulting to the memory of the royal martyr, insidious to his successor, and ruinous to his race, a thing to shame and grieve every leal true-hearted man. Their sole aim was to heap the blame of all the calamities in Britain upon an innocent martyr; to establish their abominable leagues and covenants, which had already shed so much innocent, noble, and gentle blood, not sparing even the King; and which, like the Trojan horse, pregnant with mischief, if once admitted to the citadel, would quickly pour forth on them and their descendants a fresh brood of sedition, rebellion, war, violence, rapine, and murder. If yielded to, their rightful king and supreme

---

[12] Napier, Mem., 700-705.

sovereign would have nothing left but the bare empty name of king. Even that and life itself he would enjoy only at the caprice of men beyond all others crazed with gloom and sullen frenzy, suspicious, passionate, and irreconcilably opposed in hatred to all supreme authorities. The whole power and administration would be vested in men haunted with the guilt of so many crimes against the father, and who would therefore never deem themselves secure so long as any of his race survived. To abolish the Episcopacy, under which the Church had flourished so vigorously in all ages throughout Christendom, would be to substitute the intolerable tyranny of the Presbytery, as now established in Scotland, a form of oppression which, in cruelty, pride, avarice, wantonness, and lust of power, far surpasses the worst times of Hildebrand and Borgia. The worst rebels and regicides would not only live unpunished for their execrable crimes, but invested and enriched with the plunder of the sovereign they had butchered and the Church they had despoiled, exalted to the highest honours, glorying, exulting in their triumph and supremacy. But as for the King and all his race, and the brave loyal subjects who had never faltered in his cause, they would be abandoned to the fury, hatred, insolence, and revenge of their uncontrollable enemies, were a Christian king so far forgetful of duty to parents, brothers, and friends, to God and man, as to approve, sanction, and justify those wicked edicts, whereby, under pretence of promoting their League and Covenant, all subjects had been ordered to take up arms and pursue their king with fire and sword, by which they had at last dragged him to a miserable death, hunted his devoted consort the Queen out of her husband's realms, and banished or confined those of his children who still survived in cruel exile or imprisonment. Lastly, they suspected that these idle missions served only to waste time, until that savage regicide, Cromwell, with whom they were on the best of terms, having already subdued England, might also complete the conquest of Ireland,[13] in which he was now engaged, and then, if need be, pour all his forces into

---

[13] Cromwell was appointed Lieutenant of Ireland March 15th, and directed affairs from England, sending troops and raising an army. He did not go over to Ireland till August 15th, after Jones had defeated Ormond at Rathmines.

Scotland. For these and many other reasons they unanimously declared that it was impossible for the King to accept terms from those who falsely proclaimed themselves the Estates of Scotland. If he had any regard for conscience before God, and duty to his parents and successors, for dignity at home and reputation abroad, for his personal safety, for laws human and divine, he should await very different messages and demands from them, such as should express a true though tardy repentance, and, in however slight a degree, a sincere desire to restore the King. They considered, therefore, that loyalty and due obedience could be extorted only by force of righteous war from these stubborn hardened rebels.

These arguments were so clear, striking, and conclusive that neither the Commissioners nor Hamilton and Lauderdale, who served them might and main, could offer any answer. The King was evidently moved, and inclined to accept the opinion of Montrose. But by some fatality—for it is not easy to say whose advice was followed—the expedition into Scotland was laid aside and changed for a descent on Ireland from France.[14] On his departure most of the nobles, including Montrose, accompanied the King as far as Brussels. The Commissioners, in their usual manner, were virulent and bitter in their accusations of the King, whom they blamed for not assenting to their demands and accepting their offer of peace. However, they were overjoyed as with a signal victory, to find that he had altered his intended journey to Scotland, where they dreaded his appearance, and where the people, wearied out with the greed, insolence, and tyranny of rebels, earnestly longed for his presence.

[14] It is curious that all other writers identify Montrose with the policy of sending the King to Ireland. He was first concerned to secure the King's presence for his own military descent on Scotland, and failing that to prevent his peaceful entry there as a Covenanter, in the hands of his own enemies. Ireland was preferable to this, and he would himself go to Scotland as the King's lieutenant. Montrose was appointed practically viceroy in Scotland, March 4th. The Commissioners arrived at the end of March, and argued from the 27th till the end of May. In June the King set out to visit the Queen-Mother at St. Germains, pausing at Breda and Brussels. Montrose accompanied him as far as the latter city. See letter from the King to Montrose, Breda, June 22, 1649 and his "diploma" as ambassador extraordinary, dated Brussels, July 6, 1649, with letters from the Duke of York and Queen Henrietta. Napier, Mem., 706, 707. His portrait by Honthorst (v. frontispiece) was painted between February and June of 1649, and presented to the Queen of Bohemia, who says she will hang it in her chamber to fright the "Brethern."

## CHAPTER VI.

*Montrose prepares for his descent on Scotland—State of affairs in Scotland and Ireland —His prospects of assistance from foreign courts thwarted by Scotch intrigues.*

MONTROSE was preparing for a difficult and dangerous enterprise; malicious people have even pronounced it rash and desperate.[1] But many circumstances encouraged him to hope for success. He had received numerous messages from the nobility in Scotland urging him to undertake it, and full of voluntary offers of support.[2] They assured him that almost all the Scotch were disposed to obedience, that not a man desired any other general under the King than himself. In the north Mackenzie,[3] brother

---

[1] An answer to the view expressed in Montr. Redivivus (1652), 174, 175, which must have been highly offensive to W. "But the Marquess (as is supposed), fearing lest he should have an express command to desist from his purpose, because the Treaty betwixt the Prince and the Scotish Commissioners was now very neer a conclusion, did precipitate himself, and those that were with him, into most inevitable ruine. . . . But the business being fatall, he must needs contribute his own endeavours towards that destruction which his cruell fortune had provided for him. . . . After this poor rabble of silly creatures was amazed [*i.e.*, amassed, a misprint corrected by Heath, 261, who follows the Montr. Red. verbatim] to embarque . . . the people having some experience of the carriage of his former souldierie . . . fled away in heaps." . . .

[2] See Clarendon, v. 350, and cf. Col. W. Sibbald's speech intended to have been spoken at his execution, June 7, 1650, and referred to p. 50, *n.* 16, where the month should be read June for January. A misprint of Jan. for Jun. in Montr. Red. was followed by the 1819 edit., and at first followed by ourselves. Notwithstanding Sibbald's disclaimer as to noblemen and gentlemen "keeping correspondence with his Majestie and the Marquess of Montr.," letters from Montrose were found in his "clocke bage" addressed to Rupert, Ormond, and Sir George Monro. Balf. iv. 22. For Montrose's letter to Lord Sinclair, taken in Hall's frigate, see *ibid.* iv. 33; and for other reference to his correspondence, read in Parl. "with clsose doors," *ibid.* iv. 33. On April 7, 1649, William Orde, a servant of Montrose, was arrested at Kerrimure in Angus with letters from his master (*ibid.* iii. 397, 398).

[3] Thomas Mackenzie of Pluscardine, Seaforth's brother, rose early in 1649 with Lords Reay, Ogilvy, Lewis Gordon, and General Middleton. The Act of Classes and Huntly's execution gave impetus to this rising of Gordons, Frasers, Monros, and Mackenzies to the number of 1200 men. They took Inverness in February, and David Leslie was sent against them in March. Charles wrote to Pluscardine, April 12th, referring him to Montrose for information as to his "particular desires," and again on June 3rd to the same effect, and urging him to concur with Seaforth. Seaforth archives qtd., 1819 edit. of W., 440-441. On May 4th the rising was proclaimed at Edinburgh, and on the 8th Leslie's horse "routed the most considerable pairte of the rebelles" at Balveny, killing sixty or eighty, and taking nearly eight hundred, among them Lord Reay. For Pluscardine subsequently, *v.* Ch. ix. See Balf. under dates, and Heath, 231, 232.

of the Earl of Seaforth and lieutenant of the King, was still in arms, along with Lord Reay and other Royalists, who had seized Inverness, demolished its fortifications, marched through Moray, and crossed the Spey. The prospect in Ireland was bright and hopeful. Ormond, the King's viceroy and Lieutenant-General, was acting with vigour and success; and Monro,[4] followed by others, was sent to him with the King's commands and a letter from Montrose, to stipulate for mutual assistance, as circumstances might require. Those of the English who had always remained staunch to the King, and escaped the taint of Presbyterianism, openly declared that, after being so basely deceived and abandoned by the Hamiltons, Montrose was the only Scotsman whom they could and ought to trust. With him they were ready to encounter any danger in the cause of their beloved prince. Some of the electors and princes of Germany promised their assistance.[5] The Emperor himself engaged to summon a Diet of the Empire, and represent to them how deeply the King of England's fate merited the abhorrence of all crowned heads. Of the goodwill and favour of the King of Denmark there was no room to doubt. His ambassador[6] at the Hague, both in his own and in his master's name, daily encouraged Montrose as well as the King to hope for the best.

The illustrious Queen of Sweden[7] was expected to do no less

---

[4] *Vide* p. 209, *n.* 7, and *n.* 2 above.

[5] *Vide* below, pp. 246-7, 252, *n.* 9, and Ch. vii.

[6] Clarendon, in his small sneering way, wrote that, during the Hague period, Montrose "had found means to endear himself much to Cornificius Wolfelte, ambassador extraordinary of Denmark, who promised to aid him." v. 302, 303. Ulfeldt set out for Holland before the news of Charles First's execution reached Denmark. On October $\frac{5}{15}$ Queen Elizabeth at the Hague writes to Montrose, "The Denmark Ambassador is going away." In November 1649 Turner, released from Hull, reached Hamburg, where "I found a number of Scotch gentlemen . . . attending the orders and motions of the famous Marquesse of Montrose; who, haveing trusted too much to Vlefeld, the Great Stewart of Denmark's promises of assistance, found himself disappointed by that faithles minister of estate, who afterwarde went faire to betray both his prince and countrey. This obliged the Marques to retire himselfe to Gottenburg in the Suedish dominions, where he was underhand supported, bot very inconsiderablie, by the great Queene Christina." Mem. 91.

[7] Queen Christina, daughter of Gustavus Adolphus, was at this time twenty-four years of age, and at the height of her fame and power. Her profession of the Romish faith hastened her abdication in 1654. Would W. have so written of her after this event? In her letter to the Scot. Parl., read May 20, 1650, she promises to comply with their wish, and "had commanded her ambassador Laurentius to attend the tretty of Breda, and be assistant ther for that effecte." Balf.

than any other friend or kinsman, not merely because of the ancient alliances between the kingdoms, but out of the natural goodness, justice, mercy, and magnanimity of that incomparable heroine, who had inherited these virtues from her father and grandsire. Little help was to be looked for from France and Spain,[8] then unhappily engaged in an exhausting struggle. But the King of Poland[9] and the Duke of Courland were expected to be among the first to hasten to the aid of Charles. To both these princes the King had sent special envoys to solicit their aid for Montrose. But he never received any benefit from these embassies, not so much by the fault of those princes, who were very friendly, as owing to the base arts and unaccountable treachery of the Presbyterians, who not only succeeded in destroying Montrose and ruining the King, but, unless God will it otherwise, have burdened themselves, their country, and descendants with a heavy humiliating slavery.[10]

These people with their bribes and promises had corrupted the courtiers, generally a faithless class of men, and bound them to do

---

iv. 16, 17. Baillie, iii. 256, writes: "What the mysterie may be of the Queen of Swan's [Sweden's] dimission, and why her last act should have been (without all necessitie) a strict friendship with the Protector (Cromwell) is much marvelled."

[8] The twenty-four years' war with Spain ended in 1659 by the Peace of the Pyrenees. The wars of the Fronde (1648-1654) also kept Mazarin fully occupied with internal affairs. "France is in a fyre for that unhappy Mazarin" (Spang to Baillie, March 7, 1649, iii. 69). On April 3 Baillie wrote from the Hague: "Our enemies have great confidence by the French peace to get powerfull assistance from France" (*ibid*. 88). But see Clarendon, v. 324, 325, for the relations of France to Charles in the autumn of that year.

[9] John Casimir the Fifth, born 1609, a Jesuit, made a Cardinal in 1647, and King of Poland in succession to his brother Ladislas IV. or VII. in November 1648, and crowned January 17th, 1649. In August 1649 he made peace with the Cossacks, but was again at war with them and the Tartars early in 1650, events which probably hindered the promised aid.

The Duchy of Courland was at this time a dependency of Poland.

Queen Elizabeth, October 2, 1649, writes: "Culpepper is gone for Muscovy." She adds, "The spices and aqua vitae will burn him quickly up."

Perhaps his instructions included letters to Poland and Courland. "Collonel Cochran, who had been despatched Commissioner into Poland to the Scotish Merchants, there to require their assistance, having procured very considerable summs of money upon that score, and other provision for the furthering of that expedition, dispos'd of the money for his own uses, made sale of the corn and provision, together with the vessel which was provided for the transportation of it, and did himself turn tayl to the quarrell." Montr. Redivivus, 172.

[10] From this and the absence of all allusion to events even so shortly after as Dunbar and Worcester, we may infer that Wishart wrote very shortly after the events he describes. Ruddiman's translation (reprinted in 1819) has wholly obscured this passage, and makes it appear as if written after the Restoration. See Ch. x., *n*. 1 below.

their utmost to thwart and overthrow Montrose's dealings with the King; or failing that, to throw every obstacle in his way, and prevent affairs of the utmost weight and moment. Nor was this all. To the friendly and allied princes they sent their creatures and emissaries,[11] who, under pretence of other business, had obtained passes and letters of recommendation from the King himself, in ignorance of their criminal designs, and succeeded in making them believe that Charles had been very honourably invited to assume the government of Scotland, that the terms offered by the Commissioners were just and reasonable, such as certainly ought not to have been rejected; that it was still to be hoped the King would assent without delay: it was his only chance of safety and success. Those who gainsaid this might perhaps be consulting their own interests, but did ill service to the King. Their request for arms, soldiers, pay, ships, and provisions [12] in the King's name were made for their own personal profit and advantage, and were not only unserviceable and ill-timed, but detrimental to his cause. The proper time would be when the King was established in Scotland, and could with the consent of the Estates send honourable and dignified embassies to request their aid. Meantime they

---

[11] See note 7 above with reference to their letter to Queen Christina. Their Commissioners spent the day after their arrival at the Hague in visits to the Queen of Bohemia, the Princess Royal, the Prince of Orange, the Princess Dowager, and the Estates General. Baillie, iii. 86. Their instructions contained letters to them (*ibid.* 509). Most of the English Council "are of Prince Rupert's faction, who caresses Montrose." They were favoured by Henrietta at Paris, and "Culpepper and some bed-chalmer-men [he mentions Wilmot, Byron, Gerard] are of the Queen's faction" (*ibid.* 87). See also Queen Elizabeth's letters to Montrose, which express great fear of Henrietta's influence and the intrigues of Jermyn, &c.

Sir Joseph Douglas, Robert Hamilton, William Murray, and subsequently Winram of Liberton and Will Fleming were go-betweens in negotiations of 1649-1650.

[12] On October 15, 1650, the Committee of Estates "ordaines the armes belonging to his Maiestie, that are at Bergen in Norruay, and Gottinberrey in Sueden, to be sent for." Balf. iv. 124. Had these been gathered by Montrose? The Commissioners to Breda had warrant to borrow £300,000 to give the King, "if so it was he and they accorded; wtherways to give him no money at all" (*ibid.* 6). On July 1st they petitioned Parliament for payment of 100,000 merks they had borrowed for the King at Campvere on their own surety, as they could raise none "upon the public faith" (*ibid.* 68). Charles at the time of the Breda treaty was "broght very low, when he hes not bread both for himself and his seruands, and betwixt him and his brother not ane Inglish shilling; and worse yet, if I durst wryte it." Wynram's letter, November $\frac{8}{18}$, *ap.* Baillie, iii. 523. "Canterstein is come from Suedland to attend this Treaty, and promiseth in his Master's [Mistress's?] name all assistance for a happy agriement." Wynram to R. Douglas, April $\frac{20}{30}$ (*ibid.* p. 524).

advised them to save their treasure, and not be vainly lavish of benefits which could do no earthly service to their royal friend and kinsman.[13]

· · · · · · ·

---

[13] Here there is a gap in both MSS. (*v.* Crit. Introd.). Wishart's account is continued in Ch. x. It is very necessary to emphasise this, as the tracts at the end of the Montr. Redivivus Part I. are repeatedly quoted as "Wishart's Memoirs of Montrose." This error first appeared in the 1720 edition, reproduced in 1752 and 1819 editions, though the editor of the former had MSS. before him.

## CHAPTER VII.[1]

### 1649.—*PREPARATIONS FOR A DESCENT ON SCOTLAND.*

*June.*—Montrose with Charles at Brussels—His commissions—Letters of Queen Elizabeth—He returns to the Hague—At Rhenen.

*September.*—Letters to and from Frederick William of Brandenburg—Kinnoul's detachment lands in Orkney—Leslie sent to suppress them—Montrose at Hamburg—Sends Sir J. Cochran to Courland and Poland, and Sir W. Johnston to German princes—Ulfeldt at the Hague—Montrose meets Frederick of Denmark at Flensburg.

*October.*—Proceeds to Copenhagen—The Swedish envoy's account of his doings—Sibbald, with letters to Ormond, Rupert, and Monro, arrested in Scotland—Montrose's letter to Frederick III.

*November.* — His Declaration — 10th, leaves Copenhagen for Gothenburg — Ribbing's account of his doings there.

*December.*—Second (?) detachment sent to Orkney—Letters to Seaforth.

1650.—Montrose awaits the King's messenger—Receives the George and Garter.

*February.*—Goes to Norway.

*March.*—Sails for Scotland—Letters of Charles, Henrietta, Col. Gordon, Maclear, Ogilvy of Powrie, &c.

EARLY in June 1649 the Scottish Commissioners bade farewell to Charles.[2] It was now high time for the King himself to quit the Hague, where his presence threatened to embroil the Dutch Estates with their haughty sister republic.[3] The irregular seizure of vessels on both sides, the harbourage afforded to Rupert's fleet in the preceding winter, and the recent murder of Dr. Dorislaus,[4] the English Parliamentary Commissioner to Holland, strained the relations of the two countries. All the influence of the young Prince of Orange was required to save his cousin

---

[1] In cc. vii.-ix., the Editors endeavour from contemporary records to piece together the narrative of events omitted in the MSS. (*v.* Crit. Introd.). Much of this material is now printed for the first time. The dates are all "old style." Wishart's narrative is resumed in Ch. x., with Montrose's landing at Leith.

[2] Baillie, iii. 413. They reached Scotland, June 11th.

[3] Act abolishing Monarchy, passed February 7, 1649: Walker, Hist. Indep., ii. 118. England declared a free state, May 19: Carlyle's Cromwell, ii. 2. Act proclaimed in London, May 30: Walker, *ibid.* 184, 185. Cf. Evelyn's Diary, ii. 8, "Unkingship proclaimed."

[4] *Vide* Index, Whitford. The murder occurred May 3. T. Bates, Elenchi, ii. 233. Walker, *ibid.* ii. 59, 103, 173, 174. Clarendon, with his usual vagueness in dates, says this event caused Charles to quit the Hague. Doubtless it added to his difficulties, yet he lingered some *six weeks* later.

the ignominy of a request to betake himself and his squabbling courtiers from the Dutch capital.

But before he left, Charles had definitely resolved to employ Montrose. On June 3rd he wrote to the King of Denmark, "accrediting the Marquis " of Montrose, whom he had appointed Commander-in-chief of all the forces " that can be raised."[5] On the same day he wrote to Thomas Mackenzie, of Pluscardine, brother of the Earl of Seaforth, to acknowledge his great services and sacrifices, and referred him to Montrose, as to his particular wishes, with a recommendation to concur with Seaforth in his service.[6]

On the 15th Charles left the Hague, escorted by the Prince of Orange.[7] By Rotterdam and Dort he travelled to Breda, where he took up his residence in the Prince's house, until his servants at the Hague could complete their preparations for his journey to France. From Breda he wrote privately to Montrose, to render him confident of his resolutions— "I will not determine anything touching that Kingdom [Scotland] without " having your advice thereupon. As also, I will not do anything that shall " be prejudicial to your commission."[8]

These assurances, frequently repeated, were far from needless. Among the King's partisans were many, who, from conviction or jealousy, were strongly opposed to Montrose's policy; and Montrose's party in the King's council had been much weakened by the untimely departure of Hyde on his futile embassy to Spain.[9] The Prince of Orange was well known to be in favour of the late proposals from Scotland.[10]

With so many urgent reasons why Charles should leave the Hague, the Prince may also have desired to remove him from the influence of Montrose and his friends. Their fears were roused, and Montrose followed his master. On the 24th he received a letter from Queen Elizabeth at the Hague, urging him "not to leave the King as long as he is at Breda." She had discovered "by great chance" that Orange would again press Charles to close with the Scots Commissioners.[11]

---

[5] Dep. Keeper of Public Records, Forty-seventh Annual Report, January 1886.

[6] Letter, Wishart's Montr., edit. 1819, p. 441.

[7] The details of the journey are from Heath, 236; Clar. v. 307 ff. (edit. 1717); Balf. iii. 415, &c., and letters in Napier, Mem.

[8] Letter, June 22, Napier, Mem., 706.

[9] Nicolas to Ormond, Jersey, Oct. 13-23, 1649, speaking of the New Scots Commissioners expected, and of their faction, headed by Jermyn, says: Hyde's "unnecessary and unskilful" employment in Spain has given this faction a great advantage . . . "For he was expert in all their jigs and artifices, and only [alone] understood perfectly thir canting." "Jermyn is not only entirely of the Scots Presbyterian faction, but I may tell your excell^y, he is no friend to the Marquis of Ormonde, or Marquis of Montrose."

[10] Strickland, Hagh, Aug. 30–Sept. 9, 1649, in Thurloe, i. 115. "All possible endeavor will be used from the Prince of Orange to make the Scots and thire King to close, hopeing by that means to carrie all heere; but I believe he will be mistaken for reasons I will not writt."

[11] Napier, Mem., 711.

From Breda Montrose appears to have accompanied Charles by Antwerp, —where they stayed for two days—to Brussels. Here they remained for three or four days, and Montrose received a second letter from the Queen of Bohemia, repeating her advice, and informing him that Jermyn had just arrived from Henrietta, with orders, it was said, to get Montrose's commission for Hamilton.[12] But on the eve of parting, Charles, in a formal document, appointed Montrose his ambassador extraordinary to foreign princes, with the most ample powers.[13] Charles then continued his journey to Paris, and reached St. Germains on July 12th. On September 24th,[14] after wasting much precious time in Paris, he retired to Jersey, vainly loitering for an opportunity of crossing to Ireland, attracted by the brilliant prospects of the Royalists in that country. But the watchfulness of the rebel fleet, and the news of Cromwell's rapid successes in Munster, finally "broke all their measures to the expedition,"[15] and forced him to abandon it.

His choice now lay between Montrose and Argyll. With characteristic duplicity he chose both, and eventually ruined both. But even before he left Holland, with the ink of Montrose's commission yet scarce dry, Charles had written to the heads of the dominant faction in Scotland. The messenger he selected was ominous; the persons he addressed still more so. These secret letters were conveyed by William Murray[16]—the same who, in a position of the greatest confidence, had been suspected of betraying Montrose's correspondence with Charles I.—and they were sent to Argyll and Loudon. Murray reached Edinburgh on July 15th, only four days after the Commissioners landed at Stonehaven. There he found the thinly attended Parliament still in session, awaiting the "express" from Charles. At first it was supposed that Murray was the promised messenger. But when it transpired that he brought only private despatches, the contents of which were not divulged, the Estates grew uneasy. Their jealousy was still further excited by a motion of Argyll, supported by the chancellor, Loudon, to send new commissioners to the King. Lothian was "made more willing, " with Argyll's consent, to have been sent." The House continued to wrangle over the subject till the very end of the prolonged session. It was not till August 7th, a day or two before it rose, that the messenger was "voiced" to be Libberton. The letter, however, with which "the godly Wyndram"

---

[12] Dated Hague, Jul. 3rd and 4th (*ibid*. 712, 713).
[13] Dated Brussels, July 6, 1649. Original in Montrose Charter Chest (*ibid*. 706).
[14] "In the middle of September" Clar. The date is inferred from a letter of Elizabeth, Oct. 2 (a Tuesday), wherein she writes, "They went for Jersey upon Monday [Oct. 1], was se'ennight."
[15] Clar. v. 323.
[16] See Index, Wm. Murray; and Balf. iii. 417; Baillie, iii. 97-99, for what follows.

was intrusted, being regarded by the rigid faction as "too smooth,"[17] he made shift to defer his mission till October 11th, when he sailed from Leith for Holland. Apparently it was supposed that Charles had intended to return to the Netherlands, as the letter was addressed to the King "now at Bruxells." Such had perhaps been the impression conveyed in the King's own private letters.[18] The defeat of the Royalists in Ireland now seemed to promise the Argyll faction a brighter prospect of concluding a "treaty;" and the rumours of Montrose's preparations, with the arrival in Orkney of his advance-guard under Kinnoul (September), helped to quicken Libberton's tardy movements.

From Brussels, Montrose had returned to the Hague, where he remained for about two months, doubtless engaged in preparing Kinnoul's detachment, and in attempts to procure assistance from princes friendly to the exiles. On July 22nd he wrote to Frederick William, Elector of Brandenburg, a relative of King Charles, through the House of Orange, and then resident in his duchy at Cleves, to solicit his aid.[19] From the reply, we learn that Montrose's messenger, Harry Graham, his half-brother, had already been sent on a similar mission to the Elector, while the King had employed "Lieutenant-General Adam de Karpf"[20] for the same purpose. The Elector had promised a considerable sum of money, but in his reply of the 27th, he excused himself, owing to difficulties in raising the loan. But beyond promises and professions of good-will, it does not appear that either Charles or Montrose received any material aid from the "Great Elector."

On July 23rd the Duke of York wrote from St. Germains, "I am very " glad the King, my brother, has found an occasion of employing you;"[21] and on the same date Henrietta, at Paris, acknowledged two letters from Montrose, and assured him that she felt for him an esteem "that never can " be diminished." In the light of her previous lukewarm conduct, and her favourite Jermyn's ill-veiled hostility, we may suspect that this protestation was evoked by some hint of doubt in Montrose's letters.

---

[17] Baillie, *loc. cit.* Balf. iii. 432. For the negotiations and contemporary events, see the table at the end of this chapter.

[18] On Sept. 13 Strickland wrote from the Hague, "Some apprehende the returne of P. C. [Prince Charles, *i.e.*, the King] into these parts: if he do cum hither, it will be much against the minde of the Hollanders." Thurloe, i. 121. Strickland is mentioned as the English rebel agent at the Hague in a letter Mar. 4 (N. S.) 1648-9 to Ormond. O. Papers, i. 223.

[19] Copies sent to the Editors from the Royal Archives, Berlin (*v.* Appendix, No. iv). There can be no doubt that the Elector's reply was the paper found in Dunbeath Castle (*v.* Appendix, No. ix). The sum "*decem millia imperialia*"=*Reichsthaler* (?), *i.e.*, about £2250 (?).

Frederick William I., "the Great," Markgrave of Brandenburg, Elector, &c., *b.* 1620, reigned 1640-1688, married Louisa Henrietta, Princess of Orange.

[20] See Index.

[21] The correspondence with Charles, Henrietta, Elizabeth, the Duke of York, and Seaforth, is extracted from Napier, Mem., and the App. to W.'s Montrose (1819).

From the Hague he wrote to Queen Elizabeth to inform her of his commissions. She returned his papers in a letter dated Aug. 4-14, and invited him to visit her and meet Kinnoul at Rhenen, whither she had probably retired before Montrose's return from Brussels. During this visit he must have concerted with Kinnoul some definite outline of his plans. On Aug. 15th we find him again at the Hague, writing to Seaforth, who had accompanied Charles to St. Germains. He expresses regret that he should linger there, instead of putting himself at the head of his powerful clan; "for y$^r$ presence, where you know, wold doe much goode; since you sei "affairs go so equally and on a levell. Alwayes [but] I hope thes will fynd "you goeing, and my best wishes shall accompany you alongs. I am just "now setting out, and intends to recover thir delays by the best dispatch I "can." The nature of these delays can only be conjectured. In addition to the opposition of the Hamilton-Lauderdale faction, and the divided counsels which beset the irresolute King, Montrose had to encounter great difficulties in procuring funds and ships to transport the numerous volunteers and mercenaries who besieged him with offers of service. About the end of August he left the Hague; Kinnoul probably accompanied him to Amsterdam,[22] and remained there to take charge of the first detachment. On Sept. 2nd Strickland, the newly accredited envoy of the English Parliament, wrote to Secretary Frost: "Since Montrose his absence, those, who appeared soe "much in designs against me, are seen noe more. I believe most of them "are gon, soe as I am more at liberty then I was. . . . Montrose hopes to "raise a thousand horss and thre thousand foote, and with them to visite "his cuntremen. My lord Kenowle, who is well knowne in England, I heare, "is gon to take possession of some island in Scotland. He and Montrose "perfectly hate the prævaling party in Scotland; yet the governing party "had much strenthened the hands of Montrose by makeing thire King be "received by them, whose commission to Montrose by that is more authen- "ticall."[23] Kinnoul, however, had not yet sailed, for on the 6th Strickland again wrote: "Thire is in Amsterdam a shippe in which is much armes and "ammunition, bound for Scotland, for the use of Montrose, as I am informed. "If thire be any in Scotland, who desearve such an information, it were well "they knew it. It is to be sent to some of the isles, some say the Orkades. "Those of that nation are soe excessively my ennimyes heere, that it is "high charity for me to doe any thinge, which may tend to thire service. "Montrose is expected at Hambourgh."[24] And again, in a letter of the

---

[22] Carte's Ormond papers, i. 345 ff. Nicholas to Ormond, enclosing paper of Jan. 20, 1650. We shall have frequent occasion to refer to this paper. Its authority, however, where unsupported, is very questionable, as the whole account it gives of Montrose's preparations abounds in exaggeration.

[23] Thurloe, i. 117.    [24] *Ibid.* 119.

same date, he adds, "Some armes are shipped at Amsterdam for Montrose "his use, to goe for some isle in Scotland, some say the Orcades. If thire "be any remnant good [*i.e.*, in Scotland] I wish they knew it. I am now "the man they hate most; but that is no woonder, the English doe soe to."[25]

A variety of considerations marked out the Orkneys as a suitable rendezvous for the expedition. These islands were then governed with almost regal powers by Robert, Earl of Morton, a loyal nobleman, uncle to Kinnoul. They were remote from the influences and authority of Argyll's faction, and near the country of the loyal Lord Reay and the Mackenzie clan, who had recently, under Pluscardine, Seaforth's brother, been in arms for the King. The season of the year was late; and though it exposed the expedition to great risks by storm, yet for that very reason there was less to be feared from English cruisers.[26] Moreover, the strength of the rebel navy was then occupied with Ireland, in attendance on Cromwell's movements. To them it was of the last moment that Rupert should not escape from Kinsale, either to convey Charles to Ireland, or to act in concert with Montrose. Of the two dangers the former was certainly the more imminent. Yet so ill-informed were the Scots at this time, that it was not till August, when Cromwell actually sailed, that they ceased to fear invasion[27] from the army voted for Ireland as early as March 15th. On the other hand, Montrose's descent on Scotland was likely to kindle a fierce civil war; and it is by no means certain that at that time such a diversion would have been unwelcome to the English rebels. The rise of the Independents, their repudiation of the Solemn League, the invasion of the Engagers, the execution of Charles and Hamilton, and the proclamation of Charles II. as King of Scotland, had completely estranged the rebel parties of both nations. The English were accurately informed of Montrose's movements,[28] but the event shows reason to suspect that their officers in northern waters were not disposed at this crisis to act with vigour in support of the Scottish "Estates."

Kinnoul arrived at Kirkwall about the end of September, after a perilous voyage of three weeks. The force, according to Balfour, consisted of "80

---

[25] *Ibid.* 119. It is inferred that Strickland here speaks of the ship Kinnoul sailed in, the ship so ill spoken of by Gwynne. Gordon of Sallagh (Hist. Earls of Sutherland, 550), says Kinnoul came out of Holland about the end of September, "with a number of Scots and Danish Commanders with some two hundreth Danish common souldiers." Gordon's authority for events outside his own ken is poor. He makes Montrose too come out of Holland (*ibid.* 551). The other ships in which Montrose was disappointed had perhaps, like Rupert's, taken to roving, which the needy Royalists found very profitable. Were they the three ships mentioned by Strickland, Thurloe, i. 115?

[26] The same reasons, in reference to Charles's voyage to Ireland, are urged with force by Jermyn, August 10, 1649. Orm. Papers, i. 300-302.

[27] Baillie, iii. 97.

[28] See Strickland above. They had many agents and well-wishers abroad. "It is most certain the Queen's and Prince's counsels have been long time still known to the Rebels in England as soon as resolved on." Nicolas, Orm. Papers, iii. 584. He accuses Culpepper of treachery.

## DEEDS OF MONTROSE.

"commanders and about 100 Danes and strangers,"[29] with arms and ammunition for a thousand men.[30] With Kinnoul went Captain John Gwynne,[31] whose memoirs give the following narrative of the voyage:—

"At Amsterdam, before he [Gwynne] went over into Scotland with the
"Earle of Kaynoole, upon Marques Montros his ingagement, I was told by
"those who condol'd us, (as knowing our busines better than some of our-
"selves did,) that we were all betraid; and by our proceedings it appear'd
"to be so, as thus: First, we were to have a small fleet vessel, with twelve
"guns; and instead of that we had an old one, new vamp't, without a gun;
"then we were chast at sea by a Parliament frigot, which the tempestuous
"weather kept off, and as that might soon faile us, we were prepar'd, as
"knowing the worst, to receave our doome bravely, with an attempt to board
"the enemy, sinke or swim: or had there been ever so many of them, we
"were all resolv'd, with the Earle of Kaynoole, in that desperat condition,
"rather to be buried alive with our swords in our hands, than dye any other
"way less honourable, and more cruelly, at their choice: and when, through
"the extreamity of continued stormes, we arrived (as Providence would have
"it) at our port, there had been, for three weeks, three more Parliament men-
"of-warr, impatient at our long coming; and, at the very hour we came,
"they went some other course to looke us, as though we were not out of
"sight [meaning, "as though we were out of sight?"]; but as the evening
"drew on, and the fog which obscur'd us, then we came secure ashoar."

The narrative is continued in the following letter from Kinnoul to his chief:—

"For his excellencie Lord marques of Montrose.[32]

"MY VERY NOBLE LORD,

"Your Lords: good fortune hes so much influence upon those that have
"the honour to obey your commandes, that I daere promes my self as good
"succes in the business, as your Lords: shall see hou happie wee have bein
"hitherto. After a tedious stormy on and twenty days sea jurny, wee cast
"ancher att Kirkwall, wher I found by boatmen that came from the toune
"that my unckle Mortone was att a house of his aune some 16 meiles
"from this place. bieng wery confident of his loyaltie I venterd to land,
"and without reposing I took hors and went in all heast to him, having left

---

[29] *Vide* Sallagh, *n.* 25 above.
[30] Balf. iii. 431.
[31] Memoirs, edit. Sir W. Scott, 1822, pp. 83-85. The extracts in the text are all he tells us of this expedition, beyond some verse, on the perils of the voyage, not worth quoting. He wrote probably long after the Restoration, and speaks of himself as of a sole survivor. His account is scanty, and quite deficient in dates.
[32] Original, Advocates' Libr., Wodrow MSS., fol. lxvii. 93.

" orderes to our men to land in the night, which was punctuly obeyd. I
" found my Lord more zelus to the obedience of the Kings commandes and
" your Lords: then I thoght possible a personne of his fortune in this place
" could be, in so much that efter I was bold to call us faive hundreth, he
" wisht them hartily thousants, and gave mee all asseurances that so soone
" as wee wold shou ourselves to be in capacitie to reduce the cuntry, he wold
" not faile to be assistant to us in lyff and fortune; which bieng impossible
" for us to compasse, I was forced (by my Lords desyre) to send a party
" from this to his house of Birza [*Birsay Castle*] requeirring ane positive
" answere and active assistance, which was so hartily condescended to, that
" I shall humbly desyre your excellence to considder him as the cheefest
" instrument nixt to your Lords: of the Kings service. I am confident of
" your approbatione anent my procedeur, since it was the sence of those that
" affectes the Kings service and honors your Lords: most. My unckle my
" Lord of Mortone was plaised to think he was neglected in [*that*] the Com-
" missiones for stating [*raising*] this Cuntrie were not imedeately conferrd on
" him from your Lords:. Wherupon having all asseurance of his Lords:
" Loialitie, I weavd my aune interest so much that I assind all pouer of my
" commissiones to him, which he was plaised to accept of befor the gentilmen
" of this Cuntrie, who were convocat for the receaving of his commandes and
" your excellences, which were so cheerfuly embract, that unanimusly they
" did condescend to a posteur of warre for our present defence, to consiste
" of four hundreth men presently to be levied, which is sufficient to manteane
" this place agenst all that dare call themselves Committes. I hop your
" Lords: shall feind this resignatione conduce so much to the advantage of
" the kings service, that I shall have no bleame from you, but on the
" contraire I could nether bein ansuerable to my allegence nor your Lords:
" if I had refusd it, having asseurance under my Lord his hand and seale to
" be repossesst in my commissiones, so soon as your Lords: shall think fitt
" the regement shall wait on you in Scotland. for my part I esteame it the
" greatest adventage onder the sun that I have this occasione of testiefieng
" my repect to your Lords:. This actione hes given the rebelles such a blou
" that I will tak it on my salvatione, if you fall upon them att the nick of
" ther distemper, you shall find assistance beyond all expectatione, and that
" sufficient to effectuat your ententiones. Your Lords: is gapt after with
" that expectation that the Jeus looks after ther Messia, and certenly your
" presence will restore your groaning Cuntrie to its Liberties and the King to
" his rigts. God almighty hes not only blist us thus by land, but hes made
" those we werre to expect disservice from our frindes, for the nixt day efter
" wee landed ther ancerd a shipp of 16 gunnes in another roaad of this
" same Island. the Captaine no sooner understood the reality of our inten-
" tiones and your orders, but wery galently delivred the rebelle armes unto

"us, and declared shipp and all to be at your commandes.[33] your Lords:
"knos bei what to gratifie so generus ane act, which hes maade me give
"him asseurance of your keindnes and him to think himself happy in the
"expectatione of it. I shall humbly intreat your Lords: to send my Lord
"ane absolute commissione for these Islandes, and that you wold recalle such
"Commissiones as hes Lords: conseaves to be his prejudice, as George
"Drumondes, whose father is my Lords ennimie, and is gone to the south to
"shunne ingaging in this bussines. my unckle hes proived so cordiall and
"so active, that his doings are beyond the limetes of being satisfied by
"woordes. I ame confident you will feind it fitt to befrind him in all his
"particulars. for mee, if your Lords: will doe me the honor to belive that
"ther is nothing able to alter my esteame of you, I shall be incurreged to
"serve you faithfully, and shall be still happie in being

"the most passienatte of your servantes

"K.........LE. [torn.]

".........KWAL."

Some weeks later the rumour reached Edinburgh that Kinnoul was busy in levying and arming soldiers in Orkney.[34] About the 14th of October, Lieutenant-General David Leslie, with seven or eight troops of horse, went north, "where he stayed some fifteen days, confirming the Northern shires in their obedience and weiuing [viewing] the garrisons." He returned south about the beginning of November, "finding no sture nor opposition there."[35] The season was in fact unfavourable to any active operations on either side. About the end of September both Lowlands and Highlands were visited by heavy rains and "very great snows."[36] But this did not prevent Leslie from proceeding as far at least as Ross, and he had some intention of crossing into Orkney, as we gather from Gwynne's Memoirs:—[37]

"A while after that we were in quarters in those several islands of
"Orkney, David Lesley was sent with a considerable force of horse and foot

---

[33] Captain Hall's frigate. See p. 244, n. 2, and Index. [34] Balf., loc. cit.
[35] Ibid. iii. 432. [36] "After Michaelmas" (ibid. 433).
[37] Pp. 86, 87. Nicolas to Ormond, Feb. 11-21, 1649-50. "David Lesley marched northward in November, having only with him ten troops of horse, and 700 foot, and appointed to have a rendezvous at Inverness: but first caused divulge a feigned proclamation in Montrose's name, to try the pulse of the people. But no man stirred; neither when he pressed them to rise, would they at all take arms. His intention was to have made himself strong, to have gone against Kinnoul in Orkney, but he was disappointed. Neither could he have been able to effect anything there, the Isle of Orkney being strong to the number of 8000 fighting men all loyal to the King; besides 3000 gallant men that were come from Montrose and had fortified themselves strongly in the town of Kirkwall: having also some three or four good ships, wherewith Kinnoul falls in when he pleases upon the mainland, and brings all necessary provisions for the soldiers. One of these ships belongs to Captain Ball [Hall] of Leith, who was loaded with arms and ammunition of my Lord Argyle's to go about by the North Isles to my Lord Argyle's country, for furnishing of two or three of his

"to subpres us; and before he came to the water side, which he was to "cros over first, sent a packet to Earle of Kynoole, and, amongst other "circumstances, declar'd, that by all the obligation and interest that ever "was between them, the best service he could do his Lordship, was to advise "him speedily to make his retreat into some other countrey; for his orders "were to be severely executed upon him and his party: which my Lord "Kaynoole receiv'd with so much indignation, that he commanded the packit "to be burnt under the gallows, by the hand of the hangman; and his Lord- "ship himself was [there] to see it don. Upon this so publick and general a "defiance, David Lesley presently prosecuts in his comands; and when he "had boarded several boats-full of horse and foot, to come and fall upon us, "there arros so great and sudden a storme, that they could not stirr, before "another strange relief came, by a counter command sent to Lesley, that "where ere it reacht him he was to quitt all former orders, and forthwith to "return and march to the west, against a greater invasion there; which at "last prov'd to be but false allarum, whatsoever the design was, more then "to divert them from us, and to give us a longer respiet in the countrey.

"About two months afterwards the Earl of Kynoole fell sick at Bursey, "the Earl of Murton's house, and there dyed of a pluresy, whose loss was "very much lamented, as he was truly honourable, and perfectly loyal." This event is said to have occurred within a few days after the death of his uncle, Robert Douglas, Earl of Morton, who died at Kirkwall on Nov. 12th.[38]

From Amsterdam Montrose, accompanied by Lord Napier, continued his journey towards Hamburg, which he reached early in September.[39] On the way he was well received by the Count of Friesland, who is said to have "promised him free quarter for his soldiers, and what further assistance he could be able to contribute."[40] At Hamburg he found Sir John Cochran, who had arrived there, June 11th, on a mission from Charles to raise money and induce the Senate to discountenance the disloyal proceedings of the heads of the English Merchant Company. His efforts do not appear to

---

houses there: but the captain went in with ship and all to my Lord Kinnoul. The ship carries 18 guns, and has taken since a ship of ten guns." See further, Ch. ix. Of the "feigned pro- clamation" nothing further is known.

"In the beginning of Nov. . . . Leslie came with nyne troopes of hors as far as Chanrie [Chanonry, in the Black Isle, Dornoch Firth] in Ross . . . and sent proclamations into Orknay to summond the Earl of Kinnowl and his adherents to come in and give obedience to the state. He returned south, about the midst of the same month, upon a report that there were like to be some commotions in Angus and Merns, which were quelled (if any were intended) at his return thither." Gordon of Sallagh, Hist. Earls of Sutherland, 551.

[38] Balf., iii. 433, 434, gives the exact date. He attributes Morton's death to "a displeasure conceiued at his nephew" (Kinnoul), probably a bit of idle gossip. See Napier, Mem., 727.

[39] Elizabeth to Montrose, Oct. 2nd, acknowledges a letter from him dated Hamburg, Sept. 4. Napier, Mem., 717.

[40] Nicolas, *loc. cit.*

have met with much success, to judge by his own report to Charles,[41] transmitted to Montrose, with a commission, dated St. Germains, Sept. 5, 1649, empowering him to compose these differences, and treat for a loan, half of which was to be remitted to Amsterdam for the King's use, the other half to be employed by Montrose himself. Later on we shall find similar terms in Montrose's commission to Sweden. Sir John Cochran was afterwards despatched as commissioner to the Duke of Courland, who "contributed very "nobly, furnishing six great ships loaden with corn, and what ever else was "demanded of him by Sir John Cockran, who went from thence to the King "of Poland, who is so forward that he cannot suffer to hear of a Scotsman "there (where of there are many thousands in his Majesty's dominions, "besides children and servants) "who is not honest and loyal to his King."[42] But, if we may believe the anonymous author of the Montrose Redivivus (Part II. p. 172), Sir John, "having procur'd very considerable summs of "money upon that score, and other provision for the furthering that "[Montrose's] expedition, dispos'd of the money for his own uses, made sale "of corn and provision, together with the vessell which was provided for the "transportation of it, and did himself turn tayl to the quarrell. . . . "This did much retard the Marquesses affairs." In Cochran's absence, Colonel Sir William Johnston, who succeeded in charge, was sent to the Dukes of Brunswick, Celle, and Hanover; but in the absence of more trustworthy information as to his success, there are strong grounds to suspect that the rosy prospects of help from this and other sources, mentioned in his letter from Hamburg, Dec. 14–24th, to Nicolas, were grossly exaggerated, and that the whole picture of Montrose's proceedings sent by Nicolas to Ormond (Jan. 20, 1650), owed much of its warm breadth of colour to the same touch. With naïve simplicity Nicolas owns that the rebels in Scotland professed to have little fear at such rumours, "in respect that they "know most assuredly that Montrose has neither men nor money, nor "arms nor shipping." He admits, in fact, that "during the space of two "or three months none knew but himself the particulars he intended or was "about, and those to whom he intrusted anything were men of known "fidelity and secrecy. He did not write himself to any friend, nor suffered "he any that belonged to him to touch any particular; only in general, that "they hoped all would go well and very few had that much assurance till "his business was compleat."[43]

---

[41] Dunbeath Papers. Wodrow MSS., fol. lxvii. 89 (*v.* App., No. ix.). A long windy paper, omitted by the Editors as not directly bearing on the subject. For Montrose's commission to Hamburg, see App., No. v.

[42] Nicolas, *loc. cit.* The archives at Vienna contain no record of the help offered by the Emperor, and the interview he proposed to hold with Montrose at Frankfurt-on-the-Main. This tale of Nicolas requires confirmation; but see p. 245. [43] Nicolas, *loc. cit.*

After staying little more than a week in Hamburg, Montrose hastened to meet the King of Denmark at Flensburg in Schleswig. This meeting took place on October 8th, according to the information received by Nicolas. But the Copenhagen archives have preserved a copy of Frederick's letter to Charles, September 15th,[44] wherein he acknowledges the commission of Montrose, and states that his case had been expressed *"singulari dextcritate."* As Montrose had reached Copenhagen by October 6th, he cannot have lingered long in Hamburg. Hope of the King's assistance, no less than strict etiquette and courtesy, would require him to present his credentials in person; and the King's presence in Flensburg was favourable to an early interview. Thither, Frederick is said, on the same doubtful authority, to have summoned the nobility and gentry of Holstein, "to consult of Montrose's business, and the result of that meeting was to his (M.'s) mind." Enough was promised to encourage even a less sanguine temperament; but whatever Frederick's intentions may have been, he had little power to carry them out. The real authority of Denmark was then vested in a Council of Nobles, a close oligarchy, whose powers remained supreme, till shattered by external disaster. To this council, therefore, Montrose was referred by the King.[45]

The greatest subject of Denmark at this date was Korfits Ulfeldt, the "Rigs-hofmester" (Grand Maître du Royaume).[46] His influence had been strengthened by marriage with the King's half-sister. Early in 1649, he had been employed on a special embassy to Holland, and after some delay concluded a treaty by which Denmark, in return for large sums of money, conceded to the Estates certain privileges in passing through the Sound. At the Hague he met Montrose, who, in the invidious phrase of Clarendon, "found means to endear himself to Cornificius Wolfelte." It is asserted by Sir James Turner that "that faithles minister of estate, who afterwarde went faire to betray both his prince and countrey," did little or nothing to fulfil the expectations he had kindled. It is, however, just to the memory of both King and minister to record, that as early as March 24th, Ulfeldt

---

[44] Copy of Montrose's letter to Frederick sent to the Editors, with some valuable notes, by Herr C. F. Brička, Arkivar, Rigsarkivet, Copenhagen. See App., No. iv.; and for Frederick's letter, Deputy-Keeper of Records, forty-seventh report, p. 75. Montrose's letter is holograph, and strongly characteristic of the writer.

[45] Nicolas, *loc. cit.*

[46] For the sums paid by Ulfeldt, see *Danske Magazin*, 3 *Raekke*, 55 ff. In 1653 Charles II. denied the debt. Meantime, Frederick had quarrelled with Ulfeldt, who was imprisoned, but escaped to Sweden. Ulfeldt's papers had been lost at sea, and Frederick seized the opportunity to accuse him of misappropriating these sums; but the ex-minister triumphantly produced Montrose's receipts. The scene is described in detail in *Mémoires de Chanut* (1677), iii. 342 ff. Cf. "Whitelocke's Journal" (1855), ii. 91. In 1663, Ulfeldt's widow renewed the claim; but not even wealth could make an honest man of Charles II. From notes sent by Herr Arkivar Brička. See further, Thurloe, i. 357, 473. His name appears in contemporaries as Vlefeldt, Vlefield, Woolfleet, &c.

received from Denmark a letter of credit for Charles II., and paid to Montrose the sum of 24,000 *Rigsdaler*—about £5400—and out of his own resources advanced him a further sum equivalent to £4275. On the 5th of October, Ulfeldt was on the eve of quitting the Hague.[47] He would, therefore, reach Copenhagen shortly after the arrival of Montrose.

On October 14th, Montrose addressed three letters from Copenhagen [48] to Prince Rupert, to the Marquis of Ormond, and to Sir George Monro, all three in Ireland. During his preparations he is said to have maintained an active correspondence with his friends, and to have sent messengers "every week or fortnight to Scotland, from which he received assurances " that the whole people and gentry, and most part of the nobility, were ready " to join him upon his first appearance; that there were strange changes " there, even in those that were his greatest enemies; and that the most part " of the officers and soldiers commanded by David Leslie had vowed solemnly " to render themselves for the King under his command."[49] On this occasion, we are unhappily able to trace his messenger, for shortly after his landing at Leith, Colonel Sibbald, with the letters and instructions in his cloak-bag, was arrested, and reserved for the same scaffold on which his leader fell.

These letters, "all in Montrose's own hand," were read in Parliament, May 22, 1650, but must have disappeared in the disturbances that ensued. Some details they may have contained of Montrose's progress, with, perhaps, suggestions of a scheme for concerted action. Early in the year such a scheme appears to have been on foot, as we gather from Prince Rupert's letter of April 1st.[50]

"MY LORD,

" I have received three letters from your Lordship in one day, among " which there was one sent me by Major-General Monro, whose business, " though I know not, yet whenever he shall please to let me know the " assistance I shall give, shall be set forward as much as it may. My Lord, " I find upon all occasions, that your kindness to me is the same you

---

[47] Queen of Bohemia to M., Napier, Mem., 719.
[48] Balf. iv. 22; and see p. 244, *n.* 2.
[49] Nicolas, *loc. cit.* Among these messengers, and in connection with Pluscardine's rising, were "Mr. Villiam Orde, serviter to James Grhame, sometyme Earle of Montrose quho had lately beine sent to this Countrey with letters from his master out of Holland; he was apprehendit at Kermure in Angus." Balf. iii. 397, 398, under date April 7, 1649.
[50] W.'s Montrose (1819), 446. "Kingragly" we cannot identify. Is it a mistake for "Kinsale," or is the castle "Ringrone" mixed up with Kinsale? The date of Rupert's arrival there does not appear in his Memoirs (Edit. Warburton, 1849), a valuable work, but, like Balfour's Annals, Thurloe, Carte's Ormond, and other collections on the period, a sad pickle of dates, much in need of re-editing.

"profest, and I am very sorry that as yet, there is no occasion for me to
"give a real testimony of mine, which I intend upon all occasions to do.
"Of this your Lordship may be confident, since this is from, My Lord, your
"Lordship's most faithful friend and servant,

P. RUPERT.

"KINGRAGLY, *April* 1, 1649."

As Montrose wrote to Prince Rupert on Oct. 14th, it is evident that he had not then received Queen Elizabeth's letter of Oct. 2nd,[51] informing him that Rupert was said "to be at sea again," escaped from Kinsale. She also assured him that "the business in Ireland was not so bad as was expected: Ormond had lost no towns. The King was now at Jersey, still intending to go for Ireland, if not prevented by the Parliament's ships. Culpepper had been sent to Muscovy.[52] Jermyn was expected at the Hague to meet, it was said, Lauderdale and Hamilton, and arrange to have new commissioners from Scotland. But the King remained most constant to Montrose." Again, on the 5th, she wrote to confirm her news of Jermyn, but "the King was constant. Cromwell was said to have been defeated [a false report[53]]. Those that governed Scotland made a show to wish for their King, but were not disposed to abate their terms." Her news had been brought by Patrick Ruthven, the aged Earl of Brentford and Forth, who had shown great ability in England during the early years of the rebellion.[54] At this time he entertained a project of joining Montrose, who is repeatedly assured by Elizabeth of his constancy and esteem. Clearly, when she wrote these letters, she had not heard of the massacres at Drogheda and Wexford.[55]

Among those who are recorded to have given help to Montrose, the "Duke of Holstein" is mentioned, but it does not appear which of the many Dukes of Holstein is spoken of. He contributed some ships, probably, early in 1649, "which were kept a great while at Amsterdam to no purpose, being

---

[51] Napier, Mem., 717, 718.

[52] Culpepper was sent to recover £8000 lent by James I. to the Emperor of Muscovy. Nicolas Carte's Ormond, i. 310 ff. (*ibid.* 358, 359 "lent him by the late King's means"). *Ibid.* 313, Oct. 8th, mentions that Culpepper had set out.

[53] Cf. Balf. iii. 433.

[54] See Gardiner, Hist. Rebell., Index. Charles to Ormond (Papers, ii. 376), May 16, 1649, had appointed "Brainford" to send him arms out of Sweden. Queen Elizabeth's last letter to Montrose, Hague, 7th Jan. (1650), begins "This bearer's dispatch to you, [written] by honest old Brainford, gives me occasion to write to you. You will find by his letters what he desires. I assure you he is very fast to you." In her letter of the 9th Dec. she had written, "Old Brainford will chide you, that you should mistrust his constancy to you. He says he is now too old to be a knave, having being honest ever. I am confident he is very real." He died at Dundee, Feb. 2, 1651. Napier, Mem., 721; also Ruthven Papers, Roxburgh Club.

[55] Mentioned in her letter of Nov. 19-29th (*ibid.* 720).

# DEEDS OF MONTROSE.

"three or four very fair vessels, and well mann'd. Which Prince would
"have willingly contributed more to that service, but that he perceiv'd that
"which he had given before to be so misemployed; wherein both he and
"the Marquesse were grossly abus'd." Montrose had sent Colonel John
Ogilvie "to Amsterdam to entertain such strangers as might be for his
"purpose. But he, forgetting his Commission, bestowed both moneys and
"pains in entertaining himself, suffering those who upon any termes would
"have engaged to shift for themselves."[56]

The ports of Holland and towns of Northern Europe were at this time crowded with needy English and Scottish refugees, eager from principle or necessity to embark in this—perhaps in any, cause. The termination of the Thirty Years' War, while it left the princes with impoverished treasuries, had also thrown many Scottish adventurers out of employment. Whole regiments were being disbanded.[57] It had been no mere idle boast of Montrose, that if money were forthcoming, he could land in Scotland with 10,000 men[58].

At Copenhagen, Montrose must have received the following letter from Charles. It is written from St. Germains, where the King was more immediately under the influence of the Queen-Mother and her Jesuitical faction. The warmth of its re-assuring terms was necessary to lull suspicions excited by rumours of the King's trafficking with the Presbyterian party. Evidently Charles meant the "man of the dearest honour" to believe him wholly devoted to Montrose's policy. But in the light of the King's conduct then and afterwards, the reservation implied in the words "than when I left you" . . . "upon the same principles I was," conveys an impression of astute duplicity, and surprises us only that a prince so false should have had scruples enough to insert such a saving clause.

"MY LORD,

"I entreat you to go on vigorously, and with your wonted courage and
"care in the prosecution of those trusts I have committed to you, and not
"to be startled with any reports you may hear, as if I were otherwise
"inclined to the Presbyterians than when I left you. I assure you I am
"upon the same principles I was, and depend as much as ever upon your
"undertakings and endeavours for my service, being fully resolved to assist

---

[56] Montrose Redivivus, pp. 170-172.
[57] Wishart to Lord Napier at Hamburg, Shiedame, Jan. 1, 1650 (Napier, Mem., 730-732): "The provincial Estates of Holland will needs . . . casheer ane 109 companies of foot, all of strange nations, French, English, and Scots, and most part of the cavalry, and reduce yet more those that remain." For interesting details of Scots then in foreign service, see Sir Thomas Urquhart's Mems., in Burton, "The Scot Abroad," 327, 328, &c.
[58] See p. 195.

" and support you therein to the uttermost of my power, as you shall find
" in effect, when you shall desire anything to be done by your affectionate
" friend,

CHARLES R."[59]

"S. GERMAINS, *Sept.* 19*th*, 1649.

On Oct. 6th, the Swedish resident in Copenhagen wrote to inform his government that Montrose was there, awaiting the King's return. But he waited in vain. Frederick remained in Schleswig.[60] In the Ormond paper already quoted, it is said that Montrose received great satisfaction at Copenhagen. But the following characteristic letter of Oct. 19th, shows how keenly Montrose felt the disappointment and delay. The King's letter referred to is not extant.

"SIRE, The letter with which your Majesty has been pleased to honour
" me has made me await with impatience the commencements therein
" promised. Seeing no appearance of this, I am obliged humbly to crave
" your Majesty's pardon for begging to know your intentions. Delays are
" the worst of all evils. What your Majesty shall please to do will be
" doubled by being done soon. In such affairs a refusal that sets us free
" to act, is better than a promise that ruins us. There are, I know, some
" who would have your Majesty believe that the little assistance you may
" give your royal cousin will disable you from guarding against your enemies,
" and that your neighbours may take advantage of it. But I humbly beg
" your Majesty to do me the honour to believe (and I should not make bold
" to say it, without, perhaps, sufficient assurance thereof), that your Majesty
" has never done anything which shall put your neighbours under greater
" obligations; and if you do it not, which shall give them more cause to
" take exception, and occasion worse results. I shall add no more than
" that this slight assistance to the King, your cousin, can but serve to display
" your Majesty's honour, justice and friendship, and to strengthen you on
" all sides."

On October 27, the Swedish resident again wrote that Montrose was engaging troops "in great style,"[61] but from lack of money the numbers enlisted were insignificant. Finally, on November 10, he wrote to inform his government that Montrose had left for Sweden.

Before his departure he sent the following letter to Seaforth, but neither

---

[59] W.'s Montrose (1819), p. 447, 448.

[60] Notes on the information of the Swedish envoy, and the following letter of Montrose were courteously communicated to the Editors by Herr C. F. Bricka, Arkivar, Copenhagen. See App., No. iv.

[61] "Montrose endnu er her og *i al Stilhed* lader hwerve, men at disse Hvervinger af Pengemangel kun er ubetydelige." See App., No. ix., Dunbeath Papers. " Not [note] of the Jewells and plate that is pawned."

this nor any other inducement appears to have procured for him more than "advyse" from that shifty nobleman.

"COPNAHAGEN, 27 Octobr, *veteri* [Old Style].

"MY LORD,

"Tho I heave writt many tymes to you, which seimes is not come to yr
"hands, and only receaved some tuo of yrs, yett I cannot bot tell you how
"glaid I am att the informations I receave of yr nobell and resolutt cariages
"concerning his majestie, and yr kyndens towards yr friends, which I assure
"you hes procured you so much respect mongst all honourable people as is
"not to be exchanged for a world; for what friendship you heave beane
"pleased to doe me the honor to witnes (tho it con be no more then I ever
"promised to myself,) I will make you the faithfullest returne my lyfe can
"doe, and if it please God I los it not very suddenly, I shall be sure not to
"dye in yr debt; meanetyme, I humbly entreat you be confident that wher-
"ever I be, or whatever occasions I may heave to correspond with you, or
"not, that I can never forgett what I owe you, but shall ever in all fortunes,
"places, and tymes, be faithfully and as effectually as it may please God I
"can, my Lord, yr L.'s. most faithfull cossing and servand,

"MONTROSE.

"I am useing yr advyse, and setting furth in the way that is possible,
"and I shall make you the best account that it shall please God to give me
"leave."[62]

[Directed in another hand]
"For the Earle of Seaforth this."

In the absence of certain information we may conjecture that Seaforth's advice referred to Montrose's choice of the north of Scotland for his landing, and the assistance he might expect from Seaforth's own following.

Disappointed in his hopes of Denmark, the Marquis now turned his eyes to Sweden, and the circumstances alluded to in the following letter, in his own hand, may have had something to do with his leaving Copenhagen a week later. Unhappily it is somewhat torn, and bears no address.[63]

"COPNAHAGEN, 3 *Nobi* [November], 1649.

"SR,

"I receaved yrs and a[m r]eadlie satisfy[ed] with the cours you [heav]e
"taken concerning that Lieutenant . . . as for that proposition touch-
"ing the ships and that ship of cloth and all of that kynd, Iff it can be

---

[62] W.'s Montrose (1819), p. 443, 444, from Seaforth archives.
[63] Advocates' Library, Wodrow MSS., fol. lxvii., No. 90.

" handsomely done, and be sure that it shall not misgive, I should be joyed
" with it; only Iff it be medled with, lett it be sure to carry, otherwayes It
" will give disrepuit [*torn*] to lett them come to [G]ottenberry or a [ny ?] port
" belonging to the Queene [of] Swed[en] neir it.  I will answer [for] them,
" for I he[ave] all civilities can [be] from that place.  be doeing the best you
" can in all, and expect ane express from me with all possible heast.  I am,

"Sr yr constant leall freind
" MONTROSE."[64]

As this letter was afterwards found among the papers taken by Leslie in Dunbeath Castle, it must have been addressed to one of the officers who accompanied the expedition. It refers to some proposal to seize a "cloth ship," probably belonging to the English rebels, and perhaps then lying in some port near Gothenburg.

On November 4th he wrote to Queen Elizabeth,[65] and from her reply of December 9th, seems to have expressed some distrust of Brentford, which she seeks to allay.

Early in November, probably, therefore, before he quitted Denmark, Montrose issued his Declaration. Its immediate effect was to attract to his service a number of Royalists on the Continent.[66] It was aimed, perhaps, as a counterstroke to the rumours of the King's negotiations with the Presbyterians. He must have felt that these rumours were paralysing his friends, both at home and abroad. It is certain that they contributed mainly to the ruin of his expedition.[67] The Declaration roused serious apprehensions in Scotland, where Montrose found means to publish it in December. On January 2, 1650, it drew forth a *Defence and Warning from the Commission of the General Assembly*, followed on the 24th by a long acrimonious rejoinder of the "Committee of Estates," "*in vindication of their proceedings from the aspersions of a scandalous pamphlet published by that excommunicate Traitor, James Graham,*" signed "A. Johnston, *Clericus Registri.*"[68]

---

[64] Original, holograph, now first printed. Dunbeath Papers, Advocates Libr., Wodrow MSS., fol. lxvii. 90. The letter is mildewed, and has two holes through the middle.

[65] Mentioned as received in her letter, Hague, December 9, Napier, Mem., 720. See above, p. 262, *n.* 54.

[66] Nicolas, *loc. cit.*

[67] "The people of Scotland in general are (for certain) extremely well affected to the King, and rightly disposed to join with the Marquis of Montrose, as soon as he shall appear in that Kingdom in any good posture able to secure their rising; *but some (not without reason) apprehend, that the report of the now approaching Treaty will make those of the better sort forbear to appear for him, until they shall see the issue of this treaty.*" Nicolas to Ormond, Beauvais, March 5-15, 1649-50. Orm. Papers, i. 363.

[68] For these replies, *v.* W.'s Montrose (1819), pp. 458-491. A previous proclamation against Morton and Kinnoul is mentioned in Queen Elizabeth's letter of December 9th. The expression, "that detestable bloody murderer and excommunicate traitor, James Græme," rouses her to scornful indignation.

"DECLARATION of His Excellency James Marquis of Montrose, Earl of
" Kincardine, Lord Graham, Baron of Montdieu, Lieutenant-governor
" and Captain-general for his Majesty of the Kingdom of Scotland,
" anno, 1649.

" In tanta reipublicæ necessitudine, suspecto senatûs populique imperio, ob certamina potentium
" et avaritiam magistratuum, invalido legum auxilio; quæ vi, ambitu, postremo pecunia turba-
" bantur; omnem potestatem ad unum redire pacis interfuit, non aliud discordantis patriæ remedium
" quam ut ab uno regeretur.
C. TACITUS.

"Though it may seem both a public and private injury, rather than
" matter of duty or just procedure, to do any act whatsomever, that can
" in so much as appear to dispute the clearness of this present service, or
" to hold such enemies as a party, the justice of his majesty's cause, the
" wickedness of those rebels, and my own integrity, being all of them so
" well and so thoroughly known as they are, yet, the further to confirm
" the world, the more to encourage all who are to engage, and the power-
" fuller to convince many who have harmlessly been involved, and innocently
" inveigled in those desperate courses, I do, in the name of his most sacred
" majesty, and by virtue of the power and authority granted by him unto
" me, declare

" That howbeit there have been, and still are, an horrid and infamous
" faction of rebels within the kingdom of Scotland, who most causelessly
" at first did hatch a rebellion against his late majesty, of glorious memory;
" and when he had granted unto them, by their own acknowledgement, all
" their violent and most unjust desire, they were so far from resting, not-
" withstanding, satisfied, as that, being themselves able to find no further
" pretences, they did perniciously solicit one party in the kingdom of Eng-
" land, to begin where shame and necessity had inforced them to leave off;
" and when those of the English, being by much less wicked, would have
" often satisfied themselves by his majesty's extraordinary concessions, they
" then, not intending the desperate lengths which fatal success and their
" hollow practices did thereafter drive them to, did still thrust in, as oil to
" the fire, and ganger to the wound, until they had rendered all irrecoverable;
" neither were they contented in the fox-skin alone to act this their so brutish
" a tragedy, which indeed could never have served their ends, but while they
" had received all imaginable satisfaction at home, as their own very acts of
" parliament doth witness, wherein they say, ' That his late majesty parted a
" ' contented king from a contented people,' finding their rebel brood whom
" they had begot in England beginning to lessen, and that his majesty's party
" appeared to have by much the better, they not only, contrary to the duty
" of subjects, but all faith, covenants, oaths, attestations, to which they had
" so often invoked God, his angels, the world and all, as witnesses, did

"enter with a strong army the kingdom of England, persecute their prince
"in a foreign nation, assist a company of stranger rebels, against their native
"king, and those of his loyal party, within that same kingdom, except for
"which, the whole world does know, his majesty had, without all peradventure,
"prevailed. And not ashamed of all this, which even many of their own
"party did blush to avow, when his late majesty was, by, God knows, how
"many unhappy treacheries, redacted to think upon extreme courses for his
"safety, he was pleased out of his so much invincible goodness, and natural
"inclination towards his native people, notwithstanding all their former
"villanies, to chuse that ignoble party to fall upon, thinking, that those
"whom his greatness and their duty could not oblige, his misery and their
"compassion might perhaps move with pity; yet too justly fearing their
"'Punic' faiths, he first resolved to engage them by a treaty; after which,
"when, by many intercourses, his majesty had received all manner of assur-
"ances, which though shame would make them willingly excuse, yet guilt
"will let them have nothing to say for it, it being so undeniable, and to all
"the world so known a truth, casting himself in their hands, they, contrary
"to all faith and paction, trust of friends, duty of subject, laws of hospitality,
"nature, nations, divine and human, for which there hath never been pre-
"cedent, nor can ever be a follower, most infamously, and beyond all
"imaginable expression of invincible baseness, to the blush of Christians
"and abomination of mankind, sold their sovereign over to their merciless
"fellow-traitors to be destroyed; with whom, how they have complotted his
"destruction, their secret intercourses, both before, in the time, and since
"this horrid murder, do too evidently declare. Of all which villanies they
"are so little touched with the guilt, as they now begin with his majesty
"upon the same scores they left with his father, declaring him king with
"provisos; so robbing him of all right, while they would seem to give some
"unto him; pressing him to join with those who have rigged all his dominions
"in rebellion, and laid all royal power into the dust, that in effect he would
"condemn the memory of his sacred father, destroy himself, and ruin his
"faithful party within all those dominions. These are those who at first
"entered England, soliciting all to rise in this desperate rebellion, as the
"prologue of their ensuing tragedy; who were the chief and main instru-
"ments of all the battles, slaughters, and bloody occasions within that king-
"dom; who sold their sovereign unto the death, and that yet digs in his
"grave; and who are more perniciously hatching the destruction of his
"present majesty, by the same bare, old, out-dated treacheries, than ever
"they did his sacred father's: yet the people in general having been but
"ignorantly misled to it, whose eyes now for the most part God has opened,
"and turned their hearts, at least their desires, to their dutiful obedience,
"and that there has still been a loyal party, who have given such proofs of

" their integrity, as his majesty is moved with a tender compassion for those
" righteous sakes, in behalf of all who now at last have remorse for their
" former misdemeanours, his majesty is not only willing to pardon every
" one, excepting such who, upon clear evidences, shall be found guilty of
" that most damnable fact of the murder of his father, who, upon sight or
" knowledge hereof, do immediately, or upon the first possible conveniency,
" abandon those rebels, and rise and join themselves with us and our forces
" in this present service; but also to assure all who are, or will turn loyal
" unto him, of that nation, that it is his majesty's resolution, which he doth
" assure, and promise unto them upon the word of a prince, to be ever ready
" to ratify so soon as it shall please God to put it in his power, according to
" the advice of the supreme judicatures of that kingdom, all that has been
" done by his royal father, in order to their peace; desiring nothing more
" but their dutiful obedience and faithful services, for the revenge of the
" horrid murder of his father, his just re-establishment, and their own per-
" petual happiness under his government.

" Wherefore, all who have any duty left them to God, their king, country,
" friends, homes, wives, children, or would change now at last the tyranny,
" violence, and oppression of those rebels, with the mild and innocent
" government of their just prince, or revenge the horrid and execrable
" murder of their sacred king, redeem their nation from infamy, themselves
" from slavery, restore the present, and oblige the ages to come; let them
" as Christians, subjects, patriots, friends, husbands, and fathers, join them-
" selves forthwith with us in this present service, that is so full of conscience,
" duty, honour, and all just interests, and not apprehend any evils, which
" they may fear can fall, half so much as those they presently lie under;
" for though there may appear many difficulties, yet let them not doubt
" of God's justice, nor the happy providence that may attend his majesty,
" nor their own resolutions, nor the fortunes of those who are joined withal;
" resolving, with Joab, to play the men for their people, and the cities of
" their God, and let the Lord do whatever seemeth him good; wherein,
" whatsomever shall behappen, they may at least be assured of Crastinus's
" recompense, that, dead or alive, the world will give them thanks.

"MONTROSE."[69]

About October, Sir James Turner,[70] who had accompanied Hamilton on his ill-fated march into England, was liberated from Hull, and sailing to Hamburg in a "cloth ship," arrived early in November. There he met Lord Napier, and learning that Montrose was already in Gothenburg, he enclosed a letter to him, in one from Napier, offering his services; to which

---

[69] W.'s Montrose (1819), pp. 454-458.   [70] Turner, Mem., 71, 72.

he "had a very favorable returne, and invitation from the Marques to come to him, writ with his oune hand." Turner was, however, prevented by want of means; and meeting at Hamburg with Colonel Sibbald,[71] on his way to Scotland and Ireland with despatches from Montrose, he accompanied him as far as Rotterdam, whence Sibbald set out on his fatal mission.

The Swedish service at this time was full of English and Scots, many of whom had attained high commands during the Thirty Years' War. James, Duke of Hamilton, had commanded 6000 English, under Gustavus. The two Leslies,[72] Brentford, Lumsden, Baillie, General Sir James Spence, made Earl of Orcholm, and many others had won experience and wealth in the same terrible war. Shortly after the battle of Leipzig, "in one place, at one time Gustavus had six and thirty Scottish Colonels about him."[73] From many of these, Montrose might reasonably hope for assistance in men and money; but from none more than from General James King,[74] created Lord Eythin in the Scottish peerage in 1643. This veteran officer was known to be well affected to the royal cause, in which he had fought with distinction. After the disaster at Marston Moor, he had again retired to Sweden. Montrose was led to expect that he would join "with a considerable party of Horse,"[75] and actually appointed him lieutenant-general, by warrant

---

[71] Col. William Sibbald was arrested at Musselburgh. For the letters found on him, see p. 244, *n.* 2. He was executed at Edinburgh with Dalgetty. "The other with a little more vigour [than Dalgetty], smil'd a while, and talk'd to the disorderly rabble that was about him: then with such an heroick gesture march'd to the block, as if he had been to act a gallant in a Play." Montr. Rediv., pp. 175, 187.

[72] Nicolas, *loc. cit.*, apparently quoting information from Montrose, says, that "when old General Lesley sent one thither [to Sweden] (among other things) to demand the pensions due to him and his Cousin David Lesley, her Majesty would not hear of them, and did cause signify to him that was sent, that she had nothing to do with them since they were become traitors to their King: and on the other part gave new pensions to all those officers, Scotch and English, who had been in the Swedish service before, and had been faithful to their King."

[73] Sir Thomas Urquhart's Memoirs.

[74] James King, son of Sir James King, of Barracht, Aberdeens., b. 1589 (?), entered the Swedish service in 1614 or 1615, and took part as Colonel in the Thirty Years' War. In 1634 he was Major-General, in 1636 Lieutenant-General, in 1637 Commander (*Ofverbefälhafvare*) in Westphalia. Owing to a misunderstanding with Field-Marshal J. Baner, he was recalled to Sweden in 1638. He acquired property in Germany, and later, in Sweden. In 1641 he visited Edinburgh, and appears to have done Charles I. some service there. In his will, of the year 1651, he claimed £40,000, due to him from the King for this debt, and for an unpaid pension of £1000. In the spring of 1649, King was in Hamburg; in September 1649 back again in Stockholm, where he died, January 1652. He was buried in the Riddarholms church, and the Queen attended his funeral. Notes from Herr C. F. Oehner, Kongl. Riksarkivar, Stockholm; also Gardiner, Hist. Civ. War, Index. He is said to have received a commission as Lieutenant-General, under Montrose, and "A letter of 13 March 1650 shows that *he was also engaged in some negotiations for bringing Charles II. to Sweden.*" Dict. Nat. Biogr., Article James King.

[75] Montrose Redivivus, 172. Nicolas, *loc. cit.*, was probably misinformed in writing, "Very many officers of the greatest reputation came flocking to him [Montrose]; to whom he has given commissions for the second levy, which is to be levied under *Coningsmark* [see p. 273, *n.* 88], to the

dated March 19th, 1650; but, "either he could not be ready so soon as was expected, or else delay'd the time of purpose."

Queen Christina, whatever her private sentiments may have been, had good reasons of policy for not openly supporting Charles and Montrose at this period. In April the Swedish ambassador at the Hague is said to have tendered Charles offers of help to suppress the rebels.[76] The Ormond correspondence bears evidence that high hopes were built on her support. In August strong representations were made to Charles to accept the alliance of the Swedes, as Protestants, in preference to that of Spain.[77] On August 25-September 4 Nicolas relates to Ormond, "as a secret that there is a letter "now delivered to the King from the Queen of Sweden, acquainting his "Majesty that the Scots have pressed her to intercede for them to his Majesty; "which she hath absolutely refused to do, saying she will not interpose between "his Majesty and his subjects. She hath further assured the King that she "will join with any Prince in assisting him to recover his Crowns and just "Rights, but adviseth his Majesty to forbear as yet to send any extraordinary "Embassador to her for some weighty Reasons."[78] A week later he wrote that "Sir William Balladine [Bellandine] had been left by Brainford [Brent-"ford] as agent to the Queen. She requests the King through him not to "send any extraordinary-Embassador at present. Lord Hatton is going to "be sent."[79] Sweden at this time felt itself injured by the treaty Denmark had recently concluded with Holland.[80] To offend the strong naval republic of England at this juncture would be to lose the one natural ally whose power could enable them successfully to resist this treaty. We find, therefore, that the wily Chancellor Oxenstiern looked with a cold eye on Montrose's scheme.[81] Queen Christina "supported him underhand but very inconsiderably."[82] Even at this time she may have had some leanings to the rebels, to whom she afterwards showed such marked favour in the person of their representative, Whitelock.

It was the interest of the Royalists to exaggerate the secret sympathy she may have felt for Charles. It was even a project of some to carry him to Sweden, either to join Montrose's expedition,[83] or to win the hand of the

---

number of 10 or 12000 of foot and horse, who are to be landed (God willing) about the middle of April in Scotland or England, as Montrose shall give them order."

[76] Carte's Orm. Papers, i. 277, 278. See further *id*. 345 ff., 358, 359, 455, for these dealings with Christina.

[77] Orm. Papers, i. 296. As early as May 29, 1649, Ormond, writing from Kilkenny, urged this alliance (*ibid*. ii. 376).

[78] *Ibid*. i. 306, 307.

[79] *Ibid*. i. 310. For "Brainford," see p. 262, *n*. 54. Lord Hatton was Lauderdale's brother.

[80] Thurloe, i. 463.  [81] Nicolas, Orm. Papers, i. 345 ff.  [82] Turner, Mem., 91.

[83] See p. 270, *n*. 74. On March 15, 1649 (1650), Harry Seymour wrote from Breda to Ormond, "If the Scots do not meet at Breda, of which there is a rumour, or if the treaty succeed not, his Majesty is resolved to lose no more time in idleness, and therefore must either go to you or to my

powerful and brilliant queen. But her favour to Montrose, as we shall see, did not extend to more than acquiescence in his presence at Gothenburg, with secret orders to her officers there to wink at his proceedings, and permit him to *buy* material. Even his frigate, accredited to her generosity, was sold to him, as it now appears from the correspondence obtained from the Swedish archives.

According to Sir William Johnston, quoted by Nicolas,[84] Montrose had already " sent 3000 men at several times before to Orkney," and " in the " beginning of December (N. S.) there parted nine ships of great burden, " full of men and horse, and passed the Sound to go for Scotland, but the " commander's name was kept secret. Also that Major David Grothorie " [Guthrie] took voyage with five compleat companies, the 14th of December " (N. S.) to sail for Orkney; the rest of Montrose's men being shipped at " Gottenburg, where there were 14 sail of great ships, besides small bot- " toms, waiting upon Montrose." He adds that Montrose " had shipped " to the number of 16 or 18000 arms, 24 excellent field-pieces, 9 " pieces of battery, with all things belonging, store of powder, match and " ball, abundance of corn for the provision of his army, and besides those " 3000 men long since in Orkney, he had ready 5000 foot and 12 or " 1500 horse to be shipped at Gottenberg and other places, whereof a great " part is gone in the month of December." In another letter (undated) he states that " the Queen of Sweden hath furnished the King with 10,000 arms " and munition proportionable; whereof one half is assigned to the Marquis " of Montrose; the other is designed for Ireland; but [he adds, significantly] " these are engaged for over 1000*l.*" The writer of the continuation of Wishart's history is probably nearer the truth in saying that she furnished Montrose " for the arming of such Gentlemen as should upon his arrivall " betake themselves to his partie, fifteen hundred arms, compleat for Horse, " back, brest, headpiece, Carrabines, Pistolls and Swords, all which after " his defeat in Cathanes [Ross] were taken untouch'd." The correspondence of Ribbing,[85] given in the Appendix to this volume, affords some test for the truth of these reports.

Gothenburg, or Göteborg, was peculiarly fitted for Montrose's enterprise. With a commodious harbour, rarely closed by ice, sheltered from the Atlantic by the *Skärgård*, or barrier of rocky islets which fringe the westward coasts of Scandinavia, and communicating by the river Göta with the great chain of

---

Lord Montrose; his own inclinations lean to the first; but a powerful interest press the other way whose game lies another way." Orm. Papers, i. 367.

[84] *Ibid.* 345 ff.

[85] From the Royal archives, Stockholm, courteously communicated by the keeper, Herr C. F. Oehner. To him the Editors are gratefully indebted for notes on King, Maclear, and other persons and points in this valuable correspondence, now first printed. App. vii. and viii.

lakes which form the water-way to the capital, the town was then, as now, a favourite residence for Scottish merchants. Conspicuous among these was John Maclear, already noted for his loyalty to the house of Stewart. Maclear had acquired great riches, and in 1650 was made a baronet by Charles.[86] So highly were his services to the royal cause appreciated, that he was deemed worthy of a special commendation to Christina's favour in the proposals submitted to her by Robert Meade, the King's envoy, on February 25, 1650.[87]

Leaving Copenhagen on November 10th, Montrose arrived at Gothenburg about the 12th, attended only by a few officers and servants, in all not more than ten or twelve persons. Two days later the circumstance of his arrival was notified by Per Lindormson Ribbing, the local Landshofding, or provincial governor, to Field-Marshal Count Leonard Torstenson,[88] Governor-General of Western Sweden, at Ulfsunda, his residence on Lake Mälar, near Stockholm. It was understood that Montrose had taken up his abode in Gothenburg only till the King of Denmark returned to Copenhagen. From the letters which passed between the two, we learn that, during the four months Montrose remained in Gothenburg, he observed profound secrecy in his plans and movements. At the beginning of December the local magnate's inquisitive fears were further stimulated by the arrival of a ship, with 200 men, engaged in Denmark, which came to anchor at the Billinge, a small spot below Gothenburg. Another ship had been recently hired in the town itself; and a quantity of arms and ammunition and four field-pieces, which had been consigned to Maclear, were conveyed on board.

---

[86] Herr Oehner, to whom we owe the date, informs us that Maclear's great-grandson, in 1784, took the name of Maclean (probably confused with *Maclear*) when they received the title of "Friherrar" (Freelords, Germ. *Freiherr*). For Maclear's letter to Montrose, see p. 284. On January 1, 1651, a Captain Cuninghame signs a deposition at Anstruther, that arms which he had brought from Sweden were *not* sent to the King by "Sir Jhone Macleir" (Thurloe, i. 170, 171). Apparently the ship had been seized for Cromwell, and the captain endeavours to save his goods on the ground that they were a free private speculation. Whitelocke, when he landed at Gothenburg in 1653, on his embassy, met Sir John, and, in spite of his loyalty, to which he bears testimony, was favourably impressed by his character.

[87] See Appendix, No. vii.

[88] Leonard or Linnart Torstenson, in 1641 succeeded Baner as Commander-in-Chief of the Swedish army in the Thirty Years' War. In 1642 he defeated the Imperialists at Breitenfeld, near Leipzig. In 1643 he overran Holstein and Jutland. Next year he was shut up in Denmark by the enemy, but escaped with great dexterity, and defeated Enkerfort at Jüterbok. In 1645 he marched up to Vienna, but was forced to abandon a siege for want of artillery. Gout, to which he had long been a victim, obliged him to resign the command to Wrangel in 1645, when he retired to Sweden. Königsmark, one of the boldest robbers and a most restless commander, was his lieutenant-general in the war. To him Sweden owes the famous Codex Argenteus of Ulfilas, taken in the plunder of Prague (1648), with Correggios, which Christina, with truly Gothic taste, cut out and pasted on tapestry!

For the correspondence of Ribbing, Torstenson, and Ankerhielm, see Appendix, No. viii.

On the 12th, when Ribbing again wrote, the two ships were expected to sail shortly, but he does not mention their destination.

That Montrose himself intended to sail with these ships, we learn from his own letter to Seaforth:—

"GOTTENBERG 15 *December* 1649.

"MY LORD,

"I am sory I heave not had so many occasions as I wold, to express
" unto you the joy I heave of all yr honorable and freindly cariages, both
" concerning publick and pryvatt, which I assure yr lp. is no less content-
" ment to your friendes, and satisfaction to all honest men, (evine those
" who know you not,) then it is happynes for yrself. I pray God give joy
" to preferr so vertuos and honorable a tract [trait, conduct], and be seur
" I shall be no longer happy then I be not thankfull for the nobell obliga-
" tions I owe you. I am so prest (*being to sett sayle to-morrow for Scotland*)
" as I can say littell more, only I must [give] yr l. a thousand thanks for
" yr favours and kyndness, to yr servand Mr James Woode, which I humbly
" intreat you to continue, and I will not feale, if I heave a lyfe, to caus
" returne what you ar pleased to doe to any of yr servants.

"I will say no more, but that I shall live or dye, my Lord, yr L. most
" faithfull cossing and servand,

"MONTROSE.

"[Directed] For my Nobell Lord the Earle of Siafort.

" I heare our cossing Chartrous hes gone to the King, which his maide
" me not writ unto him." [89]

The transport from Denmark with the 200 "Danes" seems to be all the foundation there is for the "nine ships of great burden" which, in the beginning of January, N. S. (*i.e.*, about December 20th), passed the Sound for Scotland, "full of men and horse." [90] Or, perhaps, in this we may recognise the "five compleat companies," which on December 4th (O. S.) sailed under Major David Guthrie for Orkney. Of this detachment and its fortunes no record appears to have been preserved. But as we shall find Major Guthrie at the battle of Carbisdale, we may assume that they reached their destination.

Meantime Montrose maintained an active correspondence with his followers, and every day Scots passed between Denmark and his headquarters.

On December 26th Admiral Ankerhielm wrote from Gothenburg to the Governor-General that a ship of the town, intended for Portugal, had

---

[89] Seaforth archives, copy in W.'s Montrose (1819), 441, 442. For James Woode and cousin Charters, see Index.

[90] Nicolas, Orm. Papers, i. 345 ff.

been purchased, and now lay at the Billinge, along with the two Scottish ships belonging to Montrose. Also the Crown had sold him the frigate *Herderinnan* (Shepherdess), which to-morrow would be handed over to Maclear, and would probably be ready to sail with the rest. Again, on January 2nd, Ribbing, impatient at receiving no orders from her Majesty or Torstenson, repeats his information. Montrose had arrived "about November 15th, kept himself secret, but presently began to assemble a number of officers, who were quartered here and there in the town. On this he had caused him to be questioned, whether he had the Queen's permission to make such a rendezvous of Gothenburg, without informing her servants." Thereupon Maclear was employed to show Ribbing a letter from Christina to Montrose, wherein she ordered her officers to pass the ammunition purchased by Maclear, whether consigned to himself or to his agents. The Queen's letter contained no further instructions. Ribbing had then written to the Queen to inform her of Montrose's conduct, and that he expected a ship from Denmark with 200 men, and that various officers gathered to him daily. To this letter there was no reply. Montrose had, however, been heard to say that General King might be expected any day. The Danish ship with the 200 men, the ammunition, and about four field-pieces, now lay with another ship out at Billinge. Montrose had also received the *Herderinnan*, a small royal ship, which Admiral Ankerhielm had been ordered to deliver, along with the guns, and two months' provisions for 50 persons. This vessel was now lying in the river, and expected to sail in a few days. Of Montrose himself he could render no account. At times he gave out that he was going to Stockholm, at times to Denmark, at times elsewhere. He studiously avoided the Queen's officers. "When he chanced to meet one in the streets, he at once turned round, and either went back or aside, so that I cannot understand the man or his designs." Yesterday (January 1st) other two "Counts came to him, but look wretchedly naked."[91] Some of his officers had again departed, and all had provided themselves with shipping. Maclear advances what they have need of. A few days ago Hannibal Sehestedt[92] was here at Bohus,[93] in the house of Mr. Ivan Krabbe; and it is thought that Krabbe is coming here to speak with Montrose. The stir of these secret preparations occasioned much uneasiness in the town, many

---

[91] "Counts" or Earls. Were these the new Earl of Kinnoul and Brentford? Many Royalists suffered extreme poverty. For instances, see Gwynne's Mem., pp. 118, 133, &c., and *n*. 114 below.

[92] Hannibal Seested or Sehested, a son-in-law of Frederick, King of Denmark, successfully defended Norway during the war with Sweden, 1643–1647, thence called in Norway "Hannibal's Feud." See further the Journal of Whitelocke, who met him on his way back to England, and Thurloe, i., Index, "Sestede."

[93] Bohus (Bååhuus in Ribbing's letter) on the R. Göta was then—as well as Marstrand—in Norway. It gave its name in 1658 to the province of Bohuslän. Extensive ruins of its castle may still be seen from the railway between Gothenburg and the famous falls of Trollhättan.

fearing that the Parliament might pounce upon their shipping as they passed English waters. In conclusion, Ribbing earnestly begged for instructions, as no faith could be put in King's coming, or in Montrose himself.

The reply to this (9th January) was briefly to let Montrose alone. Torstenson had no doubt her Majesty was aware of Montrose's proceedings, but would inquire, and take the first opportunity to let him know.

Meanwhile, before receiving this reply, a previous letter from Torstenson, dated January 2nd, had reached Ribbing, who further informed his chief on the 11th, that the "Scottish Count" had embarked yesterday on the *Herderinnan*, but the vessel was now wind-bound. And so he remained for a week, though the wind meantime changed to "the best"—and "God only knows why he lay still," Ribbing petulantly adds. "Meantime I have acted as though I had nought to do with him. Time will show what he is now after. God grant I may hit on doing what is her Majesty's pleasure" (Letter, 16th January).

Montrose had indeed the most urgent reasons for setting sail. As early as November, Captain Hall's ship, which had joined Kinnoul shortly after his arrival in Orkney, and which was reported to have since taken another of ten guns, was despatched from Orkney to Denmark. With Captain Hall were "Sir James Douglas, my Lord Moreton's brother, and one Major " Melvin (Melville) with many Gentlemen of Quality from all places of the " Kingdom, who in the name of the whole Kingdom did intreat and press " Montrose earnestly to go to Scotland, and not stay for all his men (who " might follow), for his own presence was able to do the business, and would " undoubtedly bring 20,000 men together for the King's service; all men " being weary and impatient to live any longer under that bondage pressing " down their estates, their persons and their consciences."[94]

Yet, urged as he was to depart, and with a fair wind to waft his little frigate westwards, Montrose once more turned back, and two days later, January 18th, Ribbing writes—"the Scottish General, Count von Montrose, " is back again from the ship, and lodging at the house of the 'well-born' " Hans Maclear. Most of his people are still aboard the ship. Time will " show whether they too are returning. However, they are quite frozen in."

From these extracts it is clear that Montrose might certainly have sailed under apparently favourable circumstances. The question arises, What had occurred to detain him? The answer is to be found in the Ormond paper already so often referred to.[95] Doubts of the King's double dealings, reports of which must have reached the Marquis, so far from precipitating him into a rash and desperate enterprise, as some unwise critics have represented, must have seriously hampered his movements. Immediately after describing

---

[94] Nicolas, *Orm. Papers*, i. 345 ff. [95] *Ibid.*

the arrival of Captain Hall's ship in November, Nicolas, in his report to Ormond, proceeds: "and no doubt he is parted long ere now, *if the adver-* "*tisement he has got of an express coming from his Majesty to him have not* "*stayed him:* for Colonel Johnstoun writes that *he waited at Gottenberg* "*the coming of that express*, who I believe is at him long ere now." The express, however, thus heard of *in December*, and expected to be "at him "long ere now," when Nicolas was writing (January 20th), did not even start from Jersey before Jan. 16th, and the delay must be attributed solely to the cruel vacillation of the King. That the King, however, continued up to the very last to urge the expedition is beyond question. The evidence for this is, in truth, so complete and overwhelming, that only ignorance and malignant prejudice can stoop to repeat the base forgery of Argyll.[96] Not only did Charles in his own hand write the letters quoted below, but even Henrietta assured him in the most ample terms of her deep interest in his welfare, her grateful memory of his past services; and, in spite of all rumours to the contrary, her unshaken esteem and sincerity. "My attach- "ment to you being such, that I can never divest myself of it, whatever may "befal you." So she wrote on December 1, 1649; and again, as late as March 10th:—

"MON COUSIN,

"Aiant receu votre lettre par Pooley, et par icelle veu les assurances de "la continuation de votre affection pour le service du roy, monsieur mon "fils, comme vous avez toujours eu pour celuy du feu roy [the late king] "mon seigneur, dont le meurtre commis en sa personne doit augmenter a "tous ses serviteurs la passion de chercher tous les moyens de se revancher "d'une mort si abominable; et comme je ne doute point que vous ne soyes "bien aise d'en avoir les occasions, et que pour cet effet vous ne fassies "toutce qui dependra de vous; je vous conjure donc de vouloir vous joindre "avec tous ceux de votre nation qui voudroient resentir comme ils doivent "cette mort, et oublier tout ce qui s'est passé entre vous; c'est tout ce que "j'ai a vous recommander, et de me croire avec autant d'assurance comme je "suis en effect, et serai toujours, Mon Cousin, votre bien bonne et affectioneè "Cousine et amie,

"HENRIETA MARIA R.[97]

"PARIS, *ce* 10 *Mars* 1649."

What could be stronger than this earnest appeal from the widowed

---

[96] See table, end of this chapter, under May 25th.

[97] See Wishart's Montr. (1819), 439, and for her letter of December 1st, Napier, Mem., 751. Did Montrose receive this letter, and if so, where? The letters of Charles are quoted from the same sources.

Queen, outraged by the violent death of her Royal Consort, and eagerly grasping at every means to take vengeance on his murderers?

Before returning to Montrose it will be convenient here to record the remainder of this correspondence.

"CHARLES R.

"Right trusty and right entirely beloved cousin, we greet you well. An
" address having been lately made to us from Scotland by a letter, whereof
" we send you a copy herewith, wherein they desire that we should acknow-
" ledge their parliament, and particularly the two last sessions of it, and
" thereupon offer to send a solemn address to us for a full agreement; we
" have in answer thereunto returned our letters to them, a copy whereof we
" likewise send you here inclosed, by which we have appointed a speedy
" time and place for their Commissioners to attend us: and to the end you
" may not apprehend that we intend, either by any thing contained in those
" letters, or by the treaty we expect, to give the least impediment to your
" proceedings, we think fit to let you know, that as we conceive that your
" preparations have been one effectual motive, that has induced them to make
" the said address to us; so your vigorous proceeding will be a good means
" to bring them to such moderation in the said treaty as probably may
" produce an agreement, and a present union of that whole nation in our
" service. We assure you, therefore, that we will not, before or during the
" treaty, do anything contrary to that power and authority which we have
" given you by our commission, nor consent to anything that may bring the
" least degree of diminution to it; and if the said treaty should produce an
" agreement, we will, with our uttermost care, so provide for the honour and
" interest of yourself, and of all that shall engage with you, as shall let the
" whole world see the high esteem we have of you, and our full confidence in
" that eminent courage, conduct, and loyalty, which you have always expressed
" to the king our late dear father, of blessed memory, and to us, both by
" your actions and sufferings for our cause. In the mean time, we think fit
" to declare to you, that we have called them a *Committee of Estates*, only in
" order to a treaty, and for no other end whatever; and if the treaty do not
" produce an agreement, as we are already assured that the calling of them
" a *Committee of Estates*, in the direction of a letter, doth neither acknowledge
" them to be legally so, nor make them such; so we shall immediately declare
" to all our subjects of Scotland what we hold them to be, notwithstanding
" any appellation we now give them; thereby to satisfy them and the whole
" world, that we desire to reduce our subjects of that kingdom to their due
" obedience to us, by our just and honourable condescensions, and by all
" endeavours of kindness and favour on our part, rather than by war and
" hostility, if their unreasonable demands do not necessitate us to that, as to

"the only way and remedy left us. We require and authorise you to proceed
"vigorously and effectually in your undertaking; and to act in all things in
"order to it, as you shall judge most necessary for the support thereof, and
"for our service in that way; wherein we doubt not but all our loyal and
"well affected subjects of Scotland will cordially and effectually join with
"you, and by that addition of strength either dispose those that are otherwise
"minded to make reasonable demands to us in a treaty, or be able to force
"them to it by arms, in case of their obstinate refusal. To which end we
"authorise you to communicate and publish this our letter to all such persons
"as you shall think fit."[98]

Though this document is undated, there can be no doubt that it is the "public letter" referred to in the following :—

"MY LORD OF MONTROSE,

"My public letter having expressed all that I have of business to say to
"you, I shall only add a word by this to assure, that I will never fail in the
"effects of that friendship I have promised, and which your zeal to my
"service hath so pre-eminently deserved; and that nothing can happen
"to me shall make me consent to anything to your prejudice. I conjure
"you, therefore, not to take alarm at any reports or messages from others;
"but to depend upon my kindness; and to proceed in your business with your
"usual courage and alacrity; which I am sure will bring great advantage to
"my affairs, and much honour to yourself. I wish you all good success
"in it, and shall ever remain your affectionate friend,
"CHARLES R.[99]

"JERSEY, 12*th*-22*d January* 1649-50."

That nothing should be wanting to mark his approbation, Charles, by the same messenger, sent him the George and riband of the Garter, with a letter concluding in the following terms :—

"We are most assured that as you have hitherto with singular courage,
"conduct and fidelity served us, so you will still do the same as becomes a
"Knight and Companion of so noble an Order. Given at our Court in the
"Castle Elizabeth, in our island of Jersey, this 12th day of January, in the
"first year of our reign, 1649" [1650].

---

[98] Was this or the letter of September 19 (*v.* p. 263) the one mentioned by R. Long in a letter to Ormond, Beauvais, March 2-12, 1650? Among other difficulties in the way of the Scots Treaty they have "caused a letter to be printed, which his Majesty writ to the Marquis of Montrose, as he did to your Excellency, upon occasion of his intention to treat with that nation; which though proper enough to be said to my Lord of Montrose upon that occasion, was very unfit to be published, and was accordingly ordered to be kept secret. But his Majesty commanding me to give one copy of it, it was by some practice printed in three languages, with very great disadvantage to the King, by the use the rebels of England make of it." Orm. Papers, i. 367, 368.

[99] Napier, Mem., 752.

How or when the news of this intended express from the King reached Montrose does not appear. But to this cause of delay was added the obstacle of heavy ice. He seems, however, to have succeeded in despatching three or four ships. The *Herderinnan* lying higher up stream, was either unable to clear the harbour, or was purposely retained for his own transport. At the very outset these vessels seem to have encountered severe weather. Only two ships arrived at Kirkwall. There is probably, therefore, some truth in the highly coloured reports of disaster spread in Scotland. On February 19th the following account of the little armament and its fortunes was published in Edinburgh :—

"There is more men landit this weeke in Orknay-Iylands from Montrose,
" bot the gratest pairt of his men and weshells are spoyled and lost; for
" of 1200 he shipped from the sea syde, neir Gottinburrey, ther are noe
" more then 200 landed in Scotland. (It is said heir, that thosse that cam
" last to Orknay-Iylands, are going for Irland;) for quhen they had sayled
" about tuo leaugues from the shore, they wer shattred by sticking in the
" ice; maney deyed, others after got ashore and deserted: and they wer
" much broken. *(Not a word of this in Ribbing's letters !)*
"Ther cam now onlie tuo shipes vith 200 souldiers and ther officers
" *(The Danish ship evidently)*; 12 brasse feild peices, and some small
" number of armes, with a parcell of amunitione. Montrosse himselue
" is zet at Gottenbrughe, with some Scotts, Englishe and Dutch (German)
" officers, waitting to see if he can gett aney moneyes for them : if not, they
" will desert him.

EDINBRUGHE, 19 *Februarij*, 1649 (*i.e.*, 1650, *Civil Year*).

"**A List of the Forces and Amunition that was shiped by Montrosse for "Scotland, most of wich was destroyed and spoyled.**"[100]

" Imprimis, 1200 souldiers, officers for 2 regiments, 13 frigatts fraught,
" 2 weshells for conwoyes, 12 brasse guns; the Kinges foote colors for one
" regiment, the Kinges standard and colores, Montrosses standard and
" colours, prouisions for aboute a mounthe, commissions for the officers.
" The Kinges standard was of blacke damaske, with 3 paire of handes

---

[100] Montr. Rediv. 174, which is, however, very vague in details and sequence of events, seems to allude to some such disaster: "I told you a little before of Montrose's whole Strength, which did accompany him from Germanie, whereof two ships, with neer upon a third part were sent before, but by storm of weather (which is both frequent and dangerous) amongst those Northern Islands, they were lost with all the men and arms, nothing saved." The writer does not say which islands, and speaks of this loss as preceding a "second party" which landed at Orkney, undoubtedly Kinnoul's. But there is no evidence of any detachment having preceded his.

"folded in eache other, and one eache syde of them 3 handes and naked
"armes, out of cloude, with suords drauin.

"The Kinges standard of foote was of blacke tafftay, with a mans head
"in the midele, bleeding, as if cutt off from a bodey.

"Montrosses standard was of whyte damaske, with a lion rampant one
"the tope of a rocke, with ane other steepe rocke on the other syde of a
"riuer.

"The Kinges standard of horsse had this motto — Quos pietas virtus
"et honor fecit amicos.

"The Kinges standard of foote had this motto—Deo et victricibus armis.

"Montrosses standard had this motto—Nil medium."[101]

There is a strong family likeness between this report and the tidings sent by Nicolas to Ormond, with this difference, that Montrose's enemies in Edinburgh were as little likely in magnifying delay and partial disaster to "think no evil," as his friends to communicate any really ill news. The paper to Ormond also concludes: "In the meantime I am desired from "Hamburg, Denmark and Sweden to find some faithful friend to give infor-"mation to his Majesty of all these former truths. Montrose has caused "make the King's Standart all black, all full of bloody hands and swords, and "a red character or motto above it carrying revenge."[102]

If, as seems likely, the ships reported in Edinburgh on February 19th were those which Montrose on December 16th was on the eve of sailing with, they must indeed have had a long and severe passage, and not improbably suffered delay and damage from ice and storms, before they left the coast. It is difficult to believe that the news travelled from Orkney to Edinburgh in a week. February 19th was a Tuesday; "last week" was therefore February 10–16th, within which days the party is said to have reached Kirkwall. It is, however, more probable that, as in the case of Kinnoul's arrival, the news took four to six weeks on the way to the capital, and that the ships had arrived at Kirkwall early in January. With them came —— Hay, the new Earl of Kinnoul,[103] brother to Earl George who died at Kirkwall in November. Lord Napier[104] must have left his charge

---

[101] Balf. iii. 438-440.

[102] According to Montr. Rediv. 178, the standard bore the motto, "Judge and revenge my cause, O Lord, and the portraict of the late King beheaded exactly well done." For Montrose's standard and motto, see his seal, title-page.

[103] See Ogilvy of Powrie's letter, Kirkwall, March 3, p. 286, below.

[104] Wishart's Letter "to my Lord Napier in Hamburg," Napier, Mem., 730-732, was dated January 1, 1650. But this proves no more than that he had not heard of any previous change in his residence. The letter of Charles to Napier, Breda, April 15, 1650, seems to imply that Lord Napier *had already joined* Montrose, and not merely intended to do so, as Napier (Mem. 756) infers.

in Hamburg shortly after Sir William Johnston's return in December. Secretary Nicolas tells us expressly that, when Montrose "went incognito "to Scotland,"[105] he "left behind him his Lieutenant-General my Lord "Rythen [Ruthven, Earl of Brentford and Forth] General Major Carpe,[106] "my Lord Naper and many Officers ready to make sail at such time "as he had designed." This lends some colour to the conjecture that Earls Ruthven and Kinnoul were the two "wretchedly naked Scottish Counts," who arrived at Gothenburg on January 1st.

But to return to the local record of Montrose's doings at Gothenburg, which alone, scanty as it is, can be trusted for accurate detail. On January 26th, Ribbing received a letter from Torstenson, advising his "dear brother" to give Montrose a free hand in his business, as her Majesty had not forbidden it, and requesting to be informed of further delays. Not till the 12th of February did Ribbing write again. "The royal Scottish General, Earl of Montrose, is now for the third time [107] on the point of sailing. But I have just been informed that he is coming here again. The ice is a complete hindrance to him." Finally, on the 22nd of the same month, he wrote that Montrose had at last departed. "His frigate has gone to Marstrand.[108] The general himself travelled by land to Norway, and thence to Scotland."

So much of Montrose's destination had at last become clear, even to Ribbing's penetration. Whatever other motives may have caused this change, Montrose must have been glad at last to quit the ice-choked harbour, associated with so much disappointment and delay.

To this period we must assign a letter from a Scotsman, John Gordon, colonel in the Swedish service, whom, however, research in Sweden has failed to identify. The letter is addressed to Gothenburg, and must have reached Montrose, as it was among his papers taken in Dunbeath Castle.[109] There can, however, be little doubt that the gallant colonel did find means to join Montrose, "with hazard of liffe," and lost it bravely.[110] It is probable, too, that Maclear's letter below, dated the 13th February, and endorsed in Montrose's own clear bold hand, "Colonell Gordone," was sent by the Marquis to this same John Gordon, who expresses so earnest a desire to

---

[105] There is no further evidence for this romantic visit. It was undoubtedly a false rumour. Ribbing's letters account for Montrose's movements pretty continuously down to February 22, and Nicolas's paper is dated January 20. Part of the information he sent was derived from Johnston in Hamburg, under date December 14-24. Ribbing would certainly have commented on an absence, which at the lowest computation would have lasted two to three weeks.

[106] See letter to Montrose from the Elector of Brandenburg, July 28, 1649. Appendix, No. iv.

[107] He has previously mentioned only *once*. The "third time" doubtless implies the second occasion, mentioned in Montrose's letter of December 15 to Seaforth. See p. 274.

[108] Marstrand, on an island near the mouth of the River Göta. See Index.

[109] For the evidence of this as to both Gordon's and Maclear's letters, see Appendix, No. ix.

[110] *Ibid*.

share his enterprise. As this too was found among the Dunbeath papers, Gordon must have returned it to Montrose.

" RIGHT HONOURABLE AND MOST RENOWNED LORD,

" The glorious report of your excell. matchless loialtie, together with the
" never dieing fame of your noble actiones with such incredable almost both
" sufferings and valoure performed for the service of your prince and countreie,
" hath not only amazed your enemies, but also made you both admired and
" beloued euen of those strangers, who neuer had the happines to knowe you
" otherwaies then by the deserued fame of your heroiercke uerteues: yea
" and force me (nowe by a long continued absence almost a stranger in my
" Countrie) to invie the happie fortune of those who were followers in such
" praiseworthie atcheeuements, and nowe hearing of your being at Gotten-
" burgh, and of the Continuatione of your constant resolutione, ether to see
" our iniustlie disherited king reposessed of all his Roialties, or els to
" perish in so just a quarrel, I was more inflamm'd than euer with a desire
" to spend my liffe and all I have under you Eccell: command in the persuite
" of so noble ane actione, and was nowe a good waie on my Journaie, hoping
" to have had the honour to have kissed your hands and there personallie to
" have rendred my selff and mine whollie youres, which I am forced nowe to
" doe by proxie, haueing this morning receaued my Roiall mistresse com-
" mand in all hast to gather my regiment together and to desarme them yet
" heere (?) still in a generall peac[e], to obey which being forced against my
" will to returne, I send the bearer heereoff my brother in my place, who
" hath quitted a standing companie under me to inioie [enjoy] the happinesse
" of being inrolled amongst your Eccell: followers, for whom I will request
" no fauoure least I committ ane unpardonable sinne; the generositie of your
" heroiercke nature being so universallie knowne. but so much lett me be
" bold to craue at your hands as to beleeue in what he shall deliuer con-
" cerning me; for howe soeuer now I am hindred, Yet if it shall please you
" to accept of my poore seruice, I shall by the grace of God not onlie shortlie
" be present to performe what shall be commanded me with hazard of liffe
" and fortunes but also make manifestlie appeare houe highlie I shall think
" my selff aduanced if once I maie boldlie with your excne [Excellency's]
" consent intitle my selff

" Your Eccell:
" Most humble most affectionate
and most obedient Seruuant
" J. GORDON."

[*Addressed*] " pour son Excellence Monseigneur le Marquis de Montrose
" Conte de Kincairn, Seigneur de Grahame Baron de Mucdock Capitain

284    DEEDS OF MONTROSE.

" Generall de sa Maiestée de la Grand Britaigne dans son Roiaume d'Escosse
" Mon Illustre patron
                                            A Giotteborgh." [111]

Of all the correspondence which has now for the first time been laid before the reader, no letter is so tantalising as that of Maclear. A considerable portion of it has been lost, and the writing is worse than the worst of the most paper-grudging minister of the period. Apart from the name the writer's nationality is quaintly apparent. Montrose seems to be on the point of setting out. The ships expected from the Duke of Courland have not yet arrived. Was this in consequence of the dishonesty attributed to Cochran? Or were they likewise lying ice-bound in Riga or Libau, or other eastern port of the Baltic? But we infer that others sent by the Duke had arrived, and if there is any truth in the Edinburgh rumour of disaster, these may have formed part of that ill-fated little fleet. "Abörd" was perhaps the neighbouring spot in Norway to which Montrose retired from Gothenburg; but the Editors have failed to identify it. Of William Davidson, Strachan, and Captain Law nothing further is known. The first seems to have written from Courland, one of the many Scotsman living there. The Colonel Ogilvie, now with Maclear, seems to be the dishonest "Colonel John Ogelbie" of the Redivivus, whom Montrose had left at Amsterdam, and not his namesake of Powrie, at this time in Orkney. In the postscript Maclear mentions the receipt of fresh supplies from Stockholm, and engages to maintain communications between Gothenburg and Orkney by means of frigates.

". . . uellie [Ogilvie?] [112] he mentionats as new what the Currants bringe
" of the risinge of sundrie pties [parties] in England for o$^r$ dread Soueringe.
" I sall not omite dispatche thame to yo$^r$ exellcell$^y$ [Excellency]; wisheinge
" the omnipotent god to grant ane guid feine and seasonable weather for
" yo$^r$ excellencys Speedie despatche and saife arreyvall. the port is werie
" neir frie in thee eis [ice]  The Stockholmes post is not come as yit.
" receawinge [reserving] ane part for newis before yo$^r$ excell$^{ys}$ departure [I]
" sall not omite gif [omit to give] yo$^r$ excell$^y$ notice y$^r$of [thereof]. Williame
" Davidsone shawis [shows] me [that] Colnell Ogelvie will get most of
" cabten laws [? Captain Law's] men, bot [it] will cost him great chairges
" for intertaineinge thame untill the ships be riddie. so far I can learne

---

[111] Original, Advocates' Libr., Wodrow MSS., fol. lxvii. 92. Wodrow, in his index to the volume, enters it as undated, but "probably of the same date as the last," *i.e.*, Maclear's, February 13th. But there is no evidence of this in the letters. In the "Note of the papers found in Dunbeath," Maclear's is mentioned next after Gordon's. Appendix, No. ix.

[112] See his letter below, in which he mentions the arrival of the new Earl of Kinnoul (George Hay).

" [by] Mr Davidsons letter it will be the end of this monthe or the ships
" be cleir. Herein he recomends yo' excell' in [to ?] the protectionne of
" the omnipotent god.

" remaineinge yo' excellencys

" Most humble serwante

. . . ga . . . end [? *gaten street* ?]   "JOHNE MAKCLEIR,
the 13 *febr.* 1650

[*Postscript*] " . . . I send herin Colnell Ogillvies letter . . . w' [with]
" the causes. The same had ane hard storme the last nicht; quhille [while]
" this middaye, whenas [?] the wind is sete in easterlie, [he] hopes in god
" it will continewe to further yo' excellency's voyage. The great god pros-
" per and preserwe yo' excell', grantinge yo' excell' ane saife arrayvell, qu . . .
" [which] sall be the faithefull prayer of yo' excell''s most humble servant.
" I have receavite entire [? ane letter ?] from Stockholme conserninge
" petards, matpeices [hatpieces ? or matchlocks ?], and eandgranates [hand-
" grenades]. Expecting presentlie [*i.e., immediately*] from yo' excell' a
" happie arrayvell [*i.e., news thereof*], conserning all maiters threfter [there-
" after] I sall regulate my selff and doe the uttermost in dewlie [? treuly ?]
" performing all can be in yo' excell' service. It will be newere [*illeg.*]
" requite yo' excell'. Let. cabten Strachene [Lieut.-Captain Strachan] went
" to . . . [*illeg.*] for some guid expert mariners for transportinge the 3
" ships as yit expectit from the Ducke of courlande, which . . . I conjecture
" that [?] will be in the end of aprell befoir they come here in . . . pas
" fregats betwixt for notice of all affaires. I hope we sall heave seemen and
" qut [what] ells yo' excell' stands in neid of reddie against y' [that] tyme
" on [?] receavinge tymius notice y'of for prepaireinge [*the writing was con-
" tinued over the page, which is torn at the top and blackened*]

" remaining    [*torn*]

" Most humble seruante,

JOHN MAKCLEIR."

[*Addressed in another clear German hand.*]

"For his excell' my Lord Marquis of Montrose thes Abörd."

[*Endorsed in Montrose's hand*]

"Colonell Gordone." [113]

Inquiry has failed to ascertain the exact date at which Montrose set out.
Harry May, the chosen messenger, did not start on his long journey north

---

[113] Original, Advocates' Libr., Wodrow MSS., fol. lxvii. 91.

till at least January 16th, as he brought a letter of that date from the Duke of York.[114] The same messenger brought a letter from Seaforth, which Montrose acknowledged from Kirkwall, 26th March. We may therefore assume that May's arrival was the signal for sailing. Among the many letters taken afterwards in Hall's frigate was one from Lord Sinclair, in Amsterdam, dated February 13th 1650, and this too, Montrose must have received before he left Norway. The Dunbeath papers contained a long dispatch from Thomas Ogilvy of Powrie, dated March 3rd, which must have reached Montrose about the same time. As we find Montrose in Orkney by March 26th, allowing for the transit of Ogilvie's letter, we cannot be far wrong in inferring that he sailed from Norway in the middle of March.[115]

(For the King's letters by the same bearer, see pp. 278, 279)

[The Duke of York's letter.]

"MY LORD: I would not let this gentleman, Harry May, go to you
" without writing to you. This bearer will give you a very good account
" of news, and of all the business that is here, and he will assure you how
" much I ever am your Lordship's most affectionate friend, JAMES.

" JERSEY, 16*th*-26*th January* 1650."

Letter from Thomas Ogilvie of Powrie, continuing the narrative of events in Orkney.

" MY LORD,

" In my last letter to your Lord: I forgot to show your lordship con-
" cerning my Lord marshell and Levetennent-gñall Midltone quho treulie (if
" faith and treuth be in men) ar verie loyall to his māts [Majesty's] service
" and that without any interest as they profes themselffs, aither of hamiltone
" or argetheliane [Argyll's] factionis, or ony othair quhatsoever, bot meirlie
" quhat concernes his māts hapines and service. Thairfoir let me humblie
" beg at your Lds. hands that your Ldp will be pleasit to intreat them both
" fairlie and kyndlie to adhear to ther loyall opiniones. This will conduce
" muche for your Lds interest and advantage. Your Ldp. knowes quhou
" saif and fitting ane gairisone Dunnotter is for kepeing of amonitione and
" artelliearie And belive me if your Ldp. desyre this fairlie and kyndlie you

---

[114] Even so, January 16th to *ca.* March 16th was a long time for the journey. Want of money may have delayed him. The King himself was at this time in desperate straits. On April 3-13, Nicolas wrote to Ormond from Breda, that if Charles, on his way thither, had not found an English merchant to lend him £200, he must have stayed in France for want. Orm. Papers, i. 375.

[115] King's commission of Lieutenant-General under Montrose (see p. 270, *n.* 74) was dated 19th March 1650. If Montrose signed it, he must have been on the verge of sailing, and had a very quick run to Kirkwall.

" will gett it, and for Middltone he is so far considerable that if your Ldp
" will be pleasit to make use of him quhme [whom?] indeed ye will find him
" willing eneuche to except [accept] it   He can taik of [off] the most pairt
" of all ther horss, to goe along with him any way—that he pleases to
" comand them bot cheiflie in the Kinges service   My Lord your Ldp. will
" pardoune me to be a lyttill free for my earnest wishes for the weill of his
" mats service and my best respectes for your Ldp. selff ar past all Compli-
" ment   Your Ldp. hes beine pleasit to give sume commissiones quhilk
" treulie hes beine verie detastable to verie Loyall men and hes proved hielie
" disadventagious to the advancement of your Ldps Intentiones   The par-
" ticulares I will refer to meiting your Ldp. quhilk treulie your Ldp. will find
" too clear.   My Lord since my Comeing to orknay lykewayes I am sorie to
" see authoritie and comyssiones to be put in such young handes quho
" treulie hes not witt to governe themselffes Lett alone to advance the weill
" of his māts service   And Indead if this Lord Kynnoull haid not cum
" tymouslie over with that last recreuitt thair follie had brock the verie small
" beginingis of his māts service If your Ldp sall stay any tyme from us
" (quilk god forbid) you sould aither send over sum man to comand in cheiffe
" or else send commissione to my lord Kynnoull to doe it heire and that all
" that ar heir shall not presum bot to obey him else treulie your Ldp. will
" fynd ane euill managit busines heir   My Lord I will be verie loath to be
" ane spectator to anie [thing] that mey prejudice the Kinges service and in
" troath my affectione to the weill of it hes maid m[e] thus frie with your
" Ldp. at this tyme   I sall never faill to approue my self as ever [torn] the
" Kinges interest to your Ldps selff in particular to death

" Your Ldp's obedient and
" faithfull servant to serve you

" THOMAS OGIL[UIE torn]

" KIRKWALL 3 march 1650

[Addressed] " For his excellence Lord Marques of Montrose."[116]

---

CONTEMPORARY EVENTS OF THIS PERIOD.

AUGUST 6th. The General Assembly rose.  Its last act was a letter to Charles, warning him against " malignants," especially " that flagicious person and most justly excommunicated Rebell, James Graham, who has exercised such horrid cruelty," &c.—11th. Parliament rose.—24th. Committee of Estates met at Perth, to " see the peace of the Highlands," and cause the chiefs " subscriue the band appointed by Parliament in February last" (Balf.).—SEPTEMBER 7th. " It seems Ireland is lost,"

---

[116] Original, Advocates Libr., Wodrow MSS., fol. lxvii. 94.

... "James Graham cannot come here for the King's good" (Baillie, iii. 102).—11th. Cromwell storms Drogheda.—OCTOBER 11th. Libberton sets out. Cromwell storms Wexford, and massacres another 2000 Royalists.—14th. News of Drogheda reaches Paris (Evelyn, ii. 13).—18th. Cromwell takes Ross.—*Ca.* 28th. Rupert passes St. Malo. Queen Elizabeth, letter, November 19th.—NOVEMBER 8-18th. Libberton at Campvere to R. Douglas: Charles brought very low; very poor. France unable and unwilling to help, "yet his pernitious and devillish Counsell will suffer him to starve, before they suffer him to take the League and Covenant" (Baillie, iii. 522, 523).—11th. Charles in Jersey signs a pass for R. Hamilton to Scotland (Wigton MSS., 494).—On January 1st Wishart writes to Napier, that Hamilton, Lauderdale, Dunfermline, Callendar, Sinclair, &c., in Holland, are so "darned that we hear but little of their din." "All their present hopes are of Windrum's treaty." The last two profess good will to Montrose. Sir William Fleming came this way, and went straight to Scotland (Napier, Mem., 731). Fleming passed the Hague between DECEMBER 2d and 8th. Letter of Elizabeth, December 9th, *Sunday*, in which she acknowledges Montrose's of November 4th, "received last week," and says Fleming came the day after with a letter, also of November 4th, from Charles in Jersey.—1650. JANUARY 8th. Resolved in the English Commons to recall Cromwell. The reason given was Laird Winram's dealings with Charles, and new levies of forces in Scotland (Carlyle's Cromwell, ii. 95).—12th. Charles writes to Committee of Estates for Commissioners to meet him at Breda on March 15th (Wishart, edit. 1819, p. 450). The *same day* he wrote to Montrose, and sent the George and Garter (*v.* text, p. 279).—24th. Charles in Jersey to Hamilton, requests his attendance at the proposed meeting at Breda (Burnet, Hamiltons, 414).—FEBRUARY 2nd. Libberton with letters from Charles reaches Leith (Balf. iv. 2). Heath says on 18th.—5th. Charles in Jersey to Rev. R. Douglas, Moderator (letter in Baillie, iii. 524).—12th. Committee of Estates vote to send Commissioners to Breda (Balf.).—MARCH 7th. Parliament session begins; Charles' letter and Libberton's negotiations read.—8th. Parliament gives ten instructions to Commissioners, Cassilis, Lothian, Brodie, Libberton, John Smith, Alexander Jeffra (Jaffray). For the Kirk James Wood and John Livingstone, ministers, were sent, to treat for thirty days (Balf.).—APRIL 7. "Fast for the treatie at Breda" (Baillie, iii. App. cviii.).—15th. Charles at Breda writes to Napier, "continue your assistance" to Montrose (Napier, Mem., 756).—20th. Libberton to Rev. R. Douglas, encloses the King's concessions (Baillie, iii. 523).—27th. Montrose defeated.—MAY 3rd. Charles signs the treaty. Sends Sir W. Fleming with orders to go to Orkney and inform Montrose of it. Writes to Montrose privately.—5th. His public letter to Montrose.—8th. Charles to Parliament; has ordered Montrose to disband.—9th. Charles' last letter to Montrose, *per* Sir W. Fleming.—10th. Signs Sir W. Fleming's pass.—12th. Writes to Parliament his regret at Montrose's invasion; had ordered him to disband. Read in Parliament, May 25th (Balf.). At the same time gives private instructions to Sir W. Fleming to act according to circumstances (Wigton MSS., 477).—16th. Papers from commissioners read in Parliament; new instructions sent.—17th. Montrose brought as a prisoner to Leith.—18th. Sir William Fleming lands at Leith.—20th. Charles signs a pass for Robert Hamilton to Scotland (Wigton MSS., 494).—21st. Montrose executed.—25th. Argyll in Parliament reads letter from Lothian that Charles "wes no wayes sorey that James Grhame was defait, in respect he had made that invasion without and contrary to his command."—31st. Cromwell reaches London.—JUNE. The King hears of "the murther" of Montrose (Heath, 268). This news reached Paris, June 11th (Cowley, the poet, to H. Bennet in Miscell. Aulica, 1702, p. 138).—23rd, Sunday. Charles lands at Garmouth, and signs the League and Covenant (Balf.).

## CHAPTER VIII[1]

State of Scotland in 1649–1650—Parliament, Courts, Kirk, Army—Affairs in Orkney—Montrose at Kirkwall—Orders to Hurry—Lands in Caithness—Declaration at Thurso—Caithness gentry—Effect of the news in the North—Dunbeath Castle taken—March to Carbisdale—Preparations at Edinburgh—Negotiations at Breda (Livingstone's Letter)—Lieutenant-Colonel Strachan; his letter to James Guthrie—Council of War at Tain—The local levy (Monroes and Rosses)—April 27, Strachan surprises Montrose at Carbisdale and cuts his army to pieces.

SCOTLAND, on the eve of Montrose's landing, was seething with discontent. The ruinous mismanagement of the Hamiltons and defeat of the Engagement had, with Cromwell's aid, restored the ascendancy to Argyll and the root-and-branch faction of the Kirk. Emulating the extreme party in England, the self-styled Estates were carefully managed, so as to exclude all moderate counsels. In 1648 the nobility had been represented by sixty-five peers. In 1649 never more than ten, and seldom as many,

---

[1] The sketch of Scotland in 1649–1650 is drawn mainly from Balfour's Annals and R. Baillie's Letters (iii.) for those years. To these the reader may accept a general reference, in place of citations too numerous for our text.

The description of the battle of Carbisdale is based on the very full, graphic account by Gilbert Gordon, of Sallagh, in his "Continuation of the History of the Earls of Sutherland" (fol. 1813). The style appears to be that of an old man. His entries conclude abruptly with December 1651: "Thus with the loss of the libertie of my nation I end both this year 1651 and my collections, having neither hart nor incoragement to proceed therein.—FINIS.—Laus Deo."—"This whole book was copied out of the Author's own copies in the year 1656." Hence we may infer that he was then dead. His authority is good for local events, but strongly tainted with bigotry, and warped by family pride. On events beyond his personal ken he is often very inaccurate. (The victory of Kilsyth he attributes chiefly to Aboyne, "who lead the vant-guard!") Sallagh took his name from his estate on Loch Shin. He probably fled on Montrose's advance. His account of the battle seems that of an *eye-witness*. In the main it is confirmed by the published report given in Balfour, Ann. iv. 8–12. Of its accuracy in local colour, the Editors were assured by inspection of the battle-field and neighbourhood. Dr. Joass, of Golspie Manse, a learned and accomplished antiquary, has given valuable assistance in notes, sketches of the ground, &c. He referred us to Mr. D. Cameron, of Culrain, for over sixty years a resident on the spot. Mr. Cameron was indefatigable in courteous eagerness to show all the traditional points, to which he guided us with a zeal and activity unimpaired by age. We had thus an excellent opportunity for testing the value of a strong clear tradition, confirming and confirmed by contemporary writers. This value was greatly enhanced by the fact that Mr. Cameron was unacquainted with these rare works. The mental associations of beautiful placid scenery, resigned to melancholy memories, in no way detracted from the pleasure and interest of his conversation.

took their seats. Many shires and boroughs returned no members at all; and of the seventy-two elected, the attendance sank so low that, in May, not twenty barons and burgesses were present.

The same wave of change swept the Courts, the Clerk-Register and eight Lords of Session being displaced. The most eloquent testimony to the corruption that then prevailed in the administration of the law is to be found in the fact that the equity of the judges appointed by Cromwell, after his conquest, extorted admiration from a people embittered against England by religious, political, and national hate.

The Assembly of the Kirk was even more eager to celebrate its triumph. Commissions, "sent out east, west, north and south," ousted scores of ministers from their livings. Their fury fell not only on those who had been active for the Engagement; even those who had *not* denounced it were turned adrift. In Edinburgh, Mr. Andrew Ramsay was ejected, in spite of his fifty-three years of service; and the one voice raised to remind them that he was "the painfullest minister in Edinburgh," was hotly censured by Robert Douglas, the Moderator. In Angus and the Mearns alone, eighteen ministers were deprived, five suspended, and "two expectants silenced." It is significant of the transference of authority in government, that a motion of the Assembly to abolish Church patronage was passed by the Estates, and Argyll and Loudon forced to acquiesce in a wholesale measure far more drastic than the proposal which had set the nobles in a flame against Charles I.

But with all this repression the country was bridled, not pacified. What was the tyranny of bishops and the new Service Book to the inquisitions of the General Assembly? The little finger of kirk-sessions had proved thicker than the King's loins. Many who had opposed Charles I. now yearned for his son. No heavier indictment could be framed against the Scots rebels and the tyranny of their triumph, than this new-fledged loyalty to a son who had tenfold his father's faults, with none of his virtues.

In the North, especially, only a spark of enthusiasm and success seemed wanting to rekindle the fitful loyalty of those who had shared Pluscardine's rising. Again the great Mackenzie, Gordon, and Mackay followings would rise in their thousands. Seaforth had promised all but the one thing needful—his own presence. Sir Thomas Urquhart of Cromartie, Colonels John Monro of Lemlair and Hugh Fraser, the new Lord Reay, even Lewis Gordon —despite his debt to Argyll for the Marquisate—Lord 'Ogilvie, Middleton, the Earl Marischall, and the faithful clans of Athole and Badenoch—all had been out with Pluscardine, and would rally to the King's standard. There is, in fact, reason to believe that some of these chiefs had definitely promised aid; and others were certain to respond to the call of a leader whose victories had gained fresh lustre from recent defeats. Charles himself, beggared in his hopes of Ireland, was pressed to share the expedition; and in the light of his reception two months later—two months too late— it is certain that his presence would have confirmed many waverers, now puzzled and paralysed by his intrigues with those who had pouched his father's blood-money.

The moment was propitious. Cromwell was still engaged on *his* scheme of "Thorough" in Ireland—victorious, but with forces wasted by disease and famine. Not till April 2nd did he choose to acknowledge the letter of recall, of which he had received diverse private intimations before.[2] Yet as early as December 19th the English Parliament had passed the vote, on news of "laird Wyndram's dealings with Charles." Stripped of his main support, Argyll anxiously watched and sought to guide the rising flood of national feeling, scheming busily to keep his craven head above the breakers. Even among those most deeply compromised in opposition to Montrose, there were few whom he could trust. Loudon had been a foremost Engager, and "the aboundance of teares" with which he had publicly repented of that sin would flow as freely for his next sin of failure. No longer earning English pay, and fearful of the spirit of the Engagement, the Estates had disbanded a large portion of their forces, a measure dictated as much by policy as by necessity.[3] Heavy fines and sequestrations did little to ease the intolerable burden. Taxation was imposed unequally, and provoked violent quarrels between the boroughs and Edinburgh, between the West and Fife. The country was drained to poverty. Money was scarce; the seasons bad; provisions dear beyond all precedent; the North on the verge of famine; Moray clamouring for relief.

At this time, therefore, Leslie commanded only 3000 foot (under Lieutenant-General Holburn) and 1500 horse. Some of these forces had been distributed in November as garrisons in Brahan, Chanonry, and Eilandonan Castles, the last being "the Earl of Seaforth's strongest hold. This handfull did at
" that time overawe and keep under the discontented partie, though more
" powerfull. For besides those which had been disbanded by the Earl of
" Lanerick [*now Duke of Hamilton*] and Major Generall Munroe, at the
" bridge of Striveling [*Stirling*], there flock'd daily out of England great
" companies of those who had escaped out of prison; who finding their
" estates sequestred and seiz'd upon, and withall most tyrannically proceeded
" against by the hot-spirited Ministerie, desired nothing more than an oppor-
" tunity of revenge. Besides these he [*Montrose*] had a considerable number
" of his own name and faction in the North. The Gordons, the Athole
" men who (if he had not been crush'd at his first entrie) would certainly

---

[2] Carlyle, Letters of Cromwell, ii. 95, 142, 143.
[3] For striking confirmation of this, see Strachan's letter, pp. 302, 303.

" have assisted him. This condition of the kingdome made the Marquesse
" appear like a prodigious Meteor hanging over their heads, which awaked
" those who sate at the helm of the State (whom it did indeed most concern)
" to endeavour the defeating of his attempts both at home and abroad."[4]

Beyond the meagre notices given in the last chapter, Orkney seems to have preserved scarcely a trace in local contemporary record of either of the foreign troops quartered there during those six winter months of weary waiting, or of Montrose's own arrival. Two small fragments, signed by Drummond and Kinnoul,[5] and a final extract from Gwynne,[6] with some letters referring to the flight and capture of some of Montrose's followers,[7] are all that have been recovered. It might have been supposed that events so unusual would have sunk deep in the memory of the inhabitants, and left at least a strong tradition. But no trace of this has appeared. We can only conjecture that all such memories were overlaid and effaced by the English occupation of 1651 and following years.

The two fragments alluded to are orders to John Potinger, then a leading merchant in Kirkwall, for the delivery of arms. After the deaths of George, Earl of Kinnoul, and his uncle Morton in November, affairs had fallen into confusion. At this time Drummond may have held command, in virtue of the commission which had given offence to Morton, his father's enemy.[8] To this period, therefore, we assign the first of the fragments given in the note. William, the new Earl of Kinnoul, who signs the second order, took over the command on his arrival, and we have seen that he probably accompanied the ships dispatched from Gothenburg in December or January.[9]

That Montrose had already reached Kirkwall before the close of March

---

[4] Montrose Red. 171. Their measures abroad were mainly intrigues with Charles, and letters to foreign princes, especially Christina and Orange, representing Montrose as a man of no faith, excommunicate, and hateful to the nation.

[5] These belong to Mr. J. W. Cursiter of Kirkwall, who kindly permitted the Rev. J. B. Craven, of the Rectory there, to send us the originals.

(1.) "Mister potenger delifer al the Shabers [*sabres*] you haue to this berer and get a reset [*receipt*] from him give him lykuais 2 hag botes [*hagbuts*] of found [*cast metal*].

"GEORGE DRUM̄OND."

(2.) "Jhone potinger ye shall after sight heirof deliver thes four hagbits of found which are my Lord Mortons to Captaine Wood and this shallbe your warrand March 8 1650

KINNOULE."

See the *facsimiles*. As to Captain Wood, see App. I., Noltland Letters.

A writer on Orkney of last century states that "hardly a Gentlemans house in the island but lost aither a sone or a brother" in this campaign. But see App. I. The account of Montrose's arrival at Kirkwall, by the late Mr. G. Petrie, County Clerk, Orkney (Calder's Hist. Caithness, 148), is unsupported by any reference to authority or tradition, and seems mere imagination.

[6] See App., Sequel.   [7] See App. I., Noltland Letters.
[8] See Kinnoul's letter, p. 257.   [9] See p. 281.

Mister
potinger deliver at set
Isabelth yow gave to this bearer
and got a rest from him
give him lyknais 2 garbotos of fown

George Drumond

Jeorge potinger ye shall after sight
giroff deliver his fown garbits
of fownd regies ase my lord morton
to Captaine Hood and this shall be
your warrand March 8 1650
Kinnoule

we gather from his letter to Seaforth, in reply to one which he was perhaps too busy to answer before leaving Norway.[10]

"MY LORD, "KIRKWALL IN ORKNAY, 26 *March* 1650.

"I receaved yr L. [*letter*] by Mr. May, who has confirmed me in the "knowledge of all yr nobell and freindly cariages, for which beleave I will "serve you with my lyfe all the dayes it shall please God to len me it. I "am going to the maine-land, and hes no more leasure bot to assure you I "shall tender yr freindes and interests as my aune life, and still live or dye, "my Lord, yr cossen and faithfull freind and servand,

"MONTROSE.[11]

"For the Earle of Siafort."

The *Herderinnan* could have brought little accession in numbers to the four or five hundred foreign troops who had already reached Kirkwall. But accompanying Montrose were some nobles and officers of distinction. Among these we read of the Viscount Frendraught, a kinsman of Lord Napier, and nephew to the Earl of Sutherland; Colonel Sir William Johnston, a resolute man and an old soldier, whose information to Nicolas has already been referred to; Colonel Thomas Gray,[12] a "German" soldier, who, for thirty-four years had not visited Scotland; Colonels Sir Harry Graham and James Hay of Naughton; Sir Francis Hay of Dalgetty; and, in spite of Crawford-Lindsay's dealings,[13] Major General Hurry. George Drummond of Balloch is also said to have been of the party; but we have seen reason to believe that he was already in Orkney.[14]

Two weeks were spent in organising and equipping the little force, and providing for their transport. A bond of allegiance was signed by the gentry and ministers of Orkney and Shetland.[15] Some of the ministers agreed to accompany the forces as chaplains. Leaving Sir William Johnston to act as governor in Orkney,[16] the little army, some 1500 strong, including about 1000 natives, marched from Kirkwall across to Holm Sound[17] to take ship for the mainland. For so short a voyage a fleet of fishing boats would

---

[10] Clarendon, v. 351, says Montrose arrived about the end of the year 1649. As he used English "ecclesiastical style," that gives us the date March 25 approximately. But to the same date he refers Montrose's Declaration, and adds that he "seized an old castle [Dunbeath] where he placed his stores"—both events in April, *i.e.*, 1650.

[11] Original, Seaforth archives. Copy in W.'s Montrose (1819), 443. As Montrose knew that the King and Seaforth were now at Breda, he would direct this letter to Holland.

[12] App. I., Sequel. [13] App. IX. [14] Montr. Rediv. 174. See p. 292.

[15] See Declaration below, p. 295. This is borne out by the sequel in Orkney. See App. I., Sequel.

[16] This is inferred from the omission of his name in the records of what follows, and the letter to Sir James Sinclair. App. I., Sequel.

[17] The probable point of embarkation. Calder, Hist. Caithness, 149.

suffice, convoyed by the *Herderinnan*, Captain Hall's frigate, and an Orkney vessel belonging to one Captain Love,[18] pressed into the service.

On April 9th all were in readiness to embark, and Montrose, already aboard, issued the following orders to Hurry.[19]

### "ORDERS FOR GENERAL-MAJOR SIR JOHN HURRY.

"You are presently [*at once*] after the sight hereof, to take a part of
" my company of Guard, with four of my life regiment, commanded by
" Lieutenant-Colonel George Drummond, together with other four companies
" of Lieutenant-Colonel Henry Stewart's squadron, and immediately to
" emboat yourself, with what arms and ammunition doth belong, and set
" with this evening tide for the coast of Caithness; choosing the most
" convenient place for landing as occasion shall serve; and if, according
" to your intelligence, you find not your landing opposed, nor no forces
" making in a body against you, you are to march directly to the Ord, and
" those narrow passes betwixt Caithness and Sutherland, for preventing
" the enemy's entry, and reducing such of the country people as shall offer
" to rise; according to your own best discretion, and the rule of war in
" the like cases. But if you shall find, according to your certain intelligence,
" that all the country of Caithness are in arms to resist you, and oppose
" the landing in a real way of opposition or defence, then and in that case
" you are not to hazard to force it, but to set for Stranaver [*Strath Naver*],
" and there to attempt your landing, as with most safety and conveniency
" you can. Where, if you should also find too much difficulty, as by
" appearance there cannot, you are to apply a little higher betwixt that
" and Kintail, which places are all for the King,[20] and there make your
" descent; and use your best discretion in every thing as occurs. In all
" which cases you are still to send us frequent advertisements, as falls out;
" and observe punctually the premises at your highest peril. Given under
" our hand from shipboard, near the island of Flottat,[21] this 9th day of
" April 1650."

"MONTROSE.

*Postscript.* "In regard of the shortness, and pressingness of the time,
" you are to chose five hundred of those you conceive ablest and fittest of

---

[18] Balf. iv. 41, June 4th. "The housse ordaines James Loue to be payed out of fynnes of thesse of Orknay, in respecte his shipe and goods was takin by them from him." Was this the ship said by Nicolas to have been taken by Hall's frigate? (p. 258, *n.* 37).

[19] Napier, Mem., 743; and *ibid.* 743, 744 for the Declaration which follows. The original documents were discovered in a trunk at Buchanan House. See Pref. to Nap., Memorials vol. ii. Gwynne accompanied Hurry. Mem. p. 89.

[20] He must have been assured of this. It was Seaforth's country.

[21] Flottat for Flotta. See Nap., Memorials ii. 478.

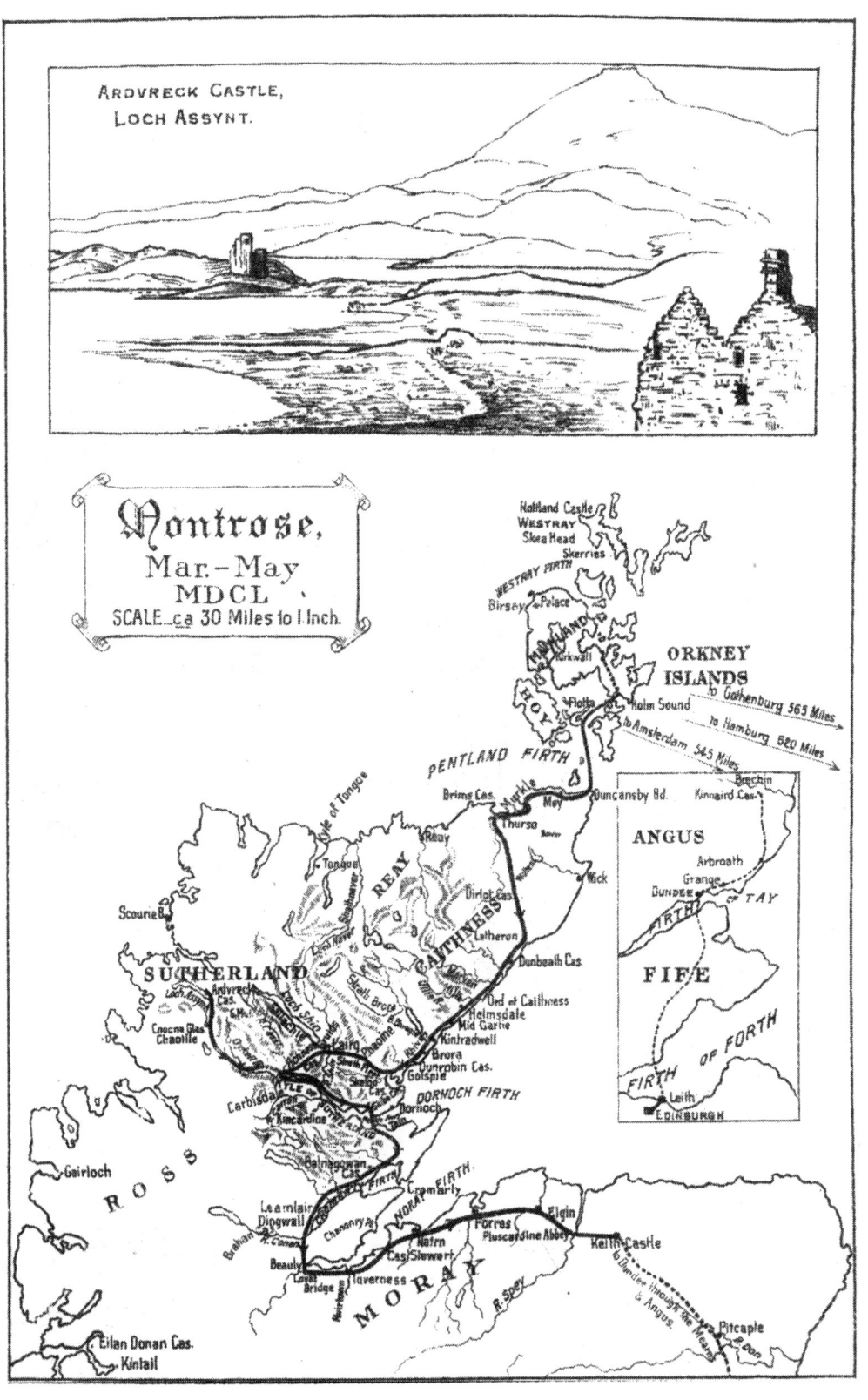

"my life-regiment, and Lieutenant-Colonel Henry Stewart's squadron,
"without looking to the equal proportion of either; as also my Company
"of guards, and such of the volunteer gentlemen and officers as are ready.
"Given *ut supra*."

A few days must have elapsed before the news arrived that Hurry had landed without opposition, and pushing on past Wick and Dunbeath, had secured the important pass of the Ord. The remainder of the forces then steered for Duncansby, where they are said to have landed.[22] Thence, skirting the north coast to Dunnet Bay, they marched to Thurso, where Montrose took up his quarters in a small house near the old church, in that part of the town called the "Fisher-biggins."[23]

The following document, his "second Declaration," must have been issued shortly after his arrival, and points to the 11th or 12th as the probable date of his landing at Duncansby.

"FOR THE GENTLEMEN AND HERITORS OF THE SHERIFFDOM OF CAITHNESS, *these*:

"GENTLEMEN: Your not appearing to us, after our arrival in this place,
"so timely as we expected, hath necessitated us (the conveniency of his
"Majesty's affairs requiring our removal from this part) to leave behind us
"some certain persons belonging to us, by whom we have thought good to
"communicate unto you such things as we judge most necessary to be done by
"you at this time, in order to the establishing and carrying on of his Majesty's
"just service in these parts, and the peace and happiness of every one of
"yourselves. For which end we have particularly commanded them to offer
"unto you, in our name, an oath of fidelity and allegiance, to be subscribed
"by all and every one of you, to his sacred Majesty; as it hath been already
"done by those of the gentry and ministry of Orkney. As we expect your
"cheerful performance hereof, and ready concurrence with us in the prosecu-
"tion of that trust his Majesty has again reposed in us, so we shall make it
"evidently appear unto you, that they could not have pitched upon any who
"should more firmly and constantly protect and defend you, in all your just
"rights and concernments, than your very affectionate friend,

"THURSO, 14 *April* 1650. "MONTROSE."

Neither the gentry nor ministry of Caithness seem to have been stimulated to any great alacrity by this appeal. Like many others they preferred

---

[22] "In the immediate vicinity of John o' Groat's." Calder, Hist. Caithness, 149. In tracing the march to Thurso, and thence to Dunbeath, we give what seems the most probable route.

Magnus Mowat of Freswick in Canisbay is styled also "of Bucholie," and has been identified with the "Balwholly" who fell at Alford. His daughter Christina was the first wife of Sir John Sinclair of Dunbeath. *Ibid.* 143. See p. 111, *n.* 20. Latheron churchyard contains curious monuments to the lady and her daughters. [23] *Ibid.* 150.

to wait, before committing themselves to open voluntary participation in the movement. It has usually been represented that the bond of loyalty they were required to sign, and which Harry Graham with a party was left to see them sign, was only extorted from them by dire threats and compulsion. Such indeed was their plea when called in question by the victors. But in the Acts of Parliament and Presbytery records there is abundant evidence to show that large numbers suffered fines, and the ministers almost to a man were deprived for their engagement.[24]

A few, however, showed themselves more forward, chief of whom were Alexander Sinclair, Laird of Brims, Hugh Mackay of Dirlot, and Hucheon Mackay of Scourie,[25] the last two being staunch partisans of the Reay interest against the encroachments of the Earl of Sutherland. These three were sent on to Tongue in Strathnaver, to assemble what men they could, and join by way of Loch Naver and Loch Shin.[26] The news of Montrose's landing must have been followed by the immediate retreat of the garrison, 100 strong, under Captain William Gordon, which had been stationed there by the Earl of Sutherland, in October 1649, in Reay's chief house at Tongue.[27]

---

[24] "Only 3 in all Cathnes that hes not takin the othe, nor subscriued the band to James Grhame, viz. Francis St. Claire, grand vnckell to the Earle of Cathnes, the Laird of Dumbethe, and William St. Clair, zounger, of May." Balf. iv. 34. See also *ibid*. 33, 35, &c. "James Graham compells the inhabitants of Cateynes to subscrybe certain new papers and bands, swearing obedience to his excellencie as to the King's generalissimo; which he presents also to the ministers there. They did all subscrybe these papers, except one, Mr. William Smyth whom (upon his refusall) he sent to his ships to be put in irnes; but this minister was afterwards released." Sallagh, 554. For Mr. Smith, minister of Bower and Watten, see Calder, Hist. Cathn., 150, and App. I., Noltland Letters. The Francis Sinclair above mentioned was a son of George, Earl of Caithness. In 1644 he arrested the laird of Drum, who, according to Sallagh, p. 579, had fled with Huntly to Caithness, and obtained part of the reward of 20,000 merks; but see note, pp. 154, 155.

[25] "Hew Mackay of Dilret" with Wm. M. of Bighous and Hucheon M. of Scourie had actively assisted Lord Reay, in 1645-1646, to oppose the claim made by the Earl of Sutherland to the lands of Strath Naver. In the beginning of 1647 the Earl procured an act against them "excepting and excluding them out of pardon, and forbidding the general persons to grant them any passes or remitts, until they satisfied him and gave him possession of the lands of Strathnaver, restored goods taken out of his Country and gave caution," &c. Sallagh, 536, 537. The same writer, p. 529, tells us that Reay in 1645 held a commission from Montrose. He mentions "John Macky of Dilret," brother to Reay, who died in 1645. Was Hugh his son, and therefore nephew to Donald Mackay, Lord Reay, who died, February 1649, in Denmark?

Hucheon Mackay of Scourie was father-in-law to the new Lord Reay. He was out with Pluscardine in 1649. After the defeat he was "licensed" to go home with the Strathnaver men. Huntly (Lewis Gordon), Ogilvy, Middleton, and Pluscardine made their peace with Leslie, leaving "Rea to suffer for the rest." Sallagh, 549.

[26] *Ibid*. 552, 553.

[27] "The garrison had the maintenance of Southerland, Cateynes, Strathnaver and Assint allowed to them for their intertainment, which the Earl of Southerland caused take up dewlie for the use of the garrison." Captain W. Gordon was a son of "Adam Gordon of Kilcalmkill that dyed in Germanie." Sallagh, 550, 551. We shall presently find the captain at Dunrobin. See p. 298, and App. I., Sequel.

Leaving a force of about 200 men[28] under his brother, to raise Caithness, Montrose proceeded to Dunbeath, some twenty-seven miles distant, by the road which strikes the coast at Latheron.

Meantime Sir John Sinclair of Dunbeath Castle,[29] on news of Montrose's landing, had hastened south to procure aid and to warn the Earl of Sutherland. The latter at once sent messengers to Edinburgh with the news, and also a request to two troops of horse quartered in Ross to come to his assistance. This they refused, on the ground that they had no orders to that effect, and their commanders were at Edinburgh. It is more probable, however, that they hesitated to venture into the mountains, where provisions for man and horse were scarce; and by so doing they may have feared to expose themselves to a rising in the rear. On this the Earl retired with 300 men to Ross-shire, leaving strong garrisons in Dunrobin, Skelbo, Skibo, and Dornoch Castles.[30]

Dunbeath Castle,[31] before which Montrose arrived about the 17th (?) of April, occupies a position of great natural advantage on a rocky cliff overhanging the sea. Seventeen years before these events additions to the southeast front had added to its extent and strength. The fortress was well victualled, and, though the garrison was small, it was not reduced till after some days' siege, when Sir John's lady, who appears to have shown great spirit in the defence, was permitted to retire with her baggage.[32] The strength of the fortress, commanding Caithness and the line by which Montrose might receive recruits, or in case of mishap retreat to Orkney, rendered it necessary to secure the castle with a sufficient force, and accordingly Major

---

[28] An inference from the numbers he landed with, those he left in Dunbeath, and those present at Carbisdale. "Harie Graham with some men." Sallagh.

[29] Sir John Sinclair of Dunbeath, with John Monro of Lemlair, among others, had brought about a "reconciliation" between Reay and Sutherland in 1649. One of the terms was the cession of Reay's lands in Strath Naver. He sat for Caithness in the anti-Engagement Parliament of 1649. When Montrose reached Dunbeath, Sir John was in Ross, according to Sallagh. Calder says, on the first news of landing he "posted off direct to Edinburgh," to give the alarm (Hist. Caithn. 149). The only authority for this is Montr. Rediv. 177, which places the battle near Dunbeath!

[30] Sallagh, 552.

[31] Dunbeath Castle is recorded as far back as 1428. The N.W. front dates 1633. The eastern portion nearer the sea was built in 1859, and large additions made in 1879. Note from Mr. W. S. Thomson-Sinclair, who now occupies the castle. In 1650 it is said to have been surrounded by a moat (Calder), but of this there are now no traces. See App. I., Sequel.

[32] "Upon very fair conditions which were ill observed." Sallagh, 552. But he gives no details, and his bias renders him of doubtful authority on such a charge. Montrose resigned an important hostage for her husband's conduct and that of others in the district. She was Catharine, third daughter of Hugh, eighth Lord Lovat (then deceased, and succeeded by a young grandson). Her eldest sister Anne was the wife of John, thirteenth Earl of Sutherland, and her second sister Mary was wife of David Ross, the important laird of Balnagown. After Sir John's death she was twice married (Douglas Peerage, Lovat). Cf. Montrose's treatment of this lady with that dealt to his sister and the Keir and Napier ladies, pp. 103, 133. He could not be guilty of an unchivalrous act. For account of castle in 1760, see Pococke, 163; Proceedings of Antiquaries of Scotland, Index.

Whitfurd and the Laird of Dalgetty, with 100 men, were detached to garrison it. With the remainder of his forces, now reduced to about 700 or 800 men, Montrose hastened to join Hurry and the van at the Ord.[33] The seizure of this pass, which a few resolute men might have made good, had been effected with skill. Some skirmishing seems to have taken place, but neither the Earl nor his followers showed much stomach for fighting, and the key to Sutherland was resigned without a serious attempt at its defence.

Following the coast, Montrose now advanced to Helmsdale and Gartie, where he encamped for the night. The next night was spent at Kintradwell. On the third day after entering into Sutherland he arrived before Dunrobin Castle,[34] the Earl's chief hold, and summoned it to yield. Captain William Gordon however, who had been withdrawn from Tongue and left in command, refused to surrender, and seized a party of Montrose's men who had incautiously ventured between the castle and the sea. A summons next day to release his prisoners remained without effect.[35] The night was spent at Rhives on the slopes of Ben Bhragie, overlooking Golspie.[36] Being weak in cavalry, and probably aware of the garrisons in the Dornoch peninsula,

---

[33] The present road over the Ord was made in 1811. The old road lay lower down, but farther out over the sheer precipice. Brand, writing in 1701, says, "The road is but narrow, and the descent steep, and if any stumble thereupon they are in hazard of falling down a precipice into the sea at the bottom of the rock, which is very terrible to behold; but who pass it for the more security use to lead their horses to the foot of the hill." "The path—for it did not deserve the name of a road—along the outer edge of the rock, and without any protection from the precipice that overhangs the sea, could not with any degree of safety be passed in stormy weather" (New Stat. Account, xv. 190. See for good account, Bishop R. Forbes' Journals, 1762-1770, p. 185, and Pococke's Tour in 1760, p. 164). Gwynne, Mem. 89, gives Hurry's force as 300, and the enemy's as treble his number.

[34] Dunrobin, the old castle, is said to have been built by the first Earl in 13th century. He died there in 1248. Pococke in 1760 says, it "is finely situated on the end of a hill which is cut off by a deep fossee, so that it appears on the south side, and next to the sea, like an old Celtic mount. Between it and the sea is a very good garden. The castle did consist of two square towers and a gateway. One tower only remains now to which the house is built." When Bishop Forbes passed it in 1762, he saw ladies and gentlemen walking on the top of the castle, and taking a view of his party with a telescope. A good drawing of the old house by the Duchess-Countess of Sutherland, is given in Statistical Account, xv. 34. See Pococke, 166; Bishop Forbes' Journal, 179.

[35] The demand was, probably, couched in threatening terms. But there is no good evidence that Montrose harried the country. Had he done so, Sallagh would certainly have mentioned it. Whereas he relates that after reaching Carbisdale, Montrose "directed word to the Earl of Southerland that though he spared to burne and spoyl his countrie, yet before it were long, he should make his own neighbors undoe him."

[36] The route he traversed is that of the railway from Golspie to Lairg. The details of the march are from Sallagh, 553, who notes the stages, Gartie and Helmsdaill, Kintredwell, the Ruiffs, Rein in Strathfleet, the Gruides in Brae-chat, Strathoikell and Carbisdaill. At Gruids, Mr. Black, the tenant, informs us that there are still entrenchments pointed out by tradition as Montrose's camp.

Montrose now quitted the shorter and more level coast route, and ascended the beautiful valley of Strathfleet to Rhaoine,[37] and thence on the following day, past Lairg to Gruids, where he halted for the night (April 23rd ?). Here the roads from Scourie by Assynt, and from Tongue by Loch Naver, converge, and the expectation of recruits from these districts was an additional reason for choosing the route up the Fleet. From the encampment at Gruids, two ways into Ross lay open to him—either to follow the course of the Shin down the narrow defile southwards to where the river flows into the Kyle, or marching westwards to Rosehall over the low hill between the Shin and Cassley, to cross the river Oykell by the fords above its junction with the Cassley and the tidal waters of the Kyle, and thence to follow the Kyle of Oykell to Carbester (Culrain),[38] a day's march of some sixteen miles. Local tradition still tells of a ford near Culrain, and within the memory of some yet living the Kyle here has been forded at unusually low tides, and when there was little water in the rivers. Such, however, is not likely to have been the case at this season of the year, and the catastrophe which here overtook some of the fugitives affords a presumption in favour of the longer route.[39] For this we have also the final authority of Sallagh, who states that, on the sixth day after his entry into Sutherland, Montrose marched from "the Gruides in Brae-chat" "to Strathoikell, and thence to Carbisdaill." Maps of the district erroneously mark the River Oykell east of Rosehall as far as Carbisdale. But it is clear that Sallagh did not consider Carbisdale in Strath-Oykell. In this he agrees with local usage, which still regards this name as proper only to the lower course of the river above Rosehall, where its waters are merged with the Cassley in the Kyle of Oykell.

The news of Montrose's landing must have reached Edinburgh about this time. It is inconceivable that his leading opponents should have

---

[37] "Rein in Strathfleet" (*n*. 34 above) is doubtless Rhaoine, between Golspie and Lairg.

[38] "Karbester," "Kerbester," or "Corbiesdale" are given by Balfour. His account makes Montrose quartered at "Strathekell in Rosse" till the 27th, with Strachan, &c., quartered ten miles distant, about Kincardine. Thence to Carbisdale (Culrain) is a good four miles, and from Culrain to Strath Oykell proper (Rosehall) another eight or nine. Balfour's authority cannot weigh against Sallagh's and local tradition, supported by other writers.

The form of the name given by Balfour suggests the common Scandinavian termination *bolstathr*. The *Car* probably refers to the "height," which is the main feature of the locality. The small loch is to the left of Culrain Station. It is still known as Carbisdale or Treasure Loch. The last name is due to a tradition that in passing it the fugitives (the party of 200 who were drowned ?) threw their arms, &c., into it. Several relics are said to have been found in it. Some years ago a shepherd on the hills "kicked up" a few silver spoons of the period, supposed also to be a relic of the event. They are now in the Museum of Antiquities, Edinburgh.

[39] Dr. Joass is in favour of the route down the Shin, and holds to the tradition of the ford near its mouth. But, ford or none, Sallagh's evidence and local usage of the term "Strath Oykell" are strongly against this. It must also be remembered that the winter of 1649-1650 had been severe (see p. 257), and the rivers were likely to be full in April-May.

delayed a single day in their measures to meet the danger. But it is matter for surprise that so little precaution should have been taken long before. Their attention was, however, at this time eagerly bent on the negotiations at Breda. At first their prospects there were bad. Their terms were in fact so high, that even the exclusion of their outspoken opponents, Nicolas and Hopton, from the King's counsels, in favour of Buckingham, Hamilton, and the Marquis of Newcastle, gave little hope of success.[40]

Eleven days after the discussion opened, Livingstone, one of the Commissioners, wrote as follows to Archibald Johnston, Clerk to the Assembly:—

"Much and most worthily Honored, I can say no more of our busnisse
"then as writen in our publick letter to Mr. Douglasse, which I know will
"be impairted to your Lp. Massie, Bunch and Titus are here, as some of
"the presbiterians of England, they do not inclyne that the king be urged
"with the league and Covenant, and, as I heare of some, say that any
"ordinance wis [which was] for it in England is expired and doeth not now
"binde, what to make of this I know not. It is like the king come to
"Scotland whether we aggree or not. O what a company is about him,
"the quintessence of all that were thought evill counsellors befor, and how
"other he will forsake them or they leave him I know not. Yesterday
"D. Buckingham and Marq. Newcastle came to him. looke to your selfe,
"and trust in God, I cannot promise what this treatie may bring forth.
"The Lord grant we may returne with a good . . .

My Lord

BREDA, $\frac{26 \, March}{5 \, April}$ 1650

yours in all service

JO. LIVINGSTONE.

[*Addressed*] "For the worthily Honored my lord Wareston."[41]

But though the King had set aside those who on the very first day of the treaty (March 15) had "fully and clearly advised that the King ought not to "approve or allow of the League and Covenant of any sort, either in Scotland "or in any of his other kingdoms, though he might give way to the national "Covenant in Scotland only," Nicolas, who wrote this to Ormond as late as May 2-12, adds: "the Scots terms are so unreasonable that they are not "published. The King and they cannot [he thinks] agree, unless the Com-"missioners have more power to recede than any of their Commissioners "yet had."[42]

---

[40] Carte's Ormond Papers, i. 378-380.
[41] Now first printed from the original, Advocates' Library, Wodrow MSS., fol. lxvii. 98.
[42] See App. X.

It is not our purpose to trace the progress of this treaty further than as it affected the fortunes of Montrose. The details belong to the general history of our country. Fanatics dreamed of binding three nations to such a spiritual slavery. To the astute politicians who directed their intemperate zeal, this infamous proposal could only serve as a means of establishing their own ascendancy among Scottish sects and parties. Small wonder that the terms were not published!

But to whatever cause we must attribute their apathy in preparing for Montrose's invasion, they could not be blind to the imminent danger that now threatened their position. Could he once reach the central Highlands, and intrench himself in his old fastnesses, among the victors of Kilsyth, Argyll and his handful of lords might for the fourth time spur off to the nearest boat; all but Loudon, who would again repent " with aboundance of teares."

Hastily collecting what forces he could, David Leslie hurried north to Brechin, where he had appointed the 25th of April for a rendezvous on Brechin Moor for 4000 horse and foot. Thence he pressed northwards by forced marches of thirty miles a day. Meanwhile he had transmitted orders to Colonels Strachan and Hackett, commanding the troops in Banff and Moray to do what they could to arrest the enemy's advance.

Archibald Strachan, lieutenant-colonel of a troop of horse, had already, with the same Colonels Hackett and Ker, whose troops now formed part of his force, done the Estates good service by the rout of Reay at Balvenie (May 2, 1649). His rising reputation as a dashing cavalry officer, and his known leanings to the " sectarian " opinions, made him no less an object of jealous suspicion to Leslie than a favourite with the extreme party, headed by such firebrand ministers as James Guthrie, Mungo Law, and Robert Traill. Early in May 1649 Leslie had resolved to cashier him, ostensibly as a " sectary," and was only deterred by Mungo Law, sent specially for that object by the Commission of the Kirk. Law " assurid him that he wold want the prayers of 10,000 saints and godlie of Edinbrughe, to accompeney hes armey: sua Mr. Mungo played hes bussines so handsomly, that he persuadit the L. G. [*Lt.-General*] that it was better for him to tollerat one sectarey (and a villane) quhom he called a godly and religious sant, then by degrading of him, disapoynt Cromwell of his intelligence, and himselue of the shoe sants [*cobblers*] of Edinbrughes prayers."[43] Balfour's suspicion, here expressed, was only too fully confirmed by events after Dunbar. But it was not till January 12, 1651, that " Collonell Archbald Straquhan was excommunicat and deliuered " to the deiuell, in the churche of Perth, by Mr. Alexander Rollocke."

In the light of subsequent events it is with peculiar interest that we read

---

[43] Balf. iii. 413, 414, and *ibid*. iv. 240, for what follows. See also Baillie, iii. 107, 111-113, &c.

the following letter to James Guthrie, his fellow "saint" and partner in treason, shortly before the events now to be described. It is written in a cramped illegible hand, more used perhaps to wield sword than pen, but glib enough in the nauseous crafty pietism, which shows who were his models, and foreshadowed his treachery. Of James Guthrie, minister of Lauder, let it suffice to quote Balfour's character of him: "a man once totally episcopall, bot now a pryme rayller, a grate fauerer of conuentickells [a crime *then* among Presbyterians!], priuey meittings and sectaries."[44] The reader will find abundant evidence to the same effect in the pages of Balfour and Baillie.

"RICHT REVEREND                               "INVERNESS 3 *Jani* [?] 1650.

"I am w$^t$ much unwillingnes now constrained to present this broken and
"rud lyne craving y$^r$ pardone for my former unkyndnes and ungratfulness
". . . I dar boldly say Sr, so it did not apear in paper it was in affectione
"in some measure knowing you will fairly . . . send [? *illeg.*] and hold me
"excused I need not make anie . . . [*longer?*] apologie then my weaknes to
"plead for me, . . . one [?] short thing I desyre may be taken notice of by
"you in the small returnes ar made by those in authoritie in the land unto the
"Lord for his matchless kyndnes and speciall [?] delyverance, wh. are not
"only meanly acknowledged and not laboured by us to walk in the power of
"his grace worthie it, . . . hale nation [?] to that called by him . . . we in
"his dispensations, badly answered his Matestie [*God*] by continewing
"wicked malignant instruments in his work, wh. obscureth the glorie and
"grace y$^r$of with ye simple and ignorant This [?] undewly greiveth his
"matestie, to behold not only in ye state very contrair returnes from those
"that will not rightly know him, but ye deadnes of those that professeth his
"name may justly be much complained of. Ther is ground of rendering great
"thanksgiving and praises to be assigned to ye most high for what he hath
"inabled you of y$^r$ calling to doe, in purging that . . . [*way?*] you have
"gone, but certainly much we yet advice especially in state and armies [?]
"I canot but acquent you w$^t$ ye lait act Assmie [*Act of the Assembly?*]
"for maner of quarterings which holdeth out and layeth ane oppressing
"burden on the comonaltie who are in manie places neir alreadie . . .
"[*crushed?*], but also injoyneth ye souldiers to live on such mentinance as
"canot be subsisted w$^t$ [*with*], the not being by you . . . sed [*caused?*] will
"neither clear the thing unto you, and show the [*ju*]stness y$^r$of, four con-

---

[44] Guthrie had held a professorship at St. Andrews, became minister of Lauder in 1638, and of Stirling in 1649. He was a leading Protester in 1650, author and presenter of the Western Remonstrance, and writer of "The Causes of Gods Wrath." For convocating the King's lieges to disturb the peace, &c., he was hanged at Edinburgh, June 1, 1661. See Life, by Committee of Assembly, 1847; also Naphtali, 66, and Baillie, Index.

"siderable things you wold be pleased to take notice of for pressing a
"r[e]d[uce]ment [?] of the [army?], first the unsupportable burdens the
"kingdom lyeth under, especially the comonaltie, 2$^{dly}$ ye gross prophanes
"and malignancie of the armie, 3$^{ly}$ unreconcilable differences amongst the
"forces who can not joyne togither against another comon enemie, being as
"much in [strife?] aganst one another as anie other enemie whatsomever,
"and last w'out additio[n of] pay to the souldiers they canot subsist on what
"is for present apoynted they live honestly [illeg., but the sense seems to be,
"so poorly paid that they cannot live honestly"], you will probably goe neir to
"loss manie if not most pairt of honest men out of the service if present
"course be not taken for preventing ye falling out of apearant inconveniences
"it is of great concernment y$^r$for requyreth much diligence and hotly a
"remedie to be sought for. I know not if orders have bein given in these
"places for ordering the rest of the levies to be in redines but we hearde of
"such order heir, And also ar secretly informed that a pressing order is to
"follow for putting the same in execution, such fears of James Grame needeth
"not, And I know not what other call you have for such doing, such desingne
"must be stoped for certanly what other [?] groanings aryseth from what
"place soever . . . ar or may be raised ar to be made use of The Lord
"hath shown what he can doe by a few [e.g., at Balvenie], undoutedly much
"more he will yet doe for himself by us. If aright we trust In him y$^r$for
"may . . . [heed?] not be given to such unlawfull courses . . . I in the
"Lords most holy name intreate you to awake and rwise [rouse] upe all ye
"Lord his freinds to be stout hairted and open [?] and rebuke evill doers be
"they of what qualitie so ever, least by neglect and more slouthfulnes our
"burden be mad more then it is, The lord is strong and mightie and as he
"hath done will doe valiantly by weak means and in small apearances So
"[Sir?] assure y$^r$ self in ye lord his strenth wh. . I know he will grant, If
"James Grhame land neir this quarters he will suddenly be de . . . ed
"[defeated?] And ther shalbe no need of the levy of knavis to the work tho
"they should be willing.
"I am yrs
"ARCHD. STRAHAN."

[Addressed] "The Richt Reverend
Mr. James Guthrie
Minister of Lather" [i.e., Lauder].[45]

---

[45] Original, now first printed (?), Advocates' Libr., Wodrow MSS., fol. lxvii. 97. In the Index (Wodrow's hand) the date (now torn) is given "3 June;" but the contents show that it must have been written before news of Montrose in Caithness. Inverness contains no record of Strachan's presence there in 1650. Had he started with Leslie from Edinburgh to reach Brechin by April 25th, and been sent on thence, as some accounts seem to imply, he could not possibly have been at Kincardine or Tain on the 27th.

This letter throws a strong light on the difficulties with which Argyll and his leading subordinates had to contend. It confirms in a measure the report of Nicolas as to the spread of *malignancy* in Leslie's forces,[46] and this alone may suffice to explain the want of preparation to oppose Montrose.

Unhappily chance gave Strachan his opportunity to show how little need there was for Leslie and his "levy of knavis to the work."

Hearing of Montrose's progress, he advanced with his own troop and Colonel Ker's,[47] then stationed at Brahan and Chanonry, to Tain, where he was joined by Colonel Montgomery's troop, Lieut.-Col. Robert Hackett with his troop, and the "Irish troop" under Captain Cullace. These five troops numbered only some 220 sabres,[48] but they were experienced troopers, well-officered, and animated by the same spirit that made of Cromwell's Ironsides the most terrible soldiers in Europe. They had also some thirty-six musketeers of Lawer's regiment,[49] under Quartermaster Shaw, which happened to be stationed in the neighbourhood; and in addition were supported by a levy of about 400 of the Monroes and Rosses living in the district, commanded by Colonel John Monro, laird of Lemlair, his son, Captain Andrew, and David Ross, laird of Balnagowan.[50] These 400 were, however, only to be

---

[46] In Ormond Papers, i. 345 ff.

[47] When Pluscardine seized Inverness, Feb. 22, 1649, Leslie, who had been sent to suppress the rising, heard at Chanonry that Ogilvy and Middleton had roused the Athole men. He hastened south, leaving Col. Gilbert Ker, and Lieut.-Cols. Robert Hackett and Archibald Strachan, with troops in Moray to "attend" Pluscardine, should they make towards Moray. In his absence Pluscardine retook Chanonry, and was joined by his nephew, the new Lord Reay, with 300 men. Leslie, turning north again, surprised Ogilvy and Middleton, who fled to Pluscardine. The Royalists (if one may call them so) advanced south to Badenoch, and were joined by Huntly (Lewis Gordon). Sutherland, who had accompanied Leslie, went north to convene the counties of Sutherland, Caithness, and Ross, with five troops under these same three colonels, who on May 8th surprised and took Reay at Balvenie, with some 900 foot, Clan Kenzie, Strathnaver, and Badenoch men. Col. Ker returned to Ross, took and demolished Reid Castle, put a garrison in Seaforth's house of Brahan, and afterwards returned to Leslie in the Mearns, and thence to Edinburgh. Neither he nor Montgomery was present at Carbisdale.

[48] Balf. iv. 9.

[49] The regiment held Inverness for the rebels in Sept. 1644. The laird of Lawers in 1650 was a minor. His father, Sir Mungo Campbell, led the van at Auldearn, where he was slain. The regiment, according to Sallagh, 525, thrice repulsed Macdonald and his Irish.

[50] On Dec. 20, 1650, Pluscardine, Balnagowan, the Master of Lovat, and Lemlair were chosen by Parliament at Perth as colonels of foot for the Inverness and Ross levies (Balf.). For references to the Balnagowan family, see "Cronicles of the Earls of Ross," with continuation from Balnagowan papers. For Lemlair's connection with Neil Macleod of Assynt, see App., No. xiii. "He was nicknamed, and is still spoken of by the country-people as, *Ian Dhu na Cioch*, 'Black John of the Breast,' in consequence of having been accessory to a barbarous mutilation of some women." MS. account of the Parish of Assynt, by the late Geo. Taylor, County-Clerk of Sutherland, written in 1832 (Dunrobin Charter-Room), kindly lent to the Editors, with the Duke's permission, by Dr. Joass. The picturesque account in it of Montrose's flight is quoted, with a few variations, in Lord Mahon's essay on Montrose. *Quar. Rev.* 157, Dec. 1846 (reprinted Essays, 1849). Mr. Taylor's narrative is too highly coloured and circumstantial for genuine tradition, and omits all mention of its sources,

relied on in case of success. Not a year had elapsed since both Lemlair and Balnagowan had been out with Pluscardine, and the circumstance lends colour to Monteith's assertion that at Glenmuick (a mistake for Carbisdale) Montrose "awaited a regiment of 400 men which he had ordered," that he advanced in the expectation of meeting these, and that he had "sent Hurry " to Balnagowan, who had espoused the cause."[50] It is at least a remarkable circumstance that in this account the number 400 agrees exactly with Sallagh's estimate of the local levy. The statement of the latter writer that Balnagowan and Lemlair were present, with the Earl of Sutherland, at the council of war held at Tain, in which it was decided to advance westwards and reconnoitre the enemy's position, is not inconsistent with the natural hope of their support entertained by Montrose. Sallagh indeed states that " the enemie, who was then at Carbisdell, was espyed and found out by " the diligence of Collonel John Monro of Leamlare, and his son Captain " Andrew Monro, who incoraged the troops to goe on, and promised to be " their leaders [*guides*], which they performed faithfullie and valiantly." Is there in this commendation an unconscious vein of surprise that men of fickle loyalty should have proved faithful to any side ? At least it is singular that in the report of the action published in Edinburgh, and probably received from Strachan, their names are entirely omitted, though we hear of Captains William and John Ross, "who came upe to the executione with 80 footte, " chosen out of the countrey forces, and did good service." After the rout these claimed and received their share of rewards.[51] Of any reward to the Munroes we find no mention, either in Balfour or the Acts of Parliament. The accounts and traditions of the battle do, in fact, tend to strengthen the suspicion that they played a waiting, treacherous part.

At the council of war in Tain it was decided that the Earl of Sutherland should return to the north side of the Kyle, to "oppose Harrie Graham

---

Where the accuracy of his details can be tested, we suspect that they were derived from *book-knowledge*, not always borne out by contemporary evidence.

[50] *Hist. des Troubles de la G. Bretagne*, par Messire Robert Mentet de Salmonet (Paris, 1661, p. 358; Eng. Tr., Ed. 2, London, 1738, p. 511). Monteith was a Scot, a Catholic priest, resident in France. His account of Montrose agrees entirely with Wishart, Part I. ; but in his narrative of 1649-1650 he is an *independent authority*, evidently unacquainted with the Montr. Rediviv. The details of the battle may have been derived from survivors, possibly from members of Pitfoddels' family, who were Catholics living in France. See p. 309 *n.* 63. On the other hand Heath, for these events, is not an independent witness ; he has transcribed bodily from the Montr. Rediviv. He makes a notable correction of a singular phrase in the Rediviv. (175), speaking of Montrose's forces : " After this poor rabble of silly creatures was *amaz'd*," for which he substitutes *amassed*. Chronicle (Ed. 2, 1676), 261.

[51] Balf. iv. 10, 37, 47. They were paid as usual, out of the "fynnes," a sure method of breeding espionage, treachery, and feuds. On the other hand, Sallagh is silent on their prowess and rewards, a silence which can scarcely be attributed to ignorance, since he mentions the rewards to Strachan and Hackett, though not local men. He also omits the thirty-six musketeers.

"with the Caithness and Strathnaver men, and to preserve his own country "from them, whose chief aim was to burn the country of Sutherland, having "command from James Graham so to do."[52] The Earl had ever shown little taste for war, and still less aptitude in his feeble defence of the Ord; and now that Montrose was in Ross, it is not improbable that he made some such excuse for again putting the Kyle between himself and the General who had so severely handled the Sutherland levies at Auldearn—where the Earl was in the reserve.

On Saturday, April 27th,[53] Strachan and Hackett marched from Tain to Wester Fearn, opposite the Dun of Criech. Above this the estuary opens into a broad lake-like expanse, contracted again by the flat alluvial beds at the Carron mouth. Beyond the Carron the ground rises into an open heathy slope, skirting the dale. Curving northward, the low range of hills sends off a spur terminating in the cold bleak heights of Craigcaoinichean. Two miles above the Carron the road passes Culrain burn, which flows to the Kyle through a deep channeled bed, fringed with broom and scrub. With the hills to the north, and the river-like estuary, the little burn encloses a triangle of level ground, admirably fitted for cavalry. Near the northern angle of this a dreary little tarn, known as Carbisdale loch, lies at the bottom of a cup-shaped depression. Beyond this the valley narrows into a pass, overhung by Craigcaoinichean.

At this point Montrose had pitched his camp, and for some days awaited news of the expected recruits from north and south. To the rear and right he was secured by the hills. His left flank rested on the Kyle. Here he guarded the pass against an advance in front by a deep intrenchment and breast-work, still clearly visible on a bluff facing south-east, towards the open ground.

In a position of such strength a few resolute men might have defied a stronger party than Strachan's. Montrose, however, in this last crisis of his career, again felt the fatal want of horse. His entire cavalry numbered only about forty, probably most, if not all, gentlemen volunteers, commanded

---

[52] Sallagh.

[53] Corresponding to May 7th of our season. Balfour gives about 230 as Strachan's numbers, in detail. They attacked in three parties, as in the text. Sallagh makes the first attack 200 men under Strachan. We follow Balfour's version as probably derived from Strachan's report. There is no real discrepancy. The second party appears to have followed hard on the first. "After prayers, said by the minister they marched about 3 a clock in the afternoone towardes the enimey, quho wer drawn vpe in a place neire a hill of Scrogie [*scraggy, rough*] Wood, to wiche, vpone the aduance of our horsses, they quickly reteired." Balf. iv. 9. In the Council it had been debated "wither to marche towardes them presently [*at once*], or to delay wntill Monday, and so declyne the hazard of ingageing vpone the Lordes day" (*ibid.*). There is a Sabbatic strain of Strachan in this, which must have pleased the "10,000 shoe-saints of Edinburgh" (*v.* p. 301). This time the minister is in evidence at a victory. Strachan and his ghostly counsellors fared worse at Dunbar.

## BATTLE OF CARBISDALE, April 27, 1650.

*(From the Ordnance one-inch Map.)*

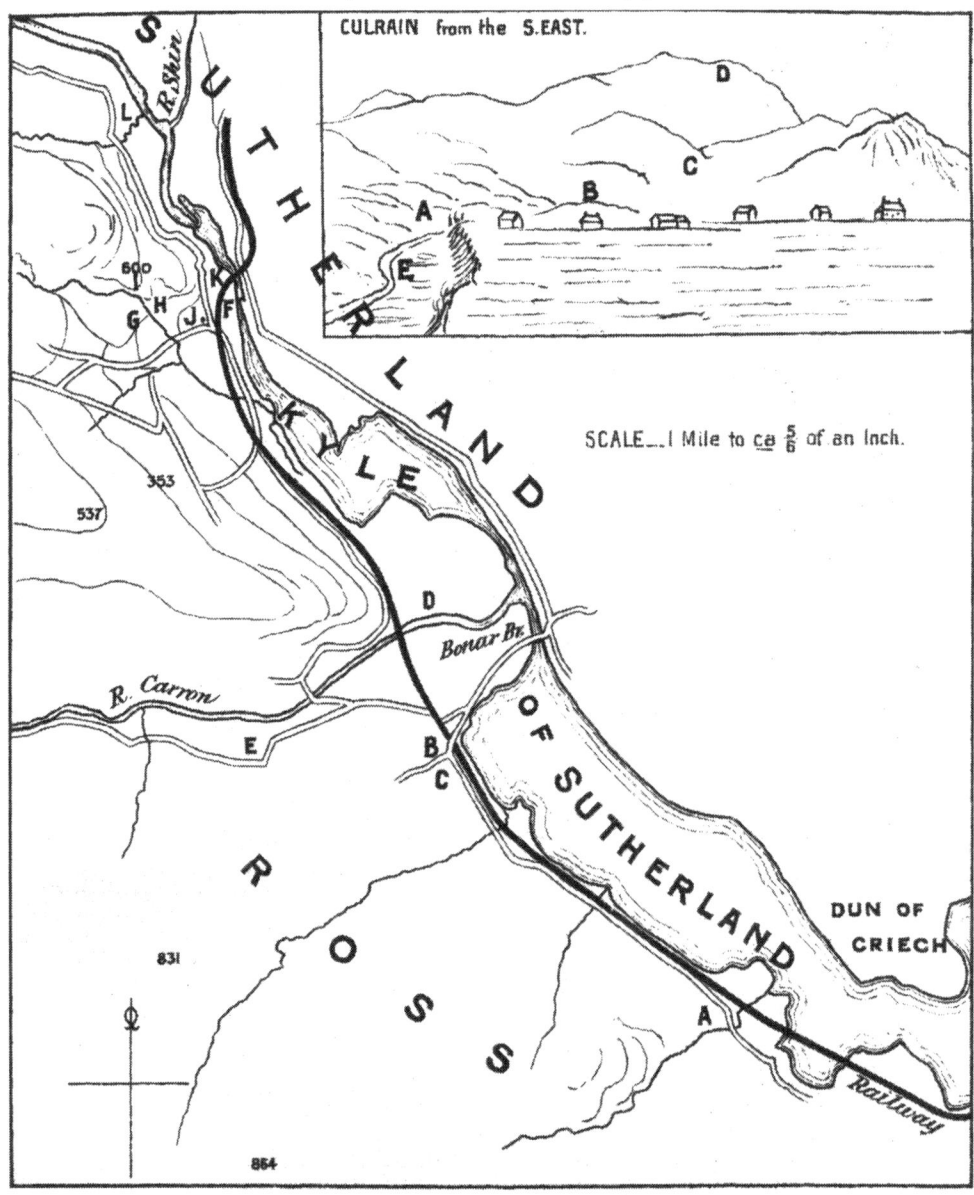

#### EXPLANATION OF THE LETTERS.

A Wester Fearn, near which Strachan hid four troops in the broom.
B Bonar Bridge Station; Ardgay Hotel; near it
C Remains of a small oblong encampment, 41 paces by 27, said to have been occupied by Strachan (?)
D Invercarron. Fords just above and below the road bridge.
E Road to the upper fords of the Carron, by which Leamlair led the ambush party (?)
F Remains of entrenchments on a bluff facing east; said to have been Montrose's Camp.' There are also entrenchments on the opposite bank of the river.
G The main battle. Broken heathy slope: "ill riding ground."
H The "scroggie wood," scattered birches on a broken slope.
I Craigcaoinichean (Craig a caoineadh?)
J Carbisdale Loch or Treasure Loch, in which arms of the fugitives are said to have been found.
K The point where 200 fugitives were drowned.
L Seven skeletons of young men found here some years ago.

The figures indicate the height.

#### CULRAIN FROM THE SOUTH-EAST.

A Main battle.
B The "scroggie wood."
C Flight. Cairns. The whole of these hills were planted with fir some 15 years ago.
D Craigcaoinichean or "Lamentation Hill."
E Culrain burn.

by Major Lisle.[54] The rest of his little army was composed of about 450 Germans and Danes, and some 700 recruits from Orkney, in all hardly more than 1200 men. But the islanders were a raw levy, undisciplined and ignorant of war. Most of them, perhaps all, had never seen a troop of dragoons, and under any circumstances could not be trusted to face a charge.

About three in the afternoon Strachan advanced as far as Wester Fearn,[55] where he concealed his force in the tall broom which covered these slopes, and was then just breaking into golden blossom. The Monroes and Rosses ascended the Carron, which they forded, and under cover of the hills which flank the valley of Carbisdale, awaited the issue.[56] Presently, Captain Andrew Monro returned with intelligence that Montrose's horse had been sent out to ascertain Strachan's position. His advice was to deceive the enemy by exposing only a single troop to view.

The appearance of this troop was reported by Lisle to Montrose,[57] and confirmed the reports brought in by Robert Monro of Achnes, who with his three sons had joined the Royalists, and, being recommended by his knowledge of the country, was employed as Montrose's chief scout-master. Robert Monro assured him that there was but a single troop of horse in all Ross.[58] Montrose quitted his position, and, ordering Lisle to halt, advanced to reconnoitre. The van was commanded by Hurry.

Suddenly Strachan, at the head of a hundred troopers, dashed out of ambush, and riding down the little party of horse, hurled the survivors back upon the panic-stricken foot, and threw the whole into confusion. The immediate appearance of a second troop of eighty dragoons under Hackett, closely followed by Captain Hutchison, with the reserve of horse and

---

[54] Monteith, 511 (Eng. Tr.), says, Montrose "ordered Major Lille, with a detachment of Musketters to march through a wood, where he might find *the Gentry of the Shire.*" This seems evidence for our suspicion that Montrose was lured out of his position by a treacherous hope, perhaps a promise, that they would join him. Beyond doubt they hung back from helping Strachan at the first; and unless he purposely omitted them in his report, in order to enhance his own achievement, only a small party of them gave him effective aid at the "Scrogie Wood." As to Lisle's musketeers, we have followed Sallagh, who makes the reconnaissance one of horse.

[55] Sallagh.

[56] The flank movement of the Monroes and Rosses is a tradition, communicated by Dr. Joass, who had it from the late Mr. Sidney Hadwen of Balblair, who had it from his old gamekeeper, "Duncan Rae, a great historian of local affairs, who died several years ago. Mr. Hadwen had an unusually retentive memory." Note from Mr. D. Cameron. The incident rests on no written contemporary evidence, but is quite consistent with the conduct of their leaders and narratives of the battle. It explains their absence and Montrose's hope. Balblair lies opposite to Culrain on the Sutherland side. Here there are said to be traces of intrenchments facing Montrose's. The Earl may have established a post of observation at this point; but we do not think that the intrenchments were connected with these events. Sallagh would certainly have mentioned the circumstance.

[57] Monteith, *loc. cit.* [58] Sallagh.

Lawers' musketeers, confirmed the rout. The Royalists fled without resistance. Only the foreigners maintained any show of order, and, retreating along the slopes, made for the wood. In the whirl of attack, Menzies of Pitfoddels, who bore the grim "royal standart," and Major Guthrie fell dead at Montrose's side; and probably the same moment was fatal to Douglas, Gordon, Powrie, Lisle, and other officers. The Orkney men, flinging aside every encumbrance, streamed past the camp in helpless flight.[59] Two hundred in one company perished in an attempt to cross the Kyle. A few gained a boat, hotly pursued by a trooper, who was drowned, the only loss sustained by the victors.

The rest of Montrose's men fell back on a "scroggie wood" of indigenous birch, which still skirts the base of the Craig. But, in spite of "ill-riding ground" on the broken heath, Strachan pursued them into the wood. He was received with a feeble random volley, which did no execution. Two troopers were wounded. One bullet, better aimed, struck him "vpon his " belley, bot lighting vpone the double of his belte and buffe coate, did not " pierce."[60] At this moment he was joined by the Monroes and Rosses, eager to show their zeal and share the plunder. Though the Royalists had abandoned all resistance, they were ruthlessly slaughtered in the wood and the hollow that passes over the hill.[61] For two hours the troops continued killing them. Scarce one hundred escaped. More than 450,[62] including ten chief officers, were slain on the field or in the flight. Hurry, severely wounded, was taken prisoner, with Colonels Gray, Stewart, and Hay, 58 other officers, 386 common soldiers, and two Orkney ministers. Montrose had his horse shot under him, and was covered with wounds. Seeing his peril, the gallant young Frendraught, himself wounded in two places, " did " an action worthy of remembrance, for he gave him his horse, and sur- " rendered himself prisoner, well-knowing that if that nobleman should get " off, the face of affairs would soon be changed."[63] As for himself he could

---

[59] Their conduct is inferred from the fact that it was the foreigners who gained the "Scroggie wood." Probably the latter kept together on the slopes, and it seems likely that the 200 drowned were islanders. Tradition marks the spot just above Culrain railway bridge (map, K). A mile beyond, and just above the junction of the River Shin, seven skeletons were found in a peaty hollow which the tenant was trenching. Dr. Joass saw the remains, and found them to be bones of *young* men, who were probably overtaken here on marshy ground (map, L).

[60] Balfour.

[61] Marked by cairns (map, H), which Mr. Cameron remembers seeing there twenty years ago. We searched in vain for them in the dense young fir with which these hills have since been covered.

[62] Inferred from the number of prisoners and those who escaped. Balfour. Sallagh says, "about 400" killed, which agrees sufficiently. For list of killed and taken, see App., No. I.

[63] Monteith, *loc. cit.* Sallagh, even if he knew it, may have thought it discretion to suppress the fact. Frendraught would observe his own counsel in seeking his uncle's protection. He was sent to Dunrobin "to be cured of his wounds." On May 23rd the Estates peremptorily ordered him and other prisoners to be sent to Edinburgh, "and if suche as hes them in custodey

count with some confidence on the powerful protection of his uncle, the Earl of Sutherland.

"This miraculous victorie hapned the twentie-seaventh of April one
"thousand six hundreth and fiftie yeares, at fyve o'clock in the afternoon,
"at Craigchoynechan, besides Carbisdell. In the verie field the victors
"gave thanks to God for their happie successe, and so returned with their
"prisoners to Tayn, where they kept them, untill the lievetenant-general
"came, who gave order for conveying them south to Edinburgh to the
"estates. He directed also the kings standart south, with all James
"Grahams papers, which were found among the baggage. The countrie-
"men of Rosse and Southerland continued the killing of such as escaped
"from the battle many dayes thereafter." [64]

---

letts them escape, the keepers to be anssuerable one ther perrill for them." Balf. iv. 23. The mothers of Frendraught and Menzies of Pitfoddels were both sisters of the Earl of Sutherland. From Sallagh we learn that Gilbert Menzies of Pitfoddels, the father of Montrose's standard-bearer, was knighted in 1639 by Charles I. at Berwick. At the beginning of the civil broils he retired to France. About July 1649, Lady Pitfoddels (Lady Ann Gordon), who was a Roman Catholic, was drowned off the coast of Holland on her way to visit her daughters, then being bred in France (*ibid.* 542). Possibly Monteith owed his information of these events to members of this family.

A report was spread that Frendraught, after Montrose's defeat, "for vexation starved himself." This news *reached London, May 25th.* Whitelock's Memorials, *ap.* Napier, Mem., 746, *n.* This rumour must have been circulated (*designedly ?*) soon after the battle. But Parliament knew better than Whitelock's informant, as the above entry *sub May 23rd* shows. The *Mercurius Caledonius*, for Jan. 25, 1661, mentions him as taking "his place in the House," and adds, "This is the Lord, who upon that fatal day when the Marquis of Montrose was defeated, and hearing that his Excellency was dismounted, came instantly and found him out, and put a constraint upon the Lord Montrose, much against his will, to make use of his horse: For, as he rightly urged, the preservation of his person was keeping life in the Cause: which without doubt it would have done, if unfortunately he had not been betrayed three days after. But the result of this brave action of the Viscount's, was the occasion of eight or nine dangerous wounds he received for his gallantry." Frendraught was present at Montrose's "True Funerals," in 1661. Napier, Mem., 841.

[64] Sallagh, 555. His mention of "Craigchoynechan" shows that the name is older than Montrose's times. "Lamentation Hill," which appears on maps, is an Ordnance misnomer, due to the likeness to *Caoinead*, "weeping," and suggested perhaps by the tradition of the battle. *Craigcaoinichean* means "mossy crag," and is descriptive. Note from Dr. Joass.

## CHAPTER IX.

### MONTROSE'S FLIGHT, CAPTURE, AND JOURNEY SOUTH.

MOUNTED on Frendraught's horse, Montrose galloped from the disastrous field and swam the Kyle of Oykell.[1] He was attended by the Earl of Kinnoul,[2] Major Sir Edward Sinclair,[3] an Orkneyman, Sinclair of Brims[4] in Caithness, and four or five others, whose names have not been preserved, and who soon separated from the other fugitives.[5] Possibly among them were Monro of Achnes and his three sons, who all escaped death or capture, and do not appear in the Parliamentary records of proceedings against Montrose's followers. But as the passage of seven or eight men through those thinly peopled regions could hardly fail to excite attention, they prudently resolved to disperse. Tradition declared that Montrose's unnamed comrades made for Kintail; and if so, they must have left him about Oykell Bridge, whence, by following Glen Einig, they could reach Ullapool, or turn south-east up Strath Cullenach and Glen More in the central highlands of Ross. For greater safety, Montrose, who had early abandoned his horse, disguised himself in the costume of a shepherd highlander. His coat, with the star or George so lately sent him by the King, and sword-belt, were afterwards found in the field.[6] The object of

---

[1] The account of Montrose's flight and capture is drawn from Sallagh, Balfour, Montr. Rediviv. and Monteith, &c. The traditions have been recorded by Mr. Taylor (Dunrobin MS.), but we have not thought it safe always to follow his picturesque narrative. The "pedie," mentioned in note 6 below, was perhaps one of the party.

[2] The Earl of Kinnoul, who had followed his brother to Orkney and succeeded to the title by right on his death, is unrecorded. His next brother, William, became fifth earl. See p. 63, note 1.

[3] There were two Edward Sinclairs of Orkney, Edward of Gyre and Edward of Ness. Their names occur together in the lists of Orkney Committees, but neither is Sir Edward.

[4] John of Brims was made Commissioner of Excise, and in other ways rewarded, in 1661.

[5] Mr. Taylor, Dunrobin MS.

[6] Balf. iv. 10. *Ibid.* 34, May 30th. A letter read in the House from Colonel Gilbert Ker, showing that he had taken a " pirat [a ship from Orkney ?] ladin with wyne and prouisione, for James Grhame in Rosse . . . also, that he had sent them a grate maney of James Grhames papers and letters wich were found in a wood neir the place of the fight, hid wnder a tree and discouered [*i.e.*, disclosed] by a pedie [servant] of James Grhames for his lyffe."

Tradition points to a hollow under a ledge in the steep northern face of Craigcaoinichean as "Montrose's cave," where he hid after the battle. But the spot is scarcely accessible for a horse, too open and near the field, and a mere *cul-de-sac*. Monteith says he swam the river. Balfour's evidence that his "coate and star wer found in the feild" is too vague to guide us.

the four fugitives, as soon as they could elude pursuit, must have been to reach Strathnaver and the Reay country, where they would be among friends, and might hope to fall in with Harry Graham, or ship to Orkney. So "they wandered up that river the whole ensuing night, and the next "day [April 28th] and the third day also [29th] without any food or sus- "tenance, and at last came within the country of Assint.[7] The Earl of "Kinnowl being faint for lack of meat," [perhaps, too, like Montrose, "covered with wounds"],—"and not able to travel any farther, was left "there among the mountaines, where it was supposed he perished."[8] Not a trace has since been discovered to mark the spot where this unfortunate young nobleman breathed his last. As the party, after wandering for two days and nights without food or shelter, were still scarcely thirty miles from the battle-field, they must either have lost their way in those desolate wilds, or been compelled to lurk for a great part of the time in the neighbouring mountains. That Montrose and his two companions, if they still remained with him, deliberately abandoned Kinnoul to his fate is more than we can believe. Spent and famished as they were, it seems more reasonable to suppose either that death had already intervened before they quitted him, or that they separated in search of food and assistance. Montrose was now alone, and would have shared his comrade's fate, "but that he fortuned "in this miserie to light vpon a smal cottage in that wildernesse, where "he was supplied with some milk and bread."[9] The traditional spot was "a small hut occasionally occupied for dairy purposes by one of the "laird of Assynt's tenants, at a grazing farm known by the name of "Glaschyle."[10]

"Immediately after the battle Captain Andrew Monro wrote to his "brother-in-law, Neil Macleod, Laird of Assynt desiring him earnestly "to apprehend any that should come in his country and chiefly James "Graham."[11] The discovery of Montrose's horse may have given a clue to the direction taken by the fugitives. It was a golden opportunity. The

---

[7] The present road up the Oykell to Assynt was made in 1823. From Tain to Culrain is eighteen miles; thence to Inveran across the Kyle two miles; thence to Inchnadamff, at the head of Loch Assynt, thirty-two and a half miles, with Ardvreck Castle about two miles further.

The ruins near Inchnadamff are those of Edderchalda House, built in 1660 by Kenneth, Earl of Seaforth, and destroyed by fire about 100 years later.

[8] Sallagh.

[9] Ibid.

[10] Mr. Taylor, Dunrobin MS. The name is common in the north, variously explained as "Grey-wood" or "Grey-pass," the former highly descriptive of the stunted lichened oaks and birches of the country, the latter peculiarly appropriate to the narrow defile, which clambers between limestone rocks and white marble quartz to the crest commanding the Loanan valley and descent to Assynt. It seems likely that the Glaschyle here mentioned was near the Cnoc na [hill of] Glas Chaoille to the left of the road, some four miles S.E. of Ledmore.

[11] Sallagh.

reward was high; and the Captain's "earnestness" might induce Neil to repair the damaged credit of his wife's kin.

Neil Macleod [12] was at this time in his twenty-second year. Descended from the Lords of Lewis, his ancestors had invaded Assynt in the fifteenth century, and established a firm hold on the district. The history of the race is distinguished, even in Highland annals, by its dark record of family feud and strife with jealous neighbours. Owing to discord in the family, the overlordship of the district passed, at the close of the sixteenth century, to Colin Mackenzie of Kintail, through whom George, Earl of Seaforth, in 1633, inherited the lands and barony. In 1646, Neil Macleod had attended his superior, Seaforth, as his "friend," at Brahan, when Seaforth joined Montrose at the siege of Inverness. Seaforth had then in his following "100 of Assints men;" and as Neil, though till 1649 still under his uncle Hugh's guardianship, was then eighteen years of age, the circumstance, admitted in Neil's own account of his troubles, lends strong presumptive evidence to the assertion of three independent Royalist writers, that Neil had himself served under Montrose's standard. It is, in fact, explicitly asserted that Montrose knew him, expected his protection, and voluntarily discovered himself to him, and that Neil was his "pretended old friend;" and, unless recent events had taught Montrose to doubt the loyalty of Lemlair, Neil's marriage to Lemlair's daughter, if he knew of it, could only serve to strengthen his hope of safety. Neil's miserable plea of an *alibi*, when called in question for the deed, will not for one moment stand against the authorities collected in our Appendix. We have, therefore, no hesitation in accepting his friend Sallagh's account, written within a few months of the event, that, on receiving his brother-in-law's letter, "the Laird of Assint was not "negligent but sent parties everywhere. Some of them met James Graham "accompanied only with one Maior Sinclare, an Orknay man. The partie "apprehends them both, and brings them to Ardwreck (the Laird of Assint "his chief residence)." Here tradition, as recorded by Mr. Taylor, confirms the Royalist writers. Shortly after leaving the sheiling where he had obtained food, Montrose was overtaken by one of Assynt's servants, accompanied, it is said, by the occupant of the hut, who inquired his purpose in those wilds, and on being told that he wished to reach the Reay country but had lost his way, they undertook to guide him. The spot where this occurred was near the head of the hill where the road, from an altitude of some 500 feet, looks northwards over wild moorland, towards the lofty

---

[12] Neil Macleod. See App. xiii. for full evidence on his conduct and its consequences to himself. The remarks on his family history are based on Mr. Taylor's MS., and notices *passim* in Hist. Earls Sutherland. See also Mackenzie's Hist. Macleods, and the 1738 account of Neil's troubles, Trans. Gael. Socy. of Inverness, xvi. 197 ff. The reward of £25,000 Scots was not the old reward offered in 1644 (p. 64, *n.* 6). Gwynne's evidence suggests that the reward was proclaimed after the battle. Did Neil hesitate till he heard of it?

peaks of Suilven, Canisp, and Coulinor. About nine miles further, passing Inchnadamff, at the head of Loch Assynt, they reached Macleod's residence.

Ardvreck Castle stands on a small peninsula on the far side of the loch, which rises slightly as it recedes from the shore. The blocks of masonry which now strew the ground still attest the strength of the original keep. "In size and accommodation this edifice was remarkably small, having only "two vaulted cellars with a narrow passage below, and two storeys above "them; while the length of the outside wall was only about 32 feet, and "the breadth 27. There is a circular tower at the south-east angle, and "some of the corner stones have been chisel-dressed, a rare ornament in "similar old buildings in the Highlands."[13]

Thither Montrose was conducted by his guides or captors, and tradition declares that he was received at the door by the laird's wife. It has been urged in extenuation of her husband's conduct to their illustrious captive, that this unhappy woman was mainly to blame for it. But for this tradition we have seen no evidence. We are not informed how they recognised Montrose. Either he had already confided himself to those who led him thither, or Macleod, "his pretended old friend,"[14] knew him in spite of his disguise and famine-wasted, fevered face, or Montrose now "willingly dis-"cover'd himself."[15] Major Sinclair of Orkney, who, according to another account, had left Montrose, was also discovered and brought in by Neil's search-parties. The two prisoners, for such they must soon have found themselves to be, are said to have been confined in one of the cellars beneath the castle.

Montrose appears to have reached Assynt on or before April 30th.[16] Entreaties and bribes were not wanting to shake his gaoler's wavering purpose; but fear of present punishment, and sordid visions of the price set upon that golden head, outweighed all that Montrose could plead or offer

---

[13] Mr. Taylor's MS., Dunrobin Charter-room.      [14] Gwynne.

[15] Montr. Rediv. 178, 179. "The Lord of Aston . . . happened on him. He had been one of his followers before. . . . The Marquesse knowing him, and believing to find friendship at his hands willingly discover'd himself. . . . 'Tis said he profered great summes for his libertie, which being in vain, he desir'd to dye by the hands of those who took him, rather than be made an object of miserie and shame (as he knew very well he should) by his enraged enemies."

[16] The dates which follow are conjectured to suit the distance to Tain, and order of events subsequently. The one certain date in Fraser's account (Wardlaw MS.) is the halt at Keith on Sunday 12th, which agrees well with his "May 4th, taken . . . and four days later delivered to Lesley at Tain" (8th), if by "taken" we understand delivered to Holburn. The following dates seem more or less probable; the distances are approximate:—April 30th (?), Montrose reaches Ardvreck. May 2nd (?), messenger to Leslie at Tain, 54 m., arrives that night. 3rd, Holburn sets out; halts at Rosehall (?). 4th, arrives at Ardvreck. Sunday, 5th, return march by Inveran, to Skibo, 54 m., on 6th. 7th, rest at Skibo. 8th, to Tain, 4 m.; Montrose delivered to Lesley; thence by Dingwall to Brahan, 27 m. 9th, by Conan Bridge, Beauly, Lovat, Muirtown, Inverness (15½ m.), to Castle Stewart, 21 m. 10th, by Nairn (10 m.), Forres (10 m.), to Elgin, 31 m.

for his freedom. Neil refused a proposal to go with him to Orkney,[17] and despatched the fatal messenger to Tain.

There is reason to suspect that in this Macleod showed some hesitation. It is not certain, though probable, that Montrose did not reach Ardvreck *on the 29th*. The course of subsequent events indicates either that the messenger took two days to reach Tain, or else he set out on May 2nd, the *second perhaps the third day after Montrose's capture*—days and nights of alternate hope and despair for the unhappy prisoner. From Ardvreck to Tain is 54½ miles, and there was then no regular road down the Oykell to Rosehall. But a fleet-footed Highlander, spurred by reward, might cover the distance on a long May day. At Tain he found Leslie, probably just arrived, who at once despatched Major-General Holburn (May 3rd?) to secure the captive. On May 4th, Holburn arrived at Assynt, and setting out with the prisoners next day, retraced his steps as far as Oykell Bridge, whence he marched, on Monday the 6th, along the northern side of the Kyle to Skibo Castle. His orders were to bring Montrose "to Sutherland;"[18] and we may conjecture that at Skibo he expected to find the Lieutenant-General on his way to crush the Royalists in Caithness and the north. The heavy marches of the last four days, not to speak of over 180 miles from Brechin[19] to Tain, covered in six or seven days, must have taxed the endurance of his men to the utmost; and for two nights they halted at Skibo, awaiting further orders across the ferry from Tain. This and the exhaustion of the party were reason enough for the two days' halt. For their prisoner they showed little consideration.

Skibo Castle was then occupied by a dowager lady named Gray.[20] "On

---

11th, to Keith, 18 m. 12th, Sunday, halt. 13th, to Pitcaple Castle, 32½ m. 14th, to about Fourdon, over 38 m. 15th, by Kinnaird Castle (14 m.) to Grange, 31 m. This was evidently a long stage, or they would not have halted within five miles of Dundee, which they reach on the 16th. Some time having been spent in Dundee, they probably advanced that day only to Leuchars or Cupar, and next day, the 17th, they proceeded to Dysart or Kirkaldy, and slept there. Saturday, 18th, by Leith, 4 P.M., to Edinburgh Tolbooth, 6 P.M.

The unhappy train of prisoners must have suffered severely from these forced marches. With Montrose were "all the prisoners of quality on foot, about 40 persons" (Wardlaw MS.); and the "281 comon souldiers" that "wer in the Canongait prisson, dismissed" (to *slavery*) on Tuesday, May 21st, probably accompanied or followed hard after the officers. [17] Sallagh.

[18] Sallagh, who knew very well that Assynt was not then part of Sutherland, in spite of the Earl's pretensions. In 1686 the estate was adjudicated to Isabella, Dowager-Countess of Seaforth, and passed by judicial sale, July 21, 1757, to the Sutherland family. Taylor MS., Dunrobin.

[19] Leslie left (?) Brechin on April 25, and marched "30 miles a day" (Balf.) to Aboyne (?), *ca.* 30 m.; thence (by Keith and Elgin?) to Inverness, 105 m.; thence to Tain, 45 m. Without a halt on Sunday, April 28th, Leslie might reach Tain at this rate in six days, *i.e.*, on the night of April 30th. Meantime he must have heard of the battle on the 27th. On the whole it seems more likely that he reached Tain on May 1st or 2nd, just in time to receive Macleod's message.

[20] Robert Gray of Skibo appears on commissions of war for Sutherland and Inverness from 1643-1645. A Robert Gray of Skibo, perhaps the son of the above, was Commissioner of Supply for Sutherland in 1655. Act. Parl. Scot.

"the arrival of the Marquis and his guards, she prepared a suitable enter-
"tainment for them. She presided at the dinner-table, at the head of which,
"and immediately before her, was a leg of roasted mutton. When Mon-
"trose entered the room he was introduced to her by the officers who
"escorted him, and she requested him to be seated next to her; but Hol-
"bourn, still retaining the strict military order he observed in his march,
"placed the Marquis between himself and another officer, and thus he sat
"down at Lady Skibo's right hand, and above his noble prisoner, before the
"lady was aware of the alteration. She no sooner observed this arrangement
"than she flew into a violent passion, seized the leg of roasted mutton by the
"shank, and hit Holbourn such a notable blow on the head with the flank
"part of the hot juicy mutton as knocked him off his seat, and completely
"spoiled his uniform. The officers took alarm, dreading an attempt to
"rescue the prisoner; but the lady, still in great wrath, and brandishing the
"leg of mutton, reminded them that she received them as guests; that as
"such, and as gentlemen, they must accommodate themselves to such an
"adjustment of place at her table as she considered to be correct; that
"although the Marquis was a prisoner, she was more resolved to support
"his rank when unfortunate than if he had been victorious; and, conse-
"quently, that no person of inferior rank, could, at her table, be permitted
"to take precedence of him. Order being restored, and the mutton replaced
"on the table, every possible civility was thereafter directed by all present
"towards the Marquis." [21]

From this point the narrative is taken up by the Wardlaw MS.[22] as follows:—

"We are now to set down the fatal preludium and parade of one of the
"noblest and gallantest generals this age saw in Britain; whose unexampled
"achievements might frame a history. Were its volumes far bigger than mine,
"it would yet be disproportionate to the due praise of this matchless hero.

"May 4th, 1650, he was taken; and the fourth day after delivered to
"David Leslie at Tain, Strachan having run south to have his reward of

---

[21] Mr. Taylor, Dunrobin MS. - Sallagh, 555, "James Grahame was two nights in Skibo, and from thence he was conveyed to Brayn and so to Edinburgh."

[22] Extracts in Napier, Mem., 773 ff.; and in the Highland Note-Book (1843, repr. 1887), by the late Robert Carruthers, LL.D. The writer visited London in 1653 and 1660; became episcopal minister of Wardlaw and Kirkhill parish, seven miles from Inverness, ca. 1662; and in 1666 chaplain to the Lovat family, at whose request he commenced to set down the history of the Frasers. He is said to have died in 1715, at a great age. He could, therefore, have been little more than a boy at the time of events which he describes at least sixteen years later. The Editors were very anxious to examine a document so important to their purpose; but the present owner, Sir William Fraser of Leadclune, curtly declined to lend it, or intrust it to a library. A further request for leave at least to see it at his residence or elsewhere failed to elicit even the courtesy of a reply. Among many scores with whom their work has brought them into correspondence, they are glad to record that this instance is solitary.

" blood from the State;[23] which did not a little gall Leslie to see an upstart
" rival risen to honour and to have so great a success: A vanity!

" Montrose, being now in the custody of his mortal enemies, from whom
" he could expect no favour, yet expressed a singular constancy; and in a
" manner a carelessness of his own condition. He was conveyed with a
" guard over the river Conan, towards Beauly. Crossing that river they
" refreshed at Lovat; such scurvy base indignities put all along upon him as
" reached the height of reproach and scorn. Which confirms the poet's *dixi*
" and *ditte*:—

'Nescia mens hominum fati, sortisque futuræ,
Et servare modum, rebus sublata secundis.'[24]

" But now I set down that which I was myself eye-witness of.

" The 7th of May, 1650,[25] at Lovat, he sat upon a little shelty horse, without
" a saddle, but a quilt of rags and straw, and pieces of ropes for stirrups; his
" feet fastened under the horse's belly with a tether; a bit halter for a bridle;
" a ragged old dark reddish plaid, a *montrer* (montero) cap, called *magirky*,[26]
" on his head; a musketeer on each side, and his fellow prisoners after him.

" Thus conducted through the country, near Inverness, under the road
" to Muirtown, where he desired to alight, he called for a draught of water,
" being then in the first crisis of a high fever. And here the crowd from the
" town came forth to gaze. The two ministers, Mr. John Annand,[27] wait

---

[23] Montr. Rediv. 175, 176, says Strachan had "a particular Commission" from the "Parliament [Committee] to command a choyce party of Horse, *which should* not be subject to David Lesleys orders" (*ibid.* 179). "Straughan having atchiev'd his businesse with great expedition, and freed the state from this much-fear'd danger, return'd to Edinburgh, leaving the rest of the businesse to Lesley and Holborn, where he received great rewards and thanks for his eminent service; not without the great *heart-burning* of David Lesley, who seeing a *rivall risen up to his honour*, and one whom he lookt upon as an *upstart* souldier, *have so great successe*, fretted not a little" (*ibid.* 180). "The Marquesse being now in the custodey," &c., to "condition," identically as in Fraser's narrative. From this it is certain that the writer of the Wardlaw MS. had the Redivivus or Heath's transcript before him when he wrote; probably the latter, as he seems to have borrowed his account of Cromwell's inauguration as Protector (1653) from him. See Highland Note-Book (repr. 1887), 235.

[24] Verg. Aen. x. 501, 502. An inept quotation borrowed from the Redivivus, where it is applied to Montrose's enemies.

[25] The date does not agree with our estimate, p. 313, *n.* 16. It is also inconsistent with Fraser's own account. If delivered at Tain on the 8th, Montrose could not have passed Lovat on the 7th. Again, he reaches Keith on the 11th, with only two stages between—Castle Stewart and Elgin. That is, he passed Lovat on the 9th, halting the night of the 8th at Brahan, a stage omitted by Fraser. We suspect the Wardlaw MS. contains a "9" for "7."

[26] "The words in italics are given as they seem to be written. The MS. is in some places very difficult to decipher." Note, Napier, Mem., 774. "John Livingstone rode to London in a gray coat and a gray Montero cap." Grub, Ecc. Hist. iii. 4.

[27] "Only one of them is named in the MS." The Rev. John Annand was minister of Inverness, and father of Mr. William Annand, Episcopal clergyman at Bellie. Hist. of Epis. in Moray, 299. The senior minister was William Cloggie. John Annand was called to a church in Edinburgh, 1647, but appears not to have accepted. Probably he got some benefit from it while he still held Inverness. He may, however, have been at Inverness on a holiday. *Scotti Fasti. Annand.*

"here upon him to comfort him; the latter of which the Marquis was well
"acquainted with. At the end of the bridge, stepping forward an old
"woman, Margaret MacGeorge, exclaimed and brauted saying,—'Montrose
"'look above; view these ruinous houses of mine, which you occasioned to
"'be burnt down when you besieged Inverness.' Yet he never altered his
"countenance; but with a majesty and state beseeming him, kept a counte-
"nance high.

"At the cross, a table covered. The Magestrates treat him with wine,
"which he would not taste, but allayed with water. The stately prisoners,
"his officers, stood under a forestair, and drank heartily. I remarked
"Colonel Hurry, a robust, tall, stately fellow, with a long cut on his cheek.[28]
"All the way through the streets Montrose never lowered his aspect. The
"provost, Duncan Forbes,[29] taking leave of him at the town's end, said,—
"'My Lord, I am sorry for your circumstances.' He replied,—'I am sorry
"'for being the object of your pity.' The Marquis was conveyed that night
"to Castle Stewart, where he lodged.

"From Castle Stewart[30] the Marquis is conveyed through Moray. By
"the way, some loyal gentlemen wait upon his Excellency, most avowedly,
"and with grieved hearts: Such as, the Laird of Culbin, Kinnaird;[31] old
"provost Tulloch,[32] in Narden; Tannochy Tulloch;[33] Captain Thomas
"Mackenzie, Pluscarden;[34] the laird of Cookstoun;[35] and old Mr. Thomas
"Fullerton,[36] his acquaintance at College. He was overjoyed to see these

---

[28] Napier identifies this with the dangerous shot Hurry received on the left side of his head when Hamilton's Engagers were routed. Turner, Mem., 65. But *dangerous shots* do not usually make a "long cut." Hurry was "wounded" at Carbisdale, and Fraser here supplies a detail.

[29] Duncan Forbes of Culloden had been commissioner to Parliament for Inverness in 1625, 1633, 1639, 1640, and commissioner to Assembly in 1639. His son John is called provost in 1646; but probably the old man retained the title in social intercourse. They were both "exempted in 1647 from public burdens and dues for their constant adherence to the cause." The stock was Puritan, but full of kindliness and courtesy. See "Culloden Papers," and "Family of Innes," Spalding Club-Book, edit. Cosmo Innes, embodying an account of the Innes by Duncan Forbes, grandson of Duncan, and father of the famous President. See also Grameid, 174, *n*.

[30] About five miles from Inverness, now a ruin, seen well from railway on left hand going south. It was full of gay company in 1665. See Grameid, 54, *n*.; Bishop Forbes' Journal, 151.

[31] Walter Kinnaird of Culbyn, the representative of a loyal family. His heir appears again in the Claverhouse rising. Grameid, 161. Act of Parl., VI. pt. ii. 33. His estate was overrun with sand in 1695, and his house now lies buried under it.

[32] John Tulloch was in Parliament for Nairn in 1639 and 1641. He is probably the old provost of Nairn.

[33] Thomas Tulloch of Tannachy was on Committee of War for Elgin in 1643-1644. His son Alexander was rewarded in 1661 by being made Commissioner of Excise.

[34] P. 245, *n* 3; 304, *nn*. and index.

[35] John Innes of Coxton and his brother James were Royalists. They were pardoned in 1647, but have still the courage of their opinions in 1650. John caused Argyll much trouble in 1655. See "Family of Innes," Index, and Grameid, 159.

[36] William Fullerton, minister of Rafford, took his degree at St. Andrews in 1628. He died in 1668. He was a Royalist. Thomas may be a mistake for William.

"about him; and they were his guard forward to Forres, where the Marquis
"was treated; and thence, afternoon, convoyed to Elgin city, where all these
"loyal gentlemen waited on him, and diverted him all the time, with allow-
"ance of the general.[37]

"In the morning Mr. Alexander Symons,[38] parson of Duffus, waited on
"him at Elgin, being college acquaintance with the Marquis; four years his
"condisciple at St Andrews. This cheered him wonderfully, as the parson
"often told me. Thence they convoyed him all the way to the river Spey,
"and a crowd of loyalists flocked about him unchallenged. Crossing
"Spey, they lodged all night at Keith; and next day, May 12th, being
"the Sabbath, the Marquis heard sermon there. A tent was set up in
"the fields for him, in which he lay. The minister, Master William
"Kinanmond, altering his ordinary, chose for his theme and text, the
"words of Samuel the prophet to Agag, the king of the Amalekites, coming
"before him delicately: 'And Samuel said, As thy sword hath made women
"'childless, so shall thy mother be childless among women,' &c. This
"unnatural, merciless man, so rated, reviled, and reflected upon the
"Marquis, in such invective, virulent, malicious manner, that some of the
"hearers, who were even of the swaying side, condemned him. Montrose,
"patiently hearing him a long time, and he insisting still, said,—'Rail on,
"Ra (?),[39] and so turned his back to him in the tent. But all honest men
"hated Kinanmond for this ever after. Montrose desired to stay in the
"fields all night, lying upon straw in the tent till the morning.

"Monday after they march through the Mearns, south.[40] By the way

---

[37] Napier adds David Leslie by way of explanation, but he had gone north. The general was perhaps Holburn, part of whose infantry formed the escort. See p. 320.

[38] "Symons" is no doubt a mistake of copyist for "Somers." Alexander Somers, parson of Duffus, was a contemporary of Montrose at St. Andrews, and a Presbyterian. He conformed at the Restoration, and latterly was a thorough Royalist. He died in 1686, aged 74. Hist. of Epis. Church in Moray, p. 194.

[39] Illegible in the MS. "Ra" is omitted in Dr. Carruthers' transcript. Napier conjectures "Rabshakeh" contracted. For Mr. William Kinanmond, see Presb. Book of Strathbogie, Index. He was appointed Sept. 6, 1649, and April 23, 1650, he got "*the Cruikit Haugh given him for grass.*" He was commissioner to the Assembly, 1649.

[40] Of the journey from Keith to Grange and Dundee no record has been recovered, except the following incident narrated by John Davidson, D.D., in his "Extracts from Inverurie and the Earldom of the Garioch" (Edinb., 1878), 297. He gives no authority for his account. "Montrose was dressed meanly, in the garb wherein he had disguised himself for concealment, and mounted on a Highland pony, having his feet tied with straw ropes, a herald, with needless parade, riding before him and proclaiming 'Here comes James Graham, a traitor to his country.' In this state Montrose passed through the Garioch, Pitcaple Castle being made his prison for a night. The laird's wife was the Marquis's own cousin, and she tried to induce him to attempt escape by a hole in the wall, which led out by a subterranean passage, but he refused." The laird was John Leslie, Baron of Balquhain. The last laird died 1757. His sister sold the castle to J. Lumsden,

"the Marquis came to his father-in-law's house, the Earl of Southesk, where
"he visited two of his own children.⁴¹ But neither at meeting or at parting
"could any change of his former countenance be seen, or the least expres-
"sion heard, which was not suitable to the greatness of his spirit, and the
"fame of his former actions, worth, and valour. *In transitu*, his Excellency
"staid one night at Dundee; and it is memorable, that though this town
"suffered more loss by his army than any else in the kingdom, yet were
"they so far from insulting over him, that the whole town expressed a
"great deal of sorrow for his condition; and furnished him with clothes and
"all other things suitable to his place, birth, and person."

But here we turn from the Wardlaw MS. to restore to history an incident which occurred at the house of the laird of Grange, some five miles east of Dundee. Doubt has been unjustly cast on the narrative from its omission in Mr. Fraser's account; but it must be remembered that in describing the latter part of this journey south, Mr. Fraser follows the fragmentary account of the Montrose Redivivus, and omits all details of the journey from Keith to Dundee, except the passing visit to Kinnaird Castle, near Brechin. His narrative here loses the value of personal testimony. What follows is related by the author of the "Memorie of the Somervills"⁴²:—

"The old Laird of Grange and his lady, a true-hearted and loyall

---

Professor of Divinity, Aberdeen, whose daughters sold it to Henry Lumsden, "grandfather of the present proprietor" (*ibid.* 417). This John Leslie and others offered, in August 1649, to submit to the Presbytery and renew the Solemn League and Covenant, "but being asked to subscrive the late acknowledgment and declaration of the General Assembly answered they could not take upon them the guiltiness contained therein." On March 21, 1650, Alex. Leslie, yr., of Pitcaple, an Engager, confessed and wished leave to "subscrive" (*ibid.* 304, 305).

If the Pitcaple tradition is to be accepted, the route taken would be by Huntly and the valley of the Urie to Old Rayne. From Pitcaple they may have crossed the country to Mills of Drum, or Craigton, and thence to Fordoun and Kinnaird. This route was probably adopted rather than that from Keith over Suie Hill and Cairn Month, because of the danger of a rescue by Farquharsons and other loyalists in Mar.

⁴¹ This passage also is borrowed *verbatim* from Heath, who had it from the Montr. Rediv. 181. The sons were then in charge of their grandfather, David, first Earl of Southesk. They were probably Robert, born *ca.* 1636, and David, born January 8, 1638. Napier, Mem., 513, *n.*, and 827 *n.* At this time therefore they were boys of fourteen and twelve. The bright face of their father, the boy-bridegroom, painted by Jamieson, still adorns the castle which witnessed this last parting from all he held dear on earth.

⁴² "Memorie of the Somervills," Edin. 1815, written in 1676, "by way of ane epistle to my sones." The writer's father made the acquaintance of Corhouse, his future father-in-law, then Lieutenant-Colonel in Stewart's regiment of horse, at Corstorphine, just before Dunbar, and met him again shortly afterwards at the laird of Grange's, where Corhouse was then quartered, and where the two remained for a fortnight. This visit occurred *within four months of the above incident*. The author's father had therefore ample opportunity for hearing an account of the lady of Grange's attempt to save Montrose, not only from the laird and lady themselves, but also from servants and neighbours acquainted with the circumstances. There appears in the narrative nothing improbable or inconsistent with other known facts.

"gentlewoman, to whose memory, for her civilitie, I ow this breif narra-
"tive.[43]

"'It was at this ladye's house that that party of the Covenanters then
"'standing armie, that gairded in the Marques of Montrose, efter his forces
"'was beat, and himself betrayed in the north, lodged him, whom this
"'excellent lady designed to sett att libertie, by procureing his escape from
"'her house; in order to this, soe soon as ther quarters was settled, and
"'that she had observed the way and manner of the placeing of the guairds,
"'and what officers commanded them, she not only ordered her butlers to
"'let the souldiers want for noe drinke, but she herself, out of respect and
"'kyndenesse, as she pretended, plyed hard the officers and souldiers of the
"'main-guaird (which was keeped in her owne hall) with the strongest ale
"'and aquavite, that before midnight, all of them (being for the most part
"'Highlandmen of Lawer's regiment) became starke drunke. If her stewarts
"'and other servants had obeyed her directions in giving out what drinke
"'the out-gairds should have called for, undoubtedly the bussinesse had
"'been effectuat; but unhappily, when the marques had passed the first
"'and second centinells that was sleeping upon ther musquets, and like-
"'wayes through the main-guaird, that was lying in the hall lyke swyne
"'on a midding, he was challenged a little without the outmost guaird
"'by a wretched trouper of Strachan's troupe, that had been present
"'at his takeing. This fellow was none of the guaird that night, but
"'being quartered hard by, was come rammeling in for his belliefull
"'of drinke, when he made this unluckie discovery, which being done,
"'the marques was presently seized upon, and with much rudenesse (being
"'in the adye's [ladye's] cloaths which he had putt on for a disguize) turned
"'back to his prisone-chamber. The lady, her old husband, with the
"'wholl servants of the house, were made prisoners for that night and the
"'morrow eftir, when they came to be challenged before these that had
"'the command of this party, and some members of that wretched committie
"'of estates that satt allwayes at Edenbrough, (for mischieff to the royall
"'interest) which they had sent for the more security, to be still with this
"'party, fearing the great freinds and well-wishers this noble heroe had
"'upon the way he was to come, should, either by force or stratageme, be
"'taken from them. The ladie, as she had been the only contryver of

---

[43] Grange House or Castle was situated half a mile north of Monifieth parish church. The old house, dating back to the beginning of the 16th century, has been replaced by the more commonplace structure. Erskine of Dun was frequently there in the early days of the Reformation, and was more successful than Montrose in making escape from it. The owner of Grange at this time was William Durhame and his wife, the lady of Grange, was Jean Octerlonie. Scott makes much confusion by placing Grange in Fife and calling the lady Somerville. Wishart had been minister of Monifieth, and could have given the story with local touches had he written.

"'Montrose's escape, soe did she avow the same before them all; testifying
"'she was heartily sorry it had not taken effect according to her wished
"'desyre. This confidence of hers, as it bred some admiratione in her
"'accusors, soe it freed her husband and the servants from being farder
"'challenged; only they took security of the laird for his ladye's appearing
"'before the committie of estates when called, which she never was. Ther
"'worships gott somewhat else to thinke upon, then to conveen so excellent
"'a lady before them upon such ane account, as tended greatly to her
"'honour and ther oune shame."

Thus far, from the time when he set forth, armed with his faithless sovereign's mandate to restore the sinking throne, down to within two days of his entry into Edinburgh, we have been enabled from scattered fragments to reconstruct the story of Scotland's most chivalrous hero. Of his progress from Dundee across Fife to Leith, not a vestige has been discovered. This singular absence of record in a county which of all others had most grievous cause to remember the victor of Kilsyth, can only, as in Orkney, be due to the obliterating tempest of trouble which swept the land a few months later. At Leith the narrative is once more resumed in Wishart's manuscript. Those who seek to know more than is contained therein, will find in Napier's "Memoirs of Montrose" a fulness of detail which has left little more to tell of the dark tragedy on which the curtain now rises.

## CHAPTER X.[1]

*SENTENCE PASSED ON MONTROSE.—HIS ENTRY INTO EDINBURGH.—SPEECH IN THE HOUSE.—LAST WORDS AND EXECUTION.*

THE Covenanting nobles and the rest, who posed as the Estates,[2] as soon as they heard that the Marquis of Montrose was betrayed[3] and in their power, resolved to judge and condemn him before he was brought to Edinburgh. They considered it necessary to avoid all delay, fearing that the reverence felt for so great a man, for his splendid birth, majestic bearing, and glorious achievements might excite in men's minds too much favour and pity for the victim they had thus condemned to death in his absence and unheard.[4] They therefore selected some of

---

[1] Here Wishart's Latin MSS. resume the narrative. He has translated freely from a tract entitled "A true and perfect relation of the most remarkable passages and speeches at and before the death of James Graham, Marquis of Montrose &c., faithfully collected by an eye-witness in Edinburgh, as they happened upon the 18th, 20th and 21st of May 1650; printed 1650" (*v.* Napier, Mem., 780, *n*). This we have not seen; but from Napier's quotations it is evidently the same as the tract bound up in the Montr. Redivivus (1652), p. 189 ff. The original, as Napier points out, is undoubtedly embodied in the Wigton Paper, xliii. 481 (Maitland Miscell., 1840), and Wardlaw MS. See note below. If, as seems likely, the Latin poem (*v.* p. 335 and 486) which concludes W.'s MS. was written after this translation of the tract, the latter must have been made within a year of Montrose's death. See p. 246, *n.* 10. W.'s variations will be noted as they occur. Grief and the rapid revolutions of the time may have prevented him from completing a history, begun to vindicate Montrose, and intended to crown his victory. Wishart in Holland was no longer in a position to give an accurate account of Montrose's preparations in 1649. The Restoration, and the return to power of such men as Middleton, Lauderdale, and Glencairn, probably induced him to abandon a theme so distasteful to Charles II. and his advisers.

[2] Wishart's characteristic refusal to acknowledge this "Rump" Parliament is based on a sound constitutional principle. Charles had acknowledged their authority by signing the Treaty of Breda, May 3-13. But Fleming, who bore his missive to the "Estates," did not land at Leith till May 18th, *the day after Montrose's sentence;* nor was the treaty finally ratified till July 4th. Balf. iv. 72. For the base double-dealing of Charles and Argyll with Montrose and the Estates, see Napier, Mem., xxxvii. 748 ff.

[3] The Latin *proditione traditus* is explicit of treachery. Wigton MS., "was apprehendit." Perfect Relation (Montr. Rediv.), "was taken." The eulogy which follows is expanded for "countenance and carriage" in the Wigton MS. and Perf. Rel.

[4] "Pity ... unheard," "known ... enemies." W.'s additions.

their own number, known as his deadliest enemies, with a commission to proceed with the needful despatch, and report at once in writing to the Estates. This was on the 17th of May. That same forenoon they gave in their report, that he should be met at the city gate by the magistrates and hangman; that he should be put upon a cart, bareheaded, and tied with cords, and so be conducted through the city by the hangman, mounted, and with his cap on; that he should be hanged till he was dead, on a gibbet at the Mercat Cross, with the book of his deeds[5] and his Declaration to the Scots tied about his neck. Thus he was to hang for three hours in sight of all the people. He was then to be beheaded and quartered, his head to be fixed upon the Tolbooth of Edinburgh, and his limbs exposed at the cities of Stirling, Glasgow, Perth and Aberdeen. Lastly, if he repented and was relaxed from the bann of excommunication, his body might be buried in a cemetery;[6] if not, it was to be buried in the place of public execution.

On the 18th of May,[7] at four o'clock in the afternoon, he was brought in at the Water Gate, and according to the sentence of the preceding day, was met by the hangman, accompanied by the magistrates and town-guard. Preceded by a long train of prisoners walking two and two,[8] he entered the gate, when his sentence was handed to him by the magistrates. He at once read it through with calmness and composure, and replied with dignity, that he was ready to submit; only, he regretted that his Majesty, whom he represented, should in his person be treated so foully and unworthily. Then with cheerfulness and alacrity

---

[5] Namely, Part I. of this Commentary—"written in Latin." The gibbet was to be "thirty foot high." Part of his sentence, if he did not repent, was "to be bury'd under a Gibbet of four Pillars, without the City." Monteith, 512 (Eng. Tr.). For the Declaration, see p. 267.

[6] "Sould be burried with pioneris [for notice of these officers, see Scot. Notes and Queries, vi. 33] in the Gray feiris [Gray-friars], if not, to be burried in the Boromoore." Wigton MS. and Perf. Rel. They add that "the new Earle of Roxburgh and Mr. Cheislye knighted at the Isle of Wight, were two of the Committee who projected this sentence." And the reason why he was "tyed to the cart was in hope the people wold have stoned him, and that he might not be able be his hands to save his face."

[7] Latin, May 20th, W.'s usual error in the Roman Calendar.

[8] Also "barheiddit." Wigton MS. and Perf. Rel. add "prisoners of qualitie, betwixt thirtty and fourty." Balfour says twenty-four, all imprisoned in the Tolbooth, iv. 34.

he mounted the cart, and was driven slowly through the most conspicuous parts of the city to the Tolbooth.[9]

Besides the guard who escorted the cart, a vast crowd thronged the streets to see him pass. Amongst them, mingled with servants and scullions, there was a large number of common women,[10] set on to harass and revile him, and pelt him with dust and filth and piles of stones. But in his bearing there shone forth such lofty majesty, dignity, and undaunted composure,[11] that even his enemies were abashed, and the spectators amazed. Their insults and curses melted into tears and prayers. The preachers, whom they call their ministers,[12] were so furious at this, that on the next day, being Sunday, they were not ashamed openly to rage against the people for not persecuting him with their abuse and filthy missiles.[13]

When he was taken down from the cart, he bestowed some gold on the hangman, as a reward, he said, for driving his triumphal chariot so well.[14] It was nearly seven o'clock in the evening[15] when he reached the prison. Immediately a number of the Estates with some ministers were sent off to examine him, or rather to torture him with abuse and impertinent questions.[16]

---

[9] "Calmness . . . composure," "slowly," W.'s additions.

[10] "Who had lost their husbandis and children in his waris." Wigton MS. "Hyred to stone him" (*ibid.*), which W. amplifies. His *congestis lapidibus* suggests preparation for this indignity.

[11] "And even somewhat more than naturall." Wigton MS., omitted Perf. Rel., but followed by W., an indication that he wrote his Lat. *before he saw the* 1652 *reprint*.

[12] "Whom . . . ministers," W.'s characteristic addition.

[13] The Wigton MS. adds, "Of many thowsand beholderis onlye the Laddie Jean Gordon, Countese of Haddington did publicklie insult and laucht at him ;" whereon "a gentellman in the streit cryed up to hir that it became hir better to sit upon the cart for hir adulltiries." Argyll, the Chancellor, and Warriston, when the cart was stopped before their "lodging," and Montrose "suspecting the bussines turned his face towards them, presentlye [at once] creipet in at the windowes;" on which an Englishman "cryed up, it was no wonder they start asyd at his look, for they durst not look him in the face thir seavin yeiris bygan." The incident was the talk of the town, and mentioned in a letter of M. de Graymond, then in Edinburgh, to Mazarin *five days after*. Napier, Mem., 781.

[14] Wigton MS. preserves his words, "Fellow, ther is drink monie for dryving the cairt."

[15] "Past seavine a'clock at night." Wigton MS.

[16] Their names were Robert, Lord Burleigh, Sir James Hope of Hopetoun, George Porterfield, member for Glasgow, for the Estates; and ministers, James Durham and James Hamilton. On their report, the three first were again sent, with Sir Arch. Johnston (Warriston), Sir Thos. Nicolson, King's Advocate, and Sir James Stewart, Provost. They replied to his question, that "ther Commissioners and the Kings Maiestie wer agreid, and the King coming heire to this countrie." Balf. iv. 13, 14.

He declined to answer a word, until they should tell him the state of his Majesty's affairs, and whether they had come to any agreement with the King, his master. His resolution being reported to the Estates, they deferred all further proceedings against him till Monday. Meantime they permitted their representatives to inform him that peace and concord were fully established between the King and the present Estates of his Kingdom. It was now late. Worn out with fatigue and hunger, exhausted by a long and arduous journey, he desired some rest and intermission. "The pomp and ceremony of his welcome that day, had," he said, "proved a trifle tedious."[17]

On the Sunday the ministers and members of Parliament gave him no rest or respite. Though he wished to fix his mind on higher thoughts, they maliciously beset him with impertinent and troublesome questions of petty import, and were unceasing in their reproaches and abuse.[18] But all their efforts failed to wring from him a single word of impatience. He told them "they were much mistaken if they thought the procession of yesterday in a mean cart had affected him with shame or sorrow. He esteemed it the most honourable and happy journey he had ever performed. His most merciful God and Redeemer had manifested his presence to him, to his great, unspeakable comfort, and had illumined and elevated his soul with divine grace, to overlook the reproaches of men, and fix his gaze firmly on him alone, for whom he suffered their indignities."

On Monday he was brought before the Estates. The Chancellor, in a long-set oration, declaimed against his crimes.[19] In the first place, he had broken both the National Covenant and the Solemn League and Covenant. Secondly, he had invaded and made war on his native land, called in Irish rebels, and shed

---

[17] "A longsome jorney . . . and he said the compliment they had put upon him that day was som thing tydeus." Wigton MS.

[18] "Who still perseued him with threatning, but they got no advantage of him" (*ibid.*). The ministers were James Guthrie, James Durham, Robert Traill, Mungo Law, and David Dickson. Patrick Simson's account, Wodrow MS. See Napier, Mem., 785-789. The General Assembly minutes also mention Hugh Mackael.

[19] "Had snivelled out a long premeditat discourse." Wigton MS.

the blood of his countrymen: wherefore God had now brought him to suffer a due and richly merited punishment.

When the Chancellor had done, the Marquis asked if he were allowed to plead his own cause, and say a few words in self-defence. This with some demur they granted, and he addressed them briefly as follows:—

"As I hear that you are in some manner[20] reconciled to the King, I regard this assembly just as if his royal majesty were here in person. For this reason only do I appear before you bare-headed, and plead my cause. In all matters and particularly in affairs of state it has been my aim to act as becomes a faithful Christian and subject. I own that I engaged in that first Covenant openly; and I adhered to it firmly, until it was clear as day that certain persons, under colour of religion and liberty, were endeavouring to wrest all authority from the King, and seize on his prerogatives. To avert this evil and clear honest men from the suspicion of a crime they abhorred, it was thought fit to form some bond;[21] firstly, to preserve religion, and secondly to maintain the royal authority. This bond I was glad to share and subscribe. As for that second League and Covenant, I thank Almighty God that I never approved it, never acknowledged it as lawful and honourable. I cannot, therefore, justly be accused of having broken it. What profit it has been to the cause of religion, thereby rent into so many shameful sects, what terrible tragedies it has occasioned, these three distressed kingdoms can witness.

"During the rebellion in England against the royal martyr, of blessed memory, the king, by the blessing of God, had almost subdued the rebels, when a certain faction in this kingdom, to their everlasting shame[22] and remorse, sent very powerful succours to their aid. His Majesty therefore resolved to send me, with his authority and commission, to use my best endeavours to divert

---

[20] "In some manner," W.'s addition. The Latin is naturally more rhetorical than the simple Wigton MS. account.
[21] The Cumbernauld Band. See p. 20. Balfour's note of this speech, iv. 15, lamely admits Montrose's contention: his wars he called "only diversione of the Scotts natione from interrupting the course of his Maiesties affaires in England;" his last invasion was by the King's command, "to accelerate the tretty." W.'s Latin here follows the Wigton MS. very closely.
[22] "To . . . shame." W.'s addition.

those rebel aids, armed against himself. I acknowledged the justice and sanctity of the command. I was bound in conscience and duty to obey promptly and loyally. How I performed this duty most of you can bear me ample witness. Even the greatest of generals have rarely succeeded on all occasions in preventing the licence of their soldiers. Where such crimes were known and clearly proved, I took care that they should be punished at once. Except in the heat of battle I have shed no man's blood, not even an enemy's; and, even then it was my maxim and my practice to spare,—and I have spared many thousands. I had taken up arms by warrant of his sacred Majesty. At his command I laid them down; and, for his sake, without regard to my own interests, retired beyond the seas.

"As for my coming to Scotland at this time, I did it by the command, the express orders of his sacred Majesty now living— and long may he live and reign happily!—to whom we all owe allegiance and fidelity.[23] It was to accelerate and ripen the treaty of peace and concord which he had resolved to make with you. His Majesty well knew that I was and ever would be ready to lay down arms at his command, as soon as a firm, lasting peace was agreed on between you. I may therefore justly venture to say, that never subject undertook more honourable warfare, in better cause, with juster authority, than that which, in the service of two of the best of kings,[24] it was my duty to undertake and carry on.

"I desire you therefore to lay aside prejudice, malice and private vengeance.[25] Consider me, as a man and a Christian in relation to the justice of the cause; as a subject in relation to my prince's commands which I faithfully performed; as your countryman,[26] who has the highest claims on your affection and gratitude, for preserving the lives and fortunes of so many of you, when I lacked neither power nor occasion, but solely the will to destroy.

---

[23] "Now living . . . fidelity." W.'s addition, here sadly out of place.
[24] For "in the . . . kings," Wigton MS. has simply "in these services."
[25] "Malice . . . vengeance," W.'s addition.
[26] "Nighboure," and for what follows, to "destroy,"—"in relation to the manie of your lyves I have preserved in battaill." Wigton MS.

And be not too rash, but judge me by the laws of God, the laws of nature, and nations, and the laws of my country. Yet if you are otherwise resolved, I appeal to the righteous Judge of the world, who one day shall be judge of all, and always gives out righteous judgment."

These words he pronounced with such solemnity, self-restraint, and calmness of countenance, the surest index of an undaunted soul, that even his bitterest enemies were moved to admiration.[27] The Chancellor then ordered his recent sentence to be read. He listened attentively, but without emotion or dismay,[28] and was on the point of speaking a second time, when the Chancellor stopped him in a threatening manner,[29] and immediately ordered him to be carried back to prison. Scarcely had he returned, when a more sullen and troublesome set of enemies,[30] the ministers, intruded, and laid siege to his composure. They thundered out anathemas. In the most tragic terms they exaggerated the terrors of their censure. They threatened eternal damnation, and sought to

---

[27] For "that . . . admiration," Wigton MS. has "as was admirable."

[28] "With a sollid and unmoved countenance" (*ibid.*).

[29] The "Chancelor stopt him" (*ibid.*); "was presently [*i.e., at once*] stopt by the Chancellour." Perf. Rel.

[30] "A more . . . enemies." W.'s addition, fully borne out by all other accounts. From "censure" to "Hell" is also W.'s addition. One of the ministers told Montrose "he was a faggot of hell, and he saw him burning already." Montr. Rediv. 182. See Napier, Mem., 786, for interesting details of the interview, described by Patrick Simson, who was present, and then twenty-two years of age. The Montrose Redivivus mentions especially Mr. Robert Traill and Mr. Mungo Law, "two such venomous preachers, as no man that knows them can mention their names without detest. The first of the two had been Chaplain before to the Marquesse of Argyle, and was his companion in his flight from the battell of Ennerlochie, and now prisoner to the States of England." The last detail is probably a mistake for Mungo Law, who was surprised with the Committee of Estates by the English under Colonel Aldrich, at Ellet (Alyth) in Angus, August 28, 1651, and conveyed to Broughtie Ferrie, Tynemouth Castle, and London Tower. Balf. iv. 314. See also p. 301.

Robert Traill, born about 1600; 1648, appointed minister in Edinburgh; 1649, proposed that ministers who had been *silent* against the Engagement should be deposed; 1650, in Edinburgh Castle and severely wounded, when taken by Cromwell; *ca.* 1655, conspicuous as a Remonstrant, of a faction in Edinburgh "inclined to frame our people to the Sectarian modell;" wrote a calumnious letter about his opponents; conversed much with General Monk, and opposed to the party of "Charles Stewart;" August 23, 1660, arrested for signing the "Supplication" to Charles. For this, for his share in the Remonstrance, his book on "The Causes of God's Wrath," and other offences, he was imprisoned 1661; tried December 11, 1662; refused the oath of allegiance; sentenced to banishment. Early in February 1663 he retired to Holland, but afterwards returned, and died in Scotland. Balfour, R. Baillie, and Wodrow (Indices). Traill's defence at his trial that he was not at the contriving or presenting of the Remonstrance, being then besieged in Edinburgh Castle, seems disingenuous. He owned that the charge on his book was "more ticklish to answer.' Wodrow, Hist. i. 200–203. Of these blind fanatics it may be said, "*disce omnes crimine ab uno.*"

frighten him with their curses. But all to no purpose. Firm in his integrity and innocence, he calmly ignored their threats as the ravings of fanaticism, a poor contrivance to overawe the ignorant mob, which could do him no harm, but were fraught with far greater dangers for those unjust and wilful keepers of the keys of heaven and hell.[31]

To the magistrates, who were watching him closely, he remarked that he was beholden to the Parliament for far the greatest honour that had ever fallen to his lot. "I am prouder," he said, "to have my head fixed on the summit of this prison, in sight of the present and all future eyes, than had they decreed me a statue of gold in the market place, or the finest portrait to be preserved in the King's bedchamber. That my loyalty and affection to my beloved sovereigns may never be forgotten, I account it the noblest of honours that in the four [32] chief cities of this realm they will erect such lasting monuments to transmit my memory even to the latest posterity. I could heartily wish that I had flesh and limbs enough to have a piece sent to every city in Christendom, as proofs and tokens of my unshaken love and loyalty to king and country."[33]

Very few of those who had had even the slightest regard for him in the past were suffered to see him, and then only for a very brief time, in the presence of magistrates, whose business was to prevent any secret conversation.[34] Meanwhile the guards and

---

[31] This is no vague reproach. R. Traill in his MS. Diary (Napier, Mem., 789-791) says that Law and he were appointed to attend Montrose on the scaffold, that "in case he should desire to be relaxed from his excommunication, we should be allowed to give it [*relaxation*] unto him in the name of the Kirk, and to pray, with him and for him, that what is loosed on earth, might be loosed in Heaven." So Patrick Simson's account :—James Guthrie said . . . "We must with sad hearts leave you . . . having the fearful apprehension that what is bound on earth God will bind in Heaven." Napier, Mem., 788.

[32] Wigton MS., "fyve of your most imminent (eminent) towns."

[33] "I could wish . . . country;" found in the Perf. Rel., not in the Wigton MS.

[34] What friends were permitted to see him? W. here is at variance with both the Perf. Rel. and the Wigton MS., which say "His friends were not suffered to come near him." The Montr. Rediv., 182, also "all access denyed to him; no, not his Father-in-law (Southesk) or any of his friends suffer'd to come nigh him." It is doubtful if the Earl of Southesk was in Edinburgh. Only *fourteen* noblemen attended this session of Parliament, and "*scarce half* of the Commissioners of Shires and Boroughs." Balf. iv. 4. On the 20th, when Montrose heard his sentence, only *eleven* noblemen were present (*ibid*. 17).

The officers in charge were Colonel Wallace and the notorious Major Weir, captain of the Town Guard. See Napier, Mem., 794 *n*.

soldiers (an impertinent and troublesome class of people) beset his chamber day and night. Their wranglings and noisy clamours scarce allowed him time or place to lift up his soul to heaven in private prayer and meditation.[35]

On the morning of the 21st of May,[36] the day on which he was to suffer death, the whole city resounded with drums and trumpets. He asked the captain of the guard[37] what this incessant din of trumpets meant. He replied that the citizens and soldiers were being called to arms. The Estates were afraid of some tumult on the rumour of his execution; nor could they disguise to themselves the fact that a large number of "Malignants" (the odious name they have attached to Royalists) were strongly in Montrose's favour. To this the Marquis replied briefly: "When living I was a terror to your good friends; am I still so terrible when on the point of death? But let them look to themselves. Even when dead I shall haunt their consciences for ever with an agony of terror." Soon after a member of Parliament, Archibald Johnston by name, a sour, crazy, sullen fellow, forced himself into his presence, and assailed him with the question what on earth he was about. The Marquis happened to be combing his hair. With a smile he answered, "While my head is my own, I dress and arrange it. To-morrow, when it will be yours, you may treat it as you please."

About two in the afternoon he put on a scarlet cloak richly laced with gold, and was led from prison to the scaffold in the market.[38] His eyes sparkled, his bearing was stately, and so majestic a beauty shone in his countenance, that all the city was horror-stricken at his cruel punishment. His very enemies were forced to admit that the age had produced no man of greater, loftier, more courageous and undaunted soul.[39] None of his friends or

---

[35] "Meanwhile . . . meditation," omitted Wigton MS. and Perf. Rel.

[36] The Latin date is again incorrect. The whole of this paragraph is omitted in the Wigton MS., Montr. Rediv., and Perf. Relation. The 1720 edition follows the Redivivus, which it states, incorrectly we feel sure, to be a "translation of the Latin MS." The editor of Ruddiman's edition, 1752, restored the passage in his Tr., reprinted by Constable, 1819. Singularly, Napier (Mem. 800) records Sir Arch. Johnston's brutal intrusion, but omits to give his name.

[37] Major Weir.      [38] By the Mercat Cross, near St. Giles.

[39] "Did acknowledge him to be the gallantest subject in the world." Wigton MS. and Perf. Rel. "His speech was full of composure, and his carriage as sweet as ever I saw a man in all my days." Brit. Mus. MS. of date *May 21st* 1650, *ap*. Napier, Mem., 805.

well-wishers was suffered to come near him. An obscure lad[40] was therefore employed to take down his last words in shorthand. In Scotland, condemned persons had always been allowed to address the people freely. But even in this he was not permitted to unburden his mind. The magistrates stubbornly denied him the privilege. His words, therefore, were not so much in the form of a set speech, as scattered remarks in answer to the occasional questions of bystanders. The substance of these replies, faithfully recorded by the notary, and transmitted to us, was as follows:—

"I am sorry if any good Christian be offended at the manner of my death. Has it not often happened to the righteous according to the ways of the wicked, and to the wicked according to the ways of the righteous? Does not a just man sometimes perish in his righteousness, and a wicked man prosper in his wickedness? Those who know me best will not esteem me outcast and miserable for my sufferings. Many far greater than I have undergone the like fate. But the judgments of God are righteous. I admit and declare the justice of all His punishments inflicted for my many grievous private sins against His sacred name. To His will I submit wholly and willingly. For the wrongs done me by men, are but His instruments, freely and heartily I forgive all men; and may God Almighty forgive them too! They have oppressed the poor. They have perverted judgment and justice. But He that is higher than they will reward them.

"What I have done in my country has been according to my country's laws. The commands of my sovereign were to defend his safety in his deep distress against wicked rebels in arms against him. It was my duty to obey. My chief study hath ever been, to fear God and honour the King, according to the laws of

---

[40] "His friends, ... debarred from coming near ... caused a young boy to sit upon the scaffold by him ... who wrote his last speech in brachography as follows. The young man's name was Mr. Robert Gordon, Cluny, my cammarad, son to Sir Robert Gordon of Gordonstoun; from whom I got the same." Rev. James Fraser, Wardlaw MS., *ap*. Napier, Mem., 806. Napier has conclusively demolished Lord Mahon's baseless conjecture that this speech was a Royalist fiction! The father of this boy was author of the Hist. of the Earls of Sutherland, continued by Gilbert Gordon of Sallagh. Wishart in the speech closely follows the account given in the Wardlaw and Wigton MSS. The last, in its quaint broken terseness, is probably the most faithful report of Montrose's *very words*.

God, of nature, and of our own nation. Nowhere have I sinned against men. Against God only have I sinned, and with Him there is mercy far above all. On this Mercy alone I rely, and shall draw near to His throne without fear. I will not seek to foretell the future, and pry into the secrets of God's providence. Yet may God, our gracious Father, grant that the wrongs I suffer this day may never turn to still greater miseries for this distressed nation and beloved country, rushing headlong to ruin.[41]

"Among you are some, and those by no means bad men, who lament that I die under the heavy censure of the church. That is no fault of mine, if I have incurred it for no other crime than because I have done my bounden duty to my lawful prince, to preserve his sacred person and maintain his authority unimpaired, according to law. This much I will say. Too rashly have your ministers excommunicated me. I grieve for their sentence, and as far as in me lies, saving always my conscience, I beg and pray them to relax and cancel it, according to God's laws. If they refuse me this, I appeal to the righteous Judge of the world, soon, I hope, to be my Judge: to the Redeemer I appeal.

"Others, to injure and destroy my fair fame and reputation even in death,[42] cry out that I am thus laying the whole blame upon the King and his royal Father. God forbid that so wicked a thought should ever enter my heart! The late King lived a saint, and died a martyr. God grant that as my fate is like his, so I too may face it with the same piety and resignation. Could a man's soul pass into another's and be united with it, I would choose his alone, before all others.[43] As for the present King, happy the people that shall live beneath his just and merciful government. His commands to me were most just. He is true to his promise, and deceives none. Though his disposition inclines to mercy, he reveres justice, and keeps his sacred word to all. I humbly pray God that he may find his subjects and

---

[41] "I will not . . . ruin," not in the Perf. Rel., Montr. Rediv., Wigton and Wardlaw MSS.

[42] "To injure . . . death," W.'s addition.

[43] "If ever I would wish my soule in another man's steid, it is in his." Wigton and Wardlaw MSS. and Perf. Rel. This singular expression is explained by W.'s Latin. The next sentence is his expansion of "For this king, never people was happier of a King" (*ibid.*).

servants no less faithful and just, that he be not at last betrayed like his father, by those whom he has most advanced and trusted.[44]

"Let none, I pray you, impute my bearing this day to dull insensibility or stubborn pride, because in some points I agree not with the most of you, and do not in all things yield to your wishes and opinions. I follow the light of my own conscience, guided by the rules of true religion and right reason, prescribed by the Spirit of God in my heart. It is for me to use the courage of faith and strength of resignation, which God in His gracious mercy grants. Armed with this strength I face death boldly. Full of faith and hope I stand before the throne of Heaven. May God be glorified, even by this my condemnation. Yet these are not words of fear and distrust, but gratitude to God and love to the people. Whenever I see you, or think of you, I must needs weep for your misfortunes, which I have sought in vain to heal, prevented by our sins.[45]

"I have no more to say, but to beg you of your charity to judge me fairly, and to desire the prayers of the good for the salvation of my soul, soon to be freed from the prison of this body. I pray for you all, and earnestly but humbly implore God to avert the wrath so long impending over this poor kingdom. Let men triumph as they will over the perishing remains of this body; but never shall they hinder me to love, reverence and fear God, and honour the King, in death as in life. I leave my soul to God and my Redeemer, my service to the King, my honour to my country and posterity, my good will to my friends, and to you all my truest love. More I could add, were I permitted, but let these few words suffice to clear my conscience."[46]

Being then asked if he wished to pray apart, he replied, "If

---

[44] "Betrayed under trust," Wigton MS., &c.—the expression used of Montrose's own betrayal in the indictment of Neil Macleod (v. App. XIII.).

[45] "Whenever . . . sins," W.'s addition.

[46] "And earnestly . . . life," and "More . . . permitted," W.'s additions. At "conscience" there is a blank in the folio MS., left probably in W.'s original for further details not given in the Wigton MS. and Perf. Rel. "The ministers, because he was under the sentence of excommunication, would not pray for him, and even on the scaffold were very bitter against him." Wardlaw MS., which then continues as above.

you do not suffer the people to join their prayers with me, my prayer alone and apart in so great an assembly will perhaps be a scandal both to you and me. I have already poured out my soul before the Lord, who knows my inmost heart. Into His hands I commend my spirit, and He has deigned in grace and mercy to assure me of full forgiveness for my sins, and peace and salvation in Jesus Christ my Redeemer." With these solemn words he closed his eyes, and lifting his hands to heaven, remained awhile rapt in silent devotions. During this it was manifest that his soul was flooded with the boundless consolation of the Holy Spirit.[47]

When he had done he called the executioner, and bestowed on him some money. The history of his deeds and his late Declaration were then brought to him, tied in a cord. He received them with a strange cheerfulness and alacrity, and himself hung them round his neck, saying, "Though it hath pleased the King to make me a Knight of the most honourable Order of the Garter, I think it less honour and glory than this cord and books. I take them with greater joy than when I received the golden chain and glorious badge of S. George. Hasten to tie them on me, as you please."

The bailies and officers of the guard then ordered his arms to be bound, and his cloak stripped off. To these he said, "Inflict on me, I pray you, what further shame and ignominy you can devise. I am ready to bear all and worse than this with cheerfulness and joy for the cause in which I suffer. God Almighty have mercy on this perishing nation!" These were his last words.[48] The sentence pronounced upon him in his absence and unheard was then executed. He suffered with undaunted courage and wonderful magnanimity. He was a man, even by his enemies' admission and esteem, without equal, and now became a candidate for immortality, changing this poor mortal life for the life of eternal bliss.[49]

---

[47] "He stood a good space at his inward devotionis, being perceaved to be inwardlye moved all the whyll." Wigton MS., &c.

[48] The simpler and truer version is, "when [the books were tied on and] his armis tyed, he asked the bailzies if they had anye more dishonour, as they conceaved, to put upon him, he was reddie [to] accept; and then, with a most undaunted courrage and gravitie, he went up to the bussines." Wigton MS. The Wardlaw MS. adds that the very hangman shed tears.

[49] For other details as to the end of Montrose, the bestowal of his limbs, &c., see App. XIV.

ENGLISH OF

THE LATIN POEM ON THE DEATH OF MONTROSE

WRITTEN ON THE FIRST ANNIVERSARY,

By GEORGE WISHART.[1]

---

In faithful Memory of
the most famous, invincible, valiant
JAMES, MARQUIS OF MONTROSE, EARL OF KINCARDINE &c.
Lieutenant-Governor and Commander-in-Chief
of all his Majesty's Forces in Scotland, both by Land and Sea,
who was inhumanly butchered by the rebel Covenanters,
this Elegy was written on the first Anniversary of his Death
by the Historian of his brilliant Deeds.
1650.[2]

Noble in birth and gifts of genius, strong of arm, and stout of heart beyond his strength, in face fair, with the fairer beauty of the soul, loyal and just, unshaken by a thousand storms, true to his King, the hero of six glorious victories, yet ever ready to give the hand of pardon to his foes, patriot, and, alas, too faithful lover of his perishing country, eternal Fame hath hallowed his memory and exalted him to glory; Virtue claims him for her own. Envy decries him, and with fierceness wilder than the fury of wild beasts seeks to stain the memory of the illustrious dead.

Ah, my countrymen, what madness burns in your hearts and fevered throats, insatiable in thirst? Will this fury never be glutted with blood, never sated with ravening—a famine fiercer with each banquet of victims, a lust that grows with feeding? Cruel, ah, too cruel is this rankling rage! Cease from wrath and stay your hands. "Stay your reeking hands:" the shriek of innocent blood cries aloud to Heaven. The vengeance of God makes ready His bow to slay; His sword is drawn to punish.

Why delight to refuse the mangled limbs and bleaching face a burial? The craven mouse insults the lion dead, and nibbles at his tawny mane. The base

---

[1] For Latin from MS. E, see end of Latin text.
[2] See p. 337. The Anniversary was of course 1651.

kestrel and carrion vulture prey on the stiffened limbs of the eagle dead. The coward hind despises the stag-hound dead. The silly lamb no longer flies in terror from the wolf that is dead. Say, ye craven mice, base kestrels, ravening vultures, hinds whose only fame is speed of flight—say, ye silly flock, is it no shame basely to destroy a man o'erwhelmed by treachery and guilt, by your crime and fury— great Heavens! is it no shame to deny a grave to the piteous mouldering limbs of him whose very name and shadow while he lived could hurl you into shameless coward flight, set you quaking with dread, fain to hide your craven heads in mountain wastes and forests, to burrow in the earth, to shun the land, to fly to ships and skulk by sea!

But if the vision of such virtue was for you no check, and served but to goad your envy on, yet the King's commands, the Sovereign's name and authority in his person, the restraints of lawful command, the rights of ancestry, the sanctity of law, and that revered Power which is held on earth most holy might have averted the crime. But in you there is no love of honour, no care for what is good. Your blind souls are utter strangers to all sense of justice, right, and truth, without duty, and without all shame.

Since reverence for the royal sceptre has departed, and it is held high honour to be traitors to the throne, and justice has been administered by slaves, and the bonds of law sundered, and leagues formed at the evil bidding of the sovereign mob, nor truth nor righteousness remains. Deceit and guile, robbery, theft, rapine, murder, are rampant; armed violence defiles our beds and desolates all with reckless lawlessness. No crime is lacking. Impious war follows on war, and in war's train pestilence and dire famine assail the wretched. New taxes grind the poor; and with new laws, new accusations, they delight to entangle loyal men, and harry the innocent with their hate. To be loyal is a crime. And, stranger wonder still, that ever racks my heart with grief and heavy dole, a terrible superstition and impious cruelty has stolen into men's wanton hearts, and hounds them on to every wickedness. God and man are assailed by the whole power of the wretched rebellious rabble and self-seeking peers. Their greedy prophets interpose no check to stay these monstrous evils. In their baseness they exult, and feed and fan the flames, eager to goad men's savage hearts to fury, to inflame their minds with wrath— haters of peace, whose dreary dirge croaks ever of war. Hell's furies seem to have sallied from the Pit to brood over our land, the deadly foes of kings, their venomous hearts swelling with rage and insolent malice, their tongues shrieking for blood, appeased by nothing save the blood of the rich, gloating most over the noblest victims. Why tell of Strafford's great and kingly soul, of Lily and Lucas, the saintly Laud, the warrior Capel, the death of hapless Hamilton, the clan Gordon and their fallen chief, the youthful Murray, the aged Spottiswood, Maxwell, Rollock, and the death of the brave boy Ogilvy, and all the long list of the fallen? Charles the matchless, Charles the good and righteous, true son of Heaven, God's own peculiar care, God's regent on earth is your chief victim, long predestined by your cruelty to bleed upon your altars. Oh, woe the deed, accursed crime, dire harbinger of coming misery!

Grant, merciful Heavens, that since fate has given the Graham to accompany the blessed Charles, who led the way assigned by fate to both, grant him his prayers and wish.[1] The King could wish no other comrade for the way, the Graham no other guide.

But you, ye base inhuman monsters, the signs of the age, the wrath of God, savages, birds of darkness, harpies, Hell's spawn, Earth's shame, Heaven's scourge, what vengeance awaits your guilt, what fury of civil war shall hunt you? I see brothers fighting, hacking, rending brothers, the yoke of slavery laid on your stiff necks, shackles of iron on your trailing feet, your throats parched with thirst, your eyes fevered with plague, your limbs wasted with resistless famine,—ah, how small, how small a part of the miseries that await you, are the penalties called extreme, the scourge, the gallows-tree! For the Avenging Angel shall haunt your guilty breasts with fresh frenzies. Never a day nor night shall yield you rest. Waking visions scare your shuddering thoughts by night, a whisper, a shadow startle you by day. A thousand cares rack your anguished hearts. Grief and horror seize your quaking souls. On this side dread, on that infamy hovering on dusky pinions; on this side the heavy wrath of man, on that the heavy wrath of God scorch your shrivelling hearts with quenchless flames, without pause, or rest, or end, until the Judge Supreme decree your sentence, and despair of the salvation it were blasphemy here to name, and ruthless Hell swallow you up, and remorse, too late! too late!

Meantime, the glorious hero Montrose, at once the shame and glory of his ungrateful country, her pride and her reproach, Scotland's love and sorrow, ascends to his starry home, Heaven's shining palaces, the stately mansions of the angels beyond the spheres. There, beneath his feet beholding the vanities of the perishing world, he has his joyous portion in the honour and love of God.

And those poor relics, the shameful monuments of impious rage, the hero's limbs exposed on high, like glorious trophies, borne on the sounding wings of fame, or reared for admiration in lofty vaulted shrines, shall tell of the virtue, loyalty, and valiant deeds of the noble hero, and adorn his spirit with fresh praise. The love of grateful posterity shall add titles and deathless records. Yea, and our Muse shall bring her gift, her all, to thee, greatest of Grahams, and year by year sing thy solemn dirge. He whom living she revered, when dead shall still, despite of bursting envy, be her constant theme.

True love is drowned by no billows of mischance: true love fears no thunderbolts of fate: true love abides immortal, firm, unchangeable. To have loved once is to love for aye.

(Written in my copy in the year 1650).[2]

---

[1] *V*. Montrose's dying speech, p. 332.      [2] Note by Wodrow.

I. G.[1]

DE REBVS

AVSPICIIS SERENISSIMI,
ET POTENTISSIMI

# CAROLI

DEI GRATIA MAGNAE BRITANNIAE,
FRANCIAE[2] & HIBERNIAE[2] REGIS, &c.

*Sub imperio illustrissimi*

IACOBO MONTISROSARVM

*Marchionis, Comitis de Kincardin, &c.*

Supremi Scotiae Gubernatoris Anno

CIƆIƆCXLIV, et duobus sequentibus praeclare gestis,

COMMENTARIVS.

*Interprete A. S.*[3]

---

[1] *I.e.*, Jacobus Graemus.
[2] These words are significantly omitted in the *Paris* edition of 1648.
[3] *I.e.*, Agricola Sophocardius, for George Wise-heart, or Wishart.

Serenissimo, Potentissimoque

# CAROLO

Dei gratiâ Scotorum, et Walliae
Principi, Duci Rothesaiae,
Magnae Britanniae, Franciae[1] &
Hiberniae[1] Haeredi &c.

S.

Pronus ac supplex, Serenissime Princeps, ad Te accedit Montisrosanus Tuus; haud totus, aut semis, nec dum

*Tantilla tanti portio miraculi.*

Qui, utut incultus, ac impolitus, et in habitu Romano barbara squallens rubigine; lucem tamen, hominumque conspectum non formidabit: si illum eo favore digneris, et gratiâ, quâ hospites, advenasque solitus es. Et hoc quidem meliore jure postulare videtur; qui non totus peregrinus est: sed in Paterno Tuo Regno genuinus natus: nec nisi fatali temporum injuriâ, quasi expositus, in externo eductus et altus solo. Nec sane desunt characteres, et notae undique impressae, quae patriam, patremque demonstrent. Illam quidem Scotiam Tuam, centenis, novenisque e Majoribus Tuis regnatam: quorum omnium sanctissimus sanguis, animaeque in Te spirant. Hunc vero antiquissimi ejusdem Regni alumnum, Patris Tui charissimi, ac clementissimi Domini sui, servum humillimum; et cultorem contra omnes fortunae casus devotissimum.[2]

Quae si minus sufficiant, ad conciliandam gratiae Tuae auram, quâ moribundo huic embryoni vitam, salutemque impertias: hoc saltem misello praestare, pro longe maximâ humanitate Tuâ, digneris, ut, rudi quamvis pencillo depicta prototypi lineamenta, ac quandam figuram agnoscas: et vel eo nomine, vitam, si non et immortalitatem largire. Enimvero quis

---

[1] Omitted in Paris edit. Previous Translations omitted this Dedication.
[2] These sentences are in apposition to *patriam patremque*, but probably W. meant the Marquis by *hunc*.

Alexandri, Cesaris, Scipionis, aut avorum Tuorum Jacobi Pacifici,[1] vel Henrici Magni[2] imaginem, quae unica extaret, ideo haberet vilem, quod obscuri cuiusdam, nec admodum periti artificis manu fuerit exarata? Non defuturum Montisrosano Apellem, non Leucippum, nec Homerum forsan suum auguror: interim Princeps Benignissime, hoc nostro utere tantisper, dum illi prodeant. Nec in sermonis impolitiam; sed in res vere Romanas, utpote nobiles, arduas, Heroicas, et quae vulgares animas longissime excedant, generosum illum et excelsum animum Tuum intende. Si enim quos deprehenderis naevos, erroresque, non genii ejus; sed ingenii nostri vitio (uti aequum bonumque est) imputaveris: equidem nec injucundum Tibi, nec inutilem fore Montisrosanum Tuum, fidenter spondeo.

Quid enim Principi, mortalium nulli post Patrem secundo, eo in loco nato, eo in statu educato, eisque ab incunabulis assueto, quae nihil quam Heroica omnia redoleant, jucundius sit, quam Heroa illum (absit invidia) nemini hoc seculo posthabendum, intueri, amplexari, observare,

*Quem sese ore ferens, quam forti pectore et armis?* [3]

Qui optimi Regum, clementissimi Patris Tui auspiciis militans, et virtuti tuae, quae tam strenue adolescit, quasi praeludens; ea gessit, quae praesens quidem admiratur aetas, grata vero posteritas nunquam conticescet. Utut enim gloriam consequatur invidia; ejusque quasi vestigia premat: caduca tamen cum sit, et mortalis, stabilem illam, ac immortalem nec assequetur unquam, nec obfuscabit.

Nullum interim Tibi hic, Serenissime Princeps, exhibemus

*Antiphaten Scyllamque, et cum Cyclope Charybdin;*

monstra nulla, aut speciosa miracula: monstris tamen simillimos hostes, et miraculis partas de illis victorias. Quid enim de Gigantum arrogantia, fabulata est Graecia mendax,[4] quod conjurati isti terrae filii, adversus Deum, pietatem, fidem, jus, et aequum in Augustissimis Parentibus Tuis, Teipso, Tuisque omnibus non sunt ausi? qui congestis mendaciorum et calumniarum montibus, ea extruxerunt propugnacula, unde immanissimis viribus in Deos depugnavere. Quid porro ab Apolline, Pallade, aut Marte in debellandis illis gestum fingitur, quod noster hic, non pari suscepit virtute, et fortuna perfecit? Si vero de perdomitis tandem, non prorsus triumphaverit, fatis Tuis omnino reputandum arbitramur; quae noluerint Patriae genium tam insignem salutem alteri, quam Tibi ipsi debere: Enceladum quippe Titanasque

---

[1] James VI. of Scotland and I. of England. "Our royal master's favourite benediction, *Beati pacifici.*"—Lord Dalgarno in Scott's *Fortunes of Nigel*, ch. xiii.; *cf.* also ch. ix.
[2] Henry IV. of France, grandfather of Prince Charles.
[3] Verg. Aen. iv. 11.
[4] Juv. x. 174.

alios, qui Patrem in vinculis detinerent; non alio quam filii fulmine, Aetneos in specus deturbandos esse censuerunt.

Maxime insuper Princeps, quid utilius Tibi ad ea tendenti, ad quae Divino Humanoque jure obstringeris; Patris, videlicet, Patriaeque ab immani tyrannide vindicationem: quam eum quasi prodromum, et viae ducem in oculis semper habere, qui et primus arcana perduellium consilia, artesque et insidias detexit, et unus ferme infandam perdomari audaciam; et coalitas prius quam cognitas vires, infringi posse demonstravit? Neutiquam enim in eo deprehendes *corpus sine Pectore*, qui, cum ne armis quidem sit, quam consilio praestantior, monstrum illud in cunis jugulandum suasit (utinam et persuasisset) et adultum, tantum non contrivit, ne virtuti tuae materies tam ampla praecideretur. Enimvero praeter insignem in eo fortitudinem, et rei militaris peritiam non vulgarem, invenies civilis quoque prudentiae documenta, quamvis tristi temporum fato parum credita; eximia tamen, et Tibi, posterisque olim profutura: dum perduelles, nimiâ optimi Regis mansuetudine, clementiâ in reos, in indignos fiduciâ, munificentiâ in ingratos, indulgentiâ in omnes, magis quam suis viribus fretos, mature occupandos, et justis armis (quando aliter fieri nequiret) compescendos censuit; prius quam vires, ex permissâ illis morâ, immodice valescerent. Quod si factum fuisset, (ut alia taceam) non civili adeo sanguine horruisset Britannia nostra, non tam impie, tam foede habita fuissent magnificentissima Domini nostri templa, non Procerum Mystarumque cruore maduissent fora, non detenti, indignâ sub custodiâ Pater Fratresque, nec, quasi vidua Mater, Tuque ipse extorris, in cognata quamvis ac hospitali, transmarina tamen degeretis terra.

*Quis talia fando*
*Temperet a lachrimis?*[1]

Cum autem in rebus gestis, etiam supra invidiam claris, Omnipotentis Dei dextera splendidissime eluceat; ut ad illum unum solida ac omnis referatur gloria: quis eum etiam non agnoscat, ornet, praedicet, et amet, quem operum ejusmodi patratorem, ac quasi thaumaturgum, clementissimus Dominus constituere sit dignatus? Si enim cum solis, et apertis hostibus Montisrosano fuisset confligendum, leviora forsan videri possent illa: quod duobus semper, plerumque vero tribus exercitibus a fronte, a tergo, a latere impetitus: quorum vel minimus copias ejus omnes, militum numero, armorum genere, et copiâ commeatuum quam longissime excedebat; sese fortiter semper, ac feliciter expediverit. Quod pulvis tormentarius, arma, aliaque instrumenta belli, nulla unquam subministrata fuerint, praeter ea, quae devictis hostibus eripuit. Quod anni spatio sex insignes, ac

---

[1] Verg. Aen. ii. 6.

plenas reportaverit victorias: omnique Scotiâ conjuratos Proceres penitus exegerit. Quod hiemem rigidissimo caelo soloque non in tabernis, ac ne sub pellibus quidem; sed plerumque sub die egerit. Quod frigidâ, ac defluente saepius ex liquente nive, sitim jugiter depulerit: nec ullo pane, aut sale; sed solâ bubulâ, atque eâ non raro macidâ simul ac macilentâ toleraverit famem, et alia belli incommoda. Verum longe difficilior illa lucta fuit, cum eis qui videri volebant Regiae Majestatis acerrimi vindices. Aliorum quidem segni ignaviâ, insolenti aliorum superbiâ, aliorum vili pusillanimitate, faedâ aliorum avaritiâ, aliorum infandâ perfidiâ: quibus omnibus tolerandis, ac corrigendis, nisi invicta prorsus constantia, et charissimi Regio indomitus amor, nunquam suffecisset.

Non enim ille severitate legum, aut poenis (quod alii Imperatores assolent) suos coërcere, aut potuit, aut debuit; qui nullis stipendiis, sed solâ charitate in Regem, et in eum benevolentiâ militabant: quibusque facillimum semper ad conjuratos fuerit transfugium, si vel levissimâ lacessiti injuriâ, aut ignominiâ notati sibi ipsis visi fuissent; viri plerique procaces, factiosi, et ad defectionem proni, si vel tantillum fuissent irritati. Adeo ut in exercitu illo authoritatem cum gratiâ conservare, res fuerit omnium difficillima. Neque aliud ejus animum violentius exercuit, quam consilia, actionesque suas aliorum modulo metiri, aut hoc saltem simulare cogeretur. Verum ille ut rem Regiam promoveret, hostium odium, aemulorum invidiam, aulicorum calumnias, amicorum querelas, vulgi contumelias, et (quod omnibus acerbius fuit, ac superstitiosae plebis animos magis perterruit) vatum prorsus furentium, diras, atque anathemata susque deque ferens, quasi ab alto despexit; omnino ille nobiliore militiâ, et feliciore seculo dignus Imperator.

Quod denique, Princeps Serenissime, e re tuâ maxime futurum spero, demonstrabit hic Tuus Montisrosanus Scotos nunquam omnes ab optimo defecisse Rege. Quod cum nominis nostri iniquissimi hostes, acerbe nimis, et malitiose calumniantur, non magis immerentibus viris, et Regis sui causâ omnia volentibus injurii; quam Patri, Tibique insidiosi et infidi. Hocque unum agunt, ut suspectos vobis, adeoque inutiles reddant amicos, servos, subditosque omnium optimos, ac fidissimos; a quorum fide et fortitudine male sibi metuunt, ne eorum ope, et operâ, ipsi pessimi consiliarii aliquando dignas proditionis luant poenas. Ne vero quis obstrepat, nos male de nobilissimâ Anglorum gente sentire, aut dicere (a quo sane scelere toto abhorremus animo) eorum quidem plurimos fidelem fortemque operam navasse Regi, ad aeternam suam gloriam, ultro agnoscimus, praedicamus, et gratulamur. Hocque unum postulamus, ut aequo jure nobiscum, et candore non minus ingenuo agant, nec factionis cujusvis, quantumvis potentis, ac validae crimen universae impingant genti: quod cum sibi fieri nolint, aliis ne fecerint. Neque diffiteantur fuisse Scotos, omnium ordinum viros praestantissimos; qui perditissimis temporibus, Regiam Majestatem ab hominum utriusque gentis pessimorum conspiratione, vel sanguine suo assertam et vindicatam voluerint.

Atque haec usque adeo manifesta sunt, ut absque omni jactatione fidenter possint praedicare, se, nullis conductos stipendiis, nullâ mercede aliâ, quam in clementissimum Regem fide, et pietate impulsos, damna longe graviora, pro rerum suarum ratione, passos esse, ac perduellibus retulisse, et nobiliores de eis acquisivisse victorias; quam illi, qui exhausto penitus Regis aerario, ad tantam ferme rerum omnium inopiam redegerunt,[1] ut sese conjuratis quasi dedere coactus fuerit. Heu, quanto, ut videtur, satius fuisset, si ad Scotos suos se recepisset; non rebelles istos, qui contra eum pro conjuratis Anglis stabant; sed pios illos, fortes, et fidos, qui sub Montisrosani imperio illi militabant. Omnino his, qui cum vicario ejus, et militiae praefecto, ea et fortiter ausi, et feliciter exsequuti sunt, quae summâ fide, hocce commentario descripsimus: nihil arduum, aut difficile videri potuisset, tam chari pignoris praesentiâ animatis. Nec quisquam, nisi rerum Scoticarum ignarus, dubitaverit praesentem illum civium animos ad sententiam suam facillime fuisse pertracturum; sponte videlicet in optimi Regis gratiam propendentium. Et hoc cum probe notum esset conjuratis proceribus, sedulo caverunt ne illi in solum natale reditus pateret: cum vix xl. passuum millibus abesset a limite.

Et Scoti quidem, utut eo potissimum tempore, durissimo servitutis jugo tyrannis istis subjecti; horrendis tamen diris eos prosequi non metuebant, qui pudendi istius consilii, de tradendo Anglis Scotorum Rege authores forent vel participes. Atque illi etiam, qui hactenus cum faederatis in aliis senserant, non obscure, quamvis cum capitis periculo praedicabant; suffecisse decessoribus Regis unicum Scotiae Regnum, suffecisse majores suos eis tutandis, ac propugnandis contra potentissimos et ferocissimos hostes: Anglos praesertim, de quibus, dum pro Regibus suis starent, multos et insignes egerint triumphos. Et quamvis cum diversis, tam externis, quam ejusdem insulae incolis, vario saepe Marte dimicassent; nunquam tamen eo redigi potuisse, ut Reges suos aliorum arbitrio et potestati permitterent ingratiis. Id vero ne sponte jam facerent, majorum umbras, sanctissimam Regii nominis reverentiam, fidem, pietatem, famam apud exteros, ad posteros exemplum, jus omne divinum ac humanum obstare. Hoc denique quam apertissime cum ipso suo faedere pugnare, quo Deum immortalem testem vindicemque invocarunt; se Regem, ejusque dignitatem, amplitudinem, ac salutem, contra omnes mortales, ad extremum

---

[1] *Sc.*, eum, regem.

vitae spiritum propugnaturos. Adeo ut (prater seditiosos, et sacrilegos, qui et malis artibus exercitum comparaverant, et in eundem summum obtinuerant imperium; ejusque armis, inermium, et imparatorum, sine duce, sine capite, civium cervicibus, et jugulis imminebant) plerique omnes Scoti nihil magis habuerint in votis, quam ut aliquando Regi optimo fidem suam, ac obsequium testatum facerent, et vel sanguine suo obsignarent. Nec sane ambigendum est, quin illi immanissimâ tyrannide oppressi, ad justissimum et mitissimum redeant imperium, ubi primum optatissimâ Paterni, aut Tui vultus praesentiâ, quasi salutari sidere fuerint afflati.

Tuum ergo est, Princeps Nobilissime ac potentissime, in hoc omnes nervos, omnem animi impetum intendere, ut laboranti Patriae Patrique succurras. Opem ad hoc operamque Tuam, omnes serio flagitant, orant, expectant, suam pollicentur. Provincia haec jure naturae, et Patrio Tua est: et in te non civium modo, sed et orbis ora, oculique intenti sunt; piique omnes precantur, ut cum bono Deo, et faustis ominibus, hoc restituendae Ecclesiae, quae tot foedissimarum sectarum sordibus inquinata jacet, stabiliendi denuo Paterni Regni, recuperandae pristinae felicitatis, et gloriae opus strenue aggressus, ad optatum pacis ordinisque finem feliciter perducas. Atque ut olim (sed sero) unum illud Europae antiquissimum Regnum, Te dominum ac Imperatorem agnoscat, amet et veneretur: aeternumque ea felicitas obtingat soboli Tuae

*Et natis natorum, et qui nascentur ab illis.*

Quo fine, Princeps Clementissime, dignare Montisrosanum Tuum erigere, amplecti, fovere; eoque uti, seu in bello duce, seu senatore in pace, tanto Principi (ut spero, et voveo) nunquam erubescendo.

*Vale. Kal. Oct. CIƆIƆCXLVII.*[1]

---

[1] The Amsterdam edition has here *die 7 Febr.* 1648.

# LECTORI BENEVOLO

## S.

PAUCULA sunt, amice lector, quae commentariolum hunc lecturos ignorare nolim: quorum alia quidem ad Montisrosarum Marchionem, cujus res in Patria biennio gestae, hic describuntur; alia vero ad operis authorem pertinent. Ac imprimis quidem constare velim illum antiquissimae ac celebratissimae in Scotiâ Graemorum familiae Principem esse; et priscâ Scotorum linguâ Graemum magnum nuncupari. Originem generis ducit a celeberrimo illo in ejus Regni Historiis Graemo, Fergusii ejus nominis secundi, Scotorum Regis socero; qui primus generi sui auspiciis, vallum illud Severi, ab aestuario Forthae, ad Glottae amnis ostium, quâ parte angustissima est Britannia, productum, et ultimum Romani imperii limitem expugnavit, et evertit: Provinciamque Romanam arctioribus conclusit terminis; unde factum est, ut non obscura ejusdem valli vestigia quae etiamnum extant, apud accolas, ejus nomen in hunc diem retineant, qui Graemi murum vocitant. Idem vero nobilissimae gentis conditor, defuncto genero Fergusio superstes, Administrator Regni, et Nepoti suo Gubernator datus, pacis non minus quam belli artibus clarus; cum Christianae fidei Doctores, recenti bello extorres, postliminio reduxisset in patriam; nec minus Ecclesiam quam Regnum optimis ordinasset legibus, adulto Nepoti regimen sponte tradidit. Floruit ille Augustorum Arcadii et Honorii temporibus, an. salutis humanae circiter cccc; a quo longâ serie, et laetâ, seri descendere nepotes, qui avitam referentis virtutem, subsequutis seculis praeluxerunt. In his enituit fortissimus Graemus; qui cum Dumbaro tempestivum admodum auxilium, periclitanti attulit Patriae adversus Danos; rerum in Anglia tunc temporis potitos, inque Scotiam cum validissimis copiis non semel frustra invectos. Majorum deinde omnium virtutes, laudesque aequavit nobilissimus Johannes Graemus, qui post Alexandri tertii mortem, interregni tempore, Brussio Bailioloque de jure discrepantibus; Patriae libertatis, cum inclyto illo Wilielmo Walla Prorege, contra Edwardi Regis Angli iniquissimam tyrannidem accerrimus fuit vindex; et post plurima praeclare gesta, pro eâdem strenue pugnans, honestissimo functus est fato. Visitur etiam hodie sepulchrum ejus in sacello, quod fanum valli, ab eodem Graemi vallo (ad quod positum est) dicitur. Ad quod etiam, agros sane amplos, et uberes, a primo illo Graemo, nepotibus quasi per manus transmissos; jure haereditario Montisrosarum Marchio possidet.

Verum ne ab obscuris modo tantae antiquitatis vestigiis, illustrissimo Heroi nobilitatem generis aucupari, ac astruere videamur; praeterire nequeo, avum hujus Montisrosarum Comitem nostrâ ferme memoriâ, amplissimis in illo Regno honoribus ornatum, ac felicissime functum esse. Qui, cum supremus esset Scotiae Cancellarius, quo tempore beatae memoriae Rex Jacobus, ejus nominis sextus, rerum in Angliâ potitus est; ab eodem in Scotiâ creatus est Prorex: et in supremo illo dignitatis gradu, Regi juxta, ac populo charissimus, e vivis excessit. Patrem vero habuit corporis, animique dotibus virum in paucis insignem; nec minus apud alias gentes, quam domi illustrem: qui cum plurimas, easque honorific-entissimas legationes pro Jacobo Rege obiisset, supremi Consilii Praeses a Carolo renunciatus, praematuro fato Patriae, bonisque omnibus ereptus, maximum sui apud omnes desiderium reliquit. Et quid tandem de ipso nepote censendum, sperandumque sit; ex eis quae hactenus gessit; cum nunc quoque sesquianno post, vixdum trigesimum et sextum annum attigerit, judicio tuo permitto.

Unum hoc in gratiam tuam addam, benigne lector; tres hactenus fuisse Scotorum Regno fatales ferme periodos: primam a Romanis, quorum jugum, Graemi illius primi ex nobilissima Brittonum Fulgentiana familia oriundi ductu, repulerunt Majores nostri. Alteram a Danis, quorum ne admitterent imperium, secundi illius Graemi praesertim eximiae debetur virtuti. Tertiam ab Anglis, et Nortmannis, quos tertius ille Graemus semel iterumque Scotiâ exegit; ac multis et gravibus affecit damnis. Adeo ut (quod de Scipionibus in Africa olim dictum fuit) fatale quasi videatur Graemorum nomen, quod Patriae, in ultimo discrimine positae succurrat: nec sine numine pessimis istis temporibus exortum hunc, qui Regi suum jus, civibus pacem, salutemque, et libertatem pristinam, familiae vero suae avitam laudem ac decus conservatum iret. Atque haec ferme ea sunt quae de Montisrosano praemittenda paucis censui.

Quod vero ad scriptorem attinet, sic habe: eum in hujusmodi studiis non admodum versatum, nec laudem ab ingenii viribus sperasse; quas nullas plane esse, vel exiguas, lubens agnoscit: nec mercedem spectasse, aut questum; qui accerrimi sunt multis ad scribendum stimuli. Verum solo propagandae, ad posteros, exterosque veritatis desiderio, opusculo huic admovisse manum. Enimvero felici sceleri plurimos; afflictae veritati perpaucos fore patronos; ex cognata huic causa, recenti, et lachrimabili experientiâ perdidicerat. Cum enim iidem in utroque Regno conjurati, suis artibus (mendaciis nimirum et calumniis) Ecclesiam evertissent; ut ex ejus reditibus, maximo sacrilegio partis, avaritiae suae litarent, posterosque dira locupletarent anathemate: non defuere tamen qui immensis eos laudibus, tanquam de patria, de Ecclesia ipsa, adeoque universo genere humano bene meritos extollerent, et sanctissimos Dei servos, Confessores Martyresque, quod illis constanter restiterint, maledictis, et blasphemiis onerarent ac proscinderent. Dubitandum itaque minime arbitratus est, quin hi qui eisdem artibus Regiam convellere Majestatem, ac destruere satagunt, ut ejus potiantur honoribus, cum Majestatis et perfidiae crimine acquisitis; invenirent quamplurimos, qui simili maledicendi libidine, in excellentissimum virum, et splendidissima ejus gesta debaccharentur: et, quod de vespis dicitur, ex fragrantissimis et saluberrimis herbis, succos, suâ linguâ, aut stilo venenatos colligerent, ac incautis, et ignorantibus propinarent. Huic malo, brevem hanc simplicemque narratiunculam, tanquam tempestivum antidotum, sincerae veritatis amatoribus offerre libuit; cujus tam pertinax voluit esse assertor, ut, quamvis hominum odium, invidiamque non levem in se derivaturum praevideret: nec illis serviliter adblandiri, nec eam obscuris et dubiis verborum ambagibus involvere decreverit. Ille enim, ut liber natus est, liberque educatus; libertatem non nisi cum anima perdere constituit. Quamvis autem aliam boni Historici laudem, ab ingenio, vel arte, vel eloquentia, nullam ambiat: unam tamen illam simplicissimae veritatis, jure suo postulare videtur; qui propugnandae illi propagandaeque, charissima hujus seculi posthabuit: ter bonis omnibus exutus, toties carcerem foedissimum ac squallidissimum passus, tertio eodem nomine exulat. Hilaris tamen est, ac laetus, quod nullius apud homines criminis reus, dignus habeatur a Domino, qui ista patiatur justitiae et veritatis ergo. Tu vero candide lector veritatem saltem in eo ama; caetera aequi bonique consule, ac vale.

---

NOTE.—In these Prefaces the original spelling and punctuation have been preserved. In the following Commentary they are slightly revised.

DE REBUS

Anno CIƆIƆCXLIV, et duobus
sequentibus ab illustrissimo

# IACOBO MARCHIONE MONTISROSARUM

IN SCOTIA GESTIS

COMMENTARIUS.

---

## CAP. I.

IACOBUS MONTISROSARUM MARCHIO, foederatorum in Scotia partes hactenus amplexus, nimis strenuam illis et infeliciter operam navaverat. Nihil enim illi quam religionem, regis honorem et dignitatem, leges patrias, libertatemque antiquissimi regni, a potentissimis hostibus Romanis, Saxonibus, Danis, Nortmannis, majorum sudore, sanguine, virtute et vita, fortiter et feliciter semper vindicatam, speciose admodum obtendebant. Et quas ipsi finxerant fabulas, ad populum per idoneos ministros deferebant. Quasi nihil aliud in aula Anglicana ageretur, quam ut libera gens, velut in provinciam redacta, veterum inimicorum imperio manciparetur. Interim etiam publicis attestationibus et solenni juramento sese obstrinxerant, non vi et armis, aut alio quovis modo, quam per libellos supplices, apud dominum Regem procuraturos, ut humillimis subditorum suorum supplicationibus clementer annueret, et authoritate sua caveret, ne carissima patria in religione aut libertate aliquid detrimenti caperet.

Verum anno demum MIƆCXXXIX, Montisrosanus comperit praeclara illa ad imperiti simul et superstitiosi vulgi animos inescandos, et a rege (tanquam religionis et libertatis hoste), alienandos praeparata. Nec enim apud illum dissimulabant foederati, nimis diu apud Scotos regnatum esse a monarchis: nec recte cum illis agi posse, Stuarto vel uno superstite (cognomen illud est regiae in Scotia familiae): in eorum vero exstirpatione ordiendum esse a Principe: adeoque regem ipsum regiamque Majestatem peti sensit. Quapropter horrendum scelus vehementer detestatus, foederatorum partes constituit deserere, consilia frustrari, opes imminuere, vires labefactare, et regem regiamque authoritatem sartam tectam pro viribus conservare. Quia vero foederati, qua vi, qua dolo, universos ferme subditos ad se pertraxerant, seque unum eorum potentiae coercendae imparem judicabat, consilium suum non statim et temere propolandum existimavit. Plerosque enim inter eos habebat amicos, viros tam satellitum et clientium multitudine, quam authoritate et opibus florentes, quos ab eis separare et secum ad partes regias revocare decrevit. Et hac arte non aspernandam manum contrahere, tam Regis, quam suae saluti melius consultum fore duxit.

Interea foederati validum exercitum contra Regem comparant. Et ad Duns oppidum in solenni conventu, absente Montisrosano, invadendam armis Angliam decernunt. Quod quidem ante sex hebdomadas in secreto suo conciliabulo conjurationis principes statuerant; adeoque libellis apologeticis (quibus expeditionis suae causas declarare laborabant) per omnem Britanniam divulgari curaverant. Hoc eorum consilium reversus Montisrosanus, cum impedire non posset, videri voluit probare. Ducebat Montisrosanus in exercitu peditum duo millia, equites quingentos: quinque vero millibus imperitabant amici, illi devinctissimi, et qui in hoc negotio operam suam pro Rege sancte promiserant. Et sane si plerique eorum non fefellissent fidem, vel omnem exercitum ad Regem secum perduxissent, vel saltem foederatorum conatus facile reddidissent irritos. Positis porro castris ad Tuedam amnem (qui finitimorum regnorum limes est), sorte inter duces proceresque jacta, Montisrosanus obtigit ut primus fluvium trajiceret. Quod quidem ipse pedes, sequentibus copiis suis pedestribus, alacriter perfecit: quo facilius consilium suum occultaret, omnemque suspicionem amoliretur. Aeque enim hominis in exercitu potentia et liberalis animi integritas male sibi consciis perduellibus formidabilis esse incipiebat: adeo ut omnes ejus gestus, dicta, et facta diligentissime observarent.

Post haec superato Tina amne, quatuor M. passuum supra Novum castrum, proditione ducum Anglicorum, qui se cum validissimo exercitu regio Eboracum receperunt, oppido potiuntur. Missis vero hinc inde arbitris qui de pace agerent, induciae secutae sunt. Dederat ad Regem Montisrosanus induciarum tempore literas, quibus fidem, debitum obsequium, et pronam voluntatem serenissimae Majestati testatus erat: nec aliud quidquam continebant. Istas per ipsos Regis cubicularios noctu suffuratas, et transcriptas, qui gratia apud Regem caeteris mortalibus praestabant, ad foederatos Novum castrum transmittendas curarunt. Illi etenim de die in diem maxime arcana Regis consilia (quorum ipsi soli vel authores fuerant vel participes) foederatis communicabant. Super istis literis Montisrosanum satis acerbe interrogare non erubuerunt perduellium quidam promptissimi. Et quamvis apertam litem intendere aut in jus vocare non auderent, quia gratia et potentia in exercitu plurimum valebat, querelis tamen et calumniis apud vulgus onerabant. Plerosque enim habebant per universum regnum obnoxios sibi praedicatores; quorum venalibus linguis ad populi animos quoquo versum flectendos abutebantur. Nec alia re rebellionem suam efficacius promoverunt, aut etiamnum promovent, quam quod popularibus concionibus boni illi oratores regem ipsum omnesque fidos sibi subditos tanquam Christi hostes (ut illi loqui amant), acerbissime proscindant; ipsi Christiani nominis scandala, et opprobria.

Montisrosano vero in Scotiam reverso, et nihil animo versanti, quam quo tandem pacto regiam Majestatem ab imminente rebellionis procella vindicaret, hanc rationem inire visum est. Primariae potentiae et nobilitatis plurimos icto foedere sibi adstrinxit. Quo sancte polliciti sunt se regem ipsum et omnia regiae Majestatis privilegia et praerogativas avitas et legitimas, cum bonorum omnium et vitae discrimine, contra quosvis tam domesticos, quam extraneos hostes ad ultimum vitae spiritum propugnaturos. Et sane eo ventum erat, ut in apertam secessionem res fuerit evasura, adeoque optatum consecutura finem; nisi quidam metu, levitate, et pusillanimitate (qui sunt pessimi arcanorum custodes), rem totam foederatis prodidissent. Hinc tumultus non exigua, et jurgia; sed pro tempore pacata. Neque enim adhuc durius quid in Montisrosanum palam decernere audebant. Postea vero foederati, novo praestito sacramento, exercitum ad obsequium suum confirmarunt. Et arctissimo foedere, adjuncto sibi Parliamento Anglicano, quamvis a privati cujusvis machinationibus satis securi sibi viderentur, de Montisrosano tamen tollendo serio consultant: cujus erectum ad alta et honesta, quantumvis ardua, animum non poterant ferre.

Ad muniendam ergo tanto facinori viam, opera quorundam Aulicorum, quos spe et largitionibus corruperant, datas a rege ad Montisrosanum literas intelligunt: easque tabellarii (Stuarti cujusdam, Trequarii comitis clientis) ephippiis insutas esse. Tabellarium vixdum Scotiae limites ingressum prehendunt, ephippium dirumpunt, literasque inveniunt. Nihil plane in illis scriptum erat, quod optimum Regem jubere, optimum subditum exsequi dedeceat. Optimi tamen illi calumniarum architecti per idoneos ministros rumores spargunt plane tragicos; deprehensa tandem et detecta regis cum Montisrosano consilia de evertenda religione et perdenda patria. Ac ne tum quidem palam in hominem animadvertere ausi, incautum ac nihil tale suspicantem, cum Naperio Marchistoniae regulo et Sterlinio de Kêêre equite (quibuscum non affinitate tantum, sed et intima familiaritate et amicitia junctus erat) in arcem Edinburgensem conjiciunt.

Pace tandem inter utriusque regni populos stabilita (inter quos nullum intercesserat bellum, praeterquam quod in clementissimum dominum et justissimum Regem communibus auspiciis meditabantur) conventus ordinum Edinburgum indictus est. Isti Rex ipse interfuit. Montisrosanus coram rege et solenni hoc conventu causam dicere omnibus votis, sed frustra desideravit. Foederati enim ejus innocentiae, et suae injustitiae sibi conscii, in hoc unum animos intendebant, ut hominem in vinculis detinerent inauditum, quoad Rex Scotia excederet, et illi in conventu omnia ex animi sui sententia transigerent cum Rege. Et sane multum metuebant ne prudentia, fortitudine, et gratia, qua tam apud aequales regni Proceres quam plebem valebat, longe plurimos ad sententiam suam pro incolumitate et authoritate Regis conservanda perduceret. Rege tandem in Angliam reverso, Montisrosanus cum suis e carcere liberatus, quia in conventu statutum erat ne in colloquium cum Rege veniret, paulisper domi suae consedit: sub finem anni MIƆCXLI.

## CAP. II.

ANNO MIƆCXLII Foederati utriusque regni larvam deponere et apertius rem gerere coeperunt. Perduelles in Anglia querelis injustis, ineptis, importunis Regem fatigare, calumniis onerare, scurrilibus cantiunculis sacrum nomen profanare, infamibus libellis (quos Pasquillos vocant) vilem facere, tumultus ciere, perditissimos quosque de infima plebe armatos magno numero in ipsum palatium immittere, extrema cuncta minitari. In quos cum ille jure regio animadvertere potuisset; rem tamen potius ad Parliamentum deferre satius judicavit, quo eos sibi devinctiores redderet. Sed frustra hoc et alia pleraque viris ingratissimis, ac horum scelerum authoribus et patronis gratificatus est Rex clementissimus. Longe enim plura illis et majora in civium suorum gratiam et (quod ab illis praetendebatur) levamen et securitatem indulserat, quam in universum omnes majores sui reges Angliae, postquam Gulielmus Nortmannus primus rerum in Anglia potitus est. Tandem ergo ut se suosque praesenti periculo subduceret, Londino cedere invitus cogitur. Reginam quidem, ut vitae ejus consuleret, in Belgicam ablegat; ipse Eboracum se confert. Parliamentorum vero ordines (ut cum illis loquar) illico, et primi quidem ad arma convolant. Et iisdem copiis quas rex (assignatis ex eorum sententia ducibus) in Hiberniam destinaverat, quaeque in procinctu erant, ad Regem ipsum opprimendum abutuntur.

Perduelles in Scotia, qui Regi satis virium esse ad coercendos Anglos probe noverant, foederatis suis in manifesto discrimine positis deesse minime voluerunt.

Et quamvis Rex clementissimus in conventu Edinburgeno, de quo dictum est supra, ex voto illis prorsus satisfecisset (quod in acta publica ab eis relatum est), ad bellum tamen illi in Anglia inferendum sese comparant.

Quo vero res suas domi in tuto collocarent, Montisrosanum (a quo ferme uno sibi metuebant) ad suas partes denuo pertrahere summa ope nituntur, Supremi in exercitu Legati munus, et quaecunque alia, quae suae forent potestatis, desideraret, ultro deferentes. Ille longe maximam procellam Regis capiti imminentem conspicatus, ut eum certiorem faceret, quo maturius occurri posset, juncto, consilii et itineris participe, Ogilvio regulo, iter in Angliam capessit.

Apud Novum castrum nuncium accipit, Reginam nuper ex Batavia reducem Berlingtoniam in agro Eboracensi appulisse. Illuc se propere confert, et Reginam omnia ordine recenset. Illa mari vehementer jactata, et nauticis molestiis aegra, respondit; pluribus de eo negotio cum illo consulturam postquam Eboracum venerint. Eo ubi ventum est, Regina Montisrosanum ultro appellat. Ille rem totam denuo explicat, et non minus periculum a foederatis Scotis, quam ab Anglis imminere demonstrat, nisi mature obviam eatur. Rogatus vero sententiam, quid potissimum faciendum arbitraretur? vim vi repellendam dixit. Non regi deesse in Scotia subditos, viros fidos et fortes; non deesse illis animos, non opes, non vires, quas foederatis opponerent, si quidquam contra Regem auderent moliri; unicum illis deesse Regis mandatum, sine quo nihil attentaturos, illo vero animatos, nihil non ausuros. Periculum esse tantum in mora. Foederatos, ubi exercitum comparaverint, caeteros, si quis vel hiscere audeat, facile contrituros. Principiis tanti mali obstandum, viperam in ovo conterendam, et seram medicinam, ubi in totum corpus praevaluerit morbus.

Consilium salubre et tempestivum; quod procul dubio prudentissima Regina probasset. Verum sic secundo vento velificantibus, ecce remoram ab adventu Hamiltonii ducis e Scotia, specie quidem ut Reginam salutaret, et sospiti felicem reditum gratularetur; reipsa vero ut Montisrosani consilia destrueret. Consciis enim et consentientibus foederatis, illuc advolaverat. Nec ille quidem periculum a foederatis Scotis dissimulavit; extenuare tamen conatus est. Montisrosani vero consilium, ut temerarium, imprudens, et intempestivum damnavit. Gentem ferocem et bellicosam non vi et armis, sed lenitate et officiis reducendam. Bellum, praesertim civile ultimum, et victoriam plerumque poenitendum remedium. Incertam belli aleam. Regi etiam victori, tristem fore de civibus suis triumphum: victo vero, expectanda quae dicere abhorreret animus. Omnia ad pacem cum ista gente conservandam experienda. Necdum eo ventum esse, ut de pace et conciliandis eorum animis desperandum sit. Totum denique negotium in se suscipere, si Rex ejus fidei et industriae rem cum vicaria potestate committeret. Regerebat Montisrosanus, nihil aliud agi, quam ut tempus traheretur, quoad perduelles coacto exercitu Regi facultatem omnem se suosque ab eorum tyrannide vindicandi praeriperent. Quod quidem verum fuisse, moestissimus probavit eventus. Succubuit in hoc certamine Montisrosanus, aulicis artibus inferior; cujus nunc toto orbe splendidissimae virtutes, reginae nondum innotuerant. Reversus in Scotiam victor Hamiltonius nullum non lapidem movere pro Rege videbatur.

Foederati interim propria authoritate (contra manifestas regni leges) conventum ordinum Edinburgum indicunt. Quem quidem Regi exitiosum fore, oculati omnes, et quotquot rebus ejus studebant, praeviderunt, adeoque ab illo horrebant, ut praesentia sua honestandum minime putarent. Hamiltonius vero nomine et authoritate Regis interposita, eosdem per literas compellat, ut conventui frequentes interessent. Nec dubitare se, quin suffragiis superiores forent, si operam suam hac vice Regi non denegarent. Quod si secus accideret, paratum se fore, cum amicis, contra foederatos protestari, et statim secedere. Nomine regio et illa spe illecti, proceres frequentes comitiis intersunt, Montisrosano paucisque illi adhaerentibus exceptis. Sed et cum Montisrosano idem per amicos egit ut pro fide et prona in Regem voluntate se illis adjungeret. Ille (qui omnia merito suspecta habebat) respondit se quidem paratum esse ad quodvis discrimen subeundum, sub ejus etiam imperio qui vicaria regis potestate et authoritate emineret; hac tamen lege, ut fidem daret, si justum et aequum in conventu impetrare non possent, se illud armis repetiturum. Ille protestaturum se respondit, non pugnaturum. Quibus perpensis, Montisrosanus ut se ipsum purum conservaret, rei eventum praestolaturus domi se continuit.

In conventu illo foederati suffragiis plus minus septuaginta superiores, regiam authoritatem penitus conculcarunt, jus vocandi comitia, scribendi milites, foedera cum exteris nationibus contrahendi, aliaque hactenus inaudita, invito rege, sibi arrogant. Et in malorum omnium cumulum, validum exercitum cogendum contra Regem et foederatis suis Anglis auxilio mittendum decernunt. In quem finem, subsidiis et novis vectigalibus populum onerant, eisque longe gravioribus, quam si in unum congerantur omnia, quae temporibus difficillimis, post duo annorum millia, centum et novem [1] Reges imposuere.

Montisrosanus ergo, qui regia authoritate Regem ipsum perditum iri conspiciebat, nec sese simul foederatorum viribus et Regis mandatis opponere poterat, tristis et anxius omnia dissimulabat. Foederati vero, propter repulsam quam Eboraci passus erat, et praelatum Hamiltonium, alienatum ejus a Rege animum rati, clam denuo per amicos tentant, si qua prece aut pretio pellectum, ad se pertrahere possent, magistratus, opes, supremas in curia et exercitu dignitates ultro deferentes. Quae quidem ille non admodum aegre audire videbatur, quo altius in intima eorum consilia penetraret. Foederati, quo certior simul et sanctior amicitia coiret, magnum illum foederis sui Apostolum, Alexandrum Hendersonium, ad eum ablegant; qui scilicet illi omnibus abunde satisfaceret. Ejus viri Montisrosanus avide expetebat colloquium, a quo profundissima foederatorum consilia expiscari neutiquam dubitabat. Ne vero clandestini cum isto viro congressus offendiculo essent aliis, qui secum regiae Majestati benevolebant, Naperium et Ogilvium regulos, Sterlinum Kerium equitem aliosque Regi impensius faventes, testes et conscios adhibere statuit. Et ad ripam Forthae amnis non procul Sterlino oppido congrediuntur.

Montisrosanus adventum tanti viri gratissimum sibi dixit, utpote cujus fidei, integritati, et in rebus arduis prudentiae plurimum tribueret. Se quidem ad amoliendam post recentes simultates hostium invidiam domi suae substitisse; rerum omnium quae in conventu transigerentur ignarum; et quomodo in tam lubrico reipublicae statu se gereret, ferme incertum profitetur. Rogare porro, ut pro solito candore, quid illis in animo sit, libere impertiretur. Hendersonius ex hac oratione inclinantis ad foederatos animi conjecturam faciens, quo hominem magis sibi obnoxium redderet, plane et sine ambagibus respondit. Statutum esse exercitum quam possent validissimum, foederatis suis Anglis auxilio, contra copias regias conscribere. In hoc acquiescere unanimiter omnes utriusque regni foederatos, vel Regem in ordinem cogendum esse, vel illis pereundum. Nihil jam optatius accidere posse, quam si ille cum aequalibus regni proceribus, adeoque caeteris ordinibus gratiam et amicitiam inire velit. Hoc omnibus gratum; ipsi vero non modo utile, sed et honorificum fore. Ejus exemplo alios (si qui sint) qui vanam regii nomine umbram revereantur, illico ad foederatos transituros. Se quidem Domino Deo suo quam maximas debiturum gratias, quod tam egregii facinoris ministrum et quasi sequestrum facere dignatus fuerit. Enixe denique rogare, ut animi sui sententiam exponeret, ejusque fidei et industriae committeret ea, quae a conventu ordinum ad utilitatem

---

[1] *Vide* Author's Dedication, p. 341.

dignitatemque suam fieri desideraret : certoque sibi persuaderet in omnibus ex voto satisfactum iri.

Montisrosanus eorum notitiam liquido adeptus, quae magnopere desiderabat, suspensos adhuc et incertos eorum animos detinere studebat. Quid enim responsi daret ? si se illis hostem palam praedicaret, hoc Regi quidem inutile, sibi vero exitiosum fore praevidebat. Ampliorem vero de se spem facere dedignabatur; eaque polliceri, quae exsequi non decreverat, manifesto dedecori fore reputabat generosus animus. Hanc ergo ingreditur viam. Interfuit isti colloquio cum Hendersonio Iacobus Rollocus eques, familiae perantiquae et opibus florentis princeps. Huic olim Montisrosani soror matrimonio locata fuit ; qua defuncta, Argathelii Marchionis, foederatorum in Scotia coryphaei, sororem secundis nuptiis duxerat. Hic pari affinitate utrique junctus, peridoneus amicitiae conciliandae internuncius videbatur. Istum Montisrosanus interrogat, utrum quae ab illis prolata essent, publica conventus ordinum authoritate, an privato tantum studio niterentur ? Ille Hendersonio a conventu data esse mandata arbitrari se respondit. Hendersonius vero negat; nihil tamen dubitare se, quin conventus rata habeat, quae ipse promisisset. Montisrosanus nihil certi statuere posse se asserit absque publica fide, dissentientibus praesertim inter se internunciis. Hic (quod in ejusmodi rebus fieri assolet) alius in alium culpam referebat; cum utrumque justius de propria incuria et negligentia queri oportuerit. Desito in hunc modum colloquio, Montisrosanus quidem voti compos ; illi vero nihil certi referentes, ad suos rediere.

## CAP. III.

Montisrosanus a colloquio reversus, rem totam sicuti gesta est ad amicos, quibus unice fidebat, defert, et simul suadet ut una omnes (ad majorem fidem faciendam) ad Regem properarent, quo plenissime de cunctis edoctus, sanioribus consiliis aurem praeberet, et adhuc, si fieri posset, ad tanta mala avertenda maturum adhiberet remedium. Plerique conclamatum hactenus esse de Rege ejusque authoritate censebant. Rem esse humanas vires penitus excedentem, ut regnum istud ad debitum obsequium reducatur. Se quidem Deo, propriae conscientiae et famae satisfecisse, qui huc usque cum ignominia, bonorum jactura, et vitae discrimine in fide perstiterint. In posterum spectatores, Deum optimum maximum meliora ardentibus votis imploraturos. Montisrosanus, qui nullis unquam rationibus adduci potuit quo minus in honestissima sententia perseveraret, communicato consilio cum Ogilvio regulo, quem unice semper diligebat, recta Oxoniam petit. Aberat inde Rex, ad obsidionem Glocestriae profectus. Reginae vero quid foederati in Scotia in Regiam Majestatem molirentur, frustra impertit. Nihil illa sibi persuaderi patiebatur, propter fiduciam quam longe maximam in Hamiltoniis fratribus collocabat.

Cum nihil apud Reginam proficeret Montisrosanus, Glocestriam proficiscitur, ipsique Regi omnia denunciat. Exercitum validissimum in Scotia comparari, diemque dictum esse quo in Angliam perduceretur. Sibi consilia eorum penitus perspecta esse; et spe conciliandi ejus animi amplissimas in eodem dignitates oblatus fuisse. Se vero tantum scelus ex animo aversatum, ad Regem accurrisse, ut ille praemonitus, si minus opportunum aliquod et efficax afferret remedium, remoram saltem et impedimentum aliquod objiceret, quoad res suas in Anglia componeret. Perduelles in hoc et illo regno seorsum facilius domandos; ubi vero copias viresque conjunxerint, rem fore difficillimam. Quamplurimos esse Scotos, qui se suaque omnia pro carissimo Rege devoverent; quorum prona voluntas illi quidem inutilis futura sit, post coactum exercitum; sibi ipsis vero perniciosa. Mature premendos esse elatos perduellium spiritus, viresque infringendas, priusquam in immensum excrescant, ne principiis neglectis, sero forsan poenitendum sit. Haec et similia indies quidem, sed frustra inculcabat. Enimvero illi non tantum cum fiducia Regis, quam in Hamiltoniis longe maximam collocaverat, sed et cum perditissimis aulicis colluctandum fuit. Qui ejus adolescentiam, temeritatem, ambitionem, et in Hamiltonios odium invidiamque Regis auribus subinde insusurrabant. De Hamiltoniorum vero integritate, fide, prudentia, potentiaque magnificentissime disserebant. Nihil proficiente Montisrosano, Rex Oxoniam ad hiberna reversus est. Et quamvis percrebrescentibus de exercitu Scoticano rumoribus, vera omnia praenunciasse Montisrosanum persentisceret, certum tamen fuit sanctissimo Regi, Scotis suis, nisi prius Angliam ingressis, ne vel levissimam querelae materiam exhibere. Se quidem datam fidem sancte colere: quam si illi violaverint, Deo et sibi poenas daturos, nihil dubitare. Dum ista Oxoniae agitantur, foederati in Scotia, nullo obstante, ex animi sui sententia omnia peragunt. Copias quam possunt maximas contrahunt. Et jam in ipso regnorum limite exercitus in procinctu stabat, qui peditum octo et decem, equitum vero duobus constabat millibus. Tandem ergo Hamiltonii adventantis infesti exercitus per literas Regem admonere non erubuerunt; hoc excusationi praetexentes, se secundum datam fidem sedulo curasse, ne qui eum ex Scotia praeterita aestate invaderent: quo vero inclinante jam hieme hoc non faciant, impedire non posse. Certo enim cum validissimis copiis jam jamque affuturos. Rex ubi se aperte ludificatum sensit, tandem Montisrosanum ultro compellat; Hamiltoniorum literas explicat: et quid potissimum agendum sit, sententiam ejus, sero quidem, sed serio postulat.

Montisrosanus refert, Majestatem regiam tandem pervidere posse, nihil ipsum ex ambitione, aut avaritia, aut Hamiltoniorum odio, sed pro debita fide et observantia dixisse. Annum jam et amplius elapsum esse, ex quo tam ipsum Regem, quam prudentissimam Reginam imminentis periculi admonere non destiterit. In hoc se infelicem, quod apud optimum dominum fidissimus servus fidem non invenerit. Rem jam deperditam videri, cui facillime mederi potuisset, nisi se illorum arbitrio permisisset, qui ejus authoritate suffulti, aliorum quidem ora obturaverint; alios vero nihil tale cogitantes, specie caritatis in Regem, ad promovendam rebellionem inscios abduxerint; quique, jam comparato exercitu, perduellibus omnia gratis tradiderint. Rex semet foedissime proditum conquestus ab eis quibus arcana, sceptrum, honorem vitamque credidisset, impensius consilium ejus rogare perstitit. Ille rem deploratam videri praefatus, verumtamen si sic domino Regi visum fuerit, se vel in reducendis popularibus ad obsequium nec impune periturum spondet, vel (quod nondum desperaret) perduelles in ordinem coacturum. Rex hominis fiducia, magnanimitate, et in rebus etiam perditis constantia non parum erectus, quo maturius de totius rei bene gerendae ordine consultaret, diem unum aut alterum indulgens dimisit.[1]

Tempore praestituto reversus ad Regem Montisrosanus indicat, se rem plane arduam et difficilem aggredi. Scotiam omnem foederatorum jugo subactam; munimenta praesidiis occupata, instrumenta militaria, commeatum, arma, stipendia, militem, cuncta denique ad belli usus necessaria abunde suppetere. Perduelles insuper Anglos arctissimo foedere ad mutua auxilia contra omnes mortales junctos esse. Sibi vero nihil eorum esse, quae ad famam saltem in belli initio conciliandam inserviant. Non militem, non stipendia, et ne arma quidem. Justissimae tamen causae et divinae opi non diffidere; et si juberet Rex rem in se suscipere, Regi quidem nihil novi detrimenti, odium, invidiam, periculum, pro caritate in Regem, in se derivaturum: modo ad paucula ejus postulata clementer annueret. Enimvero ut res melioribus auspiciis geratur, pernecessarium imprimis videri, ut Rex armatos quosdam ex Hibernia in occidentalem Scotiae partem immittat. Deinde ut Marchioni Novi castri (qui tum versus Scotiam copiis Regiis cum summo imperio praeerat) mandaret ut aliqua exercitus sui parte auxilio esset ad invadendas Scotiae partes meridionales; quorum praesertim praesidio Montisrosanus in intima Regni penetraret. Insuper, ut a potentissimo Daniae Rege aliquot equitum Germanorum

---

[1] *Demisit* in the editions, and often.

turmas impetraret. Et denique ut ratio iniretur, qua parari et ab exteris nationibus arma in Scotiam deferri possent. Ad ista etiam humanam accedere debere industriam; caetera Deo et providentiae permittenda. Rex, laudato ejus consilio, et gratiis etiam actis, quod nondum de summa rei desperasset, hortatur ut tanto operi se alacriter accingat: postulata ejus sibi curae fore.

Et sane quod ad auxilia Hibernica, Antromiae comitem accersit, et consilii Montisrosani participem facit. Est ille origine Scotus, ex nobili et antiqua Makdonaldorum gente oriundus, opibus et potentia in Hibernia clarus, plerisque etiam in Anglia primae nobilitatis affinis, juncta sibi matrimonio Buckinghamiae ducis vidua. Ditione autem sua pulsus, Oxoniae degebat. Hic negotium, quod ad Hibernos attinet, summa cum alacritate in se suscepit. Simulque foedus cum Montisrosano inire omnino voluit, quo sese ultro obstrinxit ante kal. Ap. anno MIƆCXLIV in Argatheliam (qua parte Scotia Hiberniae objacet) cum decem millibus descensurum. Agebantur vero illa mense Dec. anno MIƆCXLIII. Quod vero ad externa auxilia et arma, Ioannes Cokeramius eques legatione ornatus, cum mandatis et diplomate Regio dimittitur. Mandata ad Marchionem Novi castri in Montisrosani comitatu deferenda traduntur. Ille vero literis et diplomate Regio instructus, quo regni Scotiae vicarius gubernator et copiarum dux renunciatus erat, iter in Scotiam meditabatur. Ex improviso interim nunciatur, Hamiltonium ducem, cum fratre Lanrici[1] comite Oxoniam versus properare. Illi, quo sibi aditum facilius patefacerent ad Regem, quem hactenus consiliis suis obnoxium semper detinuerant, et pristinam apud eum gratiam recuperarent, per omnem Angliam, qua illis eundum fuit, praesertim apud provinciarum urbiumque praefectos et belli duces praedicabant, se patrio solo extorres, amissis bonis, et de vita etiam periclitantes, pro fide erga Regem a foederatis exactos, Oxoniam fugere. Montisrosanus vero et qui cum eo sentiebant, ista quidem ad eluendam recentis culpae notam magnifice jactari, verum vana et falsa esse arguebant. Illos scilicet fiducia gratiae qua dudum apud Regem, et validae factionis, qua in aula sibi addictissima pollebant, non dubitare, quo minus eundem obtinerent locum, modo vel ad salutationem admitterentur. Nec alia de causa illuc properare, quam ut denuo Montisrosano everso, extinguerent scintillulam istam Regiae Majestatis, quae adhuc in Scotia spirabat. Et Montisrosanus libere testatus est, se tanti mali spectatorem nunquam futurum. Adeoque Regis veniam humillime postulare, ut quovis gentium se recipere liceat, si isti, qui toties spem de eis conceptam frustrati fuissent,

---

[1] This represents the old Scotch pronunciation of the name Lanark, spelt *Lainrick* in Turner's Memoirs, *Lanrick* in Guthrie, etc.

## CAP. III.

in gratiam redirent. Non quod durius quid in illos decerni cuperet; sed tantum quod Regem rogatum velit, ut sedulo caveret, ne quid amplius illi rebus ejus nocerent. Rex tamen aegre consensit, ut aula arcerentur. Et omnino Lanrici comitem in civitate degere permisit. At ille nescio quibus stimulis agitatus, Oxonia Londinum ad Parliamentum Anglicanum, et mox ad foederatorum in Scotia exercitum (quod jam in Angliam irruperat) sese transtulit: et strenuam illis operam navare postea non destitit. Frater transfuga sic Regis animum perpulit, ut ducem ipsum carceri mancipandum censuerit.

Erant in aula et castris Regiis Scoti nonnulli, merito forsan suspecti quod foederatis addictiores essent, et illis arcana quaeque perfidiose proderent. Istos, ut tanquam ad Lydium lapidem probaret, hanc rationem inire Montisrosano visum est. Libellum ex Regis mandato conscribi curavit, cui Scoti quotquot fideles videri vellent, manu sua subscriberent; profitentes eo sese foederatorum consilia ex animo detestari; immissum praesertim in Angliam exercitum, contra Regem legesque patrias, tanquam Majestatis crimen damnare; et insuper sancte polliceri, cum bonorum omnium et vitae dispendio se crimen illud pro viribus in reos vindicaturos. Huic libello viri probi et honesti certatim subscripsere. Inventi tamen duo sunt, quibus Rex omnium Scotorum post Hamiltonios maxime fidebat, Trequarius comes, et Gulielmus Moravius, cubicularius Regis, qui multum reluctati, et metu detectae proditionis vix tandem induci potuerunt, ut illud praestarent. Nihilominus et illi interposito jurejurando promiserunt se in Scotia Montisrosano ad certum diem auxilio affuturos. Qua in re etiam fidem foedissime violarunt.

His peractis, et Oxonia versus Scotiam digresso Montisrosano, Hamiltoniorum amici aliique infidi aulici hominem vanum et ambitiosum praedicare, rem quae fieri plane non posset aggredi, foederatorum vires et potentiam immodice extollere, et quo plures deterrerent, qui nobilissimi facinoris participes esse desiderabant, nihil ab isto viro sperandum esse, malitiose apud omnes jactabant.

Ille vilissimorum hominum obtrectationibus nihil commotus, Eboracum, et mox Dunelmum pervenit: ubi Novi castri Marchioni mandata Regis tradi curat, et postridie congressi ad colloquium descenderunt. Novi castrensis nihil quam rerum omnium in exercitu suo penuriam ostentare. Perduelles Scotos, qui media hieme improvisi irruperant, delectum ejus pervertisse, jamque intra quinque passuum millia numero longe superiores castris suis imminere. Equitatum denique nullum sine manifesto totius exercitus periculo concedi posse. Montisrosanus contra disserebat, nihil magis ad prosperum belli eventum conducere posse, quam si equitatus (quo plurimum valebat) partem secum in Scotiam mitteret, hostesque averteret, aut saltem distraheret, et ad suos propugnandos retraheret, domestico periculo attonitos. Novi castrensis se praesenti periculo defunctum Montisrosano non defuturum amice respondit. Quod praestiturum fuisse virum nobilem et de Rege optime meritum, si diutius provinciis istis cum imperio praefuisset, nullus dubitaverit, modo ei perspectum fuerit honestum illud, et generosum pectus. Interim, quod unum pro angustia temporis potuit, ad centum equites, sed equos strigosos et male habitos (non imperatoris culpa, sed aliorum invidia) cum duobus tormentis aeneis, minusculis illis, quae campestria vocant, ei attribuit.

Mandata insuper dedit ad Regis ministros et militiae praefectos in Cumbria et Westmoria, ut Montisrosano Scotiam petenti frequentes in armis adsint, et operam ad omnia strenue praestent. Montisrosanus Carleolum versus profectus, in itinere obvios habuit Cumbros et Westmorios, pedites quidem octingentos, cum tribus equitum turmis, qui eum secundum Novi castrensis mandata in Scotiam comitarentur. Ducebat ipse equites ducentos, viros plerosque nobiles et generosos, quique in Germania, Gallia, aut Anglia ordines duxissent. Quibus copiis perexiguis quidem, nec satis fidis, instructus, Scotiam ingressus est ad Idus Aprilis. Properabat enim, ne tempore ab Antromio comite praestituto abesset.

## CAP. IV.

Scotiam ingressus Montisrosanus ad Ananam flumen pervenerat, cum, orta inter Anglos militari seditione, cui ansam praebuere Richardi Graemi satellites, plerique omnes signa deserunt, et praecipiti cursu repetunt Angliam. Ipse tamen Dunfrisium cum suis pervenit; et oppidum deditione civium in fidem recepit. Paulisper etiam illic commoratus est, ut Antromio cum auxiliis Hibernicis occurreret. Verum tempore praestituto jam pridem elapso, nullus ab eis nuncius, nulla de eis fama in Scotiam perlata fuit. Concurrentibus vero undique foederatis, nisi mature se recepisset, hostium insidiis procul dubio fuisset interceptus. Carleolum tamen incolumis cum suis reversus est Montisrosanus. Et cum nihil subsidii ab Anglis impetrare posset, nec ab exteris auxilium brevi affuturum putaret, nec de Hibernis fere ulla spes superesset, et Kalendarium comitem in Scotia novum exercitum contraxisse comperisset, quo Leslaeo subsidio esset, qui jam Eboracum cum foederatis obsidione cinxerat, ne tempus segni et inutili otio tereret, instituit illis, qui in Northumbria et agro Dunelmensi Regi militabant, operam suam navare. Nec sane ea aut illis inutilis aut ipsi indecora fuit.

## CAP. IV.

Exacto enim ex urbe Morpetensi foederatorum praesidio, arcem expugnavit. Praedam omnem Anglis permisit. Praesidiarios, accepta fide nunquam contra Regem militaturos, sine graviore paena dimisit. Munimentum ad Tinae amnis ostium foederatis (qui non ita pridem praesidium Anglorum inde deturbaverant), eripuit. Captivos eadem qua Morpetenses lege in Scotiam remisit. Novum castrum, comportatis ex Anvico et locis vicinis frugibus, commeatu non exiguo juvit. Et istis gestis, Ruperti Principis Comitis Palatini ad Rhenum literis, qui ad solvendam obsidionem Eboracensem properabat, accersitur. Et quamvis ille qua potuit celeritate ad eum contendebat, postridie tamen, quam adversa fortuna pugnatum fuit, revertenti ab Eboraco Principi obvius factus est. Et Princeps quidem mille equites Montisrosano ultro obtulit, quos secum in Scotiam duceret. Verum optimi Principis animum qui nimia apud eum gratia valebat perverterunt; adeo ut postridie illius diei quo promiserat, ne unum quidem impetrare potuerit.

Deficientibus sic omnibus, a quibus aliquid auxilii sperandum fuit, solus animus Montisrosano nunquam defecit. Carleolum ergo reversus cum paucis illis quidem, sed fidis aeque ac fortibus viris, qui illi adhaerebant, Ogilvium regulum cum Gulielmo Rolloco equite, obscuro et ementito habitu, ne ab hostibus deprehenderentur, in intima Scotiae ablegat. Illi, ante quartum et decimum diem reversi, omnia in Scotia deperdita esse renunciant. Aditus, arces, urbes foederatorum praesidiis teneri; nec quemquam inveniri, qui reverenter saltem, aut cum aliquo honore et affectu de Rege verba facere audeat. Hoc tam tristi nuncio perculsi, plerique eorum qui Montisrosano hactenus adhaeserant, ut sibi quoquo modo consulerent, alio oculos animosque convertebant, instigante praesertim ad defectionem egregio illo viro Trequario Comite. Qui votorum omnium, et dirarum, quas capiti suo coram Rege imprecatus fuerat, immemor, fidem publicam, praemia etiam, opes dignitatesque transfugientibus foederatorum nomine pollicebatur. Quasi non Regis, quod prae se ferebat, sed perduellium res procuraret: qui tamen post Hamiltonium gratia et fide apud optimum Regem praecipue eminebat.

Montisrosanus vocatos ad consilium amicos rogat, ut quid tandem in tristi hoc rerum statu faciendum videretur, in medium proferant. Suadent alii ut ad Regem Oxoniam proficiscatur, illique conclamatum esse de rebus Scoticis renunciet. Non adfuisse cum copiis Hibernis Antromium, nec ullam de eis spem fecisse. Ab Anglis parum aut nihil impetratum fuisse. De armis et auxiliis externis ne nuncium quidem perlatum; adeoque nulla ejus culpa accidisse, quod mandato sibi munere non functus fuerit felicius. Alii, ut literas apologeticas cum diplomate Oxoniam ad Regem remitteret; ipse vero ad exteras quasvis nationes pro tempore se reciperet, quoad

Deus opt. max. suggerat meliora. Omnes in hoc unanimi consensu conveniunt, nihil amplius in illo negotio attentandum esse. At ille unus et solus longe alia excelso illo et malis invicto animo versabat. Nunquam ille carissimum dominum et Regem vel in praesenti mortis periculo deserendum, nunquam de justissima causa desperandum putavit. Et si majus aliquid, quam quod in vulgares animos cadat, auderet tentaretque, sibi quidem honorificum, nec Regi forsan inutile fore augurabatur. Sicut enim dubium esset, an tandem adversam Regis fortunam clementior Deus in laetiorem commutaret, ita illud utique certum esse, quamvis excidentem ingentibus ausis, honeste tamen et cum laude moriturum. Rem tandem Dei opt. max. curae et tutelae ardentibus votis committens, sine milite, sine stipendiis, sine armis ea gessit, quae ut nobis, qui audivimus, qui vidimus, qui rebus gerendis praesentes interfuimus, plane miranda, sic et maximis in posterum ducibus cum laude imitanda et aemulanda sint. Ea vero qualia fuerint deinceps sumus descripturi.

Paucos istos, qui constantes in fide perseverabant, ad Regem perducendos Ogilvio tradit Montisrosanus. Illum enim, ut omnium, sic et praesentis consilii participem fecit. Simulque mandat, ut strenue apud Regem agat, pro maturando ab exteris nationibus, si non militum, at armorum saltem auxilio. Et ipse bidui itinere cum illis profectus, relictis apud eos equis, asseclis, et aliis impedimentis, se ipsum clam subduxit, et qua potuit celeritate Carleolum repetiit. Illi de ejus discessu nihil suspicantes, propter Ogilvium et alios carissimos praesentes, Oxoniam contendebant. Verum eo nunquam pervenerunt; plerique enim, inter quos ipse Ogilvius, Ioannes Innesius eques et equitum tribunus, Henricus Graemus frater, optimae spei adolescens, Iacobus, Ioannes, Alexander Ogilvii, Patricius Melvinus, et alii viri fortes, et Montisrosano in paucis cari, in hostium manus inciderunt. Omnesque diuturno prorsus et squalido carcere macerati; quoad vertente anno ab ipso Montisrosano armis in libertatem vindicati, fidelem illi operam postea praestiterunt. Ille Carleolum reversus, Aboinium quidem comitem consilii sui participem fecit, ne vel minimam querelae materiam relinqueret, quod inscio et inconsulto illo rem tantam aggressus fuerit, cujus utilis forsan futura fuerit in rebus gerendis opera. Verum cum justam in illo adolescente constantiam desideraret, illum ut difficillimi itineris socium non ambiebat. Facile enim persuasit, ut Carleoli subsisteret, quoad rerum gestarum fama excitetur. Et tum quidem magis opportunum fore ejus in patriam reditum.

Jamque ad iter accinctus, duos omnino itineris socios et viae duces assumpsit, Gulielmum Rollocum equitem, virum generosum, expertae fidei, et manu et consilio promptum, et Sibbaldum quendam, quem ob fortitudinis famam pari honore et amore prosequebatur. At hic postea tempore difficillimo ab eo defecit. Montisrosanus Sibbaldi servulum simulans, et habitu equisonem referens, strigoso plane equo insidebat, alterum vero trahebat manu. Et sic ad regni limites progressus est, ubi notos tutosque aditus ab hostibus diligentissime observatos offendit. Accessit etiam quod longe majorem metum incussit. Non procul a limite in clientem quendam Richardi Graemi forte inciderunt, qui eos foederatos esse ratus, et ex Leslaei militibus, qui frequentes per ista loca obequitabant, libere fidenterque indicat, Patrono suo cum foederatis Scotis optime convenire; et in se suscepisse, tanquam eorum speculatorem, delaturum ad eos, si qui ad ista loca diverterent, quos Regi favere suspicaretur. Indignum facinus propudiosi nequam, de quo non modo Montisrosanus optima quaeque sperabat, sed et qui ab infimae plebis faece, ne quid gravius dicam, ad equestris ordinis dignitatem et opes vicinis invidendas Regis gratia et male collocata munificentia evectus erat.

Non procul ab isto digressi, obvium habent militem, Scotum quidem, sed qui in Anglia sub Novo castrensi Marchione meruisset. Et iste neglectis comitibus Montisrosanum salutavit. Quod cum ille dissimulare et negligere contenderet, non dubitavit iste, sed voce et vultu ad modestiam et officium composito ingeminare, "nonne ego dominum meum Montisrosarum Marchionem probe novi? abi cum bono Deo, et vale." Ille, ubi se agnitum ab isto comperit, aureis paucis donatum dimisit. Qui rem fidei suae commissam non prodidit. Montisrosanus istis sermonibus vehementer stimulatus, quam maxima potuit celeritate famam sui antevertendam censuit. Nec jumentorum armis parcere, aut fraena ferme laxari permisit, quoad quarto demum die in agro Perthensi, qua montes pertingit, non procul a Tai amnis ripa ad aedes Patricii Graemi, Insbrakii, consanguinei sui, pervenit. Patricio ab illustrissima familia Montisrosana oriundo, et splendidissimis natalibus digno, Montisrosanus jure merito plurimum tribuebat: apud quem, interdiu in satis obscuro tugurio, noctu in montibus vicinis, aliquot dies solus egit. Comites enim ad amicos ablegaverat, ut universum regni statum accurate perdiscerent, et reversi ipsum edocerent.

Post paucos dies, rebus qua potuerunt fide et industria exploratis, nihil illi quam tragoedias renunciant. Subditos, quotquot probi et fideles essent, perduellium tyrannide oppressos jacere. Horum vero, qui sese armis vindicare ausi erant, alios pecuniis, alios capite multatos, alios in vinculis detentos, extrema quaeque indies expectare. Huntilaeum Marchionem arma temere rapta ad primum hostilis tubae sonitum deposuisse. Copias quidem illi non contemnendas adfuisse; sed defuisse copiis ducem. Amicos et clientes ejus hostium implacabili odio et vindictae expositos; ipsum vero ad ultimum insulae angulum aufugisse, et in alieno agro delitescere. Montisrosanus hoc nuncio, Huntilaei praesertim errore et Gordoniorum casu, ut par erat, valde commotus fuit. Quos ille viros, fide in Regem, fortitudinis et rei militaris gloria claros, tam insigni clade, nulla eorum culpa, afflictos ingemiscebat. Et jam tum animo versabat, quo tandem pacto eosdem ad se pertraheret; ut denuo, sed sub alio duce, belli aleam pro carissimo Rege experirentur.

## CAP. V.

SPARGEBANTUR interea apud pastores, qui gregibus suis in montibus invigilabant, incerti rumores de Hibernis quibusdam, qui navigiis advecti in septentrionali Scotiae plaga loca montana peragrabant. Montisrosano videbatur non vero absimile, istos esse de numero auxiliariorum, quos ante quatuor menses Antromius promiserat. Nihil tamen certi ea de re statuere potuit, quoad ecce literas a montanis quibusdam, intimis ejus amicis, et Alexandro Makdonaldo itidem Scoto, quem Antromius paucis istis Hibernis ducem imposuerat, ad Montisrosanum datas. Quas ad amicum quendam suum, et eundem partium studiosissimum, deferri curaverant, ut eas ille Carleolum, si qua fieri posset, transmitteret, ubi Montisrosanum adhuc subsistere putabant. Ille, cui nihil de ejus in patriam reditu subolueret, quamvis in vicinia habitaret, rem forte Patricio Graemo impertiendam censuit. Et Patricius eas sibi curae fore pollicetur, fidenterque suscipit illas Montisrosano traditurum, etiamsi illi Carleolum usque eundum foret. Et sic omni expectatione citius, favente plane et dirigente numine, ad eum pervenerunt. Ille autem, quasi adhuc Carleoli esset, respondit; jubetque bono animo esse; nec enim auxilium opportunum, nec ducem illis defuturum. Simul etiam mandat, ut quam primum in Atholiam descendant.

Erant Atholii Montisrosano multis nominibus obnoxii; et ob eximiam in Regem fidem, pietatem, constantiam cum singulari fortitudinis fama Montanorum carissimi. Et sane illi tanta viri aestimatione dignissimi ad belli exitum perstiterunt. Hiberni, et perpauci cum illis montani Scoti, qui fermi omnes ex Badenothia erant, acceptis Montisrosani mandatis, confestim Atholiam petunt. Ille, qui non supra viginti passuum millia aberat, pedes et in montano habitu, uno illo Patricio consanguineo viae duce et comite, illico illis et improvisus adest. Et sane vix sibi persuadere poterant Hiberni, hunc, quem praesentem conspiciebant, ipsum esse Montisrosanum. Verum ubi ab Atholiis aliisque, quibus probe notus erat, salutatum et tantum non ut salutare numen adoratum viderunt, incredibili gaudio perfusi sunt. Peropportunus enim illis fuit ejus adventus in summo discrimine positis. Insequebatur eos Argathelius valido et instructo exercitu. Campestris regio in armis expectabat, si in planiciem descenderent, vel equorum ungulis protrituri.[1] Navigia, quae eos advexerant, ab Argathelio concremata, ne quis effugio locus esset. Nec Atholii aut alii qui Regi favebant ullum discrimen cum illis subituri erant; quia, cum peregrini essent, non aperta Regis et cognita authoritate nitebantur. Nec ullum antiquae nobilitatis ducem ostentabant; quod montani isti imprimis venerantur, nunquam Alexandri Makdonaldi novi hominis auspiciis militaturi. Numerus denique perexiguus, qui non centum supra mille excedebat, quamvis decem millia promissa fuissent.

Postridie Atholii maxima alacritate armatos se et ad obsequium pronos numero octingentos Montisrosano exhibent. Ille hac manu stipatus, et Deo opt. max. justissimae causae tutelam ardentibus votis commendans, nihil jam desiderabat, quam cum confertissimis hostibus manus conserere. Ulterioris etiam morae impatiens, illo ipso die per Atholiae campos Iernam versus contendit. Tam ut amicis et auxiliariis (si qui rei fama excitarentur) aditum patefaceret, priusquam ab hostibus praecluderentur, quam ut perduelles rei novitate perculsos aggrederetur, antequam copias adhuc dissitas conjungerent. Wemiam ergo, Menesiorum arcem, praetergressus, cum illi fecialem, quem ad eos amico animo miserat, ignominiose, milites vero, qui extremum agmen claudebant, hostiliter tractassent, agros populari, aedes frugesque collectas immissis facibus incendi jussit, quo in ipso belli quasi limine majorem aliis terrorem incuteret. Taum deinde, fluviorum Scotiae longe maximum, cum parte copiarum illa nocte trajecit. Reliqui postridie multo adhuc mane insequuntur. Itineri accinctus, Patricium Graemum, de quo saepe, nec unquam sine honore dicendum est, Atholiis enixe rogantibus ducem dedit. Et eundem cum expeditis quibusdam, quos ex Atholiis suis delegerat, ad speculandum praemisit. Ille conspici a se armatos in edito colle ad Bukintum renunciat. In eos Montisrosanus recta ducit. Imperabant istis Kilpontinus Regulus, Taithiae comitis filius, perantiquae nobilitatis vir et de nobilissima Graemorum gente oriundus, et Ioannes Drummondus eques, Perthensis comitis filius, et hic Montisrosani consanguineus. Appellati erant illi a foederatis, ut se cum aliis Hibernis tanquam hostibus publicis opponerent; ducebantque quingentos omnino pedites; nec quidquam certi de Montisrosano adhuc inaudiverant. Ille hos quam primum occupare et vel ad partes pertrahere vel opprimere statuit. At illi, ubi primum Montisrosanum imperare intelligunt, amicorum praecipuos ad eum mittunt, qui quid in animo haberet, interrogent. Ille Regia authoritate munitum se respondit, eandemque a detestanda rebellione pro viribus vindicandam suscepisse. Rogare insuper eos, viros sibi multis nominibus carissimos, ne operam etiam suam meritissimo Regi praestare

---

[1] *Protritum iri?* But W. is expressing the thought of the Lowlanders.

graventur. Quod ut eorum natalibus dignum, et Regi gratum foret, sic et in praesentem rem[1] utile, et apud posteros exterosque eximio eorum honori cederet, si illi omnium primi ad nutantem Majestatem sublevandam accurrerent. Illi absque ulla cunctatione nec inviti quidem ad partes transeunt. Uterque enim, quamvis occulte, Regi vehementer favebat.

Ab istis edoctus Montisrosanus foederatos frequentes in armis Pertham confluxisse (secunda illa est post Edinburgum Scotiae civitas) ibique hostes ex Atholia descendentes opperiri.

Et ille gnarus Argathelium cum exercitu vestigiis suis insistere, ne inter hostiles copias opprimeretur, Pertham progredi instituit, ut hostes vel ad dimicandum cogeret, vel ut urbem vi captam redigeret in potestatem. Tribus ergo miliaribus Bukinto progressus, et perbrevi tempore militibus ad curanda corpora permisso, illucescente statim die copias educit. Nec supra totidem miliaria ab urbe aberat, cum hostes in ampla prorsus et aperta planicie (Tippermoram vocant) pugnam expectantes conspicit. Imperabat illis Elchous regulus, rei militaris, ut ferebatur, non admodum peritus. Aderant illi Tullibardinus Comes, Drummondus regulus,—sed hic, (ut fama est) invitus, qui cum universa familia paterna Regi ex animo favebat,—equestris vero ordinis plurimi, inter quos Iacobus, non minus nomine quam natione Scotus, qui, cum Venetis olim etiam cum bona fama meruisset, militari peritia eminebat. Ducebant illi peditum sex millia, equites vero septingentos. Hostesque suos praecoci spe et multitudinis suorum fiducia devoraverant. Dies erat dominicus, ipsis Kal. Sept.; et ministris curae imprimis datum est, ut militum animos, sanctissimi (scilicet) foederis memores, ad pugnam fortiter capessendam compositis orationibus accenderent. Et illi quidem vehementissima laterum contentione eo munere fortiter defuncti sunt. Ipsius enim omnipotentis Dei nomine facilem illis et incruentam victoriam pollicentur. Inter eos, opinione imperiti vulgi, eruditione et sanctimonia eminebat quidam Fredericus Carmichael, qui istam vocem pro concione edere non perhorruit: "Si unquam Deus ex ore meo quid certi aut veri protulit, ego vobis ejus nomine certam hodie victoriam spondeo."

Sacris rite, ut videbatur, peractis, aciem instruunt. Dextrum cornu Elchous ipse ducebat; sinistro imperabat Iacobus Scotus; mediam aciem Tullibardinus cogebat Comes. Cornibus equitum alae additae sunt, quibus hostem in tam ampla planicie circundari posse minime dubitabant. Montisrosanus hostium multitudinem et equitatus praesertim robur conspicatus (nec enim ille equitem vel unum, nec plures quam tres omnino strigosos

---

[1] *I.q.* "there and then," "on the spot." The editions have "in praesentiarum," a *vox nihili*, for "praesentia rerum?" or "praesentarium?"

et emaciatos equos habuit) ut par erat, solicitus, ne tam impari numero circumventus, a fronte, a latere, a tergo simul premeretur, aciem, quantum quidem fieri potuit, extendi curavit. Tresque tantum milites in singulis ordinibus[1] collocari jussit. Hi ut simul omnes jaculis[2] hostes impeterent, eos, qui ordines ducebant, genibus flexis incurvos, medios quasi illis incumbentes et pronos, novissimos, qui et proceriores erant, erectos stare jussit. Insuper mandat, ne frustra pulverem sulphureum prodigerent, cujus inopia quam maxime laborabant; et ne vel unum emitterent globulum, priusquam ad ipsa hostium ora ventum foret; sclopetis vero prima vice displosis, ut statim strictis mucronibus et obversis manubriis in eos fortiter incurrerent. Impetum eorum hostes nunquam perlaturos magna cum fiducia spondet. Dexterum cornu, quod Iacobo Scoto oppugnandum fuit, ipse Montisrosanus ducendum suscepit, sinistrum Kilpontino regulo, mediam aciem Makdonaldo attribuit cum Hibernis. Et hoc quidem optimo consilio factum fuit, ne Hiberni illi, qui nec hastis longioribus nec gladiis armati erant, in cornibus positi, hostili equitatui exponerentur.

Miserat ad hostium duces Montisrosanus Drummondum Madertaei reguli primogenitum, virum nobilem et omni virtutum genere cumulatissimum, qui ejus nomine denunciaret, Se quidem, sicut et optimum Regem, a quo mandata accepisset, a fundendo civili sanguine quam maxime abhorrere: nec aliud magis habere in votis, quam victoriam incruentam. Illam utrumque exercitum sic tandem assequi posse, si ante belli aleam, illi ad debitum domino Regi obsequium revertantur. Se non opibus inhiare, non honores ambire, non dignitatibus invidere, non vitis carissimorum civium insidiari; unum hoc iterum atque iterum per Deum immortalem obsecrare, ut tandem sanioribus consiliis aurem praebeant, et in optimi Regis gratia, tutela, fide se suaque collocarent, qui, ut hactenus in religione, aliisque omnibus, quae Scotis suis expetere visum fuit, cum longe maximo Regii juris detrimento abunde satisfecerit, sic adhuc, ut indulgentissimum patrem, quamvis infandis lacessitum injuriis, ad liberos suos poenitentes amplexandos utramque manum extenderet. Quod si vero illi contumaces in rebellione persisterent, Deum testem habere, se eorum pervicacia victum, ad imminens certamen descendere. Hostium duces ad ista quidem nihil. Verum legatum, qui sola in patriam caritate id muneris susceperat, contra jus gentium, sub custodia militari ignominiose habitum, Pertham incarcerandum remittunt. Votisque impiis sese obstringunt, parta demum victoria, caput illi amputaturos. Clementior

---

[1] Here denotes "*files.*"

[2] Probably denotes bows and arrows, as well as stones. For Highlanders armed with bows, v. Ch. vi., Battle of Aberdeen; and Spalding, sub anno 1630, Ed. 1819, p. 9, etc.

tamen Deus aliter, quam illi putabant, lectissimi ornatissimique viri incolumitati consuluit.

Ventum erat ad globi tormentarii jactum, cum hostes sub Drummondi reguli imperio, selectos quosdam praemittunt ante aciem, qui leviore pugna Montisrosanum tentarent ac lacesserent. Pauci ad istos coercendos missi eos primo insultu turbant, fundunt, et ad suorum aciem cum trepidatione non exigua pellunt. Montisrosanus momento huic instandum esse judicavit. Nec quidquam magis ad suos animandos et terrorem hostibus incutiendum conducere posse, quam si palantes et recenti vulnere attonitos confestim insequeretur, nec colligendis animis et componendis spatium permitteret. Ingenti ergo sublato clamore, universam aciem in eos immittit. Hostes primo eminus majora tormenta ante aciem collocata, majore cum strepitu quam irruentium damno, displodunt. Deinde ipsi in pugnam procedentes, equites in Montisrosani milites invecti sunt. Eos illi, deficiente iam pulvere tormentario, cum nec longioribus hastis ac ne gladiis quidem plerique essent armati, armis quae casus obtulit, lapidibus nimirum, fortiter exceperunt. Quorum ingentem vim tanta animorum corporumque contentione in eos conjecere, ut receptui signum dare coegerint non amplius redituros. Enimvero Hiberni Montanique egregia quadam fortitudinis aemulatione tam pertinaciter recedentibus institere, ut tandem praecipiti fuga sibi consuluerint. Acrius paulisper in dextero cornu certatum est. Iacobus Scotus aliquamdiu pro editiore colle acriter contendit. Verum miles Montisrosanus corporis viribus, pernicitate praesertim et agilitate superior, locum strenue occupavit. Inde strictis mucronibus Atholii insuper in hostes irruunt. Et numerum sclopetariorum globos instar grandinis emittentium nihil morantes, comminus (quod unice expetebant) aggressi, proscindunt, proculcantque. Hostes tandem eorum impetum sustinere non valentes, apertam fugam corripuerunt. Equitum plerique equorum pernicitate salutem sibi quaesiverunt. Peditum quam maxima strages, quos ad sex aut septem miliaria victores insecuti sunt. Caesa traduntur foederatorum duo millia; plures capti. Quorum alii, praestito sacramento militari, victoris arma secuti sunt, sed mala fide; plerique enim omnes defecere. Reliquos, data solemni modo fide, nunquam in posterum contra Regem ejusve duces militaturos, libertati restituit. Pertham eodem die, ne vel minimo illato urbi damno, in fidem recepit, quamvis plerique omnes fere incolae contra eum in acie stetissent; tam insigni clementia fore ratus, ut civium animi facilius Regi conciliarentur; ad quod unum consilia sua omnia dirigebat.

## CAP. VI.

Montisrosanus triduum Perthae substitit. Enimvero plurimos in locis istis, qui se Regis studiosissimos jactabant, fama recentis victoriae excitos cum amicis et clientibus armatis frustra expectabat. Solus Kinnulius Comes cum paucis ex Gaurea generosis ad partes venerunt: nec illi quidem satis constantes permanserunt. Iamque Argathelius cum valido peditum exercitu, juncto ex australibus locis equitatu, adventabat. Quapropter Montisrosanus, trajecto Tao, ad Cuprum in Angusia oppidulum, et olim egregium, nunc dirutum Monasterium, castra sub dio (ut ferme semper) locavit. Hic illi obvius fuit insignis ille adolescens, Thomas Ogilvius eques, Arlaei Comitis filius, cum aliis Angusianae nobilitatis generosis viris, qui operam suam ultro detulerunt. Quos ille benigne habitos et multum laudatos dimisit, ut ad militiam tolerandam se praepararent. Perpauci tamen eorum, praeter Ogilvios, ejus castra secuti sunt.

Postridie, incerta adhuc luce, necdum dato militibus signo ad iter capessendum, totis castris tumultuarii milites ad arma decurrere, fremere, indignari, et furiosorum more insanire persentit. Et ille, tumultum forte ex rixa inter Montanos et Hibernos exortum ratus, medium sese in confertissimum agmen conjicit. Ibi horrendum plane flagitium recens perpetratum comperit. Iacebat nobilissimus Kilpontinus regulus indigna morte trucidatus. Sceleris patrator ipsius cliens, nomine Stuartus, quem vir nobilis intima familiaritate et amicitia dignatus fuerat, adeo ut illa ipsa nocte sub eodem tegumento dormiverint. Fama est, vilissimum illud mancipium constituisse Montisrosanum ipsum de medio tollere. Et pro nimia gratia, qua Kilpontinum sibi quasi obnoxium habebat, spem concepisse pertrahendi eum ad societatem sceleris; adeoque in locum solitarium perducto, consilium suum impertivisse. Kilpontinum vero, non aliter quam par erat, facinus detestatum; et parricidam, tum metuentem, ne forte ab eo proderetur, incautum illum et improvisum, et nihil ab amico et beneficiario sibi metuentem, non uno vulnere confecisse. Perditissimus tamen sicarius, occiso eminus milite, qui ad portam castrorum excubias agebat, evasit, tam densa caligine insequentium oculis offusa, ut vix hastarum cuspides apparerent. Parricidam a foederatis, pretio alii, alii spe tantum praemii illectum vulgavere. Ut ut sit, hoc sane constat, gratissimum illis esse in hunc usque diem, et quam primum ab Argathelio ad amplissimas dignitates in exercitu evectum, hominem militiae plane rudem. Montisrosanus viri nobilis et amici casu, optime de Rege, optime de se meriti, nec minus bonarum artium, Philosophiae, divini humanique juris peritia quam fidei et fortitudinis nomine clari vehementer commotus fuit. Et corpus exanimum non semel amplexus, inter suspiria et lacrimas tristissimis amicis et clientibus tradidit ad parentes deferendum, ut pro amplissima familiae dignitate sepulturae mandaretur.

Ipse cum reliquis copiis Taodunum proficiscitur. Oppidum illud, numero civium ferox, et addito ex Fifanis praesidio confirmatum, deditionem recusabat. Nec ille victoriae recens partae famam in ejus expugnatione periclitandum ratus, versus Eskam tendit. Plerosque enim amicos suos et affines, viros in illis locis opibus et clientelis florentes, qui de se suaque in Regem caritate magnifice satis verba facere soliti erant, praesto sibi affuturos arbitrabatur. Verum illi fama adventantis excitati se subduxerunt. Unus Ogilvius, Arlaeus Comes, idemque sexagenarius, cum filiis Thoma et Davide equitibus, aliisque amicis et clientibus, expertae fortitudinis viris, sese Montisrosano adjunxit; et eximia fide et constantia usque ad belli exitum contra omnes fortunae insultus lateri ejus adhaesit; in generali ferme illa defectione, procerum Scotiae, cum Montisrosano, alterum decus et ornamentum.

Ista agenti Montisrosano nunciatur, delegatos foederatorum (quorum Burglaeus Regulus dux et praeses erat) Aberdoniam cum exercitu tenere; et septentrionales partes, in quibus ipse maximam collocabat fiduciam, prece, pretio, et armorum vi ad partes suas pertrahere. Istos Montisrosanus quamprimis expugnandos statuit, priusquam Argathelius copias cum eis jungeret. Longis ergo itineribus illuc contendit. Et occupato Deae amnis ponte, civitati appropinquans, hostes in acie stantes ante urbem invenit. Ducebat Burglaeus peditum duo millia; equites vero quingentos, quos in alis collocaverat. Et occupatis locis opportunis, majoribusque tormentis ante aciem commode dispositis, praelium expectabat. Montisrosanus peditum mille et quingentos ducebat (Kilpontini enim milites, demortui ducis corpus parentibus sepeliendum conduxerant; et ex Atholiis plerique post victoriam Perthensem, spoliis onusti domum, unde non procul aberant, se receperant) equites omnino quadraginta quatuor; quos bipartitos, et expeditissimis quibusdam sclopetariis et sagittariis (qui corporum agilitate et pernicitate equitibus propemodum aequales erant) refertos et munitos in alis constituit, ut praecaverent, ne ab hostium equitatu sui circumirentur. Quod quidem illi supra opinionem et forsan multorum fidem fortiter praestiterunt. Alae quidem dextrae Iacobum Haium, et Nathanéélem Gordonium, sinistrae vero Wilielmum Rollocum, viros fortissimos, praefecit. Sinistram hostium alam regebat Ludovicus Gordonius, Huntilaei filius, adolescens audax et praefervidus, sed desultorii ingenii, qui amicos clientesque paternos, etiam invitos, contra Montisrosanum armaverat. Hic planiciem camposque nactus equestri praelio aptos, copias in dextrum Montisrosani cornu eduxit. Quod ille conspicatus, Rollocum, cum viginti equitibus, periclitantibus in dextro cornu suis subsidio misit. Et illi, eximia virtute ducum et expeditorum peditum robore suffulti, hostium impetum tanta cum fiducia excepere, ut trecentos ipsi duntaxat quadraginta quatuor, perturbatis ordinibus et plerisque caesis, ad suos repulerint. Verum ob suorum paucitatem fugientes ultra insequi non ausi sint. Quod quidem, optimo ducum consilio factum, magni fuit ad consequendam victoriam momenti. Hostes enim in sinistrum cornu equitatu destitutum dextram suorum alam immiserunt. Montisrosanus ergo eosdem (fugato jam cum suis Ludovico Gordonio) in sinistrum cornu mira celeritate transfert. Qui cum tantae multitudini parem aciem extendere non possent, obliquato itinere primum hostium impetum evitant. Actis deinde quam dexterrime in gyrum equis in latera hostium invecti, strictis mucronibus invadunt, caedunt, fundunt, fugant. Forbesium de Kragevar equitem, insignem in hostibus virum, alterumque itidem Forbesium de Boinla, captos abducunt. Reliqui se tuto receperunt, quia tam pauci eos tuto insequi non poterant. Qui hostilem equitatum ducebant, non tam damno perterriti, quam iterato dedecore efferati, et expeditis istis sclopetariis equitatui immistis jacturam suam imputantes, et ipsi pedites ex medio suorum agmine accersunt; majoribus animis ad pugnam redituri. Hoc cum praesagiret Montisrosanus, paucos istos, quamvis fortissimos viros, equis praesertim duplici pugna fatigatis, hostibus pedestri auxilio auctis et confirmatis denuo objicere noluit. Iamque equitatum hostilem ex recenti perturbatione incompositum et procul satis a copiis pedestribus dissitum observaverat. Qua propter pedites suos (quibus damnum non exiguum a majoribus tormentis inferebatur) obequitans in hunc modum compellat: "Nihil proficimus commilitones. Quamdiu eminus res agitur, quis timidum imbellemque a strenuo fortique dignoscat? Si meticulosos istos et enerves homunculos comminus aggressi fueritis, nunquam erunt isti vestrae virtuti pares. Agite ergo, mucronibus et sclopetorum manubriis insultate, proterite, in fugam conjicite, et meritas irrogate perfidiae et rebellionis paenas." Et illi impigre[1] ducis mandata exsequentes, irruunt, et facto impetu, in ruinae modum fundunt fugantque. Equites, qui subsidiarios pedites expectabant, ubi fugientes eos viderunt, et illi citatiore cursu se subducunt. Quibus victores, nec insequi quidem nedum assequi valentes, securam fugam permisere. Peditum vero longe alia ratio fuit, quorum perpauci victorum manus evaserunt. Cum enim, quo fugerent, praeterquam in urbem non haberent, victoresque victis immisti per portas posticasque irrumperent, tota urbe acervatim cadebant. Quatuor horas pugnatum fuit tam dubio Marte, ut nemo dignosceret, in quam partem inclinaret victoria. Habuit quidem in hoc praelio Montisrosanus tormenta quaedam majora, sed nulli usui, occupatis (ut dictum est) ab hostibus locis opportunioribus. Verum hostilia non parum incommodi nostris

---

[1] Or *Nec illi pigre*. The editions have *Nec illi impigre*.

intulerunt. Inter alios Hibernus quidam tibiam ad extremam ferme cutem ictu majoris tormenti amputatam trahebat. Hic, socios ejus casu paululum attonitos cernens, clara voce et gratulanti similior proclamat: Hem socii, belli haec alea est, nec mihi, nec vobis poenitenda. Vos rem, ut decet, fortiter gerite. Quod ad me attinet, certus sum Dominum meum Marchionem me, pedestri inutilem, ad equestrem militiam evecturum. Simul his cultellum theca educit, immotusque et imperterritus, cute propria manu discissa, tibiam commilitoni humandam tradit. Et sane curato demum vulnere, equesque factus, fidelem saepe strenuamque operam postea navavit. Pugnatum fuit ad Aberdoniam pridie Idus Sept. anno CIƆIƆXLIV. Et Montisrosanus militibus ad signa revocatis, urbem ingressus, biduum curandis corporibus permisit.

## CAP. VII.

NUNCIATUR interea Argathelium cum longe validioribus copiis quam antehac adesse, Lothiano Comite, cum mille et quingentis equitibus eum comitante. Aberdonia ergo ad Kintorium vicum decem millibus passuum distantem secedit; ut Gordoniis Huntilaei amicis et clientibus, et aliis qui Regem impensius favere putabantur, aditum patefaceret. Inde Wilielmum Rollocum equitem Oxoniam ablegat, qui Regem de rebus hactenus prospere gestis certiorem faceret, et suppetias ex Anglia aut aliunde impetraret. Eum quidem bis prospere pugnasse: verum tot ac tantis copiis undique quasi obsessum imparem plane fore, nisi mature subveniatur. Interim nihil Montisrosanum magis angebat, quam quod Gordoniorum nemo se illi adjungeret; de quibus longe alia et meliora speraverat. Non defuere tamen qui pronam eorum voluntatem testarentur: sed clam adversantem Montisrosano Huntilaeum, Familiae gentisque principem, suos omnes exemplo et authoritate cohibere. Illum quidem in extrema insulae ora latitantem alienae gloriae, quam ipse frustra expetivisset, invidere. Amicis clientibusque, additis etiam minis, interdicere, ne cum Montisrosano commune haberent quidquam, aut illi consilio vel auxilio opitularentur. Quae cum ille perspecta habuisset, transferre ad loca aspera et montana copias suas statuit; ubi hostium equitatum (quo maxime pollebant) inutilem fore satis noverat. A pedestribus vero, quantavis multitudine essent, justissimae causae et militum suorum virtuti fisus, non multum sibi metuebat. Majoribus igitur tormentis, terra effossa, in palustri quodam loco reconditis, impedimentis etiam aliis molestis et praegravibus sese exoneravit. Et ad Spaeae amnis tractum profectus, non procul a veteri castello, cui Rothemurco nomen, castra

## CAP. VII.

metatus est: cum exercitu, si numerum spectes, perexiguo, sed expedito tamen et alacri, et jam victoriis etiam assueto.

In adversa Spaeae ripa Catenesios, Suderlandios, Rossenses, Moravios, et alios ad quinque millia, in armis offendit; qui eum transitu amnis, omnium in Scotia rapidissimi, arcerent, quoad Argathelius, qui vestigiis ejus insistebat, a tergo eum adoriretur. Prementibus undique tot hostibus, et obsesso similis Montisrosanus, ut se saltem ab eorum equitatu liberaret, Badenothiam, regionem asperam, montosam, nec equis ferme perviam petiit. Ubi aliquot dies gravi sane morbo laboravit. Quae res tam immodico gaudio foederatos affecit, ut penitus extinctum eum non dubitaverint affirmare, et Deo, quasi Iovi liberatori, gratias publice habendas decernere. Nec egregii eorum vates suo muneri apud populum defuere. Illi enim quasi numinis fatique interpretes, ipsius Domini Dei exercituum manu confectum cecidisse, pro oraculo disserunt. Diuturnum tamen eis non fuit illud gaudium: brevi enim convaluit, et quasi suscitatus ex mortuis, hostes magis quam antehac perterruit. Ubi enim primum per morbum licuit, in Atholiam reversus, Makdonaldum cum parte copiarum ad Montanos ablegat, qui eos ad societatem belli invitaret: detrectantes vero militiam, vel invitos cogeret. Ipse Angusiam repetit, sperans fore, ut Argathelium longis itineribus cum equitatu fatigatum, vel ad hiberna cogeret, vel quam longissime post se relinqueret. Argathelius enim tam lente et tanto intervallo insequebatur, ut plane appareret nihil minus illi cordi esse, quam belli aleam experiri. Peragrata ergo Angusia, superatoque Grampio (qui perpetuo ab oriente in occidentem jugo Scotiam quasi in aequales partes dividit) in septentrionalia regni reversus est. Cumque jam Argathelium tanto intervallo post se relictum existimaret, ut aliquod temporis spatium sibi instaurandis copiis concederetur, Strathbogiam profectus est: ut Gordonios coram ad socia arma invitaret. Sed irrito labore; Huntilaei enim mandatis praeoccupati, et ejus etiam, utpote patroni sui, exemplum secuti, sese in ignotis diverticulis occultabant. Viri enim generosi et fortes, qui principis suae gentis indignationem provocare non audebant, ad ignaviam tamen suam erubescebant. Gordonium porro Regulum Huntilaei primogenitum (heu qualem quantumque virum) Argathelius avunculus maternus sibi obnoxium cohibebat. Aboinium Comitem, natu secundum, Carleolensis detinebat obsidio. Et Ludovicus hostium castra sequebatur. Adeo ut Huntilaeae familiae nullus esset, cujus authoritatem secuti arma capesserent.

Non paucos tamen dies stativa illic habuit Montisrosanus. Quo quidem tempore, alternis ferme noctibus, cum expedita peditum manu (equites enim nullos aut perpaucos habuit) septem, aut octo, et quandoque etiam decem miliaribus confectis, hostes, quasi tertia vigilia adoriri, opprimere, fugare, viros equosque captivos abducere non destitit. Cumque suos semper salvos et incolumes reduceret, mirum est quanta fiducia militum animos accenderit. Adeo ut quamvis numerus perexiguus fuerit, nihil non, illo duce, auderent facerentque. Tandem vero, ubi omnem de Gordoniis spem deposuisset, exeunte Octobri Strathbogia digressus, Faiviam arcem pervenit occupatque. Atque inibi a speculatoribus, in quibus maximam collocaverat fiduciam, de hostili exercitu falsa omnia renuntiantibus, ad ultimum ferme discrimen adductus est. Enimvero quos Grampium nondum superasse putaverat, ad duo millia passuum improvisi castra metabantur. Ducebat Argathelius cum Lothianio peditum duo millia et quingentos ; equites vero mille et ducentos : Montisrosanus autem, Makdonaldo cum parte copiarum ablegato, pedites mille et quingentos, equites non supra quinquaginta. Cum istis copiis in planiciem camposque descendere extremae amentiae res fuisset : atqui vero in arce, nec satis munita, se continere, indecorum putavit, et famae, quam recentibus victoriis acquisiverat, derogare. Aliam ergo ingreditur viam. Copias in collem paulo editiorem et arci imminentem educit. Solum collis asperum, fossae etiam et aggeres, ab agricolis loci ad praemunienda pascua extructi, speciem castrorum exhibebant. Nondum tamen omnes in stationibus collocaverat, cum simul pauci illi ex Huntilaei clientibus, qui Strathbogia castra ejus secuti fuerant, inspectantibus omnibus, aufugiunt. Et ex adversa parte hostes collem ferociter adorti, non minimam ejus partem vi occupant. Quam si eadem virtute et constantia defendere et propugnare valuissent, conclamatum fuisset de Montisrosano. Cujus milites, tam fugientium auxiliariorum exemplo quam irruentium hostium multitudine attoniti, parum abfuit quin animos desponderent. Quos tamen ille statim praesentia sua, rerum hactenus gestarum memoria et insitae fortitudinis conscientia erexit et confirmavit. Insuper etiam adolescentem quendam Hibernum, nomine O Caenum tribunum sic compellat : "Abi tu, O Caene, cum tuis qui tibi praesto sunt, et istos aggeribus nostris penitus exue, ne nobis amplius sint molesti. Eximiam OCaeni virtutem non semel viderat laudaveratque Montisrosanus : nec ducis de se opinionem fefellit vir fortissimus. Hostes enim, quamvis numero longe superiores et equitatu suorum suffultos, aggeribus dejectos deturbavit. Et sacculis etiam quibusdam pulvere sulphureo repletis, quos hostes in praecipiti fuga dereliquerant, potitus est. Peropportuna fuit haec praeda pulveris inopia laborantibus. Nec sane reticendum hic existimavi promptissimi militum animi egregium indicium. Quidam enim, conspectis sacculis, "quid tandem?" inquit : "Nonne et globos plumbeos ministrarunt? Atqui vero et istos a parcis illis et avaris dispensatoribus repetere oportet." Quasi omnino hostium illud fuisset, necessaria ad belli usus omnia sufficere.

Equitibus interea suis, numero plane quinquaginta, in loco ad hostium impetum nimis opportuno collocatis, submissis expeditis sclopetariis mature

## CAP. VII.

subvenerat. In eos enim Lothianius quinque equitum turmas immisit: qui nondum medium interjacentis campi spatium emensi, a sclopetariis nostris eminus impetiti, actis in gyrum equis, trepide se ad suos recepere. Duplici successu elati, Montisrosani milites aegre coerceri poterant, quo minus in universas hostium copias cum impetu et clamore incurrerent. Quos ille laudatos magis, ut par erat, quam castigatos, jubet officii sui memores imperium expectare. Vesperascente tandem die, Argathelius, cum nihil operae pretium gessisset, copias ad duo miliaria abduxit: noctemque insomnem egit. Postridie vero cum nunciatum esset, Montisrosani milites pulveris globorumque penuria laborare, eductis in eundem locum copiis, collem ipsum aggeresque invasuri speciem prae se ferebat. Verum cum ad hoc praestandum animus illi deficeret, praeter privatas inter utramque aciem discurrentium militum velitationes, dum reliqui in stationibus se continerent, nihil memorabile gestum fuit. Montisrosanus interea pateras, amphorasque, et matulas, aliaque id genus vasa plumbea undique conquisita et liquefacta, in globos converti curabat. Et ne sic quidem militibus sufficere potuit. Quo tamen incommodo adeo illi non fuerunt perterriti, ut quidam, quoties globulum ex machina, accenso pulvere, in hostem torsisset (quod nunquam frustra fecisse praesumebat), toties ad socios conversus, lepide exclamaret: "Ego, inquit, certissimo ictu, proditoris os matula contrivi." Nec sane mirabitur quisquam Montisrosani milites pulveris aliarumque rerum ad bellum et usus militares spectantium penuriam saepiuscule perpessos, si animo secum reputaverit, nihil rerum istarum illis aliunde quam ab hostibus devictis suppeditatum fuisse. Et jam secundo etiam die ad vesperam inclinante, Argathelius suos trans amnem, eadem qua venerant via, ad tria miliaria Britannica (quae unum Germanicum conficiunt), subduxit. Et plures ad Faiviam dies tempus sic trahebatur: Argathelio cum tanto exercitu nihil aliud reportante, quam infamiam apud suos, et apud hostem contemptum. Ejus enim ignaviae imputatum fuit, quod illic non fuerat debellatum.

Montisrosanus tandem (ne diurno tempore extremum abeuntium agmen hostili equitatui violentius carpendum permitteret) nocturno itinere Strathbogiam repetiit. Ubi et paulisper subsistere instituit, quia et solum asperum tutiores suos praestabat ab equitum insultu, et montanis etiam locis vicinum, unde copias auxiliares cum Makdonaldo indies expectabat. Insecuti sunt eum postridie hostes, eo animo, ut ad pugnam in aperto campo ineundam cogerent. Et sane ubi primum in conspectum venerunt, explicata acie, ad proelium sese accinxere, quasi totis viribus incursuri. Verum praemissi ab Argathelio montani, qui levi proelio lacesserent, fortiter excepti, repulsique ad suos. Tum loca opportuniora a Montisrosano occupata, ad tutiora sed minus honesta consilia revocarunt. Argathelius inducias petere, colloquia, fide utrinque data, inire; nec tantum oblatis cum impunitate praemiis militum fidem sollicitare, sed et, pudendum dictu, Montisrosani caput, parricidae cuivis aut sicario, immenso pretio redimendum offerre satagebat. Quae cum Montisrosanus persentisceret (hominis enim ingenium vafrum, ad fraudes dolosque texendos, quam ad justum et apertum Martem magis natum, probe noverat), nihil antiquius habuit, quam exiguas copias quam longissime ab hostili equitatu simul et Argathelii artibus subducere.

Convocato ergo suorum consilio, sententiam suum exponit. Illi omnes prudentiam laudant, fidem operamque solitam pollicentes. Longinquo ergo itinere Badenothiam insequenti nocte petere instituit. Quo vero milites ad iter difficillimum expeditiores haberet, impedimenta cum praesidio praemisit: militesque quasi ad pugnam in diem crastinum paratos esse jussit. Jamque impedimenta in itinere erant, cum subito nunciatur Forbesium de Cragewar captivum (quem, data fide, libere in castris degere permiserat), unaque Sibbaldum illum, quem unum cum Rolloco itineris consiliique participem ex Anglia fecerat, aliosque transfugas ad hostes defecisse. Ille hominum perfidia commotus, ut majorem apud hostes gratiam inirent, consilii sui rationem indicaturos, merito suspicatus est. Confestim igitur impedimenta cum praesidio revocat, totamque sententiam mutasse videbatur. Revera tamen non mutaverat; differendum tamen ad aliquod tempus censuit, ut vana et incerta hostibus apparerent, quae a transfugis accepissent. Quatriduo tandem elapso, impedimenta denuo praemisit. Et collucentibus, totis castris, ignibus, equites quos habuit, in conspectu hostium, quasi excubias agentes collocavit; quoad pedites omni periculo procul erant: deinde et eos incolumes subduxit, omnesque cum diluculo Balveniam venere. Cumque jam ab equitatu in tuto esset, nec hostes ultra insequerentur, provecta hieme, ipso scilicet brumae tempore, dies paucos reficiendis viribus militi permisit. Et hac potissimum tempestate Argathelii artes innotuere. Plerique enim, viri nobiles et generosi, et rei bellicae periti (plures enim ille duces, si Hibernos montanosque Scotos excipias, quam milites ducebat), ad Argathelii fidem se receperunt. Causabantur alii valetudinem, alti, tantis itineribus, per loca montana, inculta, invia, saxis et vepribus obsita, alta plerumque nive cooperta, et nullis unquam mortalibus trita, hiberna illa tempestate impares sese praedicabant; adeoque invitos, et ultima necessitate adactos missionem petere. Quam quidem ille poscentibus non negavit: indignanti tamen, et degeneres animos despicienti, quam consentienti et indulgenti similior. Nec dictu facile est, quantum istorum exemplum vires ejus infirmaverit, et quam multos deterruerit, qui ut signa ejus sequerentur, se praeparabant. Unicus Ogilvius, Arlaeus Comes, quamvis sexagenarius simul et valetudinarius, cum tanto patre dignissimis filiis, Thoma et Davide equitibus, nullo unquam vel vitae discrimine adduci potuit, ut ab eo divelleretur.

## CAP. VIII.

BALVENIA Montisrosanus Badenothiam reversus, obvium habuit fidum sane nuncium, qui indicavit Argathelium cum copiis pedestribus (equites enim ad hiberna concesserant) Duncaledoniae considere; et inde omni arte Atholios ad defectionem solicitare. Ille, quamvis de eorum fide et constantia securus, incredibili tamen celeritate in Atholiam descendit. Unica enim nocte viginti et quatuor milliaria, per loca inculta, horrida, nivosa, et nullis unquam mortalibus habitata, cum copiis confecit; Argathelium nimirum equitibus destitutum aggressurus. Verum ille, sola ejus fama perterritus, cum adhuc ad sex supra milliaria abesset, milites suos sibi ipsis prospicere jussit: ipse sese fuga in Pertham (quam foederati valido praesidio tenebant), praecipitem conjecit. Redierat jam Makdonaldus, simulque Makranaldorum ducem cum suis numero quingentis pertraxerat. Addiditque Montisrosanus Patricium Graemum cum selectis quibusdam Atholiis, quibus stipatus ad lacum proficiscitur unde Taus erumpit, inde per Brodalbium Argatheliam petiturus; nusquam hostem felicius expugnatum iri ratus, quam in agro suo. Nec sane huic consilio defuerunt rationes gravissimae. Inprimis Argathelii in montanis authoritas et potentia aequalibus et vicinis formidabilis erat: adeoque totius rebellionis origo et fomes. Quotiescunque enim quis foederatis se opponere aut eorum mandata detrectare audebat, illico Argathelius coacto ex montanis (qui inviti etiam illi inserviebant) tumultuario quinque aut sex millium exercitu, miserum opprimebat. Et istam hominis seditiosi, avari, et crudelis potentiam infringendam ille jure censuit. Insuper montani illi non tantum causae Regiae favebant, sed et Argathelium, cujus tyrannidem saepius erant experti, oderant cane pejus et angue: operam tamen suam praestare metuebant, nisi illo prius debellato. Accessit denique, quod foederati inferiora Regni validis praesidiis et frequenti equitatu obtinebant. Adeo, ut nisi amicorum opes penitus atterere vellet, alio copias suas ad hiberna perducere non posset. Et hisce plane rationibus permotus, quam maximis et difficillimis itineribus et incredibili celeritate in Argatheliam defertur.

Argathelius vero tunc temporis milites in Provincia sua describebat; diemque et locum conventui indixerat. Ipse autem securus in munita Innerarae arce degebat, hostem supra centum milliaria abesse ratus. Nunquam enim antea induci potuit, ut crederet exercitum in Argatheliam vel media aestate pedestri itinere penetrare potuisse. Nec sine jactatione olim praedicare solitus erat, malle se centum florenorum jacturam facere, quam cuivis mortalium notas esse semitas, per quas aditus in ejus ditionem armatis patefieret. Nihil ergo tale cogitanti trepidi de montibus bubulci hostes vix duo millia passuum abesse denunciant. Et ille consilii incertus, et mentis ferme prae metu inops, cymbam piscatoriam nactus, fuga sibi consuluit, amicos, clientes, et universam Provinciam fortunae et hostium arbitrio permittens. Regio est montana et aspera, frugum sterilis; nullas enim, aut perpaucas colligunt. Alendis tamen gregibus, in quibus incolarum ferme opes sitae sunt, satis idonea. Montisrosanus exercitum tripartitum in agros hostiles immisit. Partem unam Makranaldorum Dux, alteram Makdonaldus, tertiam ipse ducebat. Provinciam omnem populabundi pererrant. Quotquot armatos offendunt, ad conventum a patrono indictum properantes occidunt: nec ulli, qui militiae saltem aptus sit, parcunt: aut prius absistunt, quam, viros militares omnes provincia exigant, aut ad diverticula ipsis solis nota compellant. Deinde in pagos et tugurios faces injiciunt, et ultricibus flammis humo adaequant. In hoc talionem Argathelio referentes, qui omnium primus in populares incendio desaeviit. Pecora denique secum abigunt. Nec mitius cum aliis actum est, qui in Lorna et vicinis tractibus Argathelii dominium agnoscebant. Duraverunt haec ab Idibus Decembris anni CIƆIƆXLIV ad quartum aut quintum Kal. Feb. anni sequentis.

Et sane Montisrosanus, non alias magis, singularem divini numinis providentiam agnoscere, clementiam et paternam misericordiam praedicare solitus est, quod se cum suis, ex locis istis incolumem eduxerat. Si enim vel ducenti armati angustias istas fortiter propugnassent, ejus copias aut eminus destruere aut aditu arcere facillime potuissent. Deinde, si vel bubulci armenta abegissent (quod factu erat facillimum) in locis sterilibus fame fuisset pereundum. Vel si denique hiems rigida et procellosa (qualem quotannis ferme illic experiuntur) incubuisset, vel altis nivibus immersi, vel ipso plane frigore correpti, diriguissent. Verum Deus immortalis, hostibus animum, caelo solitum rigorem ademit: soli vero sterilitatem armentorum quam maxima copia pensavit. Tandem vero Argathelia digressus, peragrataque Lorna, Glencoa, et Abria ad lacum Nessi pervenit. Et jam sane montanos omnes, vel Argathelii exemplo territos, vel ab ejus metu liberos, ad justissimam Regis causam suscipiendam et armis propugnandam contra perduelles expectabat.

Ne vero invicto Montisrosani animo nova materies aliquando deesset, nunciatur ecce Seafordianum Comitem, in illis locis longe potentissimum (de quo optima quaeque sperabat), cum Innernessi praesidiariis, qui veterani erant, adeoque Moraviae, Rossiae, Suderlandiae, Catenesiae et Fraseriorum gentis viribus, cum infesto exercitu quinque millium peditum equitumque illi occurrere. Ducebat Montisrosanus mille duntaxat et quingentos. Klanranaldini enim, et plerique etiam Atholii, nihil horum suspicati, et Argatheliae spoliis onusti, impetrata missione, domum se receperant; ad signa tamen redituri quandocunque accerserentur. Nec tamen dubitavit Montisrosanus

## CAP. VIII.

cum tumultuario isto exercitu rem proelio decernere. Quamvis enim subsidiarios veteranos esse probe noverat, reliquam tamen multitudinem ex agricolis, bubulcis, tabernariis, calonibus, et lixis recens conflatam, imbellem omnino et militiae inutilem reputabat.

Jamque nihil aliud quam in istos pugnam meditantem, fidissimus eum nuncius assequitur, qui indicat, Argathelium, coactis ex inferiori Regno copiis, et insuper additis qui adhuc illi adhaerebant montanis, cum tribus peditum millibus in Abriam descendisse, et ad vetus castellum, cui Innerlocho nomen, in ipsis lacus Abriae ripis subsistere. Montisrosanus, qui Argathelii, hominis vafri et meticulosi, ingenium perspectum habuit, consilium etiam conjectura assecutus est. Nimirum longo intervallo insecutum, ut eum primo cum septentrionalibus istis committeret, eventum pugnae ad suum commodum pertracturus; proelio tamen sponte non decertaturus. Censuit igitur rem esse majoris ad famam belli momenti, et minoris etiam periculi, si illum in montibus, ubi tanquam numen aliquod tremendum a rudi populo colebatur, vinci posse demonstraret. Exercitum vero illum septentrionalem, victoriae de Argathelio partae fama perterritum, in ordinem cogi posse augurabatur. Aberat Innerlocho Montisrosanus triginta milliaribus, nec tamen trita semita (quam praesidiis obsedit, ne quis de eo nuncius ad hostes perveniret) insistere voluit: verum recto itinere per montes Abriae invios, et incultos, solis bubulcis et venatoribus cognitos (frequentissimi enim sunt in istis montibus cervorum damarumque greges), qua nulli hactenus mortales copias duxerant, caesis eorum speculatoribus, hostibus improvisus imminet. Illi re insperata minime attoniti, illico, correptis armis, ad pugnam se accingunt. Quos ut jam paratos Montisrosanus vidit, subsistit tantisper, quoad extremum suorum agmen, difficillimo itinere fatigatum, praecedentes assequeretur. Nox erat; lunaribus tamen radiis aether illustratus diurnae lucis jacturam pensabat. Noctem in armis agunt, et levibus obscura luce velitationibus jugiter invicem lacessentes, nullum alter alteri receptui locum reliquit. Crastinum caeteri avide expectabant; unus tamen Argathelius, sibi ipsi quam[1] aliis consultior, nocte intempesta seipsum subduxit; et secundo cymbam nactus, instantis pugnae discrimen praecavit. Virtutis nimirum alienae arbiter et spectator futurus. Illucescente porro die, Montisrosanus aciem instruit: et[2] hostes impigre idem fecere. Nondum enim ipsum Montisrosanum (quod postea a captivis rescitum fuit), sed praetorem ejus aliquem, aut ducem cum parte copiarum adesse arbitrabantur.

Exorto denum sole, postr. Kal. Feb. ipso purificationis B. Mariae Deiparae, et semper Virginis die, signum tuba datum non exiguum terrorem

---

[1] The sense clearly requires the words *sibi . . . quam*, which are, however, not found in the editions.

[2] The editions have *nec* here. The same error occurs ch. vi. p. 373.

hostibus incussit. Praeterquam enim quod tubae sonus, equestris militiae index, in locis illis insolens sit, ipsum Montisrosanum adesse demonstrabat. Primores nihilominus Campbellorum (nomen illud est familiae Argatheliae gentilicium) viri fortes et strenui, et omnino digni qui sub meliore patrono justiori causae militassent, pugnam ipsi quidem alacriter capessunt. Milites tamen qui in prima acie stabant, machinis semel duntaxat displosis, Montisrosani militibus ad statariam pugnam ferociter irruentibus, terga dedere. Quos iidem, ingenti sublato clamore, tam acriter persecuti sunt, ut omnes quasi uno impetu in ruinae modum deturbaverint. Insecuta est horrenda fugientium strages, ad novem milliaria continuata. Caesi sunt hostium mille et quingenti; in quibus Campbelli plerique generosi, et qui familiam ducebant, viri apud suos clari: qui quidem pro patrono suo, nimis fortiter dimicantes, in ipso pugnae campo occubuere. Quorum sorti Montisrosanus hostis ingemuit, et quotquot potuit authoritate sua salvos fecit, et in fidem recepit: cum ipse Argathelius cymbae impositus, et paululum a ripa profectus, suos trucidatos ex alto secure aspiceret. Praefecti quidam militum et duces, quos ex inferiori Scotia illuc duxerat Argathelius, in arcem se receperunt. Eos Montisrosanus, deditione facta, fidei suae traditos benigne habuit: et non paucis humanitatis et liberalitatis officiis cum libertate cumulatos dimisit. In illa pugna, pluribus vulneratis, tres duntaxat gregarios milites desideravit Montisrosanus. Verum insignem victoriam, insignis plane viri Thomae Ogilvii equitis, Comitis Arlaei filii vulnera, quae mors paucos post dies subsecuta est, luctuosam reddidere. Erat ille Montisrosano in paucis carus. Qui sub imperio soceri sui Ruthvenii, Forthae Branfordiaeque Comitis (viri toto terrarum orbe ob res praeclare gestas notissimi) Regi in Anglia egregiam operam navaverat. Inde vero ab hujus in Scotia belli initio, Montisrosano constanter adhaeserat. Nec minus sane ille Minervae quam Martis alumnus, optimisque literis penitus imbutus, antiquissimae Ogilviorum familiae novum decus et ornamentum, et ad victoriam illam non leve momentum, pro patria et Rege honestissimo fato functus est. Hujus amissi desiderio vehementer afflictus Montisrosanus corpus in Atholiam deferri curavit: et magnifico funere (pro loci temporumque ratione) extulit. Campbellorum vero in montanis potentia, a multis retro seculis, vicinis formidabilis, hac clade penitus attrita fuit: eademque Montisrosano ad res facilius gerendas aperta est via. Montani siquidem viri bellicosissimi ab Argathelii invisa tyrannide liberati, ad operam Regi praestandam promptiores sese sponte exhibuerunt.

## CAP. IX.

MILITI immensis laboribus confecto diebus aliquot ad curanda corpora concessis, Montisrosanus Abriae montes remensus, ad lacum Nessi reversus est. Inde vero Harrigae, Arniae, Narniaeque tractus perlustrans, ad Spaeam amnem pervenit. Hic nunciatur, non contemnendam hostium manum, Elgini (Moraviae, provinciae ultra Spaeam sitae, caput est) subsistere. Ad istos vel ad partes pertrahendos, vel vi et armis perdomandos Montisrosanus properabat. Verum sola adventantis fama nubeculam istam dispulit; trepidi enim ad nota diverticula sese omnes recepere. Ille nihilominus iter prosecutus, Elginum deditione civium in fidem recepit, postr. Id. Feb. Quo quidem tempore nunquam satis ob eximias virtutes laudandus, Gordonius Regulus, Huntilaei primogenitus, ab avunculo (a quo invitus fuerat detentus) ad partes Regias palam pertransiit: et cum non adeo multis sed delectis quibusdam amicis et clientibus, Montisrosano, tanquam Regis praefecto et vicario, operam et obsequium ultro detulit. Illum Montisrosanus primo benigne et comiter habitum impensius laudavit. Postea vero penitius cognitum et probatum, sanctissimo amicitiae vinculo sibi copulavit. Quoniam vero Moravienses plerique foederatis addictissimi se in suis abdiderant latibulis, nec quidquam auxilii ab infensis animis sperandum foret, cis[1] Spaeam copias duxit, Bamphiae, Aberdoniaeque provincias, Gordonii praesentia, exemplo, et authoritate commotas, ad partes pertracturus. Et contractis quas potuit in illis locis copiis, cum peditum duobus millibus et equitibus ducentis, superato Dea amne et Grampio, in Mernium descendit. Nec procul Fettercarnia stativa habuit.

Ad Brechiniam vero septem inde milliaribus distantem, Ioannes Urraeus eques, vir strenuus et impiger, et militari gloria etiam apud exteras gentes clarus, equitum foederatorum praefectus, caeteris etiam copiis cum imperio praeerat. Ille cum sexcentis equitibus ad explorandas Montisrosani vires egressus est. Enimvero eum pedites perpaucos, equitatum vero nullum ducere ratus, si in planiciem descenderet, rei bene gerendae occasionem sperabat: utcunque vero caderet, secura sibi omnia satis fidenter promittebat. Montisrosanus, ut eum alliceret, abditis in convalli reliquis, ducentos equites duntaxat, sed, ex more, expeditissimis sclopetariis refertos objecit. Quos Urraeus conspicatus, expensa hominum paucitate, suos in aciem eduxit. Verum sero observato pedite, qui Montisrosani equites alacriter subseque-

---

[1] Ed. Paris reads *ab cis*, i.e., *ab eis cis?* The word *eis*, being so like *cis*, might easily drop out in the original MS. or first proof, and the unintelligible *ab* be omitted in later editions.

batur, receptui signum dedit: et ipse quidem Urraeus caeteros praemittens in extremo agmine strenuus se gessit. Abeuntibus Montisrosani milites instant, urgent, pellunt, quoad superato Esca amne, hostes vix nocturnis tenebris tuti, in tutum se recepere. Nec sane securos se judicarunt, quoad viginti quatuor milliaria emensi, praecipiti cursu Taodunum pervenerunt. Tum qui hactenus fuerant insecuti, Fethercarniam reversi, ac postridie Brechiniam venere. Hic edoctus fuit Montisrosanus Bailaeum ex Anglia accersitum, magni nominis ducem, cum summo imperio hostium copiis praeesse; Urraeum etiam cum equitatu illi adjunctum esse: et veteranos plerosque ex Anglia et Hiberniâ revocatos sub signis habere; jamque foederatos quasi majoribus auspiciis rem aggredi, adeoque sibi non modo cum longe alio milite, sed et peritissimis ducibus dimicandum fore.

Quapropter, ne ab eorum equitatu (quo semper praevaluerunt) circumveniretur, locorum opportuna secutus, juxta Grampii radices Taum versus tendit; Fortham etiam, si qua fieri posset, transgressurus, unde auxilia Regi non defutura sperabat. Nec fefellit hostes ejus consilium. Quapropter cum validissimis copiis duces istos objiciunt. Qui non prius in conspectum venere, quam Montisrosanus pugnae copiam offerret: verum nihil minus illis in animo fuit, quam acie decernere; adeo ut ne abeuntis quidem extremum agmen turbare tentaverint. Et ille quidem ad arcem Innercaretaeam, ac postridie Eliotam vicum profectus est. Hic denuo, relictis procul a tergo montibus, in planiciem descendit; et per tubicinem Bailaeo facultatem pugnandi offert petitque. Interfluebat infestos exercitus Ila amnis; quem neuter tuto transmittere potuit, si alter alterum arceret. Rogat ergo Montisrosanus securum transitum: quod si Bailaeo minime arrideret, se illi liberum tutumque permissurum, si modo, nulla amplius interposita mora, dimicaturos data fide responderet. Bailaeus, se suis rebus consulturum; pugnam vero suo, non alieno arbitrio, capessere, respondit. Plures dies in hostium conspectu elapsi sunt: nec hostibus in Montisrosanum copias transmittentibus, nec illo sperante transitum vi obtineri posse, prae equitum inopia. Duncaledoniam ergo progressus, Taum superare conabatur; cum inopinato malo tantum non oppressus fuit. Ludovicus Gordonius Huntilaei filius, qui in acie ad Aberdoniam contra eum steterat, nobilissimo fratre, Gordonio Regulo, sequestro, in fidem receptus fuerat. Is seu veris, seu simulatis patris literis ex latibulo suo datis, Gordonios ferme omnes, clam ipso patre, ad defectionem solicitatos abduxit: fratremque cum Montisrosano, imminente hoste deseruit. Et sane utri infensior fuerit, incertissima jactatur fama.

Montisrosanus insperata defectione multum commotus, quamvis in septentrionem necessario redeundum foret, ut novas vires acquireret, iter suum versus Fortham nihilominus simulabat. Et speculatores ejus uno ore re-

## CAP. IX.

nunciant hostes ad unum omnes Taum trajecisse, ut vadis Forthae occupatis, eum transitu arcerent. Ille, ne nihil plane superiori conatu effecisse videretur, rem praeclaram facturum censuit; si, quasi obiter, Taodunum, urbem seditiosissimam, expugnaret. Siquidem illa, fidissimum perduellium in illis locis receptaculum, nec minima rebellionis pars, non alio quam civium praesidio tenebatur. Infirmiores ergo et leviter armatos cum impedimentis secus montium radices praemissos, apud Brechiniam occurrere jussit. Ipse, assumptis quos habuit equitibus (centum et quinquaginta omnino erant) et sexcentis expeditis sclopetariis, Duncaledonia tertia vigilia profectus, Taodunum pridie Non. Ap., hora decima antemeridiana, mira celeritate pervenit. Cives vero per fecialem monet, ut urbem Regi tradant: sic saluti suae et urbis incolumitati consulturos. Secus si fecerint, ferrum flammamque minitatur. Illi tempus terere, nec respondere primo: deinde et fecialem in carcerem compingunt. Qua contumelia irritatus Montisrosanus, per tres urbis regiones milites immittit. Cives armati ex propugnaculis sese aliquandiu, sed frustra opposuerant. Hiberni enim montanique Scoti ferociter insiliunt; alii propugnaculis illos expellunt, et majoribus tormentis potiti, ea in ipsam urbem convertunt; alii portas effringunt, forum templumque occupant; alii non uno in loco admotis facibus aedes succendunt. Et sane, nisi gregarii milites ex intempestiva avaritia gulaque ad praedam potumque declinassent, opulentissimum oppidum conflagrasset. Quod tamen non minus victoribus quam victis saluti fuit. Enimvero speculatores de hostibus, quod Taum transmisissent, falsa omnia attulerant. Turmas aliquot, nec sane multas trajecisse viderant; quas illi universas hostium copias rati, seque suosque tantum non prodiderunt.

Stabat in edito colle, qui Taoduno imminet, urbanam pugnam despectans Montisrosanus, cum trepidi speculatores Bailaeum Urraeumque cum peditum tribus millibus et equitibus octingentis, vix mille passus abesse testantur. Ille suos confestim ex urbe evocavit; quod ab illis aegerrime impetravit. Milites enim hactenus de victoria securi, et vino paululum incalescentes, et opulentissimae inhiantes praedae, vix cogi poterant, ut urbe capta excederent. Et sane priusquam a praeda avelli valuere, hostes intra teli jactum abeuntibus imminebant. Caeterum, ut in ultimo discrimine fieri solet, qui apud Montisrosanum erant, sententiis variabant. Suadebant alii, ut ipse Montisrosanus suae saluti equestri fuga consuleret. Nec enim fieri posse, ut pedites istos, matutino itinere viginti et amplius milliarium lassatos, diurna inde pugna confectos, jam vero vino praedaque graves abduceret. Praesertim cum Taoduno viginti aut forsan triginta milliaria conficienda restarent, priusquam in tuto collocari possent. Belli aleam hanc esse, et forti animo tolerandam; cum longe majores clades hostibus saepiuscule illatae fuerint. Non dubitandum quin, illo incolumi, copiae brevi reficerentur: contra vero, si quid tristius accideret, conclamatum fore, et perdita omnia exclamabant. Alii rem hactenus deperditam vociferabantur, ideoque honeste saltem moriendum: et si impetu facto, in confertissimos hostes irruerent, non inglorios perire. Ipse nec his nec illis accedebat. Nunquam enim animum inducere potuit, ut fortissimos milites in ultimo discrimine positos desereret: decoram cum suis mortem indecorae securitati praeferendam ratus. Atqui vero usque adeo impares in hostem ruere, et cerebrum quasi saxo allidere, ultimum esse remedium, nec temere usurpandum. Deum immortalem, ut non ignavia nostra tentandum, sic neque de ejus ope desperandum viris fortibus et Christianis. Hortatur denique ut munera sua fortiter capesserent, eventum Deo, caeteraque suae curae permitterent.

Illico ergo quadringentos pedites praemittit, mandatque, ut quantum imperturbatis ordinibus fieri possit, gressus accelerarent. Ducentos omnium expeditissimos sequi jubet. Ipse equitibus agmen claudit. Progrediebantur equites, tanto intervallo dissiti, ut expeditos sclopetarios, si res postularet, admittere possent. Hostilem peditem suos assequi posse non putabat. Et si equites soli incurrerent, quod vix ausuros augurabatur, rem judicavit non fore usque adeo difficilem. Et quia sol jam ad occasum declinabat, nocturnam umbram non parum receptui commodam futuram praesensit. Hostes, cognito per captivos et mox perspecto abeuntium numero, ubi eos ad iter, non ad pugnam accinctos viderunt, bipartitis copiis, insequuntur. Neque id tantum ut a tergo et a latere simul aggrederentur, sed etiam ut omnem ad montes viam praecluderent. Duces vero, quo suos ad insequendum acrius exstimularent, Montisrosani caput aureorum viginti millibus licitantur. Jamque praemissi hostium equites abeuntes urgebant, cum egregii illi sclopetarii equitatui conjuncti, eorum qui acrius instabant, primum, secundum, tertiumque globulis plumbeis exceptos transfigunt. Quorum casu reliqui cautiores facti, multum de priore impetu remiserunt. Montisrosani milites, ubi se pedestri itinere superiores viderunt, recuperatis cum fiducia viribus, strenue contra equites certarunt, donec pugnam nox diremit. Et ut sese ab hostibus quoquo modo expedirent, plura milliaria in orientem secus oram maritimam confecerunt. Atqui istac illis minime eundum fuit, sed septentrionem versus ad Grampios montes, ut tandem ab infestis equitibus sese vindicarent. Verum longe maximam exercitus sui partem Bailaeus inter eos et Grampium interposuerat, ne ullus omnino receptui locus aut via pateret.

Nocte igitur intempesta, cum non procul Aberbrothia abessent, Montisrosanus suos paululum subsistere jubet. Nec diu sane substitit, cum animo reputans, vias aditusque omnes, quibus recta ad montes perveniendum erat, ab hostili equitatu interceptos esse (nec de hoc opinio eum fallebat) converso itinere, in occidentem aestivum suos acriter tendere jussit. Et hac arte, sed cum incredibili labore insequentibus illusit: quos illa ipsa nocte praetergressus, et mox in septentrionem conversus, die postero, oriente sole, Escam meridionalem non procul a Carestonia arce trajecit. Inde vero Brechiniam misit, qui suos cum impedimentis arcesserent. At illi fama istius expeditionis exciti melius et maturius sibi consuluerant, occupaverantque montes. Apud Carestoniam subsistenti speculatores subito renunciant, hostilem equitatum in conspectu esse, copiis pedestribus, cibo somnoque refectis, etiam strenue insequentibus. Montisrosanus ipse jam montibus ad tria milliaria vicinus, non multum ab eis metuebat. Verum ejus milites, qui tertium diem et secundam noctem insomnem egerant, semperque in itinere aut in pugna versati fuerant, tam altus sopor obruerat, ut vix stimulis et vulneribus suscitari potuerint. Hostes tandem levi velitatione excepti, radices montium Montisrosano occupandos permiserunt: et irrito labore, ab inutili persecutione se recepere. Ipse vero Glenescam cum suis petiit.

Et haec est celebris illa expeditio Taodunana, speculatorum quidem errore infamis, at imperatoria ducis virtute, constantia, animique in ultimo discrimine praesentia, in paucis insignis. Militum quoque in tolerandis laboribus patientia plane mirabilis fuit: ut qui saepius in pugna, semper in itinere, jejuni et insomnes, ad sexaginta milliaria confecerint, ne tantillo quidem temporis spatio reficiendis viribus permisso. Quae quidem, an apud exteros posterosve fidem inventura sint, ignoramus: verum certissima et compertissima nobis bona fide describimus. Et sane apud viros rei militaris peritos, et eo nomine, non modo in Britannia, sed et in Germania et Gallia claros, expeditionem istam celeberrimis ejusdem Montisrosani victoriis praelatam non semel audivimus.

## CAP. X.

CUM jam supra spem in tuto essent, milites corpora curare jussit Montisrosanus: ipse vero de summa belli sic statuit. Gordonium Regulum, cum illis qui post Ludovici defectionem constanter in fide et obsequio permanserant, ad suos remittit; tam ut eos revocaret quos frater perverterat, quam ut novo delectu copias augeret. Quod quidem ille strenue et alacriter perfecit; et, aliis castigatis, durius in eos animadvertit, qui fraterni sceleris authores et ministri fuere. Eoque intentius negotio incubuit, ut culpae omnem suspicionem amoveret. Nec sane Montisrosanus aut alius quisquam Ludovici flagitium magis detestatus est, quam nobilissimus frater Gordonius. Ipse vero Montisrosanus cum exigua parte copiarum (quingentos enim pedites et equites duntaxat quinquaginta retinuit) per Angusiam in agrum Perthensem contendit, ut hostes distraheret, quoad collectis undequaque copiis, exercitum repararet. Nec fefellit eum conjectura: foederati enim Urraeum, equitatus praefectum, in septentrionem cum imperio mittunt. Illi ex veteranis sexcentos pedites cum ducentis equitibus attribuunt, ut suos confirmaret, et Gordonium opprimeret. Ipse vero Bailaeus cum exercitu Perthae, quasi in umbilico Regni substitit, ad omnes eventus paratus. Duobus supra decem milliaribus aberat Montisrosanus ad pagum cui Kreifo nomen : ubi eum cum exigua manu admodum secure agere Bailaeus audiverat. Et ille ad omnem occasionem intentus, prima vigilia cum toto exercitu Pertha digressus, nocturnum iter accelerabat, ut cum diluculo, improvisum adortus opprimeret. Verum Montisrosanum rebus suis invigilantem invenit; pedites enim ad pugnam iterve paratos in procinctu habuit : ipse vero cum equitibus hosti obviam ivit, ut numerum roburque investigaret. Cumque peditum duo millia et equites quingentos comperisset, mandavit suis ut iter strenue capesserent; et observato Iernae tractu, fauces ejusdem occuparent. Ipse cum paucis quos habuit equitibus, abeuntibus praesidio fuit, ne ab insequenti hostili equitatu conculcarentur. Et sane hostes ferociter invectos tam fortiter excepit, ut caesis aliis, et aliis deturbatis, eos ad suos repulerit, quoad pedites sex milliaria emensi, angustias Iernae obtinuerunt. Et illi quidem irrito conatu semet receperunt. Montisrosanus vero illa nocte ad lacum Iernae consedit xiv. Kal. Maii. Postridie Balwidriam pervenit. Ubi Aboinius Comes ad eum accurrit, qui cum paucis Carleolo elapsus, et fama rerum a Montisrosano gestarum excitatus, sero in patriam redierat.

Balwidria profecti, ad lacum Katrinettae dictum penetraverant, cum nunciatum fuit Urraeum validas in septentrione copias contraxisse, et Gordonio imminere : adeoque periculum esse, ne vir militaris et impiger, et manu promptus, egregium adolescentem opprimeret. Montisrosanus itaque Urraeo mature occurrendum censuit, tam ut instanti periculo amicissimum virum eriperet, quam ut hostiles copias distractas seorsim carperet, et vires infringeret paulatim, quibus unitis imparem se fore, probe noverat. Longis ergo et perpetuis itineribus, Balwidria, lacuque viginti et quatuor milliarium, unde Taus erumpit, Atholia Angusiaque peragrata, superatoque Grampio, per tractum Glenmuk dictum ad intima Marriae pervenit. Gordonium in illis locis cum peditibus mille et ducentis equitibus sibi adjunxit : et confestim ad Spaeam profectus, hostem ultra deposcebat. Nec jam supra sex milliaria aberat, quem Urraeus nondum Grampium transmisisse putabat. Enimvero labore improbo et mira celeritate ipsam famam praevenerat. Urraeus, ne vel invitus ad dimicandum cogeretur, priusquam copias validissimas et frequentes auxiliarios sibi adjungeret, Spaeam festinus transmittit. Et quia suorum omnium conventum ad Innernessum indixerat, Elginum contendit. Nec lente eum Elginum insecutus est Montisrosanus. Ille inde Foressiam impigre petiit. Nec segnius Foressiam usque insecutus, et assecutus est Montisrosanus : et tam pertinaciter vestigiis ejus ad quatuor et decem milliaria institit, ut ingruentis jam noctis umbra tectus, aegre tamen Innernessum obtinuerit.

Postridie Montisrosanus apud vicum, cui Aldernae nomen, castra locavit. Urraeus vero, non secus quam speraverat, Seafordium, Suderlandiumque Comites, Fraseriorum gentem, plerosque etiam ex Moravia et Catenesia vicinisque locis armatos confluxisse repperit. Quibus cum veteranos ex oppidi praesidiariis addidisset, recta in Montisrosanum duxit. Peditum quidem tribus millibus et quingentis, equitibus vero quadringentis imperitabat. Montisrosanus (qui non supra mille et quingentos pedites, equites vero ducentos et quinquaginta sub signis habuit) recipere sese quam maxime desiderabat. Atqui vero non modo Urraeus tam acriter urgebat, ut vix ullus superesset receptui locus, sed et Bailaeus ipse, cum australi exercitu, eoque, quoad equitatum, longo validiore, Grampium hactenus longe a tergo reliquerat, et ad Spaeam magna celeritate contendebat. Quid ergo ageret Montisrosanus? Omnino vel cum Urraeo acie decernendum fuit, vel a coeuntibus hostium copiis circumvento longe gravius subeundum discrimen. Belli ergo praesentem aleam experiri statuit; eventum numini committere: et opportunitatem loci secutus, inibi hostem opperiri. Oppidulum in eminentiori loco situm convallem vicinam operiebat. Et colliculi a tergo supereminentes oculorum aspectum adimebant, nisi quam proxime[1] astantium. In istam convallem copias suas educit, hostibus minime spectandas. Ante urbem paucos quidem, sed expertos promptosque pedites cum tormentis aggeribus forte congestis tectos collocat. Dextrum cornu Alexandro Makdonaldo cum quadringentis peditibus committit: eosque in locis, aggeribus fossisque fortuitis, arbustis insuper saxisque impeditis sistit. Mandatque ut se incolumes ad omnem eventum conservarent, nec desererent stationem, natura loci munitissimam, ab omni non tantum equitatu, sed et pedestribus copiis securi. Simulque optimo consilio addidit maxime conspicuum illud vexillum Regium, quod unicum praeferre solitus erat: sic fore ratus, ut hostes, eo conspecto, potiores copias in illud cornu immitterent, propter locorum asperitatem plane inutiles; quoad ipse rei bene gerendae occasionem in sinistro captaret. Et in eum finem reliquos omnes in adversum transferens, equites Gordonio, pedites sibi ducendos assumpsit. Medii agminis (cum revera nullum esset) speciem exhibebant qui ante urbem aggeribus tecti et muniti erant. De subsidiis vero in ea paucitate ne cogitandum quidem fuit.

Hostes (quod prudentissime Montisrosanus divinaverat) ubi primum vexillum Regium conspexere, potissimam equitatus partem cum veteranis, in quibus praecipuum eorum robur situm erat, illuc dirigunt. Jamque hostium primi ante urbem et in dextro cornu dimicabant; et suis fatiscentibus subinde

---

[1] *Propissime* in the editions.

alios recentesque substituebant; quod Montisrosano pro exiguo militum numero non licuit. Statuit ergo cum suis omnibus in sinistro cornu constitutis in hostem cum impetu semel simulque irruere. Haec vero cogitanti nuncius, quem ille virum fidum et gravem noverat, submissa voce indicat, Makdonaldum cum suis in dextro cornu fugatos[2] esse. Ille praesenti animo, milites praeveniendos censuit, ne adversa fama perculsi animum desponderent. Atque illico Gordonium compellans exclamat: "Nos vero, mi Gordoni, quid cessamus? Makdonaldus noster ad dexteram hostes fusos fugatosque trucidat. Nosne segnes spectatores illi omnem victoriae gloriam permittemus?" Et simul his aciem in hostes immittit. Gordoniorum impetum Urraei equites non diu sustinuere: sed in gyrum acti, et ad fugam conversi, nuda et aperta suorum latera illis tradiderunt. Pedites quamvis ab equitibus deserti, cum et numero et armorum genere longe superiores essent, fortiter Montisrosano restiterunt, quamdiu eminus agebatur. Verum ille eos tandem cominus aggressus eo adegit, ut abjectis armis, inutili fuga sibi frustra consuluerint. At ille haud immemor eorum, quae a fidissimo nuncio acceperat, cum promptissimis quibusdam eum consequentibus ad dextrum cornu conversus, rem longe aliter quam in sinistro se habere comperit.

Makdonaldus enim, vir fortis, sed manu quam consilio promptior, in acie praefervidus et usque ad temeritatem audax, insultantibus hostibus et convitiis eum lacessentibus, sese inter aggeres et arbusta detineri dedignatus, extra stationem munitissimam (contra quam mandatum illi fuerat) se cum suis ultro objecit. Nec impune quidem; hostes enim cum et equitatu et multitudine praepollerent, et plerique etiam veterani essent, milites ejus turbatos trepidosque repulerunt. Et sane nisi mature eos ad vicinum claustrum reduxisset, omnes omnino cum vexillo Regio periissent. Ille tamen temeritatis suae errorem in reducendis militibus mira fortitudine pensavit. Omnium enim novissimus se recepit: et corpus, ingenti scuto, quod laeva gestabat, tegens, confertis hostibus se opposuit. Erant, qui in eum proximi inciderunt, hastati, qui multiplici ictu cuspides ejus scuto infixerant: quas ille ternas simul, quaternasve, ense, quem dextra regebat, amputabat. Verum et qui eum in claustro oppugnabant, supervenientem cum subsidio Montisrosanum et suos in sinistro fugatos conspicati, equites quidem in fugam se praecipitarunt: pedites vero, quorum plerique ex Hibernia veterani erant, obstinatis animis pugnantes, singuli ferme in suis stationibus occubuere. Victores ad aliquot milliaria fugientes insecuti. Caesa sunt hostium ad tria millia peditum, in quibus veterani fortissime pugnaverant. Equites fere omnes matura magis quam decora fuga elapsi sunt.

Non tamen Urraeus ipse, cum aliis promptissimis, qui novissimi campo

---

[2] We should expect *fugatum:* another mark of hasty composition.

excesserunt, effugissent[3] insequentium manus, nisi Aboinius Comes, nescio qua incuria, signa quaedam et vexilla victis et fugientibus direpta in sublime extulisset. Cumque hostes ultra non insequeretur, in suos conversus, faciem hostilem prae se tulit, et novae pugnae speciem praebuit. Quo errore tantisper implicit fuere, quoad equitatus hostilis, turbatis quamvis ordinibus, fusus in diverticula, ut cuique nota et obvia fuerunt, se recepit. Pauci cum Urraeo ante diem posterum in Innernessum pervenere. In hostibus caesis insigniores erant Campbellus Laverius veteranorum tribunus, Johannes, Gedeónque Moravii equites, aliique viri fortes, forsan et lacrimabiles, nisi laudandam alias fortitudinem infami perduellionis crimine polluissent; nec in hoc ipso judicium suum, sed multitudinis impetum, aut patronorum ambitum et avaritiam secuti. Desideravit Montisrosanus, ex eis qui secum in sinistro dimicarunt, unicum tantum, eumque militem gregarium: ex altero vero ubi Makdonaldus imperabat, ejusdem ordinis quatuor et decem. Longe vero plurimos vulneratos in tuto collocandos, et medicis tradendos unice curavit. Captivos deinde comiter et blande solatus, poenitentibus libertatem aut militiam promisit praestititque: obstinatos in rebellione, in alias atque alias custodias distribuit. In illa Aldernensi pugna Naperii adolescentis virtus magnopere enituit. Qui Naperii Reguli de Marchistona filius, Montisrosani vero ex sorore natus, non adeo pridem clam patre et conjuge Edinburgo ad avunculum advolaverat: et in isto proelio tyrocinii egregium edidit specimen, et nobilissimae indolis firmissima rudimenta deposuit. Quapropter foederatorum principes patrem ferme septuagenarium (quo praestantiorem virum hoc saeculo Scotia nullum aluit), conjugem etiam Marriae Comitis filiam, Sterlinium de Keire, levirum, praestantissimum etiam virum, familiae suae principem, et qui multa et gravia pro caritate sua in Regem passus est, cum duabus sororibus, altera quidem lectissima femina Sterlinii conjuge, altera vero virgine, in profundum carcerem conjiciunt: postmodum tamen ab ipso Naperio avunculi auspiciis liberandos. Pugnatum fuit ad Aldernam vii. Id. Maii. an. CIƆIƆCXLV.

## CAP. XI.

MONTISROSANUS, paucis diebus militi ad curanda corpora permissis, Elginum, provinciae caput, est profectus: ubi in gratiam vulneratorum diutius se continuit; quia tam medici, quam idonea pharmaca, quae in campis saepiuscule desiderabantur, prompta erant et ad manum parata. Postea trajecto Spaea, Keithum, inde Frendractum, et inde Strathbogiam pervenit. Hic

---

[3] The construction requires *effugisset: cf.* the error on p. 390, *n.*

illi Bailaeus (cui et Urraeus cum equitatu Aldernanae cladi superstite se adjunxerat) occurrit, lacessitque ad pugnam. Montisrosanus suos, immensis laboribus fractos, numero etiam et equitatu longe inferiores, quamvis pugnandi avidos, continuit, quoad copias novo delectu et auxiliis reficeret. Quapropter stationes, quas commodissimas elegerat, ad vesperam propugnare contentus, noctu Balveniam proficiscitur; quo et hostes illum insequuntur. At ille Balvenia tractum Dauniae, et Spaeae secutus, in Badenothiam adscendit. Hostes vero adversam amnis ripam tenentes, eum denuo ad pugnam lacessunt: sed frustra. Ille enim a justo proelio sedulo cavebat; frequenti tamen velitatione et nocturnis praesertim incursionibus in tantum vires animosque infregit, ut qui non ita pridem tam superbe insultassent, duces juxta et milites trepidi, et turbatis ordinibus, noctu se Innernessum receperint, nemine[1] eos insequente. Montisrosanus se ab hoc hoste liberatum non aegre tulit, hac praesertim de causa: Lindesius Comes, foederatorum post Argathelium coryphaeus, ejusque aemulus, utpote Hamiltonii Ducis levir, Argathelio vel curam, vel animum, utcunque, semper fortunam defuisse praedicabat. Adeoque imperium exercitus qui recens erat coactus in se suscipiebat; quasi rem melioribus auspiciis gerendam aggrederetur. Jamque in Angussam cum copiis transmiserat, Bailaeo quasi subsidio futurus: et si quid contra vota illi accideret, paratus tamen Montisrosanum transitu Forthae arcere. Multum enim semper metuebant, ne aliquando ille cis Fortham, propiusque Edinburgum, bellum transferret. Lindesium ergo, hactenus in Angusia ad arcem, quam Neutillam vocant, considentem, tanquam ducem militiae rudem, militesque nondum laboribus belli assuetos, quam primum debellare statuit.

Quo quidem consilio Badenothia profectus, per edita Marriae Grampium transcendit; et non minus arduis quam longis itineribus ad Arlaei fluminis tractum pervenit, hostem ex improviso aggressurus. Quod et factu facile fuit, famam enim adventus sui celeritate praevenerat; nec aberat Lindesius supra septem milliaria: et omnia ad expeditionem parata fuere. Cum (qua de causa incertum) septentrionales fere omnes clam signa deserunt; et repetita qua venerant via, ad suos sunt reversi. Erat in castris Gordonius Regulus, nec quisquam flagitium illud majore indignatione detestatus est: adeo ut eum Montisrosanus aegre continuerit, quo minus ultima decerneret in desertores, qui sub ejus clientela erant. Non desunt tamen, qui Huntilaei patris clanculariis ad Aboinium (qui valetudinis curandae gratia aberat) mandatis sollicitatos fuisse tradant. Angebat enim Huntilaeum, hominem superbum et aemulum, prospera Montisrosani fama: nec ferre plane potuit intimam filii sui primogeniti cum eo amicitiam. Ut ut sit, ille

---

[1] I.q., *nullo.*

inopinato malo perculsus, expeditionem in Lindesium differre, et praeclaram victoriam quasi e manibus ereptam patienter ferre coactus est.

Ad nova ergo consilia conversus, Nathanêêlem Gordonium, militum tribunum, virum fortem et fidum, qui gratia plurimum apud suos valebat, praemissum ipse insecutus est. Jamque Bailaeus Urraeusque Innernesso redierant, et in inferiore Marria ad Deam amnem castra locaverant. Montisrosanus per Schiae tractum et edita Marriae in intima provinciae (vulgo Cromarriam) pervenit. Cum vero adhuc edita penetraret, Makdonaldum cum parte copiarum in remotissima montana ablegavit, ut copias, quae illic parabantur, quam celerrime ad castra perduceret. Deinde et ipsum Gordonium Regulum dimisit, ut pro gratia et authoritate, qua in locis illis pollebat, Nathanêêlis delectum augeret et maturaret. Quod ille quidem impigre praestitit, et inter alios Aboinium fratrem secum reduxit. Dum haec in Cromarria peraguntur, Lindesius copias in inferiore Marria cum Bailaeo conjungit. Quibus cum Montisrosanus se longe imparem cogitaret (absentibus Gordonio et Makdonaldo cum maxima copiarum parte) ad dirutam arcem de Kargarf secessit, ne hostes in campestribus locis deprehensum equitum peditumque multitudine obruerent: illic vero montibus vicinus, nihil sibi ab illis metuebat. Hinc Aboinius, denuo valetudinarius, Strathbogiam se conferens, sub nomine praesidii non contemnendam manum secum abduxit: quos Gordonius frater aegre admodum postea ad signa revocavit. Interea Lindesius mille veteranos Bailaeo ademit; totidemque illi tirones et rudes ex suis attribuit. Et tanquam insigne aliquid suis auspiciis gesturus, per Merniam in Angusiam reversus, hoc unum tanto conatu praestitit: Atholiam cum exercitu pervagatus populatusque omnem regionem incendio vastavit. In hoc Argathelium imitatus, qui primus horrendum illud exemplum saeviendi in aedes frugesque hoc saeculo crudeliter induxit: flamma quam ferro ferocior, ubi in agros urbesque viris vacuas incidisset.

Bailaeus ea tempestate ad Bogiam, Huntilaei, et totius septentrionis pulcherrimam arcem expugnandam tendebat; ut, si minus eam in potestatem suam redigere posset, Gordoniorum, qui in vicinia habitabant, agros depopularetur, et flammis absumeret. Montisrosanus (quamvis absente cum magna copiarum parte Makdonaldo) Huntilaeo et amicis, quos omnibus officiis sibi devincire laborabat, subveniendum ratus, illuc properavit. Ubi edoctus Bailaeum milites, non omnes quidem, plerosque tamen novos ducere (veteranorum parte Lindesio concessa) nihil magis desiderabat, quam cum illo quamprimum manus conserere: rectaque in eum tetendit. Nec supra tria milliaria confecerat, cum praemissi ab hostibus speculatores sese conspiciendos exhibuere. Et ille expeditos et locorum peritos praemisit, qui hostium situm, gestum, viresque explorarent. Hi statim renunciant, peditatum in edito colle ad duo milliaria subsistere: equites vero angustiam artam et difficilem, quae quasi media inter utrumque exercitum jacebat, occupasse, et transgressos esse. In eos Montisrosanus equites, quos in promptu habebat, cum expeditis quibusdam sclopetariis immisit. Quos illi primo levi velitatione eminus excepere: mox vero trans angustiam (quam tormentariis strenue muniverant) se receperunt. Montisrosanus pedites accersit, ut hostem, si qua fieri posset, inde pellant: sed frustra; nox enim insecuta pugnantes diremit, quam uterque in armis insomnem egit. Postridie Montisrosanus per fecialem pugnae facultatem obtulit. Respondit vero Bailaeus, se conditiones pugnae ab hoste non accepturum. Ille ergo, qui angustiis istis hostem proturbare sine manifesto periculo non potuit, ut eum inde aliquando extraheret, Pitlurgum concessit. Et inde digressus ad Forbesii Reguli arcem, cui Druminorae nomen, biduum substitit. Tandemque hostem, derelictis angustiis, Strathbogiam versus tendere intelligit: et ipse ad Alfordiam vicum cum diluculo iter capessit. Bailaeus vero, ubi certam notitiam adeptus fuerat, Makdonaldum cum non minima copiarum parte in Montanis abesse, ultro eum, quasi se subducentem, insecutus est: et circa meridiem in conspectum ejus venit. Montisrosanus in editiore loco advenientem, ut videbatur, hostem opperiri statuit. Verum illo sinistrorsum ad tria milliaria declinante, ipse destinatum iter Alfordiam prosecutus, ibi noctem illam transegit, cum hostes quasi quatuor milliaribus abessent.

Postero demum die Montisrosanus suos, multo adhuc mane, in procinctu et ad proelium paratos esse jussit: et in colle, qui Alfordiae imminet, collocavit. Ipsi cum turma equitum hostium motum gestumque observanti, et vada Donae amnis, qui Alfordiam praeterfluit, scrutanti nunciatur eos, equites peditesque, ad vadum, quod mille passibus ab Alfordia aberat, properare; eo animo, ut extremum fugientis agmen opprimerent. Sic enim egregii illi augures in suam perniciem divinabant. Montisrosanus, relicta illa equitum turma, non procul a vado, cum delectis quibusdam et peritis viris, qui certiora omnia renunciarent, solus ad instruendam aciem revertitur. Et ante omnia collem illum Alfordensem occupat, unde hostium impetum exciperet, si violentius inveherentur. A tergo erat locus palustris, fossis stagnisque impeditus, ne ab equitatu circumveniretur; a fronte collis acclivis aspectum hostium intercipiebat, ut vix primos ordines oculis percipere potuerint. Necdum omnia rite ordinaverat, cum equites illi, quos ad vadum reliquerat, praecipiti cursu redeunt, renunciantque hostes amnem transgressos esse. Adeo ut neutri amplius integrum fuerit se recipere, nisi cum manifesto suorum periculo. Fama est Bailaeum, utpote ducem peritum et providum, plane invitum ad illud certamen descendisse: nec nisi Balcarisii Reguli, equitum tribuni, temeritate coactum. Qui se cum equitibus quibus imperabat, multum renitente Bailaeo, in illud discrimen praecipitaverat, unde incolumis reduci nequibat, nisi cum totius exercitus periculo.

## CAP. XI.

Montisrosanus dexteram alam (qua validior erat hostilis equitatus) Gordonio Regulo ducendam commisit: eidemque Nathanêêlem, veteranum ducem, attribuit. Sinistram vero Aboinio Comiti; cui et Wilielmum Rollocum addidit. Mediam aciem fortissimis viris, Glengario et Drumondio de Balla, juniori: quibus et Georgium Graemum, castrorum praefectum, et ipsum militiae gnarum adjunxit. Subsidiariis, quos collis penitus operiebat, Naperius ex sorore natus, imperabat. Et Montisrosanus quidem in edito, hostes vero in convalli, stagnis fossisque muniti, se aliquamdiu continuere. Nec enim vel his in altum eniti, vel illis hostes profundis stagnis et paludibus inclusos aggredi, tutum videbatur. Peditum numerus paene par erat: uterque quasi duobus millibus praeerat. Verum equitatu superior Bailaeus, qui sexcentos ducebat; Montisrosanus vero ducentos et quinquaginta. Hoc tamen intererat, quod hostes plerique mercenarii erant, ex infima plebe collecti: at qui Regi militabant, generosi, qui conscientiae justissimae causae, et gloriae, gratis, non quaestui inserviebant: quibusque mori magis quam vinci decorum. Noverat insuper Montisrosanus, veteranos plerosque cum Lindesio abesse: novos vero militari clamore et clangore tubarum perterritos, vix primo impetu pares fore. Quapropter justissimae causae et virtutis suorum fiducia primus suos deduxit. Et mox Gordonius in hostem ferociter invectus, fortiter sane ab eo, suorum multitudine freto, exceptus fuit. Jamque conferti, et cohaerentes comminus agebant; nec gradum quisquam, vel latum unguem promovere, nisi prostrato hosti; nec se recipere potuit, instantibus a tergo suis, et vestigia prementibus. Primique Gordonii, Regulus, tribunusque, hostium non exigua strage sibi suisque viam fecere. Et Nathanêêl tribunus expeditos istos sclopetarios, qui more solito equitibus quasi inserti erant, clara voce compellat: "Agite, commilitones, machinas istas, nunc inutiles, projicite; et strictis mucronibus perduellium equos transfigite, aut succisis deturbate poplitibus." Nec illi segniter tribuni mandatis obtemperabant, cum Montisrosanus repente Naperium cum subsidiariis, qui in adversa collis parte latebant, producit: quorum improviso adventu hostes territi fugam corripuerunt. Aboinius cum ala sinistra se continuit: nec, nisi levibus paucorum velitationibus, hostes tentavit. Qui cum suos ex adversa parte fusos fugatosque cernerent, integri ferme se recepere. Pedites, ab equitatu deserti, cum sese paulisper, obstinatis animis et deditionem recusantibus, opposuissent, ferme omnes ceciderunt. Equitibus fugientibus ad salutem non parum profuit Gordonii Reguli casus: qui, parta jam victoria, acrius in confertissimos invectus, a victis et fugatis globo transfixus occubuit: et suorum omnium ora animosque in se convertens, ab insequendis hostibus detinuit. Quos et Aboinius, fratris casu perculsus, admodum lente prosecutus est.

Desideravit in hoc proelio Montisrosanus militem gregarium ne unum quidem: ex generosis vero Culcholium, Miltoniumque, quorum nomina, gentemque, et familiam libenter adscriberem, si mihi certius constarent, qui pro Patre patriae et libertate et legibus fortiter pugnantes, occubuere. Nec sane debitis laudibus privandi sunt pueri quidam Scoti Hibernique, vixdum quartum et decimum aetatis annum emensi; qui positis dominorum impedimentis, et conscensis caballis mannulisque, non tantum equitum speciem exhibuerunt, sed et quasi virtutis dominorum aemuli, supra annos viresque in densissimos hostium ordines invecti sunt. Quorum quidam, sed pauci, nec impune illi, caesi sunt. Sicque egregiae indolis, et in tenella aetate, excelsi animi specimen vel viris imitandum reliquerunt. Verum Gordonii Reguli casus tam alte omnium animis insedit, ut victi potius quam victoris exercitus speciem praeberent. Pressus primo dolor stupidum imposuit silentium: qui, ubi ruptis quasi repagulis erumpere potuit, ecce omnia gemitu, singultu, ululatu, planctuque plena! Ora deinde lacrimis madentia, ut primum vocem proferre valuerunt, Deos, hominesque, et fata incusabant, quae tanto viro Regem, regnum, saeculum, seque posterosque privassent. Et victoriae praedaeque immemores, corpus exanimum intueri, ora manusque deosculari, vulnera lacrimis rigare, eximiam demortui etiam formam laudare, et nobilitatem generis, et fortunae amplitudinem cum indole comparare: et infelicem denique victoriam, quae tanti constiterit, praedicare non destiterunt. Et sane parum abfuit, quo minus victorem exercitum immensus ex hujus viri desiderio dolor oppressisset: nisi Montisrosanus sospes et incolumis, lugentium animis oculisque obversatus, jacentes erexisset. Nec tamen ipse sibi imperare potuit, ne acerbo et tristi unici et carissimi amici fato illacrimaretur. Multumque questus est, gentis suae decus, nobilitatis Scoticanae ornamentum, et firmissimum Regiae Majestatis in septentrione praesidium, virum denique sibi conjunctissimum, in ipso juventae flore praematuro fato ereptum. Interim dolorem ratione vel tempore leniendum iri confidens, nobilissimum corpus medicis condiendum tradi jubet. Quod postea Aberdoniam translatum militari et magnifico funere extulit. Et in majorum monumento in cathedrali ecclesia sepeliri curavit. Pugnatum fuit ad Alfordiam postridie Kal. Quintilis anno CIƆIƆCXLV.

## CAP. XII.

Montisrosanus sub vesperum istius diei, quo ad Alfordiam depugnaverat, ad Cluniam arcem profectus, paucas duntaxat horas militi ad reficiendas vires concessit. Et cum inde ad Deae ripam pervenisset, Aboinium Comitem, qui defuncto fratri successerat, in Buchaniam provinciam et vicina ablegavit, ut copias novo delectu resarciret. Plerique enim qui pugnae interfuerunt, cum montani essent, nec procul a suis dissiti, domum cum praeda repetiverant. Et quia nondum redierat Makdonaldus, tam hunc quam illum expectans, ad Cragstoniam stativa habuit. Verum cum auxiliares tardius quam speraverat expediri, et spem de eis conceptam fallere persentisceret, ipse ulterioris et intempestivae morae impatiens, trajecto Dea, et superato Grampio, in Merniam descendit; et ad Fordonium Sacellum (sede et sepulchro Divi Palladii olim celeberrimum) consedit. Simul his Aboinio Comiti (qui Aberdoniam venerat) mandat, ut sibi cum auxiliariis copiis, quas contraxisse dicebatur, in Mernia occurreret. Paruit quidem ille, sed copias admodum exiguas secum perduxit. Eundem igitur cum suis remisit in septentrionem, ut quantas posset, contraheret copias, et quam celerrime ad castra perduceret. Ipse per Angusiam tendens, obvium habuit Patricium consanguineum cum Atholiis suis, ad omnia sub ejus imperio paratis, et Makdonaldum cum egregia montanorum manu. Cum illa erat Maklenius, gentis suae princeps, vir fortis, et Regi in primis fidus, qui ex amicis clientibusque delectos plus minus septingentos pedites adduxit. Itidem et Makranaldorum dux, vir in montanis clarus, et qui Regi impensius favebat; et hic supra quingentos ducebat; Makgregorii insuper, et Maknabii, nullis fortitudine et laborum patientia secundi, suos duces, et gentis principes, more patrio, sequebantur: quorum certum inire numerum mihi non est facile. Glengarius, vir fortitudinis nomine, et fidei erga Regem, et obsequii caritatisque in ipsum Montisrosanum, nunquam satis laudandus: cum ipse ferme post expeditionem in Argatheliam, eum nunquam dereliquisset, per avunculos aliosque ministros suos accersiverat numero quasi quingentos. Ex edito Marriae etiam Ferchasonii non pauci, egregii viri, et spectatae virtutis. Necnon ex Badenothia pauci quidem, sed strenui, manuque prompti.

Montisrosanus illis copiis auctus et stipatus, in intima Regni penetrare statuit, tam ut hostium delectum in Fifana et Cis-forthana Regione perturbaret, quam ut Ordinum Conventum dirimeret, a foederatis non sine pompa et jactatione Pertham indictum. Nec sane quidquam in mora fuit, praeter equitatus inopiam qua semper laboraverat, adeo ut in planiciem descendere vix unquam, aut sane raro illi tutum fuerit. Quandoquidem tamen Aboinium Arlaeumque cum non aspernanda equitum manu propediem affuturos sperabat, ad Duncaledoniam Taum trajecit: et Amondiae propinquus, non minimo terrore hostes perculit, qui Pertham tenebant. Exinde vero propior factus, in silva Methvenia castra locavit.

Hostiles copiae pedestres (praeter urbis praesidiarios) cis Iernam castra metabantur. Equites oppidi conventusque custodiae destinati, cum Montisrosani speculatores conspexissent, trepidi et praecipites reversi, renunciant adesse illum, et portis imminere: nec dubitandum esse, quin admotis scalis, aggredi et oppugnare constituat. Proceribus insuper omnique conventui suadere, ut matura fuga sibi consulant : cum nihilominus Montisrosanus vix centum equites, et illi quadringentos haberent. Postridie vero, ut injectum terrorem magis magisque augeret, cum eisdem equitibus, et totidem sclopetariis, jumentis farcinariis insidentibus, ipse urbi appropinquavit; suosque ita conspiciendos ostendit, ut non exigui equitatus speciem prae se ferrent. Et quoniam hostes intra portas se continebant, illico Duplinum versus, citeriorem ripam Iernae, totumque illum tractum perlustravit; ac si equitatu omnem illam regionem sub imperio continere posset. Et sane hoc effecit, ut hostem eum non minus equestribus quam pedestribus copiis praepotentem conjectarent. Illi ergo, quotquot possunt, milites undique contrahunt, quos, si trans Fortham tendere videretur, Montisrosano objicerent. Verum, cum nec illi in planiciem descendere tutum fuerit, plures dies in stationibus se continuerunt illi, auxiliarios a regione Fifana, Cis-forthana, et ab occidente expectantes; Montisrosanus vero a septentrione. Et quia Aboinium cum suis nimis lentum impatienter ferme praestolabatur, misit qui stimulos illi adderent, priusquam rei bene gerendae opportunitatem deperderent. Questus etiam est, sed leni et blando sermone, tanquam apud fidissimum amicum, mora et cunctatione ejus factum esse, ut praeclarissima victoria, qua perduelles debellari potuisse videbantur, de manibus dilaberetur. Quam tamen jacturam celeritate ejus et industria pensari posse nullus[1] dubitaret.

Hostes, ubi eum nihil quam inanem equitatus umbram praebere resciverunt, undique comportatis auxiliis, et jam pedestribus copiis longe superiores, ultro eum ad pugnam lacessere, et invitum cogere statuerunt. Quapropter ille in vicinos montes paululum secedere decrevit, quo hostem nunquam secuturum, aut si auderet, cum suo damno facturum probe noverat. Appropinquante ergo cum omni exercitu ad Methveniam hoste, impedimenta clam in edita festinare jubet. Ipse, quasi initurus proelium, aciem disponit, aditus firmissimis praesidiis communit, equites ante aciem producit. Nec sane hostis aliud expectabat, quam pugnae aleam subiturum, quod se facturum simulabat, quoad impedimenta eo provecta fuissent, ut in tuto esse viderentur. Quod ubi factum fuit, exercitum uno agmine et confertis ordinibus iter strenue capessere jussit. Equitibus, quos habuit, et expeditissimis quibusdam sclopetariis curae datum fuit, ut extremum agmen clauderent, tegerentque ab hostili impetu. Hostis instanti, ut putabat, pugnae intentus, ex improviso abeuntes conspicatus, acriter primo insecutus est; sed frustra. Illi enim, occupatis in itinere angustiis, eos facile reppulerunt: et absque vel unius militis jactura, se in edita et ardua, adeoque hostili equitatui inaccessa recepere; a pedite, ne eos unquam aggrederetur,

---

[1] I.q., *nemo*.

## CAP. XII.

securi. Memorabile est, quod cum ad angustias Montisrosani equites appropinquarent, hostesque ulterius insequendi facultatem omnem sibi ademptam satis scirent, ne tanto conatu nihil plane fecisse viderentur, trecentos equites, fortissimos ex suis et promptissimos, in abeuntes cum ingenti clamore et conviciis immiserunt. Istos ubi Montisrosanus conspexit, viginti duntaxat expeditos, ex montanis venatui assuetis et sclopetariae artis admodum peritis, accersitos, jubet eorum insolentiam coercere. Et illi primo, incurvo corpore, et tectis machinis, discursantes, destinatis ictibus insequentium promptissimos conficiunt. Qui cum inter suos melioris notae essent, reliqui eorum casu cautiores facti, recipere sese contenti fuerunt. Verum egregii illi venatores, primo successu elati, ubi hostes perturbatos videre, in apertam planiciem evaserunt; et ultro invecti sunt in equites. Qui non aliter quam cervi damaeve a venaticis agitati, impressis vehementius calcaribus, praecipiti cursu ad suos fugerunt.

Hostes reversi in eodem loco unde Montisrosanus erat digressus, in Methvenia silva, locum castris delegerunt. Cum nihil expeditione illa memoria dignum gessissent, praeterquam quod virilem impetum sustinere non valentes, in muliebrem sexum desaevierunt. Quotquot enim Hibernorum montanorumque conjuges deprehendere, quae caritate conjugali maritos sequebantur, foedo nimis et pudendo exemplo excarnificarunt. Montisrosanus ad Duncaledoniam minorem stativa habuit; tam quia solum equitibus impeditum et impervium, quam quia ad excipiendos auxiliarios, quos indies a septentrione cum Aboinio expectabat, locus erat commodissimus. Quo tempore infesti exercitus, non procul dissiti, alii alios observabant magis quam lacessabant.

Tandem vero Aboinius cum Nathaneêle tribuno suos a septentrione Duncaledoniam perduxit; numero quidem infra spem quam de se fecerant, robore tamen et vera virtute longe supra numerum. Ducenti duntaxat equites erant, cum centum et viginti sclopetariis, qui et jumentis farcinariis aut mannulis impositi erant: pedites vero alii nulli. Simul his Arlaeus Comes, cum Davide filio, equites octoginta adduxit, plerosque ex ipsa nobili Ogilviorum familia oriundos. In quibus Alexander, Johannis equitis de Innercarita primogenitus, non modo eximia corporis forma et majorum imaginibus, sed et rerum in ea aetate fortiter et feliciter gestarum gloria eminebat. His ergo copiis auctus Montisrosanus, nec tempus amplius terendum ratus, recta in hostem ducit. Ut vero ad Amondiam venit, tentandos primo censuit, et penitus explorandum, an vera essent, quae incerta ad eum detulerat fama: plerosque nimirum auxiliarios deseruisse illorum castra, et se recepisse ad suos. Peditibus ergo ad curanda corpora dimissis, ante vesperam non procul sese cum equitatu conspiciendum exhibuit: quo illi spectaculo attoniti, in castris se continuere. Postridie, cum sub diluculo speculabundus obequitaret Montisrosanus, hostes trepidos, nocte intempesta, Methvenia profectos nunciatur; et turbatis ordinibus Iernam ponte trajecisse. Nec ille cunctatus, suos ad iter accingit; et ad sex milliaria supra pontem lapideum amne trajecto, in Iernae tractu noctem illam transigit.

## CAP. XIII.

Fifa est provincia Scotiae populosissima, opulentissima, et frequentioribus urbibus, pagis, vicis habitata. Incolae minus bellicosi: mercatores, tabernarii, nautae, agricolae. Interim novis superstitionibus addictissimi, qui tam procerum exemplo et authoritate, quam seditiosis praedicantium orationibus fascinati, se jam omnes ferme foederatis mancipaverant. Provincia ipsa paeninsula est: ad meridiem aestuario Forthae, ad septentrionem Tao jam ingentium navium capaci, ad orientem Oceano cohibetur. Nullus, nisi ex occidente, aditus terrestris: in cujus faucibus uterque exercitus haerebat. Tota provincia tumultuabatur; aliis (egregiis praesertim istis oratoribus anathemata minitantibus) omnes, cujusvis ordinis et aetatis, ad arma concitantibus, et cogentibus; aliis confluentibus frequenter; aliis huc illucque discursantibus, ut sese occultarent: prout quisque superstitione, fiducia, metuve agebatur. Montisrosanus hostes aggredi et rem proelio decernere vehementer desiderabat, priusquam novo ex Fifanio delectu vires eorum augescerent: sed frustra. Illi enim in solo tam difficili et artis angustiis se communiverant, ut nulla ratione ad eos penetrare, vel inde elicere potuerit. Cum ergo pugnae copiam semel iterumque fecisset, in intima provinciae penetrare statuit, Kinrossiamque petiit, tam ut provincialium delectum impediret, quam ut hostes aliquando ex istis angustiis extraheret; quo suis in provincia periclitantibus opitularentur. Illi ne extremum abeuntium agmen serio tentare ausi, diverso itinere, Iernae primo, et mox Tai ripam secuti, ad orientalia provinciae festinarunt. Montisrosanus in itinere Nathanêêlem Gordonium, et Wilielmum Rollocum cum exigua equitum manu praemisit. Hi (commilitonibus undique obequitantibus, ut omnia accuratius perlustrarent) decem duntaxat secum detinuere. Ex improviso autem in ducentos hostes, quorum non pauci etiam equites, inciderunt, qui milites in illis locis conscribebant. Cumque receptui locus nullus esset, duodeni, ducentos aggressi, in fugam eos praecipitarunt: et quibusdam caesis, alios captivos abduxere.

Montisrosanus sub vesperam illius diei Kinrossiam pervenit: et Fifanos a Rege quam maxime alienatos, et foederatorum studiosissimos, et superstitione insuper adstrictos, frequentes ad arma convolasse non dubitabat.

## CAP. XIII.

Nec cum tanta equitum peditumque multitudine temere congrediendum ratus, Fortham transmittere decrevit : idque hoc consilio, ut Fifanos, quos extra fines suos non nisi coactos castra hostium sequi conjectabat, longis itineribus fatigatos, sine pugna debellaret. Plerosque enim in officinis, tabernis, navigiisque natos, aut educatos, militari labori impares, statim fatiscere et succumbere augurabatur. Insuper conjurati proceres (postquam bellum ad Fortham usque translatum attoniti viderunt) in partibus Regni limitaneis, et ad mare occiduum spectantibus, milites majore quam unquam contentione conscribebant. Inter quos Lanricensis, Cassilius, Eglintoniusque Comites eminebant. Quorum delectum impedire, aut ipsos ad partes pertrahere satagebat Montisrosanus, priusquam Bailaeo et Fifanis se adjungerent. Kinrossia ergo Sterlinum versus profectus, ad tria ab urbe milliaria ea nocte substitit. Postridie, ubi pedites praemisisset, ipse cum equitatu lente subsequebatur, quia hostem vestigia sua premere putabat.

Nec fefellit eum conjectura ; enimvero quos post se reliquerat, exploratores renunciant, Bailaeum cum longe potentissimo exercitu haud procul abesse. Et illico praemissi hostium speculatores in conspectum veniunt : quorum unum incaute progressum, Montisrosani equites captum ad eum pertrahunt. Iste interrogatus, libere fidenterque respondit, existimare se Bailaeo et suis in animo esse, tota illa nocte in itinere persistere, ut eum quamprimum ad pugnam adigerent, priusquam Fifanos dimitterent : quos hactenus lassatos, vix cogi posse arbitraretur, ut transmitterent Fortham ; satis enim illis esse quod hostis ipsorum finibus excesserit. Montisrosanus igitur, ut Fortham protinus transmitteret, suos ad iter strenue capessendum hortatus, Sterlinum oppidum arcemque Regiam munitissimam (quae valido hostium praesidio tenebatur) ex adverso praetergressus, amnem vado, ad quatuor passuum millia supra urbem, illa ipsa nocte trajecit. Illucescente vero die postero, ad sex milliaria Sterlino paulisper substitit ; ubi nunciatum est hostes superiori nocte Fortham non transmisisse ; verum ad tria milliaria Sterlino trans amnem pernoctasse. At ille destinatum iter prosecutus, in fatali loco, agro nimirum Kilsythino, castris locum delegit. Milites vero corpora curare jubet, paratos tamen ad pugnam, expeditosque ad iter, prout res postularet. Hostes interim faciliori longe via et majori compendio ad Sterlinum Fortham ponte transmittunt : et sub vesperam ad tria milliaria a Kilsytha castra metantur.

Interea Lanricensis Comes, Hamiltonii Ducis frater, in tractu Glottae et locis vicinis ex Hamiltoniorum amicis et clientibus peditum mille cum quingentis equitibus coegerat : nec Kilsytha aberat supra duodecim milliaria. Cassilius vero, Eglintonius, Glencarniusque Comites, aliique conjurati proceres occidentis incolas ad eandem impiam militiam concitabant : et illi, quo magis hactenus a belli incommodis immunes fuerant, eo ad arma rapienda erant proniores. Quibus rite pensitatis, Montisrosanus praesentes cum Bailaeo copias omnino debellandas censuit. Quamvis enim numero superiores essent, longe tamen majus difficiliusque certamen immineret, si Lanricensi caeterisque unitis congrediendum foret. Atqui vero vel hoc prorsus faciendum fuit, vel irrito labore, et cum jactura famae, quam tot victoriis acquisiverat, ad montana redeundum. Hostes vero multitudine suorum freti et feroces, Montisrosanum superiorum dierum itinera praecipitem confecisse arbitrabantur: et Fortham, non consilio, sed metu transmisisse; adeo ut vel in solo, stationibusque (quas sibi commodissimas elegerat) invadendum censuerint. Hocque unum, vana spe elati, maximopere praecavebant, ne locum receptui permitterent, aut abeunti ad montana reditus pateret. Non defuere tamen qui dicerent, Bailaeum ipsum pugna abstinendum censuisse; verum Lindesii Comitis praesertim aliorumque procerum, qui in castris agebant, authoritate et suffragiis victum, invitum ferme et reluctantem eduxisse copias, et aciem pro tempore ordinasse. Ut ut sit, illucescente statim die, recta illi in Montisrosanum duxerunt. Quod cum ille cerneret, accidisse ait, quod maxime expetebat; ut militum paucitatem locorum opportunitate pensaret: priorque stationes occupare festinat. Suis insuper omnibus, equiti juxta ac pediti, imperat, ut positis molestioribus vestibus, et solis indusiis superne amicti, et in albis emicantes, hostibus insultarent. Quod cum illi alacres laetique fuissent, expediti paratique stabant, certi aut vincere, aut mori.

In campo pugnae destinato tuguria quaedam erant, hortulique rustici; in quibus Montisrosanus paucos praesidiarios commode locaverat. Et primus hostium conatus fuit, illos inde proturbare; sed frustra: ferociter enim aggressi, et non minus fortiter excepti; ubi de primo impetu paululum remittere visi sunt, propugnatores eos pellunt, fugant caeduntque impune. Quo velut omine elati montanorum animi qui propius aberant, ne expectato quidem imperio, in collem universis hostium copiis obnoxium temere se praecipitarunt. Montisrosanus, licet intemptestiva suorum fiducia commotior, non tamen prorsus destituendos judicavit. Nec sane dictu facile est, hostiumne ignavia, an subsidii celeritate, eorum incolumitati magis consultum fuerit. Montisrosanus, cum quingentis equitibus, peditum quatuor millia et quadringentos ducebat; quorum mille aut etiam plures sua culpa hostibus sese exposuerant: qui cum peditum millibus sex, et octingentis equitibus occurrebant. Verum qui ex extremo hostium agmine erant, satis tarde procedebant, eorumque adventum, dum primi segniter praestolantur, facultatem fecerunt Montisrosano maturum periclitantibus suis adferendi auxilium. Tandem tamen tres equitum turmas, quos peditum duo millia sequebantur, in temerarios istos et ferme deperditos expediunt. Quos conspicatus Montisrosanus Arlaeum Comitem (cum alii munus illud nimis indecore detrectarent) in hunc modum compellavit: "Vides, inquit, nobilissime Comes, nostros istos sua temeritate in ultimum discrimen adductos, et illico ab hostili equitatu opprimendos, nisi mature eis subveniamus. In te vero omnium oculi animique intenti sunt, te unum tanta laude dignum judicant, qui pulsis hostibus, commilitones protegas; et ut, quod juvenili eorum audacia peccatum est, matura tua adultaque virtute corrigatur." Et ille rem, quamvis perdifficilem, lubentissime in se recepit; turmaque suorum stipatus (in qua Johannes Ogilvius Baldevius, in Suecia olim militum tribunus, vir fortis juxta ac peritus, eminebat) recta in hostes duxit. Et illi quidem in Ogilvios invecti, acriter paulisper decertavere: tandem tamen virtuti eorum impares, terga dederunt. Quos Ogilvii tam pertinaciter insecuti sunt, ut in pedites suos praecipites egerint: eodemque quasi uno impetu turbatis ordinibus, proculcaverint. Et hoc egregio Arlaei Ogilviorumque exemplo Montisrosani milites magis magisque animati, detineri amplius non potuere, quo minus, ingenti sublato clamore, quasi victoriam hactenus adepti, in hostem irruerent. Nec sane perduellium equites eorum congressum diu sustinuerunt; sed deserto pedite, in profusissimam fugam se conjecere; aut pedites deserti multum restiterunt; verum abjectis armis, inutili fuga salutem sibi quaesivere. Enimvero victores eos ad quatuor et decem milliaria persecuti trucidarunt. Adeo ut peditum, qui isti proelio interfuerunt, vix centum evasisse credantur incolumes. Et ne equites quidem impune elapsi sunt, quorum alii caesi, capti alii, alii alio fusi sparsique se receperunt. Impedimenta, arma, spolia victoribus cessere; que ex suis duntaxat sex desiderarunt: quorum tres Ogilvii erant, viri fortes et generosi, qui strenue pugnantes ad praeclaram victoriam, sanguine suo, viam consignarunt. Conjurati proceres, qui frequentes isti praelio interfuerant, alii Sterlinum oppidum arcemque munitissimam matura fuga et equorum pernicitate obtinuerunt, alii ad Forthae aestuarium elapsi, naves anchoris alligatas haud procul a litore conscenderunt. In his Argathelius, jam tertio cymbam nactus, evasit in navem: nec tamen se in tuto esse judicavit, quoad sublatis anchoris, procul terra, in alto se conspexit. In captivis erant Wilielmus Moravius eques, de Blebo, Iacobus Arnottus, Burglaei Reguli frater, Dicius quidem Wallasiusque tribuni militum, et alii quam plurimi; quos Montisrosanus in fidem receptos liberaliter habuit, et data fide, dimisit. Atque haec est insignis illa victoria ad Kilsytham parta, decimo septimo Kal. Sept. an. CIƆIƆCXLV, **qua sex millia perduellium caesa traduntur.**

## CAP. XIV.

KILSYTHINAM victoriam per totum regnum nova rerum facies subsecuta est. Conjurati principes, alii Bervicum, Carleolum alii, alii Novum castrum in Anglia, in Hiberniam alii, alii alio cum summa trepidatione se receperunt. Qui vero Regi hactenus in occulto favebant, sese palam ostendere, fidem attestari, preces publice pro salute fundere, operamque polliceri non amplius metuebant. Quique prius foederatis, militaverunt, veniam deprecari, violentiam et saevum perduellium imperium incusari, se suaque omnia victori dedere, implorare humiliter fidem, et solitam clementiam expectare. Provinciae etiam et civitates quam longissime dissitae oratores mittere, fidem Regi et vicario ejus Gubernatori obsequium operamque polliceri, arma, commeatus, militem, aliaque ad bellum necessaria ultro offerre. Proceres Regni et familiarum principes frequentes accurrere, salutare, obsequium domino Gubernatori deferre, res egregie gestas laudare, gratularique. Quos ille omnes, non modo praeteritorum venia, sed et libertate et immunitate donatos in fidem recepit, bonoque animo esse jussit. Nec gravius quidquam illis imposuit, quam ut avarum et crudele conjuratorum imperium cum mitissimo clementissimi Regis patrocinio et tutela commutarent; utque inducta priorum simultatum oblivione, fidem et obedientiam, optimo Regi debitam, in posterum sanctius colerent; nec semet seditiosorum hominum consiliis deinceps immiscerent, qui, cum explendis suis cupidinibus tantum modo incumberent, Regem subditosque inter se commissos tantum non everterunt. Sibi quidem ab initio nihil unquam aliud in animo votisque fuisse, quam ut armis (quando aliter fieri nequiret) Religionem, Regem, libertatem, aequales suos Regni proceres, popularesque omnes, a perduellium tyrannide vindicatos, pristinae paci, gloriae et felicitati restitueret. Quod si effectum daret, Deo optimo maximo bonorum omnium largitori, aeternas debiturum gratias. Sin secus acciderit, eidem tamen Deo immortali, Regique, ejus in terris vicem gerenti, bonis omnibus, posteris etiam, famaeque et conscientiae denique suae, honestissimo conatu satisfacturum.

Simul his, nihil aliud quam Montisrosani laudes undique personabant. Ejus indolem, qua aequales omnes antecedebat, ejus in bello fortitudinem, in laboribus patientiam, constantiam in dubiis, in consiliis prudentiam, fidem in deditos, in rebus gerendis celeritatem, clementiam in captivos, in omnibus denique heroicam plane virtutem, omnes omnium ordinum homines ubique praedicabant. Idque plurimi fide bona et sincero affectu; alii vero dolo factitabant: et ut quisque ingenio aut arte valebat, carmine encomiastico, et panegyricis orationibus eum prosequebatur. Quaeque rerum humanarum

## CAP. XIV.

vicissitudo, et volubilis praesertim vulgi inconstantia est, foederatorum coryphaeos ducesque (quos non ita pridem numinum fere loco venerabantur et colebant) Argathelium nimirum, Balmerinothum, Lindesium, Laudonium, aliosque, tanquam malorum authores, diris publice persequi non verebantur.

Rebus vera sic prospere succedentibus, Regni partibus a tergo septentrionem versus securis, aditu in meridiem patefacto, fractis ubique conjuratorum viribus, eorumque principibus viris (qui pro scelerum conscientia de venia desperabant) Regno pulsis, et, quamvis nullo justo exercitu superstite, ad occidentem tamen tumultuabantur. Cassilius enim Eglintoniusque Comites, et alii foederatorum ministri, provincias ad renovandum bellum incitabant: et tumultuario delectu, ad quatuor millia coegisse dicebantur. Quapropter Montisrosanus postridie illius diei, quo ad Kilsytham pugnatum fuerat, copias ad Glottae amnis tractum perduxit: unde Lanricensis Comes, victoriae fama perculsus, dimissis quos coegerat militibus, aufugerat. Locum illum tanquam rebus suis in meridie et occidente commodissimum Montisrosanus delegit; Glascuamque provinciae caput est profectus. Civitatem in fidem receptam, cum faustis populi acclamationibus ingressus, milites imprimis ab injuriis coercuit; et in noxios severe animadvertens, gravius peccantes in aliorum terrorem capite multavit. In civium deinde gratiam, secundo quam venerat die, urbe excessit, ad Bothweliam castra locaturus. Ubi, quoniam ad sex duntaxat milliaria a civitate aberat, ne quid militari licentia peccaretur, civibus indulsit, ut sibi ipsis prospicerent, et suorum praesidio civitatem tenerent. Ea clementia fore sperans, ut non Glascuensium modo, sed et aliarum civitatum animos beneficiis magis, quam vi et armis, obnoxios haberet.

Bothweliae vero plures dies stativa habuit, proceres alios coram, alios per legatos, amicos, internunciosque audivit. Provinciarum et civitatum ultro omnium deferentium fidem obsequiumque confirmavit. Salutantium operamque pollicentium in illis locis primi fuere Duglassius Marchio, nobilissimae familiae et Duglassiorum gentis princeps, Limmucensis, Anandius, Hertfeldius Comites, Setonius, Drumondus, Flaminius, Madertaeus, Carnegius, Ionstonius, Reguli; Hamiltonius de Orbeston, Charterius de Hempsfeild, Tourius de Innerleith (vir meritissimus, qui postea fortiter pugnando, non segni fato functus est) Stuartus de Resyth, Dalyellius, Carnwathii Comitis frater, et alii quamplurimi: quorum nominibus recensendis, vel non undequaque sufficit memoria, vel abstinendum censui, ne ingrata forsan et intempestiva laude sub durissimo gementes tyrannidis jugo magis onerare, quam ornare videar.

Post Kilsythinam victoriam nihil prius generosum Montisrosani animum subiit, quam captivorum cura: qui nullius criminis ergo, sed duntaxat ob fidem erga Regem, in durissimo et foedissimo carcere Edinburgeno pessime habiti, ultima etiam expectabant. Naperium ergo ex sorore natum cum Nathaneéle Gordonio et expedita equitum manu Edinburgum mittit; qui civitatem deditam in fidem reciperent, captivos assererent in libertatem, et civium animos in fide et officio confirmarent: repugnantibus vero et detrectantibus imperium, ferrum flammamque intentarent. Illi cum copiis ad quartum ab urbe lapidem substitere; nec propius (nisi obstinata forsan civium pertinacia coacti) accedere statuerunt; tam ut militarem licentiam facilius refrenarent, ne injuriis miseros civis opprimerent, urbemque exosam, utpote totius rebellionis ministram, et fomitem, praecipiti ira et ultricibus flammis in cineres redigerent, quod ut modis omnibus praecaverent, Montisrosanus imprimis in mandatis dederat, quam ut suos a pestilenti contagione praestarent, quae in civitate et vicinia vehementer flagrabat, et quamplurimos in dies absumebat mortales. Ubi vero adventantium ad urbem perlatus est nuncius, tremere omnes, et de salute desperare; nec aliter ejulare, quam si hactenus enses jugulis, et tectis faces admotae fuissent. Et non pauci conscientia scelerum agitati, ingratissimos sese proditores, sacrilegos, perjuros, et omni venia indignos, sponte praedicabant. Ad captivos deinde conversi, eminus, et per occultos internuncios eorum implorare fidem, et obsecrare; ut misellae plebis et saevissimo confectae morbo miserti, victoris animum jure irritatum mitigarent: omnem in eis spem esse; et hoc unum rebus perditis superesse remedium. Protestari insuper, clementiam hac saltem vice expertos, superiorem defectionem sanctiore fide et intensiore obsequio pensaturos. Captivi vero (quibus non ita pridem vilissimi mortales acerbe nimis et contumeliose illuserant, patibulisque et crucibus devoverant) injuriarum prorsus immemores, et malorum, quae ipsi fuerant perpessi, sensu magis quam vindicta stimulati, Deo opt. max., qui libertatem salutemque minus expectatam clementer ostentaret, gratias reddidere. Inde vero ad hostes infensissimos conversi, bono animo esse jusserunt: clementissimum enim Regem, ejusque vicarium Montisrosanum populi poenitentis salutem et commodum, non internecionem et ruinam expetere. Consulere vero, ut ad Montisrosanum supplices oratores confestim mittant, qui fidem ejus veniamque deprecentur: nihil enim ad leniendum victoris animum prompta deditione validius esse. Sese etiam precibus apud eum pro eorum incolumitate non defuturos: nec dubitare, quo minus, alias invictus, precibus lamentisque miserrimorum hominum vinci se pateretur magnus excelsusque animus.

Edinburgenses hac spe erecti, consilioque adjuti, illico senatum convocant, de mittendis oratoribus consulturi. Erant inter captivos qui natalibus et gratia apud Montisrosanum eminebant, Ludovicus Craufordiae Comes, antiquissimae et nobilissimae Lindesiorum gentis princeps, militari gloria apud exteros, Suecos, Austriacosque et Hispanos clarus. Hic Lindesii

## CAP. XIV.

Comitis, consanguinei sui (qui quod honoribus tituloque Craufordiae inhiaret, ejus etiam capiti insidiabatur) arte et authoritate a conjuratis ultimo supplicio destinatus erat. Nec ob aliud omnino crimen, quam quod vir militaris, et manu promptus, strenuam fidelemque operam domino suo ac Regi navasset, et quasi adhuc navaturus metuebatur, si superstes foret. Jacobus deinde Ogilvius Regulus, Arlaei Comitis filius, Montisrosano in paucis carus, paterna propriaque virtute et potentia formidabilis. Hic etiam, cum Argathelii propter veteres simultates et recentes injurias hostis esset, ejusdem cum Craufordio criminis reus, in eodem discrimine versabatur. Illos ergo ex captivis Edinburgensis elegit senatus, et confestim in libertatem assertos, votis precibusque fatigavit, ut pro gratia, qua apud dominum Gubernatorem valebant, oratoribus suis opitularentur, urbique omnipotentis Dei flagello hactenus afflictissimae succurrerent. Seque posterosque suos omnibus diris devovent, si tanti beneficii immemores, aut beneficiis ingrati aliquando forent. Illi rem omnibus votis expetitam haud gravatim suscepere: acceptisque in comitatu suo oratoribus, ad Naperium egressi sunt. Ille, cum obiter carissimum patrem, conjugemque, et Sterlinum levirum, cum sororibus ex carcere Limnuchensi, in quem ex arce Edinburgena delati fuerant a foederatis, liberasset; copias cum captivis istis, jam in libertatem assertis, et civitatis oratoribus, re bene gesta, ad avunculum reduxit. Montisrosanus Craufordium Ogilviumque, viros amicissimos, et diu multumque desideratos, amplexus sospitesque et incolumes gratulatus, omni honore et solatio post diuturnum carcerem prosequebatur: et illi contra, liberatorem suum vindicemque gratiis laudibusque, ut par erat, efferentes, jucundissimum praesentibus spectaculum exhibuere.

Admissi postmodum Edinburgenses oratores, senatus populique mandata exponunt. Summa erat, eos civitatem Gubernatori ultro dedere, veniam supplices deprecari, obsequium fidemque in posterum spondere, se suaque patrocinio ejus et tutelae (quam humiliter postulabant) committere. Captivos insuper, qui adhuc apud eos detinebantur, secundum ejus mandata quamprimum liberandos: omniaque officia ex animi sui sententia praestanda sibi persuaderet. Et quamvis civitas dirissimo morbo exhausta jaceret, ut nulli inde milites conscribi possent, paratos tamen esse stipendia aliunde coactis pro modulo suo erogare. Hoc denique omnium maxime implorare, ut clementissimi domini Regis animum ad misericordiam inclinaret, nequando in civitatem suam, seditiosorum et praepotentium hominum arte, authoritate, et exemplo ad rebellionem concitatam gravius animadverteret. Montisrosanus de caeteris bonam illis spem fecit, nec durius quid imposuit, quam ut fidem domino Regi sanctius colerent. Perduellibus, qui contra eum tam extra, quam intra Regnum militabant, fideliter renunciarent. Arcem Edinburgensem (quam in eorum potestate sitam fuisse tunc, satis constabat)

Regi ejusque ministris redderent. Captivos denique, ubi primum oratores redierint, liberos ad castra ejus remitterent. Et sane, quod ad captivos, eos reversi dimiserunt: at caetera falsi perjurique, nisi resipuerint, olim animi usque adeo ingrati et repetitae perfidiae, Deo, veritatis et justitiae vindici, poenas daturi.

Dum ista Edinburgi agebantur, Montisrosanus Alexandrum Makdonaldum (cui et Johannem Drumondum de Balla, virum generosum et fortem, addidit) cum parte copiarum ad occidui maris oram ablegavit, ut tumultuantes illic coerceret, et Cassilii Eglintoniique conatus everteret. At illi, sola adventantis Makdonaldi fama perterriti, palantes trepidique se ad suos recepere: Comitum procerumque alii in Hiberniam contenderunt, alii in quibus nescio latibulis delituere. Provinciae occidentales omnes, Aëra urbs, Irvinaque, et aliae, certatim manus dederunt, obsequium, fidem, operamque ultro deferentes. Nec sane (quod praeter spem evenit) usquam Montisrosanus invenit animos ad Regem propensiores, quam in locis illis occiduis: quamplurimi enim generosi, equestris ordinis, familiarum principes, et nonnulli etiam primariae nobilitatis viri, ad partes laeti pertransierunt. Quorum nomina, alias cum laude praedicanda, inpraesentiarum, grato forsan illis certe, utili silentio, praeterimus: nolumus enim honestissimos viros et Regi suo addictissimos, indicio nostro, benevolentiae suae saevissimis hostibus poenas dare.

## CAP. XV.

Animum jam Montisrosanus ad limitem australem converterat: miseratque ad Humium, Rosburgium, Trequarium Comites, qui eos ad belli et pacis rerumque omnium Regis nomine et auspiciis gerendarum societatem invitarent. Erant isti, in illis locis, non modo amicorum multitudine et frequenti satellitio potentissimi, verum etiam Regiae authoritatis acerrimi vindices videri volebant. Enimvero praeterquam quod fide juxta et alii obstricti forent, non vulgaribus beneficiis ab eo erant affecti. Nec tantum ornati amplissimis honoribus, ab equestri nimirum ordine ad supremae nobilitatis dignitatem evecti, sed et praefecti quaestuosissimis provinciis, et supra aequales sortemque locupletati, sibi opes, Regi odium invidiamque conflarunt. Et hi quidem amicorum splendidissimos ad Montisrosanum ablegarunt, qui illi renunciarent, paratos esse sese, qui quodvis discrimen, ejus ductu et imperio, pro munificentissimo domino suo ac Rege subeant. Copias etiam quas possent maximas coacturos spondent: nec quidquam impedire, quo minus ad castra veniant, si ille, cum vel minima copiarum parte, ad provincias istas progrediatur. Sic tandem fore, ut non modo

## CAP. XV.

eorum amici clientesque, sed et provinciales omnes ejus authoritate et praesentia excitati et animati, alacriter ad militiam se accingant; et reluctantes cogantur, aut redigantur in ordinem. Enixe denique rogare, ut ad hoc suam illis operam impertiat; in aliis certissimam eorum fidem et promptissimam operam experturus. Splendida sane illa, et prima fronte, honesta; verum ea fide jactata, quam munificentissimi Regis beneficiarii colere assueverunt. Minus forsan eo nomine vituperandus Lanricensis Comes, Hamiltonii Ducis frater, qui a Montisrosano per amicos ad partes Regias serio invitatus, quamvis praeteritorum venia, et de impetranda fratris libertate non exigua spes illi fieret, disertis tamen verbis, et sine ambagibus respondit; Nihil sibi cum illis partibus commune fore: nec velle eum amicitiam prae se ferre, quam colere non instituisset. Atque utinam illi omnes, in quibus optimus Rex nimiam collocavit fiduciam, eodem candore et simplicitate omnia dixissent ab istorum tumultuum initio!

Eodem ferme tempore Duglassium Marchionem et Ogilvium Regulum in Anandiam Nithiamque Montisrosanus transmisit; ut junctis sibi Anandiae et Hartfeldiae Comitibus, copias, equestres praesertim, quas possent maximas conscriberent. Et insuper mandat, ut cum conscriptis versus Trequarium, Rosburgium, Humiumque tenderent: ut eos absque omni tergiversatione, ad belli societatem pertraherent. Quippe Montisrosano aulicorum mores subolurant, ut suspectus haberet, quas nectebant moras: eorundem enim, praesertim Trequarii artes, et incertam fidem saepiuscule erat expertus. Et sane Duglassius, alacri Hartfeldii Anandiique opera, non spernendam manum brevi contraxit, si numerum spectes: verum viri novi, agriculturae et pascendis gregibus assueti, militiae vero rudes; ad primum impetum prompti, mox in tantum animis defecere, ut sub signis detineri nulla ratione valuerint. Hoc cum Duglassio caeterisque ducibus certo constaret, literis Montisrosanum fatigant, ut cum veteranis quos habebat, ad se versus Tuedam properaret: ipsius enim authoritate et praesentia, cum veteranorum societate et exemplo fieri posse, ut vel sponte, vel inviti, ad officium praestandum cogerentur. Interim illi ad Galae tractum secundum mandata procedunt: Rosburgio, Trequarioque opportunitatem operamque ultro deferentes, si res ita postularet, quo facilius maturiusque suos educerent. At illi boni viri, quibus conjuratorum intima consilia erant satis perspecta, quique omnem ex Anglia equitatum, sub Davidis Leslaei imperio, jam jamque affuturum non ignorabant, nihil animo versabant, quam optimo Regi solitis artibus illudere; Montisrosanum vero (cujus gloriae invidebant) quia armis non poterant, dolo in hostium potestatem perducere. In eum ergo finem, non modo Duglassio et eis qui cum eo erant, sed et ipsi Montisrosano, per amicos frequentesque nuncios, identidem ingerunt; paratos quidem esse, qui corpora sua praesentissimis objiciant periculis : verum amicos, clientes, satellitesque contrahere, nisi ipsius Montisrosani praesentia erectos et confirmatos, neutiquam plane posse. Et quo ampliorem illi fidem faciant, infandis sese diris devovent, nisi promissis sancte et constanter steterint. Montisrosanus nihilominus, immotus ad haec omnia, Bothweliae subsistebat; si quid recti et sinceri eorum verbis subesset, Duglassium cum suis, qui hactenus in vicino tractu erant, animandis et cogendis illorum amicis et clientibus abunde sufficere ratus.

Ubi tandem diutius Bothweliae stativa habuisset Montisrosanus, montani plerique, praeda onusti, clam signa deseruere, et reversi sunt ad suos. Exinde etiam et ipsi eorum duces missionem palam ad breve tempus postularunt; praetexentes nullum exercitum hostilem intra Regni limites exstare, ideoque operam suam inpraesentiarum inutilem fore. Aedes insuper suas frugesque, quibus parentes, conjuges, parvulique instantem hiemem tolerarent, hostilibus flammis absumptas, nec ulla ex parte reparatas, querebantur : adeoque aliquot hebdomadarum veniam supplices orare, quibus suis contra frigus famemque prospicerent. Fidem vero solemniter et sponte praestare, ante quadragesimum diem, refectis viribus, longeque frequentiores reversuros. Eos Montisrosanus, cum detineri non possent, utpote qui gratis militabant, quo devinctiores sibi redderet, non modo cum venia, sed et mandatis dimittendos censuit. Militibus ergo publice laudatis, ducibus Regis nomine gratias egit: et ut strenue rem suam agerent hortatus, Alexandrum Makdonaldum popularem et cognatum (qui provinciam illam nimis ambitiose expetiverat) comitem ducemque illis attribuit, qui ante dictum diem ad castra eos reduceret. Et ille omnium nomine, composita oratione, gratias domino Gubernatori pro eximia indulgentia egit; et quasi illorum fidejussor, pro maturo reditu sponsurum se sancte juravit; Montisrosanum tamen postea nunquam visurus. Nec montanorum viribus ille contentus, qui tria millia fortissimorum militum excedebant; promptissimos etiam ex hibernis ad numerum centum et viginti clam subduxit, quasi, scilicet, ad corporis sui custodiam separatos.

Hoc potissimum tempore plures Oxonia nuncii a Rege Bothweliam diversis itineribus pervenere. In quibus unus erat Andraeas Sandilandius, Scotus, in Anglia tamen educatus, et initiatus sacris, vir integer, Regi fidus juxta ac Montisrosano carus, qui ad belli exitum ei constanter adhaesit. Robertus deinde Spotswodius eques, supremae in Scotia Curiae olim supremus meritissimusque praeses, tunc vero ab epistolis Regi, seu, ut hodie loqui vulgus amat, pro regno Scotiae ejus secretarius; qui Oxonia per Walliam in Monam insulam, et inde in Abriam devectus, in Atholiam pervenit : et ab Atholiis ad Montisrosanum fuit perductus. Nuncii plerique omnes inter alia mandata deferunt, Regis voluntatem esse, ut Rosburgium et Trequarium sibi adjungat, et eorum opera et consilio utatur : de fide industriaque hominum non esse ambigendum. Insuper, ut ad Tuedam amnem in regnorum limite properaret, et illis cum imperio praeesset, quos ad eum Rex quam primum ex Anglia esset missurus, ut eos Davidi Lesleo cum fiducia opponeret, si ille (quod suspicabatur) cum foederatorum equitatu in eum tenderet. Et haec nuncii unanimiter detulerunt; literisque suis optimus Rex, sed male credulus, significavit. Montisrosanus vero, mandatis Regiis tandem victus, ad Tuedae tractum proficisci statuit. Pridie vero, quam iter est ingressus, vocato ad concionem milite (nondum enim Makdonaldus cum montanis abscesserat) sub vexillo Regio Robertus Spotswodius in terram pronus diploma Regium Majori sigillo obsignatum Montisrosano, ille item Archibaldo Primirosio, supremi consilii (ut loquuntur) clerico, clara voce per praeconem recitandum tradidit. Deinde et militum fortitudinem fidemque erga Regem, et ejus in illos animum brevi sed magnifica oratione laudavit. Makdonaldum etiam, pro authoritate sibi a Rege concessa, pro concione, cum laudibus, tum equestris ordinis dignitate ornavit. Enimvero non modo Montisrosanus, sed et quotquot Regi favebant, optima quaeque de isto viro sperabant: quorum omnium opinionem, non tantum in causae Regiae detrimentum, sed in suam suorumque certissimam perniciem, fefellit.

Montisrosanus destinatum iter aggressus, secundis castris Calderiam arcem pervenerat, cum Aboinius Comes, frustra retinente Gubernatore, non suos tantum, sed et septentrionales alios ad desertionem solicitatos, ad unum omnes secum abduxit. Nec ullis omnino rationibus, aut amicorum precibus, qui a pudendo facinore abhorrebant, persuaderi sibi passus est, ut vel hebdomadae unius moram necteret; tum demum, non modo cum bona imperatoris venia, sed et fama et bonorum gratia et laude dimittendus. At Montisrosanus Edinburgum praetergressus, per agros Lothianae copias perexiguas quidem duxit, et in Galae tractu Duglassium caeterosque duces obvios habuit; quorum copiae hactenus multum imminutae, magis magisque indies deficiebant. In illo tractu ipse Trequarius solito alacrior hilariorque eum accurrit; qui quidem non Regi tantum, sed et ipsi Montisrosano propensissimum sese simulans, postridie filium, Lintoniae Regulum cum egregia sane equitum manu ad eum misit, quasi sub ejus signis militaturum: ut hoc quasi pignore securum de insidiis quas struebat facilius opprimeret. Nihil enim ille quam conjuratorum speculatorem, non jam primum, agebat, mortalium ingratissimus Montisrosanum, adeoque et Regem ipsum illis proditurus.

Ubi vero non supra duodecim milliaria ab Humio Rosburgioque abfuit, atque illi ne nuncium quidem praemitterent, aut levissimam officii speciem exhiberent, non parum commotus Montisrosanus, in eorum agros ducere, ipsosque, vel invitos, ad partes pertrahere constituit. Verum illi insigni arte sibi praecaverunt. Davidem Leslaeum, quem sub illud tempus

Bervicum usque penetrasse cum omni ex Anglia equitatu et plurimis ejusdem gentis auxiliariis noverant (utpote consilii ejus conscii et participes) compellarunt, eique authores fuere, ut immisso milite eos quasi captivos abduceret: quod et factum fuit pridie quam illuc venerat Montisrosanus. Sic enim fore existimavit versutus ille senex Rosburgius (qui Humium secum perduxit), ut foederatorum gratiam iniret, quod se sponte quasi eorum tutelae tradidisset: nec tamen gratia Regis excideret, dum se invitum in eorum manus incidisse simularet. Et hoc primo facinore perpetrato, Leslaeus, trajecto Tueda, in orientalia Lothianae duxit. Montisrosanus, ubi Regem seque ab istis proditum sensit, nec jam spes ulla de auxiliariis equitibus a Rege mittendis affulgeret, hostesque praevalidi reditum in septentrionem et montana obstruerent, cum perexigua manu, quam secum adduxerat, in Nithiam Anandiamque et Aerae provinciam tendere statuit; ut equitatum quam posset maximum contraheret. Quamvis enim de hostium viribus nihil illi certo constaret, in equitatu tamen praesertim positas conjectura assecutus est.

## CAP. XVI.

Kelsoa digressus Montisrosanus Jedburgum, et inde Selkirkam pervenit: ubi equites quidem in oppidulo, pedites in vicina silva collocavit. Certum enim erat locorum opportuna sequi, ne cum hoste, cujus vires prorsus erant incognitae, in iniquo solo dimicare cogeretur. Equitum deinde praefectis mandat, ut speculatores expeditos, fidos frequentesque emittant; praesidia in locis opportunis quoquo versum disponant; vigilias sedulo curent. Quae quidem omnia, more soliti, ipse coram exsequi non poterat, quia ea nocte literas ad Regem daturus, nuncium, quem fidissimum nactus fuit, ante diluculum erat dimissurus. Adeoque enixius rogavit, ut in hoc unum animos intenderent, ne hostes, qui equitatu praevalebant, improvisi suos opprimerent. Ducibus vero curam omnem industriamque spondentibus, ille scribendis epistolis occupatus, noctem insomnem egit. Cum vero subinde praetoribus suis (viris militiae peritissimis, et eo nomine apud exteras gentes claris) incertos rumores de vicinis hostibus ad se perlatos deferret, illi, seu militum et speculatorum ignavia, seu fato decepti, hostem plane nullum in illo tractu ac ne vicinia quidem fidenter nimis renunciarent. Cum prima tandem luce expeditissimi et peritissimi equites denuo ad speculandum emissi sunt; et illi quoque reversi, decem milliaria confecisse se, et diverticula quaeque diligentissime pervestigasse affirmant: dirasque capiti suo temere imprecantur, si qui armati intra decem milliaria deprehendi possent. Postea tamen, sed sero constitit, hostem cum copiis omnibus vix quatuor Selkirka milliaribus abfuisse, noctemque illam egisse in armis.

Leslaeus eo die, quo Jedburgo profectus erat Montisrosanus, in Gladsmoria, Lothianae Provinciae planicie, copias recensebat; et foederatorum primoribus, cum eo de summa belli consulentibus, Edinburgum Forthamque versus tendere visum est: ut Montisrosano in septentrionem revertenti se opponerent; et ad dimicandum vel invitum cogerent, priusquam montanos suos sibi adjungeret. Verum ille, mutato consilio, copiis universis subito mandat, ut sinistrorsum tenderent, et iter strenue capesserent: mirantibus omnibus, quibus rerum arcana nondum innotuerant, mutati itineris et tam repentinae expeditionis consilium; recta enim Galae tractum petebant. Atqui (quod postmodo, narrantibus hostibus, cognitum fuit) literas ille acceperat, quibus accurate edoctus fuit, Montisrosanum, quingentis duntaxat peditibus, eisque Hibernis, et equitatu plane imbelli nec militiae assueto, stipatum; in Tuedae amnis tractu de improviso facillime opprimi posse, si ipse rei bene gerendae occasionem peropportunam arripiat. Leslaeus ergo, istis literis monitus, propere illuc contendit: et, ut dictum est, ad quatuor milliaria Selkirka pernoctavit. Trequarium illas dedisse ad Leslaeum literas, quod constanti evulgatum est fama, ut ego non affirmaverim, dissimulari tamen non potest, eundem filio Lintonio eadem nocte mandata dedisse, ut se confestim a partibus Regiis subduceret: quod et ille laetabundus perfecit. Omnium ut ille fuerint hominum ingratissimi, et Regis optime de se meriti desertores, posteris etiam pudendi. Et sane illius diei tempus matutinum, profunda spissaque caligine plenum, hostium insidiis non minimum favit. Quos tandem instructis ordinibus in Montisrosanum tendere, nec quingentis passuum[1] abesse, trepidi ejus speculatores renunciant.

Montisrosanus, equo, qui primus occurrit, conscenso, in campo matutino conventui destinatum prorupit: ubi omnia tumultu, nihil consilio agebatur. Equites, imperio neutiquam assueti, et sparsi antea per agros, pascendis jumentis magis quam tuendae cum honore vitae intenti, vel primo hostilis tubae sonitu attoniti, palantes, incertique huc et illuc cursitabant: sed in aciem nunquam descenderunt. Pauci tamen, illique ferme nobiles et equestris ordinis viri, illuc advolarunt: et dexterae peditum alae tutelam fortiter suscepere, qui numero plures quam centum et viginti non erant. Nec pedites (qui quingenti omnino erant) frequentes aderant; plerique enim rebus privatis inter impedimenta intenti, intempestiva cura seque suaque

---

[1] The editions have *quingentis passuum millibus* (500 miles!). Did Wishart mean "a mile and a half?" If *millibus* be omitted, as in the Montr. Redivivus, Tr., 1652, correct Latin requires *passibus;* or we may read *quinque* for *quingentis*, though this would make Lesley's approach less completely the surprise it seems to have been.

prodiderunt. Quodque res hactenus turbatas prorsus perdidit, praefecti ac duces plerique aberant, et ad proelium nunquam pervenere. Nec jam, instantibus citato gradu hostibus, consilii capiendi tempus supererat. Et illi cum sex millibus (quorum plerique equites erant ex Anglice) in dextram Montisrosani alam ferociter invecti, bis quidem fortiter excepti, et ad suos cum non minimo damno repulsi fuerunt. Nec nobilem illam turmam loco pellere aut perrumpere valuerunt, quoad ad sinistram, ubi equites nulli erant, paucis qui obstabant peditibus prostratis, irrupere. Simul his duo equitum millia, quos adversa amnis ripa hostes transmiserant, generosis illis viris a tergo imminebant: qui, ne undique circumventi et eminus hostium jaculis petiti, impune caderent, qua cuique via expeditissima visa est, se subduxerunt. Pedites vero, quibus in fuga exigua spes erat, fortiter et pertinaciter pugnantes, data tandem acceptaque fide, pro vitae incolumitate, projectis armis, sese dedidere. Eos tamen ad unum omnes, inermes, nudosque, Leslaei ipsius jussu, et proculcata quam dederant fide, immaniter trucidarunt. Cujus saevissimae perfidiae notam (qua ille gloriam, si quam apud exteras gentes acquisiverat, cum aeterna nominis ignominia foedissime polluit) nullo aevo abluet. Caeterum eos, qui pugna excesserunt, hostes ultra non sunt insecuti, diripiendis nimirum impedimentis intenti : ubi sane muliercularum, calonum, ac lixarum miserandam edidere stragem ; non sexus, non invalidae aetatis miserti, promiscue omnes occidere. Caesorum numerum inire non est facile: equites ferme nulli, pedites etiam perpauci (praeter deditos istos et in fidem receptos) in pugna ceciderunt; hinc enim conjecturam facere licet, quod cum omnino quingenti tantum fuissent, et ante posterum diem ducenti et quinquaginta incolumes ad Montisrosanum perveniunt, illique omnes gladiis armati, eo numero plures non potuisse desiderari. Longe vero paucissimi capti, quoad equis fuga lassatis, viarum ignari agrestibus praeda cessere. Quos illi, beneficiorum omnium et incolumitatis recens a Montisrosano impetratae immemores, in foederatorum gratiam saevissimis hostibus, tanquam hostias inferis devotas, immolandos tradiderunt.

Nec tamen vexillis Regiis conjurati victores potiti sunt. Miles quidam Hibernus, vir fortis, et, in summa aliorum trepidatione, praesentis animi, cum hostes jam plane victores cerneret, altero, quod peditatui praetendebatur, hastae detracto pectus suum involvit. Et caetera nudus stricto mucrone per medios hostes elapsus, sub vesperam ad Montisrosanum pertulit. Cui quidem ille inter corporis custodes adscito, fortitudinis fideique ornamentum, illud in posterum gestandum dedit. Alterum vero Wilelmus Hius, Kinnulii Comitis frater, egregiae indolis adolescens (qui avunculo materno, Duglassio, Mortonii Comitis filio, pluribus et gravioribus in pugna Alfordiana saucio, quam ut isti oneri ferendo par esset, successor

## CAP. XVI.

datus), manubriis detractum secum avexit. Et ille in vicinam Angliam dilapsus, ibi tantisper delituit, quoad, pacatis utcumque in Tuedae tractu rebus, occultis et plerumque nocturnis itineribus, comite duceque viae fidissimo socio et amico Roberto Tourio, viro forti et rerum bellicarum perito, qui in Galliis centurio non sine laude dudum militaverat, in septentrionem reversus, idem illud vexillum Regium ad imperatorem laetus retulit.

Ipse demum Montisrosanus (cum suos jam fusos fugatosque cerneret, quod nunquam antehac viderat) diu nihil aliud quam honestam et non inultam mortem meditabatur: collectisque plus minus triginta equitibus, qui forte sparsi incertique oberrabant, ne vivus in perduellium potestatem veniret, decoro exitu praeveniendum statuit. Quoniam vero turmas hostiles (quae confertissime circumstabant) perfringere non poterat, a fronte, a tergo, a latere tamen lacessebat: et extra ordines progredi ausos non paucos cecidit, aliosque trepidos repulit ad suos. Verum cum nihil ad summam rei proficeret, procurante sic benignissimo numine, constantem tandem et generosum animum subiit cogitatio: jacturam illius diei perexiguam, facile recuperari posse: minimam enim copiarum partem interfuisse. Montanos, firmissimas Regni vires, septentrionales ejusdem partes adhuc integras et intactas stare. Quamplurimos etiam primae nobilitatis et potentiae viros, equestris ordinis, et familiarum principes, belli societatem palam iniisse; quos omnes sua morte attonitos, subito pervertendos; adeoque partes Regias in Scotia penitus pessundandas iri reputavit. Nunquam ergo de justissima causa desperandum censuit, ne carissimus Dominus et Rex casu ejus quam adversa pugna longe majorem faceret jacturam. Et ista quidem cogitantem peropportune exceperunt Duglassius Marchio et Johannes Dalyellius eques cum amicis, paucis illis quidem, sed fidis fortibusque viris, qui obortis lacrimis (quas vehementior extorquebat pietas) compellant, orant, obsecrant, per rerum hactenus gestarum memoriam, per carissima amicorum nomina, per Majorum manes, per lectissimam conjugem liberosque, per denique optimi Regis, patriae, et Ecclesiae salutem, incolumitatem, et pacem attestantur, ut sibi quam maturrime prospiciat: in illo uno, secundum Deum immortalem, spem sitam esse; cum eo vivendum omnibus, vel occidendum simul. Et horum tandem precibus victus Montisrosanus, impetu, patefacta per hostes via (qui jam diripiendis impedimentis magis quam insequendis abeuntibus incumbebant) se cum suis subduxit; insequi vero ausos, alios occidit, alios, in quibus erat Brussius quidam, turmae equestris praefectus, cum duobus vexilliferis, quos[1] una cum vexillis captivos abduxit. Quos liberaliter habitos, post aliquot dies, data fide, se totidem captivos ejusdem ordinis liberaturos, dimisit: quam tamen fidem ne illi quidem satis sancte coluerunt.

---

[1] The construction is mixed, and would be improved by the omission of *quos*.

Nondum Montisrosanus Selkirka tribus passuum millibus aberat, cum suorum, qui eadem via tendebant, non paucos assecutus, manum neutiquam spernendam contraxit: qua de agrestium insultibus securus, iter sensim carpebat. Dumque Trequarii arcem praetergreditur (cujus scelere proditum se hostibus necdum noverat) praemittit, qui eum filiumque ad colloquium evocent: verum utrumque domo abesse a servis renunciatur. Atqui praesentem utrumque fuisse viri generosi et fide digni testantur: et egregius ille aulicus victoriam conjuratis gratulari, et palam, Montisrosanum cum copiis Regiis in Scotia tandem profligatum cum petulantissimo cachinno proclamare non erubuit; etiam filia ejus, Queinsburiensi Comitissa, quantum per verecundiam licuit, patrem hoc nomine increpante. Montisrosanus, ubi ad oppidulum (vulgo Peblisium dictum) paulisper substitisset; quoad milites, refectis viribus, se ad iter praepararent: plurimis undique confluentibus, occidente jam sole strenue omnes ingrediuntur; et duce praesertim Dalyellio equite, postridie cum prima luce Glottam vado trajiciunt. Ubi Craufordius Arlaeusque Comites, alia elapsi via ad eum accurrunt; nihili superioris pugnae cladem reputantes, ubi illum sospitem videre. Nec ille minus amicorum incolumitate laetus, quam quod ducentos ferme equites salvos collectosque in via secum perducerent. Quamvis autem ab insequentibus hostibus jam securus esset, ad Atholiam tamen festinare decrevit: ut, facto inde initio, ex montanis amicisque aliis septentrionem versus copias contraheret. Trajecto ergo Fortha et exinde Ierna, agrum Perthensem juxta montium radices emensus, eo pervenit. In itinere Duglassium Arlaeumque cum equitatus parte in Angusiam, Areskinium Regulum in Marriam praemiserat; ut propere amicos et clientes in illis locis concirent. Ad Carnegium deinde Regulum Johannem Dalyellium, recenti affinitate conjunctum, cum mandatis ad eum finem ablegaverat. Makdonaldo insuper literas dedit, quibus mandatum illi fuit, ut secundum datam fidem ad diem a se dictum cum montanis rediret. Omnium vero maxime Aboinium per literas nunciosque fatigavit, ut amicos suos clientesque sponte pronos, authoritate sua et exemplo confirmatos animatosque reduceret.

## CAP. XVII.

AUTUMNUS erat et provectus; necdum collectae in rigido solo fruges, aedes vero et tuguria ab hostibus diruta, nec reparata contra instantem et in illis locis saepiuscule atrocem hiemem Atholios ab insita alacritate paululum distinuere. Effecit tamen apud eos Montisrosanus, ut eunti in septentrionem, unde minus periculi erat, quadringentos expeditos pedites concederent:

## CAP. XVII.

redeunti vero, ubi in meridiem tendendum foret, universas provinciae vires sancte pollicerentur.

Frequentes interim nuncii ab Aboinio deferunt, se cum suis copiis confestim affuturum; nec minorem de se et montanis aliis spem fecit Makdonaldus: Areskinius vero suos in procinctu stare, nec aliud quam vel Aboinii (qui in propinquo erat) societatem, vel Montisrosani mandata expectare significat. Percrebrescebant interea sed incerti rumores, de valida equitum manu a Rege ad eum missa; quos non procul ab australi limite abesse plerique augurabantur. Captivorum vero, nullo sexus aut aetatis discrimine, atrocissima caedes jam, non dubia fama, divulgata est: captos nimirum ab agrestibus plerosque immanem in modum trucidatos; alios (quorum et immitissimi illi homines miserti fuerant) in unum coactos, decreto conjuratorum procerum, ab edito ponte praecipitatos, et sublabentibus aquis immersos, una viros, matresque, et ab uberibus pendentes infantulos: emergentes vero fustibus acceptos, et denuo deturbatos in aquas. Nobiles etiam et equestris ordinis viros, foedissimis inclusos carceribus, ut populi ludibrio exponantur, asservari, et certo tandem capitis supplicio destinatos esse. Nihil unquam Montisrosani animum aeque affecit ac tristis ille de suis nuncius.

Quapropter ut periclitantibus quoquo modo subveniret, morae omnis impatiens mira celeritate Grampium superat, et per edita Marriae Donaeque tractum ad Aboinium contendit: ut eum praesentia sua velocius ad meridiem pertraheret. Quod eo consilio factum, ut junctis cum Areskinio Arlaeoque copiis, et accersito quamprimum Makdonaldo cum montanis aliis, additisque in via Atholiis, omnes una trans Fortham recta tenderent, ac Regio equitatui occurrerent, et hostes instanti periculo deterrerent a captivorum caede. Neutiquam enim in viros nobiles saevire ausuros putabat, pendente adhuc bello, et incerta victoria. Et sane illi anxii et solliciti, quo tandem tanta belli moles, quam parari sentiebant, inclinaret, captivorum supplicia distulere. In itinere Montisrosanus Areskinium gravi morbo correptum offendit; clientes tamen ejus (quorum fidem fortitudinemque, etiam absente patrono, non semel fuerat expertus) promptos paratosque, si Aboinius officio suo non deesset: plurimum enim ab ejus exemplo et authoritate pendebant. Jamque Huntilaeus Marchio, cum annum et aliquot menses delituisset, nescio utrum tot victoriarum ac recuperati a Montisrosano regni fama excitatus, an sideris alicujus fallaci aspectu commotus, ad suos redierat; vir infelix juxta ac inconsultus, qui ut ut Regis studiosissimus videri vellet, aut sane esset, prava tamen et occulta invidia Montisrosani gloriam imminuere magis quam aemulari nitebatur. Quod cum apud suos (utpote tam praeclarae virtutis testes et conscios) palam profiteri erubesceret, ne alienati a Rege animi aliquod proferret indicium, jactitabat tamen, se ipsum deinceps fore illis militiae ducem contra perduelles. Adeoque clientibus imperabat, amicos vero vicinosque nec sine minis hortabatur, ne sub aliis quam suis signis militarent. Regerentibus autem, quid nobis ergo ad Montisrosani mandata respondendum erit, qui vicarius Regni administrator, cum copiarum summo imperio, a Rege renunciatus est ? responsum dabat, se quidem Regi minime defuturum : interim tam eorum quam suo honori conducere, ut Regi aliisque omnibus manifestum fiat, quas illi copias viresque contulerint, quod aliter fieri nequiret, nisi seorsim militarent. Magnifice insuper potentiam suam praedicare ; Montisrosani vero imminuere. Res a majoribus suis (viris sane cum omni laude memorandis) praeclare gestas immodice extollere: formidabilem a multis retro saeculis Gordoniorum potentiam vicinis fuisse, atque etiamnum esse. Iniquissimum fore, ut eorum virtute et sanguine parta in alterius (Montisrosani videlicet) honorem gloriamque cedant. Se in posterum rationem initurum, ut nec Rex Gordoniorum opera, nec illi debita laude, gratia, et mercede fraudentur.

Aequa omnino et honorifica imperitioribus dixisse videbatur : at quotquot inter eos erant cordati, et qui penitius ejus ingenium noverant, animum plus aequo exacerbatum, et a Montisrosano prorsus alienatum viderunt : nec alio tendere quam ut quotquot posset ab illo abstraheret ; in maximum non Regis Regnique modo, sed et suum malum et perniciem : quod, proh dolor, tristis perdocuit eventus. Nec defuere in illis viri prudentes et futurorum providi, qui consilium ejus, et imprudens, intempestivum, et ipsi etiam exitiosum damnarent. Obversabatur enim eorum animis nihil unquam ab illo attentatum fuisse, cui non ratio vel fortuna defuisset. Rem jam a Montisrosano melioribus auspiciis geri ; nec secedendum sese, vano praereptae gloriae praetextu. Si enim junctis cum Montisrosano consiliis viribusque ageret, nihil impedire quo se non tantum ab injuriis tutarentur, sed et hostes etiam in ordinem cogerent, cum aeterna vindicatae Majestatis laude : seditionem vero non probrosam modo, sed et perniciosam fore. Montisrosanum quidem absque eorum ope et opera multas easque insignes reportasse victorias : ipsos sine illo nihil dum memorabile gessisse. Enixe ergo rogare, ut vicario Regio constanter adhaereat ; quod, ut Regi non minus gratum quam utile, et bonis omnibus laudandum, sic et ipsi honorificum foret. Nec dubitarunt quidam ultro profiteri, se vel cum bonorum et vitae discrimine operam et obsequium Montisrosano praestituros, si ille pertinaciter in sua persisteret sententia : quod fideliter sancteque fecerunt. At ille, repudiatis amicorum consiliis, cum Montisrosano semper contrariis sententiis pugnabat : nec quidquam hic tam aequum, honestum, pulchrum aut utile suasit, quod Huntilaeus non perverteret, vel rejiceret. Et si quando ad ejus sententiam accederet (quod saepiuscule et consulto fecit) illico ille in diversum rapiebatur: Montisrosano coram aliquando facilis, absenti semper contrarius, nec sibi satis constans.

Aboinius tamen tum temporis (ut datae fidei quomodocunque satisfecisse videretur) frequentibus a Montisrosano nunciis et amicorum suorum precibus fatigatus, cum copiis sane non spernendis apud Druminoram, Forbesii Reguli arcem, se illi conjunxit. Pedites ducebat mille et quingentos, equites vero trecentos: alacres omnes, et ad quodvis discrimen sub Montisrosani imperio paratos. Et sane, ubi primum congressi sunt, Aboinius ultro professus est se cum his iturum, quocumque Gubernator duceret: longe vero plures (quos pro angustia temporis nondum coegerat) cum Ludovico fratre subsecuturos. Montisrosanus, plurimum laudata ejus fide et industria, eadem ferme qua venerat via, iter repetit; ut additis Areskinii et Marrianorum copiis, ac superato Grampio, in Atholiam Angusiamque descenderet. Nec dubitavit ante decimum et quartum diem cum valido exercitu Fortham trajicere. Primum iter Aboinius cum suis alacriter confecit: at postridie Ludovicus frater (cui Montisrosanus Craufordiae Comitem praefecit) cum valida equitum manu, quasi hostium turmas aliquot aggressurus, noctu domum se recepit, sub specie praesidii, abductis quotquot potuit militibus. Craufordius reversus Ludovicum suos petiisse, ac postridie rediturum renunciavit; sic enim simulabat ille, qui nihil minus quam de reditu cogitabat, juvenis non hoc solo nomine famosus. Ubi vero tertiis castris ad Alfordiam ventum fuit, observatum est Aboinii milites ad conventum tardos, lentos in itinere, raris et incompositis ordinibus incedere; et singulis ferme noctibus castra deserere turmatim: tandemque dux ipse Aboinius veniam missionemque petere non erubuit. Mirantibus omnibus, et poscentibus, quaenam esset mutati tam subito consilii ratio? regerebat ille paterna mandata, quibus sibi omnino obsequendum foret. Nec patrem ejus sine justa causa mandata ejusmodi dedisse: copias enim hostiles in inferiori Marria considere, adeoque suis imminere cervicibus, si suorum praesidio destitueretur: insipiens plane fore, si milites suos alio traduceret, cum ipse in praesenti versaretur periculo. Montisrosanus ad ista; satis constare aliquot tantum hostium turmas apud Aberdoniam se continere; pedites plane nullos: pauculos istos equites nihil audere, aut posse. Nec dubitandum esse quin prima adventus sui fama, et illi etiam ad inferiora Regni tutanda a ducibus suis accersantur. Longe vero melius Huntilaei rebus consultum iri, si bellum in hostilem agrum transferatur, quam si in ejus geratur ditione. Eoque magis ad meridiem festinandum, ut molem belli a septentrione avertant. Addidit insuper copias auxiliares indies expectari ab Anglia; quas sibi adjungere nulla ratione possent, nisi cis Fortham illis iretur obviam. Multa denique cum miseratione captivorum statum exposuit (quorum non pauci ipsius erant Huntilaei affines, amici, et consanguinei) omnes nimirum inhumane trucidandos, nisi mature eis subveniretur. Quibus cum Aboinius quod responderet non haberet, rem totam ad patrem deferri rogat, impetratque. Missi ad Huntilaeum qui illi gratissimi videbantur, Donaldus Resius Regulus, in cujus agro delituerat, et Alexander Irvinius junior de Drumma, qui non ita pridem Huntilaei filiam matrimonio sibi junxerat. Uterque etiam Montisrosano recenti recuperatae libertatis beneficio devinctissimus. Resius, verecundia repulsae commotus et ille reverti erubuit, Irvinius (adolescens generosus et fortis, qui postea Montisrosanum nunquam deseruit) nihil quam literas soceri incertas et ambiguas retulit. Interrogatus vero quid de ejus voluntate sentiret, libere et ingenue respondit; nihil certi ab illo renunciatum esse; nec a prava sententia dimoveri posse arbitrabatur. Aboinius se plane invitum a Montisrosano divelli praefatus: oportere tamen carissimo patri, eidemque valetudinario morem gerere, adeoque enixius Gubernatoris veniam postulare: paucorum dierum moram tolerandam esse, quoad patris animum emolliret. Sancte insuper pollicitus est, ante elapsas duas hebdomadas se cum longe majoribus copiis subsecuturum. Cumque data sponte fide illud se facturum saepius comfirmasset, a Montisrosano multum renitente et admodum invito missionem ad praedictum tempus obtinuit.

Aboinio ad suos reverso, Montisrosanus per edita Marriae et Schiae tractum in Atholiam descendit: et inde, copiis paulo auctioribus, in agrum Perthensem, ubi per nuncium nova spe a septentrione erigitur, rogatus ab Aboinio ut se cum copiis ante praestitutum diem expectaret. Eodemque tempore Thomas Ogilvius, junior de Pouria et Robertus Nesbittus, centuriones, diversis itineribus ad eum accurrunt; uterque a Rege missus cum mandatis, ut si omnino posset, Georgio Digbio Regulo, Bristoliensis Comitis filio, cum equestribus auxiliis ad se misso non procul ab Anglicano limite festinus occurreret. Eosdem nuncios Montisrosanus ad Huntilaeum Aboiniumque ablegavit, ut eadem mandata illis impertirent: sic tandem fore ratus, ut Regia authoritate et auxiliorum spe excitati, copias accelerarent; quarum inani spe lactatus[1] in tractu Iernae diutius substitisset.

Naperius de Marchistona Regulus, integerrimae vitae et felicissimi ingenii vir, generosus, et vere nobilis, ac familiae suae perantiquae princeps, patri avoque Naperiis (toto terrarum orbe celeberrimis Philosophis et Mathematicis) in aliis par, civili vero prudentia longe superior, Regibus Jacobo Caroloque gratus juxta ac fidus, aerario olim praefectus, et ad primae nobilitatis evectus gradum, fidei in Regem caritatisque ergo a conjuratis carcerem saepius cum bonorum jactura passus, hisce diebus in

---

[1] Paris, *lactatus*. Amsterd., *jactatus*.

Atholia fatis cessit. Quem Montisrosanus puer quasi indulgentissimum parentem, adolescens monitorem consultissimum, adultus vero fidissimum amicum semper coluit: ejusque mortem haud aliter quam paternam tulit. Cujus de jure Regio, et tumultuum in Britannia Origine, eruditissimae dissertationes, utinam aliquando videant lucem!

## CAP. XVIII.

Montisrosanus, cum secundam et tertiam hebdomadam in itinere et tractu Iernae Aboinium cum copiis ex septentrione oppertus fuisset, et perduelles in captivos atrocius coepissent saevire, ulterioris morae impatiens, trajecto Fortha, in Leviniam descendit. Et in agris Iohannis Buchanani equitis, in illis partibus foederatorum coryphaei, consedit, sic fore ratus, ut propinquus Glascuae, conjuratos, qui conventum ordinum suorum illic celebrabant, a captivorum absterreret caede. Quem in finem equitatu quotidie in civitatis conspectum invectus, agros hostiles impune populatus est; quamvis illi pro Ordinum et civitatis praesidio et tutela tria equitum millia haberent in stationibus, nec ipse omnino trecentos, cum mille et ducentis peditibus. At vero ante ejus in Leviniam descensum foederati, ubi de alienato Huntilaei a Montisrosano animo audivissent, et quod Aboinius cum suis in editiore Marria ab eo descivisset, tanquam sequentis tragoediae prologum, tres egregios viros generosos et fortes capite mulctarunt.

Eorum primus Wilielmus Rollocus eques, saepius nobis laudatus, vir fortis et peritus, Montisrosano a pueritia in paucis carus, et ad ultimum spiritum fidus. Huic ante alia crimini datum est, quod foedissimo et nefando scelere seipsum non polluisset. Enimvero ille, post pugnam Aberdonensem a Montisrosano cum literis ad Regem missus, in hostes inciderat, nec destinatam evasisset mortem, nisi Argathelio, Montisrosani vitam indigne licitanti, et opes, honores, dignitatesque longe maximas pollicenti, intentatae mortis metu, assensisset, et patrandum parricidium, a quo toto animo abhorrebat, suscepisset in se. Qua arte libertate donatus ac vita, rectaque ad eum profectus, omnium illi indicium fecit, atque obsecravit, ut majori cura sibi praecaveret: non enim se solum, qui tam horrendum flagitium detestaretur, sed et complures alios ingenti pretio illectos; quorum plerique in hoc scelus artem, operam, animosque intenderent.

Secundus fuit Alexander Ogilvius, antea etiam memoratus nobis, Iohannis de Innercarita Equitis primogenitus, antiqua familia et in Scotorum historiis celebri, adolescens adhuc (vixdum enim ad vigesimum aetatis annum pervenerat) sed supra annos fortis, et erecto ad ardua animo. Nec sane quid huic objectaverint, vel conjectura assequi possum, praeter novum illud et inauditum Majestatis crimen, debitam nimirum optimo Regi fidem et obsequium. Verum promptissimi adolescentis, et eo nomine formidandi sanguine, Argathelio, Ogilviorum gentis hosti inveterato, litandum fuit. Tertius Philippus Nesbittus Eques, et ipse familiae suae perantiquae post patrem princeps, qui in Anglia Regis auspiciis cum gloria militaverat, et ad tribunatum militarem fuerat evectus. Nec aliam sane (praeter illud, ubi vera deficiunt, intentari solitum Majestatis crimen) illatae huic mortis causam investigare potuimus, quam quod virum fortem et industrium, atrocissimas patri et paternae familiae illatas injurias olim vindicaturum male sibi conscii metuebant. Atqui vero illi fortiter et constanter, ut probos et vere Christianos viros decet, nobilissimo functi sunt fato. Et his quidem merito jungendi sunt Hiberni duo, viri admodum generosi et fortes, virtute sua juxta ac natalibus clari, O Caenus Lachleniusque, tribuni militum; hoc solo nomine conjuratis invisi, quod egregiam eorum fortitudinem toties experti fuissent. Edinburgi quidem Hiberni illi excarnificati fuere; at Glascuae complures alii ad similem erant destinati poenam: verum vix expectatus Montisrosanus, et civitati ad pauca milliaria propinquus, hoc effecit, ut eorum supplicia in aliud tempus deferrent. Nunciata istorum morte vehementer commotus Gubernator, incertum est, hostiumne saevitiae, an amicorum seu ignaviae, seu perfidiae magis succensuerit. Praeter enim Huntilaeum, cujus copias cum Aboinio filio tamdiu frustra expectaverat, et ipse etiam Makdonaldus (de quo optima quaeque speraverat) saepius accersitus, et invitatus etiam vicinitate loci, quamvis dies a se dictus jampridem elapsus esset, nullam properantis spem faciebat. i Hebdomadae sex jam praeterierant, ex quo Aboinius pro copiis septentrionalibus fidem fecerat; et hiems (qua atrociorem aetas nostra nullam vidit) hactenus ingravescebat. Repulsi etiam, quos Rex miserat, duce Digbio Regulo, auxiliarii; quibus omnibus mederi facile potuissent et universum Regnum denuo in ordinem cogere, si egregii illi patroni in optima causa non fuissent praevaricati. Tandem ergo xii. Kal. Dec. Montisrosanus Levinia digressus, per Taichiae montes altis nivibus coopertos, saltusque lacusque, quorum nomina nobis haud occurrunt, emenso Iernae tractu, et trajecto Tao, in Atholiam demum reversus est. Obvios hic habuit Ogilvium et Nesbittum centuriones, quos cum mandatis Regiis ad Huntilaeum legaverat. Et illi virum contumacem et inexorabilem renunciant; qui nullam eis fidem habuerit, Regisque mandata exponentibus fastidiose responderat; omnia Regis sibi, quam illis, aut ipsi Gubernatori perspectiora: nec se, aut filios suos ullam cum eo societatem inituros. Amicos insuper clientesque, qui Montisrosano sponte operam locaverant, acerbe et minaciter increpare, duriusque cum illis quam perduellibus agere. Quae tamen omnia dissimulanda tolerandaque existimavit

## CAP. XVIII.

Gubernator; dumque cum Atholiis de ratione militiae istius provinciae transigit, ad Huntilaeum denuo Johannem Dalyellium Equitem, quasi magis idoneum amicitiae internuncium transmisit; qui de Regis Regnique discrimine, adeoque ipsius et omnium fidelium subditorum praesenti periculo doceret: et oculis ejus subjiceret, non alius quam sua filiorumque culpa accidisse, quum quod auxiliarios a Rege missos in Scotiam non intulissent, tum quod captivi, viri fortes et fidi, crudeliter fuissent mactati: superesse adhuc plures, ipsi Huntilaeo conjunctissimos, et quosdam etiam primae nobilitatis viros, quos perduelles eodem plane modo trucidaturi essent, nisi iam tandem subveniretur. Rogare denique et obtestari, ut ad amicum saltem colloquium cum Regio Gubernatore descendat: et spondere, eum illi abunde satisfacturum.

Huntilaeus, cum ad alia Dalyellio solita pervicacia respondisset, omnium maxime a colloquio abhorrebat, utpote tanti hominis (quam quod ad ejus argumenta rationesque responderet, non haberet) praesentiam, fiduciam et prudentiam extimescebat. At Montisrosanus, rebus in Atholia constitutis, ne quid intentatum relinqueret, quod aliquando eum ad saniorem reduceret mentem, dissimulatis injuriis, et coacervatis officiis, beneficiisque, occupare illum, et vel cum invito gratiam inire, et de his, quae in rem Regiae Majestatis facerent, transigere decrevit. Mense ergo Decembri aegre admodum amnes torrentesque, gelu quidem constrictos, sed nondum tantopere concretos, ut ferendis corporibus pares essent, montium juga praeruptasque rupes et altissimas nives eluctatus est: et peragrata Angusia superatoque Grampio, copias in septentrionem traduxit. Et tantum non improvisus cum paucis in Strathbogiam, ubi Huntilaeus degebat, contendit. At ille inexpectato ejus adventu perculsus, ubi primum de eo nuncium accepit, ne invitus ad colloquium pertraheretur, illico ad Bogiam arcem suam, juxta Spaei ostium sitam, transfugit; quasi amnem trajecturus esset, et suis auspiciis in Moravia adversus conjuratos gesturus bellum.

Animum jam subit, paucis indagare, unde tanta adversus Montisrosanum contumacia incesserit Huntilaeo, nulla ab eo injuria, sed e contra omni honore et officiis plerumque indebitis lacessito. Nec sane aliud quidquam fama traditum, vel conjectura assequi possum praeter impotentem tam eximiae gloriae non aemulationem, sed invidiam. Neutiquam enim alienatum ejus a Rege, sed inimicum Montisrosano animum dixerim; cujus injusto accensus odio, se in tot absurdos praecipitaverit errores; adeo ut omnia perditum iri, quam Montisrosani opera et cum ejus laude restitui maluerit. Jamque flagrantem impotenti superbia mentem plus nimis accendebat conscientia injuriarum et contumeliarum, quibus hactenus eum affecerat: eaque principalis causa (nisi ego fallor) fuit, quod illius adspectum toties evitaverit. Praeter enim ea quae nobis antehac commemorata sunt, nec pauca, nec levia in Regium Gubernatorem pater filiique peccaverant; quorum pauca per censere ab instituto nostro non erit alienum.

Majora bellica tormenta, quae superiore anno a Montisrosano humo condita meminimus, illi, inconsulto eo, effosa, triumphantibus similes, in arcibus suis disposuerant, quasi detracta hostibus spolia; nec postea repetita reddidere. Atqui vero illa in Perthensi et Aberdonensi pugna acquisiverat Montisrosanus, quarum priori nullus ex ea familia interfuerat; in altera vero Ludovicus cum suis adversa in acie militaverat. Pulverem deinde tormentarium, arma, aliaque belli instrumenta hostibus direpta et in arcibus suae potestatis, tanquam in locis tutis et idoneis, deposita, sic sibi vindicarunt, ut nec minimae partis copiam reposcenti fecerint. Ad haec Aboinius in reditu post victoriam Kilsythinam Kethum Comitem, supremum Scotiae Mareschallum (ut loquuntur), Arbuthnotum Vice-comitem, aliosque insignes in hostibus viros, in suam potestatem redactos, inconsulto Regni Gubernatore et multum refragrante, Drummio juniori, leviro suo (qui forte aderat) liberos dimiserat. Quibus conditionibus id fecerit, incertum est; hoc tamen certo constat, praeter contumeliam Gubernatori factam, arcisque Dunotriae, sane munitissimae, et magni ad illud bellum momenti, jacturam, aliaque emolumenta militiae insuper habita, nunquam ausuros fuisse conjuratos tam crudeliter in captivos grassari, si istos saltem in custodia detinuisset. Privata insuper authoritate sua, tributa, vectigalia et subsidia exigebat (quod Gubernator ipse nunquam fecerat) specie quidem promovendae militiae, reipsa tamen longe alios in usus, et in maximum causae Regiae detrimentum. Denique (quod omnium maxime deplorandum est) captivos ex hostibus superioribus in septentrione victoriis acquisitos, et in arcibus suis custodiae mandatos, alios hostili prece, alios exiguo admodum pretio libertate donarunt. Nec eos Montisrosano permisere, quos ille bello captos in eum omnino finem servaverat, ut hominum meritissimorum capita illorum commutatione redimeret. Quorum omnium conscientia agitatus Montisrosani congressum non aliter quam pestem aversabatur semper Huntilaeus.

Ac ille nihilominus, neglectis injuriis rebusque aliis omnibus posthabitis, in promovendo Regis negotio totus erat. Et in eum finem colloquium extorquere vel invito, amicitiam quibuscunque inire legibus, in omnibus consentire, et nihil non indulgere statuit, quo aegrum Huntilaei animum posset emollire. Copiis ergo in stationibus relictis, cum paucis equitibus summo mane Bogiam advolavit, omnemque fugae aut sese occultandi rationem improvisa celeritate praevenit. Ubi vero congressi sunt, Montisrosanus praeteritorum immemor, leni et blanda oratione ad belli societatem pro Regis Regnique incolumitate invitavit; illique tam abunde in omnibus satisfecit, ut quasi tandem victus manus tendere visus fuerit. Nec sane copias modo suas, sed et seipsum illis ducem fore pollicitus est, et primo quoque tempore adfuturum. Postea de belli ratione in commune consuluere; convenitque ut Huntilaeus, trajecto Spaea, per oram Moraviae littoralem dextrum iter, Montisrosanus vero per Spaeae tractum, sinistrum, et illa tempestate longe difficillimum carperet: undique scilicet Innernessum hostile praesidium oppugnaturi; et interim Seafordium Comitem, vel sponte, vel invitum et reluctantem, ad partes pertraherent. Praesidium illud, ut ut alioquin probe munitum videri posset, commeatuum tamen aliarumque rerum inopia laborabat: cui propulsandae necessaria, rigidissima hieme et procelloso mari, non adeo facile subministrari poterant. Adeoque jam in omnibus consensisse videbantur, ut Aboinius et Ludovicus fratres omnibus diris se devoverint, nisi Montisrosano constantes in obsequio et sanctissima amicitia ad ultimum vitae spiritum perstarent. Gordonii vero aliique Huntilaei amici, incredibili laetitia diffusi, patrono suo et familiae principi quasi ab inferis reverso gratulabantur.

## CAP. XIX.

Montisrosanus Huntilaei animum tandem mitigatum et ad belli societatem serio capessendam confirmatum ratus, copias suas per Spaeae amnis tractum Innernessum versus perduxit. Quo vero hostes undique suspensos teneret, Patricium consanguineum, antea non semel laudatum nobis, et Iohannem Drumondum de Balla juniorem (generosum, et probatae fidei fortitudinis virum, qui saepiuscule strenuam operam navaverat) cum imperio et mandatis ad Atholios misit; ut si qui in illis locis tumultuarentur, occasionem rei bene gerendae non praetermitterent. Quorum authoritate et exemplo Atholii excitati promptos sese alacresque exhibuere. Nec sane diu illis occasio defuit; enimvero Argatheliorum superstites, seu rerum omnium in suo agro penuria, seu praevalidi et extrema minitantis Makdonaldi metu, et potentia extorres, in Makgregorios et Maknabios, qui Montisrosano favebant, invecti sunt. Et junctis sibi postmodum Stuartis qui Balwidriam incolunt, et Menesiis, aliisque montanis, qui adhuc Argathelii sequebantur fortunam, ad mille et quingentos contraxisse dicebantur: Atholiam etiam invasuri, nisi illis mature iretur obviam. Et sane hactenus insulam in Tochertae lacu sitam, vi captam direptamque concremaverant; et in Amplae amnis tractu ejusdem nominis Castellum obsidione cinxerant. Quae ubi primum nunciata fuere, Atholii numero duntaxat septingenti, eisdem Graemo Drumondioque ducibus, ne hostes in agros suos irrumperent, praevertendos omnino censuere. Illi, Atholiorum fama perculsi, soluta Amplae obsidione, Taichiam versus sese recepere. Eos Atholii acriter insecuti, non procul a Kalendaria Taichiae arce instructos ad pugnam offendunt.  Enimvero vadum amnis occupaverant, et adversam ripam, edito colle munitam, frequentibus sclopetariis muniverant.  Quae cum Atholii conspexissent, et numerum paulo minorem quam fama divulgaverat (non enim mille et ducentos excedebant), quamvis et ipsi vix septingenti forent, ducum praesertim fiducia et hortationibus animati, non excipere, sed ultro inferre proelium decrevere.  Centum ergo expeditos milites, quasi ad vadi illius praesidium, ex adverso hostibus objiciunt: caeteri ad aliud vadum arci vicinum properant, ut illuc fluvium trajiciant.  Argatheliani, ubi Atholiorum alacritatem persenserunt, sese illico Sterlinum versus recepere.  Et Atholii primi illi, qui ad vadum inferius stabant, desertam ab hostibus ripam occupant; et mox extremum abeuntium agmen carpunt, convellunt, trudunt: et caeteri insecuti, omnes in fugam conjiciunt.  Caesi traduntur octoginta; caeteri fuga sibi consuluere.  Quibus saluti fuit, quod mane illius diei Atholii iter non minus impeditum et arduum, quam longinquum, utpote decem milliarium confecissent, equitesque omnino haberent nullos.  Illi vero re bene gesta ad suos rediere.

Celebrabant per eos dies conjurati conventum suorum Ordinum Andreapoli, quam innocuo, utinam non vocali sanguine virorum aeternam merentium laudem profanarunt.  Erant inter captivos vel ex perduellium odio viri clarissimi (non enim illi nisi in optimi cujusque capita saeviebant, a quibus vero non adeo sibi metuerent, bonorum confiscatione mulctare satis habuerunt) Ogilvius Regulus, Robertus Spotswodius Eques, Wilielmus Moravius, adolescens nobilis, et Andreas Gutheraeus, generosus, fortis, et manu promptus, quos in illa civitate mactare decreverant, ut eorum sanguine provincialium manibus parentarent: quorum supra quinque millia variis in proeliis cecidisse tradebantur.  Quoniam vero non Lege, sed sua tantum libidine in eos erant animadversuri, ad solitas artes recurrunt, immani saevitiae Religionem praetexentes.  In quem finem vates prophetasque suos Kanteum Blairiumque et alios simili spiritu agitatos coram populo producunt, qui sublimes in pulpitis cruenta depromant oracula.  Poscere scilicet Deum istorum sanguinem; nec aliter gentis peccata expiari, et averuncari posse numinis vindictam.  Et hac arte praesertim vulgi animos, alioquin ad miserationem pronos, tanquam in sacros devotosque irritabant: quasi legum humanarum authoritas aut patrocinium illis omnino nullum esse debeat, quos ipsum numen deposceret.  Nec dubitarunt egregii illi, arcanorum coelestium interpretes et arbitri, hominum animas cum corporibus aeternis poenis addicere.  Cumque hac ratione vulgum pervertissent, facile fuit iisdem delatoribus pariter ac judicibus homines innocuos, sed omni patrocinio destitutos damnare.

Verum Ogilvius, qui non modo nobilitate et potentia eminebat, sed et

## CAP. XIX.

maternum genus ducebat ab Hamiltoniis, Lindesiique erat consobrinus, cum valetudinem infirmam simulasset, difficulter impetravit, ut mater, conjunx, sororesque aegrum in carcere visitarent et solarentur. Hoc vero ubi obtinuit, cum custodes, nobilium feminarum verecundia, cubiculo se subduxissent, ille confestim amiculum muliebre sorori detractum sibi imposuit, omnique mundo ornavit. Illa etiam pileolo, quocum aeger in lecto dormitare solitus erat, caput suum circumdedit, et fratrem simulans decubuit. Multa denique salute, obortis lacrimis, invicem impertita, hora noctis octava, ipsos custodes faces cereosque praetendentes sororis specie formaque fefellit. Et confestim urbe digressus, equos (quos ad hoc habuit paratos) cum duobus asseclis conscendit, ac ante lucem matutinam in tuto se collocavit. Ubi vero postero demum die deprehensa fraus fuit ab oculatissimis custodibus, Argathelius, vindictae iraeque impotens, nobilissimas feminas, et hac ipsa pietate et industria inclitas, ad poenas deposcere non erubuit: sed frustra. Illae enim aequitate causae longe validiores patronos Hamiltonios Lindesiumque invenere: quibus conniventibus personatos istos totam egisse fabulam complurium opinio est: equidem in re incerta judicium non interponam.

Ogilvius quasi e manibus eorum ereptos conjuratos vehementer perculit; ac paene in furorem rabiemque vertit: unde factum est, ut propere de reliquis supplicium sumerent. Primus autem catastam generoso sanguine cruentavit Nathaneêl Gordonius, militum tribunus, corporis forma animique dotibus insignis. Qui morti propinquus, adolescentiam suam secius, quam fas foret, exactam multis et acerbis deflevit lacrimis. Cum vero jam morituro libellum, quo poenitentiam suam testaretur chirographo signandam obtruderent, ille nihil cunctatus subscripsit: simulque Deum, Angelos, et praesentes est attestatus, si quae essent in illa chartula descripta Regi, ejusve Majestati, aut authoritati contraria, se illis minime consentire. Solutus deinde anathematis sententia, qua propter adulterium pridem commissum perculsus erat, cum maxima spectantium miseratione cervicem securi praebuit: vir huic culpae obnoxius, sed fortitudinis et militaris peritiae gloria tam apud exteras gentes quam domi clarus.

Secundus in eandem catastam, tepenti adhuc Gordonii cruore madescentem, productus est vir aeternitate dicatus, Robertus Spotswodius, Jacobi Caroloque Regum gratia, quam eximiis virtutibus promeruerat, ad supremos honores evectus; Eques, Senatorque a Jacobo renunciatus, supremae curiae praeses, et non ita pridem in Scotia supremus ejus Secretarius (ut loquuntur) a Carolo constitutus. Hunc summum virum (quamvis quod objicerent in omni vita ipsi actores nihil haberent) Majestatis reum peregerunt: quod et eo lugendum magis, quia armatus contra eos nunquam stetisset: quippe qui pacis artibus clarissimus, ad militiam non admovisset manum. Hoc ergo solo nomine in eam animadverterunt, quod ex Regis mandato, diploma ejus ad Montisrosanum detulisset, quo ille Regni vicarius Gubernator et supremus militiae praefectus creatus erat. Atqui vero se hoc more majorum et ex legum praescripto fecisse, multis ille demonstravit. Et sane aliis, praeterquam judicibus (quos infensissimos hostes et vitae ejus inhiantes conjurati dederant) elegantissima defensione satisfecisse videbatur: adeo ut ambiguum non sit, tristem illam sententiam nunquam fuisse laturos, si vel levissimam habuissent aequi bonique rationem. Verum, ut dicam quod res est, virum optimum perdidit invidia major quam ut exsuperandae illi innocentia ejus par foret. Enimvero Lanricensis Comes, pridem in Regno Scotiae supremus Secretarius, cum ad conjuratos defecisset, clementissimum, et in universam Hamiltoniorum gentem beneficentissimum Regem compulit, ut dignitatem eam ingrato homini adimeret, inque alium conferret: nec quisquam Spotswodio dignior visus est quem amplissimo honore ornaret. Atque hinc illa vindictae invidiaeque moles, cui cum hic non sufficeret, succubuit.

Jamque moriturus Spotswodius, quum de solita gravitate et constantia nihil remitteret, ad populum more patrio verba faciebat. Verum sacrilegus iste Blairius, qui supra catastam invito adstabat, facundiam fiduciamque viri tanti veritus, ne arcana rebellionis ex venerando ore ad populum emanarent, qui morientium voces avidius accipere et pertinacius meminisse solitus est, os illi obturandum, per urbis praefectum, eundemque olim paternum Spotswodii clientem, curavit. Quam ille insolentem injuriam nihili reputans, sermone ad populum omisso, in orationibus et precibus ad Deum immortalem totus erat. Interpellatus denuo et nimis importune ab eodem molestissimo Blairio, an et se quoque cum populo pro salute animae ejus precibus apud Deum vellet intercedere, respondit, populi quidem supplicationes et vota se imploraturum; cum ejus vero impiis plane et Deo abominandis orationibus nihil sibi commune esse. Addiditque insuper, malorum quibus offensum Numen gentem istam afflixisset, longe maximum, ferro, flamma, pestilentiaque gravius esse, quod propter peccata populi spiritus mendaces in ora prophetarum immisisset. Qua liberrima simul et justissima voce correptus Blairius, usque adeo excanduit, ut a scurrilibus convitiis in patrem ejus jam pridem demortuum, et ipsum jam moriturum sibi non temperaret: egregius scilicet Christianae longanimitatis et patientiae praeco. Ea tamen omnia Spotswodius ad altiora intentus, aequo animo et cum silentio despexit. Cumque jam interritus, nec quidquam in vultu aut ore mutatus, cervicem plagae fatali praeberet, novissima ejus vox fuit: "Clementissime Iesu, collige animam meam cum sanctis tuis et martyribus, qui mihi in decurrendo hoc stadio praegressi sunt." Et sane, cum non tantum propter fidei confessionem, sed et quamcunque virtutem, qua viri

## CAP. XIX.

sancti fidem suam attestantur, subeatur Martyrium, quin eandem ille coronam adeptus sit, non est dubitandum. Et hunc demum exitum, bonis omnibus luctuosum, at ipsi maxime honorificum, sortitus est vir rerum divinarum humanarumque scientia, linguarum, praeter Europaeas, Hebraicae, Chaldaicae, Syriacae, Arabicaeque, Historiarum, Jurisprudentiae et politicarum artium peritia clarissimus, integritate morum, fide, aequitate, et constantia patriae saeculique decus et ornamentum: sibi semper constans, et aequabilis; cujus nec pueritiae adolescentiam, nec adolescentiae provectiorem aetatem puderet: antiquae pietatis intimo animo severus cultor: nec tamen apud alios ostentator vanus et superstitiosus: conciliandis amicitiis facilis juxta ac conservandis pertinax: quique jam mortuus maximum sui desiderium plerisque etiam foederatis reliquit. Exanimum corpus Hugo Scrimigerius, patris ejus olim cliens, pro temporum ratione curatum, privato funere extulit: nec ipse tanto maerori diu superstes. Paucos enim post dies catastam illam cruentam nondum loco motam conspicatus, illico correptus est animi deliquio; et a servis vicinisque in aedes suas portatus, in ipso limine exspiravit.

Spotswodio denique similis fati comitem dant Andream Guthereum, meritissimi Episcopi Moraviensis filium, et eo etiam nomine conjuratis invisum: juvenem non minus in bello fortem, quam constantem in perferenda spernendaque morte. Hic minis convitiisque ab eodem Blairio impetitus, respondit: Ampliorem sibi honorem haberi nulla ratione potuisse, quam quod honestissimam pro optimo Rege et justissima causa oppeteret mortem: quam intrepide amplexurum praesentes cernerent; et posteri forsan sint praedicaturi: de peccatis supplicem clementissimi Domini Dei misericordiam implorare, veniamque deprecari: de hoc vero, cujus reus erat peractus, se esse securum. Atque hunc quidem in modum constanter ille fortiterque fato functus est: vir, si sic Deo opt. max. visum fuisset, longiori dignus vita.

Utque jam magnae ex parte peractae tragoediae finem imponerent, post interjectam bidui moram Wilielmum Moravium, Tullibardini Comitis fratrem adolescentulum plane eodem protrahunt. Et quidem omnibus instar miraculi erat, fratrem ejus, qui gratia et meritis inter foederatos eminebat, pro unici fratris germani incolumitate et vita non intercessisse. Alii ignaviae, avaritiae alii, fraternis bonis inhianti, alii stupidissimae superstitioni imputabant: et sane omnes, etiam foederati ipsi, inhonestum et viro nobili indecorum silentium damnabant. At adolescens ipse vixdum decimum et nonum aetatis annum egressus, honesta plane et decora morte aeternam sibi apud posteros memoriam famamque acquisivit. Inter pauca illa quae ad populum profatus est, ista altiori voce prolata, qui audiverunt nobis retulere: "Reputate, populares mei, familiae Tullibardinae et universae Moraviorum genti novum idemque eximium decus hodie additum esse, quod adolescens, antiqua illa prosapia oriundus, laetus hilarisque pro patre patriae, et in familiam nostram munificentissimo Rege, in ipso juventae flore, innocentem, quod ad homines, spiritum reddo. Nec venerandam parentem, carissimas sorores, consanguineos, amicosve alios vitae meae brevioris poeniteat, quam mors honorificentissima decorabit. Orate pro anima mea, et valete."

## CAP. XX.

Montisrosanum amicorum casus, ut par erat, vehementius commovit; firmam tamem certamque pectoris constantiam convellere et subvertere non valuit. Nec sane alias generosus ejus animus, et supra communem sortem evectus, clarius resplenduit : non enim defuere plurimi, indigna suorum morte irritati, qui aegrum recenti injuria ad praesentem vindictam stimularent. Cumque justo quamvis dolori plus nimis indulgerent, et omnino aequum, utpote Talionis legem, postulare sibi viderentur, querelis multis, molestis, et importunis imperatorem fatigarunt. Indignabantur quippe, socios, amicos, consanguineos, dignissimos fortissimosque viros, de patria, de Rege, de ipso Gubernatore optime meritos, contra datam fidem, consuetudinem belli, leges patrias, ipsaque gentium et naturae jura, impune trucidari : contra perduelles a se bello captos, non tam carcere quam amico hospitio detineri, exultare, laetari, et dolori eorum illudere ; adeoque ut sontes ad poenas deposcere : nec aliter hostes ab infanda saevitia deterreri, nec suorum animos confirmari et erigi posse. Quos ille blanda oratione exceptos, ob caritatem in suos laudavit ; vindicandosque omnino, dixit, egregios illos et innocentes cives : sed eo, quo viros probos fortesque deceat, modo : non scelere et flagitiis, prout illi ; sed vera virtute apertoque bello. Perdomandos eos, non in impietate imitandos scelestissimos hostes. Nec, rem recte reputantibus, aequum esse, ut qui apud se captivi essent, adeoque suorum parricidii ne conscii quidem, aliorum peccata innocentes luant. Fidem illis datam rem esse sanctissimam, et in hoste etiam servandam. Nunquam eos in se admissuros, quod in hostibus abominarentur. Tempus affore, quo, justissimo Deo, ejusque in illis locis vicario, Domino Regi, meritas daturi essent poenas. "Interea vero capita nostra licitentur, Assassinos conducant, immittant sicarios, fidem faciant, fallantque ; nunquam tamen efficient, ut aemulatione scelerum, ac non sola virtutis gloria, cum illis contendamus."

Huntilaeus vero, cui nihil minus in animo fuit, quam quod praesenti Montisrosano promiserat, trajecto Spaea, Moraviam ingressus, procul Innernesso tempus tantummodo viresque inutiliter et indecore terebat. Enimvero praedae spoliisque nimium intentus, cum agros esset populatus, incerta fama accepit, provinciales aurum, argentum, et pretiosiora in quibusdum turriculis et obscuris arcibus condidisse. Quas dum ille frustra oppugnat, nec ullis mandatis precibusve ab instituto dimovetur, hostes immisso commeatu (qua parte arcere illos in se susceperat), Innernessum rerum omnium copia confirmarunt. Quod si ille impediisset, ut cum Montisrosano pactus fuerat, praesidiarii brevi spatio fuissent ad deditionem compulsi. Cumque jam nuncium accepisset Montisrosanus Mideltonium hostilis exercitus praefectum cum equitibus sexcentis et peditibus octingentis Aberdoniam usque venisse, et Huntilaei Gordoniorumque agris populandis imminere, Wilielmum Stuartum, militum tribunum, ad Huntilaeum misit, qui eum denuo ad Innernessi obsidionem secundum pactam fidem invitaret. Sin hoc illi minus arrideret, propter vicinum agris suis hostem, persuaderet saltem, ut junctis cum eo copiis una in illum confestim tenderent: quem levi discrimine debellandum fore non dubitaret. Ad quae contemptim ille respondit; se rebus suis consulturum; nec ad arcendos finibus suis hostes opera aut auxilio Montisrosani indigere. Post decem denique hebdomadas in obscurae cujusdam turriculae obsidione consumptas, promptissimo quoque suorum militum desiderato, re infecta, obsidionem solvere cum summo dedecore coactus fuit. Nec tam in Montisrosani quam in Regiae Majestatis contumeliam, ad Spaeam amnem, nec consulto nec conscio Gubernatore, retrocessit: pessimo omnibus exemplo, qui frequentes nec sine animi ardore ad partes Regias sese accingebant.

Inter quos opibus, potentia, et satellitum clientumque multitudine eminebant Seafordius Comes, Resius Regulus, et ab ultimis insulis Iacobus Makdonaldus Eques, potentissimae in montanis antiquissimaeque familiae princeps, Maklenius, Glengarius, Makranaldorum (ut illi loqui amant) dux, aliique plurimi; qui hactenus in Montisrosani castris, alii cum copiis suis erant, alii suas accersiverant. Atque adeo ante elapsum mensem Martium in inferiora Regni descendere potuisset Montisrosanus, cum longe majoribus copiis, quam hominum memoria eduxissent Scoti. Verum insperata tanti viri defectio non minus animos perduellibus ad perseverandum in rebellione addidit, quam viris probis et in Regem pronis offendiculo fuit, ac terrori: unde factum est, ut illi quorum copiae in castris jam erant, clam se subducere, caeteri vero moras causasque nectere inceperint. Quae quidem omnia Montisrosanum ad nova redegerunt consilia. Statuerat enim (quando lenitate et officiis apud homines plerosque vanos, leves, incertos, nec sibi satis constantes parum proficeret) authoritate, vi armorum munita, et poenarum severitate ad obsequium pertrahere: et in eum finem, cum fidissima et promptissimorum militum expedita manu, montanos omnes et septentrionales, vel invitos, ad militiam cogere. Plurimos enim provinciarum praefectos, principes familiarum, ducesque sibi obnoxios habebat; quibus pergratum fore hoc consilium probe noverat. Nec dubitavit Gordoniorum praecipuos potentissimosque viros, utpote patroni sui pertaesos, operam sibi locaturos, vel contra Huntilaei sententiam, si res ita postularet. Mitiora tamen quaeque experiri prius statuit, quam severum illud et ultimum adhiberet remedium.

Quoniam vero Innernessum erat totius septentrionis praesidium, maximi ad bellum momenti, portusque excipiendis auxiliis externis commodissimus, nihil aeque in votis habebat, quam ut illud in suam redigeret potestatem. Cum copiis igitur, quas apud se habebat, obsidione illud cinxit. Hostilis enim exercitus sub Mideltonii imperio supra octoginta milliaria aberat; et Huntilaeus Gordoniique in medio itinere sub signis interjecti erant. Montisrosanus propterea denuo cum Huntilaeo egit, ne tempus inutiliter tereret, sed prout convenerat, ad obsidendum Innernessum copias cum suis jungeret; vel saltem non procul a Spaea contineret, qua hostibus trajiciendum foret, eosque transitu arceret, si ad solvendam obsidionem progrederentur, aut ubi trajecissent, junctis secum viribus, eosdem debellaret. Ad omnia ille usque adeo contumeliose respondit, ut Gubernator omnem de eo spem ponere coactus fuerit: cautiusque sibi prospiciendum censuerit, ne tandem ab eo proderetur. Enimvero Huntilaeo diffisus, turmas equitum tres ad vada Spaeae remisit, qui hostes sedulo observarent, et si adventarent, frequentes certosque mitterent nuncios. Et illi sane occupatis ad speculandum commodissimis stationibus, diligenter invigilarunt: quoad Ludovicus, Huntilaei filius, qui Rothusiam arcem cum praesidio tenebat, facinus omnibus, quae hactenus patrasset, magis pudendum commentus est. Praefectis equitum illorum, quos ad observanda Spaeae vada Montisrosanus collocaverat, fidem fecit hostes quam longissime dissitos, nihil minus in animo habere, quam ad solvendam obsidionem amnem transmittere: atque adeo eis (qui amicissimum illum fidissimumque putarent) persuasit, ut posthabita, ad quam destinati erant, inutili speculatione, ad arcem suam reficiendis corporibus se reciperent: et ad convivium, quod in eorum gratiam instruxerat, blandissimis verborum lenociniis invitavit. Et illi quidem male creduli ad eum profecti sunt. Quos prolixa benignitate prosecutus, praeter nimis opiparas dapes, vinum, et quam vocitant, vitae aquam large promi jussit. Multisque facetiis et operosa humanitate tantisper detinuit, quoad Mideltonius cum validissimo equitum peditumque exercitu Spaeam transmisit, longeque penetravit in Moraviam. Quod cum rescivisset, eos tandem dimisit, et cum cachinno his verbis valedixit; "Ite," inquit, "ad imperatorem vestrum Montisrosanum, ferocius nunc quam in clade Selkirkana invadendum." Hostes interim recta in Montisrosanum et celeriter tendebant;

## CAP. XX.

quos equites illi aegre praetervecti, simul ferme cum illis Innernessum pervenere, adeo ut primi agminis hostilis speciem prae se ferrent: eos vero universae Mideltonii copiae intra tormenti jactum insequebantur. Verum, sic providente benignissimo numine, Montisrosanus aliunde monitus, hostilem adventum praesenserat; paululumque ab urbe digressus, copias coegerat in unum. Atque ubi hostes equitatu multis partibus superiores est conspicatus, evitata planicie se cum suis trans Nessum recepit. Hostes in postremum invecti agmen, et fortiter excepti, sese etiam continuere. Perexigua ac utrimque ferme par fuit jactura. Montisrosanus praeter Beuliam in Rossiam profectus est: quo insecuti illum sunt hostes, ut in planicie, iniquo solo deprehensum, ad conferendas manus cogerent vel invitum. Verum praeter hostium vires suis longe majores, locorum incolae infidi et inconstantes, et novi illi cum Seafordio auxiliarii catervatim signa deserentes, eum commoverunt, ut quam primum seque suosque ab hostili expediret equitatu. Qua propter lacum Nessi praetergressus per tractum Glassae, Harragaeque ad Spaeae ripam provectus est.

Statuerat Gubernator in Hutilaeum tanquam in publicum hostem animadvertere, nisi resipisceret; verum mitiora omnia prius experiri, si qua ratione ad saniorem mentem reduci posset. Quem in finem, assumpta ad custodiam corporis unica duntaxat equitum turma, celerrime confectis viginti milliaribus, ad Bogiam ejus arcem contendit. Et in itinere praemisit, qui eum de suo admoneret adventu, certioremque faceret, non alia de causa illuc sine copiis advolare, quam ut plurimum illi impertiret salutem, et de summa eorum quae ad rem Regiam facerent, cum eo consilia communicaret; quod eo desideraret vehementius, quia recentes Oxonia literas a Rege accepisset, quas illi erat explicaturus. At vero Huntilaeus primo adventantis Montisrosani nuncio perculsus, usque adeo tanti hominis praesentiam perhorruit, ut dicto citius cum unico comite equum conscenderit, et aufugerit, qua sese offerret via; nec hospitio quidem aut colloquio vicarium Regis Gubernatorem dignatus. Quod ubi rescivisset Montisrosanus, eadem viginti milliaria remensus, eodem die vi. Kal. Junii ad suos est reversus: inque hoc magis magisque incubuit, ne tam pertinax Huntilaei contumacia innotesceret, aliisque noceret exemplo. Sed frustra haec fuere; Gordonii enim ipsi aliique ejus amici, viri plerique probi et omnino generosi, cum indignatione et diris in ejus caput omnia propalarunt; quo sic indigni flagitii infamiam a se ipsis amolirentur.

Nec dictu sane facile est, quantum ejus viri exemplum septentrionales alios concusserit. Seafordius Comes, aegerrime et sero ad partes pertractus, vacillare putabatur: nec desunt qui dicant, illum nondum satis confirmatum, consilia etiam tum clam agitasse, de ineunda cum foederatis amicitia; quod tamen equidem non crediderim. Ipse etiam Alexander

Makdonaldus, nescio quid causatus, quamvis multum serioque invitatus, de die in diem nihil quam ingratas nectebat moras. Quae quidem res et dubiam de eo ancipitemque evulgavit famam: utpote illum, quamvis infensissimum Argathelii hostem, Hamiltoniorum tamen amicitia et patrocinio fretum, Makdonaldorum res privatas impendio curasse, de publico parum solicitum. Quae quidem cum Montisrosanus animo volveret, sine ulteriore cunctatione statuit, cum promptissima ut expeditissima manu, regiones omnes montanas et septentrionales praesens obire, milites conscribere, obsequentes animare; renitentes vero severitate legum et praesentibus poenis ad officium pertrahere: et quod valetudinariis infantulis fieri solet, vel invitis et reluctantibus salutem impertire. Nec deerant idonei ministri, qui ad hoc suam deferrent operam, eumque impensius hortarentur.

Dum ista ad Innernessum gerebantur, Huntilaeus, ne nihil unquam suis auspiciis et sine Montisrosano gessisse videretur, Aberdoniam, quam praesidio quingentorum militum Mideltonius tenebat, expugnavit quidem, sed cum suorum majore quam hostium damno. Praeter enim non exiguam militum fortissimorum jacturam, civium bona montanis suis diripiendis permisit. Atqui vero ex qua parte de Rege et de ipso Huntilaeo innocui illi Aberdonenses male meruerint, judicent illi, qui plerosque omnes noverint, fidei et obsequii in Regem nomine inter aequales eminuisse. Hostes vero armis belloque captos, qui et multi et in suis erant melioris notae viri, supplici blandientique quam victori similior, intactos, et integros, sine ullius pacti lege aut conditione dimisit. Nec cum plures militum tribunos et equestris ordinis viros, qui forte fortuna Aberdoniae fuere, in potestate sua haberet, vel hoc unum curavit, ut suorum quemvis redimeret, quorum non pauci arctissimis vinculis erant onerati in Scotia, vel in Anglia durissimam serviebant servitutem; semper scilicet ille hostibus quam amicis gratificari paratior.

## CAP. XXI.

Montisrosano in illa intento pridie Kal. Junii occurrit a Domino Rege (qui, nescio quo fato, se in gremium foederati Scotorum exercitus ad Novum Castrum conjecerat) fecialis cum mandatis, quibus imperatum erat, ut quamprimum positis armis, exercitum dimitteret; se ipsum vero reciperet in Galliam, inibi ampliora ejus mandata praestolaturus. Ille vero, inopinato nuncio attonitus, tristi Regis sorti (quae eum in infensissimorum hostium manus praecipitasset) efflictim indoluit. Mandata etiam illa de solvendo exercitu Regi dolo, vi, et armis conjuratorum, in quorum manibus erat, extorta fuisse non dubitavit. Verum quid consilii? si obsequium

## CAP. XXI.

praestaret, suorum bona direptionibus, cervices securibus aut restibus permitteret: sin armatus contra Regem ageret ejusque mandata, fieret perduellionis reus, quod crimen in aliis vindicandum susceperat. Ad haec vel maxime illud pertimuit, ne perduelles Regi imputarent, quae ipse exsequeretur; duriusque de eo statuerent, quem in sua haberent potestate: quod ipsae Regis literae non obscure innuebant.

Nobiles ergo, familiarum principes, et Equestris ordinis viros, in unum cogere decrevit Montisrosanus, ut arduum illud negotium, et quod omnium intererat, communi consensu transigeretur. Quem in finem, insuper habitis tot injuriis, Ioannem Urraeum, Ioannem Innesium Equites, eminentissimos in exercitu suo viros, eosdemque Huntilaeo, ut arbitrabatur, gratissimos, ad eum ablegat, qui illum ad tam seriam consultationem invitarent: diei vero locique praestituendi Huntilaeo deferrent potestatem: et praeterea adderent, paratum esse Montisrosanum ad ejus arcem se conferre, si hoc ille cuperet. Respondit Huntilaeus, Regis literas ejusdem argumenti ad se quoque perlatas esse; quibus omnino obtemperare statuerit: mandata Regis ejus generis esse, ut secundas non admittant cogitationes, nec superesse amplius consultationi locum. Regerentibus vero illis, eundem forsan esse Montisrosani animum, promptissimam quidem Regis mandatis, sed liberis, exhibere obedientiam; interim tamen omnium plane interesse, ut mature incolumitati suae et suorum prospiciant; majori fama et authoritate apud ipsos etiam hostes fieret, si in commune consulerent, ille non aliud respondit, quam se sibi hactenus consuluisse; cum aliis nihil esse negotii.

Montisrosanus igitur ad Regem responsa dedit, quibus sollicite admodum inquirebat de ejus apud conjuratos conditione; utrum tutum se in eorum potestate judicaret? atque an deinceps quoque utilis illi esset opera sua? Ac si omnino statuisset dimittendum esse exercitum, qui pro ejus salute militabat, armatis adhuc in utroque Regno conjuratis, et ferocius indies insultantibus, quo tandem pacto vitae bonisque fidissimorum et fortissimorum civium prospiceretur, qui sanguinem et carissima quaeque pro eo prodegissent? horrendum enim fore, si praestantissimi viri saevissimis hostibus non modo spoliandi, sed et excarnificandi permitterentur. Ad ista nihil aliud palam responsum fuit, quam quod ab internuncio exhibitae fuerint leges quaedam a conjuratis scriptae, quibus scilicet Montisrosano acquiescendum foret. Verum ille leges ab hostibus latas easdemque iniquissimas indignabundus rejecit; nec rem cum eis omnino transigere dignatus, denuo internuncium remisit ad Regem; testatusque est se, non nisi ipsius Regis jussu bellum illud suscepisse, nec ut arma poneret, a quoquam mortalium, quam ab ipso Domino suo accepturum leges: adeoque supplicem rogare, si ita visum sit Regi, ut quamprimum copias suas dimitteret, ne gravaretur ipse conditiones dicere, et signare; quibus, ut ut durioribus forsan, obsequentissimum se fore promisit : aliorum vero omnium, quicunque demum illi fuerint, mandata despicere.

Reversus denique internuncius leges manu Regis signatas retulit, cum mandatis jam tertio repetitis, quibus illi imperatum est, ut sine omni cunctatione dimitteret exercitum : idemque Regis nomine interminatus est poenam Majestatis, si vel tantisper detrectaret imperium. Ad Regis mandata accessit, quod qui belli societatem inierant, plerique clam et seorsim per amicos cum conjuratis de pace agebant : quod de Seafordio Comite et aliis non obscuris indiciis cognitum fuit. Huntilaeus Aboiniusque non tantum sese profitebantur apertos Montisrosani hostes, sed et minabantur insuper se armis vindicaturos, nisi confestim Regiis obsequeretur mandatis. Antromius vero recens ex Hibernia in montana Scotiae delatus, sine milite, sine armis, hoc agebat, ut montanos omnes, cognatos scilicet affinesque suos, a castris Montisrosani (quem inferioris Regni praefectum superciliose nuncupabat) ad sua revocaret ; intempestiva plane ac suis omnibus in locis illis exitiosa secessione. Quae quidem omnia rite pensitata Montisrosanum compulerunt, ut secundum Regis mandata exercitum dimitteret.

Et sane moestissimus fuit ille dies, quo militibus suis pro concione laudatis et animatis valedixit. Ut ut enim ille bono eos animo esse jusserit, et optatissimae pacis spem non exiguam affulgere praedicaret ; nec minus se optimi Regis saluti praesenti obsequio, quam praeterita fortitudine consulere, occurrebat tamen omnium animis, Regiae authoritati ultimum fore illum diem ; mandata enim illa praesentioris mali metu invito Regi quasi extorta, omnes certo statuebant. Et quamvis incolumitati suae quoquo modo scriptis legibus prospectum foret, maluissent tamen durissimo fungi fato, quam calamitosae carissimi Regis sorti segnes et viles superesse spectatores. Nec minimum generosos angebat viros adversa gentis ad exteros posterosque fama ; quasi Scoti in universum omnes foedissimae conspirationis participes una ab optimo defecissent Rege. Praesentem porro luctum maxime auxit cogitatio de fortissimo Imperatore, iniquo prorsus fato, Regi, patriae, sibi, bonisque omnibus erepto. Adeo ut ad ejus genua provoluti milites, obortis lacrimis deprecati sint, ut, quando ita Regis salus postularet, illique omnino Regno excedendum foret, se quoque in quascunque orbis terras una traduceret. Paratos enim esse, qui sub ejus imperio ubivis gentium viverent, militarent, et (si sic Deo immortali visum foret) sponte morerentur. Nec sane pauci statuerunt, vel cum manifesto bonorum vitaeque discrimine, invitum quamvis ac ignarum prosequi, operamque in ignotis gentibus ultro deferre, quam amplius navare non possent in afflictissima patria.

Legibus, quas Rex ex sententia foederatorum praescripserat, cautum imprimis fuit, ut Montisrosanus ante Kal. Sep. Scotia excederet : illi vero

## CAP. XXI.

instructa navigia cum commeatu et armamentis necessariis suppeditarent abeunti. Agebantur vero illa ad Kal. Sextilis; destinatusque est portus Montisrosarum in Angusia, quo et eis mittenda essent navigia, et unde illis solvendum foret. Ac Montisrosanus quidem, quo omnem querelae materiam praecaveret, suspicionesque amoliretur, familiaribus tantum suis et amicis plane paucis comitatus, illuc se contulit, expectavitque navigia. Hoc potissimum tempore infensissimi ejus hostes callidos fictosque rumores per idoneos ministros spargi curarunt: quibus fidenter admodum asserebatur, non permissuros Regni Ordines (ut sese nuncupabant) tam egregium civem patria expelli. Pernecessarium enim fore tanti viri praesentiam, praesertim si clementissimus Rex, qui ultro in Scotorum manus se quasi tradidisset, jus et aequum ab Anglis non posset obtinere; adeoque bello illud et armis repetendum foret: praestantiorem quippe ducem nullum exhibuisse saeculum. Et sane sanctissima fuerunt illa plurimorum vota, qui in profunda conjuratorum consilia non penetrabant: sed longe illi alias artes, alios nectebant dolos. Quid enim in Regem meditati fuerint, tristis perdocuit eventus: Montisrosano vero indignas struebant insidias. Hoc enim agebant, ut ejus modi blandimentis et inani spe lactatum, ac ultra dictum diem in Regno commorantem, tanquam rupti foederis reum, cum minore infamia opprimerent.

Elapsus ferme erat Sextilis, cum ne nuncius quis, nec levissima de navibus et commeatu perlata esset fama. Quapropter Montisrosanus (quamvis ad diem a Rege dictum eundi certus) quo foederatorum animos penitius excuteret, amicis suis permisit, ut de proroganda navigatione cum eis agerent. Verum cum hi incerta et dubia retulissent, ille nihil quam dolos fraudesque eorum verbis subesse merito judicavit. Accessit (atque hoc non leviter auxit suspicionem), quod novissimo tandem praestituti temporis die, pridie scilicet Kal. Sep., navigium ad portum Montisrosanum appulerit. Navarchus non modo ignotus, sed et conjuratorum propugnator rudis, ac pertinax: nautae militesque ejusdem farinae homines, infensi, morosi, ac minabundi; navis ipsa nec commeatu instructa, nec apta ad navigationem. Adeo ut cum Montisrosanus paratum sese ostenderet, juberetque ut quamprimum explicarent veta, navarchus responderit, dari oportere dies aliquot picandae ornandaeque navi; nec prius audere sese ventis undisque committere. Magnifice deinde de se suaque navi locutus, exhibuit diploma sibi a foederatis traditum, quo mandatum erat, ut vectores ad certos et ab hostibus designatos portus, nec alios quosvis deveheret. Simul Escae amnis ostio (quod Montisrosanum efficit portum) indies obversabantur ingentes armataeque Anglorum naves, in gratiam conjuratorum, optatissimae inhiantes praedae; ne quo pacto vitaret dolos.

Verum nec Montisrosanum latuerunt insidiae, nec defuere in foederatis ipsis amici, qui eum repetitis nunciis admonuerunt: infestum Anglicana classe mare, nec evadere incolumem posse in Galliam aut Bataviam: obsessum ferme portum, unde illi esset solvendum, ideoque navigationem rem esse periculi plenam : nec utique aliud ab hostibus quaeri, quam ut vel trahentem in Patria moram foederati Scoti, vel abeuntem, inermem et incautum, conjurati Angli opprimerent. Censuere qui cum Montisrosano erant amici, in tam manifesto discrimine, repetenda Regni montana, revocandos confestim socios, et belli aleam insidiosae paci utique praeferendam. Verum ne hanc iniret rationem, ardentissima praesertim Regis caritate distinebatur. Certo enim constabat bellum denuo renovatum Regi, quamvis immerito imputandum fore, eundemque in periculum quidem praesentissimum et forsan extrema quaeque praecipitaturum. Undique ergo pressus, insidiis hinc in suum, inde in sacrosanctum Regis caput structis, in se omnia convertere pertinaci constantia decrevit. Nec temere tamen, quasi de salute in rebus ultimis desperasset; sed prudenti consilio se subduxit.

Cum enim hostium percepisset artes, pridem miserat, qui oram maritimam portusque septentrionem versus diligenter scrutarentur: ac, si quam externam navem in illis deprehenderent, cum navarcho proposita agerent mercede, ut ad certum diem paratus ad navigandum, vectores, qui illi praesto forent, in Norvegiam cum bono Deo deferret. Commodum in portu Stanhyvio repertus est actuarius lembus Bergensis e Norvegia; cum ejus praefecto sine magno negotio transactum est: avide enim occasionem ac quaestus spem arripuit. Atque istuc ablegavit Montisrosanus Iohannem Urreum Equitem, Iohannem Drumondum de Balla, Henricum Graemum fratrem, Iohannem Spotswodium, magni illius Roberti ex fratre natum, Iohannem Lilium, expertae fortitudinis et peritiae ducem, Patricium Melvinum, eodem nomine virum clarum, Georgium Wiseheartum, S. S. Theologiae Doctorem, Davidem Gutherium, juvenem generosum et fortem, Pardusium Lasoundium Gallum, olim nobilissimi Gordonii Reguli asseclam, postea in gratam defuncti heri memoriam a Montisrosano in famulitium suum adsumptum, Rudolphum natione Germanum, probum fidumque adolescentem, cum paucis insuper servulis. Et hos quidem selegit, quos secum duceret, in quascunque demum descenderet terras, ea praesertim de causa, quod illorum plerisque infensiores nosset foederatos, quam ut vel tantillam in patria moram trahere possent incolumes. Et illi quidem iii. Non. Sept. adspirantibus ventis cursum in Norvegiam auspicati sunt. Eadem vero vespera Montisrosanus ipse, uno Iacobo Silvio, Evangelii praedicatore meritissimo, comitatus, lembum extra portum Montisrosarum anchoris alligatum, exigua vectus celoce, conscendit: vilique amictus veste patronus, pro clientis Silvii famulo fefellit. Anno Domini CIƆIƆCXLVI. aetatis vero suae XXXIV.

## PARS SECUNDA.[1]

### CAP. I.[2]

MONTISROSANUS Bergami[3] in Norvegia a Thoma Graio Scoto, arcis Regiae pro tempore praefecto, comiter quidem susceptus fuit, summoque in honore habitus: paucis vero post diebus itinere terrestri, eoque difficillimo, per juga montium ardua, inculta, horrida, multaque semper rigentia nive, Christianam[4] regni caput pervenit. Inde conscenso ✳[5] navigio in Daniam vela fecit. Ejus Serenissimum, ac beatae nunc memoriae Regem, utpote Caroli Regis ex sorore geniti avunculum, amicum certissimum et fidissimum, Christianum, visendi vehementi flagrabat desiderio. Verum quia ille tunc in Germania aberat, Montisrosanus propere transfretato Balthico, sese illuc contulit, et peragrata (opportunitatem loci secutus) ✳[6] Hamburgi paulisper quievit: praesagiebat enim animus conspiratos Scotorum proceres, qui in exercitu ad Novum castrum obtinebant imperium, cum conspirantibus secum Anglis, de perdendo, aut in ordinem redigendo rege quamprimum consensuros: dicebatque, tam probe notum sibi esse istorum hominum ingenium, ut nullis unquam rationibus ab ea sententia divelli potuerit. Multum vero rebus suis conferre posse existimabat, si facinus istud descensum suum praeveniret.[7] Augurabatur enim, peracto hactenus scelere, gratiorem sese futurum apud illos, ad quos Rex eum ablegasset; qui immanitate rei permoti, sese tandem ab insidiosis perditorum promissionibus (quibus plus satis fidebant) forsan expedirent. Experientia insuper edoctus, minime dubitabat nova bella, novos sibi imminere

---

[1] The text of this part is derived from the two MSS. in the Advocates' Library, Edinburgh—a folio, here marked D, and a MS., in the hand of Robert Wodrow, referred to in these notes as E. For some account of these MSS., and the evidence they contain of *lost MSS.*, *v.* Crit. Introd. The first translation of this part, published in 1720, is referred to as Tr. 1 in these notes; Tr. 2 denotes the revision made for Ruddiman in 1756, reprinted by Constable in 1819.

[2] The whole of this chapter is wanting in D.——[3] As though the name of this city were Berghem? But perhaps W. wrote *Bergani* (?). The old name of Bergen was Bjorgvin.——[4] *Christianiam?*
——[5] The lacuna of one word in E was supplied in the Tr. 1 by the word *Malstrand*, which appears as *Maelstrand* in Tr. 2. No such place exists. The port was undoubtedly *Marstrand*, a small town on an island near the mouth of the Göta river, about 140 miles south of Christiania (*v.* Index). The insertion of a name so unlikely to suggest itself to the translator is evidence that he had before him a MS. now lost, or the missing Ch. I. of D (?) (*v.* Cap. II., n. 46, and Crit. Introd.).
——[6] Lacuna of one word; read *Holstenia*. The Tr. 1 again supplies the word "Holstein."
——[7] *impreveniret*, E (without *suum*). There is no such word. The sense requires *suum*, a word

hostes; pessimum nimirum illud hominum genus principumque pestem assentatores aulicos et parasitos, qui calumniis et sycophantiis assuetis, in perduellium gratiam confictis,[8] viam illi omnem aditumque ad optimae Reginae gratiam praecludere conarentur, nec per istos licere, ut vel consiliis intersit, vel rerum gerendarum agnoscat rationes; metuentes quippe ne, detectis eorum artibus et dolis, perduellium quidem conatus redderentur inanes; illi vero nefaria proditionis mercede frustrarentur.

Ubi tandem tristis illi perlatus est nuncius nummos conjuratis Scotorum ducibus (stipendii sane, quod turpiter merebant, nomine, ad elevandam pudendi criminis infamiam) numeratos, traditumque simul et semel [militibus][9] istis belluis Anglis Regem, Montisrosanus continuo in Hollandiam excurrit, tempestivum jam fore ratus tam praesenti Regis sorti, quam virtuti decorique suo, si semet palam exhiberet, ad remedium aut levamen aliquod rebus usque adeo deperditis adferendum. Quo enim magis boni illi viri Regem optimum Regumque omne deprimebant nomen, eo hic erectior et majore animo ad asserendam et vindicandam ejus libertatem dignitatemque ferebatur: nec aliud illi quam cotis instar fortitudinem fidemque viri exacuebant.

Maria, Magnae Britanniae Regina, Henrici quarti Gallorum Regis filia, Lutetiam Parisiorum sibi quidem praesidium invenerat: Marito vero subsidium frustra ferme quaerebat. Enimvero, quamvis omnium Regum principumque res ageretur in rebellione ista Britannica, pessimumque exemplum in alias nationes initiaturum videretur, et in Galliam praesertim intentaret minas, perpauci tamen laboranti Carolo vel minimas ferre suppetias animum induxere. Galli vero (seu veterum cum Anglis inimicitiarum memores, seu quod Britanniam ad Hispaniarum Regis amicitiam proniorem putarent, aut aliis quibuscunque de causis alienati) mala ejus etiam laeti spectabant, flammasque quas accenderunt,[10] fovebant oleo, ipsis forsan olim nocituro.

Lutetiam vixdum fama perlatum fuit, Montisrosanum per Belgicam illuc adventare, quum solertissimi illi apud Reginam artifices, qui nihil aeque ac praesentiam ejus formidabant, omni conatu coeperunt eandem declinare. Delectus est Iohannes Ashburnhamius,[11] Regis cubicularius (idemque infaustus ejus prius ad Scotos ac postmodum ad insulam Vectim comes et deductor), qui cum literis ablegatus iter ejus averteret a Gallia. Obvius hic factus suadere occipit, ut Scotiam confestim repeteret, et bellum ibidem

---

easily obscured after "descen*sum*." Tr. 1 suggests the correction.──[8] E has no lacuna here; but Tr. 1 adds the words "to whom they were obnoxious," an absurd mistranslation, but showing that the MS. used by that translator contained the words *quibus obnoxii erant* (a favourite phrase of W.'s), *i.e.*, "to whom they were under obligations." The error is carelessly repeated in the later editions, though it was corrected in the list of *errata* in Tr. 1.──[9] *nunsitibus* (?), E, a "*vox nihili.*" Tr. 2, "to the brutality of the English army," which suggests *militibus*, in accordance with the historical fact.──[10] *accenderant?*──[11] *Ashburnnamius*, E here and elsewhere.

absque milite, armis, comitatu, stipendio, renovaret; data (sic sane videtur) opera, ut tot tantisque casibus objectum perderent, conatusque ejus omnes pro Rege redderent inutiles.

Insidiosa consilia minimo labore detexit Montisrosanus, et, repertis dolis, respondit, gratissimam quidem sibi fore provinciam illam, verum, prout tunc erat rerum status, nondum suscipiendam; nihil sibi eorum, quae ad bellum renovandum essent necessaria, suppetere, nec a Regina suppeditari;[12] amicorum ac Regi etiam fidissimorum animos recenti et ingrata armorum positione et iniquis pacis legibus fractos; occupata in regno illo a perduellibus omnia, et revocatum ex Anglia instructissimum exercitum, oppressum Huntilaeum, ac funesta Gordoniorum clade caeteros territos, nihil plane ausuros; insuper imperatum sibi a Rege (cui repugnare nefas duxerit) ut in Gallia mandata ejus ampliora expectaret; satis etiam persuasum esse non illam esse reginae mentem, ut Regia tam leviter negligat temnatque mandata; ubi vero semel Parisiis semet ostentaverit, debitumque Majestati Regiae praestiterit obsequium, novo sese eoque insigni honore cumulatum iri, si quid muneris quantumvis ardui ac difficilis a lectissima Regina illi imponeretur.

Ashburnhamius, ubi hac non successit, alia illum aggressus est via, serioque egit, ut sibi tandem consuleret, pacem et amicitiam cum conjuratis iniret, seque suosque melioribus conservaret fatis; obtulitque ultro, se a Rege veniam et facultatem, vel, si hoc praeoptaret, jussa etiam procuraturum, ut cum iisdem quacunque ratione[13] transigeret. Retulit Montisrosanus mortalem esse neminem qui paratior esset Regi suo justa et honesta praecipienti morem gerere; sed ne Regi quidem indecora, iniqua, ipsique Majestati exitiosa jubenti obtemperaturum.

Inferioris Germaniae provinciis, nomine et authoritate Hispaniarum Regis, praeerat Leopoldus Archidux; cujus bona cum venia Montisrosanus per Flandriam in Galliam profectus Lutetiam pervenit. Expectatiorem ad Serenissimae Reginae aulam venisse neminem plerique omnes judicabant; longe tamen aliter incidit. Presbyterianorum enim ac praesertim Jerminii Reguli (qui gratia in aula plurimum valebat) opera factum est, ut tanti viri dignitatem authoritatemque elevarent, ac quibuscunque possent modis deprimerent. Montisrosano Jerminius clam infensior erat hac imprimis de causa: quo tempore Carolus Rex se suaque omnia conjuratis Scotis ad Novum castrum crediderat, ut illis in omnibus satisfaceret, eorumque animos et amicitiam conciliaret, Montisrosanum jusserat exercitum dimittere. Responderat hic, iniquissimum illud fore, nisi sibi prius caeterisque proceribus, qui optima fide regi militassent, caveretur,[14] et ex Regis ordinumque

---

[12] suppeditari *posse?* "it was not in the Queen's power," Tr. 1.——[13] raᵉne, E.——[14] caveretque, E.

regni sententia honoribus, dignitatibus, agris, bonisque (quibus per summum nefas spoliati fuerant) restituerentur. Hoc Argathelius aliique perduelles (qui cum Montisrosano apertas gerebant inimicitias, ejusque simul et metuebant virtutem, et agris bonisque ditescere cupiebant) aegre tulere; nec facile consensuri videbantur. Montisrosano quidem aequa petenti gratificari volebat Rex clementissimus; verum, si invitis istis aliquid extorquere contenderet, capitis sui rem esse non dubitabat. Conversus igitur ad illum enixe rogabat, ne postulatis ejusmodi pertinaciter inhaereret, vitamque et salutem Regis sui imminenti subjiceret periculo; benigneque promisit, se ejus rationem habiturum, si quando libertati ac regno restitueretur. Interea vero honori ejus, dignitati, rebusque necessariis providisse; suadere peteret Galliam, atque ibidem legati extraordinarii munere apud Regem Christianissimum fungeretur; diploma sese literasque praemisisse, quibus munitus et instructus provinciam istam capesseret. Et quo honorificentius eandem administraret, curaturum, ne quid ad amplissimae dignitatis ornamentum desideraret, quoadusque ipse pristinam recuperaret authoritatem, eundemque, propitio numine, revocaret in patriam. Haec[15] Jerminio, qui legatum ordinarium ibidem agebat, ingrata fuere ac molesta: pertimescebat enim ne quid emolumenti aut honoris sibi cuncta ad se rapienti tanti viri interventu decederet. Eisdem igitur artibus aulicis, quibus Norvicensem Comitem non ita pridem eodem gradu dejecerat, et Montisrosanum arcere non destitit.

Nihil sane prius expectabat Montisrosanus, quam ex mandato Regis literas istas ac diploma ad se delatum iri. Verum eorum nihil in aula Reginae auditum esse referebatur, nec[16] ejus generis ulla ad eos pervenisse mandata; clam tamen Ashburnhamius indicavit, Regis quidem illam esse mentem, eandemque aulae certo certius constare, seque in illum praesertim finem ante trimestre in Galliam praemissum: verum Jerminii arte, opera, et gratia fieri, ut nihil gratum acceptumque sit aulae, quod potentiam ejus imminuere, aut commodum ullatenus laedere posse videatur.

Sensit Montisrosanus tam Regis mandata, quam postulata sua aequissima negligi et contemni: verum in vilibus istiusmodi certaminibus aulicis sordescere ac languere generosum pertaedebat animum. Reginam ergo interpellavit, rogavitque supplex, ut clementer monstrare non gravaretur, si qua in re utilem gratumque illum Domino Regi judicaret; ab ejus enim imperio (marito jam in custodia detento) totum pendere, paratumque esse jussa ejus comiter capessere, et vel sanguinis sui, vitaeque dispendio, summa cum fide et industria exsequi.

Regina ad haec anxie respondebat, nec sese expediebat satis. Virum etenim nobilem et optime de Majestate meritum fovere et erigere volebat,

---

[15] hoc, E.——[16] *haec*, E.

quoties suo ingenio permittebatur: verum aulicorum, qui Presbyterianorum opes viresque nunc minaciter, nunc blande praedicabant, quasi praestigiis irretita, in aversa abripiebatur, eundemque variis et quando repugnantibus [17] sententiis distinebat.

Audendum esse aliquid, quo perduelles absterrerentur, ne quid in salutem Regis molirentur, semper arbitratus est Montisrosanus; nec penitus ab hac sententia abhorrebat Regina; sedulo tamen cavebant aulici, ne quis sumptus ad stipendia, aut arma, aut viaticum, suppeditaretur. Obtulit indentidem Montisrosanus, semet cum decem armatorum millibus [18] in Britanniam descensurum, et cives, captivi Regis flagitium sponte detestantes, ad vindictam pronos, ad arma concitaturum, si nummorum aureorum (quos Galli pistolas vocant) sex duntaxat millia numerarentur; utque persuaderet, fidem suam vitamque, et famam omnium carissimam opponebat pignori. Sed et irrita haec omnia fuere, renitentibus nimirum helluonibus istis aulae; quorum profusissimae luxuriae quidquid reliquum fuit in Reginae thesauro perexiguum videbatur.

Interea ipsi illi conjurati perduelles (qui et primi infando foedere contra Regem sese obstrinxerant, armaverantque Scotos, et Anglos hactenus quietos ad eadem nefaria concitaverant arma, Regemque suum in tot coegerant angustias, ac denique eundem, conspirantibus secum Anglis, in certam [19] tradiderant perniciem) insigni fraude ac impudenti clam Montisrosano Reginam aggrediuntur. Prae se ferebant male se habere Regis sui captivitatem; fefellisse fidem Anglos, qui polliciti essent de eo nihil durius statuere, inconsultis foederatis Scotis: horum itaque mentem esse eundem justis armis in libertatem et pristinum splendorem asserere, si modo Ipsa eorum opera non dedignaretur, et rata haberet quae in ejus gratiam meditarentur, ac authoritate sua comprobaret; supplices itaque Reginam rogare, ut, pro longe maxima et meritissima gratia, qua apud Regem maritum valebat, Eidem consuleret et suaderet, totum sese fortunasque suas eorum fidei et virtuti committere; spondere insuper nihil illos inausum aut intentatum relicturos, nec labori unquam aut sanguini parsuros suo, aut discessuros ab armis, quoadusque ille avito impositus solio Britanniae suae restitueretur imperio.

Optima Regina, sed male credula, ejusmodi verborum lenocinio, quasi fascino quodam illaqueata, facile adducta est, ut fidem adhiberet, operamque suam (quam et praestitit) polliceretur. Montisrosano ista celari volebant; verum clandestinae negotiationes eorum non diu latuere. Ubi vero tandem

---

[17] *quandoque pugnantibus*, E.——[18] All previous translators omit *decem*. Tr. 2 notes it as in "the Latin MS.;" but the Lat. for "with 1000 men" is not *armatorum millibus*, but *cum mille armatis*; and Montrose at this time had great hopes of foreign aid, and certainly counted on raising more than the 1500 men he did actually land with in Scotland. It was his genius to be sanguine.——[19] *incertam*, E.

consilia ista evulgari oportuit, professa est apud eum Regina, tot tantisque malis, quae hactenus essent perpessi, majoribus vero ac longe gravioribus [quae][20] indies ingruerent et imminerent, victam se, victum etiam et Regem ad foederatos istos, tanquam ad secundam[21] post naufragium tabulam, confugisse, et in hac sententia firmos immotosque stare, seque suaque omnia fidei illorum permittere.

Montisrosanus (qui nullis umquam rationibus adduci potuit, ut crederet perfidos istos et suis tot sceleribus irretitos bona sinceraque fide cum Rege agere) ubi carissimum Principem vidit insidiosis hostium promissionibus confisum in profundissimum miseriarum barathrum ruere, lacrimas aegre cohibere valuit; composito tamen utcumque ac sedato vultu in haec ferme verba Reginam affatus est: "Serenissimae Majestatis est ea decernere, quae in rem vestram maxime conducant; nostrum vero est debitum promptumque obsequium exhibere; sane me [ipso][22] obedientiorem invenies neminem; officii tamen nostri ducimus, et malorum, quae Regi Regnisque ab isto consilio impendere videntur, tempestive admonere, et remedium adferre, ejusmodi saltem, quale res in ultimo discrimine positae admittere poterunt aut expectare. Satis, ut opinor, constat, ab initio istorum tumultuum bonos illos viros plus quam hostili odio et saevitia Regem persecutos esse, eundemque primos invitum militari custodia detinuisse, aditum negasse in patriam, et prodidisse Anglis; necdum a fidelium subditorum carnificina cessare, quos, eo solo nomine, avaritiae aut crudelitati suae jugiter immolare non desinunt; nec[23] sane per[duelles istos][24] omnium perditissimos[25] resipuisse vero simile nobis videtur, quos avaritiae et ambitionis stimuli, cum anteactorum scelerum conscientia, eodem semper urgeant et pellant, nimirum ut in uno laesi Regis exitio spem impunitatis securitatisque suae omnem reponant. Ultimum hoc (ut nobis quidem videtur) superest remedium, ac quasi fraenum aut capistrum indomitis belluis injiciendum, ne ad extremum pro libidine saeviant: liceat nobis (quibus ob fidelem operam Regi hactenus praestitam, nullus ad amicitiam cum conjuratis ineundam[26] relictus est locus) authoritate et diplomate Regio munitis et instructis exercitum conscribere: delectum faciamus ex Scotis illis reliquis, qui ob fluxam meritoque suspectam conjuratorum fidem, sub istorum hominum imperio nunquam sponte militabunt: sint copiae hae nostrae prioribus illis Angliam ingressis, si honeste et sincere rem gerant, quasi subsidiariae. Si vero (quod maxime metuendum est) ad indolem ingeniumque suum reversi, perturbare omnia et regem denuo prodere

---

[20] The sense requires *quæ*, omitted in E, owing to the *quæ* in the preceding line (?)——[21] This finely expressive word is omitted in Tr. 1 and Tr. 2. Montrose himself was the other "plank." The Queen had "two strings to her bow."——[22] *Me imo*, E.——[23] *ne*, E.——[24] *per*, with a blank of two words, E. Tr. 1 suggests the emendation.——[25] *Proditissimos*, E.——[26] *in eumdam*, E.——

aggrediantur, terrori illis erunt, et vel in officio conservare, vel tumultuantes aut deficientes in ordinem cogere valebunt. Quod ad nos attinet, sane vel illis,—si [27] sero, sed serio, et ex animo, ad regem redeant,—imperium, laudem, decus, gratias, omnemque ultro promittimus mercedem: nobis vero labores et aerumnas discrimina tantum deposuimus et pericula, quae, si optimo Domino ac Regi profutura videantur, neutiquam erunt ingrata.

Presbyteriani sollicitando et pollicitando, blanditiis et grandeloquentia, Reginae animum vana spe usque adeo repleverant, ut saniora Montisrosani consilia prorsus contemneret, suamque Mariti et liberorum salutem solis illis crederet, qui et malorum omnium praecedentium fuissent authores, et plura adhuc et graviora essent procreaturi. At ille, ne vel tanti flagitii impius videretur particeps, vel ignavus spectator, rogavit obtinuitque a Regina veniam, ut Lutetia abesse, et ruri animum relaxandi curandaeque [28] valetudinis gratia paulisper degere liceret.

---

[27] *quo*, E.——[28] *ruri anum relaxandi curanda in*, E.

## CAP. II.[1]

QUONIAM quidem in Presbyterianorum nec non et Independentium, novorum hominum, ac nova sibi assumentium nomina, mentionem saepius nobis incidendum erit, legentibus haec, exteris praesertim, forsan non ingratum nec ab instituto nostro alienum fuerit, paucula de iis praefari.

Usu ferme venit, ut qui a recto tramite regiaque via desciverint, in [2] plures eosdemque devios ac invicem contrarios et se mutuo intersecantes calles incidant ac incedant. Hoc sane superstitiosis novatoribus (qui reformandae religionis praetextu ecclesiam regnumque non perturbarunt modo, sed et prorsus evertere) accidisse, tristi experientia compertum est. Enimvero post legitimos ecclesiae rectores exactos, calcatam disciplinam veterem, deformatum supremi numinis cultum, excussosque summo cum sacrilegio magistratus, in innumeras illi infandasque sectas et factiones abiere, quibus sunt nomina mille, mille nocendi artes. Omnes tamen in duas quasi familias, Presbyterianorum nimirum, et Independentium, qui ambitu suo cunctas comprehendunt, distribuere licet. Primi Presbyteriani sic nuncupari volunt a novello quodam regimine ac disciplina (aut carnificina magis) ecclesiastica, superioribus saeculis inaudita, quam speciosa[3] quidem sed falso et ementito Presbyterii nomine apud vulgus efferunt. Hi in Synedrum[4] illud quod

---

[1] Here the folio MS. commences. Where not otherwise stated, the readings preferred are those of the folio (D), much the better MS. of the two in every respect (*v.* Crit. Introd.).——[2] *ut*, E.——[3] *speciosa*, E.——[4] *Synedrium*, E.

Presbyterium vocant, de populo quosque sibi addictissimos, mercatores, agricolas, fabros, nautas, sartores, veteramentarios et cerdones, nullis initiatos sacris, cooptant: quibus suffragii jus idem cum ipsis pastoribus esse volunt, eosdemque presbyteriorum laicorum aut regentium nomine insigniunt: annuus his regentibus magistratus est. Inter Ecclesiae pastores omnimodam esse debere paritatem dictis quidem astruunt, destruunt factis; perpauci enim aura populari vulgique acclamationibus praelati, in alios, non fratres tantum, sed et regni proceres, adeoque ipsum supremum magistratum plus quam Manliana[5] exercent imperia. Quae ecclesiastici juris sunt, omnia ad Presbyterium deferunt; et in[6] ordine ad spiritualia, vel sub notione scandali aut offendiculi, humana divinaque omnia. Synodos Provinciales et Nationales (quas illi appellant Generales), quae superiora quaedam sunt Presbyteria, ex eodem aere conflata, inconsulto ac invito etiam supremo Magistratu, convocant. In istis de rebus gravissimis Rempub.[7] quam maxime spectantibus non modo deliberare ac disputare, sed et decernere audent, ac resistentibus, contradicentibus, anathemata dirasque excommunicationum intentare durissimis[8] istis diris animas corporaque mortalium in impuri spiritus manus tradi docent: et hac ratione non modo plebem misellam[9] et rudem, sed et primores mirum in modum territant. Cum excommunicatis commercium omne et consuetudinem aliis interdicunt, atque ita servos a dominis, a parentibus liberos, conjuges a maritis, plebem a magistratu, nullo negotio divellunt ac dirimunt.[10] De religione aut levissimo ejusdem ritu aliter sentientes, exilio, carcere, ferro flammaque, et ultimis suppliciis persequendos censent; maxime tamen saeviunt in eos qui Presbyterii jus divinum pernegant. Si vicinus quis invisus illis fuerit, in facta omnia dictaque tam anxie et sollicite inquirunt, ut pauci admodum apud eos tuti et securi degant. Optimates, principes, adeoque et reges ipsos etiam coram in concionibus[11] acerbissime proscindunt, dicteriis calumniis onerant, invisos plebi vilesque reddunt, ac vexant impune, et hoc nomine apud populum gratiam et authoritatem aucupantur, ac eidem prophetico se spiritu afflatos esse persuadent. Nihil rite fieri praedicant ne in comitiis quidem regni, quod Presbyterii calculo non fuerit approbatum; ab uno Presbyterio judicari posse et debere Presbyteros, idque privilegium jure divino illis concessum esse dictitant, adeoque in eos seditionem quamvis rebellionemque concitantes nisi a Presbyterio praedamnatos magistratui nullum animadvertendi[12] jus esse asserunt. Ut sane quam longissime abeant a reformatae ecclesiae in Belgio et Palatinatu classibus, consistorioque Genevensi; hi enim magistratum civilem qua par est rever-

---

[5] *in auliana*, E. The expression is derived from L. Manlius Torquatus, proverbial for severity (*v.* Cic. Fin., 2, 32, 105).——[6] *cum*, E. Tr. 1 apparently read *omnia ad Synodos*, without stop.——[7] *Remp.*, E.——[8] *dirissimis*, E.——[9] *imbellem*, E; but Tr. 1, "the poor populace."——[10] *derimunt*, E.——[11] *conscionibus*, E.——[12] *animadvertenti*, E.

entia et obsequio colunt, et ab ejus nutu pendent; illi contemnunt, contradicunt, impugnant, tumultus cient, armatamque in eum immittunt plebem, quam diris superstitionibus ac juramentis obstrictam tenent. Ut denique verbo dicam, omnium ordinum hominibus graves sunt, superbi, avari, tumidi,[13] ac supra tam antiquos Druidas quam recentes pontificiorum[14] inquisitores intolerabiles,[15] ac saevi.

Presbyterianis foetum suum catulosque genuinos,—mali nimirum corvi, malum ovum,—subjicimus Independentes, quos sic dictos autumo, quod superiorem a quo dependeant,[16] agnoscunt neminem. Imperatores enim, reges, pontifices, episcopos, presbyteria, synodos, concilia, quantumvis libera et generalia, tanquam Antichristiana[17] et diabolica commenta, rejiciunt, execrantur et damnant. Et hi quidem sicut ab aliis omnibus mortalibus tanquam pollutis et profanis semet separavere, sic et illi in innumeras fere nationes[18] et familias dispersi ac discerpti sunt, quod accidisse omnino oportuit unionis et societatis conservandae vincula omnia violenter disrumpentibus. In hoc tamen mire inter eos convenit quod alii alios tolerandos, nec aliter de religione sentientes graviori poena quam segregatione[19] a sacris corrigendos conseant. Perfidia, avaritia, sacrilegio, crudelitate, et odio in magistratus, qui illis non fuerint obnoxii, cum presbyterianis consentiunt et contendunt. Ordines ecclesiasticos, manuum praesertim impositionem (cujus speciem aliquam Presbyteriani videri volunt retinere) hi tanquam malorum Daemonum inventum, ritumque magicum abominantur. Sacrorum ministros populus[20] creat, quosque heri constituere, hodie destituunt: intra privatorum conventuum parietes omnia ad cultum divinum regimenque ecclesiasticum spectantia concludunt: literatos omnes literasque, tanquam Christianae pietatis hostes, oderunt cane pejus et angue: praedicantem libenter audiunt neminem, qui se spiritu afflatum non profiteatur; in precibus temere effutitis multiloquium, gestusque magicos, oculorum vultusque distortiones, clamores horrendos,[21] et incondita omnia, tanquam certissima praesentis Spiritus pignora, laudant et mirantur. Anabaptistae fere omnes sunt: nuda utriusque sexus corpora fluminibus immergunt: Eucharistiam foedis et infandis modis polluunt: praeter Arianam haeresin[22] aliasque ejusmodi impietatis, Carpocratianorum, Adamitarum, Gnosticorumque omnium deliria[23] et obscoenitates ab Orco in orbem revocarunt egregii illi reformatores saeculi. Pontificios solos, cum illis qui cultum divinum in Liturgia[24] Anglicana praescriptum sequuntur, carcere, exilio, bonorum direptionibus, ferro et flamma puniendos censent, illis tamen quam his indulgentiores, cum

---

[13] *mundi*, E.——[14] *pontificorum*, E.——[15] *intollerabiles*, E (*v.* n. 36).——[16] *dependent*, E.——[17] *Antechristiana*, E.——[18] *factiones?* "factions and parties," Tr. I.——[19] *segragatione*, E.——[20] *populis*, E.——[21] *horendos*, E.——[22] *Arrianam haeresin*, D; *arianam heresin*, E.——[23] *diliria*, E.——[24] *Lethirgia*, E. [This by Wodrow, a theologian, in the days when the Liturgy was still a burning question!]

alios omnes quos haereticos [25] vocant, Turcas etiam [26] Judaeosque ferendos putent. Populi (quo nomine, secretis regibus principibus et proceribus, infimam tantum plebem intelligunt) jure divino in omnium vitas fortunasque imperium esse dictitant; et in hoc sane sicuti in plerisque aliis cum Presbyterianis sapiunt, nisi quod illi populo verbis attribuunt, reapse arripiant ad Presbyterium,[27] cujus placitis universum populum subjiciunt.

A primo Britannicorum tumultuum ortu Presbyteriani Independentes istos, quod numerosiores essent, tanquam [28] carissimos fratres filiosque impense coluerunt,[29] quorum operam utilem ad publicum hostem (regem ita nefarie appellabant) [30] perdomandum censuerunt. Homines enim, ut illi opinabantur,[31] fatuos et insulsos ad eorum castra quam primis transituros, aut renuentes vi ac dolis facile pertrahi potuisse putabant, ac inani illa lactati spe, eosdem modis omnibus fovere, amplecti et erigere non dubitarunt: nihil non illis indultum est, in Senatorum in Comitiis ordinem plerique cooptati sunt, alii dignitatibus aucti ad summos honores aspirare juvantur, centuriones alii, alii tribuni militum creantur, munitissimarum urbium, navalium, arcium praesidia illis traduntur, ac quaestuosissimis denique praeficiuntur provinciis; adeo ut sensim invalescentes [32] patronis suis Presbyterianis suspecti, et formidabiles esse inceperint,[33] qui sero nimis viperam se secum in sinu [34] gestasse deprehenderunt: quae justo numinis judicio debita illis persolvit nutritia, et mortales fallacissimos merita fefellit fraude, legesque dare, non accipere est ausa.[35] In infandi istius foederis (quod et sacram nuncupant ligam) arcanis, ultimum non erat quod in mutuam tolerationem,[36] quoadusque debellatum foret, quasi postmodum de controversiis inter eos ortis amice [37] essent disceptaturi, fraudulenter utrinque consensum est. Nunquam Independentes ferre Presbyteriani, nunquam Presbyterianorum tyrannidem pati Independentes, animum induxere. In Scotia Presbyteriani potiores sunt, Independentes in Anglia: ita tamen ut longe plures Scoti qui Presbyteriani audiunt Independentibus, rerum jam in Anglia potitis, quam Angli Presbyterianis faveant.

Presbyterianis Anglis regem a conjuratis Scotis traditum, et militari ac indigna custodia in arce Holmebaea [38] detentum, Independentes vi aperta eripuere, et hoc facinore quid tandem possent auderentque eosdem edocuerunt; furibundi [39] hi, fremere, indignari,[40] Dei hominumque fidem implorare,

---

——[25] *hereticos*, E.——[26] *etiam*, om. E and Tr. 1, "even Turks and Jews," Tr. 2.——[27] *presbiterium*, so regularly, and in all cognate words in E throughout.——[28] *tantquam*, E.——[29] *coluere*, E.——[30] *appellebant*, D.——[31] *oppinabantur*, E.——[32] *valescentes*, E, the *in* dropped by confusion with *im* in *sensim*.——[33] *incæperint*, (sic), D; *incaeperunt*, E.——[34] om. *se* and *in*, E.——[35] Awkwardly mixed metaphor. The remainder of this paragraph, from *In infandi* to the end of the next, *probavit eventus*, is omitted by Tr. 1 (was the passage lacking in his MS.?), but given in the Tr. 2.——[36] *tollerationem*, and so always, and in all cognate words in E.——[37] *amice*, om. D; "in an amicable and friendly manner," Tr. 2.——[38] *Holmebea*, E.——[39] *ffuribundi*, E, and wherever F occurs.——[40] *indignare*,

## PARS II.—CAP. II.

minitari[41] vindictam: ovantes illi et opima potiti praeda, victis quasi insultare, ridere, despicere, nec minas, sed armatas intentare manus. Mirum sane fuit quot quibusque dolis certaverunt. Utraque pars Regis causam tueri simulabat, libertatem, honorem, decus et regnum aequis legibus restituendum praedicabat, dolebat ab iis qui eundem detinerent, male haberi, indigne cum illo agi,[42] nec Regem modo, sed et partes ejus secutos[43] omnes amice in gratiam recipiendos praedicabant; aliter certam ac solidam pacem quam boni omnes ardentibus votis expeterent, minime coalituram. Hujus generis plurima publicis scriptis testabantur,[44] et praecipue Independentes.[45] Primus in iis Cromwellius in exercitu imperatori Fairfaxio legatus datus. Oculatiores tamen tum pervidebant,[46] nihil horum in mentem illis unquam venisse, neutiquam enim quae pars liberati assertique Regis[47] decus adipisceretur,[48] sed quae tandem de eo tanquam justis armis subacto triumpharet, et triumphati potiretur imperio, omne inter illos fuit certamen. Et sane aliquantisper Regem minus acerbe tractarunt Independentes, ac spem bonam cum eo de pace[49] multis fecere. Servis non paucis, Capellanis praesertim ac Sacrorum ministris (quod a Presbyterianis nullis precibus[50] impetrare potuit) aditum praebuerunt. Cultum divinum in Liturgia[51] praescriptum (quo ad extremum vitae spiritum unice[52] delectabatur) permiserunt; Scotos ad salutationes et colloquia absque testibus admisere. Proceribus regni aulicisque nonnullis[53] qui ei in bello etiam adhaesissent, visendi facta est copia; debitaque majestati in multis exhibita est reverentia. Verum insidiose concessa fuisse ista ab Independentibus, quoad vires factionis suae, oppressis aemulis, tam in castris, quam in comitiis auctiores firmioresque evaderent, tristis probavit eventus.

Presbyteriani Angli gradu moti, spe dejecti et quasi capite diminuti ad Scotos veteres socios confugere, et eorum implorarunt opem, fore pollicentes, ut ubi primum illi armati et Angliam ingressi fuerint, cives plerique omnes, Independentium tyrannidem[54] pertaesi, ad eos convolarent. Scoti ad bellum Anglicanum proni, oblatae occasioni non defuere, remque ad Regni Comitia detulerunt. In his, omnibus ferme expeditionem decernentibus, de belli tamen causa et exercitus duce sententiis variatum est: nam[55] alii volebant Independentium perfidiam, qui foederis et sacrae ligae conditiones violassent, ac per quos staret, quod (vi et armis oppresso jampridem Episcopatu)

---

E.——[41] *minitare*, E.——[42] *agere*, E.——[43] *sequutos* and compounds, D, E, and in all editions of Part I. throughout; so also *loquutus*, &c.——[44] *testabuntur*, E.——[45] *praec. Ind.*, om. E.——[46] *etiam*, E; *praevidebant*, D. The Tr. 1 follows D in *tamen*, but E in *pervidebant;* a further proof that the translator used a MS. now lost (*v.* Cap. I., Crit. nn. 5, 6).——[47] *regus*, E.——[48] *aedipisceretur*, E.——[49] *in eum de pacis*, E, careless copying; the *-is* of *pacis* due to *multis*.——[50] *praecibus*, D.——[51] *Leiturgia*, E (*v.n.* 24).——[52] *amice*, E. "to which he professed his firm adherence," Tr. 2.——[53] Om. *nonnullis*, E, "many of the officers," Tr 2; did the translator read *multis* in his MS.?——[54] *tyrannidem*, D.——[55] *Illam*, E. *perfidiam*, sc. *belli causam esse*.

regimen Presbyterianorum in Anglia nondum fuerit stabilitum. Argathelius cum suis, qui et seditiosissimos quosque ministros ad eandem [56] pertraxerant sententiam, hanc unicam volebant. Alii, in quibus Hamiltonii fratres principes fuere, ut ut [57] illam quidem causam belli praecipuam agnoscerent, hanc tamen addi etiam voluerunt, quod Rex, contra fidem ad Novum castrum Scotis datam, iniqua, indigna ac dura premeretur [58] custodia; quem justis armis in libertatem asserendum, et ad personalem tractatum (ut loqui solebant) cum regni sui ordinibus, vel invitis Independentibus, perducendum existimarent. Haec conciliandis animis, aucupandisque eorum suffragiis qui regi favebant, magnifice Hamiltonii prae se ferebant et praedicabant. Argathelius vero cum mancipiis suis, egregiis istis presbyteris (qui orbis et saeculi reformatores audiunt), de rege nihil audiebant, quem, tanquam pervicacem, et in impietate sua contra Presbyterium obstinatum, deserendum prorsus et immanissimis hostibus permittendum judicabant. Et hi quidem ad Synodum Nationalem, illi vero ad Ordines regni provocant.

Bina confestim, diviso in regno, suprema eriguntur tribunalia, eademque adversis frontibus arietantia. Hinc quidem diras, anathemata excommunicationis,[59] inde vero carceres, exilia, bonorum direptiones, flammam ferrumque intonant. Misera plebs superstitione et metu agitata distrahitur; nec ipsis proceribus in illa rerum confusione, quomodo se gerant, satis constat. Hamiltoniani in Comitiis superiores, ex eorum sententia exercitum conscribendum curant instructissimum; militibus duces sibi addictissimos imponunt; stipendia, arma, commeatum a civibus exigunt, cunctaque ad expeditionem maturandam sedulo comparant; ac majorem denique Hamiltonium (renitentibus plerisque ob suspectum ejus in Regis animum) Supremum copiarum omnium Imperatorem inauspicato [60] creant. Argatheliani [61] in Synodo potiores, ejus decreto expeditionem illam ab ordinibus regni imperatam,[62] damnandam execrandamque pronunciavere. Nec armis tantum suis, spiritualibus nimirum illis, populum perterrefecere, sed et plurimos in occiduis praesertim regni partibus, palam tumultuari, et ad arma temere rapienda exstimularunt.[63] Istos multitudine sua fretos et ab egregiis istis praeconibus tanquam numine afflatis animatos, imbelles quamvis ac militiae parum assuetos, Mideltonius [64] non sine discrimine compescuit. In captivis non pauci deprehensi fuere ministri, caligati quidem, et in primis ordinibus ferociter depugnantes, quibus ab Hamiltonio, Presbyterorum gratiam aucupante, flagitium illud, cum aliis laesae majestatis criminibus, inultum [65] fuit et impunitum.

---

[56] *eundem*, E.——[57] *ut* E, but *ut ut* is a favourite expression of the author.——[58] *praemeretur*, D, E.——[59] *excommunicationes*, E, with a comma after *anathemata* (but the punctuation of this MS. is extremely bad and unintelligent), followed by Tr. 2, "anathemas and excommunication."——[60] *In auspicato*, E.——[61] *Argatheliam*, E.——[62] *impetratam*, E.——[63] *extimularunt*, E.——[64] *Midletonius*, D, which comes nearer the English *spelling;* but in Part I. the name is spelt as above, namely, as it is *pronounced* (v. Cap. IV., n. 56).——[65] *multum*, E; cf. Cap. VI., n. 32.

Eisdem temporibus in longe maximam Comitiorum regni contumeliam et invidiam, Synodici illi viri solemne per omnem Scotiam indixerunt ac celebrarunt jejunium, cujus causam potissimam dixere, ordinum regni a vera rectaque religione Apostasian et defectionem, quod regem aequioribus conditionibus restituendum arbitrarentur. Hamiltonius Dux Presbyterianum se palam professus, libellis ad populum emissis, declarabat ac testabatur velle se enim[66] foedera solemnia sacramque ligam sartam tectam, contra omnes mortales conservari, et in hunc imprimis finem conscriptum esse cui imperabat exercitum. Omnes vero regias hactenus secutos partes, ac illos praesertim qui sub Montisrosano olim meruissent, longe ab omni dignitate et munere[67] militari arcebat; clam tamen et illis bonam faciebat spem, aditumque ad honores pollicebatur,[68] ubi primum Angliam fuisset ingressus. Et ille quidem hac ratione utriusque partis viris placere se posse putabat; quod neutiquam tamen consecutus est, tam illis quam his suspectus et invisus.

---

[66] *velle enim*, E. The above reading of D seems corrupt; *velle se ex animo* (?)——[67] *muneri*, E.——[68] *pollicibatur*, E.

## CAP. III.

Ad delectum quem in Scotia fecerat accuratissimum,[1] Hamiltonius ex Hibernia etiam veteranorum militum sub imperio Georgii Monroi, ducis[2] strenui,[3] non contemnendam manum advocavit. Calendarium Comitem, quem legatum illi regni ordines dederant, virum bellis tam extra quam intra insulam innutritum,[4] ac militaris peritiae nomine clarum, secum in Angliam[5] avexit; fratrem in patria reliquit, subsidia, si res postularet, tempestive allaturum. Omnibus denique secundum animi sententiam compositis, fortissimo milite, peritissimis ducibus stipatus,[6] armis ac commeatu abundans, auxiliariorum in Anglia certus, cunctorum opinione tamen lentius tardiusque procedebat; nec defuerunt sane qui clamitarent, tempus inutiliter teri, armari animarique hostes, occasionem rei bene gerendae quasi e manibus elabi, regiarum partium viros in Anglia, qui hactenus essent in armis, hostibus turpiter tradi, Regemque ipsum denuo prodi indecora illa et intempestiva cunctatione. Constat quidem Hamiltonii pollicitationibus fisos, auxilio viribusque fretos, Anglos quam plurimos, in non paucis regni provinciis, Wallia imprimis, Cantio, ac Cornubia, sub ducum regiorum imperio, praepropere ad arma convolasse, quod denique tam in Regis, quam illorum perniciem cessit.

---

[1] *acuratissimum*, D, E.——[2] *Ducis*, D.——[3] *Shemij*, E.——[4] *virum . . . innutritum*, om. E, for which it has only *innutatum et eductum*.——[5] *Anglia*, E.——[6] *stipatis*, E.

Ad Limites tandem progredienti obvii fuere borealium partium Angli non pauci, fortitudinis fideique in principem nomine clari, quique in illis regionibus illustres apud suos[7] plurimum valebant. Hi sese ultro adjungunt, ac in certissimam fidei et constantiae tesseram ac pignus, Bervicum Carleolumque oppida[8] munitissima Independentibus dudum erepta in manus ejus tradunt, eductisque quos imposuerant praesidiariis,[9] praefectum militesque accipiunt Scotos. In his Philippus Musgravius, Marmeducius Landelius, equites, aliique viri nobiles, qui gratia, authoritate, opibus, clientelis et rerum gestarum gloria eminebant, ad publicas consultationes, in quibus de rebus exigui ferme momenti disceptabatur, advocari solebant: ab arcanis consiliis, ubi graviora tractabantur negotia, procul aberant; haec cum paucis in conclavi peragebantur. Per agrum Eboracensum, utpote cujus incolae propensioris essent in regem animi, iter capesendum dicebant Angli, hominum, locorum, viarumque in patria Scotis longe peritiores. Per Lancastriam, cujus provinciales Presbyterianis addictiores noverat, ducere maluit Hamiltonius, cui quidem solemne fuit, neglectis regiis, istius factionis viros fovere et extollere. Monroum cum validissima tam equitum quam peditum manu infelici consilio in Westmoria subsistere jussit; Marmeducium etiam cum suis, non adeo multis quidem, sed fortibus ac fidis Anglis, seorsim a Scotis viam carpere[10] et castra metari voluit. Agmen vero suum longe lateque per villulas vicosque rusticos supra viginti milliaria dividi ac dissipari permisit. Quum vero contra omnes militaris disciplinae normas turpiter peccaret, ne sine ratione insanire videretur, obtendebat, se hac ratione colonis et inquilinis amicissimae provinciae consulere, et rem frumentariam, pabulationem, aquationem lignationemque militibus faciliorem ac commodiorem praestare. Hostium interim, quos acerrimos habuit et singula belli momenta diligenter observantes, securus fuit; adeo ut ille, qui alias quidem, multorum judicio, vir prudens ac providus, ac insidiarum versatissimus habebatur artifex, magno suo, regis regnique malo, inconsultus (ne quid dicam gravius) imperitus et infelix fuerit imperator.

Independentes interea,[11] qui regem vi ac dolo in Vectim[12] insulam pertractum suae potestatis fecerant, Londinensem civitatem turrimque Presbyterianis eripuerant, eosdemque tam Comitiis quam castris exegerant, facti rerum domini larvam tandem deposuerunt: nec minus his quam illi infensi ex aequo presbyterium et Monarchiam proterendam sibi et calcandam proposuere.

Fairfaxius imperator tumultuantes in Cantio et Essexia cum regiis Presbyterianos sibi debellandos assumpsit: quos, utpote imparatos, incompositos, absque ductoribus tyrones et bello inutiles, nullo ferme negotio

---

[7] *quos*, E.——[8] *opida*, D, E.——[9] *Praesidiis*, D.——[10] *capere*, E.——[11] *Interia*, E, here and often.——[12] *vectam*, E.

compescuit. Colcestria tamen, parum licet munita, Regiorum ducum et Lucasii imprimis Liliique virtute ac constantia, in omne aevum memoranda, hominum opinione diutius obsidionem toleravit. Cromwellius Legatus non absimili successu Scotos, in Lancastria sub Hamiltonii imperio secure degentes, improvisus adortus est. Primum ejus impetum exceperunt Angli illi, quibus Marmeducius dux; et hi quidem diu multumque strenue depugnavere,—quoad hostium multitudine oppressi et ferme circumventi, ac deficiente pulvere sulphureo, et desperato[13] quod frustra ab Hamiltonio petiverant subsidio,[14] fuga sibi consulere coacti fuerunt. Cromwellius de ordine et disciplina ab Hamiltonio observata per transfugas probe edoctus, et victoriae quidem facillimae[15] certa spe erectus, equitatum, quo maxime pollebat, ingenti[16] impetu in medium agmen immisit. Hamiltonius rei militaris ignarus, subitaneo hostium incursu perculsus et attonitus[17] ac consilii expers, in oppidum[18] Prestonam se cum copiis quas habebat recepit; nec illic (metu vel fato agitatus) se continuit, verum ne expectato quidem suorum adventu, qui nullis acciti nunciis, nulloque certo ducti imperio, ultro tamen alacresque ad famam rei ex agris ad eum convolabant, eadem nocte urbem hostibus permisit, et superato fluvio (cujus pontem nullo praesidio munitum Cromwellius confestim occupavit) desertis pedestribus copiis, equestrem indecoram et inutilem capessivit fugam. Pedites, Bailaei ducis exemplo et mandato, abjectis turpiter armis, victoribus semet tradidere. Equitum alii ad Monroum se receperunt, plures Imperatorem fugientem secuti sunt, et assecuti. Supererant[19] illi adhuc supra tria expeditorum equitum millia, qui trium aut quatuor dierum itinere confecto, refectis viribus, et procul a tergo relicto hoste, audendum aliquid etiamnum arbitrabantur. Aliis ad Monroum per medios hostes tentandam esse viam, aliis in Walliam ad regios, qui adhuc in armis erant, progrediendum videbatur; omnes ferme foedissimam captivitatem vel honesta morte praevertendam censebant. Unus tamen et solus Imperator belli aleam[20] esse dicebat et humiliter amplexandam,[21] nec urgentibus fatis recalcitrandum:[22] nullam in armis spem esse; de hostium clementia minime desperandum, promptamque deditionem unicam esse ad salutem viam. Quoniam vero Cromwelliani cum militibus duces non supervenerant, cum obscuri cujusdam praesidii praefecto transigere festinat; cum quo vitam pactus, semet ille cum suis dedere parabat. Vix ex inquilinis et agricolis tumultuario delectu quadringentos coegerat iste nescio quis praefectus, quibus Hamiltonius sese cum tribus instructissimorum equitum millibus traditurus erat, quum Stanfordianum[23] Comitem

---

[13] *despirato*, E.——[14] *subsidia*, E.——[15] *facillime*, E.——[16] *pollebat ingenti*, E.——[17] *atonitus*, E.——
[18] *opidum*, E, and so often.——[19] *assequuti superarunt*, E.——[20] *eam*, E.——[21] *amplexendam*, E.——
[22] *recucitrandum*, E.——[23] *Stamfordianum* (?).

(alii Lambertum tribunum aiunt) supervenisse nunciatur. Hujus potestati et arbitrio, iisdem legibus quas praefectus iste dixerat, se suosque submisit, et quam minima interposita mora in carcerem detrusus [24] fuit. Calendarius Legatus (in quem amissi exercitus et malorum omnium culpam Hamiltoniani [25] conjiciunt, utpote cui disciplinae [26] militaris curam, omnemque in castris potestatem imperator demandaverat) tantum dedecus aversatus, paulo honestiore consilio larvatus [27] Angliam peragravit, et navigium nactus, evasit in Belgicam. Captivorum opulentiores libertatem pretio redemerunt; nonnulli, elusis aut auro corruptis custodibus, effugere. In gregarios milites immani ac Christiano nomine indigna barbarie saevitum est, quos exiguo plane pretio* mangonibus venundatos ad vilissimum et durissimum servitium in Novi Orbis insulas deportarunt.

Monrous quique cum eo cladi Prestonianae [28] superstites erant, ab Hamiltonio juniore Lanricensi Comite continuo revocantur in patriam. His non procul a regni limite amicos, clientes, et regiarum partium viros magno [cum] numero adjungit. Angli etiam non pauci viri nobiles operam suam sponte offerunt, sive in Scotia, sive in Anglia bellandum foret, contra perduelles fortiter depugnaturi, et eandem cum illis utriusque fortunae sortem libentissime subituri. Proceres qui regi praesertim favebant, coactis undique auxiliis, accurrebant [29] ipsi, aut per idoneos ministros pronos animos promptamque operam denunciabant; adeo ut copias contraxerint, quae tam Cromwellio, si Scotiam forte invaderet oppugnando, quam Argathelio, si quos domi concitaret tumultus, coercendo sufficerent. Verum deerat copiis dux. In solemni ergo consessu quum de novo Imperatore in captivi Hamiltonii locum sufficiendo ageretur, frater Lanricensis ambitiosius [30] quam par erat, provinciam illam quaesivit, et renitentibus quam plurimis, invasit potius quam obtinuit. Rosburgius [31] Comes multae vir experientiae, domi nobilis, et illis in locis longe potentissimus, modesta [32] et gravi oratione contradixit, eundemque obnixe rogavit, ut in carissimi Regis patriaeque periclitantis gratiam, ab intempestiva istius dignitatis petitione abstineret. "Rebus," aiebat, "integris constat nuperam infelicem [33] istam in Angliam expeditionem multorum animos offendisse, et visam esse quasi inauspicatam, idque ea tantummodo causa, quod illustrissimus ille tuus frater imperator fuerat renunciatus. Defuisse illi fidem in rebus regiis administrandis, immerito (ut ego quidem existimo) non pauci asseruere: sane defuisse semper fortunam nemo negaverit, a quo in aestimandis ducum actionibus, humana

---

[24] *detractus*, E.——[25] *Hamiltoniam*, E; cf. Cap. II., n. 61.——[26] *disciplina*, E.——[27] *Labartus*, or *lavartus*, E.——[28] *prestonanae*, E.——[29] *accurrebat*, E.——[30] *ambitiosus*, E.——[31] *Roxburgius*, D, but spelt as above in E, and Part I.——[32] *modesti*, D, mislead by *gravi*. One of the rare instances in which E has the better reading. Om. *et* E.——[33] *infaelicem*, D, and so regularly in Part I.

* At 2s. a head! Carte's Ormond Papers, i. 177.

(perperam quamvis) pendent plerumque judicia, et recentem validissimi exercitus jacturam, cum tam insigni nominis nostri contumelia conjunctam, etsi ego libenter aliorum ignaviae, aut iniquioribus fatis ascribendam censeam, sat compertum tamen est plerosque de populo (quorum nobis gratia in hoc rerum momento modis omnibus concilianda venit) longe aliter sentire quam mihi eloqui fas sit. Quod si vero tu, Comes nobilissime, fratri tuo quasi succenturiatus substituare, clamabunt illico exacerbati et exulcerati animi de rege Regnoque conclamatum esse: eandem enim fratrum mentem, eadem consilia, eosdem conatus, eundem plane sortituros eventum. Supersunt e procerum numero plurimi viri, graves fortesque, ac rebus agendis apti, quorum majores copiis regiis non sine decore et gloria imperitaverint:[34] advocandum ex iis aliquem, et vel invitum copiis hisce praeficiendum censeo. Equidem (si sic venerando consessui[35] videatur) ad supremum imprimis regni Mareschallum, virum aetate et opibus florentem, majorum gloria et familiae splendore nemini secundum, a suspitionibus et factionibus alienum, et (quod minime praetereundum est) munus istud neutiquam ambientem, provinciam illam commendandam judicaverim."[36]

Quotquot proceres ducesque praesentes aderant, pedibus in Rosburgii sententiam ivere; quoad usque Lanricensis, magnificentius de virtutibus suis locutus,[37] et minitabundus dixit[38] minime passurum, absente jam fratre, copiarum istarum imperium a quocunque e manibus suis ereptum iri. Rosburgius, et cum eo alii qui prudenti et perspicaci mente, quo ista tandem evaderent, praevidebant, maesti ac soliciti domum sese receperunt, nec exinde rebus perturbatis et palam in perniciem ruentibus semet immiscuere.

Nihil Lanricensi Scotiam ingresso antiquius fuit quam honestissimos fortissimosque istos auxiliarios Anglos dimittere: quia, ut prae se ferebat, peregrino[39] et externo milite cinctus, Scotorum suorum animos offendere et irritare nolebat. Bonam interim mutui consilii et auxilii faciebat spem, quam illi irritam fallacemque demum experti sunt. Magno deinde apparatu, cum literis nuncios[40] in cunctas regni partes emisit, quibus omnes omnium ordinum viros, proceres praesertim et familiarum opulentiorum ac potentiorum principes, ad arma fortiter prompteque rapienda hortabatur: partem quidem fraterni exercitus, cum duce strenue repugnante, aliorum ignavia aut perfidia amissam, potiorem tamen etiamnum salvam esse et ductu suo magnis animis militare; obnixe itaque rogare, ut ad certae victoriae decus ac emolumentum participandum semet accingant. Quoniam vero fidem suam in Regem apud multos vacillare probe noverat, execrationes et vota palam addidit, dirasque capiti suo est imprecatus, si bellum illud justissimum,

---

[34] *impetraverunt*, E, with *t* crossed out in paler ink.——[35] *consensui*, E.——[36] *Judecaverim*, E.——
[37] *loquutus*, D, a more faithful copy of the author's spelling, as in Part I. (*v.* Part II., Cap. II., n. 43), but altered by the present Edd. throughout.——[38] *duxit*, E.——[39] *perigrino*, E.——[40] om. *nuncios*, E.

primo quidem pro clementissimi Regis salute et libertate susceptum, cui jam et carissimi fratris ratio accesserit, ad extremum vitae spiritum non prosequeretur. Pauci admodum fuere tam duri tamque ferrei, quos ista non movebant; pauci tam increduli, qui serio bonaque fide dicta non putarent. Transforthanae quidem regiones omnes (ne Fifanis quidem exceptis) parabant arma. Seafordius Comes, ab Aebredibus et extrema Rossiae Cathanesiaeque ora delectorum militum instructa sub signis quatuor ducebat millia. Ab ultimis Orcadibus, ductu Mortonii Comitis, praesto erant in Lothiana mille circiter et ducenti: inermes quidem illi, et quos armare bonis istis imperatoribus curae non fuit. Gordonios (cujus familiae princeps Huntilaeus indigno premebatur carcere, ac de vita Edinburgi periclitabatur), Arrollum, jure haereditario in Scotia Equitum magistrum, Marescallum Comitem, Buchanensem, Atholium cum suis omnibus, Ogilvium, Spynaeum, Carnegium, Scrimigerum, Drummondum, Tillibardinum,[41] Areskinum, Flamineum, Livingstonium, Lindesium, Sinclarium, Duglassium,[42] Queensburium, Hertfeildum, Gallovidianum, Dumfrisium, Maxwallum, Ananiensem,[43] Humium, Lintonium, aliosque quam plurimos Comites, Barones, ac familiarum principes, vel Hamiltoniis addictos, vel Regi impensius faventes, cum Montanis (uno Argathelio excepto) ad unum omnibus constabat jam jam coituros; quorum plurimi magno suo malo enses hactenus expediverant.

Coegerant quidem Argatheliani, Fanaticorum[44] potissimum ministrorum ope et opera, paucos ab occiduis regni partibus, agricolas, bubulcos,[45] opiliones, nautas, cerdonesque, id genus alios imbelles prorsus et inermes, eosdemque Edinburgum miserant sub Davidis Leslei imperio militaturos. Istos armis, quibus ferendis erant impares, non tam induunt, quam onerant; et equos, aut caballos potius, ad pistrinum pridem damnatos, nec ephippiis, sed veterinorum clitellis constratos,[46] et frenorum lupatorumque loco, capistris rusticanis cohibitos attribuunt. Sequitur hos ipse Argathelius ejusdem generis militibus ferme septingentis cinctus: ex quibus Stirlino, oppido ad ejus res opportuno, praesidium imponere meditabatur.

Edinburgum versus progrediebatur Lanricensis validi exercitus dux factus; equitum enim expeditissimorum millia ducebat quinque; peditum vero magna ex parte veteranorum sex. Milites alacres, probe instructi armatique, et peritissimis suffulti ducibus, hostes omnibus votis deposcebant; de quibus certissimam et incruentam sibi promittebant victoriam. Jamque praecursores ad quartum ab urbe lapidem Musselburgum usque pervenerant, Pontem Escae fluvio impositum[47] invadunt, praesidiarios, loco tutando a Leslaeo collocatos, pauci plurimos deturbant, fugant, caeduntque impune:

---

[41] *Tullibardinum*, E.——[42] *Douglassium*, D.——[43] *Anamensem*, E.——[44] *phanaticorum*, E.——
[45] *Bubulios*, E.——[46] *constratis*, D.——[47] *Esiae*, and om. *impositum*, E.

Lanricensi Imperatori renunciant hostes imbelles et ad militiam ineptos nihil praeter fugam aut deditionem meditari; victoriam sine caede et sanguine, adeoque minus invidiosam in manibus habere; civitatem, regni caput, Lethae navalia armamentaria, cum ingenti apparatu machinarum, tormentorum, pulveris sulphurei ac globorum, nec non et magnam commeatus vim, nullo ferme negotio, illa ipsa nocte, aut forte ante solis occasum occupari[48] posse, si instarent; nec universo quidem exercitus robore opus esse; sufficere ad illa omnia comparanda vel tertiam ejus partem.

Et sane si annuisset ille, nemini dubium fuit, recuperatam quasi Scotiam ad regis obedientiam fuisse redituram. Verum ille receptui canere, pugna abstinere, militesque suos hactenus victores revocare jubet; et declinata via regia, quae ad[49] Edinburgum ducebat, sinistrum iter carpere. Ad ista attoniti duces militesque mirari primo, dein fremere et indignari, rei bene gerendae occasionem elabi, quam si arriperent, in Scotia brevi foret debellatum; cunctationem illam intempestivam hostibus quidem lucro, sibi damno futuram; non modo spirandi sed et vires, tam intra quam extra patriam, praesertim a Cromwellio (cui militabant) colligendi spatium permitti; civitatem principem, senatus locum, nomenque, arma, armarium,[50] stipendia, gratis illis indulgeri; famam denique, quae non exigui res est in bello momenti, sibi deperire et ad eos hostes transire, qui ne in militum quidem numero censendi essent.

Interim tamen cordatiores, quo ista[51] demum spectarent, tum primum suspicare coeperunt; Lanricensem enim, peracris ingenii multaeque prudentiae virum, usque adeo desipere ac delirare, nemo sanus putaret, nisi longe alia suo versaret animo quam aliis faceret palam. Enimvero jampridem ille pacem cum Argathelianis, quibuscunque legibus inire statuerat, armaque ostentaverat, ut nocendi potestatem, non voluntatem, manifestaret, majoremque apud eos aucuparetur[52] gratiam. Compertum enim est hodie dudum eum per internuncios de rebus cum Argathelio componendis clam egisse, de militibus suis ac belli sociis, quos acciverat, parum solicitum.

Ubi ergo Lanricensem copias ab Edinburgo avertisse et per montes Pictlandicos tendere laeti hostes viderunt, suos confestim educunt, ridiculos istos homunculos et militum larvas; non quod ullam in iis spem[53] collocarent, sed ut specie exercitus dignitatem suam authoritatemque apud populum tuerentur, et viris fortissimis ducum imperio cohibitis illuderent. Veterani cum militibus ductores tristitia, pudore, ira perciti, illatam contumeliam aegerrime tulere; nec facile ab iis impetravit imperator, ne furibundi in vilissimos hostes irruerent; victi tamen authoritate viri, Stirlinum versus pergere coacti sunt. Quando ad fanum Valli[54] pervenere, primum agmen

---

[48] *occupare*, E.——[49] om. *ad*, E.——[50] *armoram*, E, *armorium*, D, and so perhaps written by W.——[51] *ea* and om. *demum*, E.——[52] *aucuparet*, D.——[53] om. *spem*, E.——[54] *v.* Author's Pref., *Lectori Benevolo*, p. 10.

cum paucis veteranis ducebat Monrous, vir integer, et qui bellum in Regis gratiam (ut ille quidem putabat) susceptum serio et bona fide administratum voluit. Subolebant huic occulta[55] quamvis et clancularia Lanricensis consilia;[56] quae cum opprimere non posset, perturbare tamen, aut in lucem efferre hac non inepta ratione cogitabat.[57] Imperatorem ultimum agmen lente cogentem procul a tergo reliquerat, cum nunciatum est Argathelium, septingentis montanis comitatum, mane illius diei Stirlinum tenuisse. Illuc cum suis Monrous quam celerrime advolat, ut si qua posset imparatum improvisus adoriretur. Portas quidem clausas et custode munitas invenit; per leporarium tamen (quod juxta pomarium amoenissimum alendis cervorum gregibus prisci reges animi gratia exstruxerant) immissus, portulam offendit, angustiorem quidem illam humilioremque quam ut equo insidens ingredi posset. Desiliens ergo vir strenuus ac impiger, effractis postibus irrupit. Enim alii arctiori aditu impediti, lente et singuli subsecuti sunt, et vix prima miscentem proelia sex sunt assecuti. Re subita perturbati Argatheliani, quidve consilii capesserent ignari, confusis ordinibus absque imperio per vias et angiportas palabundi discurrebant. Dux ipse ad primam irruentis hostis famam, eundi certus, more suo, adornabat fugam, et conscenso quem pernicissimum habebat equo, porta ab irrumpentibus aversa, pontem Forthae impositum petebat. Instat Monrous, et fugientis vestigia premit. At ille velocitate equi, tanquam cervus venatici dentibus ereptus, praeoccupato ponte evasit. Satellitum ejus, quibus fuga praerepta fuit, caeteris captis, ducenti ferme interiere.

Supervenientibus tandem cum Lanricensi proceribus, Lindesio nimirum et Glencarnio, qui soli intimorum consiliorum participes fuere, egregium illud Monroi facinus ingratissimum fuit; nec dolorem suum celare valuit Lindesius, in haec verba prorumpens, " Me miserum, qui inauspicatum hunc et calamitosum diem viderim." Male etenim metuebant, ne acerbatis[58] utrinque animis pacificandi spes et studium deponeretur.

Quamvis[59] autem Lanricensis tam apud milites quam absentes proceres, quos ad arma capessenda literis[60] indies fatigabat, solertissime dissimularet, sensit tamen Monrous, sensere et alii, quid tandem machinaretur. In his Atholii viri, montani quamvis et rudes, non prorsus tamen insensati, quique hactenus armati Ierniam usque descenderant; Imperatorem enim proceresque illi adhaerentes humiliter obnixeque rogarunt, si serio agere in animo illis esset, ut pro authoritate illis a Rege et novissimis Regni Comitiis[61] demandata resistentes, ac praesertim eos qui Edinburgi copias contraxerint, perduellionis et laesae majestatis reos pronunciarent; et hoc quasi pignore

---

[55] *oculta*, D, E.——[56] *concilia*, D, and often.——[57] *cogitavit*, E.——[58] *exacerbatis*, E. " That this should provoke *Argyll*," Tr. I, as though his MS. had *Argathelii* for *utrinque*.——[59] *Quam vero*, E. ——[60] *literis*, om. D.——[61] *Commitiis*, E.

incertas ac fluctuantes hominum mentes confirmarent. "Ut ut[62] enim nobis (aiebant) de constantia, fide, virtuteque vestra dubitare fas non sit, non desunt[63] tamen plurimi, rebus vestris non exiguum allaturi auxilium, qui hoc metu distineantur,[64] ne vos, desertis illis, cum hostibus vobis quidem turpem et indecoram, sociis vero exitiosam, pacem contrahatis. Si enim tale quid (quod dicere abominamur) acciderit, quid nobis[65] praeter diras et anathemata, carceres et exilia, rapinas et ultima quaeque supplicia ab immanissimis hostibus expectandum restat?" Haec et plura alii quoque frustra ingeminabant. Verum illi viros aequa et honesta flagitantes primo differre ac procrastinare, et mox etiam deludere nihil pensi habuerunt. Tandem vero Glencarnius Lindesiusque, hic Hamiltoniorum levir, ille frater matruelis, uterque nexu quasi et mancipio[66] illis obligatus, de pace (quam hactenus clam sociis confecerant) non tam concilianda aequis quam quibuscumque conditionibus deposcenda et amplexanda verba facere non erubuerunt. Ad illa milites indignari, murmurare, fremere. Imperator mira quadam arte, in his una virtutem et constantiam et in illis pacis studium laudare et amplecti, fronte nimirum ad horum, mente ad illorum accedens sententiam. Perplexis enim sermonibus Glencarnium ac Lindesium accusabat, et querebatur eos, inconsulto ac etiam invito Imperatore, cum hoste agere, et pacem incertam, infidam durissimisque et vix ferendis legibus deposcere; cum simul[67] oblique notaret ac increparet eos, qui tantopere a concordia abhorrerent et civilibus gauderent armis. Et quamvis iniquas istas conditiones ab hostibus obtrusas semetipsum nullatenus amplexurum profiteretur, alios tamen per parentum, conjugum, liberorum et amicorum discrimina obtestabatur, ut iisdem acquiescerent. Pauci tamen fuere tam fatui et insulsi qui crederent geminos istos pacificatores, tot nominibus illi obnoxios, quique in aliis omnibus ab ejus nutu penderent, injussu ejus quidquam de pace cogitasse, nedum transegisse cum hostibus.

Et hoc tandem modo, reluctante milite, reclamantibus aliis ducibus, regnique proceribus (quotquot regi favebant) multum renitentibus, in Glencarnii et Lindesii sententiam itum est. Milites illi tam regis quam ordinum suffragiis coacti, et duces eadem suffulti authoritate, rebus omnibus affluentibus, multis magnisque auxiliis undique accurrentibus, nullis laboribus attriti, nullis confecti morbis, ne vel minimo ab hoste affecti damno, nulla pressi angustia, incolumes, validi, optime armati et animati, leges easdemque durissimas et iniquissimas, a perduellibus paucis, invalidis, ad militiam ineptis, nullo regis mandato, nullis Comitiorum suffragiis, nulla legum authoritate innixis, latas accipere coacti sunt. Legibus[68] istis imprimis

---

[62] *ut*, D.——[63] *desinunt*, E.——[64] *destineantur*, D.——[65] *vobis*, E.——[66] *mancipiis*, E.——[67] *simull*, E.——[68] *A legibus*, D.

cautum[69] fuit, "duces omnes militesque quotquot sub Hamiltoniorum imperio meruere, ab armis discedant, qui Stirlini et locis vicinis sunt, ante elapsum biduum, qui in remotioribus regni partibus adhuc haerent, ante decimum et quartum diem; qui secus faxit perduellionis reus esto. Proceres quotquot recentis expeditionis Hamiltonianae participes fuere, aut eadem quoquo modo promoverunt, subsequentibus Comitiis sese, tanquam reos, judicandos sistant; nullum illis in iisdem suffragii[70] jus esto. Tribunis,[71] Centurionibus aliisque ducibus, insignia militaria detrahantur, nullusque ad dignitatem ullam patescat reditus, quoadusque peracta paenitentia Presbyterio[72] satisfecerint. Idem de gregariis statutum esto. Hiberni quotquot sunt quamprimum[73] Scotia excedant: qui post dictum diem inventus fuerit morte mulctator.[74] Omnes denique Presbyterio sese judicandos permittant; paenis ab eodem irrogatis comiter se subjiciant; secus qui fecerit anathemate feriatur.

Quo die militibus ista sunt palam facta, [commodum][75] plerique ferme omnes per vicos pagosque erant dispersi; alias enim non exiguum futurum fuisse tumultum satis constabat. Pauci qui aderant rem indignam aegerrime tulere, parumque abfuit quin in bonos istos pacificatores irruerent, et discerperent membratim. Et utut[76] Lanricensis Imperator culpam omnem a semetipso amoliretur,[77] furibundi tamen, nec minore cum ejus luctu quam ignominia, more patrio, ejulantes exclamabant,[78] "oh, oh, oh, oh, quis nobis reddet Montisrosanum? Montisrosane, Montisrosane, quam tristi fato tu tam intempestive abes a patria tua! Nos qui hodie tanquam inutiles et ignavi muliones, qui[79] (si diis placet) in patriam impii ac infidi, militia dejicimur, te duce, te auspice, regnum hoc pacatum, enectis aut exactis perduellibus, Regi, Regemque regno, cum bono Deo, restituissemus." Querelae, denique lamenta, imprecationes in eos qui una eademque opera Regem prodidissent, patriam perdidissent[80] militemque fortissimum ac fidissimum deseruissent, bonosque omnes hostili permisissent libidini[81] tota urbe personabant: atque ita, quasi ultimum dicentes vale, sese, quo sors aut providentia ferebat, recepere: miseri quidem omnes, omnium vero miserrime Hiberni, quibus absque commeatu, viatico, portorio, intentata

---

[69] E obscurely *tantus* or *cantus* (?).——[70] *suffragiis*, D.——[71] *Tribunus*, E.——[72] *presbyteria*, D.——[73] *quamprimis*, E.——[74] *mulctator*, D. E has here a lacuna of one word. The reading of D is so distinct that it is almost impossible that this was one of the MSS. "collated" by R. Wodrow, when he wrote E. The blank points to a copy in a difficult hand. Wishart wrote very badly, but as Wodrow noted lacunae in his folio MS., which he does not supply, it is highly improbable that he had the original before him. Tr. 1 follows D (*v.* Crit. Introd.).——[75] Om. *palam facta*, E, which has a lacuna followed by the word *commodum*. Here again D is quite clear. Tr. 1 omits *commodum*, which is rendered in Tr. 2 "luckily."——[76] *ut*, D.——[77] *amelioretur*, E.——[78] *exilabant*, E.——[79] The sense requires *quasi* to qualify *impii*, &c., perhaps dropped out between *qui si* (?).——[80] om. *perdidissent*, E. The jingle with *prodidissent* is quite in Wishart's style. He usually couples three or more nouns or clauses with only one *et* or *que*, following the English idiom.——[81] *libini*, E.

mortis paena, si vel tantillam traherent moram, remigrandum fuit; quorum alii dum reditum parant, vestibus exuti, alii vulneribus, morte alii, omnes male mulctati sunt, instigantibus praesertim occidentalium partium ministris, ad injustam et minime Christianam in innoxios immeritosque viros Hibernicae lanienae [82] vindictam.

Argatheliani [83] sine sudore et sanguine luculenta potiti victoria, et rerum in Scotia, non minus quam Independentes in Anglia, domini facti, rebus suis strenue invigilabant. Cromwellium imprimis (pendente adhuc pacis negotio) in Scotiam invitaverant. Venientem Argathelius quam potuit amicissime et honorificentissime suscepit Edinburgi. Post gratias, tanquam de Scotia optime merito, quod Hamiltonianum exercitum delevisset,[84] solemniter habitas, publico epulo exceptus fuit; in arcem majoribus tormentis multoties displosis, triumphanti similis, fuit deductus; nec prius abscessit quam cum Argathelio ejusque factionis viris, tam de perdendo optimo (qui tum captivus erat) Rege, cum omni ejus stirpe, quam de Monarchia ex omni Britannia [85] prorsus eradicanda; mutuaque opera, et auxilio ad id praestandum, occultum quidem, sed dirum et infandum foedus pactus fuisset. Qua de re Cromwellius in Angliam reversus multo magis [86] quam de Prestoniana [87] victoria apud suos sese jactabat et gloriabatur.

---

[82] *Laminae*, E. A rare word meaning "hot plates," hence "torture."——[83] *Argatheliam*, E (*v.* n. 25, &c.).——[84] Tr. 1 omits the rest of this chapter, ending "and complimented him . . . by defeating Duke Hamilton's army."——[85] *Brittannia*, E, and often.——[86] *majus*, D.——[87] *Prestonana*, E, here and elsewhere.

## CAP. IV.

Fusius paulo quam instituti nostri ratio forsan postularet ista in exterorum praesertim [1] gratiam prosecutus sum; ut illis appareat quibus artibus non Montisrosanus [2] modo, sed et ipse Rex fuerit oppugnatus, ac boni illi viri sibi perniciem et patriae servitutem comparaverint.

Sub finem Anni CIƆIƆXLVIII [3] sic illa in Scotia transigebantur. Ineunte vero CIƆIƆXLIX [4] maledictum in omnia saecula eventum sortita sunt.[5] Ante enim prid.[6] Cal. Feb.[7] Independentes successibus elati,[8] furore perciti,

---

[1] om. *praesertim*, D, and Tr. 1. Tr. 2 follows E.——[2] *Montisrosanum*, D.——[3] *CIƆIXXLVIII*, E, 1648 (*sic*) D.——[4] *CIƆIXXLIX*, E, 1649 (*sic*) D.——[5] *sortiti* (?) but perh. *illa* is the subject.——[6] *Pridie enim ante*, D.——[7] Tr. 2 adds, "That black and dismal day, scarce ever to be expiated by these nations." Tr. 1, "That black and dismal day." The reading of D can only mean January 31st. But Charles was executed on the 30th., and Wishart could hardly have erred in the date. The correct Latin for January 30 is *a. d. iii Kal. Feb.* But Wishart, as the reader may see in Part I., errs frequently in his use of the Roman Calendar (*v.* Cap. IV., n. 17), and may have written as in E, *ante enim prid.* The difficulty of construing *sortita*, and the above additions in previous translations, point to a corruption of the text in our two MSS.——[8] *successibus elati*, om. Tr. 1, rendered in Tr. 2.

ambitione et avaritia excaecati, contra jus omne divinum et humanum, regem suum, sanctissimum et justissimum, castissimum, clementissimum, et ab uno Deo judicandum, infandum parricidio trucidarunt. Londini hoc potissimum tempore degebant ab Argathelianis partibus, sed ordinum Scotiae nomine, ad parliamentum Anglicanum Oratores, in quibus Lothianus Comes, Regi (qui eum cum patre ad summos honores opesque eximia magnificentia evexerat) ingratissimus ac infensissimus hostis, authoritate et potentia primas tenuit. Hi sententiam in regis caput ut[9] juste ac legitime latam, inficias non ierunt. In[10] mandatis enim habebant a suis de jure plebis in destituendo ac morte etiam, si videatur, mulctando principe, Anglis neutiquam contradicere. Executioni tamen videri volebant intercedere, ut reversi in patriam promptum paratumque haberent quo rerum imperitis facerent fucum, quasi flagitium illud invitis iis et reluctantibus patratum fuisset. Die ergo execrandae carnificinae destinato, civitate exeunt, post paucos in eandem haud gravatim pertrahendi.[11] Oculos enim a spectaculo, Christiano nomini pudendo, avertendos astute judicabant, ad quod toto quidem pectore viri impii et infidi anhelebant.[12] Et hoc sane vel maximis optimi regis calamitatibus et infortuniis merito annumerandum videtur, quod plerosque[13] omnes quos beatae memoriae pater Jacobus, aut ipse liberalitate, gratia, donis, quaestuosissimis provinciis, et summis honoribus locupletaverat, auxerat, ornaveratque, omnium hominum expertus sit ingratissimos, ac in rebellione vel primos vel praecipuos, quum quos fidissimos invenerat, illi ferme fuerint qui ab aula, senatu, omnique administratione procul aberant et arcebantur.

Montisrosanus (cui probe nota erant conjuratorum ingenia) mala illa non tantum praeviderat sed et praedixerat palam, ac quamvis frustra, praevenire laboraverat. Verum apud animos Regum speciosis et fraudulentis Presbyterianorum pollicitationibus praeoccupatos, ac Hamiltoniorum fascinatos blandimentis[14] sanioribus ejus consiliis nullus erat locus. Quod cum ille animadverteret maerore ac luctu confectus,[15] Galliam, in qua operam suam omnem tam Regi quam sibi inutilem sentiebat, inscia quidem Regina, reliquit. Literis tamen consilii sui rationes omnes, et eundi necessitatem exposuit, ac benignum judicium, veniamque humillime deprecatus est.[16]

Ineunte ergo Aprili, duobus equestris ordinis viris comitatus, Genevam primo pervenit, et mox Helvetiis praetervectus Tirolin, Bavariam Austriamque peragravit. Vienna aberat Imperator, ad quem sese conferebat, tam ut carissimi Regis, quam suis rebus[17] apud Caesarem prospiceret. Pragae

---

[9] *utut*, D, the very opposite of the sense required.——[10] *Cui*, and om. *in*, E.——[11] *post . . . pertrahendi* om. in Tr. 1 and 2; from *die* understand *dies* with *paucos*.——[12] *anhilabant*, E.——[13] *plerique*, E.——[14] *blandiamentis*, D.——[15] *maerore . . . confectus* om. Tr. 1.——[16] New paragraph in D and Tr. 1. In general, the present Edd. have not thought fit to adhere strictly to the paragraphing of the MSS.——[17] *quam suis rebus*, om. Tr. 1 (with preceding *tam*).

eundem assecutus, gratus illi admodum acceptusque fuit, tam ob res hactenus in patria gestas, quam eximiam in Regem suum fidem ac pietatem, quae in remotioribus orbis Christiani partibus nomen famamque celeberrimam comparaverant. Paucos post dies Augustus ad iter accinctus Montisrosanum secum abduxit, et non obscuris benevolentiae et amici animi testimoniis cohonestavit. In praetorum suorum numerum cooptavit. In exercitu imperiali Mareschalli (ut hodie loqui solent) dignitate ornavit; literisque confirmavit, ac diplomate ad comparandas copias, quibus Caesaris auspiciis[18] ipse solus ac seorsum imperitaret, delectum faciendi, conscribendi milites, Tribunos, Centuriones nominandi, et emittendi Inquisitores[19] in locis ac provinciis quibuslibet S.I.R. subditis ac parentibus potestatem fecit. Germaniae partes ad Belgicam vergentes delectui facilitando ac maturando commodiores videbantur. Annuente[20] ergo imprimis Hispano legato literas admodum honorificas ad Serenissimum fratrem Leopoldum, Austriae Archiducem et pro Hispaniarum Rege inferioris Germaniae Gubernatorem, dedit, ut authoritate sua ac gratia Montisrosani negotiis consuleret eademque[21] promoveret. Hocque illi ex animi sententia succedebat; qui quum Regis sui rebus unice esset intentus, si qua occasio se offeret, nolebat procul esse remotus: prodendum[22] enim, ac perdendum prorsus a Presbyterianis istis, quibus se suaque commiserat, semper et assidue praesagiebat.

Ab Imperatore honorifice dimissus, quia expeditior via per Germaniam propter interjectos hostes impedita fuit, Vienna Presburgum in Hungaria petere fuit coactus. Inde per Terram novam[23] in Poloniam descendit, ac perlustrata Cracovia, penetravit in Prussiam, et celeberrimum Balthici emporium[24] Dantiscum venit. Inde navigio exceptus, perrexit in Daniam, a cujus Rege humaniter susceptus, post molestissimum iter dies aliquot curando corpori et reficiendis viribus indulsit. In Jutiam denique transit, ac conscensa nave Gronnigam[25] in Frisia appulit, rectaque[26] Bruxellas contendit. Tornacum[27] Archidux post recentem cladem Lansensem[28] se receperat; quo et Montisrosanus festinavit, ac Serenissimi Domini Imperatoris nomine salutem impertivit, literisque redditis, consilium auxiliumque in rebus fratrem Caesarem spectantibus imploravit. Verum quoniam, post insignem illam instructissimi exercitus jacturam, in provinciis istis,

---

[18] om. *auspiciis*, E.——[19] *et . . . Inquisitores*, om. Tr. 1.——[20] *amitente*, E, *Amritente* (?), D. "With the consent of the Spanish Ambassador," Tr. 1, which indicates the true reading. An indication that neither D nor E was used for that Tr.——[21] *et*, E.——[22] *propendendum*, E. The rest of this paragr. is omitted by Tr. 1.——[23] *Terranovam*, E, om. Tr. 1 and 2. Probably the mod. Tyrnau (*v.* p. 227, n. 5).——[24] *emporium*, Tr. 1, followed by Tr. 2, renders "Hanse-town." ——[25] *Groningam* (?).——[26] *rectaque*, om. E. A favourite word with W.——[27] *Torcanum*, E.—— [28] *Lanfensem*, D, E; *post . . . Lanfensem* om. Tr. 1. Probably the author wrote *Lanfensem* (*v.* Cap. V., n. 35). The defeat was at Lens (*v.* p. 227, n. 6).

suspicionibus ac tumultibus usque adeo laborabant, ut nihil tunc expediri potuerat, quoad Bruxellas redirent, dilata res est. Illuc ubi reversum fuit, ad Senatum ab Archiduce relatum est, ut quid e re Caesaris maxime videretur, consulerent et imperarent.

Dum ista Bruxellis [29] transiguntur, a Serenissimo Carolo, Scotorum et Walliae principe, qui Hagae Comitis [30] peregrinabatur, literas benevolentiae et fiduciae plenas [31] accepit, quibus eum accersebat ad se et invitabat. Enimvero qui apud principem erant, eidemque ex animo benevolebant, ac imprimis Serenissimus Princeps Rupertus Palatinus (qui de Presbyterianis cum Montisrosano semper sentiebat) ut illum compellaret, Carolum sponte ad hoc inclinantem impellebant.[32] Deleto enim sub Hamiltonio majore egregio in Anglia exercitu, a juniore [33] vero longe majore ac meliore in Scotia turpiter deserto ac dissipato, tam Presbyterianarum quam Regiarum partium viris utroque in regno in ordinum redactis, unum superesse Montisrosanum, qui in Scotia pro rege quidquam volet et audeat.[34] Male quidem cum illo actum esse, quod nec consilia probata, nec opera unquam, nisi rebus desperatis, advocata fuerit, ea tamen esse animi magnitudine, fide, pietate [35] in carissimum Dominum Regem, ut persuasissimum [36] habeant paratum fore, qui in ejus gratiam cuivis discrimini sese etiamnum objiciat.

De opinione principis ac fiducia quam in eo collocabat Montisrosanus certior factus (impetrata ab Archiduce venia) Hagam contendebat, cum tristissimus ille nuncius de optimo Rege, quem oculis suis cariorem semper habuerat,[37] ab Independentibus Anglis trucidato aures animumque perculit. Bone Deus, ut ad primum rei adhuc incertae rumorem totus perhorruit! Ubi vero de immani parricidio constabat, nec spei quidquam restabat amplius, non jam dolor sed maeror, non ira sed furor corripuit, subitoque generosum sic oppressit animum, ut sensus vitaeque expers rigentibus membris in medio corruerit. Quum vero ad se tandem rediisset, post altissima suspiria in has primas erupit voces; "Moriendum est, moriendum est cum meritissimo rege, testorque vitae ac mortis Dominum, vitam hanc mortalem deinceps acerbam ingratamque fore." In circumstantibus forte eram et ego qui haec describo, ut licet immenso dolori, qui et animum meum stupefecerat, ferendo impar fuerim, ad voces istas hunc in modum pro tempore occurri: "Immo vero vivendum viris fortibus, vivendum est, magnanime [38] heros, virtutemque animosque omnes advocare decet, tam ut immanes isti ac infandi parricidae meritis [39] subjiciantur poenis, quam ut

---

[29] *Bruxellas*, E.——[30] A lit. tr. of the Dutch for the Hague, *'s Gravenhagen*, "the Count's Hedge."——[31] *plenas* om. E.——[32] *impellabant*, E.——[33] *a juniorem*, E, and om. *vero* to *Presbyterianarum*, probably "skipping" a line in copying (*v.* Cap. VI., n. 86.)——[34] *volet*, obs. Indic.; his will was certain; *audeat*, subj., as expressing doubt in the circumstances. "He is sure to be willing, and may venture."——[35] *pietatem*, E.——[36] *persuasum*, E.——[37] *quem . . . habuerat*, om. Tr. 1 and 2.——[38] *magnanime est*, E.——[39] *incertis*, E.

Serenissimus filius, idemque successor legitimus, justis et piis armis avito restituatur imperio. Haec piis defuncti manibus justa debentur, haec pietate, fide, fortitudine, constantia, tua digniora sunt consilia, quam malis quantumvis maximis (qualia sane haec nostra sunt) molliter nimis succumbere et despondere animum, ac sic impiis hostibus gratificari, novamque victoriam novosque gratis indulgere triumphos." Qui alias benigne ac clementer, etiam nunc [40] patienter saltem nos audiebat, pauloque erectior (desideratissimae nimirum vindictae suavior cogitatio spiritus vehementiores a corde propemodum suffocato revocaverat) vultu pacatiore, et ad verecundiam composito, respondit; "Et ego idcirco duntaxat vivere forsan sustineam. Interim quicquid mihi superest vitae, vindicando patri martyri, ac filio [41] in paternum evehendo solium coram Deo, Angelis et hominibus sacrum votumque esto." Haec effatus, in intimum diversorii penetrale semet proripuit; nec ante elapsum biduum quenquam ad colloquium ac ne conspectum quidem admisit. Tertio demum die annuente Montisrosano, cubiculum ingressus in chartulam incidi, in qua solemne illud votum, brevi quidem sed elegantissimo carmine, ac profundissimas mentis cogitationes penitus respirante, complexus fuerat. Amoenissimi enim ingenii vir, quoties a gravioribus curis vacatio dabatur, animum poetica felicissime relaxabat. Latine a nobis utcunque redditum prima post Appendicem hanc pagina exhibebit.[42] Acumen authoris minime me assecuntum sat scio; sententiam tamen Anglicanae linguae ignaris indicasse forsan non erat usquequaque ingratum.

Carolus, ejus nominis Secundus, defuncto patri jure regio successor legitimus, quam primum per dolorem et verecundiam licuit, Montisrosanum compellavit, ac quam plurimis benevoli plane et amici animi argumentis et testimoniis copulavit sibi ac confirmavit. Imprimis enim Regni Scotiae gubernatorem vicarium et copiarum omnium terra marique Imperatorem (eodem ferme modo ac iisdem verbis, quo provinciam eandem administrandam a patre nactus fuerat) literis et regio diplomate constituit: legatum insuper, comparandis auxiliariis armis aliisque subsidiis ad bellum renovandum necessariis, ad Caesarem, Daniae Regem, principes Germaniae, aliosque foederatos affines et amicos destinavit, cum plena transigendi, foedera contrahendi, sponsiones dandi, aliaque omnia Regis sui nomine peragendi potestate, quae commoda viderentur, eisdemque enixe admodum et honorifice commendavit.

Res prospere satis succedebant, ac homines spei pleni optima quaeque sibi pollicebantur; quum Hamiltonius junior optimis initiis more suo

---

[40] *sunt*, E.——[41] *filii*, E.——[42] For the poem and W.'s version, *v.* App. According to Tr. 1, which gives both, the lines were written "with the point of his sword," probably a confusion of circumstance with the lines M. engraved on his prison window, on the eve of his death (App.).

intercessit. Cum cliente suo Lauderdalio advolaverat ille in Hollandiam profugium[43] simulans, re ipsa vero ut sanioribus Montisrosani consiliis (quod saepiuscule apud Regem defunctum cum fratre fecerat) sese opponeret, eademque oppugnaret et frustraretur. Montisrosani sententia fuit, ut Rex ipse in Scotiam iter quam primum capesseret; fidosque subditos, quorum numerus longe maximus erat, ad arma rapienda praesentia et exemplo animaret; detectas tandem populo superiorum temporum experientia perduellium tam Presbyterianorum quam Independentium funestas artes ac dolos; despectas plerisque et invisas Fanaticorum vatum in regem declamationes, quibus animos plebis fascinatos et superstitione astrictos a debito obsequi ohactenus avertere; incalescere hominum pectora recenti horridi[44] parricidii vulnere saucia et ad vindictam prona; inutiles moras, quoad concitati spiritus defervescant, non esse trahendas; conjuratis opportunitatem omnem vires vi ac dolo augendi praeripiendam; plurimos qui regibus hactenus iniquiores fuerint, mitescere, resipiscere, et ad saniorem mentem redire; principis denique praesentiam millium[45] instar esse; festinandum itaque nec ad diem aut horam producendum iter; pretiosa namque in tali rerum nexu ipsa quoque momenta.

Idem plane suadebant Seafordius[46] Comes, Kinnulius, Sinclarius, aliique proceres, qui ad hoc ipsum regi insinuandum Scotia in Belgicam navigaverant. Hamiltonius vero contra nil temere aggrediendum dicebat. Regi novo suspecta debere esse omnia; conciliandos esse hominum affectus, prius quam caput suum tanto discrimini[47] objiceret. Immodicam Ecclesiastici ordinis, Regi infensissimi, apud plebem gratiam; immensam Argathelianorum potentiam; nomen authoritatemque ordinum penes eos esse, Regique omnia adversa praedicabat; amice denique ac lente cum Comitiis agendum, nec nisi praeeuntibus eorum suffragiis quicquam[48] attentandum; quumque tragicis admodum verbis in istorum hominum saevitiam, perfidiam, seditiosos spiritus, ac sibi, principis causa, supra modum infensos[49] identidem declamaret, una tamen Regi persuadere conabatur, ut totus ab iis penderet, salutemque sibi promitteret ab illis qui perniciem patri accersiverant.

Ipse Carolus ad Montisrosani sententiam propius accedebat. Quod cum Hamiltonius animadvertisset, principis adolescentis adhuc animum ab eo, tanquam homine temerario, audace, ambitioso, bellis civilibus plus nimis intento, ac majora quam possit praestare pollicito, per aulicos alienare, sed

---

[43] *profugum*, E.——[44] *horrendi*, E.——[45] *millium* is quite clear in D. E has here a blank. In Tr. 1, also, there was either a blank, or the phrase was misunderstood, the clause being rendered "that to attack the enemy now would be more serviceable to the King's interest than the assistance of many more afterwards." Tr. 2 evidently read *millium*.——[46] *Seafordianus*, E.——[47] *discrimine*, E. ——[48] *quicquid*, E.——[49] *offensos*, E.

frustra, tentavit. Eo usque tamen praevaluit, ut plures quam optabat Montisrosanus dies consultando elaberentur, quibus novas ille morae causas, novaque impedimenta accumulabat.

Rex, qui Montisrosanum quidem amabat, ab Hamiltonio vero, ne noceret sibi, metuebat, utrumque sibi devinctissimum habere laborabat; quoniam vero dissidentes sententias impossibile erat, discordes et alienatos dissentientium animos reconciliare satagebat. Montisrosanus privatas sibi cum Hamiltoniis inimicitias nullas unquam fuisse asseveravit; de rebus majestatem regiam[50] spectantibus, in quibus parum sincere[51] versati fuerint, ortum esse dissidium, et in illum[52] usque diem productum; visos semper, praetexto officii velo, plus nocuisse regi, quam apertos hostes: consiliis enim perniciosis conatus ejus viresque labefactasse, opes animosque addidisse perduellibus, cum quibus arctissimam coluerunt amicitiam, nullis unquam rationibus induci potuisse, aut etiamnum posse, ut palam ac penitus desertis in Scotia conjuratis (quocunque tandem nomine ordinum regni aut ecclesiastici conventus sese venditent) principis partes contra omnes mortales suscipiant et amplexentur; in aliquo semper dicta, facta, fidemque haerere ac vacillare; veruntamen si vel tandem praeteritorum serio paeniteat, ultroque et ex animo ad obsequium redeant ac fidem, spondeantque in posterum nihil illis cum conjuratis commune fore, paratum se qui superiorum facinorum immemor, in sanctissimam cum iis amicitiam coeat; hac tamen lege, ut libello conscripto et in publicum emisso declarent et testentur, sese Scotorum inter se et cum Anglis perduellibus conspirationem, foederaque omnia inter subditos invito aut inconsulto Rege contracta, ut sanctissimam imprimis quam vocant Ligam detestari et damnare; bella omnia tam in Scotia quam in Anglia contra regem gesta,[53] pro nefariis et impiis habere, authores eorundem et duces laesae majestatis reos esse; Carolum ejus nominis Secundum, Dei Gratia, M. Britanniae &c. regem, si aliter nequiret, jure posse ac etiam debere justis et piis armis tam parricidium in beatae memoriae patrem perpetratum vindicare, quam viam sibi ad avitum solium[54] repetendum ac recuperandum praestruere[55] et munire; ac ad illa denique comparanda sancte polliceri fortem illi ejusque ducibus et vicem gerentibus fidelemque operam, vel cum bonorum vitaeque discrimine navaturos.

Hamiltonius cum Lauderdelio,[56] quibus ordines regni, prout tunc erant constituti, apud Reges perfidiae, saevitiae, perduellionis ac turpissimorum scelerum clam incusare sollemne erat, sedulo tamen cavebant, ne scripto aut testimonio publico ulla ex parte laederent aut offenderent, perplexe,

---

[50] om. *regiam*, E.——[51] *syncere*, E, and so often.——[52] *ullum*, E.——[53] *gestra*, E.——[54] *solum*, E. ——[55] *perstruere*, D, *prestruere*, E.——[56] so both MSS.: usu. *Lauderdalius*. But W. may have written as above, following the English sound, rather than the spelling (*v.* Cap. II., n. 64).

anxie, ambigue respondebant, nec sese expediebant satis de jure regis, quae obiter elevabant, verba facere palam detrectabant solerter; Ordinum nomen, authoritatem, potentiam, vires, pleno ore depraedicabant, et efferebant. Expedire magis regi, ac potius esse eorum expectare sententiam, ac suffragiis et authoritate in paternum evehi solium, quam ferro et flammis patriam vastare, et coronam, quantumvis debitam, civili redemptam sanguine acquirere et occupare, aiebant. Nec sententiam denique probare nec amicitiam cum illis inire posse, qui bella civilia etiam justissima suaderent; cum Montisrosano praesertim, qui ob res defuncti Regis imperio et auspiciis gestas exul, aqua domi interdictus sit et igne, bonaque relata in fiscum.

Major interea Hamiltonius post cladem Prestonianam in Anglia captivus, ab Independentibus Londini capite mulctatus est, ac justissimo quidem numinis, sed iniquissimo parricidarum judicio, trucidato regi datus successor. Sunt qui dicunt hujus modi responsum ab hariolo quodam pridem illi redditum fuisse, "Violenta morte Rex occumbet, teque illi successorem dabunt fata." Sic forsan malus quis daemon homini ambitioso illuserit, qui principi non in solio sed in carnificina succederet.

## CAP. V.

Rebus Hagae Comitis[1] hunc in modum pendentibus ab iis qui Regni Ordines[2] sese in Scotia jactabant, supervenit nuncius, qui de prono eorum in novum Regem affectu comiter praefatus, chartulam exhibuit, in qua descripta erant verba, quibus Carolum filium, patre interempto, legitimum in Regno Scotiae successorem declaraverant. Occasionem hanc non modo gratulandi, sed et quasi de Palladio caelitus demisso, exultandi, gloriandique arripuere Hamiltoniani, ac Presbyterianarum[3] partium viri; jamque palam declamabant in eos, qui non putarent pendendum plane esse regi ab istorum hominum nutu, qui tam eximiam fidem ac pietatem demonstrassent. Et sane si bona sinceraque fide, ac more majorum debito et consueto hoc praestitissent, officio hac ex parte satisfecisse, et bonam fecisse spem, nemo ivisset inficias: verum occulatioribus prima facie facinus apparuit indignum, quo Regis regiique nominis jugulum callide petebatur. Enimvero ut populo ob trucidatum patrem ad vindictam praecipiti, et filium ad suscipiendas et moderandas Regni habenas, validis clamoribus ac minacibus reposcenti fucum facerent, edictum illud emiserant; quo tamen non stabilire regem,

---

[1] *v.* Cap. IV., n. 30.——[2] *ordinibus*, E.——[3] *presbiterianorum*, E.

sed regiam omnem potestatem radicitus convellere, et evellere [4] ac sibi vindicare satagebant. Praeterquam enim quod solemnem verborum formulam, a majoribus usurpari solitam, prorsus immutaverant,[5] invexerant quoque novam.

Quod Caroli patris mortem, appellasse violentam contenti, nec parricidii ac ne homicidii quidem nomine, aut vel levissimo impietatis et injustitiae indice notaverint, quo flagitium illud se minime probare testificarentur; aliaque plurima quae sigillatim enumerari et huc congerere, supervacaneum videretur. Intolerabile [6] praesertim ac piis mentibus horrendum fuit, quod quem principem legitimum eundemque supremum agnoverint, eodem ferme spiritu ab omni legitimae potestatis exercitio arcuerint et interdixerint, quoad usque ordinibus (quos parliamenta vocant) utriusque regni satisfecerit,[7] quod quidem regem illum declarare non fuit, sed reum sibi judicandum sistere.[8] Totum enim hoc, quid aliud fuit quam imperium precarium offerre, liberum eripere,[9] potestatem in terris supremam et uno [10] minorem Deo, subditis quasi pedibus caput subjicere? Nec sibi ipsis tantum qui in tam diuturna rebellione contra defunctum regem perseverassent, sed et Anglis perduellibus ac parricidis, quorum manus paterno adhuc sanguine madentes diffluebant, filium adolescentem, innocentem, immeritum submittere, et quasi novam hostiam substituere irae et odio furiosorum hominum immolandam?[11] Hujusmodi justissimis in edictum illud observationibus ac notis Presbyterianorum inanes [12] de ordinibus suis gloriationes paululum in aula coercitae fuissent et castigatae, si novis et ejusdem [13] plane farinae subsidiis a Scotia submissis vires animosque non resumpsissent.

Perlata in Scotiam fama de eximia authoritate et gratia, qua apud novum Regem pollebat Montisrosanus, varie hominum animos affecit. Regiarum partium viris jucunda et bonae spei plena, aliis formidolosa [14] admodum et tristis. Magnopere imprimis ab eo metuebant ordines, tam ob innatam totiesque [15] expertam hominis virtutem, quam quod praeter veteres majestatis cultores, non paucos errorum paenitudine [16] ductos, ad obsequium ejus procliviores cernerent. Cavendum ergo sedulo putarunt, ne ille cum imperio vicario solus, aut etiam in Regis comitatu [17] in patriam descenderet, cives ferme omnes prout tunc erant animati, secum pertracturus in certam eorum perniciem qui in Regis caedem consensissent. Huic malo obviam ut eant, Cassilium Comitem, primae nobilitatis virum, cum aliis inferiorum subselliorum homunculis, oratores ad Carolum in Bataviam transmittunt;

---

[4] *et evellere* om. D, but the jingle is in the Author's favourite style.——[5] *immutaverint invexerintque*, E.——[6] *intollerabile*, D, E.——[7] *satisfecit*, E.——[8] "to sist him as a pannel before them," Tr. 1, using the Sc. legal term.——[9] *liberum aripere* without a comma, E.——[10] *una*, E.——[11] *immolandum*, E.——[12] *manes*, E.——[13] *ejusmodi*, E. Tr. 1, "those of their own kidney."——[14] *formidulosa*, E.——[15] om. *que*, E.——[16] *plenitudine*, E.——[17] *comiatu*, E.

qui quidem ad unum omnes cum nova superstitione qua penitus irretiti fuere, pertinaci regiminis Monarchici odio flagrabant. Legationi huic finem (quem in omnem orbem Christianum evulgandum curarunt) hunc praetendebant, ut Carolum filium ad avitum Scotiae regnum ultro invitarent; re ipsa tamen hoc agebant ut Montisrosani consilia destruerent, principemque inani pacis et obsequii spe lactatum, ab armorum bellique instituto averterent, quoad rei bene gerendae occasio elaberetur. Interim ne conjuratis secum Anglis istis parricidis res ea suspitiosa videretur, animos eorum tristi pignore confirmarunt; et quoniam Regiae dignitatis quem excarnificarent non habebant, Regibus proximum, Gordoniorum gentis principem, Huntilaeum Marchionem post diuturnum carcerem iniquissima sententia securi percusserunt. Fuit sane Huntilaeus, praeter natalium splendorem, quo nemini post regem erat secundus, familiae potentiam vicinis olim formidandam, amicorum, satellitum et clientium numerum aliaque (quae fortunae [18]vocantur) bona, vir corporis animique dotibus ornatissimus; principi autem ab ipso tumultuum initio semper fidus, hoc solo nomine conjuratis [19] tam fuit invisus, ut e medio tollendum censuerint; adeo ut, si infelix illud cum Montisrosano et Rege et Regno et sibi funestissimum [20] certamen excipias, quam paucissimos habiturus sit pares. Diem eundem quo oratores ab aestuario Forthae solverunt, principis hujus viri carnificinae dixerunt; ut vel inde rex conjecturam facere et quasi ominari potuisset, quid demum ab eis, qui optimos et amantissimos subditos indies jugulabant, expectandum foret.

Ad Regem cum venissent egregii illi oratores, incessu tardo, amictu lugubri, oculis pronis, vultu tristi, nihil quam summam humilitatem prae se ferebant. Et sane praeteritorum oblivionem et veniam, imploraturos [21] fidem, obsequium in posterum pollicitaturos, Regi justa quaeque et aequa more majorum concessuros, sinceram denique pacem inituros ac [22] concordiam, multi (quibus penitus perspecta non erant hominum ingenia et mores) speravere. Duplici legatione fungebantur, a Regni nimirum Comitiis et Conventu ecclesiastico. Utriusque princeps erat Cassilius, hujus tanquam presbyter laicus, illius tanquam primi ordinis Senator. Apud Regem altissimis suspiriis multoque praefati gemitu, veluti, ut ait ille, "Magnum si pectore possent excussisse deum," [23] chartulas demum Ordinum suorum et Synodi oracula continentes exhibuerunt. Descripta in illis honesta, humilia, pia, et ad res componendas Regemque restituendum plane necessaria postulata vocitabant: quibus si satisfieret, posse omnium suffragiis in Scotiae regnum induci.

Quum Rex de chartulis istis in concilio suo cognovisset, primo quoque

---

[18] *forturnae*, E.——[19] *conjuratae*, E.——[20] *et sibi funestum*, E. Tr. 1 and Tr. 2 omit *et sibi*.——[21] om. *imploraturos*, E.——[22] *ad*, E.——[23] Verg. A., vi. 78, "*Magnum si pectore possit*," &c., of the Sibyl.

intuitu, non tam ad regnum capessendum invitamenta, quam ad animum absterrendum terriculamenta visa sunt, nec aequa quidem postulata, sed in defunctum patrem crimina, in filium superstitem insidias laqueosque continere deprehensae sunt.[24] Summatim ut dicam, tria postulabant. Primum erat, ut rex non modo Nationale Scotiae, sed et sacram (quam vocant) Ligam Foedusque trium regnorum rata haberet, subscriptione, jurejurando ac diplomate confirmaret, finem scopumque eorundem in terris omnibus imperio ejus subditis [propagare] promovere[25] summa ope niteretur. Secundum fuit, ut ordinum Scotiae statuta et edicta omnia, foedus idem ligamque, regimen Presbyterianum, cultus divini normam (quam Directorium vocitant) fidei confessionem, Catechismum Comitiis ejus Regni Synodoque probatum stabilientia ibidem confirmaret et haberet rata; ac insuper edictis et statutis ab aliorum regnorum ejus Majestati parentium Comitiis eadem posthac forte decernentibus ultro prompteque assentiret; seque ipsum secundum illa in omnibus et cultu praesertim divino privato et publico gereret, veterem[26] Ecclesiae Anglicanae Liturgiam[27] abdicaret; novum illud susciperet Directorium, cui sese nunquam adversaturum, aut vel minimam illaturum mutatiunculam, sancte polliceretur et juraret. Tertium vero (quod et unicum suffecisset et ambitu suo complectebatur omnia) ut solemnitur declaret consensumque praebeat suum in civilibus quibuscunque praesentis et subsequentium parliamentorum. In ecclesiasticis vero negotiis Synodorum placitis standum esse; quibus nimirum tam princeps quam subditi comiter se subjiciant, ac ad obedientiam teneantur.

Pluribus cum eis egit Rex, ut si quae alia sibi communicanda in mandatis haberent, una exhiberent, quo simul ad omnia responderet posset; ut postulata illa mitigarentur paululum, nec severitati verborum praefracte nimis et pertinaciter adhaererent; ut quid auxilii ad Angliam Hiberniamque recuperandam ab illis sibi posset promittere, liquidius et clarius impertirent; ut denique de horrendo parricidio in beatae memoriae regem patrem perpetrato, et immanibus ejusdem authoribus ac ministris, de quibus ne levissimam fecissent mentionem, mentem judiciumque aperirent, et orbi facerent palam. Referebant[28] illi summam quidem eorum quae petenda essent tribus illis articulis comprehendi, nec alia habere quam quae eodem tendant, nisi nova ab[29] ordinibus submittantur mandata. Postulata sua non tantum aequa et honesta, sed et prorsus necessaria, utpote juri divino et Sacrosanctis Scripturis innitentia, adeo ut ne latum unguem[30] ab eis recedere et vel tantillulum remittere fas sit. Suppetias illi ad Angliam

---

[24] *deprehensa* (?), but sc. *chartulae*.—[25] *propagare et* (?), but perhaps *propagare* is a gloss. Tr. 1, " promote the ends of them ;" Tr. 2, " promote the ends and purposes of them."—[26] *veteram*, E. —[27] *Leiturgiam*, E.—[28] *referebat*, E (*v.* below, n. 39).—[29] *ac*, E.—[30] *unguem*, E.

Hiberniamque reducendas, quales quantasque Ordines regni legitimas ac necessarias, secundum Ligam foedusque judicabunt, expectandas esse. Ambiguis ejusmodi verborum involucris cum ad alia quoquo modo respondissent, in Regis parricidio misere haerebant. Quod cum probare et laudare erubescerent, damnare tamen nolebant, ne irritati Angli societatem criminis intempestive exprobrassent.[31] Et quamvis Rex unum hoc supra alia jugiter urgeret, praeter querimonias et expostulationes, quod quaestionibus istis ordines Scotiae quasi suspectos habere videretur, nihil obtinuit.

Inter hasce disceptationes plurimum temporis elabitur; quo illi apud principem Auriacum,[32] et eminentiores Unitarum[33] Provinciarum viros, Daniae, aliorumque principum legatos, rem suam strenue agebant, ut eis quasi sequestris et mediatoribus, Rex ad eorum sententiam perduceretur. Quibus identidem occinebant, pronum Ordinum Scotiae in Regem suum affectum; paratos esse qui in paternum solium eum[34] suscipiant et amplexentur, debitamque fidem exhibeant et obsequium; aliud nihil in mora aut impedimento esse, quam ut, abdicato regimine Episcopali, Presbyterianum admittat; idem illud (cum diversissima tamen et plane pugnantia sint[35] quod in Belgio, Palatinatu, Geneva, aliisque reformatis ecclesiis obtinet:[36] quod nisi annueret, deperditam omnem imperii recuperandi spem esse. Parum forsan apud multos profecissent illi, nisi Hamiltonius cum Lauderdelio, quasi in insidiis collocati et succenturiati, dicta eorum comprobassent, collaudassent. Quorum imprimis opera factum est, ut plerisque videretur posse Regem ac debere, habita rerum suarum ratione, postulatis eorum utcunque duris et difficilibus assentire. Exteri enim et rerum Britannicarum ignari, qui in arcana conjuratorum consilia non penetrabant, insidias tam Regi, quam omni Regio regimini instructas non pervidebant.

Carolus, ut orbi Christiano, amicis praesertim et confoederatis constaret, studio pacis et concordiae se nihil non facturum, ut Scotis suis satisfieret[37] in omnibus quae aequa ac honesta essent, et famam conscientiamque non laederent, ad ejusdem Regni proceres, quorum non pauci in Belgica erant, se convertit, mandavitque ut pro fide et obsequio debito consilium et sententiam quisque suam de postulatis istis singulatim scripto exhiberet. Operam hanc, ad quam quidem more majorum et patriis legibus tenebantur, Hamiltonius cum Lauderdelio et suis praestare inverecunde, morose, et perfracte denegarunt. Montisrosanus, Seafordius, Kinnulius, Sinclarius aliique provinciam illam non[38] detrectavere. Et hi quidem postulata ista cum jure divino et humano ac legibus Scotiae pugnantia, in beatae memoriae Regem Martyrem impia, in superstitem insidiosa, stirpi futurae perniciosa,

---

[31] *exprobassent*, E. Correct Lat. requires *exprobrarent*.——[32] *auraicum*, E.——[33] *multarum*, E.——[34] *solum cum*, E.——[35] *fuit*, E, evidently a bad copy of *sint* (*v.* Cap. IV., n. 28).——[36] *obtineret*, E.——[37] *satisfierat*, E.——[38] om. *illam*, E; om. *non*, D.

bonis et cordatis omnibus pudenda et paenitenda, multis validisque rationibus evicerunt. Nihil aliud eis peti quam ut malorum omnium quae in Britannia contigerint [39] culpa in innocentissimum Martyrem conjiciatur. Ut infanda illa foedera ac ligae, quae tantum innocui, ingenui, nobilis, generosi, et denique regii sanguinis hauserint, veluti durateus [40] equus in arce locatus, nova subinde tumultuum, seditionum, armorum, rebellionum, rapinarum et parricidiorum examina, horrendo partu, in populum posterosque effundant, ut apud haeredem legitimum, principem supremum, nomen Regis nudum et inane relinquatur, quo una cum anima tantisper frui liceat, ac viris supra alios mortales melancholicis, hypochondriacis,[41] suspitiosis, furibundis, et summis semper potestatibus implacabili odio infensis libeat; imperii vis omnis ac potestas penes eos sit, qui conscientia tot scelerum in patrem agitati, stirpe ejus superstite, sortem suam nunquam reputabunt securam. Ut abdicato Episcopatu, sub quo ab omnibus retro saeculis, in orbe Christiano, et post reformationem in Britannia, Ecclesia tantopere floruit, intoleranda Presbyterii (prout in Scotia obtinet) tyrannis invehatur; quae papatum omnem Hildebrandicum ac Borgianum crudelitate, superbia, avaritia, luxuria et dominandi libidine excedat quam longissime et exsuperat. Ut pessimi perduelles ac parricidae, non modo execranda facta ferant impune, sed et trucidati Regis, et depraedatae Ecclesiae spoliis ornati et locupletati, ac ad summos evecti honores, glorientur, exultent, triumphent, vivant et regnent. Ipse vero Rex et genus omne futurum, cum civibus quibuscumque fortibus ac fidis, qui partes ejus constanter sunt secuti, irae, odio, opprobrio, vindictae impotentissimorum hostium permittantur. Ut Rex Christianus in parentes, fratres, amicos, Deum hominesque impius probet, laudet, justificet edicta illa nefaria, quibus propagandae ligae, foederisque nomine, improba in Regem arma induere, ferro flammaque persequi civibus ac subditis imperatum est, quibus eundem ad deplorandum exitium [42] pertraxerint, et carissimam conjugem, Serenissimam Reginam, maritalibus regnis exegerunt, et liberos superstites, alios patriis ejectos terris tristi exilio, alios domi durissimo presserunt, ac etiamnum premant carcere. Denique ut vanis ejusmodi legationibus tempus trahatur, quoad saevissimus Carnifex Cromwellius (cum quo optime illis conveniebat) subacta jampridem Anglia, de Hibernia, cui nunc imminebat, triumpharet, ac copias viresque omnes, si res postularet, in Scotiam effunderet.

His itaque multisque aliis de causis uno ore affirmabant omnes Regem neutiquam posse, tam iniquis legibus, cum istis, qui sese pro Scotiae

---

[39] *contigerit*, E. This frequent error in E of singular for plural (*v.* n. 26 above, &c.) points to the abbreviation -*āt* for -*ant*, &c., in the folio Wodrow copied.——[40] *hauserunt*, E ; *duratus*, E ; *durateus* is a rare Greek word, applied, as here, to the wooden horse of Troy. It occurs in Latin only in Lucr. i. 476.——[41] *hypocondriacis*, D.——[42] *exitum*, E.

ordinibus falso venditarent, pacisci. Si conscientiae coram immortali Deo, pietatis in parentes posterosque, dignitatis apud suos, famae apud exteros, propriae salutis, juris humani ac divini haberet rationem, longe alias legationes, alia ab eis expectanda esse postulata; ut ostendant sese seria quamvis sera poenitentia ductos, vel levissima restituendi Regis cura et desiderio tangi: fidem itaque et debitum obsequium a praefractis et obstinatis in rebellione perduellibus, justis tandem ac piis armis extorquendum esse.

Ejusmodi argumentis supra modum pungentibus, quorum veritas meridiano sole clarius elucescebat, quia nec ab ordinum delegatis nec ab Hamiltonio et Lauderdelio, qui strenue illis serviebant, occursari potuit,[43] Rex ab eis alienatior, ad Montisrosani sententiam proclivior videbatur. Verum urgentibus fatis (quorum secutus consilium[44] dictu mihi facile non est) expeditionem in Scotiam meditatam, per Galliam in Hiberniam convertit. Abeuntem procerum plerique, in quibus Montisrosanus, Bruxellas usque comitati sunt. Ordinum oratores, more suo, Regem acerbis ac virulentis verbis proscindentes incusabant et criminabantur, quod eorum postulatis non annuisset, et detrectasset pacem. Laeti tamen ac quasi opimis potiti spoliis, quod iter ejus, a cujus praesentia tantopere metuebant, aversum conspicerent a Scotia, quae legitimum principem ardentibus votis desiderabat et deposcebat, jampridem avarae, superbae[45] et crudelis perduellium dominationis pertaesa.

---

[43] *potuit.* D, misled by the capital in *Rex* (?).——[44] *concilium,* D, which regularly writes *consilium*, where *concilium* would be correct.——[45] *avari superbi,* E.

## CAP. VI.

REM quidem difficilem et arduam Montisrosanus admoliebatur.[1] Plurima tamen invitabant et addebant animos, ut inconsulto, temere, et quasi desperanter (quod temere nimis et malitiose quidam[2] effutire ausi sunt) aggressus, non debeat videri; a patria frequentes nuncii, cum[3] procerum opem operamque ultro offerentium literis adhortabantur, ut provinciam alacriter capesseret: fidemque faciebant, Scotos ferme omnes ad obsequium sponte inclinantes, alium sub rege quam eum imperatorem optare neminem. Et sane septentrionem versus hactenus tumultuabantur Makaneus, Seafordii Comitis frater, idem et legatus, cum Regio Regulo[4] et aliis Regiarum partium viris Innernessum occupaverant, diruerant muros, et emensa Moravia, Spaeam amnem

---

[1] *admonebatur,* E.——[2] *quidem,* E.——[3] *eum,* E.——[4] D has here a marginal note, in the first hand, "*The Lord Rae sed haec obscura sunt.*" There can, however, be no doubt that Lord Rae is intended. In Part I., Chap. xvii., his name is rendered *Resius*, and should probably be so written here.

armati superaverant. Ab Hibernia bonae spei plurimum affulgebat; prospere agebat Ormundus pro Carolo vicarius Gubernator et copiarum Dux; ad quem omnium primus Monrous, et post eum alii non pauci cum regis mandatis, et Montisrosani literis, ablegati sunt, qui mutua subsidia, prout res postularet, peterent et promitterent. Angli quotquot regi favissent semper, et Presbyterianorum contagione[5] infecti non erant, palam profitebantur et praedicabant, se tam turpiter ab Hamiltoniis deceptos ac desertos, uni Scotorum Montisrosano fidere posse et debere: cum eo vero ad quodvis discrimen pro carissimo principe retentandum[6] et renovandum esse paratissimos. Electores quidam aliique Germaniae principes auxilia sua pollicebantur: ac ipse Caesar ordinum imperii Conventum semet indicturum, et ad eos de horrenda omnibus orbis principibus Britanniae Regis sorte relaturum spondebat. De Daniae Regis animo et affectu dubitare fas non erat; et legatus ejus Hagae[7] Comitis non modo Regem ipsum sed et Montisrosanum tam suo, quam principis sui nomine, optima sperare indies jubebat. Nec minus sane auxilii a Serenissima Suecorum Regina quam alio quovis amico et cognato expectabatur, tam ob antiqua foedera, quam ob innatam incomparabilis heroinae pietatem, justitiam, clementiam, animique magnitudinem, avo patrique simillimam. Denique (ut de Gallo Hispanoque mutuis sese vulneribus, proh dolor, conficientibus, prorsus sileam)[8] Poloniae regem, Curlandiaeque Ducem, vel cum primis ad auxilium Carolo adferendum accursuros constabat. Ad subsidia ab istis principibus impetranda et transmittenda ad Montisrosanum singuli ferme a Carolo[9] missi sunt oratores;[10] quarum tamen legationum fructum nullum[11] unquam percepit; quod non tam amicissimorum principum culpa, quam pessimis Presbyterianorum artibus et dolo inexplicabili factum est, quo non tantum Montisrosano exitium et perniciem Regi, sed et patriae, sibi, posterisque (nisi Deus opt. Max. avertat) gravissimam vilissimamque peperere servitutem.[12]

Enimvero praeterquam quod aulicos (infidum plerumque hominum genus) promissis ac muneribus corruptos sibi devinxerunt, ut pro viribus Montisrosano apud Regem adversarentur, ac destruerent, quod si minus valerent, res tamen molimine suo gravissimas retardarent; amicis foederatisque principibus exteris per idoneos ministros nimirum emissarios suos (quibus

---

[5] *contagine*, D.——[6] *receptandum*, D.——[7] *Haga*, E.——[8] *ut de Gallo . . . sileam.* This parenthesis is omitted in Tr. 1, but rendered in Tr. 2.——[9] *a Carolo*, om. Tr. 1.——[10] om. *oratores*, E.——[11] *nullam*, D.——[12] Tr. 1 has here the note, "Here there is a great Chasm in the Latin manuscript; The Remainder of this chapter is taken from a short Continuation of Montrose's History, first published about 70 Years ago" (*i.e.*, from the Montr. Rediv., 1652). This affords additional strong evidence that the 1720 translator was unacquainted with our MSS. D and E, and used a different MS., not the original; else the next paragraph, *Enimvero . . . perdant*, and others, would hardly have been omitted. See also Cap. I., nn. 5, 6, &c., Crit. Introd., and n. 15 below. Tr. 2 renders the paragraph omitted in Tr. 1.

tanquam aliud agentibus, commeatum literasque commendatitias ab ipso Rege scelerum tantorum ignaro, impetraverant) persuasere, Carolum honorifice admodum ad regnum Scotiae capessendum invitatum esse; aequa, honesta, et modis omnibus amplexanda fuisse oratorum postulata; optandum adhuc ut Rex eis quam primum annuat; unam hanc illi esse ad salutem sortemque feliciorem viam; qui aliter dicerent, rebus forsan suis bene, sed Regis male consulere; qui arma, milites, stipendia, navigia, commeatus Regis nomine deposcerent ab exteris, quaestum sibi praedamque, non principis commodum et emolumentum quaerere; cui non tantum inutiles et importunae,[13] sed et noxiae quas peterent suppetias; tempestivas tum denique futuras, cum in Regno Scotiae constitutus, amplis et honorificis ex Ordinum sententia legationibus easdem imploraret; aerario interim suo parcant, nec[14] beneficia regi amico et cognato nihil profutura prodigant et perdant.[15]

\* \* \* \* \* \* \* \*

Conjurati proceres caeterique qui pro Regni ordinibus se gerebant, ubi primum Montisrosanum Marchionem proditione traditum audivere, judicandum quoque damnandumque censuerunt, priusquam Edinburgum perduceretur. Moras enim omnes tollendas putarunt, ne tanti viri reverentia, generis splendor, majestas vultus, rerumque gestarum gloria, nimiam hominum gratiam conciliarent illi, quem absentem et inauditum extremo supplicio hactenus devovissent. Selectis igitur quibusdam e numero suo (quos infensissimos ejusdem hostes noverant) delegatis curiae dant in mandatis, ut quid[16] facto opus sit mature expediant, et sententiam quae utilissima videretur scriptam ad ordines illico deferant. Ante meridiem illius diei, qui xiiii. fuit Cal. Junii,[17] referunt illi videri quidem sibi hunc in modum

---

[13] *et importunae*, om. E.——[14] *ac*, E.——[15] E notes here, in Wodrow's hand, "Ther is here in my Copy a Page in folio Blanck." The Advocates' folio also has here a lacuna. In the Crit. Introd., and n. 12 above, the reader will find reasons to show that E was not copied from the folio D, and therefore the folio alluded to is a lost MS. Page 48 of D has space for a few more lines. Both MSS. resume with *Conjurati*, &c. The remainder of this chapter appears as Chap. VII. in Tr. 2, and as Chap. V. (corrected to VII. in the list of errata) in Tr. 1, p. 188; Chap X. in this Tr. As Tr. 2, p. 288, notes at this lacuna, "Here the bishop's narration stops," it is evident that the editor either used a more imperfect MS. than D or E, or carelessly followed Tr. 1. The latter gives the remainder of this chapter as "an old Translation of the Latin Manuscript . . . published in some Editions of Montrose's History, under the Title of a true and perfect Relation, of all the Passages concerning the Examination, Trial and Death of the most Honourable *James* Marquis of *Montrose*, Earl of *Kincardin*, Lord *Graham*, &c." (which appears in the Montr. Rediv., p. 189, ff). Tr. 2 was certainly much indebted to Tr. 1, but with (*v.* n. 8, above, and Cap. III., nn. 75, 84, &c.) independent reference to "MSS." (*v.* Pref. to that edition, p. 9). *The omissions of Tr. 1 seem not*, as the editor of Tr. 2 hastily supposed, entirely *due to* "*inexcusble inadvertency*," *but to the use of another more imperfect MS.*——[16] *dant ut quae facto*, E.——[17] Strictly this should mean May 19th. But the next day was Saturday, which in May 1650 fell on the 18th, the rendering given in the Montr. Rediv., and followed by later editors. In using the Lat. Cal., Wishart's practice follows the English method, omitting to

statuendum esse. Praetores urbanos cum Carnifice ad civitatis portas obvios habeat; nudo capite, ac loris vinctus carrucae imponatur; carnifex capite tecto et equo insidens carrucam regat et agat per civitatem. Patibulo suspensus ad crucem in foro erectam, vitam finiat. Rerum ab eo gestarum commentarius [18] cum Declaratione ad Scotos morientis collo appendantur. Ita ornatus, tres horas populo conspiciendus pendeat. Mortuo caput extremaque corporis membra amputentur. Caput quidem carceri Edinburgensi, membra alia civitatum Aberdoniae, Perthae, Glascuae [19] et Stirlini super [20] imponantur. Denique si paenitentiam egerit et excommunicationis vinculis fuerit solutus, truncum corpus in Cemiterio, secus si fuerit,[21] in publica carnificina sepeliatur.

xiii. Cal. Junii,[22] hora quarta pomeridiana, ad portam quam aquariam aut palustrem vocant, secundum latam pridie sententiam obvium habuit cum praetoribus eorumque armato satellitio [23] lictorem. Ingresso portam (praemissis aliis captivis, qui bini in vinculis longo ordine incedebant) praetores eandem sententiam in eum dictam perlegendam obtulere: arreptam ille composito animo et vultu sedato protinus perlustravit, ac graviter respondit, se quidem ultro obtemperaturum, dolere [24] tantum Regiam Majestatem, cujus vicem ipse gestaret tam foede ac indigne [25] tractari; alacri deinde animo, et gestienti similis, carrucam conscendit, ac civitatis partes quam maxime conspicuas lente praetervectus ad carcerem tandem est perductus.

Progredientem carrucam praeter armatos milites ingens obsidebat [26] hominum turba, in quibus cum calonibus et lixis plurimae erant [27] vulgares mulierculae ad hoc destinatae ac submissae, ut praetereuntem contumeliis lacesserent, pulvere, luto, stercore et congestis lapidibus infestarent, ac obruerent. Verum ea in illo enituit majestas, gravitas, fiducia, magnitudo animi, vultusque constantia, quae et ipsos hostes perculit, et spectatores reddidit attonitos, adeo ut contumelias omnes ac maledicta in preces lacrimasque converterint. Et hoc sane male habuit egregios istos oratores, quos ministros vocant; postridie enim (qui Dominicus fuit) palam in spectatores debacchari [28] minime erubuerunt, quod conviciis et foedis istis missilibus illum non fuissent persecuti. Carruca deductus Carnificem nummis aliquot donavit, inquiens, "accipe auriga recte gubernati currus mihi quidem triumphalis [29] mercedem."

Septima vespertina propemodum elapsa fuerat [30] priusquam ad Carcerem

---

count in the two "terms," namely, the 17th May and June 1st, by which the Latins made May 17th "xvi. days before the Calends of June" (v. Cap. IV., n. 7, and notes to dates, Part I., Engl. Tr.).——[18] *commentaris*, E.——[19] *Glasguae*, E.——[20] So D, E, *super portis* (?) "above the Gates at" (*Montr. Rediv.*, p. 190); or read *superimponantur*.——[21] *fecerit*, E.——[22] v. n. 17 above.——[23] *scatellitio*, E.——[24] *dolore*, E.——[25] *ac indigne* om. E, which has here a lacuna. The words are quite clear in D (v. Cap. III., n. 75; IV., n. 45).——[26] *obsidiebat*, E.——[27] *erat*, D.——[28] *debacchari*, E.——[29] *triumphatis*, E.——[30] *fuerit*, D.

pervenit. Continuo ex numero ordinum nonnulli cum ministris quibusdam, ad eum examinandum, vel magis jurgiis et importunis cavillationibus excruciandum, ablegantur. Negat ille se vel tantillum esse responsurum, quoad usque edoceant quo in loco sint [31] res Regiae, et quomodo principi ac Domino suo cum eis conveniat. Hac ejus constantia ad ordines perlata, caetera quae in illum peragenda restabant, in diem Lunae distulere. Delegatis interim suis permiserunt ut indicarent pacem Regi concordiamque plenam ac perfectam esse cum praesentibus regni sui Ordinibus. Serum diei erat et corpus laboribus, inedia[32] ac itinere non minus difficili quam longe confectum, requiem aliquam et laxationem desiderabat; dicebat enim pompam illam et apparatum quem advenienti eo die exhibuissent, fuisse paulo fastidiosiorem.

Die Dominico,[33] Ministri, Parliamentariique viri, importunis ac molestis quaestiunculis[34] jurgiis, convitiis nimis quietam[35] ac ad celsiora erectam mentem, indesinenter et morose fatigare non destitere. Constantiam tamen convellere, vel voculam unam impatientis[36] animi indicem extorquere nullatenus valuerunt. Aiebat enim, falli eos plurimum qui putarent ignominiosam illi aut[37] tristem fuisse hesternam[38] in infami carruca vecturam; semet enim longe aliter judicare; omnium nimirum quotquot in omni vita confecisset honoratissimum illud ac felicissimum fuisse iter; clementissimum namque Deum et Redemptorem manifesta numinis praesentia magnum et ineffabile solamen attulisse, mentemque gratia plane divina illustrasse et elevasse, ut despectis[39] opprobriis humanis eum unice ac firmiter suspiceret, cujus ergo ista pateretur.

Die Lunae coram ordinibus producto, Cancellarius longa et composita oratione operose exprobavit delicta in primum foedus (quod Nationale vocant) nec non in secundum (quod ligam foedusque nuncupare gaudent): deinde quod patriam infestis armis invasisset;[40] quod perduelles Hibernos advocasset, civilemque effudisset sanguinem: quibus de causis aiebat Deum justis illum meritisque subjecisse poenis. Ubi ille dicendi finem fecisset, interrogavit Ordines Marchio liceretne[41] sibi agere causam suam, et pro se pauca loqui? Quod cum (aegre) annuissent,[42] verbis istis breviter eos est affatus. "Quandoquidem Regi vos utcunque conciliatos audio, et ego consessum[43] hunc non aliter intueor, quam si serenissima Majestas simul[44] assideret, quo solo nomine hanc aperti capitis reverentiam sponte exhibeo, et causam ago, in[45] omnibus ac praesertim publicis negotiis curae mihi[46]

---

[31] *sunt*, E.——[32] *media*, E; cf. Cap. II., n. 65; Cap. V. n. 12, and n. 46. below.——[33] *Dominica*, E.——[34] *quaestiunculae*, E.——[35] *quietem*, E.——[36] *impatientiae*, E.——[37] *illam*, and om. *aut*, E.——[38] *histernam*, D, E.——[39] *despectae*, E.——[40] *inviolasset*, E, "his invasion and joyning with the Irish Rebells" (*Montr. Rediv.*) which supports the reading of D in the text.——[41] *liceretur*, E.——[42] *egre annuisset*, E.——[43] *concessum*, E.——[44] *simull*, E.——[45] *vir*, E.——[46] *initii*, E, without dots and *t* crossed, this would easily be confused with *mihi*; but D is quite clear (*v*. n. 32 above).

fuit, ut me gererem sicut fidelem Christianum ac subditum optime deceret. Primum quidem illud foedus iniisse palam profiteor, ac in eodem servando constanter perstitisse, quoad liquido ac manifeste constitit, nonnullos, obtento religionis et libertatis velo, authoritatem omnem optimi Regis manibus extortam [47] ad se rapere et quasi propriam vindicare; [48] cumque ad malum illud averruncandum, et viros probos qui a tanto scelere abhorrebant, ab ejusdem suspicione liberandos contractum quendam inire necessarium videretur, quo et religioni imprimis prospectum fuit, et insuper cautum ne quid regia Majestas detrimenti caperet, et ego ad contrahentium et subscribentium numerum lubens accessi. Deo Opt. Max. immortales ago gratias, quod secundum illud foedus ligamque nunquam probaverim, aut pro legitimo ac honesta agnoverim, adeo ut rupti istius foederis incusari [49] minus debeam. Quam vero religioni in tot exinde foedissimas discerptae sectas utilis fuerit [50] ista liga, et quot horrendas produxerit [51] tragoedias, afflictissima haec tria regna tristissimum perhibere possint [52] testimonium. Quum autem perduellibus Anglis contra beatissimae memoriae Regem Martyrem rebellantibus (quos ille benedictione divina ferme perdomuerat) [53] factio quaedam hujus regni, suppetias nimis validas et in omne aevum paenitendas ac erubescendas attulisset, visum est Serenissimae Majestati me [54] in patriam amandare, authoritate ejus instructum et diplomate munitum, ut, si qua fieri posset, copias istas perduellibus auxiliares et in eum armatas diverterem. Mandata quidem ejus tanquam justissima et sanctissima agnovi; obsequium vero promptum ac fidele ipsa mihi conscientia debitumque officium imperarunt. Uti ego provinciam illam administraverim, vestrum plurimi estis mihi luculenti testes. Maximis sane imperatoribus rara haec contingit felicitas, ut nihil uspiam militari licentia peccetur: [55] dedi ego operam, ne diu impunita forent cognita et manifesta flagitia. Extra proelii ardorem nullius, ne hostis quidem infensissimi sanguinem fudi; immo furente adhuc marte, multis millibus parcendum praecepi et curavi. Denique sicut S. Majestatis imperio pia arma capessivi, sic ad ejusdem mandata eadem seposui, et in ejus gratiam, nulla rerum mearum habita ratione, ultra oceanum me recepi.

"Quod porro ad nuperum meum in Scotia adventum attinet, imperio ac jussis S. Regis qui hodie vivit (et longum vivat regnetque beatus) et cui obsequium fidemque omnes debemus, hoc praestiti, idque ad accelerandam et maturandam actionem de pace et concordia, quam vobiscum instituerat. Certissimum enim illi fuit paratum me semper fuisse futurum qui ab armis ad nutum ejus abscederem, ubi primum de firma solidaque pace vobiscum

---

[47] *exortam*, E.——[48] *vendicare*, D, E.——[49] *mensari*, E. From this and such errors as *initii* (nn. 32, 46 above), it is clear that in the MS. copied in E the *i*'s were not dotted, and *c* and *e* written indistinctly.——[50] *fuerat*, E.——[51] *produxerat*, E.——[52] *possunt*, E.——[53] *perdomerat*, E.——[54] *ne*, E. ——[55] *percetur* (corrected?), E.

conveniret. Adeo ut merito affirmare audeam,[56] honestiorem militiam potiori jure munitam[57] et a potestate magis legitima collatam hominem subditum adeptum[58] esse neminem, quam fuit illa, quam optimorum Regum auspiciis a me gerenda et administranda suscepta fuit.

"Quapropter hoc vos postulo, ut, seposita nunc praeconcepta opinione, odio, et vindicta privata, consideretis me quod ad[59] aequitatem causae quam sustineo, tanquam hominem eundemque Christianum; quod ad mandata principis mei, tanquam subditum, qui eadem fideliter sum exsecutus; quod ad merita de vobis, tamquam civem et popularem jure carissimum et gratissimum, qui quam plurimis vitam fortunasque conservavi in quos animadvertendi nec jus nec facultas, sed unica mihi deerat voluntas. Temere iniquum[60] in me quidquam decernere nolite; verum secundum Dei, naturae, gentium, ac praesertim Regni hujus jus, et[61] leges patriae, mecum agite. Secus si feceritis, ad justum mundi judicem provoco, qui cunctis olim futurus judex est semperque juste judicat."

Haec ea gravitate, modestia et constantia oris (quae animi inturbati[62] certissimus est index) pronunciavit, ut immanissimos etiam hostes in maximam admirationem[63] pertraxerit. Cum vero breviter ita perorasset, Cancellarius sententiam in eum pridem latam, perlegi jussit; quam[64] ille diligenter quidem, sed immotus tamen ac inconcussus auscultavit. Secunda vice conantem loqui, Cancellarius et minitabundus quidem, praepedivit, illicoque[65] edixit, ut confestim in carcerem retraheretur. Vixdum regressum (morosiores plane et molestiores hostes[66]) Ministri invadunt, arcem constantiae ejus convellere aggrediuntur, anathemata intonant, censurae suae gravitatem verbis admodum tragicis extollunt, aeternas[67] interminantur poenas et diris nequicquam territant. Ille innocentiae suae innitens errantis clavis[68] terriculamenta et fanaticorum hominum deliria[69] susque deque habuit, et immeritam censuram, justo ac nihil sibi conscio minime nocituram, verum clavigeris ipsis iniquis et temerariis longe periculosiorem, aequo animo tulit.

Apud praetores urbanos, qui jugiter eum observabant, debitorem se

---

[56] *audiam*, E.——[57] *nullam*, E.——[58] *ademptum*, E.——[59] om. *ad*, E.——[60] *uñius in me* (*sic*), E.——[61] *jus et* om. E.——[62] *imperturbati*, E.——[63] *perturbationem*, E. "As was much admired even of his enemies" (*Montr. Rediv.*).——[64] *quum*, E.——[65] *ilico*, D.——[66] *morosiores . . . hostes* om. *Montr. Rediv.* "A more sullen and importunate set of enemies" (Tr. 2).——[67] *externas*, with *x* deleted, E. For Wishart's additions to the original narrative embodied in the Wigton MS., Perfect Relation, Montrose Redivivus, and Wardale MS, see notes to Pt. II. Ch. X. in our translation. In the whole of this Chap. VI. there is no evidence that any portion of it was written later than about 1650.——[68] *clavis* quite clear in both MSS. The sense requires *plebis*, or *laici*. Wishart repeatedly emphasises the terrorism exercised over the laity by the censures, anathemas, fines, and excommunications of the presbyteries and ministers. *Clavis* is probably due to *clavigeris*, immediately below. The agreement of D and E seems to indicate that the MS. from which D was copied was one of those used by R. Wodrow in his "collation" (?).——[69] *diliria*, E.

## PARS II.—CAP. VI.

parliamento praedicabat, pro longe maximo honore quo illum affecisset inquiens, "Magis eximium decus mihi[70] fore existimo, quod caput meum praesentibus posterisque conspiciendum eminentissimo carceris hujus fastigio hac de causa imponatur, quam si statuam mihi auream in foro erigendam, aut effigiem pulcherrime depictam in intimis Regiae penetralibus conservandam decrevisset.[71] Et ne fides mea pietasque in carissimos Reges oblivione aliquando oblinantur,[72] pro augustissimo honore duco, quod in quatuor celeberrimis regni civitatibus, duratura[73] tantisper monumenta erexerint,[74] quae memoriam mei ad seros possint transmittere nepotes. Si enim votis meis daretur, ex animo optarem carnem artusque meos ad hoc sufficere, ut particulatim in omnes Christiani orbis civitates dividi possent, tanquam certissimi fidei meae in Reges et in patriam caritatis testes ac tesserae."

Paucis[75] qui vel minima familiaritate illi olim fuissent grati, in conspectum ejus venire permissum fuit; quibus et tempus brevissimum fuit definitum, et adhibiti praetores qui hoc agerent, ne quos arcanos permiscerent sermones. Hostium interim satellites custodesque militares (importunum genus hominum et molestum) conclave diu noctuque opplebant; adeo ut privatis precibus ac menti ad caelos erigendae vix ac ne vix quidem tempus aut locus ab eorum cavillationibus et tumultuosis vocibus immunis concederetur.

Mane illius diei (x. Cal. Junii[76] fuit) quo morte mulctandum[77] decreverant, cum civitas omnis crepitaculorum et tubarum clangoribus immodice personaret, custodiae militaris praefectum interrogavit, quid sibi vellet immensus ille et insolitus classicorum strepitus? Respondit iste, cives militesque ad arma vocari; metuere enim ordines ne quis ad mortis illi inferendae famam exoriatur tumultus. Nec dissimulare quidem non exiguum esse malignantium numerum, quo nomine amicos omnes et fautores Regis odiose nuncupare solent, qui plus aequo illi faveant. Ad quae Marchio paucis rettulit, "**Qui vivus bonis istis viris formidatus fui, moribundus etiam sum formidabilis.**[78] Verum caveant sibi; mortuus enim conscientiis eorum jugiter obversans[79] quam maxime formidandus ero." Parliamentario dein viro, cui Archibaldo Johnstonio nomen est, homini tristi, lymphato et moroso, importune invisenti et moleste suscitanti, quid rerum ageret? (caesariem autem forte explicabat ac depectebat) subridens respondit; "Caput hoc, quod huc usque meum est, curo et ordino:[80] postridie ubi erit vestrum, pro libidine vestra vos illud pertractate."

---

[70] *meum*, E.——[71] *penitralibus conservandum decrevissent*, E.——[72] *obsumatur*, E.——[73] *diuturna*, E.——[74] *erexerunt*, E.——[75] This paragraph is briefer in Montr. Rediv., p. 193, where nothing is said of the presence of the magistrates and soldiers.——[76] *v.* n. 17 above. This paragraph is not found in Montr. Rediv. and Tr. 1, but rendered in Tr. 2.——[77] *militandum*, E (*v.* n. 49 above). ——[78] *Qui vivus . . . formidabilis* written large in both D and E.——[79] *conscientias . . . observans*, E.——[80] *ordo*, E.

Hora quasi secunda pomeridiana, paludamento coccinei coloris auro textili[81] egregie ornato indutus, in locum carnificinae destinatum perductus fuit a carcere ad forum. Is[82] radiantium oculorum visus est splendor, incessus magnificentia, vultusque decora majestas quae et civitatem omnem horrore immanis supplicii perculit, et ab ipsis hostibus invitum hoc extorsit testimonium, **majoris, altioris, fortioris, firmioris**[83] animi[84] virum nostro saeculo natum esse neminem. Quoniam vero amici quique ac benevoli quam longissime arcebantur, inventus fuit puer quidam ignotus Tachygraphicae artis admodum peritus, qui suprema ejus notis velocissime exciperet. Capite plectendis[85] libere ad populum perorare more patruo concessum semper fuit; verum et hoc illi exonerandi animi levamen a praetoribus pernegatum fuit. Ex illis tamen quae non tam continua et composita oratione prolocutus est, quam ad quaestiones ab astantibus injectas respondit, haec ferme sunt quae a notario fideliter[86] excepta et sparsim dicta congesta in[87] unum ad nos emanarunt:—

"Male quidem[88] me haberet, si cordato quivis Christiano exitus hic meus foret offendiculo. Saepiusne justis accidit secundum improborum vices,[89] et secundum justorum improbis? Caditne quando[90] justus in justitia sua, et impius in sua impietate agit prospere? Sane quibus ego probe notus sum, abjectus ac miser minime videbor, hoc nomine quod ista patiar; multis enim et me longe majoribus haud absimilia evenere fata. Justa quidem Dei judicia poenasque omnes in me irrogatas, ob privata plurima ac gravia in Sacrosanctum ejus numen delicta, aequissimas esse agnosco et praedico; voluntati ejus memet totum sponte et libenter subjicio ac permitto; mortalibus vero cunctis tanquam ministris ejus injurias in me omnes ultro et ex animo condono. Deus immortalis illis itidem ignoscat; oppresserunt pauperem, judicium et justitiam pervertere; verum qui celsior illis est, mercedem olim rependet.

"Juxta leges patrias in patria me plane gessi; et aequissima supremi principis mei mandata[91] ad tuendam ejus in maximis constituti angustiis salutem, contra illos, qui nefariis armis in eundem depugnabant, pro officio suscepi.[92] Unum hoc assidue cogitabam, ut ex lege Dei, naturae, et gentis nostrae, timerem Deum, Regemque honorarem. In homines neutiquam, in solum Deum peccavi, apud quem longe maxima est misericordia; cujus unica fretus fiducia, ad solium[93] ejus interritus appropinquabo. Futura[94]

---

[81] *texili*, D.——[82] *forum, is*, D, E.——[83] *majoris . . . firmioris*, written large in D, E.——[84] *unum*, E (*v. n.* 46 above).——[85] *plectendus*, E.——[86] *perloquutus*, and om. *est . . . fideliter*, E. Probably a line of the MS. Wodrow copied, "skipped" by oversight (*v.* Cap. IV., n. 33).——[87] *sparsum dicta congestum unum*, E, in which Wodrow has terribly mauled the passage. One knows not which to admire most—his ignorance or diligence; to have copied a MS. with such exquisite pains (in writing), of which he evidently understood next to nothing.——[88] *equidem*, E.——[89] *vicis*, E.——[90] *quandoque*, E.——[91] *. . . ndata* in D, where the page has been injured comparatively recently.——[92] *depugnabant*, and om. *pro officio suscepi*, E.——[93] *solum*,' E, as usual.——[94] *appropinquabo futura* &c., E.

praedicere et in arcana [95] D. Dei penetrare nolo.  Largiatur tamen clementissimus Pater, ut quae hodie in me perpetrantur, afflictae huic genti carissimae patriae meae in perniciem suam sponte ruenti, nunquam in graviora cedant mala.

"Sunt in vobis (homines etiam minime mali) qui de me querentur, quod gravi illa censura ecclesiastica notatus moriar.  Culpa haec mea nulla est, siquidem illam alio crimine non promeruerim, quam quod debitum legitimo principi [96] praestiterim obsequium, idque ad religione sacrosanctum [97] ejusdem caput authoritatemque sartam tectam juxta leges conservandam.  Dolet sane temere nimis (ne quid gravius dicam) mihi a viris istis interdictum sacris, quantumque in me est, salva semper conscientia, ut sententiam illam secundum Dei leges revocatam velint et cassam, peto ac voveo.  Quod si minus impetravero, justum mundi Judicem (quem propediem mihi futurum judicem spero) ac Redemptorem appello.

"Obstrepunt alii (ut morientis etiam famam et existimationem modis omnibus laedere et elevare valeant) me hac ratione culpam omnem in reges conjicere.  Procul absit [ab omnia mea] [98] tanta impietas.  Beatissimus ille Rex defunctus vixit omnino sanctus, mortuusque est Martyr.  Utinam et ego, prout non prorsus absimili fato, sic et simili sanctitate et patientia vitam finiam [99] meam.  Equidem si animam meam in cujusvis vicem transire liceret, aut cum alia conjungi aut componi, unicam ejus seligerem et praeoptarem.  Quod vero Regem vivum spectat, omnium sub sole felicissimum fore populum existimo, qui sub justissimo et mitissimo ejus imperio vitam sit traducturus.  Quaecunque mihi in mandatis dedit aequissima fuere.  Promissis stat firmiter, nec fidem fallit.  Et quamvis ad misericordiam et clementiam genius ejus sit propensior, justitiam tamen in omnibus religiose colit, et cum omnibus sancte observat.  Deum Opt: Max: veneror supplex, et oro, ut non minus fideles et justos servos subditosque inveniat; ne forte (ut pater) ab illis aliquando prodatur, de quibus optime fuerit meritus, et in quibus nimiam collocaverit fiduciam.

"Nemo, quaeso, bruto stupori aut superbae contumaciae tribuat, quod hunc in modum me hodie geram, quod in nonnullis aliter quam plerique vestrum sentiam, et in omnibus ad vota sententiasque vestras non accedam.  Conscientiae meae ad verae religionis et rectae rationis normas compositae lumen sequor, quod benedictus D. Dei mei Spiritus (qui cordi insidet meo) praemonstrat.  Strenue mihi utendum est fidei virtute et patientiae vigore,

---

[95] *arcanis*, E.——[96] *legitimi principis*, E.——[97] D ends here with the catchword *sacrosanctum*, showing that some written pages of this MS. have been lost.  As it contains sixty pages, and the folio sheets are arranged in quires of eight pages, probably four pages, or one sheet, have been lost—enough to have contained the remainder of Part II., but not the poem copied by Wodrow in E (*v.* pp. 486 ff.).——[98] *omnino ab me?* or *abominata mihi?*——[99] *fineam meam, Equidem*, E.

quem ille benigne et clementer largitur.[100] Ita armatus morti fortiter occurro, ac spei fiduciaeque plenus solio caelesti me sisto. Glorificetur Dominus[101] in caelis vel hac mea condemnatione in terris. Quae quidem timoris ac diffidentiae verba non sunt, verum gratitudinis in deum et dilectionis in populum ejus plena. Quoties enim vos cerno, aut cogitatione complector, non possum non illacrimari malis vestris, quibus ego tempestive mederi, renitentibus peccatis nostris, frustra conatus sum.

"Plura dicere non habeo quam quod caritatis vestrae judicio recte ordinato memet permittam, et piorum preces pro salute animae meae ex hoc corporis carcere hactenus evolantis postulem. Ego sane pro vobis omnibus oro, et Omnipotentis Dei iram pridem excitatam ac misello[102] huic regno imminentem serio sed submisse et humiliter deprecor. De putrescentibus corporis hujus reliquiis triumphum agant homines quantumlibet; nunquam tamen efficient[103] ut Deum meum non timeam, non colam, non amem, Regemque meum tam in morte quam in vita honorem. D. Deo ac Redemptori spiritum, obsequium Regi, patriae posterisque famam, benevolentiam amicis, et vobis omnibus propensissimum affectum commendo. Plura forsan, si liceret, adderem; verum ista breviter liberandae conscientiae meae dicta sufficiant."[104]

Rogatus postmodum solusne ac seorsum precari vellet, respondit, "Si quidem preces mecum communicare populo non permittitis, tam vobis quam mihi forsan erit scandalo in tam frequenti concione separata et solitaria oratio. Coram Domino, cui penitus perspectum est cor meum, hactenus effudi animam meam; in manus Ejus spiritum meum tradidi, et Ille mihi plenam remissionis peccatorum, pacis ac salutis fiduciam in Jesu Christo, Redemptore meo, clementer et gratiose obsignare dignatus est." Haec graviter effatus, obseratis oculis, erectis in caelos manibus, aliquantisper in spiritu supremum Numen veneratus est. Quo quidem tempore ingenti divini spiritus solamine desuper perfusum fuisse non obscura prodiderunt indicia. Isto defunctus officio lictorem advocatum nummis[105] aliquot donavit.

Allatum mox rerum ab eo gestarum commentarium cum declaratione ad Scotos funiculo[106] appensum, mira quadam alacritate et vultu ad hilaritatem composito, collo suo imposuit, inquiens, "etsi munificentissimo Regi visum fuerit in numerum equitum nobilissimi ordinis Garterii me cooptare,

---

[100] *largetur*, E. (*Largietur*)? "had supplied him," Tr. 2, in which this whole speech is rendered, with extraordinary want of taste, in the third person.——[101] *sisto, Glorificaetur dominus*, E, the punctuation of which throughout, where there is any, is very wrong, even, as here, with a capital to guide the copier. Tr. 2 renders *sisto*, "to sist himself before the throne of God," using the Sc. legal term. The Montr. Rediv. gives here, "Let God be glorified in my end, though it were in my Damnation," a sentiment explained by the Latin words *in terris*.——[102] *missello*, E.——[103] *efficiant*, E.——[104] "Here yr is a leafe in folio Blank," note in E.——[105] *numinis*, E (*v*. n. 49 above).——[106] *fruciculo*, E.

longe tamen majori decori et ampliori honori funiculum hunc cum appensis libris cedere existimo. Eos itaque intensiore gaudio amplector quam torquem aureum, aut ipsum D. Georgii gloriosissimum insigne olim susceperim. Confestim,[107] quaeso, annectite, prout vobis maxime arridebit."

Praetores denique et satellitum praefectos, cum brachia vinculis constringi et paludamentum detrahi curassent, hisce verbis compellavit; " Agite, obsecro, adjicite quicquid dedecoris (ut vos quidem putatis) aut ignominiae superest, quod in me comminisci[108] valeatis; paratus enim sum qui sponte, comiter et hilariter plura ac tristiora omnia hac de causa perpetiar. Deus immortalis pereuntis hujus gentis misereatur!" Atque ita tandem secundum sententiam pridem in absentem et inauditum latam, invicta constantia et miranda animi magnitudine, vir, vel hostium confessione et suffragio, incomparabilis, immortalitatis candidatus vitam hanc miseram ac mortalem cum beata illa ac aeterna commutavit.

---

[107] *Confesti in,* E.——[108] *me-comminisci (sic)* E.

## MANIBUS BEATISSIMIS

Illustrissimi,[1] Invictissimi, Constantissimi, Jacobi MONTISROSARUM MARCHIONIS, Comitis[2] de KINCAIRNE &c.: Gubernatoris vicarii, et copiarum omnium terra marique in Regno Scotiae pro Regia Majestate supremi Imperatoris, a Conjuratis perduellibus immaniter trucidati, Versus sive Elegia,[3] anniversaria prima, authore eodem, qui commentarium rerum ab eo praeclarissime gestarum fidelissime descripsit.

CIƆIƆCL.

QUEM genus, et genius, quem mens in corpore firmo
    Firmior, et pulchro pulchrior ore lepos,
Quem pietas, quem alma Themis,[4] constantia nullis
    Expugnata (licet mille petita) malis,—

Quem Regi servata fides, victriciaque arma,
    Sextaque palmatae gloria rara togae,[5]
Hostibus et toties ultro data dextera victis,
    Quem nimius patriae (proh pereuntis) amor

Extulit ad superos, et fama aeterna sacravit,
    Et totum virtus vendicat[6] una sibi,
Deprimit invidia et, rapidis truculentior ursis,
    Gestit adhuc manes (heu) violare pios!

Quis furor, o cives, urit jecur, oraque siccat,
    Atque verecundam non sinit[7] esse sitim?
An Pharii[8] nullo rabies extinguitur haustu
    Sanguinis, an nullis morsibus atra jacet

2. Exsaturata fames? epulis sed crescit adauctis,[9]
    Crescit et infandae dira libido dapis.
Saevitum nimis est, nimium crudelibus iris
    Hactenus indultum. Jam cohibete manus,

---

[1] *Jaustrissimi*, E. This MS. is our only authority for the poem.—[2] *Comes*, E.—[3] *Lessus sirelegia*, E.—[4] *Themes*, E.—[5] cf. Martial, vii. 2, 8.—[6] *vendicat*, E; cf. Part II., Cap. VI., n. 48.—[7] *non sinit et esse*, E.—[8] *Pharii*, an allusion to the Ministers, compared to the mad dervish priests of Isis (?); cf. Tib. i. 3, 32.—[9] *adunctis*, E, a word without authority. For *adauctis*, cf. Plaut. Stich. ii. 2, 62.

## MANIBUS BEATISSIMIS.

"Carnifices, cohibete manus," vox horrida clamat
    Et penetrat caelos sanguinis innocui;
Lethiferosque arcus tendens ensemque coruscans
    Intentat poenas vindicis ira Dei.

Crura, manusque ambas, exsanguiaque ora sepulchro
    Et laceres artus quid prohibere juvat?
Extincto pavidus mus[10] insultare leoni
    Assolet, et torvas rodere dente jubas:
Extinctae rigidos aquilae depascitur armos
    Degener et milvus, foedaque vultur edit:
Extinctumque fugax contemnit dama Melampum,
    Et formidatum vana capella lupum.
Dicite vos pavidi mures, vos dicite milvi
    Degeneres, et vos dicite carnivori

3. Vultures, solaque fuga[11] vos dicite damae
    Insignes, vanae dicite, quaeso, caprae,
Proditione, dolo, scelere atque libidine vestra
    Oppressum indigna perdere morte virum,
Atque (immane nefas) tristi pallentia tabe[12]
    Membra arcere suo semisepulta rogo
Non pudet, ad vivum cujus modo nomen et umbram
    Non puduit turpem praecipitasse fugam,
Et trepidasse metu toties et montibus altis
    Aut timidum silvis occuluisse caput,
Et vertisse[13] solum, et totis diffidere terris
    Et petiisse rates et latuisse mari?
Si vos non tenuit tantae virtutis imago,
    Invidiae stimulos sed magis ursit acres,[14]
Regia jussa tamen, nomenque vicesque supremi
    Principis, imperii legitimique modus,
Jura patrum, legesque sacrae, et veneranda potestas,
    Qua nihil in terris sanctius esse solet,

4. Avertisse scelus potuit. Sed nullus honesti
    Est amor in vobis, curaque nulla boni;

---

[10] *unus*, E, but *v. mures*, six lines below.——[11] *atque fuga sola*, E.——[12] *labo*, E, in which *o* and *e* are often confused, *e.g., ferme* appears frequently as *forme*.——[13] *vertisse solum*, meaning, to dig hiding-places in the earth (?), or, like *mutari caelum*, "to seek other lands" (?).——[14] *ācres* always; but probably Wishart wrote the line as it stands.

Et procul a caecis animis jus, fasque fidesque
    Exulat, et pietas et pudor omnis abest.
Regalis postquam cessit reverentia sceptri,
    Et majestatis laus fuit esse reos,
Jusque datum servis, et rupta repagula legum,
    Et populi auspiciis foedera juncta malis,
Sinceri rectique nihil; fraudesque dolique
    Cumque latrociniis furta, rapina, neces;
Visque armata toros pertentat, et omnia vastat,[15]
    Et nihil illicitum jam putat esse sibi.
Nullum crimen abest. Instant bella, improba bella,
    Et belli comites, pestis et atra fames
Invadunt miseros. Nova vectigalia vexant,
    Legibus atque novis criminibusque novis
Illaqueare pios juvat, et nil tale merentes
    Exercere odiis. Quam nocet esse pium!

5. Quodque magis stupeas,[16] et quae mihi maxima semper
    Viscera corrodit cura dolore gravi,
Dira superstitio mentique illapsa protervae
    Impia crudelitas[17] provocat omne nefas;
Inque deos hominesque ruit miserabile vulgus
    Seditione potens, ambitione patres
[Flantur],[18] avaritia nihil (heu) moderabile suadent,
    Nec finem tantis imposuisse malis.
Vecordes gaudent, accensis pinguia flammis
    Pabula conjiciunt, sufficiuntque novas[19]
Egregii imprimis vates; qui sponte furentes
    Exagitant stimulos, et fera corda cient,
Accenduntque iris animos, pacemque perosi
    Carmine ferali nil nisi bella crepant.
Eumenides[20] credas Stygio emersisse profundo,
    Et nostro Furias incubuisse solo
Regibus infensas, queis ira odioque superbo
    Livida corda tument,[21] lingua cruenta tonat;

6. Nec nisi purpureo placantur sanguine ditum,
    Gratior ante aras victima nulla cadit.

---

[15] *vustat*, E.—[16] *Quod m·igis stupeas*, E.—[17] *crudēlitas.*—[18] *Si Flamen*, E, with *si* deleted. The capital F shows that *Flamen*, or some word like it, began the line. *Flantur* is conjectural.—[19] *novat*, E.—[20] *Eume*, or *Sume*, or *Eumet* (in different hand, and partly obliterated) *Indies*, E.—[21] *sument*, E.

Quid memorem ingentes animos regnique capaces,
  Straffordi magni, cum Lilioque Lucam,
Et Laudem pietate insignem, et marte Capelum,[22]
  Atque infelicis funera Hamiltonii,
Gordoniosque alios ipso cum principe gentis,
  Moravium juvenem, Spotswodiumque senem,
Maxwallum, Rolocum[23] et nimium praecocis Ogilvi
  Fata [Lethum]?[24] ast omnes longa referre mora.
Carolus unus adest, et Carolus omnibus unus,
  Carolus ille bonus, Carolus ille pius,
Carolus ille Deum soboles, et maxima magni
  Cura Dei, et magno proximus ille deo,
Major adest testis, quem vos immanibus aris
  Devotum pridem non jugulasse pudet,—
Heu scelus, heu facinus, monstrum execrabile cunctis,
  Nuncia venturi prodigiosa mali!

7. Di bene, quod Carolo comitem dent fata beato
    Graemum, quod Graemo fata dedere ducem
  Ingentem Carolum, votis date, et optio fiat,
    Ille alium comitem nollet, et ille ducem.
  Sed vos humani generis portenta, Gigantes
    Terrigenae, saecli testis, et ira Deum,
  Cyclopes, ululae, Harpyiae, Stygiaeque paludis
    Excrementa, soli probra, flagella poli,
  Quanta manet vindicta reos ultricibus armis,
    Atque intestinis Mars furibundus aget!
  Fraternas acies fraternaque vulnera cerno, et
    Eruta fraterna viscera saeva manu,
  Et servile jugum duris cervicibus atque
    Imponi pedibus ferrea vincla pigris,
  Arentesque siti fauces, et torrida peste
    Lumina, et indomita languida membra fame.—
  Parva loquor; vestrum quota pars est ista malorum
    Quos majora vocant termina, flagra, cruces.

8. Conscia corda novis furiis agitabit Erinnys,[25]
    Nulla dies requiem, nox quoque nulla dabit;

---

[22] *et laudem . . . Capelium*, E.—[23] *Rocolum*, E.—[24] *Lethum*, so E. *Equitum?*—[25] *Erimnis*, E.

Conterrent noctu pavidas insomnia mentes,
　　Conterrent tacitum murmur [26] et umbra diu;
Anxia mille graves distorquent pectora curae,[27]
　　Solicitosque animos luctus et horror habet;
Hinc metus, hinc atris volitans infamia pennis,
　　Hinc gravis ira hominum, atque [28] hinc gravis ira deum,
Livida [29] perpetuis urunt praecordia flammis,
　　Nec mora, nec requies, nec modus ullus erit,
Donec ab immota Supremi Judicis urna
　　Sors cadet, illa meis non referenda modis,
Desperata salus et inexorabilis Orcus,
　　Seraque vos Nemesis, vos metanæa [30] premet.
Interea Rosei Montis [31] fulgentius Heros,
　　Ingratae patriae dedecus atque decus,
Ornamentum ingens, ingens infamia terrae,
　　Idem amor atque dolor, Scotia moesta, tuus, [32]

9. Sidereasque domos nitidique palatia caeli,
　　Astra super, Superum tecta superba petit;
Sub pedibusque videns pereuntis inania [33] mundi,
　　Gaudet honore dei, gaudet amore frui.
Atque illae (infandi monumenta pudenda furoris)
　　Reliquiae, tanti pendula membra viri,
Clara trophea velut, famaeque sonantibus alis
　　Imposita, aut celsis suspicienda Tholis,
Virtutemque fidemque et fortia facta loquentur
　　Magnanimi Herois, laudibus atque novis
Ornabunt manes. Titulos fastosque perennes
　　Adjiciet gratae posteritatis amor.
Quodque potest unum, tibi, maxime Graeme, quotannis
　　Solemnes elegos [34] nostra Camena dabit;
Quem coluit vivum (rumpantur ut invida Codro [35]
　　Ilia) defunctum non minus illa colet.

---

[28] *murimur*, E.——[27] *cura*, E.——[28] *et*, E.——[29] *Levida*, E.——[30] i.e., μετάνοια, repentance, remorse.——[31] *Rosei montis*, i.e., *Montis rosei*, Montrose.——[32] *messa tua*, E.——[33] *mania*, E.——[34] *Elogos*, E.——[35] *Codro*, E. From Verg. *Ed.* vii. 26. Codrus was a worthless poet, envious of Vergil. Hence often, as in Juvenal, typical of a bad tedious poet. Perhaps Wishart means to suggest that his writings had aroused the envy of some poor scribbler. Certainly the success of his "Commentary" was most distasteful to the Covenanters.

## MANIBUS BEATISSIMIS.

10. Verus amor nullis fortunae extinguitur undis;
 Nulla timet fati fulmina verus amor;
 Immortalis amor verus manet, et sibi semper
 Constat, et aeternum, quisquis amavit, AMAT.[36]

Anno 1650 scripsi in copia mea.[37]

---

[36] The pathos and beauty of the last four lines form an exquisite monument of Wishart's love for his slain hero, which deserves the immortality it claims.——[37] Note in the same hand as the poem and the rest of E, namely, Robert Wodrow's. The date shows that it was a note of the author himself. But as the preface to the poem says that it was written on the "first anniversary," it must have been written on May 21st, 1651, and probably "Anno 1651" should be read here. If the lost original MS. contained it, and in this order, immediately after Part II., we should have strong evidence that Part II. was written before May 1651. The numbers at the side of the above lines occur in the MS. They have nothing to do with the sections of the poem. Possibly they refer to the pages of the MS. from which Wodrow copied. The numerous corruptions and erasures indicate that this was written in an obscure hand. As the numbers do not occur to the same number of lines regularly, possibly in this lost MS. lines had been scored out. The normal number of lines to a page seems to have been eighteen. Hence the page of the lost MS. was a small one, not the folio "Book" "collated" by Wodrow, which had over forty lines to the page. See Crit. Introd.

# APPENDIX.

## APPENDIX I.

### BATTLE OF CARBISDALE. See Part II., Chap. viii.

#### LIST OF THOSE KILLED AND TAKEN PRISONER,

from Balfour, Ann. iv. 11, 12, &c., supplemented from the History of the Earls of Sutherland (Sallagh's Continuation), Montr. Rediv., Monteith, and Acts Parl. Scot.

Balfour's list is given in the 1756 edition of Wishart's Montrose, with variations, which show that the editor derived it from some MS. list, the source of which we have been unable to trace.

#### KILLED.

Thomas Ogilvy, Laird of Powrie.
Gilbert Menzies, Laird of Pitfoddels, yr., standard-bearer.
John Douglas, youngest son of William, Earl of Morton.
Col. J. (?) Gordon (Sallagh). See pp. 282–284.
Major Lisle (Monteith, 511).   Captain Erskine.
Major Biggar.   Captain Garrie.
Major Guthrie (Monteith, 511).   Lieutenant Home (Holme).
Captain Stirling (Monteith, 517, says he was executed—a mistake).   About 450 common souldiers killed, and 200 drowned.
Captain Powell.
Captain Swan (?). In Acts Parl. Scot. Swan is banished. Was the report of his death incorrect, or were there *two* of the name?

#### PRISONERS.

Viscount Frendraught. See p. 308, n. 63.

General Major Hurrie, "pleaded the benefit of quarter, and a great charge of children." Montr. Rediv., 186. *Executed* May 29th.

Colonel Thomas Gray, petitioned the House, May 31st, "quherby he shew that he had beine out of the countrey 34 zeires, [p. 26, " 33 zeires"] and wes cousined and circumveined by James Grhame." Balf., *ibid.*, p. 26, says, "It wes expected some moneyes should haue bein gottin out of him, bot that failled." Was this the Colonel Thomas Gray of Part II., Chap. 1, n. 2? Herr Koren, keeper of the

Throndhjem archives, informs us that on October 13, 1649, the army in Norway was reduced; and July 20, 1650, a successor was appointed to his lieutenant-colonelcy of the Throndhjem infantry. Previously he had served in the war between Sweden and Denmark-Norway, under Hannibal Sehestadt, the Statholder in Norway. In a fit of intoxication he had insulted Sehestadt, for which he was court-martialed, September 1645, but dealt with leniently. Saml. Norske Folks Sprog og Hist., iii., iv. (Chr. 1835–1838), 400, and *ibid.* v. 302.

Lieutenant-Colonel Stewart.

Lieutenant-Colonel James Hay, brother to the laird of Naughton. Detained in the north either by wounds, or friends anxious to screen him. May 23rd, the House ordered him to be sent to Edinburgh. He was afterwards employed by Charles II. and the Perth Parliament to deal with Monk on currency questions. Balf. iv. 329.

Major Affleck. "Cap: Androw Afflecke, a Scottsman borne, quho had beine out of this countrey 29 zeires, . . . the housse by woyces sentences him to be banished the kingdome for euer, vnder the paine of death, and not to returne without licience of the parliament." Balf. iv. 27; Act Parl. Scot., VI. ii. 569.

Captain John Spottiswood, son of the laird of Darsie, grandson of the Archbishop of St. Andrews (p. 187, n. 8). *Executed* May 29. See his craven petition, as given in Balf. iv. 28–31; but comp. Montr. Rediv., 187: "a compleat young Gentleman, and very worthy of pitty (if any had been shown), being very young, but an excellent spirit, and a good Scholar." Cf. F$^r$ Hay's genealogy of Fam. of Spottiswoode, Spot. Mis. i. 13.

Captain William Ross, banished for life; sent to France. Balf. iv. 26, 37. He appears as "Lieutenant" in the first account of the battle (*ibid.* 11). A Lieutenant William Ross, in Glencairn's expedition, was taken by the English at Dunkeld, February 10, 1654. Gwynne's Mem., App. p. 247.

Captain Mortimer.

Rittmaster Wallensius (Rootemaster Vallensius, Wallensen, a Dane?).

Peter Saues, Captain of Dragoons (probably a foreigner).

Captain Warden (Englishman?).

Captain Auchinleck (probably identical with Major or Captain Affleck—same name).

Captain Lawson.

Captain-Lieutenant Gustavus (*al.* Gustar, a Swede?).

Lieutenant Verkin (foreigner).

Lieutenant Andrew Glen (Osen in 1756 edition).

Lieutenant Rob. Touch. Acts Parl. Scot., VI. ii. 580.

Ernestus Buerham (Dane or Holsteiner?).

Laurence Van Luitenberge (*al.* Luttenberg. Hollander?).

Lieutenant David Drummond. "The parliament pardons his lyffe, and ordaines him to be sent to France, and banished this kingdome, and to act himselue neuer to returne thither bot licience of the parliament." Act Parl. Scot., VI. ii. 571; Balf.

iv. 37. Was he the Colonel Drummond who, in December 1653, shipped from Holland with 150 volunteers for Glencairn? Gwynne, Mem., App. 221.

Lieutenant John Drummond.
Lieutenant James Dun (*al.* Din).
Lieutenant Alexander Stewart.
Cornet Ralph Marlie (*al.* Murray).
Cornet Henrick Erlach (Holsteiner?).
Cornet Daniel Bennicke (Holsteiner?).

Ensign Robert Graham. Cf. Acts Parl. Scot., VI. i. 669. "Reserved for punishment, with one Grime, servant to Jas. Henderson." Balf. iv. 19. Robert Graham, the Elder, of Cairnie, attended Montrose's "True Funerals" in 1661; also Robert G. of Morphie.

Ensign Adrian Ringwerthe (Holsteiner?).
Ensign Hans Boaz (Holsteiner?).

| | |
|---|---|
| 2 Quartermasters. | 2 Trumpeters. |
| 6 Sergeants. | 3 Drummers. |
| 15 Corporals. | 386 Common soldiers. |

2 Ministers, Mr. Kiddie and Mr. Meldrum. No trace of them has been found in Orkney records; but they appear to be "the deposed ministers of Orkney, quho had landed with James Grhame." Balf. iv. 31.

Besides these, Captain Alexander Charters, brother to the laird of Empsfield, was taken and *executed*, June 22nd. "Of an honourable and antient family in that "kingdome. The ministers having dealt with him to acknowledge his fault "publikely, and dehort all others from it (which from no others of his companions "they could extort) he, though resolute enough and a good Scholar, yet partly "by the perswasion of his friends, and partly by weaknesse which was occasion'd "by his wounds, agreed to their desire, and was content to make a publique "Manifesto in hopes his life might be saved. With this conquest of conscience "the Ministers (to produce their great work to the Common people) came vaunt- "ing upon the scaffold . . . " And so he made a "long and tedious Harangue," which they had "very energetically pend for him;" and then they "fairly cutt off "his head and seal'd his confession with his blood." See Balf. iv. 50, 52, 53, 56, who omits all these details, but shows that he begged hard for life.

The English officers were sentenced to be sent to France, probably to recruit Sir Robert Murray's or other regiments there. "The Dutche (*i.e.*, foreign, mostly "German) officers with a Dutche minister to be dismissed home to ther auen "countrey." Balf. iv. 35, 36. June 4th, the German and Dutche officers offered their service to the state, desiring some maintenance and subsistence in the meantime to supply their necessity (*ibid.* 40).

Of the common soldiers, most of the foreigners probably fell in the battle. We read of "five Englishmen" dismissed, (*ibid.* 50). Two hundred and eighty-one were confined in the Canongate by May 21st. Forty of these "being forced from "Orknay were dismissed"—that is, as it appears, given as *slaves*—six to David

Leslie, "being fishers;" 6, also fishers, to Argyll; 6 "zoung lustie fellowes" to Sir James Hope, "to his lead minnes." The rest were given to Lord Angus and Sir Robert Murray "to recreuit ther French regiments" (*ibid.* 18). If this was "dismissal," one wonders what became of the rest!

A mystery also hangs over the fate of the 105 prisoners who had *not* reached the Canongate prison by May 21st. Some, severely wounded, may have been left in the north, or succumbed to the hardships of the march south. Others may have been among the prisoners peremptorily ordered south by the House, May 23rd, but more probably the last were officers.

### Fate of the Detachments left in Dunbeath, Strath Naver, and Orkney.

This narrative would be incomplete without some account of Montrose's followers who were not present at Carbisdale.

Having despatched the prisoners south, Leslie, with five troops, some of Holburn's regiment, and some of Sutherland's men, proceeded to Caithness, and having examined into the offence of the local gentry, directed them south to be censured by Parliament. He then laid siege to Dunbeath Castle, which was valiantly defended for some days, till the water supply of the garrison was cut off, and they were forced to surrender. (For Montrose's papers found there, see Appendix IX.) These were all sent south to Edinburgh, and Sir William Hay of Dalgetty was there *executed*, June 8th. Balf. iv. 23, 36. See his Eulogy in App. to Wishart (Ed. 1819), 521. Major Whiteford, a Scotsman, narrowly escaped the same fate, but was ordered to depart the country before July 31st. It is said that he owed this clemency to the part he had taken in the murder of Dr. Dorislaus at the Hague,[1] a year previously, an act of revenge on one of the regicides, which was counted to him for righteousness.

Meantime, the Earl of Sutherland had sent Captain William Gordon with 300 men towards the heights of Caithness to try what Harry Graham was doing, but before he could overtake him, he had heard of the overthrow, and shipped with all his men for Orkney. Captain Gordon arrived at Thurso just in time to see him sailing. But Orkney was no refuge, and hurriedly they prepared to abandon the islands, soon to be visited by Lesley's fury, in the person of the ruffian Cullace. Thus far from Sallagh. The narrative is continued in a letter we have found in the Wodrow MSS. (fol. 67, n. 95, now first printed). Unhappily, the end is torn, and gives no clue to the writer of this interesting document.

"Honbl and Loving,

"Heaving the ocatione of ane bearer, I thought good to aquant you hou
" buissines gois heir. our Governour Sir William Johnstoune hes takine ane
" shipp and gone to the sea with the wholl monitione and arteyllarie. at his

---

[1] Heath, 236; Clarendon (1714) v. 356; Acts Parl. vi. 594.

# APPENDIX.

"entrie in the shipp thair was one Junes [James ?], Borroustouns[2] good sone,
"a kynd of a leiftenant to George Drumond. the governour dreu a pistoll and
"shott and killed Junes. My Lord Mortoune . . . (*illeg.*) gen to sea and his
"doughter, Mr. James Aickine[3] thair ar all gon alongis with the Governour.
"they heave my Lord of Mortouns wholl Jeualls and pleatt with them; yit it hes
"pleassed god that the shipp that the Governour and his traine was in they ar
"rune on upone the Skerries of Skea [*v. Map*] in Wastray firth, and will never
"winne off. I pray you doe that ye can to obtaine a warrand from the Leivtentant
"generall to tak them, since they ar so suir upone the Skerrie. Yee will not want
"aid in this cuntrie more then any other man will geatt. ane it be weill considerit
"it is a mater of conserinment. spair me ane answer to this, and what ells yee
"knou about . . . essent [*torn, ? the laird of Assynt ?*] . . . [*torn*] . . . egence
"[*locality ?*] . . . 6 . . . 1650 [*torn*] your . . .

"J [*? torn.*]"

[*Endorsed*] "Ffor Sir James Sinclair[4] off Murkill, These."

The date of this was probably May 6th, 1650.

That the fugitives fled in haste we gather from the narrative of Gwynne, left behind, to his no small discontent. He had perhaps remained in Orkney with Johnston, and did not know their cause for haste.

"Soon after, Montros marcht further into the Highlands, and Collonel
"Grymes (his natural brother) [Harry Graham], was coming up with a recruit of
"five hundred more men to him, and were come something near the place where
"he was defeated, which made Collonel Grymes to retreat, and march back into
"Orkney, where one Sir William Jonson was left governor: and upon a debate
"amongst them what best to do, they only talk'd (and that was all), as if they
"would go by sea, and rescue Montros, which they easily might have don, as
"there was no fear of an enemy thereabout, since the party of horse which beat
"him had don their work, and were gon far enough from those parts, and himself
"in the custody of a pretended old friend, who had few or no more for a guard
"upon him then were the family and servants of the house wherein he was in
"restraint, and in a manner conceal'd too, untill there came fourth a declaration,
"that whosoever should apprehend and secure him should have such a summe of
"money for his reward: But, in the meantime, had we don ony thing, we could
"not have done less then endeavour to fetch him off; having had time enough,
"and to spare, for it, and the house he was in so very near the sea, as an oppor-

---

[2] Borrowstoun, a hamlet in Reay, seven miles west of Thurso. "Good-son," Scotch for son-in-law.

[3] Mr. James Atkine was son of Harie Atkine, Commissary of Orkney. He was minister of Birsay and Harray. He drew up declaration of loyalty for the presbytery of Cairiton, 1650. They were all deposed, and he betook himself to Holland. Fasti 393. Note from Mr. Wm. G. T. Watt, F.S.A. Scot., of Skaill House, Stromness, who also informs us that George Graham, son of Bishop Graham, was deposed with most of the ministers for signing Montrose's bond.

[4] See Calder's Caithness, 105, 140, 143 (?).

"tunity offred for it: but the governor of Orkney choos'd rather to take some of
"the merchants' shipps out of their harbour to carry himself, and others whom he
"pleas'd, away with him, leaving some of us behind a sacrifice to Lesley, and
"others our foes in the countrey. Howsoever, I mett with the best of the worst
"luck, for, by a kindnes which I had don not long before to a gratefull person,
"came so home to me as to preserve me strangely; and my last faire escape was
"an opportunity to get in an open boat for Shetland, and from thence in a herring-
"bus for Holland, when your Majesty was under sayle for Scotland." Mem. 91–3.
Gwynn reached Holland so destitute that "upon Amsterdam iron-bridge, after I had
"come from Montrose his ingagement, I sunk down dead with meer hunger; and
"had it not been for the great charity of strangers that reviv'd me, I had gon (for
"ought I know,) the way of all flesh, insinsible of any further paine." *Ibid.* 133.

It appears from Balfour's notices of proceedings in Parliament that Johnston and Harry Graham sailed off in Captain Hall's frigate, and in spite of the Skerries of Skea did "win off" and reached Norway. Hardly had they set foot on shore when they were arrested by the natives; and the crew in the absence of the captain mutinied, under the leadership of one Vanderson or Waterston, a native of Anstruther in Fife, and carried the ship with all Montrose's valuable papers, compromising to many in Scotland, and not least of all perhaps to Charles himself, back to Leith, where Waterston and his crew received the thanks of Parliament, and a present of the ship, to be employed in their service. We read of "15 strangers" whom they brought in, probably foreign soldiers who had escaped with the Governor from Orkney. These were dismissed.

Happily for the credit of Scotsmen, an offer made by the natives to hand over their prisoners to Scottish vessels, then on their coast, was refused—an act of generosity which brought down on the captains a Parliamentary inquisition.[5]

Sir Harry Graham survived to occupy a prominent place at the "True Funeralls" of his brother, May 11, 1661.

Gwynne was not the only officer deserted in Orkney. George Drummond of Balloch and Colonel Melvin were shortly afterwards seized by a party of enthusiasts for the Covenant and confined in Noltland Castle, on the extreme north-west point of Westray Island. The neighbourhood of this castle to the accident which had befallen Johnston's ship on the Skerries [see Map, and letter, p. 497], leads us to hazard the conjecture that these two officers had gone ashore, despairing perhaps of the vessel floating clear, and were surprised by the party. The same chance which threw in our way the Dunbeath and other letters enables us to trace their further course, and assign a date to these events. Wodrow's untiring zeal has rescued the following letters (MS. Fol. 67, No. 101) giving the names of their captors:—

"Loving Sone, These ar showing that William bridges böot is cum home out
"of Shetland and reports that thair came serttain Intelligence with the buchen

---

[5] The above is given as the most probable account to be drawn from Balfour's obscure notices.

"[*Buchan?*] merchandes to Shetland upon Thsday last [*Thursday, May 9th?* *May 17th below was a Friday*] of the defeat of the armie and that the generall was takin and the levie was to be upon waddinsday thaire efter [15th?] and the heill gentrie of Shetland with the Comons ar all in armes and will not gane [?] a man that way thrupon Lovetennent Cornell Wood[6] hes ane mynd to dispache him selff in all heist out of Shetland this is all I can learin (learn) that way Yee sall wit that the Lovetennent generall send word with Magnus essen that yee sall return him ane answer with all diligence. Lykewayes wrytt to me with this bearer q$^t$ [*what*] is done in Wastrey or Kersten [?] or q$^t$ uther neuis yee have not farther for the present I still continowe

          yor Loving Father

"BRABAST[7] *the* 17 *of May* 1650.     WM. SINCLAIR."

[*Addressed*] For his Sone be [*by*] ane loving sone
  [Geo. Sinclair, *v.* next letter]
    MAJOR EDWARD SINCLAIR[8] THESE."

Enclosed in the above letter is the following, addressed on the back:—

"For The much honored David Leslie Leivetennent generall of the Scottish Armie these"

"MUCH HONORED AND NOBLE SIR,

"Haveing formerly wrytten our mynd to your Lp w$^t$ Colonell Jon Stewart, wherin wee did relate our condition [condit nou? i.e., *conduct?*] w$^t$ in the Castle of Noutland, which nou is keiped for the ends of the Solemne League and covenant, and you . . . [r Lordship's?] service under the comand of Captain Jon Pollock, and by the assistance of the gentlemen of the Isle under subscribed, but hearing that our letter hath not come to your hands, wee have nou resolued to send this gentleman George Sinclar (who hes been still [*continually*] with us since the taking of the castle, and is privie to all our intentions, to whom wee have given comission by tounge, seeing ther is no saue convoying of letters) to declare our condition. wee doe expect a partie of ane hundreth men at most to be sent for the receiveing up of the Castle, and till then wee intend to keep it out. we give your Hie [*Highness*] to know y$^t$ [*that*] wee have Leiutennant Colonell Drumond, sone to Baloch, and Captaine Leiutennant Melvill our prisoners. noght [*what?*] farther wee have to say we refair to this bearer, whom

---

[6] See Kinnoul's order of March 8th, p. 292, n. 5.

[7] Brabusta occurs as a name in Westray, Sanday, Durness, and Hoy. There was a William Sinclair of Greenwall in Holm about this date, and associated with him a *James* Alen (*v.* Peterkins' Rental, 49).

[8] Edward Sinclair of Essinquay (?), a person of some importance; or Edward Sinclair of Clumby, Sandwick (?), or Edward Sinclair of Ness (?); but none of these are known to have been in the army. Notes by Mr. William G. T. Watt.

500 APPENDIX.

"wee intreat to be returned sauely and speedily, and that he be gra [*graciously?*]
"repaed for his paines. Thus till your He [Highness], a sure . . . tainting [?]
"of us, by which wee sall continew

Your humble and faithfull servants<br>
W [M. ?] SMITH [9] minister<br>
Pollok

"From NOUTLAND CASTLE,[10] *the* 18 *of May* 1650

                          Will Sinclar [11]

Ja. Soullar [12] (?)        Thomas Alen

                          T. M. Abercrombie        Fogon (?) Balfor."

As the writers of the above had had time to send a letter and hear that it had miscarried, the seizure of Noltland Castle must have been effected some time previously, probably at once, on news of the defeat at Carbisdale. The demand for so strong a force as 100 men is indication that they were hard pressed by those of the natives who heartily sympathised with Montrose. Captain Cullace with his troop was sent over to Orkney, too late to prevent the escape of Hall's frigate; but he secured the prisoners in Noltland. "The countrey people gave Captain Cullace
" all obedience, and assisted him to apprehend such of James Graham's followers
" as had remained in that countrie. George Drummond of Ballach was taken,
" with divers others, whom Cullace carryed south with him out of Orknay, except
" Drummond of Ballach, who hade dyvers times escaped before. So being returned
" to Cateynes, he caused him to be shot at the post, least he should escape from
" him."

The fate of Captain Melvin, Melweill, or Melvill we have been unable to trace. As Lesley's letter, informing the House that "George Drumond, Ballows brother, and Capitane Melweill were apprehendit in Jutland castle, in Orknay," was read on June 4th, Cullace must have arrived at Noltland very soon after the above letter to Lesley was sent off.

---

[9] In the same hand as the letter. Possibly the same as Henry Smith, minister of Shapinshay.

[10] Noltland Castle, here spelt as locally pronounced. "At the head of the bay which forms the harbour stands a stately Gothic ruin, called the castle of Noltland, part of which has never been finished. This house is built at a small distance from the shore, and stands on an eminence gently declining towards the sea. The face of the ground between this ruin and the sea is a beautiful green, covered with the richest pasture in the summer season. There is a traditionary account here, that this house was intended as a place of retreat for Mary Queen of Scots and Bothwell . . . but upon Mary and Bothwell's defeat, the castle of Noltland, and some adjoining lands, were granted to a gentleman of the name of Balfour, who put the Balfour's arms on this house." He was a brother or a near relation of Sir James Balfour, then Governor of Edinburgh Castle. Old Statistical Account of Scotl. xvi. (Edinb. 1795).

[11] See letter, p. 499.

[12] Probably James Scollay of Strynie Tofts and Papa Stromay, a man of some estate, and representative of one of the oldest Orcadian families. For these notes on Orkney names we have been indebted to the kind researches of Mr. William G. T. Watt. Nothing is known of the rest. But we may conjecture that Fogon or Hogen [*i.e.*, Hucheon?] Balfor was of the family that owned the castle. See above, note 10.

# APPENDIX.

Major Sinclair of Orkney, the companion of Montrose in his flight and imprisonment at Ardvreck, is mentioned among those whom the House, on May 23rd, ordered to be sent south. In the absence of any information to the contrary, it is to be hoped that this demand was disregarded; but he may have taken his place among the numerous sufferers on "the altar of bloody sacrifice" in Edinburgh. See Skinner's Eccles. Hist.

Sinclair of Brims also escaped capture. Perhaps he is to be identified with "Captain Breams," who accompanied Gwynne to join Middleton in Skye, after the collapse of Glencairn's expedition, 1654. Gwynne's Memoirs, 102.

### Rewards to the Victors.

Strachan and Hackett each "received one thousand pound sterline and ane gold chain." Sallagh, 557.

Neil Macleod, besides his £20,000 Scots and 400 bolls of meal (see App. XIII.), obtained the command of the garrison at Tongue, in Strathnaver, with the consent of the Earl of Sutherland (*ibid.*).

Baillie, iii. 113, January 2, 1651, says, Strachan's "eminent service, first against "Pluscardie, and then against James Grahame, got him the Church's extraordinarie "favour, to be helped by 100,000 merkes out of their purses for the mounting "him a regiment."

After performing good service against Cromwell, assisted by Lawer's regiment (Balf. iv. 89), he joined the Remonstrants, and in 1651 went "into the publicke enimey of the kingdome" (*ibid.* 269), "a pryme actor against the stait" (*ibid.* 271). See Baillie, iii. Index.

---

## APPENDIX II.

(See pp. 96, 97, 104, 105).

I.—Two Letters from Montrose extracted from *Mercurius Aulicus*, May 10 and June 2, 1645.

The first of them appears to have been slightly altered in spelling in order to fit it better for English readers. The second is prefaced thus:—"The expresse is written with my Lord Montrose's owne hand which (we seriously protest) is here made publicke to the world without the least mutilation or alteration of word or syllable from the original."[13]

II.—Also Extract from *Carte's Ormonde Papers*, I. 73 (Ed. 1739).

### I.

#### No. 1.—[*Montrose to ——*].

Since my returne to yours with James Small I received one of the 20th of February desiring to know the condition here of His Majesties service; I shewed

---

[13] Kindly communicated by C. H. Firth, M.A. Oxford, lecturer in Modern History, Pembroke College.

in my former that what had past before the Winter-time Sir William Rollocke had made you ane very faithfull account and true in all circumstances, and as for what hath intervened since, mine (which I hope will reach your hands before this) I am confident shall do it;* only thus much I must tell you (to decline in short all your doubts) that had I had but for one moneth the use of those 500 horse, I could have seene you (before the time that this can come to your hands) with twenty thousand of the best this Kingdome can afford; though I may justly say I have continued things this halfe yeare bygone without the assistance of either Men, Armes, Ammunition, or that which is the Nerffes of warre; so that had we not beene supported by divine providence Our Army could not have subsisted, and I cannot chuse but think it strange that this unhappy Country which had beene the bane and cause of all your woes, being now in so faire a way of reducing, that not onely the ordinary but easy meanes should have been neglected. Howsoever though you have not assisted me, I will yet still do my best to barre all assistance coming against you, and to the better; for besides all their new Levies and Recruits are barr'd, they have beene forced presently to draw 4 Regiments of Foote from Newcastle downe here to oppose me, notwithstanding the weaknesse of their numbers there already. So (though above all things I should wish an happy Accommodation 'twixt his Majesty and His Subjects) let nothing that may be apprehended from this, move the King to any thing that is dishonourable; for so long as it pleases God I am alive and free, there shall nothing trouble His affaires from this: Wherefore let Him be pleased to make His Conclusions from the face of things there, which I pray God give an happy Aspect to, and so I will cast me into your hands, and seigne myselfe,

Your most faithfull and humble Servant

DOUNE *April* 20, 1645.

MONTROSE.

No. 2.—[*Montrose to Lord Digby* (?)].

MY LORD,

Since Sir William Rollack's returne I received one from you and ane other two nights agoe of the 20 of April, the Carier whereof shewes me that ther ar ane other upon the way which is not yet come to my hands. I made returne to them all bot I heir some ar intercepted. All heir praised be God goes weale, Inderlothy and the burning Dundee I am confident you heave particularly heard. The Rebels being somewhat strong, they heaving brought five or six Regiments more from England and Ireland, I thought it not safe to hazard to deale with all their forces together, but resolved to make a fraction to devide my forces to make them doe the liken, which when I got them to doe and at a good distance one with another, I marched from Forth to Spey (night and day) with long marches, to force Urrey to feight, who was then lying at Spey to raise the North, against Bailly and all other forces should come from the South and joine; At my first aproch he tooke the Retrait, but I persued him so hard as I beat up his Rear for 14 miles, and put him to Innernesse, and marched againe backe to Oldharne some 14 miles from him;

---

* A reference perhaps to the letter of February 3rd. See Napier, Mem., 484.

wherefore he finding himselfe a little concerned, did not stay till Bailly and all those forces should come to him, but heaving Larers and Buchanans Regiments in Indernesse, and Lothiens with himselfe, together with Lowdons, and some 300 horse, he conveined Seafort, Lovet, Sudderland, and all the whole Country thereabouts, and caime marching backe upon me from Indernesse to Oldharne, 'twixt foure and five thousand, whereof there were four of the best trained Regiments they had in the three Kingdomes: I wes horse and foot about fourteene hundred men, allwayes finding myselfe ingaged, and that the longer I delayed they should increase and I diminish, I resolved to feight, but chosed my posts and all advantages of ground, and to bide them at the defence, So they being confident both of their men and their number fell hotly on, but being beat backe, seimed to coole of their fury, and only intended to blocke us up (as it wer) till more number should come, which perceiving, I divided my selfe in two wings, (which was all the ground would suffer) and marched upon them most unexpectedly, and after some hot salvyes of musket and a litell dealing with sword and pike, they tooke the chase, where they left three thousand of ther foot slaine in the place, and had all ther horse killed and scattered; and I am now making for Bailly. For your Armes and Ammunition I heave as yet receaved nothing, neither heave I heard; for the Enemy is my best Magazine, for I never laicke but it pleases God I beate them and supplies my selfe: I am instantly dispatching . . . who I must remit you to in all I can say, as if I waited on you my selfe, which is one of the most longing desires of

Your most affectionate Servant

CULLEN ABOYNE, 17 *May* 1645.   MONTROSE.

## II.

News from his Majesty's Army in Scotland, to be presented to the most Honourable the Lord Lieutenant General of Ireland; written at Inverlochy in Lochaber the 7th of February 1644; by an Irish officer in Alexander Macdonald's Forces.

*[Ormonde Papers.]*

When the Irish forces arrived in Argyle's bounds in Scotland, our General-Major Alexander Macdonnel sent such of his Majesty's commissions and letters to those to whom they were directed; although for the present none was accepted on: which caused our General-Major and those forces to march into Badenogh, where they raised the country with them; and from thence to Castle-Blaire in Athol, where the Lord Marquess of Montrose came unto and joined them with some other small forces. From thence they marched to St Johnston, where the enemy had gathered 800 horse with nine pieces of cannon; his Majesty's army not having so much as one horse: for that day the Marquess of Montrose went on foot himself with his target and pike; the Lord Kilpunt commanding the bowmen, and our General-Major of the Irish forces commanding his 3 regiments. The armies being drawn up on both sides, they both advanced together, and although the battle continued for some space, we lost not one man on our side, yet still advanced, the enemy being 3 or 4 to one: howsoever, God gave us the day; the enemy retreating with their backs towards us, that men might have walked upon the dead corps to the town, being two long miles from the place where the battle was pitched. The chase continued from 8 a clock in the morning till 9 at night: all their cannon, arms, munition, colours, drums, tents, baggage, in a word, none of themselves nor baggage escaped our hands, but their horse, and such of the foot as were taken prisoners within the city. This battle to God's glory and our Prince's good was fought the first day of September.

From thence we marched straight to Aberdeen, only surprizing such as withstood us, with little or no skirmishing till the 13th of the same month. At Aberdeen the Covenanters of the North had gathered themselves together to the number of 3000 foot and 500 horse, with 3 pieces of cannon. We had then about 80 horse. The battle being fairly pitched, it continued for a long space, and the enemy behaved themselves far better than they did at St Johnston. Yet we lost not that day above four, but the enemy were altogether cut off, unless some few that hid themselves in the city. The riches of that town, and the riches they got there, hath made all our soldiers cavaliers. This battle being ended, only our manner of going down to battle, and how each commanded I omit, till it be drawn and set down in a more ample manner; now tendering only a brevity of our proceedings; for if I should write the whole truth, all that hath been done by our army would be accounted most miraculous; which I protest I will but show in the least manner I can, leaving the rest to the report of the enemy themselves.

After this battle we marched towards the Highlands so far as to Castle-Blaire, where I was sent to Ardamuragh, with a party to relieve the castle of Midgary and the castle of Langhaline; Midgary Castle having a leaguer about it, which was raised 2 or 3 days before I could come to them: at which time the Captain of Clanranald with all his men joined with the Clan Coo men and others who had an inclination to his Majesty's service.

In the mean time, while I was interested upon those services, the M. of Montrose marched back to the Lowlands, almost the same way he marched before, till they came to a place called Fivy in the shire of Aberdeen; where Argyle with 16 troops of horse and 3000 men marched up: and upon a very plain field Argyle was most shamefully beaten out of the field, and had it not been for his horse, they had suffered as deeply as the rest; so that there was not on our side any hurt done, but on their side they lost many of their best horse, and most of all their commanders hurt, and the Earl Mareschal's brother killed. After the armies separated, the Lord Marquess marched again to Castle-Blaire in Athol: where I met again with him and such of the Highlands as had joined with me. The day of Fivy was Oct. 28.

From Castle-Blaire we marched to Glanurghyes, called M'Callin M'Conaghig, which lands we all burned, and preyed from thence to Lares, alias Laufers; and burned and preyed all his country from thence to Aghenbracke's, whose lands and country were burned and preyed; and so throughout all Argyle, we left neither house nor hold unburned, nor corn nor cattle, that belonged to the whole name of Campbell. Such of his Majesty's friends as lived near them joined with us. We then marched to Loughaber, where Mʳ. Alane came and joined with us, but had but few of his men with him. From thence we marched to Glengarry, where the Lord of Glengarry joined with us. At this place we got intelligence that Argyle, Aghenbracke, and the whole name of Campbell, with all their forces, and a great number of Lowlandmen, with them, were come to Inverloughy in Loughaber following of us. This caused us to make a countermarch the nearest way over the mountains, till we came within musket-shot of the castle of Inverloughy; it then being night, so that the enemy stood to their arms all night, the sentries skirmishing together. By this place of Inverloughy, the sea comes close to it, and that night Argyle embarked himself in his barge, and there lay till the next morning, sending his orders of discipline to Aghenbracke and the rest of the officers there, commanding the battle. Which on both sides being pitched and their cannon planted, the fight began; the enemy giving fire on us on both sides, both with cannon and muskets, to their little avail. For only two regiments of our army playing with musket-shot, advanced till they recovered Argyle's standard, and took the standard-bearer: at which the whole army broke; which were so hotly pursued both with foot and horse, that little or none of the whole army escaped us, the officers being the first that were cut off. There Aghenbracke was killed, with 16 or 17 of the chief Lords of Campbell; their other Lowland commanders (only two Lieutenant-Colonels) all cut off; four others of the name of Campbell taken prisoners, as Bearbrick, the young Laird Carrindel, Inverleeven Capt. son of Enistesinth, and divers others that got quarter, being men of quality. We lost but two or three that day. This was fought the second of February.

## APPENDIX III.

VERSES WRITTEN BY THE MARQUIS OF MONTROSE UPON THE MURDER OF KING CHARLES I., WITH DR. WISHART'S LATIN VERSION. [See p. 229.]

> Great, good, and just! Could I but rate
> My griefs to thy too rigid fate,
> I'd weep the world to such a strain,
> As it should deluge once again:
> But since thy loud tongu'd blood demands supplies
> More from Briareus' hands than Argus' eyes,
> I'll sing thy obsequies with trumpet sounds
> And write thy epitaph with blood and wounds.[14]

---

[14] "Set to music among Songs for one, two, and three voices, with some short Symphonies, collected out of the Select Poems of the incomparable Mʳ Cowley, and others, and composed by Henry Bowman, Philomusicus." Ed. 2, Oxf. 1679. W.'s Montr. (1819) 495.

Carole, si possem lachrymis oequare dolorem
Ipse meum fatumque tuum, tua funera flerem,
Ut tellus nitidis rursum stagnaret ab undis :
Sanguis at ille tuus, quum vocem ad sidera tollat,
Atque manus Briarei mage quam Argi lumina poscat,
Exsequias celebrabo tuas, clangore tubarum,
Et tumulo inscribam profuso sanguine carmen.

## APPENDIX IV.

The following two letters are now printed for the first time from the *Königlich Preussisches Geheimes Staats-archiv*, Berlin, kindly communicated by the keeper, Herr Friedländer.

PRAESENTAT. CLIVIS DIE 26 *julii* [1]649.

SERENISSIME PRINCEPS,

Cum nec paucis nec leuibus argumentis propensum Celsitudinis vestrae animum erga Dominum meum magnae Britanniae, Franciae ac Hiberniae regem penitus perspectum habeam, hinc est, quod Celsitudinis vestrae (etiam in fidos regis ministros ac subditos) fretus beneuolentia, non dubitauerim aliquid hoc titulo Celsitudini vestrae litterarum dare ut et quo loco res Britanniae in praesentiarum sint breviter exponam et Celsitudinis Vestrae auxiliatricem manum humiliter implorem. Cum enim iam apud nostrates susque deque eversa sint omnia et eo rebellionis evaserit furor, ut sine externo auxilio negotia regis domi confici nequeant, Rex in Galliam discedens, mihi una cum suprema rerum Scotiarum cura in mandatis dedit ut ad Celsitudinem vestram Dominum Hennericum Gremum domesticum suum quamprimum remitterem, hic et regis animum, et in presenti rerum statu ad tantum perficiendum negotium meam Celsitudinis vestrae auxilii necessitatem accurate exponet, et ut verbo multa complectar omnia a Celsitudine tanquam a filo pendent, quod si et regiis votis et mihi humiliter supplicanti faveret Celsitudo vestra ausim polliceri Regem cum ad propria fauente deo et auxiliantibus amicis pervenerit, Celsitudini Vestrae pro tot tantisque beneficiis gratissimum extiturum, nec autem tanto (seruitio suo) vinculo astringet ut prius desinam quam obliuiscar me infinitis titulis

HAGAE COMITIS
22 *Julij*
1649

Serenissime princeps
Celsitudinis Vestrae
humillimum et obsequentissimum servum
MONTROSE.

[*Address*]

Serenissimo, ac Celsissimo Principi, Domino FREDERICO GULIELMO MARCHIONI BRANDENBURGICO Sacri Romani Imperii archimarescalco ac principi Electori, Duci Borustiae [*sic*] Puliaci Cliviae et montium nec non Stetini,

Pomeraniae Cassubiaeque Wandaliae, Silesiae, Crossiae ac Paegerdorfii, Burgrauio Normbersensis [*sic*], Comiti Marchiae et Rauensburgi Domino Rauenstenii Cliuiae.

[*Reply to the Above.*]

Kanzleinotizen [Endorsement] ist von Sr. Hochwurd[en] dem Herrn oberkammerherrn also angeordnet worden. (ad Marchionem de Montrosse per Dn. Henricum Gremum.)

ILLUSTRISSIME DOMINE, AMICE DILECTE.

In quo statu res Britannicae pro tempore versentur, quaeque ea propter illustrissimae Vestrae dominationi ad nos deferre, visum fuerit, ex literis eius ad nos perscriptis satis intelleximus. Non immemores, qualiter Regiae dignitati Magnae Britanniae, non ita pridem per militiae suae equestris locum tenentem Generalem Johannem Adamum de Karpf, opem auxiliumque a Nobis poscenti responderimus: speramus, quemadmodum Regia eius dignitas propensissimam animi nostri voluntatem desuper luculenter perspexit, ita illustrissimam Vestram dominationem etiam nunc Nos, habituram exinde excusatos, caussa, quae auxilii nostri dilationem flagitabat, nondum sublata. Recordamur equidem, superiori tempore Nos Henrico Gremo indicasse, aliquantam pecuniae vim Nos aliunde mutuo sumpturos Regiaeque eius dignitati exinde decem millibus imperialibus gratificaturos; Verum cum ii, quos eiusmodi mutuum nobis daturos putabamus, nonnullas difficultates circa numerationem fecerint, aegre ferimus, quo minus voluntatem nostram modo dictam, illustrissimam Vestram dominationem aequo laturam animo, quod postulatis eius pro tempore annuere nequeamus. Certo vero sibi persuasum habeat, quamprimum res nostrae permiserint, Nos in ferendis suppetiis pro virili Regiae eius dignitati non defuturos. Interim illustrissimam Vestram dominationem bene valere cupimus, datae ex Arce nostrae Clivensi die xxvii. julii anno Salutis MDCXLIX.

Ad illustrissimum Dominum Marchionem Montrosse.

[From the original-copy in the K. G. S. archives, Berlin.]

## APPENDIX V.

COMMISSION FROM KING CHARLES II. TO THE MARQUIS OF MONTROSE, FOR SETTLING THE DIFFERENCES WITH THE TOWN OF HAMBURG, AND BORROWING A SUM OF MONEY FROM THE SENATE. [From W.'s Montr. (1819) 446].

CHARLES R.

Right trusty, and right entirely beloved cousin, we greet you well. We send you herewith a relation which we have lately received from our trusty and well beloved Sir John Cockeran, knight, of his proceedings with the town of Hamburgh; and being justly sensible how unnecessary it is for us, at this time, to make new enemies, or to be severe in our resentments of such things, as in time of more prosperity we ought to insist on; we therefore desire, and we hereby require and authorise you, to employ yourself by such ways and expedients as you shall think fit, to compose the differences, and to settle a better understanding between us and the said town of Hamburgh, only in that particular of their resolution, to receive a public minister from the bloody rebels in England, we cannot but believe it to be inconsistent with all amity and alliance with us, which, our pleasure is, shall be so represented to them, but without any menaces or threats on our part, to the end, that if they shall avowedly receive any such public minister, we may be at liberty to take such resolution as shall be fit for our own honour and interest. In the mean time we desire you to press the senate to give us some present testimony of their good affection, by supplying us with the loan of a considerable sum of money, upon such assurance of repayment as we can for the present give them. And if any money can be gotten from them, our pleasure is, that one half thereof shall be for your employment, and that the other half be remitted for our use to our trusty and well beloved John Webster of Amsterdam, merchant; some proportion being first deducted out of the whole, for the supply of our trusty and well-beloved servant Sir John Cockeran, Knight: And so recommending this business to your care and good endeavour, we bid you heartily farewell.

GIVEN AT ST GERMANS *the 5<sup>th</sup> September* 1649.

[See text, pp. 258, 259. Inquiry in Hamburg has failed to elicit any account of these proceedings.]

## APPENDIX VI.

LETTER FROM MONTROSE TO FREDERICK III. KING OF DENMARK. [From the Royal Archives in Copenhagen. See p. 264 and n. 60.]

SIRE, COPNAHAGEN 19 *Octobr.* 1629.

J'ay receu celle dont vostre maiesté a pleu m'honorer, ce que me fait avec impatence attendre l'honneur de ses commensements, lesquelles m'ont esté promises par celle la; de quoy voyans nul apparence, je suis necessité de supplier le tres humble pardon de vostre maiesté de prier de çavoir ses resolutions, car les delayes sont pires que tous maux, ce qu'il plaira a vostre maiesté de faire, quand il et tost et fait au double, et en des telles occasions un negatiue, que nous resoud, et bien meillieure q'un assurance que nous ruine. Je say qu'il y en a qu'ils feront croire a vostre maiesté, que la pittite assistance, que vous donneray au roy vostre cousing, vous incommesera pour estre sur vos gardes contre vos ennemyes, et que vos voisings en peuvent prendre leur auantages; mais je prie tres humblement vostre maiesté de me faire l'honneur de croire (et je ne prendray la hardiesse de le dire, sans que je pusse peutestre asser assuré), que vostre maiesté n'a jammais rien fait, que obligira plus vos voisings, et en ne le faisant pas, que les donnera plus des

exceptions, et que peut occasionner des pires effects ; a laquelle je n'ajouteray plus, mais que cette pittitte assistance au roy vostre cousing ne fera que monstrer l'honneur, la justice et l'amitié de vostre maiesté et vous assurer de toutes partes.   Je suis,
Sire,
de vostre maiesté
le tres humble, tres fidele
et tres obeissant serviteur
MONTROSE.

Pour sa majesté le roy de Dennemark.

# APPENDIX VII.

This paper and the following twelve letters or extracts from letters relative to Montrose's proceedings at Gothenburg, along with some valuable notes on the persons, &c., alluded to, have been kindly communicated by Herr C. F. Oehner, Keeper of the Royal Archives, in Stockholm. To his courtesy our history is greatly indebted for so much new and original information. Want of space obliges the Editors to omit translations. The substance of the documents will be found in the text, Part II. chap. vii. pp. 273 ff.

### Proposals on Behalf of Charles II. submitted by Robert Meade to Queen Christina of Sweden.

Serenissimae ac potentissimae Principi Majestaté suae Reginae Sueciae, de parte Majestatis suae Magnae Britt$^{iae}$ humillime proponenda per Robertum Meade a D$^{no}$ suo Rege M : B : isti muneri ablegatum.

1 : mo. Quod Dominus meus Rex M : B : singularia Ma$^{tis}$ suae Reginae Sueciae erga Causam Eius Benevolentiae Testimonia gratissimo animo recolat, obnixeque roget Ma$^{tem}$ suam Sueciae pro certissimo habere, non unquam defuturam Ma$^{tem}$ suam M : B : quin omnibus omnino modis conata semper fuerit dignas favoribus collatis, et dehinc conferendis per Ma$^{tem}$ suam Sueciae Grates retribuere.

2 : do. Quod, quo certior fiat M$^{tas}$ sua Sueciae de Regio in hunc finem proposito (scilicet gratissime restituendi quicquid per Ma$^{tem}$ suam Sueciae ad promovendam Causam eius Afflictissimam aeque ac Justissimam, impensum sit vel dehinc fuerit) M$^{ti}$ suae Sueciae proponat D$^{nus}$ meus Rex M : B : ut (si pro re fuerit M$^{tis}$ suae) dignaretur admittere Legatum aliquem extraordinarium instructum in Officium istud plena cum potentia instructum de parte M$^{tis}$ suae M : B :

3 : tio. Ut vellet dignari Ma$^{tas}$ sua Sueciae secundum pollicita sua gratiosissima, Regique Domino meo acceptissima, vires et Consilia sua interponere, ut subditi isti Scotiae vellent omissis rigidis istis immo iniquis de Rege suo Legitimo, Indubitato, Agnito, Postulatis ; debitam Ei fidem et Obedientiam praestare, et (si visum fuerit) ut dignaretur M$^{as}$ sua Sueciæ Legatum aliquem, eum in finem, versus Scotiam delegare.

510 APPENDIX.

4 : to. Ut vellet Ma^{tas} sua Sueciæ (quod hactenus semper fecerit) Subditos illos Coronae Britannicae sub dominio Coronae Sueciae in praesentiarum commorantes, qui se bene affectos erga Causam Regiam monstrarunt, benigno vultu usque intueri, et non solum faventiores sui Radios Aspectus in Ipsos continuare sed e contrario Supercilium suum contrahere adversus istos (si qui sint) Anglos vel Scotos tanquam Omni Monarchico Regimini Hostes infensissimos.

5 : to. Ut particulatim dignaretur M : sua Sueciae nobilem Virum Joannem Mackleire Gotteburgi commorantem gratioso oculo intueri, tanquam optime de Rege suo D^{no} meo Rege M : B : meritum, et ut insuper permitteret M : sua Sueciae si per Naves aliquas M^{tis} suae M : B : Mercimonia aliqua dicto Viro Nobili I : M : per Regem aut Ministros eius transmittantur in satisfactionem Impensorum pro Rege suorum, Huius modi Mercimonia in manus eius tradantur et exinde distribuantur non imposito gravi aliquo Vectigali.

6 : to. Si sine praeiudicio M^{tis} suae Sueciae fieri possit, ut vellet concedere liberum Navigijs Belli M^{tis} suae M : B : Ingressum et Egressum cum licitis suis prædis, portubus istis Regni suecici occidentalibus versus Gotteburgum.

7 : mo. Quod dignaretur M^{tas} sua Sueciae praemissa gratiose pervolvere & de ijs Statuta suo humillimo Ma^{tis} suae servo exhibere; Ipsique exoptatissimum istum Honorem indulgere ut vivat & moriatur

Maiestatis Suæ
Humillimus ac devotissimus Servus
ROB: MEADE.

STOCKHOLMI, *Febr:* 25, 1650.

A tergo [endorsed]: Nuncii Regis propositio et postulata nonnulla oblat. Stocholmiae *d. a.* 1650.

---

## APPENDIX VIII.

FROM PER LINDORMSSON RIBBING, PROVINCIAL GOVERNOR IN GÖTEBORG, TO PRIVY COUNCILLOR FIELDMARSHALL COUNT LINNART TORSTENSSON, GOVERNOR-GENERAL OF VESTERGÖTLAND, DALSLAND, WERMLAND AND HALLAND.

1. (*Extract.*)

Presenterat Ulfsunda den 20 Novemb: A° 1649
Suarat d. 24 ejusdem
Datum Götheborgh den 14 Novemb: 1649.

*Höghwellborne Grefue, Her Feltmarskallk
och General Gouverneur . . .*

P.S.— . . . för 2 eller 3 dagar sedan ehn Skotsk greffwe hiitkommen ifrån Dannemark Graff de Montrose, haffwer någre officerer medh sigh, doch inthet alla

# APPENDIX.

i hopp medh tienare och altt öffwer 10 eller 12 personer, höller sigh nästan hembligh, och skall alenast whara till tids fördriff hiit rest, [effter som konungen i Dannmark inthet ähr hemma i landet, uthan i Holsten], tils thes konungen komme tilbakar igen, mehr weth jagh inthet aff honom . . .

H. Greff, Exlt.

tienstwilligste Wen

Per linnormson

Ribbingh.

2. (*Extract.*) The same to the same.

Presenterat Ulfsunda den 18 Decemb: Anno 1649.
Datum Gjötheborg den 12 December 1649.

. . . Den Skottskie General och Greffuen ligger her ähnnu, och reesa daglig Skotter emellan Dannemark och her. För 8 eller 10 dager sedhan kom ett Skepp med 200 man werffuade ifrån Dannemarch och ligga her wed Billinge. Jagh mener dee löpa sin kooss sampt med ett annat Skepp, som her hijrdt är i dessa dager. 4: Regementz Stycken sampt en Cuantitet af den Munition och Geveer Mackeleer ähr lefuererat, är nu der upå fördt. Greffuen begiärer elliest inga Conversera medh, Skall wara förfahrlig rädder för Banditer, Så att han inthet troor sig sielff. Och will her med haffua Hans Grefl. Excell! jempte dess höga wårdnat Gudh den alldrahögste befallat, till all stadig wellgång. Och förblifuer etc.

3. (*Extract.*) From Admiral Ankerhielm to the same.

Present. Ulfsunda den 1 Januari 1650.

*Nådigeste Greffve och Högvälborne Herre, Herr Fältmarschalck och Generalgouverneur Linnardt Thorstensson gunstige Herre, mechtige befordrare och högtährede patron.*

. . . Nytt ifrån denna ortten är innthet synnerliget skrifnotabelt, uthan stadjens skiep som haffva ährnat åt Portugal liggia nu uthom Billingen til lijka medh de 2 skotske skiep, som Grefve von Montrose tilhorer; och kan lätteligen hända, at Fregaten Herderinnen bliffver och segelferdigh medh, som försåldh är aff Cronen, huilken och i morgon bliffver Her Hans Machelier öffuerleffuererat. . . .

Gottenburg den
26 *December* 1649.

E. Grefl. Excellentz

ödmiuke och underdånige
tiänare

M. Thyssen-Anckerhielm m.p.

512                    APPENDIX.

4.                    Ribbing to the same.

Preesent Ulfsunda den 8 Januarij åhr 1650.
Suaredt den 9 ejusdem

*Högwellborne Grefue, H: Feltmarsk:*
*och General Gouverneur.*

Nest tienstlig helssan, och all welmågas önskan Aff Gud alzmechtig tilförende. E. Ex: kan iagh på dett tienstligaste ey underlåta, Uthan mig förfråga om denne Skotskee Grefue Montroses actioner, efter som mig tijker dett wehrer så lenge, och iag inga order Huarken uthaff H : K : M:t Sielff eller aff Hans Ex:t om Hans Pehrson hafuer. Och såssom iagh tilförende hafuer några gånger Hans Ex: her om tilkenna gifuet, Nl. att förbemelte Greffue kom Hijtt ungefehr den 15 Novemb. och hölt sig Her så heembligh in till dess Han begijntte, att sambla her een hoop officereer, som logiera sig her och der i Staden, Huarföre iag war förorsakader att låta fråga Honom, om Han någon order Hafuer ifrå H : K : M:t att Hålla Her een sådan Sambleplatz och inthet gifua H : K : Maij:tts betienndte her inne der om tilkenna, Huarföre Han då först sende mig H : K : M:s breff medh Hans Mackeleer, deruthj Hennes K : Maij:t befaller, iagh skulla låta föllia den Ammunition och Stijcken, som aff Hans Mackeleer wohre uphandlade, antingen honom sielff eller Hans uthskickadhe, och sedan skaffua honom Skeep der till, för billig prijs, Her uthur Staden. Mehr förmeltas der inthet uthj. Derupå iagh då Skreff Hennes K : Maij:t till, att Han för sin pehrsohn war Her, doek höllt sig Heembligh och ingen wille Han tala medh (: som Han giör ähnnu :) I lijka måtta att Han förwentter edt Skepp Hijtt frå Dannemark medh 200 Mahn i Skjären, och att daglig åthskiellig officerer sig till honom Samblade. der upå iagh ingen swar Haffuer bekommit, uthan samme General Hafuer alltidh låtit sig Höra, att General Kinngh skulle Huar dag förwenttas Hijtt med widsere Order ifrå Hennes Kongl. Maij:t. Samma Skepp med follck, Neml. dee 200 Mahn, och den inlastade Ammunition och Stijcken på 4 när, [samt] Ett annat Skepp liggier uthför Billinger och hafuer Han och bekommit ett Cronones litet Skepp som Her lågh, Herderrinnan benemd, Huilket Ammiral Ankerhielm Hafuer Order Honom att lefuerera, med Stijcken och Prowianth till 50 Pehrsohner uthj Tuå Månader, Huilket och nu ähr uthlagt på Strömen, och förmenas att dee löpa i desse dagar sin kooss. Men Hans Pehrsohn kan man ingen synnerlig beskedh haffua om. Stundhom låter han sig förnimma, att willia åth Stocholm, Stundom åth Dannemark, och Stundom annorstädes. Om een öfficerere möter honom på gatan eller annorstädes, så wender Han strax om, går tillbaka eller afsijdes, att iagh inthet förstår mig på den Mannen, eller Hans Desiegner. I går kommo åter twå Grefuer till honom, Men see illa Nakotta uth några Officerere åhre och igien borthreste, och Somblige Hafua ärnet sig med Skeppen. Mackeleer förskiuter Huadh dee behöffua. I desse dage Hafuer och Hanibal Seestedh warit her på Bååhuuss hooss H:r Jfuer Krabbe, Och förmenas

APPENDIX. 513

att Jfuer Krabbe Kommer Hijtt, till att tala medh förbemelte Grefue. Och alldenstundh iag inthet wett H:s Kongl. Maij:tt willie Herom, och een stoor deell i Staden befahra sig för sine Skepp, Så frampt parlamentet blifue öfuerlegne, Orsaken att dee moste dee Engelskie kooser förby, Huarföre bedher iagh hans Ex:t på dhet tienstligaste, Han wille Her uthj öppa mig sitt höga betänkiande, Huru iag best mig Her uthj förhålla skall, alldenstundh Huarken på Kinngz ankompst eller honom åhr något adt lijta. Och förwentter hans Ex:t suar med neste Post, huru Her med erhålles skall. Och befaller Hans Gref: Ex:t medh des höge wård nat uthj Gudz Craftig beskijdd till all welgång. Och forblifuer

Hans Greff Ex:ts.
tienstwilligste Wen
Per linnormson
RIBBINGH.

DATUM GIÖTHEBORG
den 2 *Januarij* 1650.

5. (*Extract.*)   Torstenson's Reply to the Above.

*Edell och Wälborne Hr Landshöffdinge,*
*Käre Broder och sijnnerlige gode Wän.*

. . . *P. S.* Ahnlangande dhet min Kare Broder förmähler om Montrose twiflar iag [ej] Hennes Kongl. Maij:tt allaredan om haus ferdh skall wara witterligit, doch det ware sigh huru dett will, så lärer iag inthet underlåta at nempna derom, och min Käre broder medh första widare derpå suara . . . Och befaller, etc. etc.

LINNARDT TORSTENSSON.

DATUM ULFSUNDA
den 9 *Januarij Anno* 1650.

6. (*Extract*).   Ribbing to the same.

Present Ulfsunda den 18 Januarij Anno 1650.
Suaradt den 19 ejusdem.

. . . Elliest monde iagh för otta dagar sedan, aff den 2 Huius Mensis, Hans Ex:t tillskrifua om den Skottskie Greffuen General Montrose. Men nu åhr Han sedermehra i gåhr afreester och till Skeps steegen upå Skeppet Herderrinnan, som dem Updragit och försåldt åhr. Men nu åhr Contrarie windh, sa at dee inthet kunna uthlöpa. Om Han kommer Hijtt in i Staden igien, eller på Skeppet förblifuer och upwachter winden och så afsegler, kan iagh nu inthet wetta. Han reeste elliest uthj stillheet aff, lijka som Han Kom Hijtt. Huilket iagh Hans Ex:t uthj tienstlighet ey Hafuer kunnedt underlåta. Och befaller etc.

DAT: GIÖTHEBORG
den 11 *Januarij* 1650.

7. (*Extract.*)     The same to the same.

Presenterat den 22 Januarij A̱° 1650.
Suaradt den 26 dito.
Datum Giötheborg den 16 Januarij 1650.

. . . Montrose kommer ifrån skiepet hiit igen. Han haffwer nhu legatt i 8 dagar snardt på skepet och hafft den besta winn. Hwarföre han haffwer legat stilla må Gudh wetta. Jagh wentar hans Echcells: gode betenkiande, om iagh så altt skall låta passera. Her till dags haffwer iagh [gjort] liika som iagh inthet haffwer hafft till att bestella medh honom, uthan låtitt så altt passera. Hwadh han nhu tager sigh före her effter, gifwer tiden. Gudh giffwe iagh kunde hiitta på att göra hwadh H. Kong. Mtz. behager.

8. (*Extract.*)     The same to the same.

Praesent: Ulfsunda den 26 Januarij A̱° 1650.
Suaradt samma dagh.
Dat: Giötheborg den 18 Januarij 1650.

. . . Den Skottske Generalen Graf von Montrose ähr nu hijtt in igien från Skeppet kommen, och logerar hooss Wellborne Hans Mackeleer. Hans follch ähr mestepartten ähnnu uthe quar på Skeppet; Om de och inkomma, gifuar tijden, Men dee ähre elliest Heelt infrossne, huilket iagh Hans Greff: Ex̱ḻ i all tienstligheet ey hafuer kunnat aflåta. Och befaller etc. etc.

9. (*Extract.*)     Torstenson's Reply to the Above.

Datum Ulfsunda den 26 Januarij A̱° 1650.

. . . Ahnlangandes Skotske Grefue Montrose så wille min käre broder låtha honom icke desto mindre frijtt beställa sina saker, effter han intet är förwägrat af Hennes Maijestett, och om han något skulla fördröja, will min Käre broder mig om hans företagande altijd gifua part . . .

10. (*Extract.*)     Ribbing to the same.

Present: Ulffsunda den 12 Februarij Anno 1650.
Datum Giötheborgh. den 6 Februarij 1650.

. . . Den Konglige Skottskia Generalen Graf von Montrose ähr nu tridie gången till wegz att afsegla. Men som iag rätt nu förnam, så segs kommer Han Hijtt in igien. Jsen ähr fuller Honom till hinders. Huilket iagh Hans Greff: Excelḻḻ ey hafuer underlåta kunnat. Befaller her med etc. etc.

APPENDIX. 515

11. (*Extract.*)　　　　　　The same to the same.

　　　　　　　　　Present: Ulffsunda den 28 Feb: A.° 1650.
　　　　　　　　　Datum Giötheborgh dhen 22 Februarij 1650.

. . . Den Skottske Generalen Graf von Montrose åhr nu mehr afreest. Hans frigaatt åhr lupen till Mastrandh, Men Generalen siellff i Pehrsson förrest landwegen till Norwegen, och genast der i från åth Skottlandh. . .

Och förblifuar etc. etc.

## APPENDIX IX.

### List of the Dunbeath Papers.

[Now first printed from the Advocates' Library, Wodrow MSS. fol. lxvii. 88.]

A not of the Letteris that lievtennent generall gate out of the trunke that came to Dumbeath.

[1] A letter that came from the King of Denmarke to the king 15 Septr 1649 referring to James Grahame. [*Lost?. See* p. 264.]

[2] A letter of the Marques of Brandeburgh to James Grahame 28 July 1649 mentioning Carp to be his Lieutennent gñall and acknowledgeing his promise of decem millia imperialia bot his impossibilitie for the present to performe it. [*Lost? See* p. 252.]

[3] Sr. Johne Cochrans relation of the particulars of his negotiation since his comeing to Hamburg wherein to his hand (?) . . . [*illeg.*] he shewes that some wold have stopped a pryse taken by vertew of the kings Comission upon the pretence that the king was no king He shews the great difficultie he had to get a publick audience and what contempt hee had from ye English company agt quhom he gives in his complaint He tells of a contract made [?] betwixt the English Rebells and the town of Hamburg He gives his advise that the king should declair against it [*Original preserved in same vol.* No. 89. *See* pp. 258–9.]

[4] A letter of propositions from on [one] Gordoun a Suedish Corlonel [*Original, ibid.* No. 92. *See* p. 259 and n. 41.]

[5] Ane other letter from the king of Denmark to the king referring all to James Grahame. [*Original lost? Copy, Copenhagen Archives. See* p. 260, n. 44.]

[6] A letter of Johne Mcleirs. [*Original, ibid.* No. 91. *See* pp. 284, 285.]

[7] A letter from James Grahame consenting to the takeing of some ships. [*Original, ibid.* No. 90. *See* pp. 265, 266.]

[8] A paper called the pedigree of my Grandmother subscryved by Alexr Charteris [?] and thear is tuo letters of Wil[?] Chambers written from Paris. [*Lost?*]

[9] A letter of ane Robert Hay. [*Lost ?*]

[10] James Grahams warrand subseryved under his hand that he was come to Caithnes to releive the Cuntrey from burdens and that hee wold proceed ag$^t$ all as Rebells who did not concurre with him. [*Lost ? See* p. 295.]

[11] A paper of Hurries Resolution to follow James Grahame. [*Lost ?*]

[12] A Recommendatioune of one Molleson from Brandeburgh and Bei the Citie of Elben [?] [*Lost ?*]

[13] Thear is a paper written in James Graham's hand called a Not of the Jewells and plate that is paūned. [*Lost ?*]

[14] Thear is the beginning of a Declaration set doun on a leafe of peaper. [*Lost ?*]

[15] Thear is a ler [*letter*] of Craufurds unto Hurry complaining of Montrois great undertakings w$^{th}$out effects. [*Lost ?*]

[16] Thear is a Comission to quarter M$^r$ Rob$^t$ Feueing [? *illeg.* Fleming ?] [*Lost ?*]

[17] Thear is a great Bunshe of Dutch peapers. [*Lost ?*]

[18] Another bunshe of papers of P . . . not worth reading. [*Lost ?*]

[*Endorsed.*] Not of the peaporis come out the trunck that was at Dumbeathe.

This paper with Nos. 3, 4, 6, 7, and others not referred to in the above were found by the Editors in the Wodrow folio lxvii., in consequence of Napier's vague reference to Powrie's letter in that volume, Mem. 736. It is strange that Napier should have missed so much, especially as the folio is indexed (in Wodrow's hand). But until a *systematic catalogue* of this great Wodrow collection is undertaken, much valuable material will remain sealed to History.

## APPENDIX X.

TERMS OFFERED TO THE KING (see p. 300) BUT REFUSED PUBLICATION, EXTRACTED FROM THURLOE STATE PAPERS, I. 147, 148.

*His majestie having received the propositiones following from the commissioners of the kingdome of Scotland:*

Wee [desire ?] that your majestie shall sweare, subscribe, and seall the nationall covenant of Scotland, and the solemne league and covenant of Scotland, England, and Ireland, in the words following to be subjoined to boith:

I Charles, King of Great Britane, France, and Irlande, doe assure and declare by my solemne oath, in the presence of the almightie God the searcher of hearts, my allowance and approbatioune of the nationall covenant, and of the solemne league and covenant above-written; and faithfullie oblige myself to prosecut the ends thereof in my station and callinge; and that I for myself and successores shall consent and aggree to all actes of parliament enjoyning the nationall covenant, and the solemne league and covenant, and fullie establishing presbiteriall government, the directorie of worshipe, confession of faith, and catechismes, in the kingdom of Scotland, as they ar approven be the generall assemblie of this kirk and parliament of this kingdome; and that I shall give my royall assent to acts of parliament, bills, ordinances past or to be past in the houses of parliament, enjoyning the same in the rest of my dominions; and that I shall observe these in my owne practise and familie, and shall never mack opposition to any of these, or endeavour any change thereof:

His majestie doth consent to this whole proposition *in terminis;* and for performance thereof his majestie doeth declare *in verbo principis*, that so soon as he sal be desyred by the parliament and the general assemblie, or by ther Commissioners, he shall solemnlie swear, subscribe, and seale the nationall covenant of Scotland, and the solemne league and covenant of Scotland, England, and Irlande, in the words preceiding, subjoyned to both.

*His majestie lykwyse haveing receaved the propositions following:*

Wee desire that your majestie wold acknowledge the authoritie of this and former parliaments, that hes bein since the tym your royall father or his commissioners wer present therin; and that your majestie give such ane allowance of the acts made in this and the thrie last imediatlie preceiding sessiones of this current parliament since the fourth of January 1649, as your majesties royall father gave in 1641, unto the acts maid in the sessione of parliament 11<sup>th</sup> June 1640; and that your majestie wold consent and agrie, that all matters such as ar or shall be authorized by them, and maters ecclesiasticall by the ensewing assemblies of this kirk, and such as ar or shal be authorized by them:

His majestie doeth consent to this whole propositione *in terminis.*

*His majestie haveing also received the proposition following:*

Wee desyre, that your majestie wold recall and disclame all commissions ishued furth for acting any thing by sea or land to the prejudice of the covenant, or of this kingdome; or of any, who doe or shall adhere to the solemne league and covenant, and to monarchicall government, in any other of your majestie's dominions, and all other declarationes made by any in your majesties name, or by your warrand against the samen; and further, that your majestie wold disallow, and disclame or declare null and voyd all treaties and agriements whatsoever with the bloodie rebells in Irland; and to declare that your majestie wold never allow nor permitte any libertie of the popish religion in Irlande, or any uther part of your majesties dominions:

His majestie doeth consent to this whole proposition *in terminis.*

*His majestie haveing received the proposition following:*

Wee desire, that your majestie wold be resolved to sweare at your coronatioune by and attour the oath of the covenants aforsaid, the oaths appoynted by the

8th act of the first parliament of your royall grandfather King James VI. and ratified therefter by manie acts, and insert in the nationall covenant, to be sworne by all kings and princes of Scotland at ther coronation; and that your majestie wold then declare, that you will in maters civill fallow the counsell of your parliaments, and such as ar or shall be authorized by them; and in matters ecclesiasticall by the counsell of the generall assemblie, and such as ar or shall be authorized by them:

His majestie doeth consent to this whole proposition *in terminis*.

## APPENDIX XI.

### No. I.—Extracts from Records of the Presbytery of Dingwall. (Communicated by Mr. W. Mackay, F.S.A. Scot., of Inverness.)

*Meeting at Dingwall, 9th April* 1650 —"The breyren report y$^r$ making vse of the declara$^{ones}$ of Estate and Kirk [15] against Ja: Grahames declara$^{on}$ by reading and explaining the same in ther severall c'grega$^{ones}$."

*Meeting at Dingwall, 16th April* 1650 —"The breyren being informed of Ja: Grahames landing in Cathnes with forces and comeing forward for furder supplie for carieing one his former bloodie rebellions and perfidious courses and considdering the act of the g'nall [*assembly*] for receiveing of malignantes to publick satisfac$^{on}$ to import y$^t$ all who formerlie were vpon the rebellions and malignant insurrec$^{ones}$ in the land and professing y$^r$ repentance of the same and desyre to be received to satisfac$^{on}$ that if anie such suld furder promove anie rebellious course against God's work and people they suld [*be*] exc'municat, They doe y$^r$fore for preventing anie associationes considera$^{ones}$ or correspondencie with the s$^d$ excommunicat bloodie traytor or his forces Ordayne all the breyren to make intima$^{on}$ out of y$^r$ severall pulpits that anie who shall associat or correspond with the s$^d$ Rebell or his forces shall be sentenced with exc'munica$^{on}$ sumarlie, and the severall breyren are appoynted to performe accordinglie in cace anie breach fors$^d$ shall happen to be comitted."

*Meeting at Dingwall, 28th May* 1650.—"The Brethrein report y$^t$ they keiped the Thanksgiveing [16] for ye victorie at Corbisdell obtained against James Grahame and others enemies to ye cause and people of God, his adherentes."

The Editiors have been greatly indebted to Mr. William Mackay of Craigmonie, Inverness, for permitting them to see his copy from the Dingwall Presbytery Records, in addition to the extracts which he kindly sent them, as bearing more directly on Montrose in 1650. These records began to be kept 19th June 1649, with a notice of the thanksgiving observed for the "wictorie at Balvenie." Thereafter they abound in references to the prevalence of "Malignancy" in Ross-shire.

---

[15] For the text of these see W.'s Montr. (1819), pp. 458–491. The counterblast, the Commission of the General Assembly, was issued January 2nd, that of the Committee of Estates, January 24, 1650.

[16] "There was a solemn day of thanksgiving appointed through the whole Kingdome, Bonfires, shooting of Ordnance, and other testimonies of joy." Montr. Rediv. 180.

# APPENDIX.

The names of offenders, according to the Act of Classes, appear in many entries, chiefly Mackenzies, Monroes, and Rosses. So prevalent had been the vice of loyalty to chief and king, that in some parishes (Urray, Kintail, Lochalsh, Lochcarron) there were no elders not incapacitated by Malignancy. The offences were various in degree—complicity in "James Grahame's rebellion," or in the "unlawfull ingadgement," or in the late "insurrection in the North" (Pluscardine's).

In September 1649 the parishes of Urray and Kilchreist contributed seventy-six names, Kilterne twenty-two, Urquhart and Loggie fifteen. And these were by no means all, as it is evident from repeated entries to that effect, that the "Brethren" charged to make up the lists had great difficulty in getting the offenders to "compeir" and confess.

Of special interest we note that on September 11, 1649, in the meeting held at Dingwall "Jo$^n$ Monro of Lemlair compeiring before the Presbyterie acknowledging his error and professing great greife and sorrow for his accession to the unlaw$^{ll}$ ingadgment and the late rebellion in the North and c'sidering y$^t$ according to the act of the gr̄all assemblie none above the degree of a leivetenant guiltie as he was, can be received on repentance untill they have their recourse to the gr̄all assemblie or their commissioners, Therefore supplicated the Presbyterie to grant him a certificat of his cariage before the unlaw$^{ll}$ ingadgment and since his coming off the late rebellion, to be proported to the Commission of the gr̄all assembly, to which he intended to have his recourse with all c'venient diligence for receiving such censure as they would be pleased to enjoyne . . .

"Sickly Captaine Androw Monro acknowledging his accesse to the unlaw$^{ll}$ ingadgment for England and professing his greife," &c. (applied for a similar certificate on the same terms).

In the list from Kilterne, given in, Sept. 18, 1649, we read "Robert Monro, Lemlair his sonne."

Dec. 11. Kenneth M'Kenzie of Assint and others "confessed their accession to Ja: Grahame's rebellion," &c.

Jan. 22, 1650. Keneth M'Kenzie, laird of Gerloch, confessed to the same.

Feb. 5, 1650. Letter from the Commission of the General Assembly "appoynting Jo$^n$ Munro of Lemlayre to c'peir before them at Edin$^r$."

Aug. 28, 1650. "John Monro of Lumlaire presented ane Testimoniall bearing y$^t$ he had made satisfac$^{on}$ for his malignant courses according to the ordinance of the Commissioners of the Kirk qlk certificat wes subscryved be M$^r$ Jo$^n$ Annan, to whom he wes recommended to y$^t$ effect."

Space forbids us to quote more from these interesting records. The above is perhaps enough to show to what extent Montrose was justified in expecting aid from the levies of Ross.

### No. II.—ADVOCATES' LIBRARY, Wodrow MSS., fol. lxvii. 102.

[*Extract.*] A letter signed J. Smythe off Braco, dated Meall the 18 off Maij 1650, addressed to Lt. Generall Lesley, wherein the writer excuses himself for his "ingadgement" [to Montrose] on the ground that he had been forced to return to his house for fear his house and tenants should be plundered. "I wald nogt have returnit for any thing they could have don to my self so I migt have been frie off the Ingadgment. it is many tymes it repentit me since that I did return but I could not mend me for I could nogt win away efter that tyme they were so jelous off me and kepit still ane watchfull ei ouer me."

## APPENDIX XII.

No. I.—LETTER FROM LOUIS XIV., KING OF FRANCE, TO THE ESTATES OF SCOTLAND. (From Monteith, Hist. des Troubles, 366, 367.)

On the news of Montrose's capture Cardinal de Retz hastened to Court, to procure the intercession of Louis on his behalf. "But before the messenger could set out, news arrived of Montrose's murder." (June 11th. See p. 288.)

*"Les Lettres du Roy estoient conceues en ces termes."*

"TRES-CHERS ET GRANDS AMYS, Aiant sçeu que le sieur Marquis de Montrose estoient demeuré prisonnier au dernier combat qu'il a rendu en Escosse, et considerant que ce malheur luy est arriué par le sort des armes, en executant la Commission de nostre tres-cher et tres-amé frere et cousin le Roy de la Grand' Bretagne, qu'il s'est tousiours conduit auec beaucoup de prudence, d'honneur et de vertu, et qu'il en a merité nostre bien-veillance et nostre affection particuliere, ayant mesme esgard à la tres-humble priere nous a esté faite en sa faueur, par le sieur Euesque de Corinthe Coadiuteur en l'Archeuesché de nostre bonne Ville de Paris. Nous nous sentons conuiez de vous escrire celle-cy par l'aduis de la Reine Regente nostre tres honorée Dame et Mere, pour vous prier de mettre ledit sieur Marquis en liberté, et de ne pas souffrir qu'il luy soit fait aucun mauuais traittement. Nous nous promettons que vous aurez esgard à nostre recommendation que nous vous faisons très affectionnée, et que vous voudrez preferer les douceurs de la clemence aux rigeurs du chastiment qu'on peut dire qu'il n'a pas merité, puis qu'il a genereusement satisfait à son premier deuoir, en obeissant au Roy son Souuerain et le vostre, qui se pourra souuenir vn iour de la faueur que vous aurez faite à vn de ses seruiteurs, pour lequel nous enuoions exprés ce Gentilhomme qui vous assurera de nostre affection, auquel vous donnerez creance en tout ce qu'il vous dira de nostre part, et vous fera connoistre que nos instances se font, pour ledit sieur de Montrose, d'aussi bon coeur que nous prions Dieu vous auoir, TRES CHERS ET GRANDS AMYS, en sa sainte et digne garde. Escrit à Compiegne le 10. iour de Iuin 1650."

Monteith adds: "Le mesme Prelat [Cardinal de Retz] . . . a tousiours dit, que Montrose estoit l'homme du monde qu'il eust iamais veu, qui luy representast le plus parfaitement l'idée des grands hommes de l'ancienne Grece et de l'ancienne Rome tout ensemble."

# APPENDIX.

### No. II.

The following details as to the personal appearance of Montrose are taken from the rare Montr. Rediv. (True and perfect Relation), pp. 196-198.

"The death of the noble Marquesse was not bewailed as a private losse, but rather as a publique calamitie. The greatest Princes in Europe expressed no small sorrow for his unhappy end. And indeed wee have not had in this latter Age a man of more eminent parts either of body or of mind. He was a man not very tall, nor much exceeding a middle stature, but of exceeding strong composition of body, and incredible force, with excellent proportion and feature; Dark brown hayr'd, sanguine complexion, a swift and piercing gray eye, with a high nose, somewhat like the antient signe of the Persian Kings Magnanimitie. He was of a most resolute and undaunted spirit, which began to appear in him, to the wonder and expectation of all men even in his childhood. Whom would it not have startled to attempt as he did at his first entrie into Scotland, a journey wherein he could not almost escape discovery, all passes being so layd for him, but even when he was known, and almost made publike, he proceeded in his intention? He was a man of a very Princely courage, and excellent addresses, which made him for the most part be us'd by all Princes with extraordinarie familiaritie; A compleat Horseman, and had a singular grace in ryding, Nor is it lesse wonderfull how in so great scarcity of all things when warre in that Country is but tedious with the greatest plentie it can afford, he could patiently endure so much distresse. Nor is it lesse to be wondred at, how he could win so much upon those Irish, who had no tye to him either of Countrie, Language or Religion, as he did. More especially when they wanted not all manner of temptation, that either their own miseries and intolerable duty could suggest, or the wit and sagacitie of the enemie could invent to make them leave him, and abandon the service. Besides the many examples shown upon them and their continuall want of Pay, either of which accidents in an Armie is ground enough, and has been many times the occasion of mutiny and desertion. Nor had he only an excellent and mature judgement for providing and forecasting of businesse, but a prompt and readie spirit likewise in matters of present danger and sudden calamitie, and these things which might have confused another mans understanding, as such sudden chances often doe, were a whetting to his wit. There are many stratagems in severall Histories related, which in the heat of action have been put in practice for the regaining of a day already lost, or in danger to be so. As that of Jugurtha, a politick and valiant Prince, who in the heat of a battell betwixt him and Marius the Roman Consull rode up and down in the head of the Armie, showing his bloudie sword, and affirming that he had slain Marius with his own hand, which word did so encourage the Numedians, and amaze the Romans that had not Marius in time appeared, that day had been in hazard. It is likewise reported of one of the Roman Captains, that he flung his Standard amongst the middle of the enemie, that his own souldiers by pressing forward to rescue it, might break and disorder the enemie. Likewise of another

522                              APPENDIX.

that took the bridles off the horse-heads, that every man might be alike valiant, and charge, as we say, without either fear or wit. But beyond all these in my opinion was that device of the Marquesses, who at Alderne being in a great strait, one wing of his Armie being routed, and the other in a very staggering condition, he did so incense that which was yet whole, with the feigned success of the other, that [it] valiantly charged the enemie, and put the business again in an even ballance. And very like was it to that device of Tullus Postilius [Hostilius], who being deserted by Metius King of the Albans told his souldiers that he had don 't of purpose to try them, and by that means turn'd their fear into indignation. He was exceeding constant and affable to those that did adhere to him, and to those he knew very affable, though his carriage which indeed was not ordinarie, did make him seem proud; Nor can his enemies lay any greater fault to his charge, than this insatiable desire of honour which he did pursue with as handsome and heroick action as ever any ever did, and such as had neither admiration of avarice or self ends, though he was therewith by some most unworthily branded. For these, and the like vertues of which he was the rich possessour, he was lamented all Christendome over, by all sorts of men, and since his death too by those who had the greatest hand in't, though their success at that time did animate their crueltie.

>    Nescia mens hominum fati sortisque futurae
>    Et servire modum rebus sublata secundis.[17]

---

## APPENDIX XIII.

### DID NEIL MACLEOD BETRAY MONTROSE?

This question has been much debated,[18] with some confusion on the various issues. We propose to cite the evidence of original authorities. Much of it will probably be new to some of those who engaged in the controversy.

(1). Balfour, Annals, iv. and (2) Acts Parl. Scot., both contemporary in the strictest sense, attest the fact that Macleod of Assynt claimed and received a reward for the apprehension of Montrose, and was thanked therefor by the Parliament.

(3). Gordon of Sallagh, whose account was written probably in 1650, certainly not later than 1651, bears evidence as quoted in our text. Pt. II. Ch. ix.

(4). The anonymous author of Part II. of the Montrose Redivivus alleges that Montrose, "knowing him and believing to find friendship at his hands, willingly discover'd himself," and was handed over to Lesley by "the Lord of Aston," "being greedy of the reward."

This work was published in London in 1652. The expression "Lord of Aston,"

---

[17] These lines are here appositely quoted in reference to Montrose's *enemies*. The Rev. W. Fraser, who doubtless borrowed them from the above passage (see p. 316 and n. 24), applies them with feeble point to Montrose. Probably he misunderstood their application above.

[18] *Nat. Observer*, Mar.-April 1892.

# APPENDIX.

with other indications, points to an English author. The narrative depreciates Montrose's last attempt, and could not possibly have been written by Wishart.

This account is copied *verbatim* by Heath in his Chronicles.

(5). Ian Lom, "the Bard of Keppoch," present at Inverlochy in 1645, who lived till after 1715, wrote a Lament for Montrose, in which he explicitly accuses Assynt of basely selling Montrose. We are indebted for our note of him and the following literal version of the passage to the late Mr. Alexander Nicolson, an eminent authority in Celtic literature, who infers that it was probably written not long after Montrose's execution.

LAMENT FOR MONTROSE, BY IAN LOM.

V. 8.

"I'll not go to Dunedin
Since the Graham's blood was shed,
The manly mighty lion,
Tortured on the gallows.

That was the true gentleman,
Who came of line not humble,
Good was the flushing of his cheek
When drawing up to combat.

His chalk-white teeth well closing,
His slender brow not gloomy;
Though oft my love awakes me,
This night I will not bear it.

Neil's son of woful Assynt,
If I in net could take thee,
My sentence would condemn thee,
Nor would I spare the gibbet.

If you and I encountered
On the marshes on Ben Etive,
The black waters and the clods
Would there be mixed together.

If thou and thy wife's father,
The householder of Leime [*Lemlair*],
Were hanged both together
'Twould not atone my loss.

Stript tree of the false apples,
Without esteem, or fame, or grace,
Ever murdering each other,
Mid dregs of wounds and knives.

Death-wrapping to thee, base one!
Ill didst thou sell the righteous,
For the meal of Leith,
And two-thirds of it sour!"

The Gaelic is in Mackenzie's "Beauties of Gaelic Poetry" (1841), 50.

(6). John Gwynne, a survivor of Montrose's expedition (see Index), followed Glencairn in 1653 on his Expedition. He spent the winter of 1653 in the Reay country (p. 100), whence he proceeded from Strath Naver to Skye (102). Page 92 he speaks of Montrose after his defeat as "in the custody of a *pretended old friend*."[19]

---

[19] See also above, App. I. Gwynne's Memoirs, a record of services ungratefully neglected by Charles II., are undated. But from prefatory letters to various noblemen we infer that the work must have been written after 1675, and probably before 1683. One is to the Duke of Grafton, born 1663, made Duke, 1675. Another, to the Duke of Monmouth, speaks of distinctions, gained probably in the Dutch War, 1672-74, or at Bothwell Brig, 1679. Monmouth was exiled in 1679, and again, in 1683, for complicity in the Rye House Plot. There is apparently an allusion (p. 19) to the Popish Plot, 1678. At the time of writing Gwynne had served over forty-two years, and was therefore probably over sixty years old. He had been in Charles I.'s Guards before the Civil War (1642), and engaged in drilling the Princes (Charles II., born 1630) and Buckingham (born 1627).

(7). In the MS. account of Glencairn's Expedition by an eye-witness, supposed to have been John Graham of Duchrie, edited with Gwynne's Memoirs (1822, Maitland Club), 180, 181, we read that Glencairn, on a quarrel with Sir George Monro, "marched [with 100 horse] straight to the Laird of Essen's bounds. . . . His Lordship having arrived in safety at the Laird of Essens, he [Macleod] offered his services to secure the passes, so that the whole army, though they were pursuing, should not be able to come near him that night. My Lord was *obliged to accept of this favour, though this gentleman was said to be the person who betrayed the great Montrose; yet others affirm it was his father-in-law, he [Macleod] being very young at that time.*"

(8). "J: E. Miles Philo-Gramus Po," about the time of Montrose's funeral in 1661, wrote, in an elogium to be inscribed on his tomb, *nequissime hostibus traditus.*

(9). Dr. George Bates, chief physician to the King, writes in his "Elenchi Motuum nuperorum in Anglia" (London, 1663), Part II., 82, "Fugit Comes Montisrosanus, vestibusque cum montano quodam commutatis, per tres dies quatuorve delituit, unico servo comitatus; donec *Toparchae de Aken* jejunio fractum *se tradidit, qui etiam si olim sub signis ejus meruerat, mutata jam cum fortuna fide, ad Lesleium deduxit, mille librarum* [pounds sterling] *corruptus.*" The spelling of the name, the fact that he makes Sibbald taken in the battle by "Straughan," and other slight variations, show that Bates was unacquainted with the Montr. Rediv. His evidence, therefore, is entitled to the full value of *independent testimony.*

(10). *Mercurius Caledonius*, by Saintserf, a friend of Montrose, Jan. 25, 1661. Montrose would have escaped "if unfortunately he had not been *betrayed* three days after." Napier, Mem., 841.

(11). The sole (contemporary) evidence against this is Monteith's omission of Macleod's name. He says (Eng. Tr. p. 511) Brim (Sinclair of Brims) "betray'd him," and a Party of the Country People came upon him immediately, who, after having promis'd him all manner of good Usage, basely sold him to David Lesly.

Balfour, Ann. iv. 10: Montrose "fled, bot was afterwards taken by the Laird of Assins people."

Acts Parlt. May 17th, 1650. "The Estaitts of pliament Remitts to the Committee of dispatches To think upoun a recompence to be given to the laird of assint for his good service and ane effectuall menes of reall pay^t w'out delay lykas the l/ Chancelar in name of the parliament and be thair warrand gave him hartie thanks for his faithfull service, and intimat the pliaments intentione to him."

May 23, 1650. Argyll, Burghley, and others, appointed as a Comm^tte "to meitt and think upoun a way of payment et satissfac°ne to the l/ of assint for his good service."

24th. "Report anent the l/ of assint redd and remitted to the several bodyes."

(Balf. iv. 35). May 30th. "The parliament appoynts a Committee . . . to consider of the fynnes to be impossed on" . . . those who had joined Montrose

# APPENDIX.

... "and that the Laird of Assin, that tooke and apprehendit the said James Grhame, be payed the soume of 25,000 lib. Scotts, out of the first, and be for all others of these fynnes."

(*Ibid.* 41.) June 4th. The house assigns the Lord St. Clair's fine to sundrie ... "quhat they want of that, to haue it out of the first and reddiest of the fynnes of Orknay and Cathnes men, nixt after the payment of the Laird of Assin, and the officers" [victors at Carbisdale].

(*Ibid.* 52.) June 8th. The Committee of Fines and Process to meet on Monday [10th] ... "annent the ending of the Laird of Assin Mr. Rob: Farquhars bussiness."

(Acts.) June 11th. Assint "supplicates."

(Balf. iv. 52). June 11th. "Bill this day exhibit to the housse by the Laird of Assin, shewing that for his good seruice to the countrey, the Clan-Kenzie, Clan-Kay, and the Laird of Glengarey, had spoyled his countrey." (This is the only mention we find of this).

(Acts). June 14th. Report concerning l/ assint.
,,        ,,   21st.    ,,       ,,      ,,

(Balf. iv. 56.) June 22nd. "The Com: of Proces report anent Assin to have 20,000 lib. from Mr Robert Farquhare, quho shall be collector of the fynnes of the lait ingagers with James Grhame; approuen and ratified by the housse."

(Acts.) June 25th. Argyll and others ordained to speak with Sir James Melvill anent the l/ assint to report to morrow.

(*Ibid.*) June 28th. Sir Jas. Melveill in presence of parlt. in name of M$^r$ Ro$^t$ Farquhar "undertook that the l/ of assint should be presentlie satisfied in money or securitie of what is appointed to be given him."

Act in favour of the l/ of assint.

We have seen that Assynt was first to have 25,000 lib. Scots (=*ca.* £1360); then 20,000 lib. There can be little doubt that he accepted the 400 bolls [20] of "sour meal," still so infamous in Highland tradition, as payment in kind for the odd 5000 lib. Balfour tells us that in July 1649 oatmeal sold in Edinburgh at 15 lib. the boll; in Fife at 13 lib. 6s. 8d., and, again, in December 1651, when prices were high, "Comon ottemeall" sold in Fife at 10 lib. (*ibid.* 334). In 1649–50 the North suffered from famine, a circumstance which would render Assynt the more disposed to deal in kind. Assuming a medium value of $12\frac{1}{2}$ lib. per boll, 400 bolls would equal exactly the odd 5000 lib. due to him; and he might even hope to profit on it in the famine-stricken North. Such an attempt to trade away his damaged goods would account for the strength of tradition on the subject. But this is pure conjecture. Whether he ever succeeded in extorting the 20,000 lib. (=*ca.* £1088) from Mr. Robert Farquhar does not appear. His receipts for the meal were extant after the Restoration.

(12). Burnet (1643–1715), Hist. of his own Time (1883), 34. Montrose "was

---

[20] A boll was two bushels.

betrayed by one of those to whom he trusted himself, Mackloud of Assin." See below, p. 528.

In the face of this evidence it must be considered beyond all further question

(i.) *That Assynt seized and delivered up Montrose.*

(ii.) *That he claimed a reward, that his claim was allowed, and, in part at least, paid, and himself thanked for his service, and given priority over all other claims for reward.*

Without such evidence it might have been possible to cavil at the Royalist authorities already quoted. But, as the case stands, the two propositions above rest on the authority of Neil's friends and Montrose's enemies, and must be regarded as facts proved as certainly as anything in history. This evidence alone would suffice to outweigh the *alibi* which Macleod's apologists declare that he successfully maintained before a Royalist jury when impeached for this crime after the Restoration. But on examination of the records we find that

(iii.) *Macleod did pretend an* alibi *when threatened with trial for the betrayal of Montrose.*

(iv.) *That he was never tried on this count, but liberated in virtue of an Act of Indemnity—which he pleaded.*

(v.) *That at his subsequent trial in 1674 the charge was repeated in "aggravation" of other offences, but waived; and no defence made except on those other charges, and on those other charges alone he obtained acquittal.*

To an impartial reader this plea of *alibi* must appear one of the worst features in Assynt's case. For either he lied egregiously to the Parliament of 1650, or he lied egregiously to the Parliament of 1660. Some element of truth there may have been in the assertion, sufficient perhaps to suggest the plea. But even if there were a shred of truth in the statement with which he is credited (13) by the MS. of 1738 (see p. 529), that he was not at Ardvreck when Montrose was brought there, but "60 miles away," and if, as has been suggested, it was his wife who seized Montrose, he must have suppressed the fact in 1650, when he claimed and obtained full credit for the deed.

As to the proceedings against him in 1660-63, and again in February 1674, the following references and extracts should effectually dispel all doubts as to the real issues and results in question.

23rd June, 1663. "Personall Protections" granted to Neill M'cleod "of Assint" and others during this Session of Parliament (Scots Acts).

17th Aug. 1663. "During the sitting of parliament, and I think by order of it, Angus and Neil M'Leod were denounced and put to the horn, being, as was alleged, the persons who had taken the marquis of Montrose, May 1650. This was done, August 17$^{th}$, this year" (Wodrow, Hist. Sufferings, i. 381). Even the martyr-monger Wodrow cannot make a saint of *him*, and has no comment to add.

# APPENDIX.

### *Letter to Charles II. from the Parlt.*

8 Oct 1663.

"MOST SACRED SOVERAIGN,

"Ther being a criminall processe depending befor yor Parliament at the instance
"of yor Majesties Advocat with the concurrence of the Marquis of Montrose as
"his informer against Neill McLeod of Assint for his alledged betraying and giveing
"up of the late Marquis of Montrose to those who murdered him and for takeing
"a sum of money from them in recompense of that same treacherous act   And he
"being brought to the Bar and the dittay with his answer thereunto the reply made
"to your Advocat and his duplys being at lenth red and considered Wee find he
"denyes the mater of fact alledged against him   Bot supposeing the same wer
"true he grounds his defence upon the indemnity granted be yor Majestie to your
"Scots subjects in the treatie at Breda in the year 1650 and the ratifications of the
"same passed be your Majestie at your being in this Kingdom in the year 1650
"and 1651   Tho it wes instantly offered to be proven under his hand that he
"had receaved the money above mentioned and that this treatie could be no
"securitie to him it not being produced, and being (if any such thing be) befor
"the deeds quarrelled   And Wee considering that in all former processes dureing
"this Parliament it was yor Majesties expresse pleasure and accordingly all those
"crymes which wer lybelled against any persone as done before that treatie and
"these assureances Or which had any ground of defence from them wer layd
"aside and not insisted on   Have conceaved it suteable to our duetie and your
"Majesties Commands to forbeare further procedor in this particular till your
"Majestie wer acquainted therewith That your Majestie upon consideration of
"the bussines may be pleased to give order either for the prosecution thereof befor
"your Justice or for sisting of all further proceiding Or for any other cause therein
"Which your Majestie in your Royall judgement shall think fittest for your honour
"and service   This is in name and be warrand of your Parliament signed be
"your Majesties most humble most obedient and most faithfull Subject and
"Servant."

The treatie of Breda, here pretended in defence, was signed 13 May and
11 June, ratified by Act, 4 July, confirmed by the Declaration of Dunfermline,
16 Aug. 1650 (Balf. iv. 73 and 92). The last provided expressly for "an act of
"oblivion to all, except the chieffe obstructers of the worke of reformatione, and
"the authors of the change of gouerniment and the murthers of his royall father."

1st Dec. 1663.   "At a Sitting of the Privy Council in Edin. on 1st Dec. 1663
"a petition was presented by Neil; stating that he had been been a prisoner in
"the Tolbooth of Edinburgh for over three years 'upon groundless allegations of
"the accession to the betraying of the late Marquis of Montrose, by which
"imprisonment,' &c., he is redacted to that condition by sickness that it is impossible
"to him to escape death if he remain any longer in that place, and craving to be
"relieved from prison and to have the liberty of the city of Edinr, upon sufficient

"surety being found for his appearance when called upon. Medical certificates "having been laid before the Council their Lordships ordered him to be set at "liberty upon finding sufficient caution for his reappearance, and bound him not "to leave Edinburgh under a penalty of £20,000 Scots." Register Privy Council, Acta Decreta 1663.

On the same date the bond of caution was granted by Macleod and others. *Ibid.*

Note the sum. These grim Lords of Council are ironical. We could almost pity the man, grown familiarly "Neil" in his troubles, caged in his prime of 30, three years spent in that loathsome prison, for the youthful crime that wrecked his stormy life. Yet Burnet—no friend to Montrose—says he made a merry time of it. Hist. of his own Time, 85.

"The gross iniquity of the court appeared in nothing more eminently than "in the favour showed Maccloud of Assin, who had betrayed the marquis of "Montrose, and was brought over upon it. He in prison struck up to a high "pitch of vice and impiety, and gave great entertainments: and that, notwith- "standing the baseness of the man and his crimes, begot him so many friends,— "that he was let go without any censure."

But what with courtesans and dilettante science "the Merry Monarch" forgets enemies as well as friends, sometimes with equal discomfort to both. Three years elapse before his "tender," "gracious" reply is made. At last, on February 1666, the following letter was read by his Majesty's Commissioner to the Privy Council.

"CHARLES R.—Right Trusty, &c., . . . forasmuch as by one letter dated at "Edinburgh, the eight of October 1663, &c. . . . we were informed that the "criminal process depending &c. . . . [repeating the preamble of the letter] . . . "And we, considering also that by the public indemnity made in the second "Session of our first parliament there is no exception of the said Neil Macleod "but that he is included within our first general pardon and indemnity, whereby "all manners of treasons murders and offences done by any person by virtue "of any power or warrant from any pretended Parliament, &c. . . . Since January "1637 until September 1660, or by any their abettors and assisters, are pardoned "and discharged, And it being also represented to us that, notwithstanding all "the foresaid Acts of Indemnity, and sure pardon and the sisting of proceedings "against him before the Parliament as is mentioned in the said letter, yet the "said criminal process was of new again intended before the Justice, and the said "Marquis of Montrose with the concourse of our Advocate, insisting therein.—

"And having considered the said letter . . . and . . . general Act of Indemnity, "and being most tender and careful that the public security and free pardon which 'we have so graciously indulged to our subjects for liberating them of their minds 'and composing their minds to cheerful affection for our Royal person and government should [*not?* singular omission!] be violat broken or impeached in 'any case wherein there may be any ground or defence from the said Act of

"Indemnity granted in the second session of the first Parliament, or from any
"pretended act of indemnity granted at Breda or in Scotland in the years 1650
"and 1651.

"Wherefore it is our will and pleasure that the foresaid process against the said
"Neil Macleod for the alleged betraying of the late Marquis of Montrose and
"taking of the said recompense therefor, should be sisted and no further proceeded
"in before our justice, and that our judges civil and criminal should be discharged
"to meddle or proceed in the said matter,—

"And that the foresaid Act of Indemnity ought and should free and liberate
"the said Neil from any          for the deed aforesaid,—

"And that this our will and order be intimated by you our Commissioner, &c.

"Subscribitur sic by his Majesty's command

"LAUDERDALE.

"Given at our Court at Whitehall the 20th day of Feb. 1666, and of our reign
"the 13th year."

"The said Lords of Council . . . ordain the same (letter) to be recorded in
"the Books and to be intimated and the Judges therein discharged [*commanded*]
"in manner appointed" (Acts of Privy Council, 1666–7, p. 546).

The Angus Macleod mentioned in the extract 17th Aug. 1663, above, was Neil's cousin. Their connection is shown thus:—

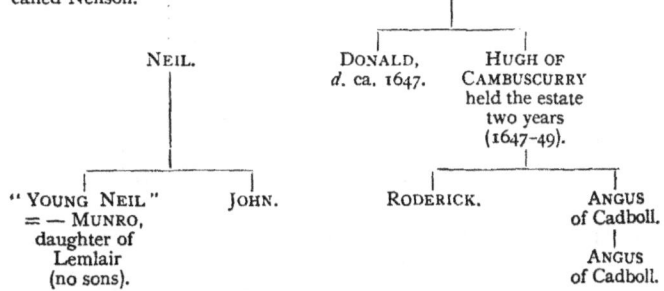

Donald's sons, Neil and Donald, died before their father. Hugh administered the property for "young Neil" during his minority, and appears to have involved the estate in obligations which caused Neil life-long litigation. On Sept. 12, 1649, Hugh "disponed" the estate to his nephew on his majority, and the instrument of infeftment was registered 8th Jan. 1650. Neil was therefore born probably in the autumn of 1628, and was between twenty-one and twenty-two years of age when he seized Montrose. These facts are from the paper written in 1738 on Neil's troubles ("How the Macleods lost Assynt," by Mr. William Mackay, Transactions, Gael. Soc. Invern., xvi. 197 ff.). They dispose of the doubt expressed by

Graham of Duchrie (?), *ca.* 1655, that Neil in 1650 was too young for the deed. They have also an important bearing on the question—

### WAS NEIL EVER A FOLLOWER OF MONTROSE?

Undoubtedly the fact would constitute a grievous aggravation of his crime. It is asserted definitely by the Montr. Redivivus, 1652, and Bates, in 1663. It is implied vaguely in Gwynne's "pretended old friend." The silence of the Acts Parl. in 1650 cannot be alleged in his favour.

If we ask at what period he could have served under Montrose, it appears that the only probable time was in 1646, when Seaforth joined Montrose. It is admitted in the 1738 document that "*in that year Seaforths men haveing joined* "*Montrose at Inverness,*" there were "*likewise a* 100 *men of Assints under his* "*Superior Seaforth's command,*" and further, "*Neil of Assint himself then a minor,* "*being a friend in Seaforth's house at Braen* [*Brahan*] *Seaforth ordred his men to* "*fall upon Assints Estate, where yey made fearful Havock,*" &c. On this it is to be noted that Neil was then eighteen years of age, and therefore older than many who had borne arms in this war. It is difficult to account for his presence at Seaforth's house of Brahan, near Inverness, when Seaforth's and his own men were with Montrose at Inverness, unless we suppose that Neil himself had come down with his 100 followers. When Middleton nearly surprised the Royalists there, Montrose retreated by "Beauly into Ross" (Wishart, 1647, 179 above), and must have passed close by Brahan. Wishart, then an eye-witness, tells us "the natives were treacherous and inconstant, and Seaforth's new levies were deserting by companies."

It might be urged that as Neil could have little friendship for Seaforth, who in 1640 had invaded and harried Assynt (p. 200), he attended his superior in 1646 on compulsion. But the document which we are quoting, though strongly hostile to Seaforth, does not mention this among his acts of oppression. Unless his friendship for Seaforth in 1646 is a fiction, to heighten Seaforth's alleged treachery, we have here what is in effect Neil's own admission of the fact. The narrative explicitly declares that it is "taken from some old papers write for Neil McLeod of Assint."

Finally, we have the statement, written in 1650 or 1651, by his friend and neighbour, the local annalist, Sallagh (p. 555), who regarded him as a *protégé* of the Earl of Sutherland, that Neil showed diligence in the search for Montrose, and resisted "great offers" which Montrose made to him, "if *he would goe with him to Orknay*, all which he refused."

*"Che fece per viltate il gran rifiuto!"*

On these statements we incline to believe that there is here presumptive evidence in favour of the assertion that (vi.) *Macleod had served with Montrose, and that Montrose knew him, and expected to find protection from him.* He would hardly have asked an avowed uncompromising enemy to go with him to Orkney. Lemlair had been out with Pluscardine not twelve months before; and unless Montrose had seen reason to suspect Lemlair of treachery in the recent battle, the knowledge

# APPENDIX.

of Neil's marriage to Lemlair's daughter must have strengthened his hope of safety.

It remains to consider how far the accusation of treachery appeared in Neil's trial in 1674, since it is on his acquittal by the jury that his apologists found their only strong plea in his favour.

We have ourselves examined the account of the trial in the Book of Adjournalls, a strictly contemporary diary of unimpeachable authority, preserved in the High Court of Justiciary.

### TRIAL OF ASSINT FOR TREASON.

Endorsed "found clean by ane assyse."

[*Extracts*] "Neill M$^c$cleod of Assint now prisoner in the Tolbuith of Edinburgh,

"Feb. 2 1674 before Lord Collintoun, President, John Lockhart of Castlehill, John Baird of Newbygh (?) [Newbyth], Thomas Wallace of Craigie, Comm$^{rs}$ of Justiciary. Persewer, Sir John Nisbet of Dirletoun, Kt., the King's Advocate; Informer, Alex. Grhame of Drynie; Sir George Mackenzie, Advocate. The prisoner was defended by Mess$^{rs}$ John Elles and Robert Colt." After a preamble on the Statute of Treason, the "libel" or indictment proceeds:—

"Nevertheless it is of veritie that the said Neil Mcleod of Assint having
" shacken off all fear of God dewtie and alleadgance to his prince, and respect and
" regaird to his Majesties person and Lawes did in the moneth of March Appryll
" May June July or August 1649 years [date singularly vague and inaccurate!]
" upon ane or other of the dayes of the sed moneths or ane or other of them
" *most perfidiouslie treacherouslie baslie and Inhumanelie* UNDER TRUST[21] take and
" apprehend the person of James late Marquis of Montrose his Majesties hye
" Commissioner and Lieutenant general whilst he wes invested under his hynes
" seall for that effect and delyvered him prisoner to the Rebells his Majesties
" enemies then in armes ag$^t$ his hynes Majestie by whom the s$^d$ Marquis wes
" cruellie and inhumanelie murdered for the which the s$^d$ Neill Mccleod receaved
" the number of ffour hundreth bolls of maill as the reward of the s$^d$ treason-
" able act and which maill was delyvered to him be Sir Robert Ffarquhar of
" Mounzie. . . ."

Then follows an accusation of treasonably assisting the English under Morgan in 1654, and harrying Seaforth's lands. Then follow various acts of violence alleged against Neil in 1669–70, as the imposition of illegal taxes on ships touching in Loch Inver, his violent seizure of one Captain Keir, with threats to murder him on his refusal to pay these imposts. He garrisons and "stuffs" his house of Ardbrack with 20 Neillsons *alias* "Clecheanbricks"[22] against the Sheriff of Sutherland, with a commission of ejectment given at the instance of Sir George M'Kenzie of Tarbet and John M'Kenzie, son to the Earl of Seaforth . . . "the s$^d$ Neill M'Cleod did

---

[21] The italics are our own.  [22] See below, p. 533.

"most proudlie contemptuouslie and treasonablie fortifie and mantaine the said "house with his Majesties Rebells" . . . 27 Dec. 1671 he was required to surrender; 28 Feb. 1671 [*i.e.*, 1672] "declaired fugitive." "Commission of fyre "and sword directed by the Lords of his Majesties privie Counsill to the Earle "of Seaforth, Lord Lovitt, Laird of Ffoulis and others, who gathered eight "hundreth men and went against the house with cannon," &c. Neill had fled to the mountains with 300 men. The garrison on a summons answered they "cared not a plack for the King." The siege lasted fourteen days. Neil fled to Caithness and Orkney, but was arrested by Sir William Sinclair of May, and sent prisoner to the Tolbuith of Edinburgh by the Counsills order, where he now lyes.

Neil Macleod petitioned for trial. The Lords of Privy Council granted an order for a trial, 5th Aug. 1673.

At the trial "His Majesties Advocat declaires he does not insist upon the first tuo Crimes lybelled [*i.e.*, those committed in 1650 and 1654] but only as aggravations" . . .

" My Lord Advocat answers [to Mr. John Elies for the "pannal" or prisoner] "that Instruments are taken that no defence is proponed ag$^t$ any of the other "articles of the dittay except only the tuo last contained in the same and therfor "his Majesties Advocat declaires that as to the tuo first articles anent the treason- "able taking and delyvering his Majesties Commissioner the Marques of Montrose "and the pannals joyning with and assisting the English Rebells under Morgan "he does not insist upon the samen at this tyme bot as aggravations of the other "Crymes and articles contained in the dittay" . . . and asks for a trial on the "remnant articles."

On February 3rd and 9th the trial was "continued;" on the 16th "debated;" and "continued" till the 18th, when it was "remitted to ane Assise" (jury—the names given).

On the 19th the sentence was :—"The Assyse all in on voyce (on only excepted) "assolyied the pannall Neill M$^c$cleod of Assint from the crymes contained in the "tuo members of the last article viz that the pannal after the publica$^o$n of the "commission for fyre and sword did raise and levie ane hundreth men and "upwards in armes and patt them under officers and militarie discipline and "defend Arbraek."

The taking of Captain Keir not proven.

Other charges not proven.

Finally, to complete his miserable career, we have on 5th August 1690, order of removal of Neil Macleod from out of lands of Assint. Mackenzie's Hist. Macleods, 418.

We cannot here enter more fully into the records of these trials. The extracts cited are all that concerns Montrose directly. It is, however, to be noted that even on the other counts we have the testimony of Burnet (see p. above) as to the means Neil employed to secure his acquittal. It is hardly possible to read through that trial without feeling that Neil's acquittal was a miscarriage of justice. The King's advocate seems to have had a growing suspicion of the line the jury would take, and pointedly hints to them that on the evidence a verdict for the defendant would render them liable to prosecution for misprision of treason. No further proceedings seem to have been taken. A month later, Lauderdale, as High Commissioner, published a fresh Act of Indemnity, 24th March 1674. (The text is given in Wodrow, Hist. Sufferings, ii. 266.)

That Neil in betraying Montrose was actuated by any motive beyond base greed does not appear. No evidence has been brought to show that he was a conscientious bigot, or even pretended to be so. Religion, apart from self-interest, was not a ruling passion in those remote Highlands. Amidst bewildering changes of allegiance, fidelity to their feudal chiefs was the only steady influence on the northern clans. The garrison with which Neil "stuffed" his castle "cared not a plack for the King," and probably cared as little for the Parliament. Force they could appreciate. Whether in 1672 they said this or no, the words represent the lawless feeling of the Highlands long before and long after Montrose's days.

Neil's tribe, an invading offshoot from Lewis, had for two centuries been torn by family feuds and bloody quarrels with their neighbours. It would be difficult to find a darker record of violence than the history of his family and the "Sioleanbrice," or Sleaght-ean-Aberigh,[23] "Seed of John the Grizzled," a fighting sept of Macleods, among whom Neil recruited his followers. Neil was oppressed by his neighbours, Mackays and Mackenzies. The latter in turn were harassed by the Gordons of Sutherland; and from their land-grasping, Solemn-Leaguing chief, the Earl, Neil's father had obtained effectual aid in 1646, when besieged by Seaforth "*for favouring the Earl of Sutherland*" (Hist. Earls Sutherland, 534). It is in the obscure and repulsive annals of these petty feuds that we must seek the mainsprings of Highland politics.

The evidence of tradition points to the same conclusions. Where there is strong presumption that tradition has been unbroken, its evidence is entitled to weight, and its value is greatly enhanced, when, as in the present case, it accords with contemporary documents. Of its general tenour there can be no doubt. The local traditions have been embodied in the MS. by Mr. Taylor, and the bolls of sour meal are still a by-word.

The fame of the illustrious victim has lent a peculiar interest to this tale of sordid avarice and treachery. But no one who has read the writings of Spalding, Sir Robert Gordon, Gilbert Gordon (Sallagh), and Patrick Gordon, and Fraser of Wardale will recognise in Neil's miserable history more than one among the many lawless lives of greed, rapine, treachery, and bloodshed with which Highland annals in the seventeenth century abound.

---

[23] See Hist. Earls Sutherland, 60. The reference and derivation we owe to Dr. Joass. The name, like that of Macgregor, was a by-word. See *ibid.* p. 529, &c., and above, p. 531. Ian Lom's seventh stanza above (p. 523) is forcible, but not exaggerated.

## APPENDIX XIV.

### Relics of Montrose.

"*Verses wrote by the Marquis of Montrose with the point of a diamond upon the glass window of his prison after receiving his sentence.*"

> Let them bestow on every airth a limb,
> Then open all my veins, that I may swim
> To thee, my Maker, in that crimson lake,
> Then place my par-boil'd head upon a stake;
> Scatter my ashes, strow them in the air.
> Lord, since thou knowest where all these atoms are,
> I'm hopeful thoul't recover once my dust,
> And confident thoul't raise me with the just.

Montrose was a prisoner in the Tolbuith which stood just above St. Giles', and was executed at the cross which stood then a few feet north-east of the present cross lately erected.

"In his doun going fra the Tolbuith to the place of execution, he was verrie rychlie cled in fyne scarlet, layd over with riche silver lace, his hat in his hand, his goldin hat-ban, his stokingis of incarnet silk, and his schooes with their ribbenes on his feet, and sarkis provydit for him with pearling about, above ten pund the elne. All these war provydit for him be his friendis; and ane prettie cassik put upone him, upone the scaffold, quhairin he was hangit. To be schoirt, nothing wes heir deficient to honour his pure carcage, moir beseiming a brydegroom nor a criminall going to the gallowis" (John Nicoll (an eye witness), Diary, p. 13, quoted by Napier, Mem., ii. 453, where see notices of the stockings and other relics preserved in the Napier family). It is believed that Lady Napier (Lady Elizabeth Erskine) provided these garments for the Marquis, and it was she who had the heart removed and embalmed. For its romantic history see Napier, Mem. Nicoll (Diary, p. 12) says, "He hung full three hours, thairefter cut down, falling on his face, nane to countenance him but the executioner and his men."

It was ordered that the dismembered limbs should be sent to Glasgow, Stirling, Perth, and Aberdeen. If Sir Edward Walker's eyesight was good, it would appear that an arm and hand had been substituted for the leg and foot appointed to Aberdeen. In 1650, when accompanying Charles II. on his way from Garmouth to Edinburgh, Sir Edward was lodged in Aberdeen at a merchant's house opposite the Tolbooth, on which he "saw affixed one of the hands of the most incomparable Montross." Sir Edward appears to be the only witness as to the limb at Aberdeen being an arm instead of a leg as had been ordered. In all official references it is called "limb" or "member" only. Fraser says he saw an arm over the "South Port" of Dundee, but as there was no "South Port" in Dundee, and that town was not named in the order as to the distribution of the remains, he must be wrong. He may have meant Perth. We know of no other references to the limbs in other towns. Cromwell's officers had more decency than those of the "King of Scots," and had the relics taken down. The "member" at Aberdeen was placed in Huntly's vault till 1661, when it was raised with ceremony and conveyed to Edinburgh.

### Minute of Council of Aberdeen.

*25 Februai*, 1661.

The said day, the counsell haveing informatione from Doctor James Lesly, Doctor of Medicine, that it was signified to him from Edinburgh, by Capitane George Melvill, that it wes the desyr of ane noble and potent Earle, James, Marques of Montrose, that that dismemberit part of the bodie of the lait murtherit Marques of Montrose, his father, suld be soucht out of the place of the Church of this Burghe, wher the samen was interrit efter it wes taken doune from of the pinacle was put up by the enimies of the said Marques, and that the samen suld be taken up and preservit, till order suld come for transporting the samen to the bodie; and the Magistrates and Councell haveing givin order for the forsaid effect, and report being maid to them that the said member wes fund out in the place of the said Church where it had beine interrit; and, being most willing and desyrous to tack up and preserue the same in the most decent and convenient maner culd be gone about—Have appointit, and does appoint the inhabitants of the burghe to be warnit be beat of drum and sound of trumpet, for conveining this day, about twelff a clok, in ther best armes and array, for accompanieing the Magistrates and Councell to the Church, for tacking wp the said member. And that the samen be taken up and put in ane coffin, to be coverit with ane reid crimpsone velvit cloth, and caried be Harie Grahame, sone to the Laird of Morphye, from, the Church doun the Braid Street to the Toun's publict house, accompanied with the Magistrats and Counsell, and with the inhabitants of the toune goeing before in armes to the Toun's publict house with sound of trumpet and beat of drum, ther to be kepit under custodie of the Magistrats in the hich Counsell Hous, till such tyme as order suld be sent for transporting theroff, and appoints the inhabitants to discharge their guns, and shoot volies at and about the mercat croce at their comeing thervnto, and delyverie of the said member to the Magistrats. (Council Register, vol. liv, 248–9.) quoted Spalding Miscel., v. 35.

### Letter from James, second Marquis of Montrose, to the Magistrates of Aberdeen.

Right honourable,—Being informed by your commissioner and his ascessor that yee have, witht much solemnitie, reased that member of my fathers, which was erected in your cittie by the comand of some barbarous and disloyall persons pretending the authoretie of a parliament. I have urett this to returne you manie heartie thanks, and, withall, to assure you that I have a most reall recentment of that action, quherby ye have not onlie testefied your constant adherance to his Majesties service, bot also have, in a verie singular maner, wittnessed your respects to the memorie of him quho was your faithful freind, and have lykvays putt a verie high obligation upon

Your most affectioned friend and servant<br>MONTROSE

EDR., 30*th March*, 1661.

I shall desyre ye will be plesed to deliver that member to the lairds of Morphie and Fintrie, or to anie having ther warrant, for I have writt to them theranent.

Ffor the right honourable the lord provest, balzies, and toune counsell off Abberdeine.

### FROM THE LAIRD OF MORPHIE.

MORPHIE, *the 9th of Apryll*, 1661.

RIGHT HONORABILL,—The Marquess of Montross hath writen to me of laite, showing that he hath sent yow a letter of thankes for the great respectes ye hawe wittnessed to him towardes the raising of that member of his fatheres [24] that was erected in your towne, and that he hes desyred of you that it may be delywered to the laird of Fentrie or my selfe, or to anie hawing our warrent, quhairfoir I hawe directed this bearer to yow for that effect, to whom ye will be pleased to cause delywer the samen. I hawe noe moir to adde for the tyme, sawe that I ame, and do subscrywe my selfe,

Yours verie humbill serwant<br>A. GRÆME, of Morphie.

For the right honorabill the prowest, bailezies, and counsaill of Aberdeine—Thess.

---

For the drawings of Montrose's right-hand and fore-arm and sword (p. 537), the Editors are indebted to the courtesy of Mr. J. W. Morkill, of Killingbeck, near Leeds. The ghastly relic is probably unique. It is labelled "Montrose's arm," in the writing of Dr. Thoresby, a well-known Yorkshire antiquary at the beginning of last century, with whom it was deposited by a Dr. Pickering,[25] on his leaving this country for Spain (in 1704?). From that date its history is clear and continuous. Mr. Morkill submitted the arm to Sir William Turner, the eminent anatomist, who describes it as "mummified, bearing evidence of having been at one time impaled.

---

[24] See Spalding Miscel., v. 385, 386. This member was certainly "gathered to the body" at Holyrood, there awaiting the great funeral. Cf. "Relation of the True Funerals of the Great Marquesse of Montrose," &c., given in W., 1819, and other editions.

[25] A. Pickering was among the Roundhead officers, and was in communication with the officers in Scotland who were in local commands. One or more of them owed him money. Was he curious in relics, and obtained this arm and hand from its post. It is not unlikely. See Letters of Roundhead officers.

APPENDIX. 537

The hand is small and well proportioned, and obviously not that of a big man, or of one accustomed to manual labour. In the palm is a hole such as would be made by driving a nail through it, and on the inner side of the fore-arm is an appearance which could have been produced by pinching up the skin when soft and flexible, and driving a nail through it." The sword, which appears to have

always accompanied the arm, is double-edged, with a small basket hilt. On both sides of the blade, damascened in gold, is the quartered coat of Montrose, 3 escallop shells on a chief quartering, 3 roses, 2 and 1, with date 1570, and "Hermann and Keisserr" (makers' name). Scratched on the hilt are the initials I. S. (I. G. ??).—From notes kindly furnished by Mr. Morkill.

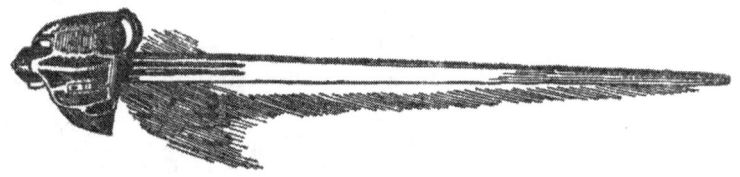

# INDEX OF PERSONS AND PLACES.

*⁎* *n* denotes special reference to a biographical or descriptive note.

ABERCROMBIE, T. M., 500.
Aberdeen, xxv.–xxvi.n, xxx. xxxviii., liv. lv., 18, 19, 49, 66, 70 & n, 88 & nn, 91, 98, 100, 112 & n, 113nn, 114, 154 & n, 155, 163n, 167n, 176, 180 & n, 181, 323, 534-6. Battle, 66nn-7nn, 69 & n, 504. Braid St., 535. Bp. of (1637), xvii. Hardgate, 69n. University, 59n.
Aberdour, 168n.
Aberfeldy, 56n.
Aberfoyle, 160n.
Abernethy, 104n.
Abörd (?), 284-5.
Aboyne, Jas. Gordon, Viscount, 18, 38n, 50 & n, 73, 88n, 97 & n-8n, 101, 106, 109-10 & n-11, 113 & n-14 & n-15, 118, 140, 148-51, 153-7, 160, 162 & n-3 & n-4, 184 & n, 284n, 314n.
Adair, Rev. Wm., 206n.
Advie, 165n.
Adwallon Moor, 43n.
Affleck, Major or Capt., 494.
Aikenheid, James, xxiii. George, xxiii.
Airlie Cas., vii., 19, 30n, 50n. Earls of, v. Ogilvy. River, see Isla.
Airth, Earl of, 23, 57n.
Aithry, 121n.
Aken, see Assynt.
Alane, Mr., 505.
Aldbar, liv.
Aldrich, Col., 328n.
Alen, Jas., 499n. Thos., 500.
Alexander, John, son of the Earl of Stirling, 97n.
Alford, xxxiii., 88n, 115n, 123n, 145, 150n, 153, 167n, 295. Battle, 108-12 & nn-13.
Alloa, 148n. Castle, 121n.
Almond, 115, 118 & n. See Lord Livingstone of, & Logie Almond.
Alnwick, 46.
Alvey, Yeldard, Vicar of Newcastle-on-Tyne, xix.
Alyne, Loch, 54n.
Alyth, 90 & n, 163n, 328n.
Amisfield or Hempsfield, v. Charters of. Tower of, 130n.
Amond, 20.
Ample, 166 & n, v. Strathample.
Amsterdam, xliii.–iv., 253-4, 258-9, 262-3, 284, 286, 498.
Amulree, 56n.
Ancrum, Rob., Earl of, 70n.
Angus (district), vi., 19, 72, 88n, 96-7-8n, 105, 114, 148, 153, 161, 258n, 290, 328n. Earls of, v. vi. & n. Wm., 11th Earl of, v. Marquis of Douglas.
Ankerhielm, Admiral M. Thyssen, 274-5, 511-12.
Annan, Rev. W., 168n. River, 45.
Annand, Jo., minr., Inverness, 316 & n, 519. Wm., minr., Bellie, 316n.
Annand, W., xxxii.n.
Annandale (district), 136, 141. Jas. Murray, 2nd Earl of, 129 & *n*, 136-7.
Anstruther, Fife, 273, 498.
Antrim, Earl of, 38 & n, 44-5, 48, 51n, 54 & n, 114, 184 & n.
Antwerp, 43n, 251.
Appleby, 209n. Cas., 210n.
Arbroath, 94. Adam, Abbot of, vi.n.
Arbuthnot, Sir Rob., 1st Visct. of, 162 & n-3*n*.
Ardamuragh, 504.
Ardlogie, v. Jo. Gordon of.
Ardnamurchan, 54n.
Ard, Loch, 160n.
Ardvoirlich, v. Stewart of.
Ardvreck Cas., Assynt, 312-13 & n-14, 501, 526, 531-2.
Argyle country, xxv., 17n, 38, 80ff, 115, 216, 257n, 503-4. v. Argyll, Campbells.
Argyll, Arch. Campbell, 8th Earl, 1st Marquis of, xii., xxx., xxxvii.-xli. 18 & n, 19, 21-3, 27n-8-9n, 30n, 32 & n, 38n, 47n, 49n, 50n, 55-6n-7 65 & n-6 & n-7n, 74-5, 79 & n, 80-3 & n-7n-8, 105, 107, 121n, 123n, 125, 127, 129nn, 132, 137n, 158 & n-9 & n, 165, 168, 175n, 178n, 180, 191n, 193, 205, 207n, 214, 217 & n-20, 223, 230n, 251, 254, 277, 286, 290-1, 301, 304, 322n, 324n, 328n, 496, 504-5, 524-5. v. Campbells.
Arnot, Jas., of Ferney, 125 & n. Rob., of Ferney, v. Burleigh.
Artamford, v. Alex. Irvine of.
Ashburnham, John, xlvi., 190n-1 & n-2, 194.
Ashley (Astley), Governor of Newcastle-on-Tyne, xix., 20.
Assynt, Loch, 299. Parish, 296, 311 & n-12, 530, 532. v. Neil Macleod.
Aston, v. Neil Macleod.
Athole (district), 19-20, 54n, 55-7, 72-3n, 79, 85, 97-8n, 107, 139, 147, 150n, 153, 155-6, 160 & n-1, 165 & n-6, 503. Clans of, 290-1, 304. John Murray, 2nd Earl of, 216 & *n*.
Atkine, Harie, of Orkney, 497n. Jas., 497 & n.
Auchinbreck, v. Campbell of.
Auchinleck, Capt., 497. Andrew, minr. xvii.n.
Auldearn, 82n, 89n. Battle, 98-103 & nn, 306, 502-3, 522. Deadman's Wood, 100n.

538

# INDEX OF PERSONS AND PLACES.

Avon, R., nr. Linlithgow, 150n.
Ayr, 126n, 134, 167n–8n.
Aytoun, 2n.

BACHILTOUN, 60n.
Badenoch, 54n–5, 72, 76, 79, 104–5, 115, 304n. Clans of, 290, 304n.
Baillie, Rev. Rob., of Glasgow, xxx., 120n, 148n, 168n, 207n, 237n. Sir Wm., of Lamington, 89n. Gen. Wm., of Letham, 47n, 83n, 87n–8n–9 & n, 90–1n–2 & n, 94, 96, 98 & n, 104 & nn–5 & nn–6–7 & n–8–9–10 & n, 115n, 121–3n, 129n, 209n, 211n–12 & n, 270, 502–3.
Baird, Jo., of Newbyth, 531.
Bala Cas., 165n.
Balblair, Sutherland, 307n.
Balcarras, Alex. Lindsay, 2nd Lord, 1st Earl of, 88n, 109 & n, 115n, 123n.
Baldovan, 158n.
Baldovie, v. Jo. Ogilvy of.
Balfour, Fogon (?), 500 & n. Sir Jas., of Denmylne, 125n. Lyon King, 254.
Balfours of Noltland Cas., Orkney, 500n.
Balgavie, xxxiii.
Ballantyne, Major, 38n.
Ballindary, v. Wishart of.
Balloch, v. Drummonds of. Cas. 17n, 21.
Balmedy, 60n.
Balmerino (place), ix. Lord, xiv., xv., 17n, 21, 63n, 102n, 127.
Balquhain, v. Leslie of Pitcaple.
Balquhidder, 97 & n. See Stewarts of.
Balvenie, 77 & n, 79, 104, battle, 244n, 301, 304n, 518.
Balwholly, 111n, 295n.
Baner, J., Swed. Fieldmarshal, 270n, 273n.
Banff, 301. Lord, 31n.
Barnard Cas., 210n.
Barnbougle, 139n.
Baron, of St. Andrews, xvi.n.
Bass, The, 132n.
Bates, Dr. Geo., 524.
Batten, Admiral, 25n.
Bearbrick (?) yr, Laird of, 505.
Beauly, 179, 313n, 316, 530.
Beaumont, George, xxix.n.
Beauvais, 266, 279n.
Bellandine, Sir Wm., 271.
Bellie, 87n.
Belstane, Col., v. Lindsay of.
Belton, East Lothian, 122n.

Bennet, H., 288.
Ben Etive, Ben Nevis, &c., v. Etive, Nevis, &c.
Bennicke, Cornet Dan., 495.
Benwell, xxiii.
Bergen, Norway, 187, 189 & n, 247n.
Berwick-on-Tweed, 18, 27n, 126, 137n, 141, 150n, 209 & n, 309.
Bhragie, Ben, Sutherland, 298.
Biggar, Major, 493.
Birsay Cas., Orkney, 256, 258, 497n.
Billinge, The, Gothenburg, 273, 275, 511–12.
Blackadder, Capt., 143.
Blackhall, 22–3. v. Stewart of.
Blackness, 31n, 103n.
"Black Pate" Graham, v. Pat. Graham.
Blair (place), 150n, 156n, 160n. Jo., of, 38n. Col. Laur., 189n. Rob., 167 & n, 170–2.
Blair Athole, 79n.
Blairgowrie, 105n, 184n.
Blebo, v. Sir Wm. Murray of.
Blythnooke, liv.
Boaz, Ensign Hans, 495.
Bog of Gight, 87n, 161 & n, 163, 179.
Bogie, Cas. of, 107.
Bohemia, v. Elizabeth Qu. of.
Bohus, 275, 512. Bohuslähn, 275n.
Bolsover, 43n.
Borders, The, xix., 36, 50–1, 120, 135, 139, 149–50n, 156, 167n, 209, 213, 218.
Borrowstoun, 497n.
Borthwick, Col., 176n.
Bothwell, xxv. xliv., 127n, 128 & n, 138–9 & n. Brig, battle, 523n.
Bowden Hill, xix.
Bower, Caithness, 296n.
Bowes, 210n.
Bowness, 22.
Boyd, Lord, 20–1.
Boyndlie, v. Alex. Forbes of.
Boynton Hall, 26n.
Brabast (?) & Brabusta, Orkney, 497 & n.
Brae-chat, 298n.
Braes of Angus, 19.
Braemar, 88n, 150n, 157.
Brahan Cas., Ross, 291, 304 & n, 312–13n, 316n, 530.
Brandenburg, Frederick William, Elector, Marquis of, 252 & n, 282n, 506–7, 515–16.

Breadalbane, 79n, 80 & n.
Breams, Capt., 501.
Brechin, vi.n, 89, 91, 94, 301, 303n, 314 & n, 319. Family of, v. n.
Breda, 41n, 243n, 245n, 247n, 250, 271n, 281n, 286n, 288, 293n, 300, 322n, 326n, 527, 529.
Breitenfeld, battle, 273n.
Brentford and Forth, Earl of, v. Ruthven.
Bridge, Wm., 498.
Bridge of Dee, xxxvii., 8, 66, 113n, 175n.
Bridge of Esk, 217.
Bridlington, 25 & n.
Brims, v. Sinclair of.
Bristol, lvi., 70n. Earl of, 156.
Brodie of Brodie, xxxii., 176n, 288.
Broughtie Ferry, 328n.
Browne, Sir John, lvii.
Brownlee, Rob., 167n.
Bruce, Capt. Harry, yr. of Clackmannan, 146n. King Robert the, vi.n.
Bruce of St. Andrews, xvi.n.
Brunswick, Duke of, 259.
Brussels, xlv., 227 & n–8n, 230n, 243n, 251 & n–3.
Buccleuch, Earl of, 169n.
Buchan, 113–14n, 498. Jas., 7th Earl of, 216n.
Buchanan, 160n. Geo., 157n. Sir Geo., 157n. Sir John, 157. Buchanan's regt., 503.
Buchanty on the Almond, 56 & n, 58, 148 n, 150n.
Buckie, v. Gordon of.
Buckingham, Duke of, 26n, 49n, 51n, 191n, 300, 523n. Dowager Duchess of, 38.
Buerham, Ernestus, 494.
Bull, John, x.
Bunch, 300.
Burleigh, Rob., Lord, 65 & n–6, 123n, 125, 324n, 524.
Burley, 65n.
Burnet, Dr., xxxii.n.
Burns, Rob., of Glasgow, 47n, 158n.
Byers, v. Lindsay of.
Byron, Lord, 210n, 247n.

CAIRITON, Orkney, 497.
Cairn, 319n.
Cairnburgh, 114n. Capt. of, 114n, 123n.
Caithness, 71, 82, 294–5–6n–7 & n, 304, 306, 314, 496, 516,

## INDEX OF PERSONS AND PLACES.

518, 525, 532. Geo., Sinclair, Earl of, 154n, 296n. v. Sinclairs. Bp. of, xxxiii.
Calder Cas., 140.
Calderwood, vii.
Caldhame, 88n, v. Middleton of,
Callander (place), 150, 166. Cas., 166n. Earl, xxi., 45 & n, 46, 129n, 206, 208–9n, 213 & n, 230, 288.
Cambo, v. Myreton of.
Cambridge, Earl of, v. Hamilton, Jas., Duke of.
Cameron clan, 79n.
Campbell, clan, 54n, 79n, 83n, 84–6, 505. of Auchinbreck, 83n, 85n, 504–5. Laird of Bearbrick (?) yr., 505. Lady Mary, 32n. Patrick, of Edinample, 8on, 166n. Sir Rob., of Glenurquhy, 8on, 166n. v. Argyll.
Canongate, v. Edinburgh.
Cant, Andrew, 66n, 167 & n, 206n–7n. Junr., xxxi. & n.
Capel, 27n, 194n, 335.
Car, Robin, 182n.
Carbester, v. Carbisdale.
Carbisdale (battle), 49n, 63n, 89n, 155n, 188n, 274, 298–9 & n, 305, 309, 317n, 493, 500, 518, 525. Loch, 306.
Cardross ford, 97n.
Careston, 94. Cas., 95 & n.
Carisbrook Cas., 191n.
Carlisle, 27n, 44–5, 47–8, 50 & n–1n, 55, 63n, 73, 77n, 88n, 97 & n, 126, 209 & n.
Carmichael, Fred., 59 & n. Wm., of Monifieth, x.
Carmyllie, 95n.
Carnegie, 216. Sir Alex., 95n. Sir Dav., 1st Earl of Southesk, 319 & n, 329. D., Master of Lour, 20. James, Lord, liv., 2nd Earl of Southesk, 129 & n, 148. Sir John (1622), vi.n.
Carnwath, Rob., 2nd Earl of, 22, 129n–30 & n, 169 n.
Carpe, v. Karpf.
Carrickfergus, 38n.
Carrindel, Laird of, yr. 505.
Carrington, Arch. Primrose of, 139n.
Carron R., Ross, 306–7.
Carstairs, John, xiii.
Cartowis, 66n.
Cary, Sir Rob., 135n.
Casimir V., John, King of Poland, liii. 246n, 259.

Cassilis, John, 6th Earl of, 120 & n–1n–2, 128, 134, 169n, 217n, 237 & n–8, 288.
Cassley, R., Sutherland, 299.
Castle Blair, 503-4.
Castle Campbell, 121n.
Castle hill, 92n.
Castle hill, v. Edinburgh.
Castle Stewart, Moray, 313n, 317 & n.
Castleton, 150n.
Cawston, 168n.
Celle, Duke of, 259.
Cessnock, 47n.
Cessfurd, v. Roxburgh.
Chalgrove Field (battle), 89n.
Chambers, W., 515.
Chanonry, 258, 291, 304 & n.
Charles I., King, xiv. xv. xviii. xx. xlvi.–vii., 3ff, 10, 14–18, 22–29, 34–41, 48, 135–6, 138–9, 149, 151, 156, 160, 169–70, 179, 182–5, 190–1, 193–6, 203–4, 207, 210, 220, 224–5, 267–8, 326–7, 336–7, 505, and notes *passim*.
Charles, Prince of Wales, King Charles II., xl.–i.–vi.–vii., 1, 7, 26n, 227–233, 235–43, 245, 249–54, 259–60, 262–4, 266, 271–4, 276–9, 287–8, 290, 300, 327, 331–2, 506–10, 516–18, 528–9, 534, and notes *passim*.
Charters of Amisfield (Hempsfield), 129, 130nn, 142n, 143n, 274. Capt. Alex., his brother, 495, 513.
Chelmsford, 210n.
Cheriton (battle), 211n.
Chester, lvi.
Chieslie, Sir John, 323n.
Choicelee Wood, 19.
Christian IV., King of Denmark, 37, 189–90n.
Christiania, 189 & n.
Christina, Queen of Sweden, 245 & nn, 247n, 266, 270n–1 & n–2–3n, 275, 282, 292n, 509, 512–14.
Clackmannan, v. Bruce of.
Clarendon (Hyde), 260.
Clanranald, 79n, 82, 123n. Capt. of, 79n, 176, 504.
Claverhouse, 79n.
Claversham, 204n.
Clayhills, Rev. Andr., of Monifieth, viii.
Clecheanbricks, *see* Macleod.
Cleves, 252, 506–7.
Cliftonhall, Wishart of, xxxv.
Clova, 98n.
Cluny, 114n. Cas., 113 & n. v. Sir Alex. Gordon of.

Clyde R., 9, 147, 150n.
Clydesdale, 122, 128.
Cnoc na Glas Chaoille, v. Glaschyle.
Cochran, Col. Sir John, liii., 22, 38 & n, 246n, 258–9, 284, 507–8, 515. Wm., of Cochrane, 38n.
Cockburnspath, 17n, 22.
Coe, clan, 504.
Coitts, 49n.
Colchester, 194n, 210 & n–11 n, 213n.
Coldingknows, v. Home of.
Coldstream, 20.
Collace, Kirk of, 64n.
Collinton, Lord, 531.
Colonsay, v. Macdonald (Coll Keitache) of.
Colt, Rob., 531.
Colville, W., xxxii.n.
Colvin, Lord, 41n.
Compiegne, 520.
Comrie, 97n, 150n.
Conan R., 316. Bridge, 313n.
Congreve, Rev. Fr. G., xlvi.
Conveth, vi.n.
Conway, Gen., xix., 20.
Cookstoun, v. Coxton.
Copenhagen, 260 & nn–1, 264–5, 273, 508.
Corbie Hill, 92n.
Corbiesdale, v. Carbisdale.
Corhouse, Laird of, 319n.
Corinth, Bp. of, v. de Retz.
Cornhill, 20.
Corrieyairack, 83n.
Corsare, John, 45n.
Corstorphine, 319n v. Forrester of.
Cossacks (war with), 246n.
Coulinor, 312.
Courland, James, Duke of, liii. 246, 259, 284–5.
Cowie, 88n.
Cowley, the poet, 288.
Coxton, 49. v. Innes of.
Crabston, 113n.
Cracow, 227 & n.
Craigcaoinichean, Culrain, 306, 308–9 & n–10n.
Craigievar, v. Forbes of.
Craigston, 113 & nn.
Craigton, 112n–13nn–14n.
Cranston Kirk, xxvi., 140n.
Crathes, liv., 63n.
Craven, 211n, Lord, xxix.n.
Crawford, Ludovic Lindsay, 16th Earl of, xxi., xxiv., 22–3, 46n–7n, 52n, 105n, 123, 132 & n–4n, 147, 153, 179n, 184n, 195n, 216n, 516. Craw-

## INDEX OF PERSONS AND PLACES.

541

ford-Lindsay, Earl of, 216n, 293.
Crichton, Lord Wm., of Sanquhar, 1st Earl of Dumfries, 216n.
Crieff, 96.
Cromar, 106.
Cromwell, Oliver, xxx., xl.-i. 26n-7n, 46n, 100n, 122n, 129n, 141n, 154n, 204 & n, 211 & n-12 & n, 214, 216n-17n-18, 223 & n-4n, 234n, 242 & n, 246n, 251, 254, 273n, 288-9, 291, 301, 316n, 328n, 501.
Culbyn, v. Kinnaird.
Culcholy, 111, 295n.
Cullace, Capt., 304, 500.
Cullanach, Strath, 310.
Cullen Aboyne, 503.
Culpepper, 246n-7n, 254n, 262 & n.
Culrain, 299, 306-7n-8n, v. Carbisdale.
Culterferry and ford, 114n,
Cumbernauld House, 20. Band, 20, 326 & n.
Cuninghame, Capt., 273.
Cunningham, Anne, 27n.
Cupar, in Angus, 63 & n, 105n. v. Elphinston, Lord of.

DAIRSIE, viii. xi. xiii. *See* Spottiswoode.
Dalgettie, v. Hay of.
Dalstoun, 51n.
Dalkeith, 216n.
Dalmeny, 139n.
Dalyell, John, of Glenae, 130 & n. Sir John, 146-8, 161.
Darwen, 211n.
Danube, R., 226n.
Dantzig, 227.
Davidson, Wm., 284-5.
Deadman's Wood, v. Auldearn.
Dearn, R., 98n. Strath, 87 & n.
Dee R., 88, 98n, 106, 113 & n-14. v. Bridge of.
Dempster, 176n.
Denbigh, Wm., Earl of, 26n.
Denmark, 296n. v. Copenhagen; Frederick III., K. of.
Denmylne, v. Balfour of.
Denny, 121n.
Derby, Countess of, 216n.
Dick, Col. Wm., 125 & n.
Dickson, Capt., 111n. Dav., xxx., 159n, 207n, 217n, 325n.
Digby, Lord George, lvii., 149n-50n, 155n-6, 160, 209, 502.
Dingwall, 313n, 518-19.

Dirleton, Earl of, 40n.
Dochart, Cas. and Loch, 165 & n.
Dochray, Mr. S., xxviii.
Doddington, Col., 49n.
Dollar, 121n, 130n.
Don R., 98n, 108 & n. v. Strathdon.
Donaldson, Margt., 60n.
Dornoch, 297-8.
Dorislaus, Dr., 249, 496.
Dort, 250.
Douglas Cas., 129n.
  Douglas, son of Morton, 145. Geo., 111n. Sir Jas., Morton's brother, 188n. John, youngest son of Wm., Earl of Morton, 308, 493. Sir Jos., 235n, 247n. Lady Marion, 31n. Lord Rob., xii. Sir Rob., 126n. Rob., minr., xxx.-i.n, ii.n, 207n, 247n, 288, 290, 300. Wm., 11th Earl of Angus, 1st Marquis of, 129 & n, 136-7, 140, 146, 148, 216. Sir Wm., 20. v. Angus; Morton.
Doune, 502.
Dover, 24n.
Downs, The, 210n.
Drogheda, 234n, 262, 288.
Dron, 119n.
Drum, 67n, 113n, 155n. *See* Mills of, Irvine of.
Drumcross, xxxv.
Drumlithie, 88n.
Drumminor Cas., 108 & n, 150n, 153.
Drummond, Hon. Catharine, 32n. Dav., Master of Maderty, 60 & n. Lt. Dav., 494. Lt. Col. Geo., Balloch's brother, 257, 292 & n-5, 497-500. Jas., Lord, lvii., 20, 58, 61, 129 & n, 216. John of Balloch, 109 & n, 134, 187 (?). John, yr. of Balloch, 109 & n, 150n(?), 165 & n, 166-7n. Lt. John, 495. Sir John, liv., 57 & n. of Hawthorndean, xxvi., 127n. of Logie Almond, 57n. *See* Maderty.
Duart, 123n. v. Maclean of.
Dublin, 234n.
Duchrie, v. Graham of.
Dudhope, 92n. John Scrimgeour, 3rd Visct. of, 216n.
Duffus, 318 & n.
Dumbarton, 21, 83n, 121n.
Dumfries, xx., 45 & n, 109n, 130n, 149n-50n, 159n. Earl of, v. Crichton.
Dun, Castle of, liv.

Dun, Lt. Jas., 495. *See* Erskine of.
Dun of Criech, 306.
Dunaveg, 141n.
Dunavertie, 54n, 141n, 206n.
Dunbar, 9. Battle, 141n, 246n, 301, 306n, 319n.
Dunbeath Cas., 252n, 282, 293n, 295 & n, 297 & n, 496, 515-16.
Dunblane, xxx.
Duncrub, 32n. v. Rollock of.
Dundas, Thomas, xxxv. James, xxxv. Thomas, junr., xxxv. of Newliston, xxxv.
Dundee, xlv. liv., 65-6n, 89, 91 & n-2 & n, 95, 124n, 169n, 262n, 314n, 318n-19, 321, 502-4. Earl of, 216n. East Port, Law, Nethergait Port, Seagait, Overgait, West Port, 92n, "South Port," 534.
Dundonald, Earl of, 39n.
Dunfermline, Earl of, 19, 169n, 288. Declaration of, 527.
Dunglass, 19.
Dunkeld, xxxi., 52n, 79, 90 & n-1 & n, 115, 117n, 494. Little, 117-18n.
Dunnavertie, v. Dunavertie.
Dunnet Bay, 295.
Dunneveg, 54n.
Dunnottar Cas., 163, 286.
Duns, 14, 18, 19.
Duns Law, xxvi..n, 135n.
Dunrobin Cas., 296n-8 & n, 308n.
Duntreath Cas., 157n.
Duplin (Dupplin), 116, 118n. Lord, 63n.
Durham City, liv., 42, 49n, 89n. Jas., minr., 324n-5n.
Durham, Wm., of Grange, x., 329n. Family, of Grange, viii. Rev. Pat., of Monifieth, viii.
Durie, 21.
Dutch War (1672-4), 523n.
Dysart, Countess of, 41n. Earl of, 15n, 41n.

EARN, Loch, 64n, 97 & n, 166n. R., 97n, 115, 118, 120, 147.
Easington, xx.
Echt, 319n.
Edgehill (battle), 51n, 132n.
Edglie Moor, 20.
Edinample, v. Campbell of.
Edinburgh, xix. xxiv.-v. xxx. xxxvii., 17-19, 22, 25, 28 & n,

30n-1n, 41n, 45n, 49n, 50n, 52n, 67n, 79n, 85n, 87n, 89n, 102, 105, 113n, 115n, 128n-9n, 130-2 & n, 134, 140-1n, 143, 154n, 159, 167n, 216 & n-17 & n-18, 220, 223, 244n, 251, 270n, 280-1, 290, 297 & n, 299, 302n, 305, 308n, 316n, 321-2, 328, 494, 501, 519, 525, 527, 535. Borough Moor, 323n. Bp. of (1637), xviii.; v. Wishart. Canongate, xxxii.-iii. Prison, 314n, 495-6. Castle, 102n-3n, 130n, 133, 145, 217n, 223, 328n. Castlehill, 92n. Cross, 50n, 236n-7n, 323, 330n, 534. Grayfriars, 30n, 323n. Luckenbooths, xxiv. Parliament House, 206n. St. Giles Ch., 2n, 28n. Thieves' Hole, xxiv.-v. Tolbooth, xxv. xxxii., 49n, 130, 132n, 314n, 323 & n-4. University, vi. Water Gate, 323.
Edward I., K. of England, vi.n, 10.
Edzell, Laird of, 95n.
Eglinton, Alex., 6th Earl of, 121 & n-2, 128, 134, 169n, 217n. Rob., his son, 217n.
Eil, Loch, 83.
Eilandonan Cas., 291.
Einig, Glen, Ross, 310.
Elben (?), 516.
Elcho, Lord, 23n, 58-9.
Elgin, 66n, 82n, 87n, 98, 104, 150n, 313n-14n, 318.
Elibank, Pat., 2nd Lord, 101n.
Eliot, nr. Arbroath, 90n. Water, 95n.
Elizabeth Cas., Jersey, 279.
Elizabeth, Princess, 135n.
Elizabeth, Qu. of Bohemia, xxviii. xxix.n., 234n, 238n, 240n, 243n, 245n-6n-7n, 250-1 & n-2n-3, 258n, 261n-2 & n, 266n, 288.
Elliot, W., xlviii.
Ellis, Sir John, 531-2.
Ellon, xxxi.n.
Elphingston, 47n.
Elphiston, Jas., Lord of Cupar, 63n.
Elswick, xxiii.
Enistesinth, 505.
Enkerfort (battle), 273n.
Emperor of Germany, v. Ferdinand III.
Erlach, Cornet Henrick, 495.
Errick, 179. Strath, 87 & n.

Errol, Gilb., 10th Earl of, 216 & n.
Erskine, Capt., 493. of Dun, 320n. Lord John, 20, 148 & n-51, 153, 216. Lady Elizabeth, 102 & n.
Esk, Bridge of, 217. R., 65, 89, 94, 186.
Essen, v. Assynt.
Etive, Ben, 523.
Eyellandtirrem, v. Macdonald of.
Eythin, v. King, Gen. Jas.

FAIRFAX, xx., 49n, 204 & n, 210 & n-11n.
Fairfoul, Bp., xxx.
Falconer, Sir Alex., 88n, 162n.
Falkirk, 10, 217n, 219.
Farg, Glen, 119n.
Farquhar, Sir Robt., 525, 531.
Farquharson, clan, 115. of Mar, 319n. Donald, 88n, 100n.
Federate, Rob., Irvine of, 134n.
Ferdinand III., Emperor, 226n-7, 245, 259n.
Ferney (Fernie). Jas. Arnot of, 125n. Rob. Arnot of, 65n.
Fettercairn, 88 & n-9n, 314n.
Feueing (?), Rob., 516.
Fiddich, 77n.
Fielding, Lady Mary, 26n.
Fife, lv., 65, 115-6, 291, 314n, 321, 525.
Fincastle, 150n.
Findhorn, 87n, 165n.
Finlater, 47n.
Fintrie, v. Graham of.
Fleet, Strath, 299.
Fleming, Archibald, 126n. Lord, 129, 216. Sir Wm., 197n, 247n, 288, 322n.
Flensburg, 260.
Fletcher, Mr. W., xlvi.
Flotta, Orkney, 294 & n.
Forbes, Alex., of Boyndlie, 68 & n. Castle, 108n. Duncan, of Culloden, Provt. of Inverness, 317 & n. Duncan, his grandson, 317n. John, Provost, 317n. Of Craigievar, 67, 76. Lord, 108 & n, 153. President, 317n. Patrick, v. Caithness, Bp. of.
Fordell, lvii.
Fordoun, 114n, 319n. Kirk, 114.
Fords of Lyon, 21.
Forfar, 95n.
Forres, 98 & n, 313n, 318.

Forret, Dav., minr., xvii.n.
Forrester, Lord, of Corstorphine, 89n.
Fort Augustus, 82n.
Fort William, 83n.
Forteviot, 118n.
Forth, Earl of, v. Ruthven.
Forth, R. and Firth, 9, 19, 27n, 31, 90-1, 105, 115-16, 119, 120-1 & n-2, 147, 150, 153-4, 157, 215, 219, 238, 502.
Forther, 30n.
Foulis, Laird of, 532.
Framlington, Long, 20.
France, Qu. Dowager of (1650), 520.
Frankfurt-on-the-Main, 259n.
Fraser, 87n. Ann, Countess of Sutherland, 297n. Catharine, wife of Sir John Sinclair of Dunbeath, 297n. Col. Hugh, 290. Rev. Jas., of Wardlaw, 313n, 315n, 331n. Mary, wife of Balnagowan, 297n.
Fraserburgh, 154n.
Frederick III., K. of Denmark, 227, 245, 250, 259-60 & nn, 264, 508, 511, 515.
Frederick William, Elector, v. Brandenburg.
Frendraught, Visct., 104, 293, 308 & n, 310, 493.
Freswick, 295n.
Frieland, Laird of, 41n.
Friesland, Count of, 258.
Fronde, Wars of the, 246n.
Frost, Secretary, 253.
Fullarton, Thos., 317-18n.
Fyvie Cas., lv., 50n, 73 & n, 75, 504.

GALA, v. Strath Gala.
Galloway, 20. Alex., 1st Earl of, 216 & n. Bp. of, xxx.
Garden, Jas., 188n.
Garmouth, 178n, 288, 534.
Garrie, Capt., 493.
Gartie, 298 & n.
Gartmore, see Graham of.
Gateshead, xix. xxi.
Geddes, Jenny, xv.
Gela, or Gella, see John Ogilvy of.
Geneva, xlv., 226.
Gerard, 247n.
Germany, v. Ferdinand III. Princes of, 245.
Gicht, or Gight, v. Gordon.
Gisburn, 211n.
Gladsmuir, 143.
Gladstanes, Geo., Abp. of St.

# INDEX OF PERSONS AND PLACES.

Andrews, vii. xvi.n, 30n.
Dr. Alex., Archdean of St. Andrews, xvii.n, xviii.
Alex., son of the Abp., vii.
Alex., minr., St. Andrews, xi.
Glanurquhyes, 504.
Glaschyle, 311 & n.
Glasgow, xxx. lvii., 32n, 47n, 49n, 126n, 128 & n, 150n, 157, 158n, 159, 160n, 323, 534. Assembly (1637), xvii. xviii. Bishops of, v. John and Robert Wishart. Cathedral, 27n. College, 40n. Cross, 47n.
Glen, St. Andrews, 494.
Glenae, v. Dalyell of.
Glenalmond, 148n, 150n.
Glenavon, 71n.
Glencairn, Wm. Smith, Earl of, xxix.n, xli., 122 & n, 169n, 175n, 216n–17n, 220–1, 322n, 494–5, 501, 523–4.
Glencoe, 82, 83n. v. Coe. Laird of, 79n.
Glendochart, 81n.
Glenesk, 95 & n, 98n.
Glengarry, 115 & n, 176. clan, 79n. Donald, chief of, 79n, 109 & n, 505, 525.
Glenisla, 30n, 98n.
Glen Livet, 104n.
Glenmark, 98n.
Glen More, 310.
Glenmuick, 98 & n.
Glenmuick, Sutherland, 305.
Glen Nevis, Laird of, 79n.
Glen Roy, 83n.
Glenshee, 106, 150n, 155, 184n. Spital of, 105n.
Glenurquhy, v. Sir Rob. Campbell of.
Gloucester, 34 & n–5.
Golspie, 298.
Goodie, 166n.
Gordon, clan, 53, 71n, 74n, 123n, 244n, 290–1, 336. of Sutherland, 533. Lt., 38n. Adam of Kilcalmkill, 296n. Lady Ann, wife of Menzies of Pitfoddels, 309n. Sir Alex., 38n, 113n. Sir Alex., of Cluny, 134n. Lord George, 66n–7n, 71n, 82n, 87 & n–8 & n, 91, 96–100, 105–6, 109–10 & n–12n. of Gight, 134n. yr. of Gight, 111n. Gilbert, of Sallagh, 254*n*, 298n–9, 312, 522, 530. Lady Jean, Countess of Haddington, 324n. Sir John, of Haddo, 52n, 154n. Col. John, 282–3, 285, 308, 493, 515. Lord Lewis, 2nd Marquis of Huntly, 67 & n, 73, 87n–8n, 91 & n, 96, 153, 162, 164, 177–8n, 244n, 304n. of Logie, 52n. Lady Mary, 154n. Col. Nathaniel, liv., 66 & n, 82, 87n–8n, 103n, 106, 109–10 & n–11n, 118, 120, 128n, 130, 169 & n. of Newton, 216n. Robert of Cluny, 331 & n. Sir Robert, of Gordonstoun, 331n. of Struders, 100n. Capt. Wm., 296 & n, 496. See Aboyne — Huntly — Sutherland.
Goring, Lord, 194n.
Gorm, Donald, 79n.
Gorthie, v. Graham of.
Götha R., Sweden, 272, 282.
Gothenburg, 188n, 245n, 247n, 266, 269, 272–3n, 277, 280, 282, 284, 292, 509–15.
Gowrie, 63.
Grafton, Duke of, 323n.
Graham, Alex., of Drynie, 531. Lady Beatrice, 60n. Dav., son of the 1st Marquis of Montrose, 319n. Lady Dorothea, 32n, 156n. of Fintrie, 536. of Gartmore, 57n. Geo., 109 & n. Geo., of Inchbrakie, 52n. Geo., of Inchbrakie, son of Patrick, 52n. Rev. Geo., son of the Bp. of Orkney, 497n. of Gorthie, 52n, 184n. Harry, son of the Laird of Morphie, 535. Sir Henry (Harry) Graham, 49 & n, 134n, 187, 252, 293, 296–7n, 305, 311, 496–8, 506–7. **Jas. Graham, Earl, and 1st Marquis of Montrose,** *passim.* John, 21. John, of Duchrie, 524, 530. Lady Lilias, 134n. Lord Graham, 82n, 87n–8n, 134n. Lady Margt., 156n. of Morphie, 163n. A., of Morphie, 536. Patrick, of Inchbrakie, 52 & n, 55–6, 80, 109n, 114, 129n, 165 & n–6–7n. Patrick, his son ("Black Pate"), 52n. Sir Rich., 45 & n, 51 & n. Rob., son of Montrose, 319n. Rob., elder, of Cairnie, 495. Rob., of Morphie, 536. Ensign Rob., 495. See Montrose.
Graham's Dyke, 9, 10.
Grampians, 72–3, 88, 90, 94, 97–8, 105 & n, 114 & n, 150, 153, 161, 184n.
Grange, nr. Dundee, 314n, 318n–19 & n–20 & n. Laird of, v. Durhame.
Grant, clan, 71n, 87n. Cas., 165n. Laird of, 54n, 67n, 71n, 87n.
Grantully, v. Stewart of.
Gravesend, xxix.n.
Gray, Lady Agnes, 57n. Patrick, Lord, 23, 57n, 66n Rob., of Skibo, father and son, 314n. Mrs., of Skibo, 314 & n–15. Lt. Col. Thos., 189 & n. Col. Thos., 293, 308, 493–4.
Graymond, Mons. de, 324n.
Grey, Lord of Groby, 212n–13n.
Grey, Lord, lvii.
Grime, 495.
Groby, v. Grey.
Groningen, 227.
Guelderland, xxvii.
Gruids, Sutherland, 298n–9.
Gunnerson, Jens, 188n–9n.
Gustavus, Capt.-Lt., 494.
Gustavus Adolphus, K. of Sweden 27n, 245n, 270.
Guthrie, in Forfar, 95n. Andr., 167n, 172n. Cas., 167n. Major Dav., 188 & *n*, 272, 274, 308, 493. Hen., Bp. of Dunkeld, 167n, 172. Jas., minr., xxx., 207n, 301–2 & n–3, 325n, 329n.
Gwynne, Capt. John, 254–5, 292, 497–8, 501, 523 & *n*.

HACKETT, Sir James, lv., Lt.-Col. Rob., 301, 304 & n, 305n–6–7, 501.
Haddington, 17n, 22, 217n. Lady, 67n, 324 (Lady Jean Gordon).
Haddo, v. Gordon of.
Hague, The, vi. xliii., 25n, 82n, 227–8 & n, 230n, 232n–3n, 235, 237n, 245 & n, 247n, 249–50, 253, 260–2, 288, 464n, 498, 506.
Hairshaw Wood, 130n.
Halden, John, 126n.
Hall, Capt., 49n. Capt., of Leith, and his frigate, 244n, 256–7nn, 276–7, 286, 294 & n, 498.
Halkerton, 162n. Cas., 88n.
Haliburton, Bp., xxxi.
Hamburg, xxviii. xlv.–vi., 43n, 190 & n, 245n, 253, 258 & n–9, 263, 269–70n, 281 & n–2 & n, 507–8, 515.

## INDEX OF PERSONS AND PLACES.

Hamilton, Anne, Duchess of, 40n.   Geo., minr., xvii.n.   Jas., 3rd Marquis and 1st Duke of, xviii. xxxvii.–viii., 15n, 18, 22–3, 26 & *nn*, 27n–8 & n–9, 34n–5n, 39 & n, 40, 46n–7, 122, 136, 154n, 191n, 197n, 205–8 & n, 209 & n, 211 & n–12 & n–13 & n–14, 223, 227, 230 & n, 233 & n, 243, 245, 253–4, 269–70, 289, 336.   Dowager Marchioness of, xvii.n.   Jas., minr., xxxi.n, 324n.   John, 2nd Duke of, v. Lanark.   Of Orbiston, 129 & *n*.   Rob., 247n, 288.   Bp. of, xxx.
Hammond, Govr. of Carisbrook Cas.,191n.   Chaplain, 204n.
Hampden, 89n.
Hampton Court, 24n, 203n–4n.
Hanover, Duke of, 259.
Harehead Wood, 142n.
Harray, 497n.
Hartfell, Earl of, 129n–30n, 136–7.   James, his 2nd son, 129n.
Harthill, 179n.   v. Leith of.
Hartlepool, xxi.
Havre, xlv.
Hatfield, 204n.
Hatton, Lord, 271 & n.
Havre de Grace, xlv.
Hawthornden, v. Drummond of.
Hay, "Crouner," 50n.   Col., liv., 308.   Sir Francis, of Dalgetty, 111n, 179n, 270n, 293, 298, 496.   Jas., 66 & n., Col. Jas., brother to Naughton, 293, 494.   Jas., of Muldavat, 66n.   Col. of Linplum, 66n.   Rob., 516. Wm., 63n, 145 & n.   Sir Wm. (?), of Dalgetty, 496, v. Sir Francis.   v. Kinnoul.
Heath, Jas., author, 244 n.
Helmsdale, 298 & n.
Helvoetsluys, 24n.
Hempsfield, v. Charters of.
Henderson, Alex., minr., xv. xvii.n, xviii. xx. xlvii., 22, 28n, 30 & n–2, 34n, 38n. Jas., 495.
Henrietta Maria, Queen, 15n, 24–5 & n, 28, 34 & n–5, 38n, 43n, 49n, 129n, 190 & n–3 & n–4 & n–6 & n–7n, 225, 242–3n, 247n, 251–2 & n, 263, 277–8.
Henry IV., King of France, 2, 191.
*Herderinnan* frigate, 275, 280, 282, 293, 511–15.

Herriot, George, xxxiii.
Hilton, xx.
Holburn, Lt.-Gen. or Major-Gen., 291, 313n–15, 496.
Holland, xxvi.–vii.–ixn. xlv.–vi., & n, 191n, 210n, 241, 309n, 322n, 328n.   v. Amsterdam—Hague, &c.
Holland, Lord, 27n.
Holm Sound, Orkney, 293.
Holmby House (Cas.), 197n, 203 & n.
Holstein, 273n, 511.   Duke of, 262.
Holyrood, xxix. xxxi.n–iii.–iv., 22, 59n, 97n, 536n.
Home (place), 136, 140.   Sir Jas., of Coldingknows, 3rd Earl of, 20, 135 & n, 141, 216.   Mary, Countess of, 223 nn.   Lt. (Holme), 493.
Honthorst, 243n.
Hope, Sir Jas., of Hopetoun, 324n, 496.   Sir Thos., of Kerse, 17n, 23, 28n. Sir Thos., yr., 19.
Hopton, 300.
Hornby, 211n.
Howie, Dr. Rob., Provt. of St. Andrews, vii. & n., xiii. xviii.
Hoy, Orkney, 294n.
Hull, 245n, 269.
Hume, Lt.-Col. Sir J., v. Home.
Huntingdon, Rob., Earl of, v.n.
Huntly (place), xxxviii. & n, 319n.   Geo. Gordon, 2nd Marquis of, 29n, 49n, 52 & n–3, 65n–6n–7n–70–1n–2, 87 & n–8n, 91, 105n–7, 113n, 150n–3n–4n–7, 160–1 & n–5 & n, 175 & n–6 & n–80, 182n–4 & n, 192, 216 & n, 237, 244n, 296n, 336, 535. v. Aboyne Gordons.
Hurry, Col., later Gen.-Major, Sir John, 23, 49n, 82n, 87n–8 & n*n*–9, 92, 96–8 & n–101, 104 & n, 106, 182, 184n, 187, 206n, 293–5, 305, 307–8, 317 & n, 493, 502, 516.
Hutchison, Capt., 307.   George, xxxi.n, xxxii.n.
Hyde, Chancellor (Clarendon), 193n, 228n, 233n, 250.

INCHBRAKIE on the Earn, 52n. v. Graham of.
Inchiquin, Lord, 54n.
Inchnadamff, 313.
Innes, Alexander.   James, John of Leuchars, John of Coxton, Lt. Col. John, Robert Innes of Innes, 49 & *n*.   Sir John, of Leuchars, 49n, 182 & nn.
Inver, 114n.   Loch, 531.
Inveran, 313n.
Inverary, 19, 79n, 83n.   Cas., 80.
Inverleith, v. Towers of.
Inverleven, Capt., son of Enistesinth, 505.
Inverlochy, 79n, 82n–3nn, 85n, 87n, 159n.   Battle, 109n, 328n, 502–3, 505.
Inverness, 82, 89n, 98 & n, 101, 105 & n–6, 164–5, 175 & n–8 & n, 180, 244n–5, 257n, 302–3 & n–4n, 312–13n–14n–15n, 317, 502–3, 530.   County, 314n.
Inverquharity Cas., 90 & n. v. Ogilvy of.
Inverurie, 318n.
Ireland, xxxix. lvi.. 242 & n, 245, 254.
Isla, 105 & n.
Ireton, 224n.
Irvine, town, 126n, 134. Alex. Irvine, of Artamford, 134n.   Sir Alex., of Drum, 31n, 52n, 134n, 155n, 162n–3, 296n.   Alex., yr of Drum, 52n, 134n, 154 & *n*–5, 163.   Lady Mary, 134n. Robt., of Federate, 134n.
Isla, R., 90, 105n, 184n.
Islay, 54n.
Ives, Richd., ix.

JAFFRAY, Alex., 288.
James VI. & I., vii., 10, 156, 169–70, 225.
Jamieson, painter, 319n.
Jedburgh, 142–3.
Jennison, Rob., S.T.P., xviii.n.
Jermyn, Hen., Lord (Earl of St. Albans), 190n, 193–4, 247n, 250n–2, 254n, 262.   Sir Thomas, his father, 193n.
Jersey, 234n, 250n–1, 279, 288.
John o' Groats, 295.
Johnston, Jas., of Johnston, 129*n*. Lord Johnston of Lockwood, 19, 129 & *n*.   Arch., of Warriston, 18, 20, 266, 300, 324n, 330 & n.   Col. Sir Wm., 259, 272, 277, 282 & n, 293, 496–8.
Jones, Col., lvi., 242n.
Joyce, Cornet, 197n, 203n.
Junes (?), 497.
Jüterbok, battle, 273n.
Jutland, **273n.**

# INDEX OF PERSONS AND PLACES.

KARGARF, 106.
Karp or Karpf (Carpe), Lt. Gen. John Adam de, 252, 282, 507, 515.
Karr, Thos., xix.n.
Katrine, Loch, 97.
Keir (place), 97n. 109n. Sir Geo., of Stirling, 17, 20-3, 31n, 97n, 103 & n, 134n, 204n. yr. of Stirling, 97n. Lady, of Stirling, 134n; Keir Ladies, 297n. Keir, sea-captain, 531-2.
Keiss, Cas., 154n.
Keith, town, 104, 108n, 314n, 316n, 318n. Kirk of, 107n. Lady Mary, 57n. Wm., 7th Earl of, 162 & n, 163n. Mr. William, xxxi.n.
Kelso, xx., 142.
Kendal, 209n, 211n.
Kennedy, Jas., 178n. Capt. Rob., 23.
Kennermony, 165n.
Keppoch, 83n. v. Ian Lom — Macdonald of.
Ker, A., lv., Col. Gilb., 301, 304 & n, 310n. Lord, 22, 135n. Sir Robt., of Cessfurd, v. Roxburgh.
Kerrimure in Angus, 244n, 261n.
Kerse, see Sir Thos. Hope of.
Kersten (?), 499.
Kettler, House of, liii.
Kid, Grissel, x.
Kid, James, xxxi.n, xxxiii.
Kiddie, minr., 495.
Kilbirnie, 47n.
Kilchreist, 519.
Kilcummin Bond, 82n.
Kildrummie, 162n.
Kilgraston, 115n, 118n-19n.
Killiewheemen, 82n.
Kilmahog, 150n, 160n.
Kilmartin Glassery, 81n.
Kilpont, John, Lord, liv., 56 & n, 60, 64 & n, 166n, 503.
Kilsyth, xxv. xliv-v., 31n, 40n, 49n, 54n, 65n, 103n, 109n, 121n-3n, 125-6 & n, 128, 130 & n, 132n, 135n, 139n, 147n, 154n, 162 & n, 167nn, 289n, 301.
Kilterne, 519.
Kinanmond, Wm., minr. of Keith, 318 & n.
Kincardine Cas., 102n, 109. Town, Ross, 299n, 303n.
Kingcausie, 113n.
Kineil, 27n. House, 22.
King, Sir Jas., of Barracht, 270n. Gen. Jas., Earl Eythin, 270 n, & 272, 275, 286n, 513.

Kinghorn, Earl of, 20, 169n.
Kingragly (?), 261n.
Kingston, 210n.
Kingussie, 79n.
Kinloch, Col., xxxiii.n.
Kinnaird, Walter, of Culbyn, 317 & n. Cas., Forfar, 314n, 319n.
Kinnoul, Geo. Hay, 3rd Earl, liv., 18, 63 & n, 241n, 252-4, 257 & n-8 & nn, 266, 276, 280n-1 & n, 287, 292. Hay, 4th Earl (d. Ap. 1650), 275n, 282, 292, 310 & n-11. Wm. Hay, 5th Earl of, 145 & n, 310n.
Kinross, 119 & n-121.
Kinsale, 234n, 254, 261n-2. v. Rupert.
Kintale, 294, 310, 312, 519.
Kintire, 54n.
Kintore, 70-1n.
Kintradwell, 298 & n.
Kirkcaldy, xxxii.n.
Kirkcudbright, 20, 47n.
Kirkhill, 315n.
Kirkwall, 49n, 63n, 155n, 254-5, 257-8 & n, 280-1 & n, 286 & n-7, 292 & n-3.
Kleish, Laird of, 41n.
Knaresborough, 211n.
Knox, John, xxxviii.n. 30n,
Königsmark, Genl., 270n, 273n.
Kowdoun, 47n.
Krabbe, Ivar, 275, 512-13.
Kyle of Sutherland, v. Sutherland.
Kylochy, 165n.

LACHLAN, Col., liv., 159.
Ladislas, IV. or VII., King of Poland, 246n.
Ladywell, v. Stewart of.
Lairg, 298n-9.
Lambert, 27n, 210n-11n-12n-13 & n, 217n.
Lamington, v. Baillie of.
Lambye, John, Montrose's Pursebearer, xii.-xiii.
Lanark (Lanrick, Lanerick), William, Earl of, and 2nd Duke of Hamilton, lvi., 22, 27, 34n-5n, 39 & n, 40 & n, 47n, 120, 122, 128, 136, 169n, 170, 205, 207n, 208, 213-15, 217 & n, 218-20, 222, 230 & n-2, 241, 245, 251, 262, 288, 291, 300.
Lancashire, 31n.
Langdale, Sir Marmaduke, lvii., 208n-9 & n-11 & n.
Langhaline Cas. (?), 504.
Lansdown, 132n.

Lanton, Jane, xix.n.
Lares or Laufers (Lawers?), 504.
Largo, 230n.
Lasound, Pardus, 188 & n.
Latheron, 295n.
Laud, Abp., xiv. xv. xviii. xxxvii.-viii.n.-ix., 336.
Lauder, 302 & n-3.
Lauderdale, John, 2nd Earl of, xxx.n, 175n, 207n, 230nn, 232, 241, 243, 253, 262, 288, 322n, 529, 533. Duchess of, 41n.
Laurentius, 245n.
Laurie, Andrew, xxxi.n.
Law, Mungo, minr., 301, 325n. 328n. Capt., 284.
Lawers, v. Campbell of.
Lawers' Regiment, 304 & n, 308, 320, 501, 503.
Lawson, Capt., 494.
Learmont, Andr., of St. Andrews, xvi.
Ledmore, 311n.
Leeds, 211n.
Leicester, Lord, xxix.n.
Leighton, Bp., xxx.
Leipzig, battle, 270, 273n.
Leith (town), v.n, xxix.n, 27n, 35n, 218, 252, 261, 288, 314n, 321-2n, 498, 523. of Harthill, 216n.
Lennox, district, 157, 160. Duke of, 17n.
Lens, battle, 227 & n, 463n.
Lenny, Pass of, 160n.
Leopold, Archduke, 192 & n, 197n, 226-8. I., Emperor, 192n.
Leslie, Alexander, Earl of Leven, Alex., of Pitcaple, yr., 319n, xix. xx.-i. xxiv. xxvi.n, lv.-vi., 16n, 17n, 18n, 19, 21, 35n, 43n, 45n-7n, 51, 54n, 135n, 167n, 217n, 270 & n. David, Lt. Gen., afterwards 1st Lord Newark, lv., 137, 139, 141 & n, 143 & n, 144, 159n, 175n, 184n, 206n, 217 & n, 244n, 257 & n-8 & n, 261, 270n, 291, 296n, 301, 303n-4 & n, 309, 313n-14 & n, 316 & n, 496, 498-9, 515, 519, 522. Jas., M.D., 535. John, Laird of Pitcaple, 318n. Col. Ludovick, 22. Robin, brother of David Leslie, yr., 184n.
Letham, v. Baillie of.
Lethin House, 165n. Cas., 176n.
Leuchars, 49n. Kirk of, 30n. v. Innes of.

## INDEX OF PERSONS AND PLACES.

Leven, v. Leslie, Earl of.
Lewis Island, 312, 533.
Libau, Courland, 284.
Libberton, see Winram.
Lillie, Major John, see Lisle.
Lily, 336.
Linplum, v. Hay of.
Lindsay, 47n, 106-7, 110, 123n, 127, 216-17n, 221. Col., of Belstane, 102n. Lord, 168-9, 220. Alex., 2nd Lord, v. Balcarras. Geo., 3rd Lord Spynie, 167n, 216 & n. Lord John, of Byers, xvii.n, 19, 21, 105n, 132n, 216n. Master of Spynie, 63n. v. Crawford.
Lingen, 210n.
Linlithgow, 3In, 103n, 128n, 133, 150n, 217. Palace, 129n. Earl of, 45n, 129 & n.
Linton, 147n, 216. Lord, lv., 140, 143.
Lintz Cas., Austria, 226n.
Lisle, Sir Geo., 211 & nn. Major John (Lillie), 188 & n, 307 & n-8, 493.
Little Dunkeld, 117-18n.
Littlekeny, v. Ogilvies of.
Livet, Glen, 104n.
Livingstone, 216. Hon. Jas., 45n. John, 288, 300. Lord, of Almond, 45n.
Loanan R., 311n.
Lochaber, Jan, 82-3 & n, 87, 139, 503, 505.
Loch-an-Eilan, 71n.
Lochalsh parish, Ross, 519.
Lochbuy, v. Maclean of.
Lochcarron parish, Ross, 519.
Lochearnhead, 97n. See Earn.
Lochearnside, 150n.
Lockhart, John, of Castlehill, 531.
Logie, v. Gordons of.
Logie Almond, 118n. See Drummond of.
Logie Wishart, v.-vi.n. xxxiii.
Lom, Ian, The Bard of Keppoch, 83n, 523.
London, xvi. xviii., 18, 19, 21-2, 24, 30n-1n-5n, 40, 67n, 155n, 204n, 210n-11n, 213n, 233, 288. Bow Bridge, 210n. Tower of, vi.n. 19, 204n, 210, 216n, 230, 328n.
Long, R., Secretary, 279n.
Lorn, 81, 82. Lord, 76n.

Lord (9th Earl of Argyll), xli.
Lothian, East, vi., 122n. Lothians, 91n. Wm., 3rd Earl of, 18, 70 & n, 73-4, 224 & n, 251, 288. Lothian's regt., 503.
Loudon, Chancellor, xv. lv., 19, 122n, 127, 217n, 235n, 251, 290-1, 301, 324-5 & n-6, 328 & n. Loudon's regt., 503. Cas., 126n.
Loue, Jas., sea-capt., 294 & n.
Louis XIV., King of France, 520.
Lour, 20.
Lovat (place), 313n, 316 & n. Lord, 503, 532. Hugh, 8th Lord, 532. Master of (1650), 304n.
Lucas, Lord, 210n-11n. Sir Richd., 211 & n, 336. Sir Thos., 43n.
Luitenberge, Laurence van, 494.
Lumisden, Ch., xxxi.n.
Ludlow Cas., 35n.
Lumley Cas., xxi. liv.
Lumsden (in Thirty Years' War), 270.
Lumsdens of Pitcaple, 318n.
Lyon, Fords of, 21.

MACALAIN, Angus, 80n.
M'Callin, M'Conaghig, 505.
M'Culloch, Capt. John, 46n.
Macdonald, clan, 38, 81n, 123n. Alex. (Alastair Coll Keitache or "Colkitto"), 54 & n, 56, 60, 64n, 72-3, 75, 79, 81, 99, 100-1n-2,106-8,113-14,121n, 126n, 134, 138-40 & n, 148-50, 160, 165, 180, 184n, 304n, 503. Capt., 178n. Angus, 109n. Coll Keitache MacGillespick, of Colonsay, 54n. Donald Glas, of Keppoch, 79n. J., of Eyellandtirrem, 79n. Sir Jas., 114n. Sir Jas., of Sleat, 176 & n. John, 79n. Ranald Og, of Mull, 101n.
Macdonell, Eneas, 79n. Lord Macdonell and Aros, 79n. v. Antrim.
MacGeorge, Margaret, 317.
Macgregor, 97n. Clan, 80n, 115, 165, 533n.
MacIdowie, Allan, of Lochaber, 83n.
Mackael, Hugh, 325n.
Mackay, clan, 290, 525, 533. Hucheon, of Scourie, 296 & n. Hugh, of Dirlot, 296 & n.

John, of Dirlot, brother to Lord Reay, 296n. Wm., of Bighous, 296. v. Reay.
Mackenzie, clan, 54n, 244, 254, 290, 304n, 519, 525, 533. Colin, of Kintail, 312. Sir Geo., Advocate, 139n, 531 (the same?). Sir Geo., of Tarbet, 531. John, son of Seaforth, 531. Keneth, laird of Gerloch, 519. Kenneth, of Assynt, 519. Capt. (Col.) Thos., of Pluscardine (Seaforth's brother), 175n, 244 & n, 250, 254, 261n, 290, 296n, 304n-5, 317, 501, 519, 530. Murdoch, (Bp.), xxxi.
Mackintosh, 87n. clan, 71n.
Maclean, clan, 79n, 123n, 130n. Maclean, 114, 121n, 176. Sir Lachlan, of Duart, 114n. of Lochbuy, 114n. Macleans (of Gothenburg Sweden), 273n. Of Torloisk, 114n. of Treshnish, 123n.
Maclear, Sir John (Gothenburg), liii., 272-3 & n, 275-6, 282, 284 & n-5, 510-12, 514-15.
Macleod, clan, of Assynt, 312, 533. of Lewis, 312. Angus, of Cadboll, Neil's cousin, 526. Angus, of Cadboll, father and son, 529. Donald, called Neilson, of Assynt, 529. Donald, son of Donald Neilson, 529. Hugh, uncle of Neil, 312. Hugh, of Cambuscurry, 529. John, the Grizzled, 533. "Young" Neil, of Assynt, the traitor, 304n, 312-13 & n-14 & n, 333, 497, 501, 522-33, 529. Neil, his father, 529. Roderick, cousin of Neil, 529.
Macnabs, clan, 80n, 115, 165.
Macpherson, 87n.
Macranalds, chief of the, 79, 81, 114.
Maderty, v. John, 2nd Lord, 32n, 60, 129 & n. v. Drummond.
Mälar, Lake, 273.
Man, Isle of, 139, 149n, 155n.
Mar (district), 98, 105n, 148, 319n. Braes of, 105 & n, 106, 115, 150, 155. Lower, 106, 153. 9th Earl of, 20, 102n-3, 121n, 148n, 217n.
Marischall, Earl, 18, 20, 28, 214,

# INDEX OF PERSONS AND PLACES. 547

216, 290. his brother, 504. Lands of, 88n.
Markinsch, Fife, 59n.
Marley, Sir John, Mayor of Newcastle-on-Tyne, xx.-i.n, xxiv. & n. Cornet Ralph (*al.* Murray), 495.
Marston Moor, xxi., 43n., 46n, 89n, 121n, 270.
Marstrand, xlvii.-li. 189, 275n, 282 & n, 435n, 513.
Martin, Dr. Jas., Provt. of S. Salvator's College, vii. xiii.
Mary Culter, 113n-14n.
Massie, 300.
Matray, Walter, 59n.
Mauchlin, 206n.
Maule, Wm., in "Giuldie" (Dundee?), xi.
Maurice, Prince, 35n, 39n.
Maxwell, Bp., xviii. Lady Elizabeth, 52n. Gabriel, minr., 206n. Sir Jas., Provt. of Dumfries, 45n. Lord, xxi. Rob., 216 & n, 2nd Earl of Nithsdale, 38n, 216n. ? 52n, 336.
May, Harry, 285-6, 293.
Mazarin, Cardinal, 246n, 324n.
Meade, Rob., 273, 509-10.
Meall (?), 519.
Mearns, The, xxvi.n, 88 & n, 107, 114, 162n, 258n, 290, 304n, 318. John of the, vi.n.
Meldrum, minr. (of Orkney?), 495.
Melgund, 95n.
Melvin, Major Patr., 49 & n, 188 & n, 276, 498-9.
Melvill, Melville, Andrew, Principal of S. Andrews' Univ., vi. Capt. Geo., 535. Sir Jas., 525. Major Patrick, v. Melvin.
Menmuir, 88n.
Menstry, 121n.
Menteith (district), 109n, 160, 166-7n.
Menzies, clan, 165. of Weem Cas., 56 & n. Alexander, 56n. Lady Ann Gordon, wife of Pitfoddels, 309n. Gilbert, of Pitfoddels, 309n. Gilbert, yr., of Pitfoddels, 188n, 308-9n, 493. Family of, 305n.
Merchiston, 103n. v. Napier of.
Methven, xv. 21, 52n, 54n, 115-18. Wood, 118n.
Mey, v. Sinclair of.
Midcalder, 140n.
Middleburgh, xlv.

Middleton, Lt.-Gen. John, of Caldhame (afterwards Earl), xxxii. lvi.-vii., 49n, 52n, 88n, 102n, 109n, 122n, 146n, 150n, 153n, 175 nn-6 & n, 178 & n, 184n, 206 & n, 209n, 244n, 286-7, 290, 296n, 304n, 322n, 501, 530.
Middleton Haugh, 20.
Midgary, 504.
Millfield, 20.
Mills of Drum, 114n, 357n.
Milton, v. Ogilvy of.
Minch-Moor, 147n.
Mingary, 54n. Mitau, liii.
Mitchell, Dav., xvi. xxx., & n.
Molleson, 516.
Moncrief, Sir James, xxxiii.n.
Monifieth, vii.-ix. & n., x. & n, xi., 320n.
Monikie, xi.
Monk, Col., later Gen. (Albemarle) xxx., 122n, 175n, 217n, 328n, 494.
Monro Clan, 244n, 304, 307 & n-8, 519. Capt. Andrew, son of Lemlair, 304-5, 307, 311-12, 519. Genl. Sir Geo., xlv.-lvi., 19, 38n, 51n, 72n, 122n, 208-9, 211n-13, 217n, 219-20, 244n-5, 261, 291, 521. Col. John, Laird of Lemlair, 290, 297n, 304 & n-5, 312, 514, 524, 529-31. Lemlair family, 523. Daughter of Lemlair, Neil Macleod's wife, 312-13, 526. Robert, son of Lemlair, 519. Sir Robt., 210n, 217n. Robert, of Achnes, and sons, 307, 310.
Monmouth, Duke of, 523n.
Montgomery, Col., 145n, 304 & n.
Monteith, Robert, of Salmonet, 305 & *n*, 309n, 520. Wm., 2nd Earl of, 52n, 57n.
Month, 319n.
Montrose, town, 83n, 154n, 160n, 185-6, 188. Roads, 187n, 188n. Old Montrose, 88n. **Jas., 1st Marquis of,** *passim.*
James, 2nd Marquis, 535. Marchioness of, 146 & n, 160n. v. Grahams.
Mor, John, 79n.
Moray, xxxi., 71, 82, 88, 245, 291, 301, 304n, 317. Bishop of, 172. House, 223n. Lord, 223n. Margaret, Countess of, 223n.
Morgan, Col., 531.

Morpeth, xvi. xx., liv., 46 & n.
Morphie, v. Graham of.
Mortimer, Capt., 178n, 494.
Morton, Rob. Douglas, Earl of, xii., 111n, 129n, 135n, 145, 216 & nn, 254-6, 258 & n, 266n, 276, 292. His successor, 292n, 497.
v. Douglas.
Mowat, of Balwholly (Bucholie), 111n, 295n. Christina, his wife, 295n.
Moydartach, Donald, 79n, 123n.
Muckart, 121n, 130n.
Mugdock Cas., 157n.
Muidartach, John, 81n.
Muirtown, nr. Inverness, 313n, 316.
Muldavat, v. Hay of.
Mull, 121n. v. Macdonald of.
Munster, Ireland, 251.
Murray, Earl of, 167n. Sir David, lv. Sir Gideon, 101 & n. Sir John, of Philiphaugh (?), 101 & nn. Cornet Ralph, v. Marley. Sir Robert, 495-6. Robert, xxxvii., 21, 41n. Thomas, 41n. Wm. (Gentleman of the Bedchamber to Charles I.), 15n, 22, 41 & *n*, 197n, 230n, 247n, 251. William, brother to the Earl of Tullibardine, 167, 169n, 172, 336. Sir Wm., of Blebo, 125 & n. Murrays of Sudhope, 101n. v. Annandale—Athole.
Muscovy, Emperor of, 262 & n.
Musgrave, Sir Phil., 91n, 209 & n, 210n.
Musselburgh, 217.
Mylne, John, 92n.
Myreton, Thos., of Cambo, 167n.

NAIRN, 87, 98n, 313, 317n. Strath, 87n.
Napier, Archibald, 1st Lord of Merchiston, xxviii. & n, xlv., 17, 20-3, 30 & n-1 & n, 102 & n, 109n, 134n, 150n, 156 & *n*, 160n, 230n. Lady Elizabeth, 103n. Lady Elizabeth, 134n, 297n, 534. Lilias, xxviii.n. Lady Margaret, 31n, 103n, 297n. Archibald, Master of Merchiston, 2nd Lord, xlv., 97n, 102*n*-3 & n, 109n-10, 128n, 130, 132, 258, 263n, 269, 281 & n-2, 288, 293.

Naseby, 130n, 135n, 209n.
Nassau, William of, 240n.
Naver, Loch, 296, 299.
  Strath, 15n, 52n, 216n, 294, 296 & n-7n, 304, 306, 311, 523.
Neilsons, 531-3.
Ness, Loch, 82, 87, 179.
Netherwitten, 20.
Nevay, John, 206n.
Nevis, Ben, 83n.
Newark, 1st Lord, 141n.
  -on-Trent, 40n, 159n.
Newbattle, 167n.
Newburn-on-Tyne, xix. xxi., 20, 89n.
Newbury, battle, 132n.
Newbyth, v. Baird of.
Newcastle-on-Tyne, xvi. xviii. xix. & n, xx.-i. & n, xxiii.-xxxii. lvi., 15, 17n, 20-1, 25, 27n, 30n. 38n, 45n-6 & n-7n, 49nn, 52n, 126, 132n, 154n, 167n, 182, 184n, 190 & n, 193 & n, 205, 502. *See* Ashley, Governor of.   All Saints' Ch., xviii.n, xxi.n.   Mayor of (1640), 20; *see* Marley. Sandgate, xxi.n.   St. Andrews Ch., xix.   St. Nicholas Ch., xix. xxi. Westgate, xxi.n, xxxiii.
Newcastle, Wm. Cavendish, Earl, later Marquis and Duke of, xix. xx., 26n, 37, 39, 42-3n-4, 46n, 51, 300.
Newmarket, 197n.
Newton, of Eglesham, 20.
  v. Gordon of.
Newtyle Cas., 105 & n.
Nicolas (Nicholas), Secretary Ed., 17n, 250n, 253n-4n, 259, 266n, 271-2, 277, 281-2, 286n, 293, 300, 304.
Nicoll, John, 534.
Nicolson, Sir Thos., King's Advocate, 324n.
Niddrie, 129n.
Nisbet, Capt., 150n, 160.
  Sir Alex., 155n, 159n.
  Sir John, of Dirlton, 531-2.
  Sir Philip, of Nisbet, 134nn, 155n-8n-9 & *n*.   Sir Rob., 155 & *n*.
Nithsdale, 136, 141.   Rob. Maxwell, 2nd Earl of, 38n, 216n.
Noltland Cas., Orkney, 498-500 & *n*.
North Berwick, xi. xxx.
North Esk, 95n.
Norway, xxvi. xlv., 494, 515.
  v. Bergen, Christiania, Marstrand, &c.
Norwich, 210n-11n.   Earl of, 194 & n, 210n.
Nottingham, xx., 132n.
  Cas., 209n.

O'CAHAN, v. O'Kean.
Octerlonie, Jean, Lady of Grange, 320n.
Og, John, 79n.
Ogilvy family, 123n.   Alex., 49 & n, 118.   Alex., of Innerquharity, 118, 157n. Sir Alex., 158 & n-9. Capt., 150, 160.   Sir Dav., of Clova, son of 1st Earl of Airlie, 65 & n, 78 & n, 118.   Jas., 8th Lord, and 1st Earl of Airlie, 63n, 65 & *n*, 77, 84n-5n, 88n, 115, 118, 123n-4, 132-3-4n, 136, 137n, 147-8, 150, 167 & n-9. Jas., Lord, and 2nd Earl of Airlie, xxiv. lvii., 23, 25, 30 & *n*, 34, 47-9 & n, 50n, 65 & *n*, 244, 290, 295n, 304n. Lady, 30n.   John, of Baldovie, 49n, 124 & n. Col. John, 263, 284-5. Sir John, 90n.   John of Gela (Gella), 49n.   Sir John, of Inverquharity, 49n, 118, 159.   Alexander, yr. of, liv., 336   John of Littlekeny, 49n.   Margt., wife of Geo. Wishart, vii. of Milton, 111n.   Lady, 134n.   Sir Thos., son of 1st Earl of Airlie, liv., 63 & n, 65 & n, 78, 85 & n.   of Powrie, 134n, 142.   Capt. (Col.) Thos., yr., of Powrie, 155 & n, 281, 286, 308, 493, 516.
Ogle, Glen, 97n.
O'Kean (O'Cahan, O'Kyan), Col., 74 & n, 85n, 159 & n.
Orange, Dowager Duchess of (1649), 247n.   Louisa Henrietta, Princess of, 252n. Wm., Prince of, xxvii., 24n, 240 & n, 247n.
Orbiston, v. Hamilton of.
Orcholm, v. Spence.
Ord, The, Caithness, 294-5, 298 & *n*, 306.
Orde, Wm., 244n, 261n.
Orkney, xxx., 49n, 63n, 252-4, 257 & n, 272, 274, 280 & n-1, 284, 286-8, 292 & n, 294n, 297, 307-11, 321, 495-6, 498, 525, 530, 535.   Ministers at Carbisdale, 308.   *See* Birsay - Kirkwall - Noltland- Wastray, &c.
Ormond, Marquis of, 242n, 244n-5, 250n, 259, 261-2.
Osbourn, John, xxiii.
Oxenstierne, Swed. Chancellor, 271.
Oykell Bridge, 310.   Kyle of, 299, 310.   River, 314. Strath, 298n-9 & n.

PAISLEY, Black Book of, xi.
Panbride, 95n.
Panmure House, 95n.
Pantes, Dr., of St. Andrews, xvi.
Paris, xlv.-vi. & n, 43n, 191-3, 197n, 198, 247n, 251-2, 280.
Paterson, John, xxxi.n.
Peebles, 147, 150n.
Pembroke, Earl of, 203n.
Pendennis Cas., 27n, 35n.
Pentland Hills, 218.   Battle of, 46n.
Perth, 19, 20. 54n, 57-8, 60 & n, 62-3, 66, 79, 91n, 96, 109n, 115 & n, 287, 301, 304n, 323, 494, 503-4, 534.   Earl of, 57 & n.
Peter Culter, 113n.
Petrie, Alex., xxvi.
Petty, 165n.
Philiphaugh (battle), xxvi. lvi., 31n-2n, 40n, 47n, 49n, 52n, 54n, 63n, 66n, 113n, 129n, 130n, 132n, 139n, 141n, 150n, 167n.   v. Murray of.
Philipston, Dundas of, xxxv.
Pickering, 536 & n.
Pitarrow, vi.n., v. Wishart of.
Pitcalney, v. Ross of.
Pitfoddels, v. Menzies of.
Pitlurg, 108 & n.
Pitscottie, Gen., 52n.
Pitsligo, 68n, 167n.
"Plotters," The, 21.
Pluscardine, v. Mackenzie of.
Poland, King of, liii., *see* Casimir.
Pollock, Capt., 499-500.
Pontefract, 211n.
Pooley, 277.
Popish Plot, 523n.
Porle, 132n.
Porterfield, Geo., Commr. for Glasgow, 47n, 324n.
Pottinger, John, of Kirkwall, 292 & n.
Powell, Capt., 493.
Powrie, v. Ogilvies of.
Prague, 226.
Presburg, 227 & n.

## INDEX OF PERSONS AND PLACES.

Preston (town), xlv., 27n, 89n, 175n, 209n, 211 & n, 213. (battle), 230n, 233.
Prideaux, Ed., lv.
Primrose, Sir Archd. of Carrington & Chesters, 139 & *n*. Viscount, 139 n.
Prince of Wales, v. Charles II.
Prince Charles Edward Stuart, 66n.
Princess Royal, 24n, 247n.
Prynne, xix.
Pym, 191n.
Pyrenees, Peace of (1659), 246n.

QUARRENDON Hill, xx.
Queen, The, v. Henrietta Maria. of Bohemia, v. Elizabeth. of Sweden, v. Christina.
Queensberry, Earl of, 147n, 216. Countess of, 147 & n. arms of, vi.n.
Queensferry, North, 217n.

RAE, v. Reay.
Ramsay, minr., xvi. Andr., minr., 290. Michael, of Monifieth, x.
Rathmines, 242n.
Rattray, 184n.
Rayne, 319n.
Reading, 132n.
Reay, Donald Mackay, 1st Lord, xxi., 52, 134n, 154 & n-5, 176, 244n-5, 254, 296 & n-7n, 529. Master of, 2nd Lord, 290, 296n, 301, 304n. parish, 311, 523. *See* Mackays.
Reid Cas., Ross, 304n.
Remonstrants, 328n, 501.
de Retz, Cardinal, Abp. of Paris, 520.
Rhaoinne, Sutherland, 298n-9 & n.
Rhenen, 253.
Rhives, Sutherland, 298 & n.
Ribbing, Per Lindormson, Govr. Gothenburg, 272-3 & n-5, 282 & nn, 510-15.
Ribble Bridge, xxiv., 49n, 211n.
Riddarholms Kirk, Stockholm, 270n.
Riga, 284.
Ringwerthe, Ensign Adrian, 495.
Ripon, 21.
Robertson clan, 54n, 79n. of Clermonth, xvii.n. John, xxxii.n.
Rog, Sir W., lv.
Rogers, Sam., xlvi.
Rollo or Rollock, Alex., minr., xvi., 301. Lord, 32n. Sir Jas., of Duncrub, 29n, 32 & n, 47n, 83n. Sir Wm., 32n, 47 & n, 50 & n, 66-7, 70, 77 & n, 109, 120, 150n, 157n-8 & n, 336, 502.
Rosebery, v. Primrose.
Rosehall, 299 & n, 313n-14.
Ross county, 71, 82, 257, 297, 299, 304n, 306, 309-10 & n, 518-19, 530. (town), Ireland, 288. clan, 304, 307 & n-8, 519. Dav., Laird of Balnagowan, 304 & n-5. Capt. John, 305. Capt. Wm., 305. Lt. or Capt. Wm., 494. of Pitcalney, father and daughter, 529.
Rosyth Cas., 130 & n. *See* Stuart of.
Rothes Cas., 178 & n. Earl, xv. xxxvii., 18, 120n-1n.
Rothiemurchus, 71 & n, 162.
Rotterdam, 50n, 233n, 235n, 250, 270.
Row, vii. xxvi.n.
Rowton Heath, battle, 209n.
Roxburgh, county, 136, 140. Sir Rob. Ker, of Cessfurd, 1st Earl of, 135 & *nn*, 139, 141, 214-5, 223n. 2nd Earl of, 323n.
Roy Bridge, 83n. Glen, 83n.
Rullion Green, xxxii., 125n.
Rupert, Prince, xlvii., 43n, 46 & n, 89n, 159n, 227 & n, 233n, 234n, 244, 247n, 249, 254 & n, 261 & n-2, 288.
Rushworth, 49n.
Rusky, 166n.
Rutherford, John, minr. of Dairsie and Monifieth, xi. Samuel, minr., xxx., 168n.
Ruthven, Patrick, Lord, and Earl of Forth and Brentford (Brainford), 19, 21, 41n, 63, 85, 105n, 114n, 262 & n, 270-1, 275n, 282. Lady Patricia, his daughter, 63n.
Rye House Plot, 523n.

SAINTSERF, 524.
Sandgate (Newcastle), xxi.n.
Sandilands, Andr., xxv.n, 137-8n. Sir Jas., xiii.
Sanquhar, v. Crichton of. Declaration of, xl.
Saues (Saves), Capt. Peter, 494.
Scarborough, 43n.
Scheveling, 25n.
Schiedam, xxvii.-viii.n, 263n.
Scollay, Jas., of Strynie Tofts and Papa Stromay, 500 & n.
Scone, 21, 76n.
Scotston, vi.n.
Scott, Helen, of Monifieth, x. Sir Jas., 58-61. Wm., 30n.
Scourie, 299. See Mackay of.
Scouring Burn, 92n.
Scrimgeour, Hugh, xiii., 172 & n. John, 3d Visct. of Dudhope, 216*n*.
Seaforth, Geo., 2nd Earl of, 20, 82 & n*n*-3, 87n, 98, 164, 176, 179, 184, 188n, 215, 230n-1, 233n, 241, 245, 250, 252n-3, 264-5, 274, 286, 290-1, 293-4n, 312, 503, 530, 531. Dowager Countess of, 314. Earl (1672), 532.
Sehestedt, Hannibal, 275 & *n*, 494, 512.
Selkirk, 142 & n-3, 147, 178.
Seraphim, Herr, liii.
Seton (place), 237n. Lord, Chancellor, 73n, 129 & *n*. Lord, lvii.
Settle, 211n.
Sevenbergen, Holland, 227n.
Seymour, Harry, 271n.
Sharpe, Abp., xxx.
Sharpe's Gravenhagen, v. the Hague.
Shaw, Quartermaster, 304.
Shaws, 71n.
Sheirglass, v. Stewart of.
Sheldon, Chaplain, 204n.
Sherburn, 209n.
Shetland, 101n, 293, 498-9.
Shields, S., liv.
Shin, Loch, 289n, 296. River, 299 & n, 308n.
Shuttleworth, Col., 49n.
Sibbald, Col. Wm., xlvii., 19, 47n, 50 & *n*, 66n, 77, 244n, 261, 270 & n & n, 524.
Sideserf, Bp., xxx.
Simson, Pat., minr., xxxviii.*n*, 325n-6n, 329n.
Sinclair, Alex., Laird of Brims, 296 & *n*. Major Sir Ed., of Orkney, 310 & n, 313, 499, 501. Ed., of Clumby and Ed., of Essinquay, Orkney, 499n. Ed., of Gyre and Ed., of Ness, Orkney, 310n. Francis, grand-uncle of Earl of Caithness, 296n. Geo., 499. Sir Jas., of Murkle, v., 497. John, Laird of Brims, 310 & n, 510. Sir John, of Dunbeath, 295-6n-

2 N

# INDEX OF PERSONS AND PLACES.

7 & n.   Wm., 499-500. Wm., of Greenwell, in Holm, 499n.   Sir Wm., of Mey, Caithness, 296n, 532.   See Caithness.
Sioleanbrice, 531, 533n.
Skärgård, The, 272.
Skea, Skerries of, 497-8.
Skelbo Cas., 297.
Skene, 98n.   Loch, 114n.
Skibo Cas., 297, 313n-14 & n-15 & n.   v. Gray of.
Skipton, 211n.
Skye, 501, 523.
Slain-Man's-Lee, 144n.
Sleaght-ean-Aberigh, v. Sioleanbrice.
Sleat, v. Macdonald of.
Sma' Glen to Buchanty, 56n.
Small, Jas., 501.
Smith, Col., 176n.   Hen., minr. of Shapinshay, 500n. John (London), 38n. John, minr., Commr. to Breda, xxxi.n, 288.   Wm., minr., 296n.   Wm., minr., 500 & n.
Smythe, J., of Braco, 519.
St. Albans, Earl of, 193n.
St. Andrews, vii. viii. xi.-xvii. xxviii.-ix.n-xxx., 30, 31, 40n, 66n, 103n, 129n, 139n, 166-8n, 318 & n.   University, vi., 59n.   See Gladstanes, Abp. of.—Wishart, Bp. of.
St. Germains, 7, 234n, 251-3, 259, 263-4, 508.
St. Giles' Church, see Edinburgh.
St. Johnston, see Perth.
St. Malo, 288.
St. Margarets, Westminster, 34n.
St. Michael's Mount, 27n.
St. Neots, 210n.
St. Nicholas (Newcastle), xxi.n, xxix.
St. Ninians, 217n.
St. Salvator's College, St. Andrews, vi.
Somers, Mr. Alex., parson of Duffus, 318 & n.
Somerville, Lt. Col. Jas., 46n. Jas., Author of the " Memorie of," 319n-20n.
Soullar, v. Scollay.
Sound, The, 260, 272, 274, 500 & n.
Southesk, Earls of.   See Carnegie.
Southwark, 27n.
Southwell, 70n.
Spang, Wm., minr., 207n, 235n, 240n.
Spean, R., 83n.

Spence, Gen. Sir Jas., 270.
Spey, R., 54, 71, 82n-3n, 87-8, 98, 104 & n, 161, 164-5n, 175-7, 178 & n, 179, 184n, 245, 502.   v. Strathspey.
Spital of Glenshee, 105n.
Spottiswoode, Abp., viii. xi. xii. xv. xvi. xviii. xxx. xxxvii., 139n, 494.   Laird of Dairsie, 494.   John, of Dairsie, 187 & n, 494.   Sir John, xiii.   Sir Rob., President, xiii. xxvi. lvi., 139 & n, 140, 167 & n, 169 & n, 171 & n-2, 336.
Spynie, v. Lindsay,
Stafford, and Governor of, 212n.
Stamford, Earl of, 213 & n.
Stewart, clan, of Atholle, 54n. of Ardvoirlich, liv., 64 & n, 97n, 166n.   Lt. Col. Alex., 22. Lt. Col. Alex., 495. Stewarts of Balquihidder, 165. of Blackhall, 21.   Lt. Col. Hen., 294-5, 308, 491, Sir Jas., Provt. of Edinburgh, 324n.   John, and John, yr., of Ladywell, 21-2.
John, of Sheirglass, 148n, 150n.
Col. John, Covenanter, 499n.
Lady Margt., 147n.   Sir Thos., of Grantully, 17n, 57n.
Lt. Col. Walter, 17, 21-2.
Col. Wm., 176 & n.
Stewart's reg. of horse, 319n.
See Stuart.
Stirling, town, xlv., 31 & n, 109n, 121 & n, 133, 166, 217 & n, 219, 291, 302n, 323, 534. Bridge, 122.   Castle, 115n, 125.   Capt., 493. Earl of, 40n, 97n.   Sir Geo., of Keir, 17, 21, 31 & n, 97n, 103 & n, 134n, 197n, 204n.   Lady, of Keir, 134n.
Stockholm, 273, 275, 284-5, 510.
Stockton-on-Tees, Cas., xxi.
Stonehaven, 49n, 88n, 114n, 187-8n, 251.
Stonyhurst Park, 211n.
Stormont, Lord, 20-1.
Strachan, Jas., minr. of Fettercairn, 88n.   Lt. Col. Archibald, 299n, 301, 303-8 & nn, 316 & n, 501, 524. Lt. Capt., 284-5.
Strafford, xxiii., 49n, 336.
Strathample, 165-6 & n.
Strathavon, 162n.
Strathbogie, 57n, 67n, 72 & n-3 & n, 75-6n, 88n, 104, 153n, 161, 318n.

Strathdon, 71n, 104 & n, 150, 162n.
Strathearn, lv., 56, 97, 118, 156-7, 160 & n, 222.   Earldom of, 57n.
Strath Gala, 137, 140, 143.
Strath Glass, 179.
Strathnaver, see Naver.
Strathspey, 71n, 87n, 98n, 104, 164, 165 & n.   v. Spey.
Strathyre, 97n.
Strickland, Sir Wm., 26n. Parliamentary envoy to Holland, 250n, 252n-3-4.
Struders, v. Gordon of.
Stuart, 79n.   (Clan), 144n. of Rosyth, 130 & n.   See Stewart.
Suie Hill, 108n, 319n.
Suilven, Ben, Sutherland, 312.
Sunderland, Lord, 142n-3n. Town (Durham), xx. liv.
Sutherland, county, 71, 82, 294, 298, 304n, 309, 314 & n. Earl of, 22, 38n, 98, 293, 296, & n-7 & n-8 & n, 304-5, 307n-8n-9n, 496, 501, 503, 530, 533.   Kyle of, 299, 305-6, 308, 314.
Swan, Capt., 493.
Sweden, Queen of, v. Christina.
Symons, see Somers.

Tain, Ross, 303n, 305-6, 309, 313n-14 & n.
Tarff, 83n.
Tartars, war with, 246n.
Tay, R., ix., 52 & n, 56, 63, 80, 90-2, 115, 117n, 119-20, 160. Loch, 81n, 97.
Teith, 121n.
Teviotdale, lv., 70n.
Tewes, Sir W., iv.
Thompson, Will., lvi.
Thame, 89n.
Thoresby, Dr., Antiquary, 536.
Thott, Henrik, 189n.
Throndhjem, 189n.
Thurso, 295 & n, 496.
Tippermuir, battle, xxv. liv., 58, 118n, 162, 503.
Titus, 300.
Tolbooth, v. Edinburgh.
Tomintoul, 71n.
Tongue, in Strath Naver, 296 & n, 299, 501.
Torloisk, v. Maclean of.
Torphichen, Lord, 140n.
Torth, 143.
Torstenson, Fieldmarshal Count Leonard, 273 & n, 275-6, 282, 510-15.
Tournay, 227 & n.
Touch, Lt. Rob., 499.

# INDEX OF PERSONS AND PLACES.

Tower of Amisfield, 130n.
v. Charters of.
Towers, Lady Jane, 130n.
Rob., of Inverleith, 145 & n.
Sir John, of Inverleith, 130 & n.
Traill, Robt., minr., 301, 325, 328n-9n.
Traquair (place), 136.
House, 147n. 2nd Earl of, 17, 18, 41, 47, 135 & n, 137, 139-40, 143 & n, 147 & n.
Treasure Loch, Carbisdale, 299n.
Treshnish, v. Maclean of.
Trewick, 20.
Trollhättan Falls, 275n.
Tromp, van, 25n.
Tullibardine, Earl of, 47n, 58-9, 123n, 172, 216.
Tullybelton, 47n, 52n.
Tullibody Wood, 121n.
Tulloch, Alex., son of Thos., of Tannachy, 317n. John (?), Provost of Nairn, 317 & n.
Turner, Sir Jas., xlv., 50n, 206n, 211n, 245n, 260, 269-70. A., xxxi.n.
Tweed, R., xx., 15, 20, 22, 137, 139, 141, 143, 150n, 217n.
Tweedside, 145.
Tyne, R., xxi., 15, 46.
Tynemouth, 46n. Cas., 328n.
Tyrnau, 227 & n, 463n.

ULFELDT, Korfits (Cornificius), 245 & n, 260 & n.
Ulfsunda, 273, 510-15.
Ullapool, 310.
Umphraville, Gilbt. de, p. v.
Urie R., 319n.
Urquhart parish (Ross), 519.
Sir Thos., of Cromartie, 290.
Urray parish (Ross), 519.
Ury, 88n.
Uttoxeter, 212n.

VALLENSIUS, see Wallensius.
Vanderson, see Waterston.
Vane, Sir Harry, xix., 30n, 34n.
Venachar, Loch, 160n.
Verkin, Lt., 494.

Vienna, 226-7, 273.
Villiers, Eleanor, 193n. See Buckingham.
Vlefeld, see Ulfeldt.

WALKER, Sir Ed., 534.
Wm., minr., North Berwick, xi., xxx.
Wallace, Col., 125 & n, 329n.
Capt., 38n. Thos., of Craigie, 531. Sir Wm., vi.n, 10.
Wallensius or Wallenson, 494.
Waller, 211n.
Warden, Capt., 494.
Wardlaw, 315n. MS., see 315-16nn, and Fraser.
Warrington, 211n. Bridge, 212n.
Warriston, v. Johnston of.
Waterston of Anstruther, 498.
Watten, Caithness, 296n.
Webster, John, merchant, Amsterdam, 508. Isobel, of Monifieth, x.
Weem Cas., 56 & n.
Weems, Jas., xxviii.n. Dr. Ludowich, xxviii.n.
Weir, Major, 329n-30 & n.
Wellbeck, 43n, 149n.
Welden, 46n.
Wemyss, Earl of, xii., 130n.
Sir Patrick, 17n.
West Chapel Shade, 92n.
Wester Fearn, Ross, 306-7.
Westgate, v. Newcastle.
Westphalia, 270n.
Westminster, 30n.
Westray Firth, 497, 499.
Wexford, 262, 288.
Whitford, Whiteford, Whitfurd, Major, 298, 496.
Whitehall, 24n, 27n, 63n, 529.
Whitelocke, 271, 273n, 275n.
Wick, 295.
Wigan, 211n.
Wight, Isle of, 323n.
Wigton, Earl of, 20, 129n.
MS., 322-34nn.
Wilkie, John, xxix.n.
Wilmot, Lord, 247n.
Wilson, John, 158n.

Winchburgh, 129n.
Windsor, 24n, 27n, 49n, 204n. Cas., 216n.
Winram, Geo., of Libberton, 237n -8n, 247n, 251-2, 288, 291.
Winton, Earl of, 129n.
Winwick, 212n.
Wishart, barony of, vi.
Geo., the martyr, vi.n, 114n.
Rev. Geo., the author, Bp. of Edinburgh, Pref. v.ff., xliv.-vi. 16n, 168n, 178n, 188, 248n, 263n, 288, 322n.
Huego, the author's son, xiii.
Sir Jas., of Pitarrow, Justice-Clerk to Qu. Mary, vi.n.
Jean, the author's daughter, xi. xxxiii. John, Archd., and Bp. of Glasgow, vi.n.
Sir John, of Logie Wishart, v. xiv. Margt., the author's daughter, xiii.n, xxxiii.
Patrick, the author's son, vii. xiii.n, xxxiii.-v. Rob., Bp. of Glasgow, vi.n.
Rob. and Thos., the author's sons, xiii.n., xxxii. Thos., of Ballindarg, xi. Wm., Bp. of St. Andrews, vi.n.
Wm., minr. of Leith, v.n, xxix.n. Wm., of Logie W., xxxiii.n. John, Com., xxxiii. Jean (or Dundas), xxxv.
Wolfelte, v Ulfeldt.
Worcester, xl., 40n, 175n, 216n, 230n, 246n.
Wrangel, Fieldmarshal, 273n.
Wynram, v. Winram.
Wood, Rev. Jas., xxvi.n, 188 & n.
Wodrow, Rob., xxxv. xl. xlviii. l. li.-ii.-iii.

YARMOUTH, 210n.
Yarrow, R., 147n.
York, city, xx., 15, 24 & n, 26 & n, 29, 31n, 42, 46, 49n, 51n, 159n. Abp. of, 135n.
Jas., Duke of, 227n, 243n, 252 & n, 286.
Young, Hen., 92n.
Ythan, R., 75.